Lectures on medical jurisprudence : edited by Francis Ogston, Junior.

Francis Ogston

Lectures on medical jurisprudence : edited by Francis Ogston, Junior.
Ogston, Francis
collection ID ocm25669849
Reproduction from Harvard Law School Library
London : Churchill, 1878.
xi, 663 p. : ill., forms ; 22 cm.

The Making of Modern Law collection of legal archives constitutes a genuine revolution in historical legal research because it opens up a wealth of rare and previously inaccessible sources in legal, constitutional, administrative, political, cultural, intellectual, and social history. This unique collection consists of three extensive archives that provide insight into more than 300 years of American and British history. These collections include:

Legal Treatises, 1800-1926: over 20,000 legal treatises provide a comprehensive collection in legal history, business and economics, politics and government.

Trials, 1600-1926: nearly 10,000 titles reveal the drama of famous, infamous, and obscure courtroom cases in America and the British Empire across three centuries.

Primary Sources, 1620-1926: includes reports, statutes and regulations in American history, including early state codes, municipal ordinances, constitutional conventions and compilations, and law dictionaries.

These archives provide a unique research tool for tracking the development of our modern legal system and how it has affected our culture, government, business – nearly every aspect of our everyday life. For the first time, these high-quality digital scans of original works are available via print-on-demand, making them readily accessible to libraries, students, independent scholars, and readers of all ages.

The BiblioLife Network

This project was made possible in part by the BiblioLife Network (BLN), a project aimed at addressing some of the huge challenges facing book preservationists around the world. The BLN includes libraries, library networks, archives, subject matter experts, online communities and library service providers. We believe every book ever published should be available as a high-quality print reproduction; printed on-demand anywhere in the world. This insures the ongoing accessibility of the content and helps generate sustainable revenue for the libraries and organizations that work to preserve these important materials.

The following book is in the "public domain" and represents an authentic reproduction of the text as printed by the original publisher. While we have attempted to accurately maintain the integrity of the original work, there are sometimes problems with the original work or the micro-film from which the books were digitized. This can result in minor errors in reproduction. Possible imperfections include missing and blurred pages, poor pictures, markings and other reproduction issues beyond our control. Because this work is culturally important, we have made it available as part of our commitment to protecting, preserving, and promoting the world's literature.

GUIDE TO FOLD-OUTS MAPS and OVERSIZED IMAGES

The book you are reading was digitized from microfilm captured over the past thirty to forty years. Years after the creation of the original microfilm, the book was converted to digital files and made available in an online database.

In an online database, page images do not need to conform to the size restrictions found in a printed book. When converting these images back into a printed bound book, the page sizes are standardized in ways that maintain the detail of the original. For large images, such as fold-out maps, the original page image is split into two or more pages

Guidelines used to determine how to split the page image follows:

- Some images are split vertically; large images require vertical and horizontal splits.
- For horizontal splits, the content is split left to right.
- For vertical splits, the content is split from top to bottom.
- For both vertical and horizontal splits, the image is processed from top left to bottom right.

LECTURES

ON

MEDICAL JURISPRUDENCE

LECTURES

ON

MEDICAL JURISPRUDENCE

BY

FRANCIS OGSTON, M.D.

PROFESSOR OF MEDICAL JURISPRUDENCE AND MEDICAL LOGIC IN THE
UNIVERSITY OF ABERDEEN

EDITED BY

FRANCIS OGSTON Junior, M.D.

ASSISTANT TO THE PROFESSOR OF MEDICAL JURISPRUDENCE, AND LECTURER ON
PRACTICAL TOXICOLOGY IN THE UNIVERSITY OF ABERDEEN

LONDON
J. & A. CHURCHILL, NEW BURLINGTON STREET
1878

June 27, 1905.

By R & R CLARK, Edinburgh.

PREFACE

The following Lectures on legal medicine are offered to the profession in the hope that they may supply the long-felt want of a work containing the various forms of Scottish medico-legal procedure, differing as they do in many respects from those of England, for which country the books of Drs. Taylor, Guy, etc., have been specially written. But though thus intended primarily for Scottish practitioners, no pains have been spared to fit them for a wider sphere, by the addition of the legal forms in use in England and other countries, where these have been found to differ from those of Scotland.

While retaining the lectures on General Toxicology, the Editor has thought it better to omit Special Toxicology from the work, as this subject has been so often and so ably treated of in books devoted to that department of legal medicine.

The Editor here desires to thank several kind friends for valuable assistance and suggestions in the preparation of this book for the press, especially Mr. George Cadenhead, Procurator-Fiscal of Aberdeen; Mr. J. M. Thomson, barrister-at-law in Edinburgh; and Dr. John G. Hall of Aberdeen; and also Mr. James Cadenhead of Aberdeen, who etched the illustrations for the work.

ABERDEEN, *January* 1878.

CONTENTS.

LECTURE I
Medical Evidence 1

LECTURE II
Medical Evidence—*concluded* 17

LECTURE III
Age 33

LECTURE IV.
Sex—Doubtful Sex 44

LECTURE V.
Personal Identity 57

LECTURE VI.
Impotence and Sterility 75

LECTURE VII.
Defloration and Rape 88

LECTURE VIII.
Rape—*Continued* 99

LECTURE IX.

Rape (*concluded*), and Sodomy . . . 115

LECTURE X

Pregnancy . . . 131

LECTURE XI

Delivery . . . 152

LECTURE XII

Birth . . . 170

LECTURE XIII.

Criminal Abortion . . . 192

LECTURE XIV

Infanticide . . . 206

LECTURE XV

Infanticide—*continued* . . . 217

LECTURE XVI

Infanticide—*continued* . . . 237

LECTURE XVII

Infanticide—*continued* . . . 253

LECTURE XVIII.

Infanticide—*concluded* . . . 266

LECTURE XIX

Insanity . . . 277

LECTURE XX.
Insanity—*continued* . 287

LECTURE XXI.
Insanity—*continued* . 301

LECTURE XXII
Insanity—*concluded* . 323

LECTURE XXIII.
Feigned, Factitious, and Latent Diseases . 334

LECTURE XXIV.
Death in its Medico Legal Aspects . 346

LECTURE XXV
Death—*continued* . 360

LECTURE XXVI.
Death—*continued* . 373

LECTURE XXVII
Death—*concluded* . 385

LECTURE XXVIII.
Medico-Legal Inspections . 397

LECTURE XXIX.
Homicide . 409

LECTURE XXX.
Wounds . 414

LECTURE XXXI.

Wounds—*continued* 429

LECTURE XXXII.

Wounds—*continued* 443

LECTURE XXXIII.

Wounds—*continued* 460

LECTURE XXXIV.

Wounds—*concluded* 478

LECTURE XXXV.

Death by Drowning 495

LECTURE XXXVI.

Death by Drowning—*concluded* 507

LECTURE XXXVII.

Death by Hanging 521

LECTURE XXXVIII.

Death by Strangulation 537

LECTURE XXXIX.

Death by Suffocation 547

LECTURE XL.

Death from Cold, Heat, Lightning, and Starvation . 555

LECTURE XLI

GENERAL TOXICOLOGY 565

LECTURE XLII

GENERAL TOXICOLOGY—*continued* 580

LECTURE XLIII.

GENERAL TOXICOLOGY—*continued* 594

LECTURE XLIV

GENERAL TOXICOLOGY—*continued* 608

LECTURE XLV

GENERAL TOXICOLOGY—*concluded* 622

APPENDIX.

I CERTIFICATES OF INSANITY 637
II VARIOUS FORMS OF MEDICO-LEGAL REPORTS . . . 640

LIST OF AUTHORITIES 647
INDEX 649

LECTURE I.

MEDICAL EVIDENCE.

PRELIMINARY REMARKS.—Designations of Medico-legal Science—Occasions for its Application—Evidence of the Ordinary Witness—Evidence of the Scientific Witness—Limits of Legal Testimony—Limits of Medical Testimony—Forms of Legal Procedure in Criminal Cases—Criminal Institutions of Scotland, of England, of the Colonies and United States, of France, of Germany—CRIMINAL AND ECCLESIASTICAL COURTS—Position of the Expert at the Investigation of Criminal Charges—In his strictly Medical Capacity—At the Precognition in Scotland—On the Coroner's Inquest in England, in America—The Written Report—The *Viva Voce* Examination—Rules for the guidance of the Expert—Examination for the Defence—Cautions to the Medical Witness

THE department of medical science to which it is my province to draw your attention here is rather unfortunate in its usual designation. Little fault indeed could be found with the titles of Forensic Medicine or Legal Medicine, which some have chosen whereby to characterise it; but I cannot say so much for that by which it is best known, namely Medical Jurisprudence, an unfortunate misnomer, which, however inappropriate, can scarcely now be got rid of.

Of the scope of the science generally, it will not be necessary to say much. You must be aware that occasions arise in the course of a professional career on which the medical man will have to step beyond the sphere of his ordinary avocations as the attendant on the sick. Such occasions occur in the case of those judicial proceedings, civil or criminal, which are found to bear more or less directly on medical science, and in which the administrators of the law require for their guidance facts and opinions which are only to be procured from the medical practitioner in his strictly professional capacity.

In all such inquiries at law there are two leading forms in which evidence to this effect may be called for on the part of the legal authorities—forms which, though not always kept apart in practice, need to be distinguished, and borne distinctly in mind by the scientific witness.

Thus, evidence may be called for from the witness as to the

mere facts of the case, or he will be required to state the conclusions at which he has arrived from the consideration of these facts, whether observed by himself or supplied to him by others

When he has merely to speak to the *facts* of the case, the professional is in the same position as the ordinary witness. In common with the latter, what is chiefly demanded of him is, a memory sufficiently retentive to enable him to recall what he has seen or heard, sufficient intelligence and acuteness to enable him to discern the usual import of deeds and words, and enough presence of mind to bring out the result of all this at the proper moment, in answer to a well-directed system of interrogatory. In proof of this, it has been remarked, that boys and girls under puberty, when not too bashful, usually make the best ordinary witnesses, from the superior acuteness of their observation, the instinctivity of their perceptions, and the readiness of their memories at that early age

Further, when called on to speak to the facts of the case, it will be expected of the witness that he confine his testimony to what has fallen under his own observation, or it may be occasionally, where words have been heard by him, as well as actions witnessed, to state, when so required, what he understood at the time of the occurrence in question to be the import of the expressions made use of, or the purport of the actions performed

In connection with this department of testimony it may be proper to add, that though, in common with others, the medical witness may be interrogated as to the *res gestæ* of the case, it is usual, unless on special occasions when no other evidence can be procured, to confine his testimony to the occurrences which only a medical man is supposed to be competent to observe

The same restriction applies to the case of the medical practitioner, when, occupying a higher capacity than that of an ordinary witness, he is called on to adduce the inferences naturally flowing from and built up on the facts and circumstances either observed by himself or merely reported by others. Here too the facts and inferences with which he will be permitted to deal must be such alone as bear on the purely medical aspects of the case. The administrators and interpreters of the law consider it to be their exclusive function to interpret facts and draw conclusions in all circumstances, except those in which their own incompetence must at once be admitted, that is, where the questions before them are of a purely technical or scientific character, such as the greater number of the medical points coming before them for settlement and adjudication.

Now, whether in his less ambitious character as a mere observer, or in his higher position as a judge and interpreter of the value and bearing of the facts of his science, or, as usually happens, in both combined, the medical jurist has a sufficiently important part to play within the department of legal practice, in which his aid may be at any time sought, where legal principles have to be settled or legal decisions pronounced based on purely medical facts and conclusions; and beyond this the medical practitioner, in his official capacity, does not require to travel in seeking to fit himself for such exigencies as these, a circumstance lost sight of by most of the earlier writers on medical jurisprudence, and which if duly attended to would also disencumber many of our existing medico-legal works of much superfluous matter having but an indirect bearing on the science which they profess to elucidate. Of this sort are many discussions on purely legal questions with which the practitioner or medical jurist, as such, has little or nothing to do, and the introduction of which could only have arisen from ignorance on the part of the expert of the practical object of his science, and the proper position he is found in practice to occupy in inquiries at law bordering on medical topics.

Equally superfluous and still more mischievous are many of the details, still frequently reproduced from the older writers in our modern treatises, of medical inquiries which would now be repudiated by the existing judicatories, and the discussions of questions which are now settled on evidence, and on principles of a sort altogether foreign to those which medicine is capable of supplying. The inquiries with which the modern expert has to concern himself occupy a less extended field than was formerly believed to be the case, while the evidence required to substantiate the points which they embrace is not now required to be of that strictly demonstrative character, which demanded that each single fact advanced should be incapable of explanation by any other view than the one taken of it by the witness, and thus put it out of the power of the judge or jury to arrive at moral conviction on any point whatever, unless each and every link in the chain of proof was not only indisputable but undisputed,—a thing perfectly unattainable in such a science as medicine, in fact in any science whatever, if we except that of pure mathematics.

Thus narrowed and restricted within reasonable and practicable limits, the series of topics falling legitimately to be discussed by the medical jurist, as his subject is now viewed by its most enlightened cultivators, embraces such points and such only, as are either purely medical in the wider sense of the term, or arise directly out of medicine proper, and consequently which can only be satisfactorily dealt with by the magistrate after he has acquired a knowledge of their medical aspects.

Of this class of topics and inquiries in forensic practice we are constantly being presented with examples, where points are broached and judgments given, the consideration and settlement of which rest upon data and arguments altogether foreign to the usual sphere of the legal functionary, and which the medical practitioner is alone competent to furnish; data and arguments drawn from professional sources, at times pretty widely apart, and demanding for their correct appreciation and application a familiarity with several of the more recondite of the departments of medical science.

Before proceeding to enumerate the topics with which the medical jurist has to deal, and to the study of the details thus opened up to the profession of medicine, where it comes into contact with certain departments of law, the formal elucidation of which constitutes the science of medical jurisprudence, it may be useful and instructive, as a fitting introduction of the whole subject, to direct your attention at the outset to the two following topics :—*Firstly*, To the ordinary forms of procedure followed by the administrators of the law in this and other civilised countries, in so far as these are found to bear on and demand the co-operation of the practitioner in his medical capacity; and *Secondly*, To the precise character of the testimony which the medical witness is expected to be able to produce in the course of such proceedings towards the furtherance of the ends of justice.

This I shall attempt to do as briefly, and in terms of a character as little formal and technical as the subject will admit of.

I. In proceeding to notice the forms of legal procedure, in so far as they are found to affect the medical practitioner, your attention has to be directed

1*st*, To the Criminal Institutions of Scotland, differing as they do, in form at least, from those of the sister country, and in not a few important particulars from those which regulate legal procedure amongst the other European nations.

In Scotland the prosecution of crime is not left, as in England, to the injured individual or his friends, but is intrusted to a public officer, who conducts the prosecution at the public expense;

failing which the individual or his friends may press the criminal charge as in the sister country.

The Lord Advocate, or his deputies, the Advocates-Depute, are the public prosecutors for crimes over the whole of Scotland. The Court before which these public officers appear is the High Court of Justiciary, whose powers extend over the whole of Scotland, and whose Circuits travel twice a year through its most populous counties.

Besides the Court of Justiciary, there is in each county the Sheriff-Court, and in each considerable town a Burgh Court, both for lesser offences. The Justices of the Peace also take cognisance of the smaller crimes.

In each county or burgh a public officer is appointed, whose duty it is to receive all complaints from individuals who have been injured in their persons or estates within the limits of his jurisdiction, and to prepare such cases for prosecution before one of the above courts, according to their nature and the degree of criminality of the action.

The Justices of Peace in each district have also a Procurator-Fiscal, as this officer is termed, who prosecutes before them in cases fit for their decision.

In the event of a crime which is of a serious complexion, such as murder, rape, etc., occurring in any county or burgh of Scotland, the proceedings are as follows:—Upon the information of the injured party or his friends, a complaint is made out by the Procurator-Fiscal of the burgh, county, or district where he resides, and the party offending, after being judicially examined, is committed to prison for further examination. The whole of the evidence on the case is brought together and reduced to writing, with the view of being immediately submitted to Crown Counsel, and of serving for their brief on the trial.

The written report of the medical man engaged in the case forms part of this investigation, or *precognition*, as it is termed.

The precognition, or *procès-verbal*, being concluded, the Sheriff or magistrate who has superintended the Procurator-Fiscal in the collection and investigation of the evidence, or who is cognisant of its nature, commits the accused to stand trial if there be sufficient grounds for committal, when the accused may apply for bail if the crime admits of it.

The accused party being committed for trial, the precognition is transmitted to the Crown Counsel in Edinburgh, who determine on the propriety of a prosecution, and who have power to terminate the proceedings and liberate the prisoner, to remit the case to an inferior judge for immediate trial, or to direct the accused to be detained for indictment before the higher courts.

When it has been decided by the Crown Counsel that the prosecution is to be gone on with, the trial takes place at the High Court, at the circuit, or at the Sheriff-court, and the indictment is made out and the trial conducted by the Lord Advocate or one of his deputies.

The indictment or criminal charge narrates minutely the nature of the crime, the place where it was alleged to have been committed, and must specify all articles to be used in evidence, and contain a list of the witnesses.

At the commencement of the trial the witnesses are locked up in the charge of an officer of the Court, and are separately called and examined publicly on oath.

2*d*, The English practice in criminal matters is in many respects different from the Scottish. Except in some particular classes of State and political offences, and in a few cases which have drawn on themselves much public attention from their rarity or importance, the English law recognises no public prosecutor, the prosecution being left to the individual who has sustained the injury, or to his friends.

The party or parties concerned having resolved to prosecute, the depositions of the witnesses are taken, in presence of the accused, before a Justice of the Peace, who, if he thinks the case of sufficient importance, grants warrant to commit the prisoner to stand trial.

The prisoner—when once committed—must be kept in prison if the offence is not bailable, or if he cannot find bail, till the next quarter sessions or assizes if the offence was committed out of London, or till the next term if it was committed within it.

When the Grand Jury meets, the indictment is preferred against the prisoner. If twelve of them, on hearing the evidence, find a true bill, the prisoner takes his trial before the Petit Jury, either immediately or at the next term.

A portion of the duties which fall to our Procurators-Fiscal is, in England, discharged by a coroner, or paid magistrate, and a jury. In all cases of sudden death or death under suspicious circumstances, the coroner sits as a judge, and has the power of summoning witnesses, of directing a post-mortem examination of the body, and a chemical analysis of the contents of the stomach; and if the finding of the jury leads to ulterior proceedings, he binds over the witnesses to appear at the next assizes.

The course of *Oyer and Terminer* in England, corresponding to the Scotch High Court and Circuit Courts of Justiciary, are those courts of commission or assize in which Crown cases, such as treasons, felonies, and misdemeanours, are disposed of.

The medical witness when subpœnaed to attend must do so under a heavy penalty, and, until lately, was not allowed his expenses. Now, however, this privilege has been accorded him in all cases of felony, and in certain cases of misdemeanours.

3d, In India and the British colonies the forms of criminal procedure are those of England; while the United States of America adopt these, with some slight modifications to be noticed further on.

4th, In France, since 1808, the machinery of the criminal law has been as follows:—

The Court of Simple or Ordinary Police takes cognisance of offences involving a slight fine or a short imprisonment, like our own Burgh Courts.

The Court of Correctional Police hears appeals from the above-mentioned court, and condemns slight crimes to a severer fine, or to longer, though still limited, imprisonment.

The Criminal or High Criminal Court is the tribunal for the trial of offences to which a greater punishment is annexed than that of temporary imprisonment. It is held, like our own Courts of Justiciary, in courts of assize, in Paris monthly, and four times a year on circuit in the provinces. The *Procureur-Général*, or *Procureur de la République*, or one of his substitutes, like the Scotch Lord Advocate and his deputes, fills the place of public prosecutor.

The Court of Appeal hears appeals from the Court of Correctional Police, and pronounces on the validity of the accusation.

The Court of Cassation (or Repeal) annuls sentences, judgments, and decrees attacked on the score of incompetence, informality, or undue severity. But the decree of this court is not final; the prisoners may be detained in custody, and the trial carried anew to a court of assize.

But if the courts of justice in France bear a resemblance to those in Scotland, the modes of procedure of these tribunals present points of striking contrast with them. It would be out of place to dwell here on the want of anything like the Habeas Corpus Act, which deprives the prisoner of any security against apprehension on unjust or frivolous charges. The power of the counsel for the defence is also much more limited than with us, while the witnesses on the same side are sometimes handled in a very rude and unbecoming way by the judge and public prosecutor. The evidence, too, against the accused is drawn from him in prison by a forced system of continued and repeated interrogatory, which in many instances amounts to a species of moral torture, while again the declarations thus obtained from the prisoner are liable to be turned against himself, and he may be at any time confronted with the witnesses, and required to explain away, if he can, their testimony or the discrepancies in his declarations.

5th, The criminal law in Germany, if differing in form from that of France in the prominence so largely assigned to documentary evidence, has so many points in common with it, that the remarks bearing upon the position of the accused which I have adduced in regard to the one apply in substance to the other.

Thus in Germany the same system of interrogatory is pursued as in France, and this for periods not unfrequently of several years when the suspicions of guilt are strong, and the proof defective. As in that country, the evidence is often chiefly drawn from the admissions and contradictory statements of the prisoner. He is confronted with the witnesses, and every effort which ingenuity can devise is had recourse to, in order to draw him into admissions which are to be employed against himself.

The contrast which this presents to the practice of our own courts of criminal law has been thus put by an eminent Scottish barrister:—"In this country no attention is paid to anything beyond the circumstances *directly* connected with the commission of the crime, and what has been heard or seen by the witnesses present at the time, or immediately before; and if these throw no light on the motives of the prisoner, the law takes no further steps to clear up the doubt. No inferences are drawn from the past to the present; the former life of the prisoner, his general character, habits, and inclinations, are excluded from consideration. But in Germany" (and the same remark applies in substance to France) "the inquiry stretches backwards over an indefinite period. The accused is traced, perhaps, from his cradle to his prison; his early passions and youthful errors, as well as his matured opinions and habits, are all considered as so many circumstances from which presumptions as to his guilt or innocence of the particular charge against him may be drawn."

"In this way, although much must necessarily be left to the

discretion, good sense, and perspicacity of the judge, whether any, or what, weight is to be given to such presumptions; and although instances of gross abuse, arising from judicial blindness or wilful prejudice, do not unfrequently occur from the admission of much that is not evidence at all, in any legitimate sense, it cannot be denied that the ample and circumstantial detail, which is the result of these comprehensive examinations, gives to the annals of German and French criminal jurisprudence a completeness and connection, a regular and progressive interest, which it is vain to expect from the reports of similar proceedings in our own country."

You are no doubt aware that on the Continent, and in Germany especially, the subdivision of professional labour is carried much farther than amongst ourselves. There the management of criminal cases is entrusted mostly to a *special* class of medical men, singly or in conjunction. But what I think it most to the point to notice here is the very different position which the medical practitioner occupies in France and Germany to what he does in our criminal cases. In place of being subjected to a *viva voce* examination on the precognition or trial, at the preliminary investigation a series of written questions is put into his hands along with the written depositions of the witnesses and of the accused, and from the study of these he is required to give in writing his opinion of the case, with his reasons adduced at length, and the grounds on which he has based them; so that, in fact, their medical reports bear a close resemblance to the charge of the judge in our courts when summing up the evidence for the guidance of the jury.

This latitude allowed to medical jurists abroad renders the perusal of their accounts of criminal trials so instructive, particularly to the younger practitioner, that nothing which we possess on this subject can fill up the blank which our medico-legal literature presents so far as practical details are concerned. This, if nothing else, makes it the imperative duty of the teacher of medical jurisprudence to recommend to his hearers the study of the French and German languages if they should wish to reach eminence in this department of their profession.

In the above very brief outline of the forms of procedure in courts of law, my remarks have been confined to the practice of its criminal department, with which chiefly, though not exclusively, the medical practitioner has to do. There are other courts before which he is liable to be cited, namely, the Civil and

Ecclesiastical Courts. In these, however, the forms of procedure are not so peculiar, and differ so little in essentials from those to which I have just adverted, that, passing them over, I may at once proceed to the remaining point which I proposed to consider, namely—

II The precise character of the evidence, including the form it will have to take, which will be expected of the medical practitioner at the different stages of the legal investigations to which he is liable to be summoned

The points which fall to be discussed under this head, it may be well to premise, must necessarily be passed in review in a manner somewhat desultory and unconnected; but as it is a matter of notoriety that the want of familiarity with the points which I shall include under it, has been the cause of many a professional failure, leading to future regret on the part of the practitioner, I have to bespeak your special attention to the observations which succeed, while I attempt to follow the steps of the medical man from his first connection with a criminal investigation, up to the time of his leaving the witness-box, when his duties terminate; noticing *first*, the part of the investigation entrusted to the expert; *second*, his appearance at the precognition before the public prosecutor; and *third*, as a witness at the trial subsequently, when the proceedings are carried out by the law authorities The medical jurist is employed in criminal investigations in order to the elucidation of the strictly medical points of the case, whether as regards the living or the dead. Occasions of the former sort arise in connection with the charges of rape, abortion, pregnancy, etc, and of the latter kind with those of homicide, poisoning, etc In either case the expert, whether he has been previously connected with the case or otherwise, is directed by a warrant from a magistrate to follow out or to commence his inquiries into the facts and circumstances coming within his proper province, and to report in writing such facts and circumstances as he has thus acquired, and the conclusions which he has arrived at in regard to them. This report has to be drawn up in the form of a solemn affirmation, that is, to be given on *soul and conscience;* while abroad the oath is tendered to the expert at the outset of the proceedings, and is not again repeated during the investigation as amongst ourselves.

This investigation concluded, and his report handed in to the public prosecutor, the expert is usually called on to appear before him at the precognition or preliminary legal investigation

Whether a medical practitioner has thus already been connected with a criminal case, or from his acquaintance with it otherwise, he is able to throw light upon it, he cannot withhold his assistance at the precognition when duly cited for this purpose.

In this country (Scotland) the judge-examinator may grant warrant for calling witnesses for the precognition, and if necessary may put them on oath in order to elicit the truth. In case of their refusing or contumaciously declining to appear, fresh warrants may be issued to compel their attendance. When brought before the judge in like manner they may be coerced with imprisonment if they either refuse to answer questions at all, or answer in a manner plainly evasive or illusory.

This, it will be seen, renders it impossible for the practitioner to evade this duty in any instance of the least importance, though it is well known that some medical men are anxious to avoid it when they can succeed in doing so. The examinator on such occasions may tender a fee to the medical witness, but he rarely does so in this country in criminal cases.

In England the coroner and justices are in much the same position as the judge-examinator in Scotland. Till lately, medical men were summoned to the coroner's inquest, as other witnesses are, and were not allowed their expenses, nor were they expected to attend this court unless they chose. A recent enactment, however, while it empowers the coroner, on refusal to obey his summons, to sue the medical practitioner before the nearest justice and inflict a fine of £5 on him, secures to the medical witness, *when specially summoned*, a fee of one guinea for simple attendance, or two where a post-mortem inspection or a chemical analysis is required.

The only exception to the payment of the medical witness secured by this Act, is in the case of a person dying in a public hospital, lunatic asylum, or other public institution endowed or supported by voluntary subscriptions, in which circumstances the medical officer of such institution is not entitled to claim payment for his services (6 and 7 Will. IV cap. 89).

The fees paid to medical men for investigations ordered by the English magistrates are not fixed by statutes, but are subject to local regulations. Unless a party charged be committed for trial fees are not commonly allowed, except where a previous arrangement to that effect has been made. A magistrate in England can compel a medical practitioner to attend before him to give evidence of the facts within his knowledge. He cannot, however, compel him to make an analysis or undertake any extraordinary investigation demanding time and skill. If an analysis be made without any previous stipulation, and the prisoner be not committed for trial, the medical practitioner will probably receive no fee for the analysis. If the prisoner be committed for trial, the fee is secured by an order from the judge at the trial.

Unfavourable as is the position of the medical witness occasionally in this country—liable to be called away from his home and stated avocations, it may be at some pecuniary sacrifice—that of the practitioner in the United States appears to be worse. His attendance while compulsory, does not entitle him in criminal cases to any fee, whether cited either for the prosecution or the defence.

In that country the medical man may be called in for the elucidation of the case in certain instances. Thus we find it stated by Croker, that where the attendance of the coroner cannot be procured within twelve hours after the discovery of a dead body under suspicious circumstances a Justice of the Peace is authorised to hold an inquest, and where the cause of death is not apparent, to associate with himself a regularly qualified physician, to make a sufficient examination for the discovery of the cause of death.

The scientific evidence on the precognition in Scotland usually consists of two parts—the written report of the medical men engaged in the case, and their answers to interrogatories put to them with the view of further eliciting the whole of the particulars.

In some cases the report alone is called for. This document is also made a production on the trial. It must, as I have said, bear to be on soul and conscience, and embrace a distinct statement of the facts of the case so far as they came under the personal notice of the reporters, with their opinions strictly deduced therefrom, succinctly but clearly stated. A little consideration as to the aim and destination of the report suffices to show the absolute necessity of attention to all this. Intended as it must be to come before non-medical persons, and to serve for their guidance, its language must be such as they can follow, and its facts and inferences must be clearly stated and very carefully kept apart, so that the latter shall be readily seen to be such as are built upon and logically flow from the former.

It is advisable in every case to preserve a duplicate of the medico-legal report, as after it is once given into the hands of the law authorities, the witness will have no opportunity of seeing it again till it is given to him to be read to the court and jury at the trial, it may be six or seven months afterwards, should the case be proceeded with.

When, as is usual, the medical witness, besides delivering his written report, is further interrogated along with the other witnesses, the evidence thus elicited is taken down in writing, and the whole signed by him.

In any case of importance, or where the precognition has embraced topics or opinions of a doubtful or difficult kind, it is well for the witness to note down as soon after as possible the substance of the evidence then given. This will assist his memory and may prevent discrepancies appearing at the trial, originating in forgetfulness or subsequent impressions—discrepancies which would be immediately detected by the public prosecutor, who holds in his hands and examines from those very notes of evidence formerly given and signed by the witness. It is chiefly from ignorance of, or inattention to this, that we are to trace several of those complaints on the part of medical witnesses of the harshness or want of consideration of the public prosecutor or the bench, and it is scarcely to be wondered at that the examiner should have his temper tried, and vent his spleen on the witness when his testimony is seen to conflict with or not to bear out his previous deposition.

Before the precognition takes place the medical witness should take care to make himself fully master of the case in all its bearings, and not leave this necessary duty to be completed when the trial is coming on, as is too often done; for it is not unusual for the medical jurist to be even more closely examined on the precognition than at the trial, and hence he may be called upon in court to go over again the evidence previously adduced, as occasionally happens, in a careless and unguarded manner, and without due consideration on his part. Besides, it is not an unfrequent thing for the disputed points, or those on which the whole of the proof ultimately turns, to be broached at the precognition. Hence it may happen that opinions advanced by the witness on that occasion may require to be modified or even departed from at the trial, a procedure certain to call down on him the censure of the Bench.

An instance in point occurred in Aberdeen some years ago. A person was murdered by one of a gang of gipsies in the county. The two medical men who were called to the deceased were shown at the precognition a pocket anvil with which they testified that the mortal wound might have been inflicted. One of the medical gentlemen, however, when examined in court, declared that, on reflection, he had altered his previous opinion, and now thought that the wound could not have been inflicted by the anvil. For this vacillation he was severely reflected on by the presiding judge, though this gentleman had been highly complimented in the same quarter for his appearance in a case of importance previously.

The error here lay in the witness not having sufficiently weighed the evidence before adducing his opinion at the precognition.

As an additional reason for enforcing a due preparation for the duties of the medical witness at the precognition, it may be proper to mention that his evidence will be reviewed critically by the Crown Counsel, who very frequently submit it to the judgment of an experienced medical jurist at head-quarters before deciding to take up the case. Should the evidence therefore be imperfect, or the opinions elicited be unsatisfactory or incorrect, the Crown Counsel have it in their power to summon additional medical testimony, and thus a skilful practitioner may be brought forward to complete the imperfect, or overturn the erroneous, testimony of the original witness, rendering the position of the latter, if incompetent, a very undesirable one.

If all this were kept in mind, we should find medical witnesses coming to investigations of this kind with something of the same special preparation with which we find them provided in other departments of the profession. The general practitioner, for instance, does not, as a matter of course, undertake a rare and difficult surgical or obstetrical operation where his previous training and professional routine have lain in a direction altogether different, though he will not hesitate to engage in a medico-legal case with whose bearings he has had no opportunity of making himself previously acquainted. This arises from the circumstance of medical men in ordinary practice failing to perceive any speciality in the class of questions likely to come before them in inquiries at law bearing on medical science; inquiries often very different from those with which they are apt to be conversant in the ordinary sphere of their strictly professional avocations.

As it is indispensable for the interests both of public justice and private freedom that the public should have no means of knowing what is going forward at the precognition, the medical witness should consider the evidence he has given as a matter to be kept private till the trial is over

I once heard a very trying question put to a medical witness in court who had been rather free beforehand in discussing the character of the crime as gathered from his knowledge of the Crown proceedings. The question he was compelled on oath to answer, though very mortifying to himself.

It is of the very highest importance both to the success and expedition of a criminal trial that the witnesses should be able to speak at once, and without hesitation, to the articles produced in evidence against the accused, which they have previously identified when examined in precognition. There is no method of securing this which can be relied on but by signing sealed labels affixed to the articles, when they can speedily identify the signature, and thereby feel assured that it is the article to which their declaration, whatever it may be, bears reference.

A lethal weapon, for example, is exhibited to the medical man on the precognition. His signature or initials on sealed label at once convince him that it is the individual instrument which he formerly saw, when produced to him again at the trial.

Once more it may be proper to mention that, in addition to the precognition by the Crown lawyers, the agent or counsel for the prisoner is entitled to precognosce the medical witness, nor is he at liberty to refuse to answer any interrogatories thus put. It may not be amiss for him on this occasion to procure an exact copy of his evidence, and of the questions then put to him, in order to obviate the chance of his words being twisted or distorted by the agent for the defence.

The remarks adduced for the guidance of the medical jurist on the precognition apply in substance to the professional witness called to the coroner's inquest in England. These inquests are not conducted in a way to satisfy the profession. Their grand defect lies in the very imperfect data on which the judgment of the jury is mostly founded. By the provisions of the Coroners' Act, no test of skill and experience, nor any proof of the possession of medical and legal knowledge, is demanded of the candidate for this important office; while again it is left to the discretion of the coroner and jury to employ medical testimony or to dispense with it, as they think fit. Further, the law has made it an onerous charge to the coroner to receive medical evidence under any circumstances, and accordingly it is scrupulously avoided when the omission to call for it can be passed over with any show of decency

The consequences of this are such as might have been anticipated. Thus we find by the Registrar General's reports in a single year (1841) as many as 6708 sudden deaths becoming the subject of coroners' inquests, in which the causes of death were not ascertained.

When he does happen to be called to such courts, the medical practitioner should be aware of the importance of his position, which is often a more serious one than he is apt to imagine from what he may frequently witness taking place around him. "The appearance of the jury," remarks Dr Cumming, "often a set of tradesmen hastily collected, and in their working clothes; the place, perhaps a village alehouse; and the coroner, some obscure county attorney, are all circumstances liable to throw the medical jurist off his guard. If the case is reported for trial, however, the evidence then and there given will have to be gone over before the assizes, the judge sitting on which will have the former depositions of the witness before him, comparing them with the testimony now adduced." In accordance, too, with the "Prisoners' Counsel Act," to which I lately alluded, his depositions are now in the hands of the prisoner's advocate. It may be conceived in how peculiar a situation the medical man is liable to be placed should his second thoughts prove to be at variance with those hastily given by him in the first instance, and especially if, through his means, the prisoner have been in jail perhaps for months on a charge of which it now turns out that he is not guilty. Nor will the compunction of the medical witness in such a position be lessened by the consideration on his part, that had he died between the inquest and the trial his depositions might have led to the condemnation of the accused.

LECTURE II

MEDICAL EVIDENCE—*Concluded*

POSITION OF THE EXPERT ON THE TRIAL—Refusal to give Evidence—Fees for Attendance—Nature of the expected Evidence—Hearsay Testimony—Parole Evidence—Dying Declarations—Evidence tending to Degrade or Criminate the Witness—Evidence which may subject him to Civil Liabilities—Reference to Notes or Memoranda—Volunteering Evidence—Agreement on Points of Evidence—Willing and Costive Witnesses—Use of Technical Language—Demeanour towards Counsel and the Court—Position of the Witness in Court

At last lecture our medico-legal course was commenced with a brief notice of the occasions on which the medical practitioner may have to assist in the elucidation of legal questions, and the kind of evidence which may be expected of him under such circumstances.

Having touched on these topics, I proceeded to another, which, though preliminary, required to be adverted to before intelligently entering on the discussion of the various individual questions which make up the science of Forensic Medicine. With this view I had to notice, in a general way—*First*, The criminal institutions of Scotland; *Second*, Those of England; *Third*, Those of our colonies and of the United States of America; *Fourth*, Those of France; and *Lastly*, Those of Germany.

Proposing next to follow the course of the medical jurist on the separate occasions in which his services as an expert are likely to be required, I had only time to advert to his part in the precognition in Scotland, and at the coroner's inquest in England. I now come to the consideration of his position on his appearance at the trial.

In Scotland the medical witness is summoned by a writ delivered at his residence. If the fact of a witness having been duly cited, and failing to appear, is made out to the Court, they will, on the application either of the procurator or of the panel, who may desire his testimony, grant warrant for his apprehension or incarceration till he finds caution to appear and give evidence, in order to secure his attendance at the next diet of the trial.

The witness who, after due citation, fails to attend, or offer a sufficient excuse, is in the first instance subjected to a fine or *unlaw*, as it is called, of a hundred merks Scots (about £5), and that equally whether he has been cited personally or at his dwelling-house. In addition to this the court, upon such *prima facie* evidence being submitted to them of disobedience to the law, will grant warrant for the apprehension of the witness, and his imprisonment, till liberated in due course of law. From this imprisonment he can only be delivered by the judge on his setting forth his contrition, and offering caution to appear and give evidence.

The fee for attendance on the High Court, Circuit, or Sheriff Criminal Courts, is a guinea a day if held in the town in which the medical witness resides. When he is summoned from a distance two guineas are allowed him for each day of attendance, as well as for each day occupied in coming to and going from the Court to his place of residence, and a guinea a day additional for travelling expenses.

In England witnesses are summoned by what is called a *subpœna*, that is, a summons issued by the proper authority, which must be attended to under pain of consequences.

The fees allowed for attendance at the Assizes are one guinea, and in some cases two guineas per diem. A small sum per mile is allowed under the head of travelling expenses. Special fees of a higher amount can be obtained only by an order from the judge. Very strong reasons, however, must be shown for departing from the usual course.

When called into court to give evidence, the witness is first sworn to tell the truth, the whole truth, and nothing but the truth, words admirably calculated to impress him with the solemnity of the occasion, as well as to prevent concealment on his part. Those of the Protestant Church, whether Episcopalian, Presbyterian, or Dissenter, are all sworn standing uncovered, with the right hand held up, but Roman Catholics are sworn holding the right hand on a cross drawn in pencil or chalk on the gospels. It used to be incumbent on every witness, excepting Quakers, to take the oath, and if he declined he might be summarily imprisoned by order of the court, but now, by 26 and 27 Vic. cap. 85, sec. 1, any person alleging conscientious scruples against being sworn, may make a solemn declaration instead.

In Scotland the form of swearing, the administration of the oath being entrusted only to the judge, is much more solemn and impressive than the brief and flippant fashion of imposing this obligation by a police officer or crier in an English court.

Immediate or direct testimony, and the inferences flowing from it, as formerly stated, constitute the kinds of evidence received in law on the part of the medical witness; hearsay evidence, or testimony at second-hand, being in the general case inadmissible. It is, however, admitted under certain exceptional circumstances. (*Vide* Alison, *Criminal Law of Scotland*.) Hearsay is allowed, for instance, in our practice, in regard to the account which a person who has received a mortal wound has given of the manner in which he was injured, and that not only on a death-bed, or under the impression of death, or the sanction of an oath, but at any time between the wound and the death, provided only it was done seriously and deliberately, and at a time when the deceased appeared to be aware of what he was saying, and in the possession of his faculties.

In England, likewise, the dying declaration of the deceased in cases of murder, that is to say, the declaration made under the apprehension of death, has always been regarded as admissible evidence, but with this exception, English law does not admit verbal proof of the statements of the deceased unless these were made before a magistrate, and in the presence of the prisoner.

The principle on which this exception from the general rule of evidence is founded is partly that the awful situation of the dying person is considered to be as powerful on his conscience as the obligation of an oath, and partly that the absence of interested motives in one who is on the verge of the next world is supposed to dispense with the necessity of cross-examination.

The correctness of this principle, in the general case, may perhaps be conceded, but it should be borne in mind that exceptions are liable to occur occasionally, however rarely.

In one instance which came under my own notice, a female, who died from the action of abortives, on her deathbed accused a clergyman of being the father of the child with which she had been pregnant, though he was able to establish an *alibi* at the time the conception must have taken place.

Mr Amos refers to a melancholy illustration of the same point, that of Richard Coleman executed for the rape and murder of Ann Green in 1749. Coleman was convicted on the dying declarations of the woman, but his innocence was established two years afterwards, when another person was executed for the same offence upon the clearest evidence. This mistake, Mr

Amos thinks, was most likely a mistake of identity, but he adds this important remark, that some persons, even in their dying moments, will exaggerate and blacken the offence of an individual to whom they attribute the loss of life. Human passions, he justly remarks, do not always quit their empire over man though upon the verge of the grave.

Dying declarations are usually proved by medical men, and the proof of them imposes great responsibility on the medical practitioner. Every word said to or by the deceased, and the order of the conversation, ought to be related with the greatest precision, and the *ipsissima verba* of the statement should be given as nearly as possible. Hence every medical man who is aware of this will not fail to have his attention more alive on such awful occasions than one who does not know the necessity for such very accurate observation, and he will seize the very earliest opportunity, while the circumstances are fresh in his memory, to commit them to writing, for he will be allowed to refresh his memory with such memoranda in the witness-box, provided they are made out at the time of the transaction, or as soon after as possible. In every instance too in which the dying declaration is heard by a third party, if a person of any intelligence, he should be asked to adhibit his signature to the writing at the time it is made out.

On occasions of this sort however the medical man should be careful not to overdo his part. "From my experience in courts of justice," says Mr Amos, "I am enabled to say that on such occasions medical men are sometimes not only too inattentive, but they are on the other hand sometimes too officious, interrogating the dying man as to the facts connected with his death, suggesting circumstances, and pressing him to a fuller account. All this," he adds, "has a bad look, and exposes the medical man to much unpleasant remark and thwarts the object of justice."

To be entitled to weight, dying declarations ought to be voluntary, and least of all should they consist of a mere assent to circumstances suggested, mere answers of yes or no to the questions of others, called *leading a witness*, and which would not be allowed even when a witness delivers his testimony, subject to all the checks upon it, when he comes forward in the court.

I will merely further add on the subject of dying declarations, that to make them receivable it is not necessary that the deceased should have expressed any apprehension of danger for his consciousness of approaching death may be inferred from the nature of the wound, or the state of illness, or other circumstances of the case. This imposes upon the medical man who has to give evidence respecting a dying declaration the necessity of being able to give a very clear account of the precise situation and degree of danger of the deceased at the time the declaration was made.

In adducing his testimony, the medical witness is not at liberty to withhold any information which may bear on the case, in whatever way it has been acquired. On this principle it has been held that a practitioner is even bound to disclose the secrets divulged to him in the course of his professional attendance, however much it is to be lamented that such disclosures should be made the subjects of judicial publication.

There can be no doubt that the medical man who voluntarily violates the confidence reposed in him by his patient acts dishonourably, but it is equally clear that he cannot withhold the fact if called upon to disclose it in a court of justice; an appeal to the bench is the only safeguard to the medical man's honour, and by its decision alone can he be guided as to how much of the information thus acquired is to be disclosed, and what, from its irrelevancy, he can be allowed to withhold.

Both in Scottish and English practice it is settled that a witness cannot be compelled to answer any question which may expose him to a penalty, or to a criminal charge.

A surgeon who goes out with parties about to fight a duel is liable to be punished criminally if it can be proved that he knew the duel was to take place. He is supposed in that case to be an aider and abettor of the crime, a charge against which the plea of his having acted merely in his professional capacity will not shield him. In giving evidence on the prosecution of the survivor, where death has followed, he may refuse to criminate himself.

A witness may also refuse to answer any question tending to degrade either his moral or professional character, unless the question forms any part of the issue, in which case he is obliged to give evidence, however strongly it may reflect on his character; but in all matters irrelevant to the investigation at issue he may legally refuse to answer.

The competency of asking these questions on the one hand, and the witness's privilege of declining to answer them on the other, seem to be established.

A medical witness on a trial for rape, was asked on cross-examination, if he had been in the way of having connection with the woman said to have been ravished. He hesitated for some time whether to answer or not, when it occurred to him to ask if he must answer the question, and on being assured that he need not do so unless he chose, as if feeling relieved, he spoke out· 'Then I refuse to answer"

It is frequently made a question whether a witness on a trial may refer to notes or memoranda to assist his memory. On this subject the rule in law is, that notes or memoranda made up by the witness at the moment or recently after the fact may be looked to in order to refresh his memory, but if they were made up at the distance of weeks or months afterwards they are not admissible. It is accordingly usual for the witness to look to memoranda made at the time, of dates, distances, appearances on dead bodies, and the like, before emitting his testimony, or even to read such notes to the jury as his evidence, he having first sworn that they were made up at the time, and faithfully done.

It is not necessary that the memoranda should be made up by the witness himself, if made at the time under his inspection. But a witness cannot assist his memory by a memorandum which another person has made, and which he did not inspect at the time it was being made, or at least speedily afterwards. The not adverting to this distinction occasioned a great deal of floundering in Dr Granville's evidence at the celebrated Gardiner Peerage case. On that occasion it was further settled that the production of notes could only be allowed when the witness used them merely to refresh his memory, and that if the transaction or facts noted had completely escaped the witness's memory, so that all he could testify to the court was as to what he found in his notes, they could not be allowed. The admissibility of reference to a written paper here would be held as annihilating the value of parole evidence, and converting a jury trial into the consideration of written instruments.

The general rule as to the inadmissibility of written evidence is however departed from in the case of medical or other scientific reports or certificates, which are lodged in process before the trial, and libelled on as productions in the indictment, and which the witness is allowed to read as his deposition to the jury, confirming at its close by a declaration on oath that it is a true report.

The reason of this further exception is founded on the consideration that the medical or other scientific facts or appearances which are the subject of such a report, are generally so minute and detailed, that they cannot with safety be entrusted to the memory of the witness, but that much more reliance may be placed on a report made out by him at the time when the facts and appearances were fresh in his recollection while the medical or scientific witness has no personal interest in the matter, and from his situation and rank in life is much less liable to suspicion than those of an inferior class, or those intimately connected with the transaction in question. Such reports to be admissible must not contain other than scientific points, such as conversations with the deceased, or the like, nor does their reception excuse the practitioner from being examined like the other witnesses on the other facts of the case.

Where the report is found to embody a series of circumstances or transactions, such as the narrative of a protracted case of illness, the account will be received as more trustworthy if made out from day to day as the symptoms occurred than if only drawn up at its conclusion. The report should be written by the medical witness in his own handwriting.

It has now become a matter of notoriety that on occasions of interesting and important trials there are found medical men who, when their evidence has neither been sought nor desired, will step forwards to volunteer their services on the defence. Now, without stopping here to remark on the despicable character of the motives which in many instances prompt to the seeking of such displays in the courts of law, I shall at present content myself with merely suggesting a few reasons wherefore the medical man who values duly his comfort and respectability, not to speak of the good opinion of his professional brethren, should hesitate before rashly and unadvisedly committing himself to a course which must necessarily lead to the pitting himself at a great disadvantage against the medical witnesses on the opposite side.

As the prosecution of crime is now managed in Scotland, no cases are brought forward in courts of law by the public prosecutor but such as he has reason to believe admit of proof of a kind that will carry conviction to the minds of an intelligent jury, and satisfy the judge that he has acted fairly by the culprit. On the other hand, in undertaking the defence the defending barrister only concerns himself with the task of finding out flaws in the evidence or obtaining conflicting opinions on the facts of the case. It is in the latter direction especially that he looks for his chance of success, and here it is, above all in cases involving medical questions, that success is oftenest secured. Having no concern with the truth of the matter, he is careful to mould the witness to his purpose by drawing him into admissions based not upon the whole of the data possessed by him, but upon partial or garbled statements such as alone he is careful to bring forward and arrange in his own way. Wherever the profession has been found to differ as to the interpretation of facts, he will endeavour to bring such conflicting views into strong prominence if he cannot further get the witness to commit himself to the side, whether correct or not, that best serves the interest of his client. Now, as the medical witness for the defence has not the facilities of the Crown witness for arriving at the truth, nor even the data on which a full and correct judgment can be formed on the points in question, he is almost certain either to come short of the truth or to take the wrong side; and, once so committed, he must be ready either to modify or reverse his judgments on the cross-examination, or to stick to his previous opinion in the face of facts and circumstances brought out before him in a more complete form, or as counterbalanced and overborne, it may be contradicted, by others of which before he was not at all aware. In circumstances such as these some honesty of purpose, as well as readiness of mind, and no slight intimacy with the bearing of difficult and disputed points in medicine, are demanded of the witness in proceeding on the spur of the moment, with no time for reflection, and under the jealous eyes of the judge, prosecutor, and jury, to rearrange his ideas and modify or alter his previous judgments, qualifications for the exercise of which task few medical practitioners have had favourable opportunities of acquiring.

By the way, it may be proper to warn you here, that although the chances of getting into a false position are chiefly on the side of the witness for the defence, the Crown witness, with less excuse, may fall into the same snare. He too must take care that the public prosecutor does not lead him to speak decisively upon points which rest at best on a doubtful foundation, or to become a partisan on the side on which he is cited. If he does so the counsel for the defence will at once perceive his error and avail himself of it in the cross-examination which he will institute.

The question has been frequently mooted as to what is the proper line of conduct to be pursued by a medical witness towards his professional brethren when summoned to take the opposite side from them in a trial. I shall suppose that the citation has not been procured at the solicitation of the witness himself. Cases may indeed occur in which the practitioner would not only be justified in coming forward in this way, but would even be culpible in shrinking from a task required of him by a sense of public justice and honour; as where the parties entrusted with the management of a case have been guilty of culpable negligence, have displayed gross ignorance of their duty, or have been actuated by improper motives, to the danger of perverting justice or injuring innocent individuals.

In every other conceivable situation the professional man will best study his own comfort and respectability as well as the public interest, by reserving his services till they are called for on sufficient grounds. When they are so, and he comes to be placed in opposition to his professional brethren, even in the worst imaginable case, some delicacy is called for on his part in dealing with the character, the opinions, and the practice of his medical opponents. In such a position everything savouring of triumph or gratification, or having the appearance of contempt or disrespect, should be carefully avoided, particularly where the parties on the side of the prosecution are known to have done their best to arrive at the truth.

The workings of that contemptible rivalry and jealousy which are so readily fostered betwixt village practitioners was exhibited some years ago at a circuit court in which I was present.

A country surgeon had been called into consultation by a rival practitioner in the case of a man who died soon afterwards, from a blow received in a quarrel. On the trial he was asked, "When called in, did you approve of the treatment which had been adopted?" His answer was, "No!" "Did you disapprove of it, sir?" "No!!" By the judge—"What! did you neither approve nor disapprove of it?" "No!!!"

By his demeanour it was sufficiently evident that this witness looked with contempt on his colleague, in this case a rather dissipated and low character, and that his conduct was dictated by a desire to exalt himself at his expense. If so, the reception of this part of his evidence must have shown him his mistake; it was indeed anything but complimentary.

It must be obvious that consultations betwixt witnesses previous to the trial would not only add to the value of their evidence but tend also to secure a better feeling and more mutual respect among the parties. When summoned upon *opposite* sides it is perhaps hardly to be expected, in the present state of the profession, that they should thus meet and voluntarily explain their respective views of the case in hand, though we can see no good grounds for excusing the distrust and jealousy which constantly arise between the parties opposed to each other on such occasions. When summoned on the same side there are no obstacles to their meeting together and discussing the bearings of the case before tendering their evidence. It is not at all meant by this that there should be any collusion or agreement in a story, but merely that the witnesses should have the opportunity of comparing their respective opinions and the grounds on which they have been formed. "Intelligent and honest men," says Dr. Percival, "fully acquainted with their respective means of information, are much less likely to differ than when no previous communication has taken place."

Much mutual forbearance is necessary in such cases when the parties hold different opinions upon important points. This, however, is only likely to be the case where the individuals contrast widely with each other in mental endowments and acquired information; and where such is the case, if the better informed and more intelligent can succeed in overcoming the prejudices and avoid exposing the deficiencies of his colleague without offending his *amour propre*, the differences between them may disappear and unanimity be happily secured.

A good plan for getting rid of such disagreement is to go over the facts of the case, with the assistance of the best authorities, when, by referring to them at every stage, a wrongheaded and obstinate colleague will give in to those who might not be disposed to yield to anything that might be advanced by one who, though better fitted to deal with the points in question, was deemed by him as otherwise, at best, but his equal in professional rank and reputation.

In referring to the use of authorities in coming to a common understanding amongst witnesses in consultation before appearing to give evidence at a trial, it is necessary to warn you against the mistake of trusting too much to these, or expecting more from such references than merely to ascertain what the inferences are to which the facts of the case would legitimately lead, if properly understood and appreciated, in the hands of men of skill in this special department.

Authorities, it should be known, in the hands of counsel on a trial are two-edged weapons, and may be turned against the witness. For while barristers are very ready to parade an array of authors wherewith to confute the facts and opinions advanced by the expert, the latter may not always be permitted to strengthen his evidence from the same source. On the contrary, it may be

...opted to cut him off altogether from such appeal, and to restrict him to the fruits of his own individual observation and experience. I need not say that this course is scarcely a fair one on the part of the legal profession. They are not entitled to expect in every instance that the expert, in tendering evidence, should state nothing but what has come to him through his own experience. Were professional witnesses always thus restricted, their sphere would be a very narrow one, for who, it has been asked, could or should venture to offer an opinion on any difficult point that has not been adopted from or confirmed by the experience of others.

The professional witness who has to appear in courts of law, should be aware that those employed in the conduct of the case strictly limit themselves to bringing out those points in it which they expect to bear upon the conclusions they hope to establish to the satisfaction of the judge and jury. Hence the witness, remembering this, should confine himself to tendering that part of the evidence which is asked of him, without concerning himself with the purport of his testimony. This should be done by him patiently, distinctly, and tersely, neither indulging in a flow of words, nor unduly attempting their restriction within too narrow bounds. The object of the inquiry will thus be answered, his testimony will be taken down by the presiding judge accurately and readily, and extraneous matters excluded from the trial. Should, however, it thus happen, that after having replied to the several questions put to him by the counsel on both sides, the court, and the jury, the whole truth had not been elicited, and any material points had remained to be disclosed by the witness, the course for him to follow would be to disclose these to the judge, who, in the circumstances, would be found readily to admit and gratefully to receive any additions and explanations which might be really essential to the ends of truth and justice.

Again, the language of the witness under examination should not only be direct and concise, and any qualification which it may demand reserved till after the evidence has been given. It must also be uttered in a tone of voice sufficiently loud, or, rather, clearly enunciated, to be heard by all in court, and in terms intelligible by those to whom it is addressed. An eminent judge, we are told by Dr. Taylor, has been known to declare that there are no witnesses so difficult to be heard and understood as those of the medical profession.

On this last point—intelligible language—a pertinent piece of

as has been intended to Dr. Amos, namely "that the witness should drop, as much as possible, the language which is known only to scientific men, and adopt that which is in popular use. If you have occasion to speak of a person fainting," he continues, "do not say, as I have heard it said, that you found the patient in a state of *syncope*, and you must not expect a Court of Justice to understand you if you talk of a person being *comatose*, or of the appearance of his stomach being *highly vascular*, or of your having discovered poisonous ingredients in his stomach by means of a *delicate test*. The judge and counsel are generally very shallow men of science, and it is a great advantage to them to raise a laugh at persons whom they would represent to be using hard names for common things. Veterinary surgeons are a great game for counsel, as I remember in particular a veterinary surgeon who, when cross-examined by Serjeant Vaughan, was so unfortunate as to make use of the term *suspensory ligament*, which the serjeant interpreted a *hangman's noose*."

Such hard names for common things continue to be the rule rather than the exception in medical reports coming before Courts of Law. Out of a number of such reports, I may cite a few illustrations in one I perused lately, where, within the compass of a dozen short sentences, no fewer than thirty-one such terms were encountered, as abdomen, cuticle, clavicle, scrotum, mesial line, sutures, periosteum, fontanelle, dura mater, arachnoid membrane, etc., terms for which equivalent expressions in English might readily have been obtained, such as belly, scarf-skin, collar-bone, etc.

With the notice of one other point and the reflections to which it gives rise, I shall conclude these introductory remarks. I refer to the circumstance of medical witnesses losing their temper and retaliating by abuse, when subjected to what they consider rude and unbecoming treatment from the counsel.

The witness should remember and make allowance for the latitude conceded in practice to the examining counsel, who has, moreover, usually the sympathy of the court and jury on his side. The respective positions too of the witness and counsel are *different*, the former being in court to speak on oath to facts, and to the inferences founded on them, when this is sought from him; the latter is expected, as a part of his duty to his client, to negative if possible the one and to twist the other, moulding both to the interests of the person he represents.

Frequent of late, in England, and especially in Ireland, as has seen the occurrences of bickerings betwixt the barrister and the medical witness, and the often really insolent tone of the one towards the other, yet truth compels me to say that, on these occasions, the blame has been mostly attributable to the practitioner, who has either gone farther in his evidence than was justifiable by the facts of the case, or has enunciated his opinions without their being sought for, or pressed them too positively or dogmatically on the court. Faults of this kind on the part of the practitioner have been committed in ignorance of much that it behoved him previously to have known and considered, and which are seldom taken into account by the inexperienced witness.

In the *first* place, the fact should not be overlooked that while, by the constitution of the British law, medical evidence is less required, and has less importance assigned to it here, than in most other European countries, and in theory, at least, is ignored in certain mixed questions, such as the existence of insanity in connection with criminal charges, and the capacity of individuals so affected for the management of their affairs, medical men, on the other hand, have gone to the opposite extreme, and have been disposed to exact for professional testimony a degree of importance, and a directness of bearing on legal inquiries, which neither the Bench nor the community has been disposed to concede to it.

Secondly, the value and directness of medical evidence have been lessened by the facility with which differences of opinion have often hitherto been elicited from professional witnesses on questions even of the very highest importance; discrepancies which have been at once set down to the defects of the science itself, instead of being looked on as evidence of partial acquaintance on the part of some of the witnesses with the subject on hand, or their inexperience of the real bearings of their evidence on the expected event of the trial.

Thirdly, it has been remarked, to the prejudice of the profession, that unbiassed testimony has been less easily procurable in the case of medical questions in law than in others of a different kind. This has, as we have already seen, has been but too prominently exhibited in the demeanour of the witness towards his professional brethren on the opposite side at the trial, and in their total neglect of previous consultation and comparison of opinions. On some occasions, however, the bias of the witness has been markedly exhibited in a shape unfortunately still more unfavourable to the weight of his testimony, as where the medical practitioner has shown an undue anxiety to procure the investigation of a case which has come under his notice in the course of his ordinary practice, whether from motives of humanity, from love of justice, or from the less excusable desire on his part of thus obtaining a little notoriety. Now I need scarcely say that the medical man is deserting his true place in society when, leaving his duty of attending the sick, he seeks to usurp the place of the public prosecutor, by urging on, or taking a part uninvited in a criminal prosecution, or in the collection of evidence. All that he is called on to do when he has become cognisant of crime in his professional capacity, and where he would be in danger of being held as a *socius criminis* by concealing what he knows of it, is at once to intimate his suspicions or information to the nearest relatives of his patient, or, failing them, to the nearest magistrate, with whom it would properly rest to give information to the authorities, by whom his evidence would be sought for officially if wanted.

In ignorance of such circumstances as these, and of one or two others to which I had occasion previously to advert, it has happened, as was to have been anticipated, that the position of the inexpert and inexperienced witness has occasionally been anything but a desirable and comfortable one, though on this point there has been some exaggeration on the part of medical writers. Take, as an example, the published sentiments of Dr Gordon Smith, which have been quoted with approbation by other medical authors:—"I fear not to assert,' he writes, "that the instances in which it has happened that medical witnesses have come down from any judicial examination of importance without suffering more or less injury, have not been many; that those in which credit has been actually gained have been fewer still; and that I know of no instance in which it can be satisfactorily shown that an individual reputation has been thereby established."

"There is hardly a situation in which a medical man can be placed that so powerfully menaces his reputation, and none where so much personal uneasiness is endured. The medical witness is too frequently rendered miserable and inefficient for the purposes of justice from the novelty and perplexities of a situation so different from that in which he is generally placed in the ordinary exercise of his profession. There is often but little apparent difference, it has been said, between the situation of the witness and that of the criminal."

What admixture of truth there may be in the above statements, and in others to the same purport in other medical authors, after they have been cleared of their over-colouring, is not, however, to be got rid of by the easy process they have had recourse to, of casting all the blame on the lawyers. Not a little of it is, as we have seen, attributable to the witness himself, whose fault it must have been, not that of others, if he has come into court to speak on a subject on which he was but partially informed, and to emit judgments, *ex cathedra*, on questions, the grounds of which he was unprepared for explaining and defending. It may be true, as contended for, that the lawyers may attempt to browbeat the medical witness, or to draw out from him admissions of a self-contradictory kind, which they may use with effect against him; but all the time the examining counsel is under the eye of the court, whose duty and interest it is to see that the witness has fair play, and that his testimony is not twisted into the support of falsehood and error.

That, on the other hand, undue advantage is not sometimes taken of the inexperience of the medical practitioner, and the necessarily unsettled character of some of the opinions elicited from him under examination, I am by no means prepared to deny, though I think it is our duty to see that the conclusions drawn from such an admission should not be strained too far. It rests with ourselves to obviate, as we best may, such defects, so far as they are avoidable and removable; and, while we seek to take advantage of opportunities, as they arise, of accustoming ourselves to speak in public on fitting occasions, we should also strive to acquire the necessary lessons of how best to discriminate clearly in our own minds, and how we may most readily enable others to discriminate between what is certain and what is uncertain in medicine, and so to conduct ourselves in these difficult circumstances when placed in the witness-box, as to exhibit clearly the distinction betwixt the evidence of the qualified and the unqualified practitioner when bringing forward their respective testimonies; and much, I am happy to say, has been done, and is daily being done, in these directions by medical jurists. For, although there are points still unsettled in forensic medicine, and of these not a few, there are many others which have been clearly traced out and settled on a more secure basis than that on which much of our knowledge in medical science generally has hitherto been seen to rest. This has been accomplished, I need scarcely say, in this department of our science by the careful sifting of its difficult and doubtful points, by the painstaking endeavours which have been employed in the elimination of every possible source of error in its conclusions, in laying down with precision the boundaries which mark off the positive on the one side from the uncertain on the other, and in thus placing in separate and distinct categories the probable, the possible, and the actual, alike in fact and in opinion.

LECTURE III.

CLASSIFICATION OF THE SUBJECTS EMBRACED BY A COURSE OF LEGAL MEDICINE

Age, in its Medico-Legal Relations—Occasions for the Inquiry—Periods fixed in Law for Special Purposes—Data for the Determination of the Age—In the Dead—Arbitrary or Artificial Data—Physiological Data—At and before Birth—From Birth to the Forty-fifth Day of Extra-uterine Life—From Early Infancy to Manhood or Womanhood—At Later Periods—In the Living—In Infancy—In Childhood—In Pueritia—In Adult Age—In Declining or Old Age.

THE general scope of the topics, the sum of which constitutes the science of Legal Medicine, may be seen at a glance by a bare enumeration of the subjects which will have to be passed under review by us in all their details, and which, for all practical purposes, may be classed under one or other of the following heads:—

I. We have the class of medico-legal questions arising in connection with the *Age* of different persons.

II. Those bearing upon their different *Sexes*.

III. We have a set of inquiries which originate in differences between individuals at diverse periods of life, or the means we possess for fixing the *Identity* of the living and dead.

IV. We have the large class of questions relating to the generative functions—namely, *Impotence* and *Sterility* in the male and female; and in the latter, the investigations connected with charges of *Rape*, and with the occurrences of *Pregnancy*, *Delivery*, the *Birth* of children, and the *Destruction of the New-born Infant*.

V. We have to encounter a set of questions relating to the *Intellectual* and *Moral Powers*, in their varied states of derangement, as affecting the mental capacity and responsibility of individuals.

VI. We have to take into account *Diseases* in one of their special aspects, and to determine the best methods of discriminating betwixt *actual* and *assumed* disorders.

VII. and lastly. The subject of *Death* opens up numerous

D

and important classes of inquiries—namely, the various *modes* of death, whether it has been natural, suicidal, accidental, or violent, the mixed agencies by which it has been brought about, as hanging, drowning, strangulation, suffocation, poisoning, etc.

To this order of the inquiries coming within the province of the medical jurist I shall adhere pretty closely in following out the details of our subject, as being, on the whole, the most convenient arrangement of our materials open to us, and as the one which some familiarity with the teaching of this department of Medical Science has led me to adopt as best fitted to lead onwards from the less difficult to the more complicated and important topics and discussions which will have to claim our attention in the sequel.

Permit me only to add here that the above classification of medico-legal topics had been employed by me some years previously to the announcement of the scheme followed in the teaching of medical jurisprudence by the School of Medicine of Paris, with which it will be found closely to correspond.

I. AGE IN ITS MEDICO-LEGAL ASPECTS.

This topic will not detain us long. In discussing it I propose to notice, *first*, those periods of life which the law has fixed for certain purposes; and *secondly*, the means we possess for the determination of the age of persons alive or dead, when no record of this is otherwise to be had.

First, Legal questions respecting age.

The question of age may have to be settled in cases of birth, criminal abortion, and infanticide. It may also arise indirectly in charges of rape, early marriages, and the affiliation or maternity of infants. The age of the parties may have to be settled in a few instances fixed by statute, as in the Acts for the Regulation of Factories and Workshops. It may also form an element in regard to the identification at any age of a person either alive or dead. In law, certain periods of life are fixed in order to the determination of certain rights or immunities, as also in regulating the degree of culpability attaching to crimes against the person, or done by a particular agent.

The distinction which holds in Medicine between the ovum or embryo, and that betwixt an abortion and a premature birth, does not hold in law. The legal statute uses the term miscarriage of a child, whatever be the age of the fœtus or the period of its expulsion from the uterus

The distinction, which till lately was held in law, between the criminality of causing the premature expulsion of an infant previously or subsequently to the period of the mother's quickening does not now exist. By the law, as it stands at present, capital punishment, which formerly depended on whether the female had quickened or not, is abolished. In all cases it is left to the discretion of the Court to inflict transportation or imprisonment

The question of quickening may come up in law, however, in another connection. Thus, after a woman has quickened, if condemned to death, the sentence is deferred till after her delivery, though not otherwise, unless it may be occasionally at the discretion of the judge

If, at the time of delivery, the fœtus appears not to have lived in the uterus to the full age of seven months, the mother, it is said, ought not to be convicted of concealment of the birth of a child under the statute

Under seven years an infant is considered in law incapable of committing any crime. As regards evidence, children under the age of twelve years cannot be put on oath; but they may be examined on declaration, if they appear to be intelligent and to understand the obligation of speaking the truth, though without that sanction

The recent Acts for the regulation of factories and other works, as a rule, prohibit the employment of children under eight years. From eight to thirteen years, boys or girls cannot be employed for more than six and a half hours a day. Betwixt the ages of thirteen and eighteen years no one can be allowed to work more than sixty hours a week, or ten and a half hours on each of the first five days, and seven and a half hours on Saturday. This last restriction applies also to females of any age

The carnal knowledge of a female infant under ten years of age, till recently a capital offence, is now considered in England as a crime punishable by transportation for life, and this although the hymen be not broken, and although emission be negatived. Even the solicitation of the infant herself affords no palliation of the crime

Carnal knowledge of a female between ten and twelve, with her consent, is a misdemeanour punishable by imprisonment with hard labour

Above the age of twelve years the consent of the female

does away with any imputation of legal offence, as females who have passed this age are considered to be capable of offering some resistance to the perpetration of the crime

Puberty in the female is, in law, fixed at twelve, at least two years too early

Under the age of fourteen both sexes are presumed not to have been guilty of any crime, but proof of sufficient knowledge between good and evil makes them liable for offences; so that, unless great weakness of intellect appears, they are liable to criminal punishment for crimes of commission after the age of seven, but in no case for a rape or sexual crime under fourteen

Males after fourteen, and females above twelve, are allowed to marry

Eighteen is the earliest period for service in the army, and experience proves that it is injurious to the State to enlist recruits under twenty-three

By the 1 Victoria, c 26, no will made by any person under the age of twenty-one years shall be valid. In connection with this subject, however, it is proper to state that the day of a person's birth is, in law, included in the computation of his age; and as there is, in law, no fraction of a day, a will may be made at any time on the day before that which is usually considered the twenty-first anniversary of his birth, and yet be held valid

The same thing holds good in other cases of majority, as has been proved in formal legal decisions

Let us notice, in the *second* place, the data which we possess for the determination of the age of the party at the different periods of life

Some of these, formerly relied on, are of an artificial character, others, and such as are now in use, are based on physiological changes, following each other in the natural development of the human system. Thus, the ancients believed that very important changes took place in the animal economy at the end of the seventh year and its multiples, and although the theories advanced by them on this subject are now known to be untenable, and too vague and uncertain for the purposes of the medical jurist, yet an examination of this doctrine will account for many of the present divisions of time, as well in fact as in law

It will be observed, for instance, that the foetus which has reached the seventh month may survive its birth Dentition, again, commences at the seventh month after birth, and the second dentition at the end of the seventh year. Twice seven, or fourteen, is the age of puberty; three times seven adult age; four times seven to seven times seven the period of maturity; ten times seven the supposed natural term of life

These periods, though of an arbitrary and artificial character, are nevertheless found to correspond with the physiological division of human life into the six principal periods or epochs—1st, Infancy; 2d, Childhood; 3d, Pueritia, or boyhood and girlhood; 4th, Adolescence; 5th, Adult age; and 6th, Declining or old age

It will be seen, however, that they fail to take in the period of fœtal life, one of considerable importance to the medical jurist; while, besides, they are too lax and indefinite for his purposes, which necessitate a different arrangement of the periods of life during and after birth

The necessity for the determination of the periods of fœtal life up to its termination at birth arises in connection with certain inquiries bearing on the *live* or *still* birth of the infant both in civil and in criminal cases, and particularly in connection with charges of criminal abortion and infanticide, and they form an important element in legal medicine

Such of those points as fall to be determined in the living fœtus or infant will come before us afterwards under Birth and Maternity. Those which will be best discussed here embrace those points the determination of which is possible from the examination of the dead fœtus or infant

1 At and before birth, the settlement of the age is made to rest mainly on the *weight*, the *measurement* of the entire body or its parts, and the progressive *ossification* of the *bones*

Thus, the average *weight* of the infant, according to the latest calculations, is

At 5 months 5 to 7 ounces
„ 6 „ 1 lb to 2 lbs 2 oz
„ 7 „ 2 lbs to 4 lbs 5 oz
„ 8 „ 3½ lbs to 5 lbs 7 oz.
„ 9 „ 4 lbs 5 oz to 7 lbs

The average *length* of the infant is

At 5 months 6 to 10½ inches
„ 6 „ 8 „ 13½ „
„ 7 „ 11 „ 16 „
„ 8 „ 14 „ 18 „
„ 9 „ 16 „ 20 „

Again, the middle of its length is found to be

At the 6th month at the lower end of the sternum
" 7th " a little below the end of the sternum
" 8th " nearer the umbilicus than the sternum
" 9th " at or close to the umbilicus

Once more, points of ossification are first observable

At the 5th month in the pubes and os calcis
" 6th " " four divisions of the sternum
" 7th " " astragalus
" 8th " " last sacral vertebra
" 9th " " lower end of the femur

In addition to these sources of information, there are some others which will occasionally assist us in ascertaining approximately the age of the fœtus, thus —

Comparative measurements of the head at the different periods, though not much attended to here, are relied on by our German brethren. Again, the existence of the pupillary membrane, or its disappearance, points to the infant's being, in the one case, under, and in the other, beyond, its seventh month. Further, the state of the nails, the sebaceous coating on the skin, the down on the surface, the advance of the meconium, the liver, the kidneys, and the testes, will afford data, the valuation and approximation of which will come before us under Infanticide.

2. The changes taking place in the living infant, immediately *after* its birth at the full time, and up to the forty-fifth day of extra-uterine life, enable us to fix its age at this period with sufficient accuracy for most practical purposes. These changes are,—the closure of the fœtal vessels following the establishment of respiration, the discharge of the meconium, the shrivelling and fall of the umbilical cord, and the desquamation of the cuticle. The details connected with these changes have so close a connection with the subject of live birth, that it will be necessary to reserve their consideration till we come to treat of Infanticide.

In cases of death in infants, where the child may have perished or been destroyed immediately after birth, a few additional points call for our attention. Thus, it may be well to notice, whether the child has or has not been washed, and the sebaceous coating, or the blood on its surface, got rid of, or otherwise; the cord may or not have been tied; or the child may or not have been dressed partially or entirely; operations usually requiring the assistance of a third party. Again, the air is believed not to enter the stomach of the infant for some minutes after its complete respiration, while the finding of saliva in this viscus has had considerable stress laid upon it, of late, in Germany, in proof of the same circumstance having happened. As matters of common observation, again, it is known that the infant does not empty its bladder or intestines for a short time after its birth; though it should be remembered that the bladder has been found empty in still-born children, and that the meconium is occasionally passed in utero, or at least partially, if not entirely, during delivery. The presence of milk in the breasts of the infant, though but an occasional occurrence, does not usually last beyond the first week, although it has been known to persist to the third week.

3. Beyond the forty-fifth day after mature birth, the best means which the medical jurist possesses for deciding as to the time of life betwixt early infancy and the epoch of manhood, are those deducible from the state of the *osseous system* in general, and the progress of *dentition*—the latter available in the living, the former, of course, only in the dead body.

The growth of the skeleton to maturity, and the appearances and changes of the teeth, are less subject to variation than the other parts of the system, and may be taken in connection, as laid down by Beclard, Devergie, Briand and Chaudé, Tardieu, etc.

Thus we have the following approximations more or less definitely laid down:—

At 4 months—Cornua of the os hyoides ossified
„ 5 „ Cornicula of the os hyoides ossified
„ 6 „ Point of ossification at the anterior arch of the atlas, alæ majores united to the sphenoid bone

From the 7th to the 8th month—The eruption of the lower central, then of the superior central, incisor teeth

From the 9th to the 10th month—Eruption of the lateral incisors

At 1 year—Points of ossification in the epiphyses at the lower end of the humerus, and at the heads of the humerus, femur, and tibia. Posterior arches united to the bodies of the vertebræ, and the separate portions of the temporal bone to each other. The four anterior molar teeth appearing in succession, sometimes the canines

At 2 years—Points of ossification at the lower ends of the

radius, tibia, and fibula. Epiphyses of the metatarsal and metacarpal bones ossified.

At 2½ years.—Patella, lesser tuberosity of the humerus, and the four smaller metacarpal bones ossified. Eruption of the canines and the four posterior molar teeth.

At 3 years—Union of the odontoid process with the body of the axis. Ossification of the cuboid bone, and the larger trochanter femoris.

At 4 years—Ossification of the trapezoid, and of the second and third cuneiform tarsal bones. Bony union of the styloid process with the temporal bone.

At 5 years—Ossification of the semilunar and scaphoid carpal bones, of the epiphyses of the bones of the fingers, and of the upper end of the fibula. Bony union of the rami and the body of the vertebra dentata.

At 6 years—Bony union betwixt the descending rami of the pubes and the ascending rami of the ischii. Ossification of the proximal epiphyses of the four smaller toes.

At 7 years—Ossification of the trochlea of the humerus.

Between the 6th and 7th year—Shedding of the milk teeth, and appearance of the two first permanent molars.

From the 7th to the 9th year—Ossification of the olecranon and the scaphoid bone. Union of the two bony points at the head of the humerus. Appearance of the eight permanent incisor teeth.

At 9 years—Bony union of the three portions of the os innominatum at the bottom of the acetabulum.

At 10 years—Eruption of the anterior permanent bicuspids.

At 12 years—Bony point at the inner border of the trochlea of the humerus. Ossification of the os pisiforme. Eruption of the posterior bicuspids, canine and second molar teeth.

At 13 or 14 years—Ossification of the neck and of the lesser trochanter of the femur.

At 15 years—Bony point at the inferior angle of the scapula. Consolidation of the last four sacral vertebræ. Bony union of the coracoid process with the body of the scapula.

4. The period of *Puberty* in both sexes is, of course, indicated by the evolution and completion of the sexual characters and organs—viz., besides the expansion of the genitals in the *male*, the enlargement of the chest and depth of the voice, the growth of hair in different parts of the trunk, and of the beard; and in the *female*, the expansion of the pelvis and the growth of hair at the pubes and axilla.

5. After puberty, from 15 to 20 years—Bony point at the sternal end of the clavicle. Ossification of the coccyx. Eruption of the dentes sapientiæ. Bony union of the trochanters and head of the femur with the shaft of the bone, and the two ends of the bone as with the shaft of this bone.

From 18 to 25 years—Union of the body of the sphenoid to the basilar process of the occipital bone. Bony union of the three pieces of the tibia, of the first and middle portions of the sternum, of the osseous points at the extremities of the transverse and spinous processes of the vertebræ, and of the epiphyses of the ribs.

From 25 to 30 years—Bony union of the first with the other sacral vertebræ.

From 40 to 50 years—Consolidation of the ensiform cartilage with the sternum.

The chief of these points may be seen at a glance in the table at the end of the lecture.

I need not do more than allude briefly to a few vague indications of mature and advanced age which have been proposed, such as the condition of the teeth, the depth of the lower jaw, the inflexibility of the spinal column, the colour and quantity of the hair, and the state of the genitals.

Such, then, are the various sources available to the medical jurist for the determination of the age, where this question may have to be decided. Of these, the indications derivable from the teeth and the sexual organs and peculiarities are accessible in the living. In judging from any or all of them, it is essential to observe that they ought only to be regarded as affording *approximations* to the real age, and that, in availing ourselves of the averages they would authorise us to lay down, the extreme ratios which are liable to be encountered must not be lost sight of. It is known, in fact, that the periods thus deducible from the least fluctuating of these data, though in general not likely to mislead very far, are, we must be prepared to admit, not so constant in every instance as might be desired.

To take, for example, the eruption of the teeth, alone available in the living; it is well known that this natural process is liable to considerable variations, both as regards the *time* of the appearance of particular teeth, and as to the *order* of their eruption. Thus, even in a limited experience of midwifery practice, I have met with children with incisor teeth fully formed at birth—with the first incisor making its appearance in a girl of 16 months—and with the entire absence of teeth in a boy of two years, affected, however, with chronic hydrocephalus. Scanzoni, again, has recorded a case where none of the teeth appeared till the seventh year.

Again, as regards the ossification of the skeleton, some differences of opinion exist among the physiological and medico-legal authors from whom our data have been borrowed, as to the precise dates of these several changes, though these differences are neither many nor important.

The value of any or all of our data for this end, however, I may remark, in conclusion, becomes less as the age of the parties has advanced beyond the conclusion of the first dentition; while the completion of puberty, and the advance of years, increase their vagueness and uncertainty.

TABULAR VIEW OF THE DEVELOPMENT OF THE SKELETON AT DIFFERENT PERIODS AFTER THE FORTY-FIFTH DAY OF LIFE.

AT 4 MONTHS.	AT 5 MONTHS.	AT 6 MONTHS	FROM THE 7TH TO 8TH MONTH.	FROM THE 9TH TO 10TH MONTH	AT 1 YEAR
Cornua of os hyoides ossified.	Cornicula of os hyoides ossified.	Point of ossification at the anterior arch of the atlas. Alæ majores united to the sphenoid bone	The lower central incisor teeth appear, then the upper	The lateral incisor teeth appear	Ossific points at the humerus and first cuneiform bones, heads of tibia and femur. Posterior vertebral arches united to the bodies and the parts of the temporal bone to each other. The four first molars appear in succession, sometimes the canines
AT 2 YEARS	AT 2½ YEARS	AT 3 YEARS	AT 4 YEARS	AT 5 YEARS.	AT 6 YEARS
Epiphyses of metatarsal and metacarpal bones ossified. Ossific point at lower end of radius.	Patella and lesser tuberosity of humerus ossified. Canines and four second molars erupted.	Body of axis united with the odontoid process.	Trochanter major, trapezoid, and second and third cuneiform bones ossified. Styloid process united to the temporal bone	Trapezium and semi-lunar ossified. Rami of the vertebra dentata united to its body. Upper end of fibula and epiphyses of finger-bones ossified	Ossification of proximal epiphyses of the bones of the four small toes
AT 7 YEARS.	FROM 7 TO 9 YEARS	AT 10 YEARS	AT 12 YEARS	AT 14 YEARS	AT 15 YEARS
Trochlea of humerus ossified. Between 6 and 7 years the milk teeth drop and the first molars of the second dentition appear	Ossification of the olecranon and scaphoid bones. Union of the two bony points at the head of the humerus. Appearance of the eight incisor teeth of the second dentition	Eruption of the anterior bicuspid teeth	Appearance of the posterior bicuspid, canines and second molar teeth. Ossification of the inner border of the trochlea of the humerus and of the pisiform bone	Ossification of the trochanter minor	Ossific point at the inferior angle of the scapula. Consolidation of the sacral vertebræ. Union of the coracoid process with the scapula
FROM 15 TO 20 YEARS	FROM 18 TO 23 YEARS		FROM 27 TO 30 YEARS	FROM 40 TO 50 YEARS	
Ossific point in the sternal end of the clavicle. Ossification of the four coccygeal vertebræ. Eruption of the dentes sapientiæ. Bony union of the head and trochanters of the femur with its shaft. Union of the lower end of the femur, and of the two extremities of the humerus with the shafts of these bones	Union of the body of the sphenoid to the basilar process of the occipital bone. Consolidation of the three pieces of the tibia. Union of the first to the middle portions of the sternum. Union of the osseous points at the extremities of the transverse and spinous processes of the vertebræ, and of the epiphyses of the ribs		Union of the first sacral vertebra with the others	Consolidation of the ensiform cartilage with the sternum	

LECTURE IV.

SEX—DOUBTFUL SEX

MEDICO-LEGAL INQUIRIES ORIGINATING IN CASES OF THIS SORT. MEANS OF DECIDING ON THE SEX. WHEN THE SYSTEM IS NORMALLY DEVELOPED—In the Foetus—At Birth—From Infancy to Puberty—After Puberty—From the Figure—From the Skeleton. WHEN THE SYSTEM IS ABNORMALLY DEVELOPED—Hermaphrodism—False Hermaphrodites—Androgynæ, from Enlargement of the Clitoris, from Prolapsed Uterus—Gynandri—Hypospadia—True Hermaphrodites—Lateral Hermaphrodism—Transverse Hermaphrodism. RULES FOR THE INVESTIGATION IN CASES OF DOUBTFUL SEX.

THE question of the sex of an individual, either dead or alive, not unfrequently arises in Juridical Medicine, and from the earliest foetal period at which a separate existence may be maintained, the sex may fail to be settled, either as an independent question, or as an element in other inquiries.

The question of the father's *tenancy by the courtesy*, or his right to the management of its property, depends on the sex of his new-born infant, whose sex may also regulate the order of succession to property. The validity of marriages, too, has not unfrequently been tried by determining whether the individual belonged to the sex alleged at or before the time of the union; while again the question of sex may arise in questions of personal identity.

In the great majority of cases, as may be readily supposed, the settling of the sex to which a person belongs is a very simple affair. The sexual peculiarities suffice for this. But cases occasionally occur which present difficulties of a more or less serious sort, thus :—

It may be necessary for the identification of a dead body, to determine the sex to which the individual belonged, where it has suffered mutilation and the sexual organs are wanting, or where only portions of the skeleton have been found.

Even where the body, alive or dead, is entire, its imperfect development may leave the real sex difficult to be ascertained, or even impossible to be made out. Of this last, a striking instance occurred in the practice of Dr Wilson, of Oldmeldrum, to whom I was indebted for an opportunity of examining the child, and of obtaining a wax cast, of which Fig 1 is a representation When seen by me, in May 1867, the child was in its eighth month, and had been treated as a female. The urine and fæces passed out by a small cloaca betwixt the pubes and umbilicus As will be seen, there was no anus. A soft body of the size of a large pea in front of the pelvis might have been taken for an abortive clitoris, or a very diminutive and imperforate penis Two folds of integument, with but very little prominence or distinctness, might have passed for labia, or mere vestiges of a split scrotum. In one of these folds a soft kernel was indistinctly detectable, which might pass for the rudiment of a testis

From this, Dr Wilson and I were shut up to the conclusion that the sex of the child could not be determined, at least during life, if even an examination after its death might assist in the determination of the point. This latter event, however, left the case in nearly its previous obscurity. The infant, which was in a sickly state at the time of our examination, died eight months afterwards without any obvious cause. With considerable difficulty and hesitation, a sight of the dead body was obtained; and during our stay with it we were repeatedly ordered, in a very peremptory manner, out of the house. We were only able, therefore, in these unfavourable circumstances, to determine that the descending colon distended to double its natural diameter, ended by a large opening at the fundus of the bladder; that there was no trace of uterus or rectum in the pelvis, and that the two minute rounded eminences in front and at one side of the exterior of the pelvis were merely structureless masses of fat

In those instances, again,—and they are of more frequent occurrence than is usually suspected.—where what may be termed *genital malformations* in the ordinary sense exist, some of the most eminent physiologists and medical jurists have been at sea as regards the determination of the sex; while, on not a few occasions, it has only been after death that the real sex has been accurately determined.

In discussing the points arising for solution in cases of doubtful sex, I shall arrange these under two heads:—

I The means of determining the true sex, where the sexual apparatus and sexual conformation are naturally, though imperfectly, developed, and

II Where these are malformed

First, Of the natural development of the sex.—To begin with the *fœtal state*. According to Velpeau the fœtus has no sex for the first fifty-five days, and it is not till between the second and third month that the genitals can be distinguished. In fact (Kobelt) there is a time in the earliest period of fœtal life when the distinction betwixt the sexes is impossible, from the temporary co-existence in each individual of all the elements of the reproductive organs.

Even between the fifth and seventh month of intra-uterine life —the earliest moment in legal medicine at which the inquiry as to the sex of the fœtus can arise—mistakes may readily occur from the close resemblance at that period of the penis to the clitoris.

At birth at the usual time, the non-descent of the testes may give rise to doubts of the sex. The *eighth* month is the time usually assigned for entrance of these bodies into the ring, and the *ninth* month for their arrival in the scrotum. Wrisberg, however, "upon an examination of 97 (*sic*) infants at birth, found that only in 67 both testes had reached the scrotum, in 17 one or both were still in the canal, in 8 one testis, and in 3 both testes remained in the abdomen."

After birth, and up to the establishment of puberty, inspection of the genitals is the only means we possess for the discrimination of the sexes. When these are wanting after death, or where only the skeleton is discovered, we have *no* marks for our guidance on which we can rely.

After puberty the differences between the male and female figure, even independently of the genitals, are sufficiently marked in the well-formed person. There is in general more plumpness in the female than in the male; the muscles are smaller and less strongly marked, the integuments are more abundant and softer, the connective tissue is more largely provided with a supply of fat, the nails are smooth and semi-transparent, the hair of the head fine and long, and that on the other parts of the body comparatively scanty.

The *proportions* also present some remarkable contrasts. Thus the female is usually not so tall as the male, and the whole figure makes an approach to the oval not witnessed in the case of the masculine form. Other differences equally distinguishable come to be readily observed when we pass from the general conformation to the separate parts. The upper part of the female body is proportionately more developed than that of the male, half her length corresponding with the upper part of the symphysis pubis, and his striking the middle of this bone. The lower limbs of the female are thus proportionately shorter than those of the male, while the trunk is somewhat longer, enlarged at its fore and upper part by the prominent mammæ, and exhibiting a furrow extending to the sacrum along the back, with a lateral depression on each side from the ribs to the nates peculiar to the sex, especially as modified by the civilisation of the present day. The chest of the female has a larger antero-posterior and a smaller bicostal diameter than that of the male. The upper and lower parts of the trunk respectively in the two sexes have opposite characteristics, the breadth of the chest, including the upper part of the arms, being less than that of the pelvis in the adult female and rather exceeding it in the male. The comparative breadth of the pelvis gives a fuller contour to the tops of the thighs in the female than in the opposite sex, and a greater obliquity to the thighs, rectified in her by the elongation of the inner condyle of the femur.

Minor differences present themselves in the smaller and more delicate head and limbs in the female, and a less degree of fulness of the lower jaw and projection of the larynx.

These particulars not unfrequently call for attention as in cases in which portions of bodies are found under suspicious circumstances, of which we meet with instances in medico-legal records both here and on the Continent, some of which will be noticed by and by. Again, particular attention to the differences between the male and female skeleton comes to be demanded of the medical jurist where the corpse has not been discovered till after the destruction of the soft parts.

I have already remarked that the examination of the bones alone can afford no indication of the sex to which they belonged, prior to the establishment of puberty. The same observation applies *a fortiori* to the fœtus before birth. What follows, therefore, must be understood as applicable solely to the adult skeleton.

With regard to the osseous structure in general, it may be observed that there are some very striking peculiarities belonging to the bones of the adult female. They are less firm and lighter than those of the male. The flat bones are thinner, the round bones more cellular or spongy, and the long bones more smooth and tapering, while those rough lines or ridges, which result from the repeated and more powerful action of the muscles in the male, are less perceptible. The processes are but feebly marked, the joints generally less bulky, and in short there are everywhere discernible in the general bony structure marks of a more delicate conformation.

But to come to particulars. The female skull is smaller, more oblong, and less flattened at the sides than that of the male, the face is more oval, the frontal sinuses less developed, the nasal apertures smaller, the jaws shorter and more elliptical, and the chin less prominent.

The shape of the chest has been already noticed, but some minor points in addition are here available, such as the shorter and more convex sternum in the female, the thinner and more flexible xyphoid cartilage, the more delicate and uniform ribs, with longer cartilages.

I need but remind you of the striking differences in the shape and size of the pelvis in the two sexes. In the well-formed female the ossa ilii are more expanded, the sacrum more capacious from its greater convexity, a less acute angle is formed by the union of the descending rami of the pubes, the distance is greater between the ossa ischii, and the sub-pubic foramina are larger than in the male, and the different measurements of the brim and outlet of the pelvis, are points with which you must be familiar. The greater distance between the cotyloid cavities in the female, and the proportionate length of their inner condyles, already adverted to, give rise to the peculiar position of the femurs.

The chest of the female, as best seen from behind, is narrower and less convex than that of the male, while it is not so deep, leaving a greater distance between its lower border and the crest of the ilium.

In cases calling for an examination of the skeleton, some familiarity with the bones of the human subject as compared with those of the lower animals, is needed on the part of the medical jurist, since, in recorded cases, these have been found intermingled, as in a Parisian instance, in which there were parts both of a male and a female, and some bones of oxen.

We now come to consider in the *second* place, the determination of the sex in those cases where the organs of generation are malformed.

What adds to the difficulties of the medical jurist in these inquiries is, that the malformation is seldom confined to the genitals alone but often extends to the conformation of the body generally, and even to the distinctive mental faculties, while the sexual desires are either wanting altogether, or point in a wrong direction, the male considering himself and acting as a female, and the female as a male. It has occasionally happened that in such instances nothing short of actual dissection after death has discovered the true sex of the individual.

To the whole of this class of malformations the generic term *Hermaphrodism* has been applied. Not that it is meant that such a being as an hermaphrodite, in the strict sense of the word—that is to say, a being possessing both the male and female organs in such a state of perfection as to be competent to perform the functions of either sex indifferently—has ever existed in man or any of the higher classes of animals. No one now asserts this.

Following in this some of the latest and best authors, we shall consider these imperfect beings—imperfect from defect on the one hand and excess on the other—under two specific appellations —namely, that of *false* and that of *true* hermaphrodites.

In the first or *false* species of hermaphrodism, the genital organs and general sexual conformation of one sex approach from imperfect or abnormal development those of the opposite.

In the second species, the *true* hermaphrodism, there actually co-exists upon the body of the same individual more or fewer of the genital organs and distinctive sexual characters both of the male and female.

With proper care and attention, it is always easy to discover the true sex in the different varieties of false (*spurious*) hermaphrodism. It is chiefly in regard to the so-called *true* hermaphrodite that the mistakes referred to have arisen, even in the hands of competent observers.

To facilitate your comprehension of this difficult and important subject, I subjoin the table (slightly altered) given by Sir James Simpson in the second volume of the *Cyclopædia of Anatomy*, p. 685, which I prefer for our purpose, as less elaborate than that of Geoffroy Saint-Hilaire.

Simpson's table will convey a clearer idea of the varieties of these beings than could be conveyed in words.

It will not be necessary under the present subject to examine in detail all the varieties laid down by this author, two of which will come before us again under Impotence and Sterility.

LECTURE IV.

HERMAPHRODISM

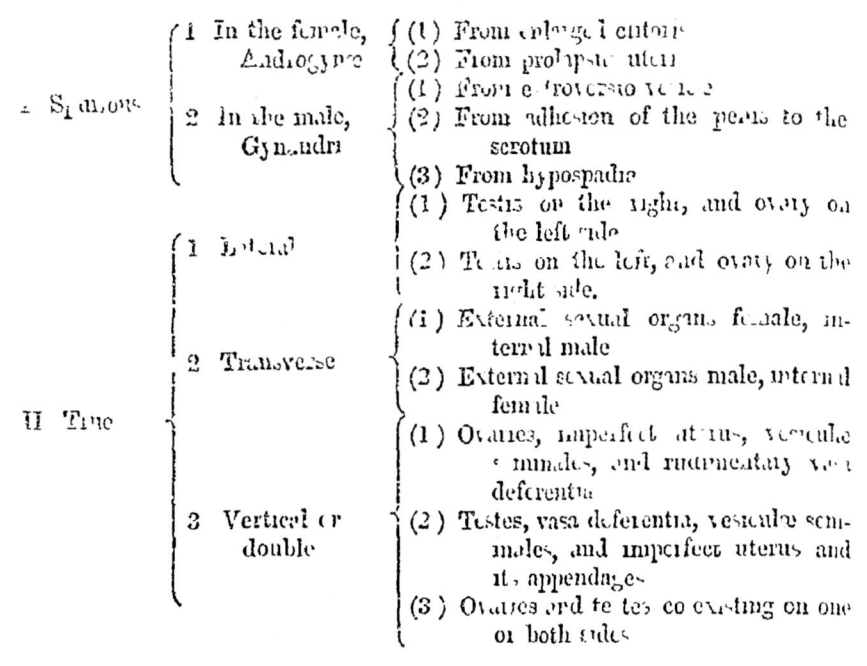

I. Spurious
- 1 In the female, Androgyne
  - (1) From enlarged clitoris
  - (2) From prolapsed uterus
- 2 In the male, Gynandria
  - (1) From e[pi]trovers[i]o ve[sic]?
  - (2) From adhesion of the penis to the scrotum
  - (3) From hypospadia

II. True
- 1 Lateral
  - (1) Testis on the right, and ovary on the left side
  - (2) Testis on the left, and ovary on the right side.
- 2 Transverse
  - (1) External sexual organs female, internal male
  - (2) External sexual organs male, internal female
- 3 Vertical or double
  - (1) Ovaries, imperfect uterus, vesiculæ seminales, and rudimentary vasa deferentia
  - (2) Testes, vasa deferentia, vesiculæ seminales, and imperfect uterus and its appendages
  - (3) Ovaries and testes co-existing on one or both sides

Let us consider the *spurious* female hermaphrodism—androgyne—as existing occasionally in the female. This variety of spurious hermaphrodism has been known to arise from two causes, either (1) from a preternatural growth of the clitoris, or (2) from prolapse of the uterus, the enlarged clitoris in the one case, and the protruded uterus in the other, having been repeatedly mistaken for the male penis.

(1) The size of the clitoris is said to be greater than usual in some tropical climates, while travellers have related that among certain tribes this increased development is nearly universal in their females. Even in Europe it is not unfrequent. I have had occasion to notice it in a girl of thirteen, who was believed to have yielded herself for some years previously to libidinous practices. In Arnaud's case the organ is said to have been 10 inches long, and in Beclard's case 27 centimetres (10½ inches). In Ramsbotham's case there was a sulcus ending in a cul-de-sac at the summit of the clitoris. In Beclard's case the vulva was blocked up by a dense membrane, and the entrance of the vagina would only admit the passage of a sound of moderate size, the labia were narrow and short, and the bodily conformation more masculine than feminine.

The worst of the features in certain of the recorded instances of this form of hermaphrodism is the marriage of the parties as males, and that others of them, on account of their noxious commerce with both sexes indifferently, have drawn upon themselves the notice of the law authorities.

(2.) The remaining form of spurious female hermaphrodism is that in which a prolapsed uterus has been mistaken for a penis, a mistake which, however unaccountable, has been made even by the profession, as in the instance recorded in the *Philosophical Transactions* (XII. 232), where a female passed herself off as a true hermaphrodite with the Faculties of Toulouse and Paris, till one member of the latter body detected her true sex. Other instances of the same mistake are given by Sir James Simpson.

In the *male*, the varieties encountered in the false or spurious hermaphrodites—androgyni or gynandri—are the malformations (1) from extroversion of the bladder, (2) from adhesion of the penis to the scrotum, and (3) from hypospadia.

(1.) The first of these forms of hermaphrodism has less bearing on the subject we are considering than on that of impotence, as only a very careless observer could confound the protruded bladder above the pubes with the vulva of a female. This bodily conformation seems to be not infrequent, as I have met with it thrice in males, in addition to the instance above referred to in the child (p. 15). Two of the males were shown to the class in former sessions, and the third is presently in the Infirmary (1875), where his cure is being attempted. The subjoined figure shows very well the appearance these individuals present. (Fig. 2.)

(2.) "Adhesion of the inferior surface of the penis to the scrotum has," says Sir James Simpson, "occasionally given rise to the idea of hermaphrodism, the penis being so bound down as not to admit of erection, and the urine passing in a direction downwards so as to imitate the flow of it from the female parts."

A long narrative of a case of coalition of the penis to the scrotum is given in the twenty-first volume of Eulenberg's *Vierteljahresschrift für gerichtliche Medicin*, p. 77. The peculiarity of this individual was the position of the penis, not in front, but behind the scrotum, which appears from the woodcut to have been partially cleft.

(3.) The remaining variety of spurious male hermaphrodism is that arising from hypospadic cleft of the penis. In these malformed persons, termed hypospadians, the urethra, instead of being continued to the summit of the glans penis, is found to terminate by an opening in the median line somewhere along the lower surface of the penis nearer to the bladder. Where the orifice thus misplaced is but small and in the vicinity of the glans, no mistake can arise

In a patient who presented himself to me with gonorrhœa in 1839, the opening was close behind the attached border of the prepuce, and though the glans was really imperforate, it did not appear so at first sight, from there being two or three blind openings near where the urethra usually terminates

Cases, however, not unfrequently occur of a more puzzling kind. In these the glans is imperforate, the penis is diminutive in size, resembling an enlarged clitoris, the urethra opens further back towards the perinæum, the opening not being a mere foramen, but a fissure of some length, so as to give the idea of the entrance to the vagina in the female. When the fissure is thus situated, the scrotum is frequently found split into two lateral halves, giving no indistinct approximation to the form of the labia majora in women. Should the testes not have descended from the abdomen, as in some men who are otherwise normally formed, the deception would be still more complete.

Dupuytren in his *Leçons Orales*, mentions an extraordinary instance of this kind :—' A person affected with hypospadia was married for fifteen or twenty years, and during all that time was treated as a female. Sexual intercourse was regularly effected by the canal of the urethra, nor was it until the period just mentioned had elapsed that it was discovered that the individual was a man."

Three different cases, in several respects similar, are given by Arnaud, Caspar, and Geoffroy St Hilaire, in two of which the supposed female was in the practice of cohabiting with the male sex, while in the other instance the party lived for a long time on good terms with a husband. A person with this conformation of the genitals exhibited himself here (Aberdeen), some years ago, to several of the medical practitioners. The testicles could be felt in the two divisions of the cleft scrotum, but the urethral fissure, which was lined with mucous membrane of a red colour at its lips, was large enough to admit one or two fingers to about the depth of half-an-inch, and was copiously moistened with mucus. The penis was small, and the glans imperforate. The masculine character of the body generally was pretty well developed.

Of a wax cast given me by the late Professor Lizars (Aberdeen University) I have but an imperfect account. It was said to have been taken from a Lascar in Guy's Hospital some years ago. It appears to be that of a person of the same form of sexual malformation as the last. The penis was imperforate, one testicle had remained in the groin, and the other was evidently present in one of the divisions of the split scrotum. (Fig. 3.)

Such are the different varieties of the spurious hermaphrodism, the forms of genital malformation of most frequent occurrence, and about the existence of which there is no dispute amongst authors.

There is, however, no such unanimity as to the existence among the mammalia of such a being as a *true* or real hermaphrodite; but the differences on this point have turned on the reality of the alleged instances of persons possessing, not the *organs*, but the *functions*, of both sexes. Such bi-sexual powers are met with in union with the bi-sexual conformation in the greater number of the phanerogamous plants, and in certain classes of animals in the low grades; but, unless among some of the older authors, this claim is generally abandoned in the case of man and the higher animals—the term "true hermaphrodism" being, as I have said, restricted to those cases in which there actually co-exist in the same individual more or fewer of the genital organs and distinctive sexual characters both of the male and the female. Far from agreeing with the plants and animals to which I have just alluded in prolific power, I am not aware of a single authentic instance of such mixed beings possessing even the generative functions of *one* sex, resembling in this the sterility or impotence of the mule amongst animals.

The first variety of this species I shall notice is that which has been called *lateral* hermaphrodism. The peculiarity of the sexual organs in these persons has been, that, in the same individual, there has been found on one side of the mesial line a testicle and its appendages, or what has resembled such, and on the other an ovary and its appendages. In such cases, the organ which has been found most frequently on the left side has been the ovary, and *vice versa*. In these instances, also, along with a testicle on one side and an ovary on the other, there has generally co-existed a more or less perfectly formed uterus, while the external parts of generation, and of the body generally, have differed in their sexual characters—in some instances being female, in others male, and in others again of a neutral or indeterminate type.

The second variety of true hermaphrodism is what has been termed *transverse*.

In the variety last considered we found that the male organs were placed on one side of the median plane and the female on the opposite. In the present variety, on the other hand, the external organs are male and the internal female, or the external genital organs are female and the internal male. By external and internal I do not mean those parts placed superficially or more deeply in the body; I employ the words external and internal in the sense in which they are employed by St Hilaire, followed by several anatomists. Those parts of the genitals which are covered by the common integument, or are lined by mucous membrane and thus communicating with the external air, are by them classed as external organs, in which are included the vagina and uterus, though hidden deep in the pelvis. The testis, though more exposed from being placed outside the pelvis, is termed an internal organ.

This being understood, I proceed to remark that there is only one form of this variety with which, as medical jurists, we can, even if in this case we can, have anything to do, namely, the one in which the external genital organs are female and the internal male, and in fact even here little more than mere suspicion could in any case be entertained during life, as the true state of matters can only be guessed at by our finding a body which resembles a testicle in size and form in the groin or labia. You will readily perceive that the medical jurist would only be called in to clear up the doubts as to the sex of such an individual during the lifetime of the party. The existence, in this case, of a body which might be a testicle in the labium, is too slight evidence whereon to form a decision. Nothing short of dissection after death can lead to the discovery of the transverse form of hermaphrodism.

The third and last variety of true hermaphrodism does not fall within our province to investigate, as the existence of two ovaries and two testes in the same individual cannot even be suspected, much less verified, during life.

The subject of hermaphrodism will be fully concluded with some directions for the guidance of the medical jurist when called upon for a decision as to the sex of an individual affected with any of those malformations we have considered.

An hermaphrodite is recognised in law, and is allowed to inherit property by descent or otherwise, according to the prevailing sex. In ecclesiastical courts, the sex of such persons requires to be fixed in questions relating to the validity of marriage.

It must be abundantly obvious that nothing but an intimate acquaintance with the prevailing varieties of hermaphrodism will assist the medical jurist in investigations of this kind, particularly in cases of true hermaphrodism, in which the greatest difficulties occur. For these, or indeed for any of the varieties, to specific rules can be given. True, we have a few general rules applicable to all such inquiries, which it is of consequence to keep in mind.

Those which are given by Marc in the article "Hermaphrodisme" in the *Dictionnaire des Sciences Médicales*, and adopted by Orfila and Cummin, are the best we possess, and are as follows:—

1st, The examination of all the external organs of generation must be performed with exactitude and caution; every opening is to be sounded to ascertain its depth and direction, taking care to use no force.

2d, The inspection of the whole surface of the body is no less essential, with a view to determine the prevailing character, and hence the probable sex. We should also strive to make ourselves acquainted with the tastes, habits, and propensities of the individual under examination. This, however, will often require time; and care must be taken not to confound the habits which may have originated in the artificial position held by the party in society with those which result from organic structure or development.

3d, Ascertain whether, from any opening, especially about the genital parts, there be any periodical sexual discharge, a circumstance of great importance, and which will be of itself almost decisive as to the feminine nature of the person examined.

4th, When the individual submitted to our scrutiny is very young—suppose a new-born child with irregular sexual organs—nothing is more likely to mislead than precipitation. We must avoid haste by all means. Perhaps the utmost we can or ought to do, in the first instance, is to give a formal notice of the dubious nature of the case, and to take time, years if necessary, in order to be able to observe the progressive development of the physical and moral characteristics; this we should do deliberately rather than hazard any opinion which subsequent facts might stultify.

Lastly, No attention ought to be paid to the declarations of the individual himself or of his relations; at all events it will be necessary to weigh well such declarations, in order that we may form a correct judgment of the possible motives by which they may be dictated.

CONCEALED SEX

Under the head of concealed sex some writers on medical jurisprudence have treated of those persons, who, without any such malformations as we have considered, have purposely assumed the dress and occupations of the opposite sex from their own. There have been individuals who have done so from caprice, or from other than criminal motives; others have done so deliberately as a screen for the commission of the most execrable and abominable actions.

These cases present no difficulty in investigations bearing on the sex of the individual. The dress and occasionally some of the general sexual characteristics are usually all that favour the deception, and when the former is laid aside the ambiguity ceases.

LECTURE V

PERSONAL IDENTITY

PERSONAL IDENTITY.—Legal Questions bearing on the Identity of Particular Persons IN THE LIVING.—Occasions for the Inquiry—Means employed for concealing the Identity—By changes in the Personal Appearance—By changing the Colour of the Hair, methods for darkening the Hair, means of detecting this change, methods for changing Dark Hair to Light, detection of the change—By the obliteration of Tattooed Marks—Difficulty of identifying Individuals occasionally—From close Personal Resemblances—Where the parties are related—Where they are nowise related—Cautions required in testifying to Identity—Occasional facilities of Identification under unfavourable circumstances. IN THE DEAD.—Immediately after Death—During the progress of Putrefaction—Where the body is Mutilated or Incomplete—Where only the Skeleton is found—General Rules for the Identification of Individuals—The Moral Proof—The Proofs from Physical Appearances.

THE question as to the identity of certain persons may arise in law both in civil and criminal proceedings, in the living and in the dead.

I. Identity of the living.—The instances of this sort in which the medical witness may be called on to take part are those where the proofs are found to rest almost entirely or altogether on such physiological facts as he alone can satisfactorily supply; otherwise, as happens in the majority of cases of confusion of persons, or suspicious claims, the relatives and connections of the party in dispute are examined, and failing these, witnesses who have been personally acquainted with the individual in question; while, in addition, as in the late famous Tichborne trial, the claimant's memory may be tested regarding facts and occurrences to which no impostor could be in a position to speak in a clear and connected manner.

The occasions on which medical evidence may be demanded will vary with the circumstances, as where a person is suspected to be the party who committed a crime, whether recently or at a remote period; or again, where the individual had been abstracted or left home in infancy, and had reappeared in adult age to claim recognition by his friends, or a lost possession or privilege. In some of these cases the evidence will turn on the existence of corporeal defects, marks upon the skin, traces of former wounds or diseases, etc., and in others on the effects of the natural growth of the body to maturity, or that of time and the accidents of life, climate, occupation etc., in changing the personal appearance.

In some instances, to avoid identification, a criminal or escaped convict may have sought disguise by more summary measures, as by change of dress, shaving the head, or altering the colour or the style of adjustment of the hair, allowing the whiskers to grow or removing them when previously worn, or by varying his previous carriage or deportment.

With only one of these ready methods for escaping detection, however, is the medical jurist called to deal. To this and some of the others to which I have referred I will now have to call your attention.

1st, In cases of disputed identity the question has arisen in legal medicine as to the possibility of the *disappearance* of a scar. We believe that, as a general rule, all scars resulting from wounds and from cutaneous diseases which involve any loss of substance are indelible, the only exception that can be made being in regard to trifling punctured wounds, where but little violence has been done to the skin, and where there has been no loss of substance. Considerable light has been thrown on this last class of alterations on the surface of the body by researches on the Continent some years ago.

A body was found at Berlin in 1856 so disfigured and mutilated that its identification could not be made out satisfactorily, though the probability was that it was that of Gottlieb Ebermann, a cattle-dealer. But though this individual was known to have been scarified in the operation of cupping eight or nine years before his death, and to have had the initial letters of his name tattooed into one of his forearms, no trace of either could be detected on the body, examined with every care by magistrates and medical men.

This and some subsequent occurrences led to an investigation by Caspar in Germany, and Hutin and Tardieu in France, as to the possibility of effacing such marks, the common belief being that such marks are indelible. The result arrived at by these inquiries was that the popular opinion is in the general case correct, yet that exceptions occasionally occur. Thus, in 37 persons examined by Caspar the marks had become in time effaced in 6; in 509 per-re-examined by Hutin they had disappeared in 27, in 76 inspected by Tardieu the marks had become effaced in 8—or about 11 per cent of the whole.

It has also been found that the substance employed by the tattooer influences the permanence or otherwise of the markings. Vermilion, which is used, is the least permanent colour. China ink, which is often employed, though not absolutely indelible, rarely disappears. But what is more to our purpose to remark is that it has been shown that tattooing, besides being occasionally known to disappear naturally, may be got rid of, in no lengthened period, by artificial means, such as the application of blisters, tartar emetic ointment, or other means of producing suppuration of the skin.

A criminal in one of the French prisons, according to Tardieu, got rid of extensive tattooed marks on his body in six days by the use of the following means, a fact which was verified in another case by the reporter. He first applied to the parts a paste of pure acetic acid and lard; they were then rubbed with potash, and lastly with dilute hydrochloric acid. In repeating the experiment, Tardieu left the paste on the tattooed part for twenty-four hours, by which time the cuticle was raised and the true skin reddened. After this the part was rubbed five or six times in the course of the second day with potash, which occasioned very little pain. The day after a thin but closely adherent crust was left at the place which fell off on the seventh day, leaving the marking but partially obliterated. This, however, was immediately succeeded by a new crust, which did not drop off for fourteen days more, leaving a superficial smooth scar without the least vestige of the tattooing.

From the researches thus undertaken some very curious disclosures have resulted, and it has been shown that in the lower ranks of life special marks are chosen by particular trades, which might be of assistance occasionally in establishing a doubtful case of identity. *Vide Ann. d'Hygiène*, 1849-50, and 1862.

I may add that Casper has found that the marks left by the scarificator in cupping, if not deep, may disappear in from two to three years.

I have directed your attention particularly to these facts and conclusions, as they seem to have been overlooked in the famous Tichborne trial, where the professional evidence was confined to surgeons and physicians, evidently unacquainted with forensic medicine, who were called to speak on the permanence or possible disappearance of tattooing and the cicatrices of wounds in venesection and cupping.

2d, In a case of rape, tried in Aberdeen, evidence in defence was brought forward to show that, in the female, soft chancres could not have existed after the period of intercourse, as no mark of their previous presence was visible about the genitals of the prisoner six weeks afterwards. My testimony at the prosecution was that I and another physician had seen them at the time alleged. I am now the more confirmed in this opinion, from the fact that in a subsequent case in private practice, where several such chancres were met with and treated by me, all trace of them was found to have disappeared six weeks subsequently.

3d, The attention of the profession was first prominently called to the attempts at evading the means of ready identification by dyeing the hair on the occurrence of the following case:—A man, named Benoit, was suspected of having committed a murder. Certain witnesses deposed to having seen him in Paris at *two* o'clock on the afternoon of the day in question with *black* hair, and others to having seen him at Versailles, with *fair* hair, at *five or six* o'clock the same evening. The man's hair was naturally jet black (and it does not appear that he wore a wig). The question, in consequence, proposed by the law authorities to M. Orfila was whether black hair could be dyed fair? One of the first hairdressers in Paris, who was also consulted, declared that it was impossible; but Orfila stated that it was not only possible, but had been effected twenty-six years before by Vauquelin by means of chlorine.

We notice—

(1.) The means of darkening the hair. There are various methods in use for altering the colour of the human hair. In general the object is to change red or sandy hair to a darker hue, i.e. to brown or black.

Preparations of lead, silver, and bismuth are employed for the purpose, lime or ammonia being first used to remove the fatty matter of the hair. A very common agent is a mixture of lime and oxide of lead in equal parts, or three parts of litharge to two of lime, the litharge being sometimes replaced by carbonate of lead. The mixture, made into a paste with hot water, is applied to the hair for four or five hours. The lime combines with the fatty matter of the hair, while the lead forms with the sulphur of the hair a black sulphide of lead.

The use of bismuth, at one time employed in place of

lead, appears latterly to have been abandoned if we may trust the investigations of Chevalier, who recently investigated this subject.

This author mentions that in Paris the hairdressers and perfumers who keep articles of this sort for sale trust to the use of litharge or nitrate of silver, which latter they dissolve in about nine parts of water, and vend under the names of Persian, Egyptian, Cyprian, or Ebony waters, with a solution of the same strength of sulphide of potassium, to be used to remove the grease previous to the application of the silver.

It should be known that the above preparations for darkening the hair are not unfrequently attended with dangerous consequences to the individuals employing them, such as erysipelas, excoriation of the skin, inflammatory swellings of the face, cerebral disturbances, and even permanent insanity.

In one instance in which severe effects followed the dyeing of the hair and beard, the powder which had been made use of for this purpose was found to contain 1 part of quicklime, 3 of red lead, and 1 of carbonate of iron.

But in the case of dyeing the hair of a dark colour, as it is not difficult to attain the desired end, so neither is it difficult, by means of close inspection or by chemical re-agents, to detect what has been done. The metallic sulphides thus formed can be decomposed and the metals extracted by means of nitric acid for testing.

(2) When, on the other hand, the object is to render dark hair of a lighter colour, the end is obtained by the employment of *chlorine*, first washing the hair with ammonia to remove the greasiness. One part of strong liquid chlorine diluted with four parts of water will change, in the course of *two* hours, according to Orfila, *black* hair to *dark chestnut*. By successive immersions in a solution of the same strength it will be brought to a *bright chestnut*. If the same hair be brought to a *deep blonde* colour, it may ultimately be brought to a *bright yellow*, or to *white* with a yellowish tinge.

Devergie differs from Orfila thus far, that he has never been able, in his trials, to produce the full effect of whitening in less than twelve, fifteen, or twenty hours. Further, he has noticed that chlorine does not destroy the colour very uniformly.

This last circumstance might enable us to decide in most cases whether or not the hair had been artificially changed, even independently of chemical experiments. Besides, as the hair grows, the new growth will be of the previous colour. Moreover, it should be borne in mind, that as persons dyeing their hair to avoid recognition would scarcely think of going farther than to alter that of the head and whiskers, by comparing the hair of these parts with that of the pubes and other parts of the trunk, a ready means of detecting the change presents itself to the examiner.

(3.) A point has been adverted to by our continental brethren, as calling for the special attention of the medical jurist, namely, the means of identification of individuals by the examination and measurement of the footprints left by them on the ground. I notice this, however, chiefly for the purpose of pointing out the circumstance, that it has been contended by Mascar of Belgium that the prevailing opinion, that the impression of the foot on the soil *always* corresponds exactly with the foot making it, is not by any means a correct one; but that, on the contrary, while in fact instances may occur in which the footprint may be even larger than the foot itself, from the peculiar shape of the shoe, boot, or slipper worn, or from the depth to which the foot had gone, as a general rule, it is found that the print in the ground is *smaller* than the foot which made it.

Mascar is here so far borne out by Caussé, who has also given much attention to the subject, as to the fallacy of the common opinion of the invariable correspondence in size between the foot and its print. His conclusion, however, is not that the latter is most frequently smaller than the former, but that the impression in the soil is usually *larger* than the foot making it.

This difference of opinion, especially when taken in connection with the statement common to these two jurists, lessens the value of the proposals which have been made by different parties, of means for securing a permanent record, if we may so term it, of such impressions on the soil, for future comparison with the armatures of the feet of parties who afterwards may be suspected to have made them, in the case of murders or other crimes.

The most ingenious of these is that of M. Hougolin, which consists in raising the temperature of the impressed ground to about 220° Fahr., by holding over it a sort of warming-pan filled with incandescent charcoal, and then dusting stearic acid, in fine powder, over the footmarks, which melts and sinks in at the part taking so exactly the form of the footprints, as that, when allowed to cool, it may be detached and used as a mould for the production by plaster of Paris of a facsimile of the feet of the parties who had left their traces in the soil. The advantage of this

Pl IV

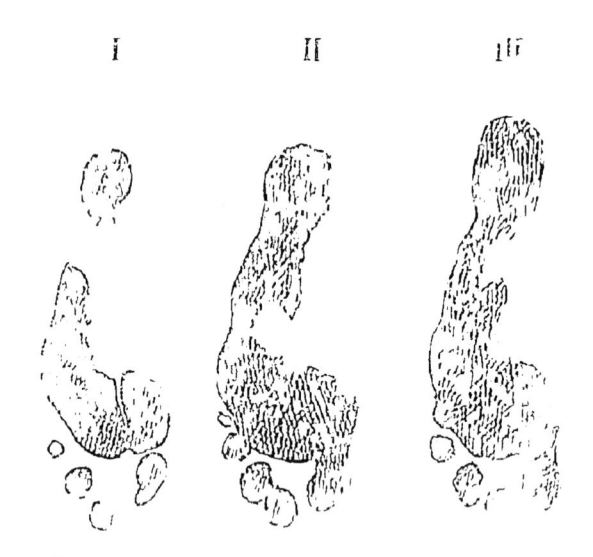

I   II   III

FOOTPRINTS

SHOWING THE DIFFERENT SIZE OF THE PRINT OF THE SAME FOOT

I PRINT OF FOOT LEFT IN RUNNING
II   ,,   ,,   ,,   ,,   ,, WALKING
III   ,,   ,,   ,,   ,,   ,, STANDING

To face page 60

plan is that, however loose the soil, except in the case of snow, all such evanescent traces can be, as it were, stereotyped and preserved.

(4) Another point connected with identification has likewise attracted attention—viz, the impression left by the naked foot when covered with blood on the floor of an apartment. The result of the attention which has been given to this subject, however, is that such impressions can only lead to the identification of the suspected criminal when the conformation of the foot or toes of the party has been so peculiar as to have left traces of such peculiarity on the stain.

Nothing could be accurately determined from the size of the stain, as only a part and not the whole of the foot, would have been in contact with the ground. It might be useful, however, to preserve a stain of this kind for future reference, as in the case of the boarding of a wooden floor, which could be taken up at the stained part and its identity secured.

The conclusions of our continental brethren seem to have been overlooked or ignored by our own jurists on the occasion of a remarkable trial in Glasgow, in 1862. In this instance, impressions from the feet of the woman on trial for the murder (M'Lachlan) were compared with others from the floor, left by the victim, and also with impressions from the feet of an old man (Fleming), on whom the crime was attempted to be shifted by the defence.

To demonstrate the futility of trusting to such evidence, I set on foot some experiments at the time, the results of which I show you — (Fig 4)

You will observe the varying sizes of the different impressions, on the paper, of the foot of the *same* person, produced by differences in the mode of bringing down his foot, 1st, In a rapid progression, 2d, by standing on the spot, and 3d, by a slow advance.

(5) There are, further, cases which present obstacles to the identification of living persons, which are partly to be considered as legal curiosities, and partly involve points bearing more or less directly and exclusively on legal medicine. Thus our legal records contain instances of mistaken identity, from the resemblance which one individual is occasionally found to bear to another, and that whether in the case of relatives or otherwise. Passing over these—of which some striking cases are adduced by Dr Montgomery, calculated to teach the necessity of studying

accurately the grounds of such decision on the part of witnesses, and the extreme caution by which they should be guided in their decisions—it is of more importance to remark, on the other hand, how readily witnesses will succeed at times in identifying persons whom they have seen, it may be only once, and that in situations extremely unfavourable for noting the personal peculiarities by which alone they can be guided. The flash of a pistol, or the gleam of lambent lights, in a dark night, has more than once sufficed for this.

A trial which occurred in France in 1808 gave rise to some proceedings calculated to throw light on the effects of fire-arms in leading to the identification of the persons discharging them in the dark.

A gentleman's servant, while riding along with his master, was wounded by being fired at from behind a ditch, and through a hedge. It was an hour and 43 minutes before the rising of the moon, and the night was dark, yet both the gentleman and his servant swore that they recognised the assassins by the light of the discharge. One of the persons accused was arrested, tried and condemned, but an appeal was taken to the Court of Cassation. This led to the question being referred to M. Gineau, Professor of Physics in the Imperial College, whether it was possible that the priming on being inflamed could produce sufficient light to discover the face of the person firing. Gineau, in consequence, with several friends, had guns fired on in a dark room, and in a courtyard, but found the light so fuliginous, and so rapidly extinguished, that those placed around could not distinguish the person firing. The condemned was therefore acquitted.

The erroneous nature of this decision was shown by a case subsequently reported in the same country by Foderé, as well as by the experiments of Dr Desgranges of Lyons, which led the latter to the conclusion that on a very dark night, and away from any source of light, the person who had fired the gun might be identified within a moderate distance. He states, however, that if the flash were not very strong, the smoke very dense, and the distance great, the person firing the piece could not be identified.

A case in point is adduced by Dr Taylor, where a gentleman in England, in 1839, identified a person who fired at him while driving home in his gig during a dark night.

Some further light has been thrown on this point, and previous opinions have received certain modifications, from the result of a numerous and varied series of experiments undertaken at Constantine, by M. Cauvet, in December 1873. His conclusions are, (1) that the person firing a pistol may be recognised if the observer is placed very near him, say five paces, and at the side of the line of fire. (2) that he may be recognised when the discharge has been in a close place of small dimensions, and the observer is in a stooping posture, or squatting; (3) that the chance of distinguishing the person firing is affected by the quality of the powder employed, the best English powder enabling the observer, when in or by the side of the person firing, both to see and identify him.

The identification of persons has been often accomplished by attention to minute circumstances, easily overlooked by a careless observer. Thus, identity may be established by observing that the party is left-handed, in cases where a particular wound or injury could have been inflicted only by a person thus circumstanced. Thus, in a case in which Sir Astley Cooper was concerned as a witness, the prisoner when pressed to say whether he was left-handed, protested that he was not. When called on, however, to hold up his head and plead to the indictment, he unconsciously held up his left hand. Dr Cummin, again, has referred to the following cases:—That of a butcher, detected from the mode in which the throat of his victim had been cut; the mark left by a blow with a large key, with which in self-defence the attacked had struck his assailant; and certain impressions on fruit, corresponding with the absence of two front teeth, which led to the detection of a thief who had this peculiarity.

Instances of a like kind might easily be multiplied, but these may suffice.

Lastly, Certain continued influences, chemical and physical, seldom fail to leave their imprint on different parts of the bodies, particularly on the hands and feet, of workmen engaged in various trades and occupations. These have been studied, to some extent successfully, by Devergie, Tardieu, and Vernois.

It now only remains for us to consider the medico-legal points turning on the question of—

II. Identity in the dead body.—It becomes necessary occasionally to identify the dead, in cases of murder, accidental or sudden death, poisoning, etc.—cases which not unfrequently present themselves under very embarrassing circumstances. There is no period after death at which this investigation ceases to be requisite, or at which it can be declined by the medical jurist as unnecessary. We shall therefore have to advert to the identification of the dead

—1st, Immediately after death and previous to the commencement of putrefaction in the dead body. 2d, After decomposition has begun in the body, before the soft parts have disappeared, or previously to the completion of the process of putrefaction. 3d, Where the body has been previously mutilated, or where fragments of it only are found; and 4th, After the body has been reduced to the state of a mere skeleton.

1st, Of the identification of the body soon after death, and before the commencement of putrefaction. I need scarcely remind you of the change the features undergo soon after death in any case, at periods varying, according to circumstances, from a few hours up to some days. No one can have been present at the post-mortem inspection of a person whom he had attended or known during life but must have been struck with this. The change is made more striking when the examination takes place under circumstances which otherwise yield no assistance to the ready recognition of the party. Thus, in the summer of the year 1831, the body of a boy of fourteen was discovered in a stable attached to the dwelling house of a medical man in Aberdeen. It was enclosed in a sack with a rope about the neck, and the sack was wet, as if newly taken out of water. A clamour having got up about his having been *burked*, I was sent to make a judicial inspection of the body. From the appearances on dissection I had no hesitation in reporting that the boy had died from natural causes, and that his death had resulted from extensive disease of the knee and hip joints. It was afterwards discovered that the body had been disinterred from the churchyard of Banchory-Devenick, and that, enclosed in the sack, it had been dragged, at the stern of a boat, through the Dee opposite the churchyard. What I would notice in this case is, that the boy had been my own patient, in the Boys' Hospital, from the 19th of February to the 9th of May in the same year, and had only been in the country for five or six weeks before his death; and yet, so altered were his features, that not having heard of his death, I had not the slightest idea at the time of the inspection of having ever seen the boy before.

The following occurrence took place when I was a student. The details I give from memory.

A medical student of the name of Downie, who died about two years afterwards, had, in company with some others, disinterred a body from the churchyard of Newhills. On the night after that of the disinterment, they were bringing it to town from a place where it had been temporarily concealed, near Donmouth. They had scarcely, however, moved from the spot when the Coastguard suddenly came upon them. Downie's companions fled, leaving him with the body, which he attempted to defend, but was overpowered and captured. The Coastguard brought the body to town with the prisoner, whom they lodged in gaol. A day or two after this the wife and sons of a weaver in the 'Spital,' who had been some days amissing, came forward and claimed the body as that of their relative. But as this person had been in good health at the time of his disappearance, and as no reason was known for his absence, the relatives of the weaver, who had sworn most positively to the identity, accused Downie of having enticed him away and murdered him.

Downie now seeing the serious nature of the charge thus preferred against him, found it necessary to state where he had actually procured the body in question. A party was then sent out to Newhills, to search the grave there, which they found empty.

But here a new difficulty arose. The relatives of the Newhills dead person, when shown the body, offered to make oath to it, while the Spital people refused to acknowledge their mistake.

At this stage of the proceedings, however, the case assumed a new aspect. The Spital weaver reappeared in life, but so incredulous were the people of the neighbourhood, that he had to be paraded through the streets to satisfy them, and many even then would scarcely believe the evidence of their senses, but insisted that it was only a figure dressed up in the weaver's clothes that was shown them.

Downie was tried for the violation of the churchyard, and fined heavily.

In the *Edinburgh Monthly Journal* for February 1854, Dr Kinloch has related a case of mistaken identity under the following circumstances :—

The body of an old man was found on the bank of the Dee at Drumoak. The left ear and the first finger of the left hand were wanting—the mutilation apparently of long standing. Two young women claimed the body as that of their father, who had been in the habit of leaving home for weeks at a time, and who had lost his left ear and left forefinger. On the return of the daughters and friends of the supposed party from his funeral, the boatman of a ferry which they had to cross, asked them for whom they were in mourning, and on receiving their answer, laughingly informed them that he had only half an hour before ferried them father over alive and well, which, on reaching home, they found to be true. Whose the body was which they had interred was not discovered

2d, The dead body may require to be identified after the commencement of the decomposition of the soft parts In cases of this sort medical men are obviously the only persons qualified to assist in establishing the identity

The subject of the changes undergone by the body after death, during the several stages of its decomposition, is one which will have to be discussed afterwards in detail in another connection (*Vide* Death.) Meanwhile, it will only be necessary to observe here that some striking instances have occurred, in which, contrary to what is usual, even the features have been known to escape alteration for long periods, so as to be still recognisable

Thus, the remains of Hampden were supposed to have been identified in Buckinghamshire in 1828, and the body was said to have been at the time in a high state of preservation

In 1813, the coffin of Charles I. was opened in St George's Chapel, Windsor, in presence of Sir Henry Halford, who states that, on removing the cerecloth, the complexion of the skin was observed to be dark and discoloured He adds that the forehead and temples had lost little or nothing of their muscular substance, the cartilage of the nose was gone, but the left eye, in the first moment of exposure, was open and full, though it vanished almost immediately After describing the pointed beard, the oval face, and the teeth, which were all characteristic, he sums up The countenance, in short, notwithstanding its disfigurement, bore a strong resemblance to the coins and busts, and especially to the picture of Charles by Vandyke

Further, we may remark here that, although there can be no doubt of the occasional, though certainly extremely rare, occurrence of such instances as the above, the difficulty of identifying the dead body after the commencement of decomposition is extremely great

In a trial which took place at Edinburgh in 1823, of resurrectionists for stealing dead bodies, one of these was sworn to by a witness as that of his sister, which he knew by a decrepitude, and certain marks which characterised the person of the deceased On the ground of the change wrought by putrefaction (the body having been interred nine weeks before the recognition took place), it was attempted to throw a doubt over this statement, and medical men were called on for their opinion The late Dr Barclay, who was examined for the defenders, stated that the longest period he ever knew during which the features remained recognisable was a fortnight, in the instance of a Lascar. He mentioned in evidence that a case had occurred the previous winter, in which some friends of a lame person, understanding that the body had been brought to his rooms, came to claim it. Dr Barclay ordered it to be delivered up; but Dr. Thatcher, his assistant, caused an artificial subject, made of leather, to be set before the applicants, and they claimed this instead of the real subject.

Occasionally bodies are found to mummify naturally, when the identification cannot be made out. A child's body was examined in the Aberdeen dead-house in 1874. It had been found in a servant's chest in an outhouse, which led to an inquiry by the authorities. From its dry and shrivelled state the sex could not be determined, and from the bulk of the bones and the ossification of the lower epiphyses of the femurs, the only point which admitted of settlement was that of its being a child born at or near the ninth month of its mother's pregnancy.

A similar natural mummy was found on pulling down a dry-stone wall in the country a few years ago, where nothing but a slight leathery coating covered the bones.

3d, The question of identity may have to be settled after the body has been mutilated, or where fragments of it only have been found.

A curious case of this kind was communicated to me by a legal gentleman who was agent for the defence. An idiot boy in Aberdeen, who died about sixty years ago, was disinterred for dissection by some medical students. After a considerable portion of the body, including the face, had been dissected, it was discovered by his relatives that the body had been carried off from the churchyard, and a search having been established, it was traced to the custody of the students. They were accordingly brought to trial. The body of the boy, when found on the dissecting-table, was so disfigured that there was only one means left of proving its identity. The boy had a whim during life of permitting his nails to grow, and had not allowed them to be cut for many years previous to his death. They had consequently curled round the tips of his fingers and toes till they had thus come to extend along the palmar and plantar surfaces in a strange way. The counsel for the prosecution availed himself of the knowledge of this fact, and his proof seemed to be complete, when a late shrewd and intelligent member of the profession came forward and gave in evidence that it was not an unusual circumstance for the nails to grow for several inches after death. This astounding statement so nonplussed the jury that the case was allowed to drop, is not proven.

The case of some resurrectionists tried at Edinburgh several years ago for stealing from a churchyard the body of a lady which was not traced to the dissecting-room till a great part of the corpse was destroyed, the body in question was identified by a dentist, who produced a cast of the gums which he had taken before her death.

A still more striking case of identification by a person of the same profession occurred in the American case of Dr P——. An attempt had been made in this instance to consume the body by fire in an assay furnace, but a set of mineral teeth remained, though the gold plate in which they had been fixed had been melted; and by an examination of the teeth a dentist recognised them as of his own manufacture, as those which he had supplied to the murdered gentleman.

The following is one out of the many foreign cases which might be quoted of the identification by the profession of mutilated bodies.

On the 18th of November 1814 Auguste Dautun was assassinated in Paris by his own brother. On the day following some boatmen found in the Seine a human head wrapped in a dish-cloth, in the corner of which were the letters A. D. Other portions of the victim, with two entire thighs and legs, were discovered the same day near a public *fosse d'aisance*.

It became of importance to ascertain if the person thus discovered were actually Dautun, and, as that individual had been lame, it was necessary to demonstrate that one limb was shorter than the other, which could not readily be known from the appearance of the fragments.

The examiners, of whom the celebrated Dupuytren was one, after describing the height, the complexion, the colour of the hair, the teeth, the wounds present, and the situation of a wart on the face, carefully inspected the lower extremities, and especially the bones and soft parts entering into the formation of the hip-joints, from which they were led to draw the following conclusions:— 1st, That the man examined must have had, when a child, disease of both hip-joints. 2d, That these diseases, although of remote period, and cured, must have left a remarkable degree of deformity of the hips and pelvis, and have led to difficult progression, and probably lameness, and certainly to a painful and disagreeable moulding of the body on the lower limbs. An exact comparison of the two limbs in regard to their length, and an examination of the soles of the feet led them to believe that the right lower extremity was shorter than the left, and that the individual must have supported the weight of the body in progression and in standing on the ball of the toes, not on the whole sole.

The case of Greenacre, in London, deserves to be noticed. In 1837 the trunk of a woman was discovered in a sack, the head and legs being wanting. The persons who examined the mutilated body could find nothing to serve for its identification but a malformation of the uterus, the mark of a ring on one finger, and the horny cuticle of one who had been engaged in household work. The bloodless state of the body, however, pointed to the mutilation having been effected before the corpse had cooled. The head, when afterwards found at a different place, exhibited the profile peculiar to the sex and order of birth. The lower extremities when discovered at a still later period, exhibited as their sole peculiarity a dyeing of the skin over the legs, as from the wearing of black stockings. The sections of the bones of the thighs and neck when now compared, were found exactly to correspond. This examination assisted the detection of the murderer when subsequently arrested on suspicion.

In November 1857 the public in London was kept in a state of high excitement for some weeks by the discovery on one of the bridges of parts of a body in a basket, which the utmost activity of the police failed to identify, while no clue was obtained to the party or parties who had exposed it, the greatest care having been taken to destroy all traces of its identity. But here, though the head was wanting, as well as the greater part of the spine, the hands and feet, portions of the left side of the chest, and the whole of the viscera of the chest, abdomen, and pelvis, and most of the muscles, Dr Taylor clearly made out the sex from the bones and from a portion of the corpus cavernosum of one side left attached to the ischium, as also the probable age of the party, his height, the colour of his skin and that of his hair—these last from fragments of skin left on the wrists and one knee—and the date of death approximately. He also showed that the mutilation must have taken place while cadaveric rigidity continued in the body, from eighteen to twenty-four hours after death, but the individual had received a wound in the left side of the chest over the seat of the heart while alive or only recently dead, that after death the limbs had been in the distorted state usual in cases of violent death; and that the muscles had been exposed to boiling water, and afterwards salted

A case of the identification of a mutilated body under very unfavourable circumstances occurred here (Aberdeen) in September 1875 A lad of sixteen, while bathing at the sea-beach, was drowned, and the body carried out to sea The weather at the time was tempestuous, and the body had been tossed about amongst the rocks at the mouth of the harbour for ten days before it came ashore The naked body was disfigured, the skull being bare, and the soft parts of the face destroyed by the erosive action of the water, or by the ravages of fishes, so that the father of the missing boy failed to identify him. This was not the case with the mother, who claimed the body as that of her son from detecting two small pimple-looking projections on the front of the chest, which, at the inspection, were found to be supplementary mammæ

4th, It now only remains for us to notice lastly that the dead body may be required to be identified after it has been reduced to a mere skeleton

Trials at long periods after death, and when nothing but the bones remain, are not unusual on the Continent, and cases of this sort occasionally occur in this country

In 1759, Eugene Aram, the famous scholar, was tried, condemned, and executed for a murder committed fifteen years before, chiefly on the evidence of the skeleton, found in a cave, with the skull beaten inwards

In a case investigated by MM Laurent, Noble, and Vitry, at Versailles in 1818, the bones of a man who had been murdered, and had lain buried for three years, were identified by noticing a malformation, which must have produced a certain degree of lameness

In such instances as these, where only the bones remain, unless some peculiarity exists in the skeleton, such as those just referred to, or where there are indications of injuries inflicted on them during life, the only data we can furnish towards their identification must obviously rest on the approximations we can obtain as to the age and sex of the inspected party, on the principles already laid down under Age and Sex

It may not be out of place here to advert to a question put to me, in connection with a criminal case, as to the earliest period of fœtal life at which the buried remains might be sought for with the chance of finding them, where the exact spot of sepulture was known. The answer obviously was that they could scarcely be looked for too soon, even before the third or fourth month.

In the autumn of 1862 I had occasion to examine the mutilated remains of an infant, born in the eighth month, consisting of bones of the left arm, left side of the chest and abdomen, and left thigh and leg, kept together by the integuments, along with some of the bones of the head and face, and the right ulna and femur, partly acted on by fire. The other parts of the infant were believed to have been destroyed in the fire by the father of the child.

I have merely to add on this point, that the medical examiner will occasionally be expected to discriminate readily between the bones of the lower animals and those of man, whether found together or separately.

An interesting case of the former kind is given by Tardieu in the *Annales d'Hygiène*, tome xx page 114, from a Roman case.

An instance of the latter occurred here, which is so far interesting, as that had it not been found that the bones were entirely those of the sheep, it might have given rise to some curious conjectures and suspicions. The mutilated and partly charred bones were found under the hearthstone of a house in Aberdeen, which had been occupied by a woman (Humphrey) who was executed in 1824 for the murder of her husband, by pouring oil of vitriol down his throat when drunk in bed.

I have now laid before you the various circumstances under which the question of identity may be brought under your notice. As both in the dead and the living body each individual case has its own peculiarities, it has been necessary to illustrate the subject by actual cases, no other course being open to us, since in most of the illustrations the narrative has included the prominent points to be attended to in such investigations, and I have been spared the necessity of much general remark. I shall now, however, in conclusion, give a comprehensive review of the general principles applicable to the cases which are apt to arise in medico-legal practice. These deal either with general or special physical appearances, i.e. applicable to the whole of these cases, or limited to only a portion of such inquiries; but all or many of them are applicable, as well to the living as to the dead.

Such physical appearances—following Orfila—may be summed up as follows:—

Attention has to be directed to—1*st*, The *age* of the individual, or the nearest approximation to it which can be obtained. 2*d*,

His *height*. 3d, The *head*, and especially the shape of its bones; the hairs, their number and colour, the forehead, which may be prominent or compressed; the eyebrows, which may be far apart, or may meet at their inner extremities, the eyes, whether large or small, prominent or sunk; the nose, which may be short, long, etc; the lips, large or small, with or without trace of cicatrices; the teeth, few in number, irregularly placed, small, or *vice versa;* the mouth, large or small; the chin, full or pitted, round or pointed; the beard, thin or bushy, the face, broad or long 4th, The *neck*, whether short and thick, or long and thin. 5th, The *chest*, whether well-formed or otherwise, the shoulders, whether high or the reverse, the sternum, whether flat, sunk, or prominent. 6th, The *pelvis*, whether large or small 7th, The *limbs*, including the hands and feet, whether large or small; the fingers, whether short or long, or of mutually proportionate lengths, the knees, if turned in, the ankles, whether more projecting than usual, the lower limbs and feet, whether of equal length, and free or not from deformity. 8th, The *genitals*, if free from any defects of conformation 9th, Whether or not any *marks* exist on the *skin* 10th, *Cicatrices* which may have followed burns, wounds, or tumours, marks which seldom become effaced, and which may sometimes, from their seat, their form, their direction and extent, etc, afford valuable indications 11th, Traces of *dislocations* or *fractures*

Of these characteristics, those upon which Orfila lays most stress are the four following—viz the *height;* the *state* of the *bones* and *form* of the *skeleton;* the state of the *teeth*, and lastly, the *hair*

LECTURE VI

IMPOTENCE AND STERILITY

Impotence as a Disqualification for Marriage—Impotence as a Ground for Divorce—Impotence as distinct from Sterility—IMPOTENCE IN THE MALE—Physical Causes—Absolute Causes—Absence of the Penis—Absence of the Testes—Congenital Deficiency of the Testes—Eunuchs—Extrophy of the Bladder—Hermaphrodism—Doubtful Causes—Hypospadia and Epispadia—Bifurcation of the Penis—Adhesions of the Penis to the Scrotum or Abdomen—Excessive or Diminutive Size of the Penis—Abnormal Direction of the Organ—Contraction of the Urethra—Phymosis and Paraphymosis—Scrotal Hernia—Hydrocele—Sarcocele—Monorchides and Polyorchides—Polysarcia—Occult Causes—Moral Causes—Functional Causes—IMPOTENCE OR STERILITY IN THE FEMALE—Physical Causes—Absolute Causes—Absence of the Vagina—Absence of the Uterus—Absence of the Vulva—Doubtful Causes—The Extremes of Age—Irregularity of the Vagina—Occlusion of the Vulva—Excessive Constriction of the Vagina—Irritability of the Sexual Organs—Bicorned Uterus—Amenorrhœa—Occult Causes—GENERAL CONCLUSIONS

IN previous lectures we discussed the *structural* differences in the sexes, bearing upon legal questions. The study of the *functional* relations of the sexes, to which we have now to turn, opens up to us many important medico-legal topics—Impotence in the male, sterility in the female, the crimes of rape and abortion, pregnancy and delivery in the female, various questions connected with the birth and maturity of the infant; and infanticide, or the destruction of the viable infant, which will close this division of our course.

The first of these topics, connected with the exercise of the genital organs, is that of Impotence, or inability for sexual intercourse, closely connected with which is that of Sterility, or unfitness for procreation and conception.

Sexual incapacity, in the form of impotence, though usually attributed to the male alone, may exist in either sex, as may such incapacity in the form of sterility, though commonly imputed to the female alone.

The question of sterility in either sex is in a great measure inferential, and the fact is oftenest dependent on internal organisation, of which the medico-legal examiner cannot in general have sufficient cognisance in the living body. It is so closely connected with the question of impotence that the law has not attempted to separate them, and, to be understood, they must be treated of together. It is to be kept in mind besides that, though there may be sterility without impotence, yet that impotence necessarily implies sterility.

Impotence in the male may be set up as a sufficient plea to invalidate a charge of rape or bastardy, but the importance of this condition in either sex, medico-legally considered, has its bearing mainly on the validity of the marriage contract, since in law, unless the parties are in a condition to fulfil that contract— the procreation of children—it becomes *ipso facto* void, and a divorce may be sued for and obtained on that plea. This may be done from whatever cause the impotence has arisen, provided that such impotence is not relative merely, or removable, but virtual and irremediable, and that it had existed previous to marriage, and had not occurred only after the marriage had been contracted.

But before this forcible separation of the parties, or divorce, can be obtained, the fact of the impotence must be incontestably established, and this can only be done by inspection of the parties, and by medical testimony, which it behoves the medical practitioner to be able to produce when required. For although other than medical evidence is justly demanded in such cases, yet the latter throws the preponderating weight into the scale.

Impotence in either sex, employing this term in its wider sense as including sterility, may arise from various causes, either *physical* or *moral*. Some of these of the former class are at once obvious to the examiner, and decisive of the question of impotence, others of them are of a character at best but inconclusive or uncertain. Hence the division of physical causes into *absolute* and *doubtful*. Other causes again, though physical and actual or real, lie beyond the reach of the examiner, and hence have been termed *occult* or hidden. Besides, in either sex, the causes of impotence may be of a purely constitutional kind, and merely inferential, as such not admitting of medical or legal proof or evidence, to which consequently the designation *moral* causes has been assigned. These, though they should be recognised by the medical jurist, obviously lie beyond his province.

Taking up in order the various causes of impotence we have just enumerated, firstly in the male and secondly in the female, we proceed to notice—

The Physical Causes of Impotence in the Male.

Impotence in the male may be either absolute or relative, the former being a real, permanent, and irremediable inability, the latter being but temporary, relative to one particular female, and removable by time alone or by curative means.

We begin then with the absolute causes of male impotence. The *first* of these is,—the *absence* of the *penis*.

The absence of the penis from whatever cause it may have arisen, necessarily implies impotence. This deficiency must, however, be in every case complete; for if a sufficient portion of it be left to enter within the external parts of the female, to excite the venereal orgasm in her, and to deposit the semen within the vagina, fecundation is possible, and the impotence cannot be admitted. Cases of mutilation of the organ short of this, which were not followed by impotence, are recorded in sufficient number. Of this, I encountered an instance early in my own practice. A gentleman from Edinburgh, though, when seen by me, he had lost his glans and part of the penis from phagedena, subsequently married, and had children. Other instances of more extensive mutilations are on record.

A wax cast in our museum represents the case of a seaman who recovered from a fall on a hunting knife at Greenland, causing a large penetrating wound in the abdomen, and the complete loss of his penis. In this instance, however, the man confessed that, though he had venereal desires, he could not effect copulation.

The absence of the *testicles* is an absolute cause of impotence, but nothing except their entire absence is to be reckoned as such. It is not enough to enable us to decide that there are no testes that we find none in the scrotum. If no trace of a local cicatrix, or marks of mutilation, be discoverable, the probability is that they have not reached the scrotum. In those individuals termed "crypsorchides" these bodies often remain for life above the inguinal ring. It is necessary, therefore, to be able to distinguish between these crypsorchides and persons in whom there exists a congenital atrophy, or entire absence of the testes, and the following marks will answer this purpose:—

Those who, from birth, have no testicles, or very imperfect and inert ones, have the genitals but little developed; the mons veneris is loaded with fat, they have little bodily and mental energy, and no sexual desires, their skin is fine and soft, the figure approaches the feminine character, they have little or no beard, the voice is shrill, the breasts bulky, the hands short and plump, and the limbs slender.

Crypsorchides, on the contrary, have the usual development of the sexual organs, and possess the usual masculine characters, though in a few cases even they approach the general feminine character.

Where the absence of testes combined with the local cicatrix points to the extirpation of these organs, the distinction should be noticed between those who have been castrated in infancy and those who have been thus mutilated after puberty. In the former, the same characters will present themselves which we have noticed as peculiar to those who have congenital want of the testes. When the castration has been effected later than puberty, erection still occurs; and coition, though not, of course, with emission of semen, may be effected. The masculine character otherwise is still retained as before.

To this, however, I have known one exception, and Devergie mentions others known to him. Several years ago I extirpated a testicle for soft fungus from a patient. The opposite one soon afterwards atrophied, so as not to exceed the bulk of a horse bean. About two years after the operation, when I again saw him, his beard had almost disappeared, and he had acquired a feminine voice and general appearance, to a very considerable extent. The penis had shrunk to the dimensions of boyhood, and the scrotum was shrivelled. He had no sexual desires nor potency.

Apathy, moroseness, want of sensibility, pusillanimity, and incapacity, are said to be mental qualities of all eunuchs.

The opinion has been maintained, especially on the Continent, that those eunuchs who are made so after puberty may retain, for indefinite periods of considerable continuance, the power of generation, in proof of which facts are appealed to. Thus, a man who was castrated by Sir Astley Cooper stated that he retained the sensation of emission for *twelve* months, and the power of copulation for *ten* years after the operation. Otto mentions that he found the vesiculæ seminales still full of semen in a man who died *nine* months after he had castrated himself. Ricord, again, refers to the case of a man who was castrated on account of disease in both testes, who had, nevertheless, erections and the most violent sexual desires. Besides this, it is asserted, on grounds which are not questioned, that animals have been known to propagate after castration. All this, however, comes short of the proof of potency after the loss of the testes, and only proves that erection, copulation, and even the emission of some fluid, may take place occasionally under these circumstances

Some of the differences of opinion amongst authors as to the effects of certain genital defects and mutilations admit to a certain extent of reconciliation, if we take into account the fact that such impotent, or supposed impotent, persons, whether we term them eunuchs or not, present considerably diversified defects; whether these have been caused by atrophy of the testes, the effect of these organs being crushed artificially, as is done by veterinary surgeons in animals; the removal of the testes leaving the penis entire; or the deprivation, not only of the testes, but also of the penis and the rest of the external organs of generation. These last alone are truly eunuchs, and undoubtedly impotent.

When the external genitals are not developed, the individual is generally set down as impotent. Previously to puberty, the impotence is undoubted, but it should be kept in mind that cases occasionally occur both of its unusually early and unusually late appearance in the male. *Fourteen* years is the earliest age at which we have any authentic instance of a boy being prolific. On the other hand, Mr Farr records an instance of a man of forty-two, whose sexual organs had remained in an infantile state.

In such a case as this last, it is not necessarily to be inferred that the individual is incurably impotent. Mr Curling mentions a person of twenty-six whose penis and testicles little exceeded the size of a boy's of eight years, but who married and became the father of a family, the genitals in the course of two years attaining their full adult development.

Extrophy of the bladder, as usually encountered, is a manifest cause of impotence. This malformation is characterised by a bramble-like tumour placed above the symphysis pubis, whose bulk is liable to considerable increase, formed by the bladder turned out through an opening in the abdominal parietes, the consequence of arrested development. (*Vide* Fig 2, p 51.) The ureters open on the surface of the tumour; the penis is imperforate, short, destitute of urethra, and sometimes dilated and hollowed out into a groove on its upper surface. Frequently the testicles remain in the abdomen, and the scrotum is empty and shrunken.

Real hermaphrodites are undoubtedly impotent, though not so regarded in law, they being permitted to marry. All the divorce cases we read of have been in consequence of the parties choosing the sex to which they did not properly belong.

The remaining physical causes of impotence in the male may,

for distinction's sake, be termed *doubtful* causes. Amongst these we have Hypospadia and Epispadia. The conformation of the former of these, already noticed under Doubtful Sex, though presenting obstacles to connection, has not been found in every case to lead to sterility. Thus we have authentic cases of the transmission of this malformation from the father to the son. In the celebrated case of John Hunter, mentioned by Sir Everard Home, where the opening was below the scrotum, injection of semen was had recourse to with effect; though in one instance of Truset, impregnation took place in the natural way.

Epispadia, or that defect in which the opening is on the dorsum of the penis, betwixt the glans and pubes, is much more rarely met with than hypospadia, and would interfere still less with the potency or virility of the individual. I had once occasion in practice to treat a young gentleman in this condition for gonorrhœa.

Bifurcation of the penis, though it might present an obstacle more or less surmountable to penetration, would not of itself necessarily lead to sterility; the experiments of Spalanzani, and others, having shown that in animals complete intercourse is not necessary to impregnation.

Examples of attachment of the penis to the abdomen or to the scrotum, if they do not properly belong to the province of the surgeon, are rather to be regarded as medical curiosities, than as likely to give rise to practical difficulties in their legal relations.

The same may be said of excessive and diminutive size of the penis, either by themselves, or in relation to the dimensions of particular females. Abnormal direction of the organ, and contraction of the canal of the urethra, phymosis, paraphymosis, scrotal hernia, and hydrocele, are circumstances which in the majority of instances admit of relief. Sarcocele, if both testes were completely diseased, would involve impotence; but those cases are admittedly rare, and the diagnosis would not in any case be difficult.

Monorchides, or persons possessing only one testicle, are now excluded even from the doubtful causes of impotence; though the Parliament of Paris, in 1665, decreed that the marriage-contract should not be held valid unless two testicles were producible.

The same remark applies to Crypsorchides and Polyorchides; neither these persons, nor Monorchides being necessarily impotent, as has been proved by the fact of their occasionally fruitful marriage.

Polysarcia, when excessive, has been mentioned as an

occasional cause of impotence, from the mechanical impediment it might present in some instances to the venereal congress

Physiologists have been unable to fix with any precision either the earliest or the latest period of virility in males, hence the impossibility of correctly judging of potency from the mere age of the parties. Hence too it is that the Ecclesiastical Courts look rather to the habit, strength, and constitution of the parties, than to their age

Again, amongst the doubtful causes of impotence must undoubtedly be placed that large list of cases, enumerated by some authors as a separate class, under the designation of *functional causes*, and originating in debauchery, intemperance, the abuse of narcotics or other drugs, diseases of the nervous system, or of the urinary organs, etc. As all these causes are relative, and can scarcely in any instance admit of being satisfactorily demonstrated, they have only an indirect bearing on medical jurisprudence

In the same category must be placed a set of cases which have been recognised, in which the male is, from causes which are not obvious, if not impotent, at least powerless to effect the impregnation of some one female, but not of others In the *Causes Célèbres* an amusing twofold instance of such want of sexual harmony is given by Pitaval. Two gentlemen of rank, very much of the same age and personal appearance, were married to wives who proved unfruitful after several years of marriage The two couples at last determined to proceed to a celebrated watering-place, in the hope of deriving some benefit from the change and the use of the springs On the way they put up at an inn, and retired for the night But the two wives had preceded their husbands to bed, and each of the latter mistook his friend's room for his own. In consequence of the mistake, each of the ladies proved with child

To the doubtful causes of impotence we must refer a set of cases, closely allied to the last, which are distinctively known (in contrast with physical defects) as *moral causes* of impotence in the male. The causes of impotence which we have considered were either such as produce permanent impotence, or those disturbances of the system, and obvious diseases, which, during their continuance, have the power of suspending the generative functions. Those to which we have now to advert are such as, even in a sound constitution, and in males with perfect genital organs, are capable of suspending the genital functions for a time, their cessation leaving the genitals free to fulfil their office.

G

Of this sort are strong mental emotions, such as too ardent desire, fear of not being loved, or of being incapable, shame, timidity, jealousy, hatred, disgust—in short, anything by which the mind is forcibly arrested. A temporary impotence from this class of causes is by no means of rare occurrence.

Of all the causes just mentioned, the fear of incompetence is most frequently productive of impotence. It was a knowledge of this fact that led Hunter to adopt the remarkable mode of cure which proved so successful in a case of impotence which came under his notice. He prevailed on the person to promise, on his honour, to pass six nights in bed with a young woman without attempting sexual intercourse; and, before the allotted time had expired, the patient's only fear was lest the force of desire should induce him to break his promise.

The facility with which the most vigorous man is rendered impotent by working on his imagination, or his superstition, was well known to the ancients, and may be still witnessed occasionally amongst the ignorant in more than one European country.

Lastly to the classes of causes of impotence brought forward by some writers, under the denominations of *occult* and *functional*, we need not refer, as these, even more than the last, have little or no bearing on Legal Medicine, as neither admitting of proof or refutation.

We now come to the subject of impotence or rather sterility, in the female. Here as in the case of the male, the physical causes are those only with which we have directly to do.

The organs of generation being naturally more complicated and deeper seated in the female than in the male, the causes of impotence in them are at the same time more numerous, and in general less apparent.

I shall enumerate all those physical causes which have been well authenticated, in the same order as I formerly pursued in treating of impotence in the male, giving, first, those which are generally admitted as absolute or certain causes; and, secondly, those which are only relative, temporary, or dubious.

Of the *certain causes*. I commence with congenital absence of the vagina. An instance of this occurred in the Old Meldrum case, noticed above (p   ) under "Doubtful Sex." This defect may or may not, as in the instance again brought forward, be coupled with absence of the uterus; but cases are more numerous of the combined deficiency of both organs.

In some instances, too, the defect in question has been coupled with the total want of the external organs of generation. Foderé gives an instance of this kind. A female, aged 25, for six years married without consummation, was examined by Dejours. She had never menstruated, but was in good health. A tumour, pierced by a small hole, was all that was found by him at the site of the vulva. He made an incision two inches deep, expecting to reach the vagina, but in vain. The artificial opening was kept patent by means of tents, but the husband, in despair, procured a divorce, and on the death of the woman, ten years afterwards, neither vagina nor uterus was discoverable on dissection. Beck refers to a similar case.

Another of the absolute causes of female sterility is absence of the uterus. In this instance, which is not of frequent occurrence, the vagina usually terminates superiorly in a *cul de sac*, the female does not menstruate, but her health does not suffer from the want of this evacuation. The absence of the uterus may be suspected, when, on introducing the finger into the vagina, it is found to terminate in the way we have described. To be certain of the existence of this deficiency, however, it will be necessary at the same time to introduce a catheter into the bladder. It can thus be ascertained that there is no organ interposed between the bladder and the finger at the place where the uterus should have been.

As we have seen, however, some authorities deny that this defect can be known during the life of the party.

Andral, in his *Pathological Anatomy*, mentions a case of complete absence of the uterus which occurred to M. Dupuytren at the Hôtel Dieu, in a woman aged 27. The vagina did not exceed an inch in length, and behind the *cul de sac* in which it terminated the rectum only was to be found. Above and behind the bladder were found the broad ligaments, containing, as usual, the fallopian tubes and ovaries. Where the tubes met there was a small solid tumour, with a resemblance to the uterus. The mammæ were well developed, the external genitals well formed, and there was nothing masculine in the appearance of the woman. She had never menstruated.

Stein gives a similar case in Hufeland's Journal, and has adduced others from several authors.

A third absolute cause of female sterility is total absence of the vulva. This confessedly rare malformation is usually coupled with absence of the vagina, or uterus, or both, as in the Old

Meldrum case, or with a defect to be noticed by-and-by, namely, irregularity of the vagina.

Fourthly, among the absolute causes of sterility in the female might be placed the extremes of age. But here almost as great latitude must be allowed for in judging absolutely of the fertile period, as in the case of the male sex. If we are to rely on reported instances, pregnancy must be admitted as having happened at all periods between the ages of 10 and 60 years, while its occurrence earlier or later than these ages must be considered as barely possible, if we are not prepared to call in question the authenticity of the narratives of female infants, on the one hand, exhibiting all the marks of puberty at 3 years or under, and on the other of women continuing to menstruate to their sixty-sixth or even their ninety ninth year

This brings us, in the second place, to the admittedly doubtful causes of sterility. Of these, I may notice first, one which I alluded to in speaking of the absence of the vagina—viz., irregularity of the vagina. By irregularity, I mean here an unusual course of the vagina, this canal having been known occasionally, in place of taking its usual course and opening at the vulva, to terminate at the perineum, the rectum, or even at the umbilicus. Briand is the only author who, so far as I am aware, would place this unnatural state of the canal amongst the absolute causes of impotence. In the first volume of the *London Medical Gazette*, there is a case related of copulation having been effected and followed by pregnancy where the vagina terminated at the rectum. The labour pains were suspected by the woman herself to be merely colic, and the medical man thought they were from retained menses, as the vulva was known to him to be wanting, and the vagina to have no outlet in that direction. On introducing his finger into an opening which he made with a scalpel in the direction of the vagina, he was astonished to find the membranes presenting. The delivery of a living child followed. The wound was subsequently kept open, and the woman again became pregnant. It is only necessary to add, that the minute opening through which the impregnation in the first instance had taken place was discovered in the rectum. It was only sufficient in size to admit a small probe

A similar case is given by Siebold

Barbaut relates two further cases of the same sort, where pregnancy occurred and delivery was effected, in one of them through laceration, and in the other by an incision in the direction of the internal parts

One more still striking instance remains, related by Morgagni. He states that a contemporary, Gianella, was called to a pregnant woman, 40 years of age, whose vagina opened on the anterior wall of the abdomen. He had to dilate it before delivery could be completed.

Another of the doubtful causes of sterility is occlusion of the vulva. We have a number of curious stories in reference to this matter, not to mention the older narratives of Beckman of jealous husbands on leaving home locking up their wives by padlocks passed through the labia. It is said in some parts of Africa to be the practice to this day to procure adhesion between the contiguous surfaces of the labia to secure the female slaves against impregnation. This practice, however, if it really exists, would be quite ineffectual in producing the desired security, unless it was also so complete as to close the vulva so perfectly as at the same time to prevent the escape of the urine, and to this extent it would scarcely be attempted. Though it might interpose an obstacle to delivery, it assuredly would not secure, in all cases, against impregnation.

The same remarks apply to those occasional adhesions of the labia which arise from inflammation produced by natural causes. Such an obstacle to the generative functions could easily be removed by operation.

Amongst the doubtful causes of female sterility must be placed excessive constriction of the vagina. This defect is fortunately not incurable, and cases are given in which the canal was successfully dilated by the introduction of bougies. Besides, even where the constriction has been considerable, impregnation has been accomplished, as in a case, related in the memoirs of the Academy of Sciences of Paris, of a woman who had a vagina so narrow as scarcely to admit a quill, and to render the escape of the catamenia difficult. After being married eleven years she proved with child, and the vagina then dilated of itself sufficiently to admit of delivery at the full term.

Excessive irritability of the sexual organs, rendering coition too painful to be permitted, is a removable cause of sterility, depending, as it usually does, upon some local cause, as in the cases mentioned by Dr Cobbam, where it depended upon piles, and ceased on their removal, and by Mr White, where the cure of a fistula obviated the impediment. Early in my own practice I was called to the wife of a watchman who was in the eighth month of pregnancy, but who from this circumstance, protested that she could not be pregnant, and persistently remained unconvinced of it up till an hour or two of her delivery at full time. The woman had been several years married.

Bicorned uterus has been mentioned as a cause of sterility in those instances in which the septum has been known to be prolonged even to the vulva. This might prevent intromission, but it is now known that it has, at least on two occasions, been compatible with impregnation.

Be this as it may, it is known that women with a bilocular state of the uterus are not sterile. Andral gives one case of this kind, where the woman died in giving birth to a child at the full time. Ollivier, in the *Archives de Médecine*, brings forward the case of a woman with this malformation, who died of peritonitis in giving birth to her fifth child.

A case strictly parallel has been given by Dr Lee, in the *Transactions of the London Medico-Chirurgical Society*. The woman had previously borne several living children. Another case has been lately reported from Norway.

Amenorrhœa has been considered as a cause of sterility in the female. The sexual functions in the female being regulated by the catamenia, it is commonly asserted that they cannot become impregnated either before their occurrence or after they have ceased to appear. As a general principle this may be true, but exceptions to this rule are known to have occurred, and cases are recorded of impregnation previous to the establishment of this function, and after its natural cessation.

The few causes of sterility in the female which remain to be noticed are all occult ones, and therefore, for the purpose of the medical jurist, must be placed amongst the doubtful causes, as, whether real or not, they are undiscoverable during the lifetime of the parties. Of these I may class together the obliteration of the cavity of the uterus, and of the canal of Fallopius, either complete, or limited to the inlets or outlets of the tube.

Some years ago I met with a case on dissection, which combined several such defects, not usually found co-existent.—

Mary Clark, a girl of the town, had poisoned herself with laudanum. At the *post-mortem* examination there was found a fibrous tumour of small size, which occupied the cavity of the uterus, whose mouth was plugged up. Both fallopian tubes were sealed up, except about the middle of their length, where a serous cyst was found in each about the bulk of a pigeon's egg. Similar cysts were found in both ovaries

If I may judge from what I have since met with in the dead-house, these last affections, and also obstructions of the fallopian tubes, seem to be usual in prostitutes, and may account in these instances, independently of other alleged causes, for their frequent sterility

Other organic causes I pass over, from their being occult ones I also omit the discussion of other reputed causes of impotence and sterility in women, such as prolapse of the uterus and of the vagina. They are so reputed without any sufficiently good reason Conception has been known to take place in such conditions of the female, as well as when gonorrhœa, fluor albus, immoderate menstruation, and even a carcinomatous state of the uterus were present

To sum up our remarks on the causes of impotence and sterility, both in the male and female, in the words of M Orfila:

1 There are certain causes of impotence in both sexes appreciable by us, which are absolute and irremediable It is sufficient to point out the existence of these causes in order to prove the individuals impotent

2. Certain other malformations, cognisable to the senses and remediable by art, give rise to temporary impotence

3 Mental causes are not sufficient to establish the existence of impotence.

4 When the excuse of temporary or relative impotence is set up for any reason—as to repel a charge of being the father of a child, for instance—if the impotence did not exist at the moment, nothing but medical proof to this effect, and that taken at the time of the alleged copulation, could safely be admitted in law.

5. Sterility can only be admitted in the case of incurable impotence

6 In every other circumstance, all that we are entitled to assume amounts to mere suspicion, insufficient to lead to the dissolution of a marriage, or to the disinheritance of an infant.

LECTURE VII.

DEFLORATION AND RAPE

DEFLORATION AND RAPE.—Preliminary Remarks.—Defloration and Rape contrasted—What constitutes a Rape in Law—Difficulty of repelling a Charge of Rape—The crime of "Intent to Ravish" VIOLATION OF THE FEMALE UNDER PUBERTY.—Occasional amount of injury in such cases—Absurd notions as to the effect of such connection—Indecent practices on female infants—Relaxation of the legal proof in the case of infants—False charges thus facilitated—Coition without penetration, and its effects on the female genitals—Diseased states liable to be mistaken for the effects of Impure Connection—Peculiar inflammatory affection of the Pudendum—Spurious Gonorrhœa—Instances of children laying themselves out for Libidinous practices—Effects of such practices on the Person and Genitals

THE subjects which have hitherto occupied our attention have all been referable to one class of questions, those which affect the civil or social rights of individuals. The one which we now approach belongs to a different class of questions, namely, those which relate to the division of Injuries against the Person.

The first of these which I shall notice comprises the subjects of Defloration and Rape.

These two topics, though in reality separate, are usually discussed together by writers on medical jurisprudence, and necessarily so, as the former of these, defloration, possesses no further interest for the medical jurist beyond the bearing of the proof of that act on the alleged forcible violation or rape of the female's person.

Defloration means simply, as the term implies, the act of depriving a female of her virginity, and as such it does not of necessity come within the meaning of a criminal action. When, however, this has been done forcibly, or against the will of the female, or in circumstances which rendered her incapable of withholding her consent, the violation is regarded as a crime of the deepest dye. But force is not in law regarded as a necessary element to constitute the crime of rape. A woman under the influence of bodily terror, from the use of threatening language, may yield her assent. This, however, may be regarded as moral force, and it is so in fact regarded in law   Again, under the influence of narcotic drugs, or in the states of syncope or of coma, the woman is incapable of giving or withholding her assent, in any of which cases the connection, though it may have been accomplished without the use of violence, is still considered as virtually forced, and as such is severely punishable

In charges of rape moreover, by the law of Scotland the quality of violence is only required in females above the age of twelve years, below that age it is held that consent cannot be given, and that the connection must have been involuntary   In the case of females below the age of puberty, which you will remember is fixed in law at twelve, there is only a constructive force, or force in the estimation of the law; a girl of these tender years being held to be incapable either of desire or discretion, so that the deed is said to be without her will even when she makes no resistance   On this account, and on account of the greater depravity implied in such an attempt on an innocent and helpless infant, the pains of law have always been more rigorously applied in such cases than in ordinary rape.

In England it has been decided that consent does not excuse or alter the nature of the crime when the female is under ten years of age, and the carnal knowledge of such a female is considered rape in law   Even the solicitation of the child does not excuse it.

In all these instances the force has been merely moral, and the proof of the crime rests upon the fact of the sexual intercourse having been effected, without the necessity of establishing the having had recourse for this purpose to actual violence or physical force.

There are, however, cases of rape in which the circumstance of sexual intercourse having been admitted or proved, something further must be established to bring the case within the range of a criminal prosecution   The criminality of the act in these cases consists alone in the physical force which has been employed to effect the sexual intercourse   Thus it has been laid down in our (Scotch) law that a rape may be committed even on a common prostitute, provided clear and decisive evidence of the act having been perpetrated by violence is laid before a jury, while in England not only does this hold good, but it is further decided that the same crime may be committed on the concubine of the ravisher, these circumstances being only held as clogs on the prosecution

This being understood, you will be prepared to perceive the

degree of confusion which has arisen in regard to this subject from the incautious use of the terms forcible violation and forcible defloration as synonymous with rape in some of our works on medical jurisprudence. If they are still to be retained, it should be clearly understood that in the majority of such cases the sense in which they are employed is that of moral or constructive force and not merely as implying physical violence only.

Up to the date of our earlier works on medical jurisprudence, English lawyers were by no means agreed as to what it was that constituted a rape. By a recent Act (9 Geo IV, c. 31, § 18) it is now settled that the crime is established on the proof of actual penetration, or *res in re*, as it is termed, without the proof of actual emission, thus assimilating the law of England to that of Scotland, which says that rape is completed by proof of contact of the privy parts and entry of the body, without any proof of actual emission

It is also agreed on in both countries that this penetration does not require in every instance to be complete. A slight penetration, and such as does not rupture the hymen, is considered sufficient, even in adults, while, in the case of the injured party being below the years of puberty, it is enough that the body had been entered, though not to the degree which takes place with a full-grown woman.

The facility with which a woman who has yielded willingly to the embraces of a man may get up a charge of rape against him, and the difficulty of disproving such a charge, render more than ordinary attention necessary in respect to the evidence adduced. The principal point to attend to is whether the statement in regard to the violence used is duly corroborated, and this is done in the most unexceptionable way by such physical appearances as afford real evidence of the truth of her story.

Accordingly it is of more importance in such cases to substantiate the marks of violence which may be detected on the *body* than even those on the genitals. The marks of blows, or of struggling, or of grasping the throat, would scarcely be produced with the woman's concurrence, while the usual physical appearances about the genitals consequent upon rape are by no means decisive of the charge, because they are produced equally by voluntary and involuntary connection, where, as usually happens, it occurs for the first time

In connection with the legal aspects of this crime, it is only necessary to add here that the law regards as a lesser crime the attempt to ravish, if the party, in addition to the violence on the female, have gone no farther than having made evident preparation for connection.

In now proceeding to follow out the different medical points arising out of these legal dicta, it will conduce to clearness if I arrange my remarks, as I purpose to do, under three divisions.

1st, The violation of the female *under* the age of puberty

2d, After puberty, and previously to her having otherwise had sexual connection.

3d, After puberty, and when the person had been accustomed to such connection

1st, Of violation of the female under puberty, i.e., as fixed in law at 12 years. Under 10 years, as we have seen, we are at liberty to disregard the circumstances of assent, or non-assent, on the part of the child. From 10 to 12 years, her assent, though it mitigates the crime, does not excuse it. In either case, however, the proof is generally a more simple affair at this period than in the case of the puberant female. From the undeveloped state of the sexual organs in the female, copulation as it is ordinarily understood, cannot take place without producing extensive injury, from the disproportion between the adult male organ and the narrow canal of the vagina. In every case, therefore, such extensive marks of local injury should be looked for, and unless they are found, we can in no case admit that coition has been complete. Instances are met with of violence produced in this way on children sufficiently serious to prove directly fatal, or indirectly so from the unhealthy constitution of the parties. An Irish case of the former sort was published in the *Medical Gazette*, April 1840, in which a child of 11 years perished after 24 hours, where the post-mortem examination disclosed the external organs of generation and perineum torn and violently inflamed, the vagina torn away from the uterus, and a large rent in the peritoneum, with bloody fluid effused into the abdominal cavity. Of cases indirectly fatal in this way there are several instances in Dr Taylor's Manual

The known frequency of such violations of children is believed to have arisen from the idea entertained by the profligate and uneducated that gonorrhœa is readily cured by connection with a healthy female, and infants are sacrificed for this purpose as least likely to make resistance. In 1836 two cases were tried in England, and the parties convicted and sentenced to death. The rape in one case was on a child only 4½ years of age, and the other on a girl under 9. The former child died of the injuries received; the latter was alive nine weeks after. The details of these as of other cases of rape, but rarely, however, come before the public.

The class of cases we have just noticed stands in remarkable contrast to another class of cases of the violation of female children under puberty, in which the medical proof may not only be difficult, but frequently impossible. I allude to those instances of the rape of infants, where there has been no penetration in the sense in which the term is usually employed by physiologists, that is where the male organ has not penetrated within the vagina, but merely within the external parts. By the English law it is not now as it was till recently, held necessary that there should be penetration beyond the vulva to constitute a rape; penetration to the bottom of the vulva, without entrance into the vagina, or injury to the hymen, being sufficient. This decision has assimilated the law of England to the practice which has been acted on in Scotland since 1841, at which time the law on this point was distinctly laid down.

It is the more imperative on me to direct your attention specially to this point, as it must be evident that by thus relaxing the stringency of the proof of violation, the law has opened up a wider door than before to the admission of those false charges of rape which were by no means unknown under the less recent statutes. It behoves the medical witness, therefore, that in examining children under puberty he take special care that he does not become a party to the prosecution of a male person charged with this crime on insufficient grounds, as is known to have been attempted sometimes for the most nefarious purposes, sometimes without any known object, and sometimes for the purpose of gratifying revenge.

Instances of this sort are related by Foderé, Davis, and Caspar, and three such cases have occurred in my practice. In Foderé's case, a woman, besides suborning a witness to the alleged fact, excited redness around the pudenda, prior to the examination of her child. In Davis' case the infant had syphilitic sores, while a clergyman accused was free from disease and of unimpeachable character. In the latter of these cases the child, herself an infant of mendacious habits and of low connection, appears to have been instructed how to play her part in the prosecution. The same preparatory training seemed to have been gone through in one of my own cases.

In 1839 a decent married tradesman, aged 50, was apprehended in Aberdeen on a charge of rape, alleged by the mother to have been committed on her child 8 years of age. When examined separately, in less than an hour after the alleged rape, the child told a most feasible story, which tallied in every particular with the mother's account. The child's person, however, afforded no proof of any attempt having been made on her, and the accused was able to show that he had merely passed in and out of the woman's apartment, and had not spoken to the child.

In one of the two remaining instances suspicion was at once aroused, from the glib statement of a child of 9 years, whose familiarity with the usual details connected with sexual intercourse showed that she was no stranger to the subject, and she turned out to be one of those precocious children who are known to go about at night to solicit libidinous practices on the part of inconsiderate youths.

One further case cannot be passed over, as it illustrates a new phase in sham cases, fortunately not likely to be often paralleled. A tradesman of irreproachable character, we are told by Caspar, was accused by a woman of having violated her daughter of 11 years, and having communicated a gonorrhœa to her. The child was scrofulous, the clitoris unusually developed, the entrance to the vagina inflamed and painful to the touch, the hymen obviously stretched, and there was a copious urethral discharge. On examination, the defender was found to be free from disease, and the cross-examination brought out the fact that the mother, after having fruitlessly endeavoured to extort money from the tradesman, had delivered the child to her own paramour, who she knew was affected with gonorrhœa.

It will be observed that in none of these sham cases, with the exception of the last, was there any trace of violence at all corresponding with what we have described as the necessary consequence, to a greater or less extent, of the entrance into the vagina of an infant of the adult male organ. How far such a case of connection could happen, as might be effected by the mere penetration of the penis within the labia or nymphæ, is a difficult question. The entire absence of marks of injury about the external genitals would not of course negative the possibility of such connection, or afford good grounds for affirming that it could not have been effected. The proof in such charges has hitherto been made to rest mainly on purely legal grounds, yet the results of the increased attention which has been of late directed to such libidinous practices has shown that medical evidence may throw much light upon them. Of their frequency there can be no doubt. In Paris alone Tardieu tells us that he has had no fewer than 181 cases brought under his notice by the law authorities, and although in rather less than one-third of these no traces of the practice were left on the genitals, the remaining two-thirds, or rather more, left some such positive indications as the following.

In the simpler cases slight irritation of the vulva, characterised by moderate redness and heat of the parts; more frequently swelling and contusion of the labia, intense redness of the hymen and vaginal outlet, and the whole of these parts so painful as to make any examination of them difficult, if not impossible It was not unusual, he tells us in his cases, to meet with excoriations, superficial erosions, or even real ulcerations The sign, however, on which this jurist places most reliance, in instances of this sort, is the abundant purulent discharge which succeeded the local inflammation in 88 out of 103 of his cases, with what he considers characteristic rapidity and severity, the discharge in some of these appearing in a few hours after the violence, often on the second or third day, rarely later, attended with severe smarting, increasing heat, pain on walking, and constant desire for friction of the parts

But this brings us to the consideration of one other point connected with the subject of rape in females under puberty, to which it is necessary to advert pointedly before taking leave of this section. I allude to the occasional existence in female children of diseases of the genitals naturally occurring which are very liable to be confounded with the effects of local violence on the one hand, and on the other with venereal affections, the results of impure connection. The diseased states in question agree in nothing but their common seats on the genitals

The first of these is an unhealthy inflammation of the pudendum, speedily ending in sloughing of the external parts, and generally proving fatal The inflammation, previous to the separation of the sloughs, if the child survives this, is not attended with any discharge, which circumstance will serve to distinguish it from the affection next to be described. I met with some cases of this sort in female infants in dispensary practice, and it seems to be not uncommon, occurring occasionally in endemic form. It is usually preceded by febrile symptoms for two or three days, and when the genitals are examined they are found inflamed and swollen. The colour is dark, and ulceration, with gangrene, quickly follows. The fever now assumes a typhoid character, and death shortly takes place

The attention of the profession, so far as I am aware, was first called to this subject by the occurrence of the following case, related by Dr Percival in his Medical Ethics —

A girl of 4 years of age, and in good health, was suddenly seized with inflammation of the pudendum and symptoms of defloration, with pain on making water. She had slept two or three nights in the same bed with a boy 14 years old, and complained of having been very much hurt by him during the night. The symptoms increased in violence, and the child died on the ninth day. An inquest was held on the body, and Mr. Ward, under whose care the patient had been in Manchester Infirmary, deposed that death was caused by external injury A verdict of murder was returned against the boy by the coroner, and he was accordingly taken into custody. A very short time afterwards, however, several similar cases occurred in the same neighbourhood, in which there was no ground for supposing that violence had been offered. Fortunately for the boy, his trial had not come on, and Mr Ward now informed the authorities of the mistake he had committed, and the prisoner was discharged.

The other form of local disease in young females, which may be confounded with the effects of violation, consists of a form of catarrh or purulent discharge from the genitals, closely resembling the gonorrhœa of the adult. Like the same complaint in boys, it is not unfrequently encountered in the female children of scrofulous parents, especially amongst the poor and uncleanly, and occasionally in connection with ascarides in the rectum. In two instances of this kind in my own practice the female servants in charge of the children were suspected of having communicated real clap Dr. Beatty mentions the case of a gentleman in Dublin, charged with the rape of a female child of 8 years who had this infantile discharge, and who narrowly escaped being executed

In addition to a similar charge against a boy, recorded by Ryan, we have notices of this affection by Capuron, Briand, Orfila, and Devergie, while Sir Astley Cooper has referred to it in his own peculiar characteristic and forcible manner One of his cases I must quote for your edification "A gentleman," he says, "came to me and asked me to see a child with him, who had a gonorrhœa on her. I went and found that she had a free discharge from the preputium clitoridis I said there was nothing so common There was considerable inflammation, and it had even proceeded to ulceration, which I told him would soon give way to the use of liquor calcis with calomel Do you tell me so? he replied, why, suspicion has fallen on one of the servants, but he will not confess If he had appeared at the Old Bailey, I should have given my evidence against him, for I was not aware of what you have just told me. I told him that if the man had been hanged by his evidence he would have deserved to have been hanged too."

In addition to the constitutional peculiarities of the children affected with this disease, and their habits in their homes, the rapidity of its appearance, the severity of the inflammation, and the amount of the discharge, will, it is said, usually be such as are more characteristic of the spurious than of the true gonorrhœa. But, as we have seen already, the gonorrhœa of infants has the same exaggerated character as compared with the disease in the adult. It should be borne in mind, besides, that we have no diagnostic marks sufficiently certain for our guidance in arriving at a decision which shall be beyond challenge on all occasions. From not attending to this, much obloquy was incurred by members of the profession in Dublin, in 1855, by two crown cases breaking down from this cause

But while we conceive it to be the duty of the medical jurist to keep in view the possibility of mistaking between these two forms of disease, and, if necessary, to make the public prosecutor aware of such a chance of mistake on his part, he ought not on the other hand, to be ignorant of the undoubted fact, that real or ordinary gonorrhœa easily and speedily follows libidinous practices on female children In my own practice four such instances occurred within two years, two of which may be noticed here.

At the Autumn circuit of 1840, a person was tried for attempted connection with a child of 9 years. From his own declaration, it seemed that he had had emission of semen, though, from the uninjured state of the child's genitals there could have been no entrance into the vagina, but only penetration within the labia He was labouring under gonorrhœa at the time, and the child became affected with the same disease two days afterwards He pled guilty to the attempt to ravish, and was sentenced to seven years penal servitude.

At the circuit court in autumn 1842 a more aggravated case of the same sort was tried A groom in Aberdeen had practised this kind of connection with no fewer than four children of from eight to ten years of age, while himself affected with gonorrhœa, and to three out of the four females he communicated the disease

In one of these the redness and discharge were very slow in disappearing, while, in a second, the occurrence of a bubo in the groin soon after was noticed. No instance of this last sequela of the disease has been recorded after spurious gonorrhœa, though reasoning *à priori* there is nothing to hinder this from happening in the one form of disease more than in the other. The man pled guilty to the charge of indecent practices, and was sentenced to 10 years penal servitude; and the judge (Lord Justice Clerk Hope), in his address, stated that in addition, he was almost inclined to revive the old practice of whipping through the streets.

Before taking leave of this subject it will be necessary to direct your attention to a kindred but opposite topic. I formerly alluded to the existence of a class of young females under puberty, who devote themselves to the infamous trade of going about the streets at night to solicit young men and boys to the commission of libidinous practices. These young females are known to the police here (Aberdeen), but their number is very limited. It is different, however, in some of the large cities of Continental Europe, where the trade has become so notorious, in combination with that of the kindred vice of Sodomy, as to have called the attention of magistrates and jurists to this disgusting subject.

Tardieu states that he has examined judicially in Paris no fewer than 60 such females, 29 of them rising eleven years, 26 from eleven to fifteen years, and 5 from fifteen to twenty years of age. On these cases he founds his description of the state of the genitals in such subjects, where from their habitual submission to lascivious touches on the part of the male, before the parts are sufficiently developed to admit of ordinary penetration, a character and condition is acquired by them which they never afterwards lose. "The first thing," he states, "which strikes the observer in these young females is the contrast betwixt their general development and that of the genitals. While the former preserves its infantile character, the labia are enlarged and parted below, the vulva patent, the nymphæ elongated, and projecting beyond the labia, the clitoris very bulky, exposed, often red, and readily erectile. But the chief peculiarity which distinguishes these precocious females, is the shape assumed by the vulva, which is that of a funnel-shaped cavity of some depth, capable of receiving the penis, the bottom of which is formed by the hymen, more or less worn or attenuated, its borders frequently fringed, and leaving the entrance to the vagina open and dilated."

With this description the observations of Tolmouche are in

essential accordance, and such a state of genitals, either before or after puberty, could leave little room for doubt as to the non-virginity of females, on whom such appearances were readily to to be detected, at all events at such early periods of life.

Several such cases have come under my notice in medico-legal practice. One of these was (in October 1859) in a gul of no stated occupation, or ordinary means of livelihood, of a wretched appearance, and ill dressed, who, though she appeared younger, gave her age as thirteen. She had lodged a charge of rape against a man of between fifty and sixty. Her statement of the circumstances, however, was of a highly improbable kind, to say the least of it. She alleged that the man had drawn her aside into a wood in the country, and there had thrice forcible connection with her, betwixt two of which acts he had slept for a short time, after which they came to town together, when before parting he treated her to a cup of coffee On examining this girl, some blood was found at the vulva, which she herself stated was menstrual. The hymen was entire, the vulvar cavity had a considerable depth, the clitoris was larger than usual, and the nymphæ projected for about an an inch beyond the labia. The girl admitted too that she was not a stranger to sexual intercourse, which had commenced with a boy two years previously. Of course in such a case no charge of rape would lie, and the man was set at liberty.

LECTURE VIII.

RAPE—*Continued.*

VIOLATION OF THE PUBERANT VIRGIN. SIGNS OF VIRGINITY—The state of the Labia—The state of the Nymphæ—The condition of the Clitoris—The state of the Fourchette—The existence of the Hymen—The Carunculæ Myrtiformes—The Vaginal Orifice—The condition of the Pubic Arch Uncertainty of these signs, singly or in combination. SIGNS OF DEFLORATION—From the state of the Genitals, variable extent of these, not dependent on Coition alone—From the presence of Seminal and other Stains on the woman's clothes—Blood stains—Stains from Urine, Fæces, etc—Seminal stains—Physical character—Chemical character—Microscopical character—Separation of the Zoosperms—Occasional failures in their detection—Inference deducible from their absence—Mistakes regarding them—Trichomonas Vaginæ—From the subsequent occurrence of Gonorrhœa or Syphilis—From the subsequent occurrence of Pregnancy

2d, Passing from the subject of the violation of female children under puberty, we come to that of violation *after* puberty in virgins

Here the proof of the alleged rape becomes more difficult and complicated than in children.

As by far the greater number of actual cases of violation occur in this class of females, *i.e*, women after puberty, and who have never had previous sexual connection, in order to prove the charge we must have evidence—

(1st), That previous connection could not have taken place.

(2d), That connection had taken place at the time alleged.

(3d), That the connection had been forced, and not voluntary on the part of the woman

The first of these inquiries regards the point as to whether or not the puberant female has had previous sexual intercourse; or, in other words, what are the signs respectively of virginity and of previous unchastity. This inquiry, though in some respects a twofold one, and although it admits, to some extent, of being discussed from two opposite points of view, is yet practically one and the same As such then we shall here consider the subject of *virginity*, as far as the signs of it are concerned.

The attention of the profession was first called to the uncertainty of the signs of virginity, adduced by authors prior to his time, by the following occurrence related by Duchatelet.

Two young women were insulted in the streets of Paris by some young men, and reproached with prostitution. They brought their accusers before the magistrate, and as the young men persisted in their charge, they offered to submit to an examination as to their virginity. A very able physician undertook the investigation. After a most careful examination, he deposed that, in respect to one of the girls, he could not determine whether she was or was not a virgin. As to the other, he suspected that she was not a virgin, but he could not swear to it. It was afterwards ascertained that they were common girls of the town, and that one of them had been two or three times in the hospital for syphilis.

This occurrence led Duchatelet, with the assistance of practical and experienced colleagues, to investigate with the aid of the speculum into the usual state of the genitals in prostitutes. The result was as follows—The genitals do not present any particular alteration or appearance in these different from married or modest women. They frequently found that young girls, who had very recently become prostitutes, had vaginas as large as women who had borne several children, and, on the other hand, they often examined women who had been twelve or fifteen years on the town, who evinced signs of premature decrepitude, and yet the vagina and other parts of the genitals presented nothing at all remarkable. They examined a woman aged 51 years at the Pension of Madalenettes, who had been on the town since the age of 15, and yet the genital organs, in her case, might have passed for those of a maid just turned 18. These observations, which were made with much care, and verified on a large scale, are well calculated to lead us to examine with some distrust the alleged proofs of virginity, especially those of them which have been handed down from earlier writers, and reproduced on their authority without its being deemed at all necessary to submit them to any fresh scrutiny.

In virgins before the decline of life the labia are said to be bulky, smooth, vermilion-hued, elastic, and in contact with each other, concealing the orifice of the vulva entirely. Now, though this does usually hold true in these circumstances, the facts advanced by Duchatelet are sufficient to show that this state of the parts is not peculiar to virgins, but may also be found at times

DEFLORATION AND RAPE. 101

in prostitutes; while, on the other hand, it has been admitted that these characters may all be lost in virgins, from ill-health, or from the continued effects of leucorrhœa, or other irritating discharges

The last circumstance noticed has been most relied on by the latest observers, who have drawn attention to the circumstance, that on the separation of the thighs the entrance to the vagina comes more readily into view in women accustomed to coition than in virgins.

Little reliance is to be placed on the colour, smoothness, and plumpness of the nymphæ, as a test of the virgin state of the genitals. There is no doubt, however, that in healthy virgin females these bodies are smaller in proportion, and consequently be more concealed by the labia, when the thighs are nearly in contact, and that in prostitutes and others accustomed to intercourse with the male, they speedily become subject to enlargement and project farther beyond the labia. It can readily be imagined, nevertheless, that indulgence in libidinous desires and manipulations would produce the like effect without the necessity of sexual intercourse.

The normal size and condition of the clitoris affords a presumption of virginity, and its enlargement, facility of erection, and the laxity and mobility of its prepuce, exactly the reverse, but these indications are with great difficulty judged of, while it is to be borne in mind that the practices we have referred to may have no little effect in bringing about the changes in question.

In the healthy virgin adult, the fourchette forms a sharply-defined bridle, stretched across the lower border of the vaginal orifice, behind which lies the cul-de-sac, of more or less depth, known as the fossa navicularis. In prostitutes and women who have borne children, both these peculiarities cease to be observable, giving a greater degree of enlargement to the vulva behind and below than in virgins. It is to be observed, however, that the fourchette is not necessarily interfered with in coition, while, on the other hand, it has been known to be ruptured from disease, the effects of a fall, or from the forcible separation of the thighs. The existence of the fossa navicularis, again, is dependent on that of the fourchette, and disappears with its rupture or relaxation.

The most opposite conditions of the parts referred to can alone authorise even probable conjectures as to the virginity or non-virginity of the female under examination.

Conflicting statements are to be met with in authors as to

the state of the hymen in the virgin female. The existence of the hymen, in any case, has even been doubted by writers of note, such as Paré, Dionis, Buffon, and Mahon Recent researches have, however, dispelled all doubts on this subject Devilliers, for instance, found in 150 cases, Orfila in 200, Tardieu in 300, examined with this object, that the hymen was constantly present in each instance, while no unequivocal case of its absence has been lately produced. In children this membrane lies deep, and can only be readily seen in them on the forcible separation of the thighs, when it is found to consist of two lateral and vertical folds of integument at the entrance of the vagina, which it almost closes A very common form of the membrane, after the age of infancy especially, is that of an irregularly circular diaphragm, broken at its upper third by an opening more or less large, and placed more or less distant from the lower border of the vaginal orifice In a third set of cases the hymen has been described in late observations as a sort of diaphragm, exactly and regularly circular, pierced by a central opening A fourth form assumed by it, and that its most common appearance, is that of a semicircular fold of integument stretched across the lower border of the vaginal orifice, its free border concave and notched (echancré), and its extremities losing themselves in the labia minora. Lastly, the hymen has been occasionally encountered in the shape of a mere narrow fringe around the entrance to the canal of the vagina, in one case as a sort of bridle across the vagina, with a passage on each side; in another, as a complete septum, pierced by numerous minute openings, and in a third instance as a double septum, without any opening whatever into the vagina. The entrance into the vagina is thus practically closed or narrowed by the hymen, which in early life is most usually vertical, but by the natural development of the parts gradually assumes a horizontal direction. Towards puberty more firm and consistent than in early life, as menstruation becomes established, it becomes more or less flaccid, presenting less resistance to their flow, and is more easily lacerated

That the hymen is ruptured or lacerated in ordinary intercourse is undoubted in the general case, but it must be conceded that in some females it may be at the time in so lax a state, or so moistened by the discharges, as to permit the introduction of the penis within the vagina, particularly when the former is small, without the rupture of the membrane In proof of this, Mauriceau, Ruysch, Meckel, Walter, Baudeloque, Capuron, and Davis, have adduced cases in which the hymen was found uninjured at the commencement of labour

The last named author quotes an instance, which used to be related in the following humorous terms by Dr Haighton, in his lectures.

"The lady was the wife of one of the physicians of St. Thomas' Hospital in London The hymen closed the orifice of the vagina, leaving only some small apertures, and it was so strong as to have resisted all the efforts of her husband to effect its rupture The lady, however, sickened, the abdomen enlarged, and the legs became œdematous. She went to Bath to get cured of her dropsy, but soon returned worse than ever, and desirous to die at home. She had not reached London, however, before pains, which she considered colicky, obliged her to stop at an inn, where in less than half-an-hour she was radically cured of her dropsy by becoming the mother of a well-grown living child The incorrigible hymen had ruptured spontaneously at the proper time"

But if it must thus be conceded that intercourse to such an extent as even to lead to conception may take place without the destruction of the hymen, the opposite assertion that the membrane may be ruptured in virgins, from other causes than connection, would require more proof than has yet been furnished Ulceration of the parts, or the forcible introduction of a foreign body into the vagina would undoubtedly suffice for this ; but we take leave to doubt how far some other assigned causes, such as acrid discharges, rough riding, leaps, or falls, would satisfactorily account for an effect of this sort

The importance of the carunculæ myrtiformes or hymenales, as enabling us to judge of the condition of the genital parts, will depend on the view we take of these bodies. By a few anatomists, the carunculæ are regarded as the rudiments of an imperfectly developed hymen, and, as such, as a real though imperfect sign of virginity. The commonly received opinion, however, is that these bodies are the remains of the torn hymen, and, as such, it regards them as indications, in every case in which they are found, of previous sexual connection on the part of the female It should be borne in mind that these bodies vary considerably in their number and character in different women, presenting themselves as vegetations, tubercles, crests, filaments or polypi, forming excrescences, placed in varying numbers at different points of the circumference of the vaginal orifice

The external orifice of the vagina is usually very narrow in virgins, especially where the hymen is well developed, in these cases even in the adult female, rarely admitting of the entrance of more than the point of the forefinger. This narrowness, however, may be naturally present in prostitutes, or may be produced in them by contraction of the sphincter, while in virgins the hymen may be imperfect, and the orifice naturally large, or in a state of unusual relaxation from the effects of leucorrhœa, menorrhagia, or the abuse of the warm bath.

In a similar way the dimensions and state of tension of the vaginal canal may vary, without affording any reliable indications of the virginity, or otherwise, of the female, as shown by Duchatelet.

Lastly, in some rare instances, the infantile condition of the pubic arch may persist after puberty, in which case the rami of the pubes and ischium may be so approximated that full penetration cannot be effected.

It will be seen from the above examination of the signs of virginity that the character of uncertainty attaches with more or less force to each and all of them.

The presence of the hymen is the one on which most reliance is to be placed; but even this sign is not in every case to be depended on, while all the others are of a more or less equivocal character, and, as such, could only authorise us to form, from their combination, opinions which may rise from plausible conjectures to more or less strong probabilities.

Before leaving this part of our subject, it is also necessary to remind you of some of the changes which may be effected on the state of the genitals, which in the virgin adult female may simulate certain of the consequences of sexual connection. I refer to the effects which may be produced by the practice of the solitary vice of masturbation, by no means a rare one with respectable females. It must be obvious at once that any foreign body introduced into the vagina whose volume sensibly exceeds its diameter, may rupture the hymen, and give rise to the carunculæ myrtiformes if introduced briskly and forcibly; and that a foreign body of the same diameter as the vagina, introduced gradually and without force, may dilate the hymen without producing the carunculæ; this latter being the usual effect produced by those bodies which are employed in cases of masturbation, while it may also be the consequence of the use of the speculum, pessaries, etc. In such cases as these the examiner will find that the hymen has disappeared; it would be rash, therefore, to conclude, without the closest previous inquiry, that such effects are to be attributed to sexual connection.

One word more in connection with this part of our subject. In making an examination, it should be borne in mind that, in most instances, from being placed not at the very entrance of the vagina, but slightly behind it, the hymen, as in the case of the infant, may be present, but may not come into view till after the wide separation of the thighs, a procedure which is frequently unwillingly submitted to by the female.

Still more importance attaches to the next point for notice, namely, the signs of recent defloration in the previously intact female.

I have had occasion already to observe that in children below the age of puberty the signs of a recent connection, when it has been fully effected, are too evident to be mistaken, owing to the disproportion between the adult penis and the impuberant female genitals. Where both parties are above puberty, it is obvious that the same disproportion may still exist, though in a less degree, and produce effects in the female proportionate in degree, though the same in kind. In these circumstances, however voluntary the act may have been, the venereal congress may leave considerable local injury on the female parts, particularly when the parties have been actuated by strong and ungovernable desire. The same thing may occur when there is disproportion between the ages, the male being in the vigour of manhood, and the female just past the period of puberty, and her sexual organs not so fully developed as they afterwards become. In such instances the following, or several of the following, appearances may be encountered, namely—bruising of the clitoris and labia, excoriations of the clitoris and nymphæ, laceration of the mucous membrane of the external parts, with ecchymoses under the membrane, vascular injection in the vicinity of the excoriations, rupture of the hymen, sometimes of the fourchette, and even excoriations of the lining membrane of the vagina within its external orifice. In addition to this the vulva may appear swollen, and be tender or painful to the touch, while the shift may be stained in front with seminal spots, and behind and in front with blood.

These appearances on the genitals must be looked for early. In almost every instance they will have become obliterated by the third or fourth day, by which time the lacerations will have healed, the cicatrices disappeared, and the torn hymen be in such a state as to make it difficult to say whether it had been divided recently or at an earlier period.

I have hitherto supposed that the male party to the connection had the advantage over the female in age, in the development of the genitals, and in vigour generally. Now it must be apparent that, though the occurrence will not be so frequent, the reverse of all this may happen. In these circumstances the effects resulting from a first connection to the female may be much less marked, though still some of them ought naturally to be expected. These indications would be still fainter when, from more advanced age, the female genitals become relaxed, and when this relaxation has been increased by the long-continued existence of leucorrhœal discharges, or profuse menstruations. I have some grounds for thinking, however, that the local consequences of these have been exaggerated, as I have examined women who had long been subject to profuse discharges, and in them the genitals were as firm, and the diameter of the opening as narrow, as where no such causes had been in operation. The observations quoted from Duchatelet go to strengthen this assertion.

There is one drawback to the assumption of the injuries to the genitals just described as a proof of a first and recent connection, which is, that where the disproportion between the bulk of the penis and the entrance to the vagina is very great, they may all be produced in a female who has had frequent previous connections, or even in a woman who had borne children, as has occasionally though certainly very rarely happened. This occurrence is not, however, a very puzzling one to the medical jurist. An examination of both parties could not fail to make him aware of such a situation of affairs, and enable him to avoid this chance of mistake on his part.

It is the more necessary to warn you that we possess no certain means of distinguishing between these local injuries, which may be produced by a first coitus, and those which may be caused to the same parts by the forcible entrance of foreign bodies. It is not likely, however, that a female would produce those upon herself voluntarily unless it were her interest to do so, a case which we shall have to consider in the sequel.

Besides, it should be borne in mind that the mechanically produced injuries of the genitals, with difficulty distinguishable from the effects of a first intercourse in a previously chaste female, may be produced by the female herself, or by the assailant not in the usual way, but by other means on his part than by the entrance of his penis. Of this I met with an illustration several years ago.

A young man of 18 one morning attacked an old woman, with the design of forcing her, in a common lodging in Aberdeen

The woman, though worthless, and formerly a prostitute, after he had seized her and thrown her on a bed, began to make such an outcry as threatened to bring the neigh' s to her assistance. Seeing this, the young man desisted after fruitless attempt, but, at the same time, thrust his forefinger into the vagina, and, as the woman said, hurt her very much. The external parts, when examined some hours afterwards, had a raw and bruised appearance, from a rent which extended a short way into the vagina.

Granting then, an admission which we would not be justified in withholding, that we cannot always certainly distinguish between the effects on the genitals of the entrance, for the first time, of the penis and that of a foreign body of equal bulk, we come now to inquire what other indications of recent sexual connection we possess, which may serve to remove the ambiguity occasionally attending those just discussed.

I have already briefly referred to the existence of *seminal* and *bloody* spots upon the female's linen. These will now have to be noticed more particularly. If, in addition to the finding of such stains, we also discover semen in the vagina and about the vulva, we shall be able to say with some confidence that the genital injuries were produced not by any foreign body, or the manipulations of the woman herself or others, but by coition alone.

The stains on the woman's linen are usually of two sorts—one pale, and the other coloured.

The coloured stains are found generally on the back part of the shift. They are mostly from blood, differing however in appearance; one sort of them of a *deep* red, rich in colouring matter equally diffused over the stain, the second sort of a much *lighter* red, or rather a *reddish yellow*, but coloured at the centre of the stain, and their margins having a defined reddish line. The former of these stains arises from pure blood, the latter from a sero-sanguinolent discharge, becoming gradually less and less red.

Besides these reddish stains arising from blood, other coloured stains may be met with on the woman's linen, such as the broad diffused yellowish ones caused by urine, those of yellow or greenish yellow colour, traceable to fæculent matter, the light yellow diffused and stiffened patches from muco-purulent or mucous discharges, greasy stains, stains of mud, etc.

Seminal stains, when found on the linen after coition, are usually situated in front, at a point corresponding with the vulva, though they may occasionally be met with behind.

They will usually be in a dry state, of a *greyish-white* colour, circumscribed, and rounded in their form, and their circumference ending in a greyish line of a deeper tint than that of the disc, while the stuff at the part is stiff, as if starched. If recent, the spermatic odour may be detected, or it may be reproduced by merely moistening the cloth. These seminal stains can readily be distinguished from most of those we have mentioned. Blood stains, besides their red colour, possess certain characteristic chemical and microscopical characters, which will fall to be noticed at another period of our course. The colour and the peculiar odour emitted by urinary and fæcal stains sufficiently discriminate these, while the microscope would assist the diagnosis where the stain had arisen from purulent matter. Stains caused by leucorrhœal matter or other discharges containing albumen differ from seminal stains, which *alone* among stains produced by fluids of animal origin are found to contain no albumen. To bring out this distinction Lassaigne proposes a simple method. This consists in moistening the suspected stain with a drop or two of plumbate of potash (obtained by dissolving oxide of lead in liquor potassæ), and keeping the stuff for eight to ten minutes in a temperature of 68° Fahr. If no albumen be present, no change of colour will result; but if any be present, a sulphur-yellow colour will be produced. Of course this test is not applicable to stains on wool which usually contains sulphur. Its value besides is restricted. All that it can determine is, that where the test fails the stain is not an albuminous one. It cannot assist in determining that it has been caused by *semen*, a defect which attaches equally to all the other distinctions betwixt seminal and other stains we have passed under review.

In the admitted absence then of any positive test of the presence of semen in suspected stains, we are compelled to have recourse to the careful and judicious employment of the microscope, and to the search by means of it for the presence of the *seminal animalcule*. The possibility of readily detecting the seminal animalcule, or zoosperm, even in dried and old seminal stains, though denied at first by Orfila, and by Donné, a practised microscopist, has been placed beyond doubt by Devergie, John Dury, Bayard, and Roussin. The successful prosecution of this line of proof dates from the occurrence in Paris of a case of considerable interest. A man, named Beugnet, had assassinated his mistress, whom he had accused of having, either on the night or the morning preceding the murder, had sexual intercourse with a stranger. His motive for this act was jealousy, their marriage having been fixed to take place a few days afterwards.

The examiners, MM Bayard and Ollivier, were required by the law authorities to inspect with particular attention any fluid which they might be able to detect within the sexual organs of the female, in order to ascertain if traces of semen were by any possibility mixed with them.

From experiments instituted by Bayard, he found, as Orfila had done previously, that on diluting seminal spots the slightest friction sufficed to crush the animalcules, rendering them a confused mass under the microscope, that between plates of glass these zoosperms preserved their life and motion as long as the mucus in which they swam retained its fluidity; and that in proportion to its cooling or drying, they mostly lost the power of motion, which ceased altogether at the end of two or three hours on the complete agglutination of the mucus

Bayard now sought for the best means of disengaging the animalcules from the muco-glutinous matter of the dried sperm, without injury to these. This he found could be accomplished by several solvents, such as saliva, urine, or blood, and milk previously diluted with water, but with most facility and readiness by alcohol, and solutions of soda, potash, and ammonia, previously diluted with distilled water, in proportions varying with each of these fluids

Finally, Bayard advises the following process for the verification of seminal stains on clothes —

1. Cautiously cut away the suspected stain from the rest of the cloth, without rubbing the tissue.

2 Macerate the suspected tissue for twenty-four hours in as much distilled water as will merely cover it, when the water is to be poured off and filtered.

3. Heat the fragments of cloth in freshly distilled water, till the temperature reaches to from 140° to 150° F, when the water is again to be poured off and filtered

4 Treat the stained cloth with water, to which a tenth part of alcohol has been added, or in ammonia diluted with sixteen parts of water, when these liquids are to be filtered

5 The various filtrations being over, the apices of the filters are to be cut away, spread upon a plate of glass, and moistened with the alcoholised or ammoniated water, which dissolves the mucus and entirely detaches the deposit Should fatty matters be present, these may be removed by the addition of ether

Lastly, The solution thus obtained, when examined by a microscope magnifying 300 diameters, exhibits the spermatic animalcules in an entire and unbroken state, and completely detached from mucus.

Bayard claims to have completely succeeded by this process in detecting the zoosperms in healthy vaginal mucus, collected 8, 10, and 72 hours after coition, and on pieces of cloth stained with sperm and dried, and that after intervals of one and even of nearly three years.

Ritter objects to this process as too complicated, and only likely to succeed where the semen happens to be abundant. He advises in preference the modification of it proposed by Schmidt, which is as follows:—

The cloth is to be carefully examined to ascertain on which side the stain is. When this is learnt, it will be seen that within, and generally near its edge, there is an elevated and thickened part, with a slightly glistening appearance, which he says is formed by a layer of dried spermatozoa, and which may be further distinguished from the thinner portion of the stain by the touch, or better, by holding the whole opposite the light, and noticing that this part is opaque.

This part of the stain is then made to form the apex of the cloth by folding it with the stained side outwards, dipped below the surface of as much water as will half fill a watch-glass, and kept there for three or four hours. On this, after the previous addition to the water of a few drops of ammonia, the watch-glass is to be warmed with the minute flame of a spirit lamp, and the thickened apex of the stained stuff to be moved about in it, and finally lightly squeezed between the thumb and fingers.

If the fluid does not now exhibit the zoosperms, it may be concentrated by allowing a portion of the water to evaporate spontaneously by exposing the watch-glass for a few hours, or this may be done with a few drops of the fluid on a slip of glass.

One source of failure in the detection of the spermatic animalcule, on clothes stained by sperm, by these and other methods, has been recently advanced by Roussin, after an elaborate series of experiments with the fresh and dried fluid, both by itself and on articles of dress. Three prominent facts were brought out by him—

(1.) That if carefully handled, and dried at a moderate temperature, the zoosperm may be preserved unchanged for an indefinite period.

(2) That by mere dilution with water, the zoosperm can be readily made out, in the dried sperm, by the microscope, though this is much facilitated by the previous addition to 100 parts of water of 1 part of iodine and 4 parts of iodide of potassium

(3) That in stains produced by the drying of sperm on articles of clothing, the zoosperms are found to be so entangled in the fibres of the cloth that very few of them can be detached by water and other fluids, and they must be sought for amongst the meshes of the fibres.

To facilitate this search for the zoosperms in the tissues of the cloth, Roussin advises to proceed as follows :—

With fine scissors cut from the centre of the stained part a square portion not exceeding a quarter of an inch in size, avoiding as far as possible any crushing or friction. This is to be placed gently on the surface of a little water (two drops) in the bottom of a watch-glass, covered by a slip of glass to prevent evaporation, and left there for two hours, during the interval taking care to reverse the fragment with the aid of two fine needles. The threads of the stuff are then to be carefully separated from each other, the threads taken up with pincers and pressed against a slip of glass to expel their moisture; the glass slip is then to be covered with a cover-glass, and the slide placed in the field of the microscope. Should no zoosperms be detected, the portion of the stuff thus tested is to have its fibres carefully disentangled, these fibres one by one placed on a second glass slide, with the previous addition of a drop of water, covered with a cover-glass, and examined leisurely. Where the result of this second trial is doubtful, Roussin recommends the addition of a drop of the iodic solution, followed up instantly by the microscopical examination.

Before leaving this subject it may be necessary to observe that, however carefully gone about, the search for zoosperms in stains of this kind may result in failure; copious dilution, for instance, may render the search futile, even where their presence in the stain cannot be doubted; as where, besides the seminal fluid, there had been a simultaneous discharge of blood, or leucorrhœal secretion intermingled with it.

Farther, the researches of Caspar have shown that the zoosperm is not *always* present in the seminal fluid ejaculated from the penis, or in the fluid of the vesiculæ seminales, even in young and potent individuals; and that their absence is *not unusual* in the seminal fluid in the old and feeble, and, what is more to the point, in those who have previously to its examination had recent or repeated sexual connection.

The failure of the search for the seminal animalcule, then, cannot in itself be held to invalidate a charge of rape. On the other hand, it should be equally borne in mind that the discovery and discrimination of semen about the genitals of the female, or on her linen, either moist or dry, only proves the fact of previous connection, without by itself determining anything as to its voluntary or involuntary character.

It should be known that though, as formerly noticed, the front of the woman's shift nearest to the genitals is the part usually stained by the semen, exceptions to this may be encountered. This may occur, as remarked by Roussin, from the possibly unnatural positions of the parties, the disorder of the dress, and the attendant violence and agitation, leading to the deposit of the sperm on the different parts of the clothes of either party, on the bedding, or on objects in the vicinity. A case in point is given by Roussin.

Once more it is necessary to warn you against mistaking for the spermatic animalcule the ciliated epidermic cells, and above all the trichomonas vaginæ—particularly in the broken and dried state in which these bodies may present themselves to the observer.

Still, with all these deductions from its value—where connection otherwise was known to be impossible; where the alleged forcible violation was complete and recent; and where this source of evidence may come in corroboration of the proof from the state of the genitals and other parts of the woman's person—the medical jurist would not now be justified in neglecting to avail himself of its assistance.

The examination of suspicious stains may be further called for where only a *negative* result is expected, or likely to be reached by it, as in Bayard's case, already referred to. Of this I have had several instances in my own practice. In one, which turned out to be a sham case, the stains proved to be simply leucorrhœal. In the case of James Robb, tried here (Aberdeen) for the violation and rape of an old woman (Smith) at Auchterless, the absence of semen from the linen and vaginal mucus corroborated his own statement before his execution, that the sexual intercourse had not been completed. Once more, in the investigation of the case of a woman Harvey, at Cults, where the search was equally unsuccessful, the evidence pointed out that the genital injuries had been caused by stabbing, and that no rape or sexual connection had taken place.

Another sign of sexual intercourse is of some importance, namely, gonorrhœa or syphilis, as a consequence of intercourse with a person affected with either of these diseases. I have already had occasion to refer to a prevalent vulgar notion, that a clap may be cured by a carnal connection with a healthy virgin. Such a connection, or indeed the connection of one labouring under gonorrhœa or syphilis, may give rise to these diseases in the female, and thus lead to one other proof of the venereal act having been accomplished. This additional indication of recent connection requires, however, to be guarded against so many sources of fallacy, as to lessen very much its value. We have seen that female children are liable to spurious gonorrhœa of spontaneous occurrence. Adult females are not exempted from a discharge having the same appearance, and arising, among other causes, from the approach of the menstrual period, when the menses have been suppressed or retained, as also from the practice of masturbation, from the abuse of irritant injections, from calculi in the bladder, from some diseases of the skin, etc.

Besides, the female may have received the venereal affection from other sources than impure connection or sexual intercourse. It would, moreover, be requisite to have proof that the female was previously free from any form of venereal disease.

Sores arising from injuries inflicted by the voluntary introduction into the vagina of hard bodies different from the male organ, and ulcers of the hymen, naturally arising, might in some cases be confounded with venereal chancres.

The purulent discharges from chancres, and that from common sores, are confessedly too much alike to be distinguishable, unless we were at liberty to test the two by inoculation, which we could scarcely venture to do in a case of this sort. The assertion of Donné and Ricord, that vibriones exist in such syphilitic primitive sores and chancres as have not been treated by topical applications, and in sores of no other kind, requires confirmation before it could be made available by us. Besides it is not every one who could be expected to detect such extremely minute objects, barely distinguishable by a magnifying power of 670 diameters.

Gonorrhœa occurring at the exact time of an alleged forcible intercourse with an infected male is not without some weight in the proof of rape, otherwise it would assist the case but little, unless it could be shown that the woman was previously free from the disease, and could not have contracted it subsequently

I

through any channel, while again we possess no test for distinguishing between gonorrhœal and other muco-purulent discharges. Donné's proposed test of the *acidity* of morbid vaginal discharges, as contrasted with the *alkalinity* of the natural mucus from this canal, does not promise much assistance in this direction

Lastly, one more sign of the woman's having had sexual connection at the time alleged, is the subsequent occurrence of pregnancy.

Curiously enough it has been strenuously denied that pregnancy could follow a connection involuntary on the woman's part, and at one time in this and other countries a charge of rape could not be sustained if the alleged forced intercourse were followed by conception. This position, however, must be abandoned as untenable

The point, however, is not one of much importance either way, as to constitute impregnation an available sign of rape, proof would require to be had of the female's chastity, both before and subsequently to the alleged violation, almost an impossibility in the general case

In connection with this subject, a curious case was currently credited some years ago in Ireland—that of a gentleman's having forced two sisters in succession, and both the females being impregnated in consequence That such double connection was at least not an impossibility was shown by the investigation of a rape case here (Aberdeen) in 1849, it having come out that the party, after forcing one female, adjourned to a house about a hundred yards off, and had a voluntary connection with another

LECTURE IX.

RAPE (Concluded) AND SODOMY.

SIGNS OF RAPE OR INVOLUNTARY CONNECTION — Physical Signs—In the Living—Genital Injuries—Injuries on other parts of the Person—Seminal and Blood Stains—Gonorrhœa or Syphilis—Pregnancy—Marks on the Ravisher's Person or Clothes—State of the Woman's Clothes—Indications of Narcotism or Insensibility from other causes in the Female—Moral Proofs—Sham Cases—Previous Character of the Woman—Power of Resistance on her Part—Influence of terror, narcotics, anæsthetics, etc., in overcoming resistance—Intercourse during sleep—The place where the alleged Crime was committed—The fact of cries having been heard in the vicinity—Improbabilities or inconsistencies in the Woman's statements—Relative Age and Strength of the Parties—The Female being dead—Violation in Women accustomed to Connection—Physical proofs—General Rules for the Investigation of cases of alleged Rape. SODOMY.

THE last topic connected with sexual intercourse in the female above puberty and previously intact I stated to be the question as to whether the connection was voluntary or involuntary on her part. As in a charge of rape the proof rests mainly on the decision of this point, it will require to be examined with some particularity.

I may remark at the outset, that though the signs of defloration at periods remote from the time of the alleged involuntary or forced connection, may form an element in the inquiry we are entering on, yet it is in almost every case where the crime has been recently committed that we are likely to be called upon to undertake the investigation.

In the ancient law of Scotland it was held indispensable that the woman who had been ravished should not delay making her complaint *ultra unam noctem*. If she did so her complaint was no longer listened to. This strictness is not now preserved as a legal bar to the charge, and a delay of *three* days has been permitted. But any undue delay in communicating the outrage, at least to the most confidential relations, still does form a serious objection to her testimony. The omission to communicate the disaster, even for twenty-four hours, will in general form an important feature in the case.

By the English law, as it at present stands, there is no time of limitation fixed, yet public opinion demands an early discovery, and an accuser who has postponed her complaint for any unreasonable length of time is listened to with great caution by a jury

This state of the law is the more fortunate, for, as we have found in discussing the signs of a first sexual intercourse, the most trustworthy of these are very speedily effaced, that after the third or fourth day they are scarcely to be looked for and that insuperable difficulties attend upon the practical application of the signs of sexual connection at all remoter periods, unless in women who have borne children

When called in these circumstances to investigate an alleged rape, or case of involuntary or forced connection, the proof that it was involuntary does not rest entirely with the medical witness, Much of this depends on the moral bearings of the case Those, however, which chiefly concern the lawyers, sometimes admit of being elucidated by the physical appearances, which are the peculiar province of the medical jurist, and as such cannot be safely overlooked by the latter

First then, of the Physical Proofs of Rape.—If called to investigate the case earlier than the third or fourth day, we are entitled to look, in the great majority of cases, for those appearances on the genitals which were formerly adverted to, as consequent on a first connection, namely, bruises or excoriations, or both, on the clitoris, labia, and nymphæ, or at least fulness, heat, and tenderness about the vulva, with rupture of the hymen where it has existed, and perhaps of the fourchette

The absence of some or all of these, you are prepared to understand, is not so conclusive as to permit us to state that, even in a previously intact virgin, sexual intercourse has not taken place recently On the other hand, the presence of them all only proves that there has been some body lately within the vulva What that body has been, whether the penis or a foreign body of the same or greater bulk we are not yet in a condition to prove, and where no further evidence of the cause of the local violence has been obtained, the law authorities should be distinctly made aware that these marks of defloration might all be produced by other causes than connection Besides, even admitting that they had arisen from sexual intercourse, we are not prepared to testify that the intercourse had been involuntary or forced

There are some other physical marks of connection which, if found on the person, will lead pretty certainly to the conclusion that the connection has not been with the woman's consent. The party who has been violated will frequently present bruises on different parts of her body, such as she would not be likely to inflict on herself, but which are easily accounted for on the supposition that she has struggled against the embraces of her ravisher. These bruises are most likely to be found on the groins, thighs, wrists, or breasts, or about the throat.

If, in addition to this, seminal or bloody stains were discovered on the female's linen and verified by microscopical investigation, the proof of the criminal nature of the connection would be as complete as it could be expected to be by anything short of moral proof or ocular testimony.

We have seen the extent to which the local injuries to the genitals will usually be carried in children. But even in young and healthy adult virgins the injury inflicted by the ravisher is occasionally fearful, involving danger to life, or even speedy death. Cases of this aggravated sort occur from the party being insensible at the time, or when she has been beset by such a number of ruffians as to render resistance impossible, and when it may be that two or more have had forcible connection with her in turn. One atrocious instance of this kind I shall relate, which was tried in Scotland in 1830.

Margaret Paterson, an unprotected female, was making her way on foot one evening from Edinburgh to Dalkeith, when she came up with a cart driven by two Gilmerton carters. She was taken into the cart by these villains under the pretence of assisting her on her journey. There they forcibly held her down, and repeatedly violated her person; and not only so, but they afterwards took stones from the road, coals, straw, prickly plants, and everything they could immediately find, and forced them into the vagina. When she fainted under her tortures, they threw her out of the cart into a ditch by the roadside, where she was found next morning, with only life enough remaining to linger out three days of agony, luckily, however, with the power to disclose the names of her murderers.

On examining the body after death, the substances just mentioned were found in the vagina and rectum, for both passages were broken down into one, the perinæum being dreadfully lacerated. All the abdominal viscera were in a high state of inflammation.

The two carters were convicted and executed.

In such cases as this, and more of the like sort might be adduced, there would be little chance of mistake in assuming that the intercourse had not been voluntary on the woman's part. But even in instances of a less likely sort serious local injury may be encountered.

Thus, in two cases tried at Aberdeen in 1849 where penetration in the physiological sense had not taken place, copious hemorrhage in both females had followed the attempts at entry, from superficial injuries of the external genitals and entrance of the vagina.

I need but remind you after what has been said, that gonorrhœa or pregnancy following sexual intercourse affords no proof of its having been involuntary on the part of the woman.

It may strengthen the proof both of intercourse and of its having been effected by violence, if the *accused* be carefully examined as speedily after the occurrence in question as possible. It is not unlikely that where the woman has struggled against his approaches, indications of the struggle may be left on his person.

Thus in the case of Archibald Fraser, tried at Aberdeen in the spring of 1839, for attempt to ravish, besides a scratch on the dorsum of the penis, similar scratches were noticed by me on his face, with blood on his knuckles and fingers.

Blood on the man's linen, coincidently with blood from the female's genitals, would also assist in connecting him with the woman's injury. Semen in the prisoner's urethra, or seminal stains on his linen, should likewise be sought for, though but equivocal signs. Soon after intercourse, if the male have not passed water in the interval, semen may be expressed from the urethra by compressing the penis from its root to the glans.

As likely to afford some indications of a struggle where it has taken place, the *clothes* of both parties should be examined, in order to detect rents in them, or soiling from the ground.

In the case of Robb, one of those referred to as having been tried at Aberdeen in 1849, the man had forced his way into the woman's house by going down the chimney, and the corded trousers he wore had left their impression on the sooty walls, while particles of soot had adhered to the trousers. The traces of soot on the trousers were so slight as to have escaped the notice of the prisoner before his apprehension, but sufficed for discrimination chemically. These circumstances, strengthened as they were in this instance by the discovery in the woman's bed of a button torn from his clothes in the struggle with her, and of his walking stick outside the door of the cottage, proved important links in the chain of evidence which led to his conviction.

But to return to the woman. If she were found immediately after suffering sexual violence under the influence of narcotic drugs, this circumstance would afford a strong presumption that the intercourse had been constrained.

Insensibility from other causes, and lasting for some time, though more equivocal than narcotism, would not be without its importance as likely to have arisen from terror or shame, and to have facilitated the perpetration of the act.

In the case of Fraser, lately alluded to, though she had made a stout resistance and ultimately foiled her assailant, yet the woman lay for some hours after he left her in profound hysteric coma.

It is well known that deep intoxication has been tried to facilitate the commission of rape. The presumption afforded by this state of the female would in the general case, however, be rather against than for the accusation.

The *moral* proofs of involuntary intercourse or rape, I have said belong in general rather to the lawyer than to the physician. Still there are some of these, the investigation of which is best followed out by the medical jurist, and others which may assist him in ascertaining and settling the question of consent or non-consent on the part of the woman, upon which often hangs the detection of sham cases.

We have seen that rape has been feigned in the case of children under puberty. After puberty it is much more common, as, according to Mr Amos, there are probably in England a dozen or more met with on circuit for every genuine case that comes to be investigated.

The previous character of the woman who has charged a man with the commission of a rape on her is allowed considerable weight in law in determining the assent or non-assent. "The character of unchastity," says Mr Alison, "is, without doubt, the strongest possible presumption against a charge of rape; because it is natural to suppose that a woman who has once yielded, and, still more, who has made prostitution a trade, will not seriously resist on another occasion. But this is only a *presumptio hominis*, though without doubt one of the strongest kind; and as such, may be elided by distinct and unequivocal evidence of actual violence on the occasion libelled."

In 1839 I had to examine a charge of this kind against a non-commissioned officer in the Aberdeen barracks, who had borne a very high character in his regiment. The female, a woman of the name of M'Beth, related a very circumstantial story, which was borne out to some extent as to place and circumstances. It was found, however, on examining the woman, that she had an abundant gonorrhœal or gleety discharge, and a bubo in one of her groins, and had otherwise the character of a notorious prostitute. The man, who was detained in custody some weeks, showed no trace of infection from the alleged connection. The prosecution was ultimately dropped when the woman's character was found out.

At the Derby Spring Assizes in 1836, a lad of the name of Dolman, aged 17, was capitally indicted for a rape on Sarah Baxter, aged 21. The complainant proved to be a woman of coarse character, who, as appeared from the evidence, seduced the prisoner to the act of sexual intercourse on a public road. The prisoner was acquitted.

Some authorities go so far as to hold that no violation can ever take place without some consent on the part of the female, arguing that she has it generally in her power to foil her assailant. It must be admitted that a woman with strength of body and presence of mind has a great deal in her power. The arguments advanced on this point, however, apply rather to the case of entire penetration of the vulva than to the partial entry, which is now admitted in law as amounting to the crime of rape. That such entry may be forced in an ordinary case I had the assurance of actual fact in at least one serious case (Robb's case); but, after all, the question is rather a legal than a medical one.

The question assumes an altogether different aspect when the woman has been rendered insensible by the effects of terror—such, for example, as to bring on syncope or hysteric coma—where she has been beset by such a number of ruffians as to render all her efforts at resistance fruitless, as in the case of Margaret Paterson, already related; or where she has had narcotics or intoxicating liquids administered to render her insensible.

A case occurred in Dublin in 1831, in which a gentleman was tried for a rape, and convicted, chiefly in consequence of the impression that some soporific had been administered by him to the young lady, by means of which he was enabled to effect his purpose.

In France, a dentist was convicted of a rape upon a female to whom he had administered ether.

Chloroform is said to have been used successfully for the same nefarious purpose.

An intense excitement was shown in Berlin some years ago in

consequence of a lady of rank having been ravished in a state of *mesmeric coma*

Again, a woman may yield to a ravisher under threats of death or duress, when the consent will not excuse the crime

The same remark applies to the cases of *imbecility* and *insanity*, or a great natural feebleness in the female

It has been made a question whether intercourse could be effected with a woman during natural sleep, and thus a charge of rape originate

A case in point is referred to by Dr Taylor as having occurred in London In this instance, however, the female, who alleged the charge against a gentleman, was a prostitute, and its improbability led to the abandonment of the prosecution

That intercourse might be effected with a female during a lethargic sleep, the effect of overpowering fatigue, has been argued for on the strength of two occurrences, the one related by Gooch, the other by Dr Montgomery The cases, however, are so strictly parallel, that I need adduce only one of them —

A servant woman at an hotel in Nenagh proved pregnant, and solemnly declared that she was not conscious of having had intercourse with any man Suspicion, however, fell upon an ostler in the establishment, who subsequently acknowledged that he believed he was the father of the child ; that, having found the woman in a deep sleep from fatigue, caused by long-continued exertion and being kept out of bed two or three nights in succession he had connection with her, and, as he believed, totally without her knowledge, as she did not evince the slightest consciousness of the act at the time, or recollect of its occurrence afterwards The parties were married with mutual consent

The following occurrence from Dr Guy bears out the probability of the circumstances just noticed —

"In the year 1840, I was consulted," says this author, " by a poor woman, who, after mentioning other complaints of little importance, stated that she was somewhat alarmed by the fact of her sleep being so heavy that she was with difficulty aroused She added, by way of illustration, that her husband had assured her that he had frequently had connection with her during sleep"

I need scarcely warn you, however, that extreme caution is necessary in admitting statements to the above effect from pregnant females, remembering the occasional effrontery of women in that state in denying or palliating their pregnancy, and the doubts which attach to their statements.

There are few accoucheurs who have not seen the expected mothers of illegitimate children denying their being pregnant even during labour, and up to the expulsion of the infant.

The place where the crime is alleged to have been committed is considered in law one of the most important indices of the inquiry as to the want of consent on the woman's part.

"Undue weight is frequently attached," says Mr Alison, "to the fact of cries having been heard. If the woman was aware that she had been discovered, or caught in the act, her screams cannot be relied on because they may have been uttered to give a colour of violence to a voluntary proceeding. If they took place *before* any discovery, to her knowledge, had been made, and alarmed persons at a distance, they are the strongest evidence of resistance."

Two very interesting illustrations of these remarks are brought forward by Mr Alison; but the following case, for which we are indebted to Mr Amos, is preferred for its brevity.

A bailiff, who was tried at Leicester, was charged with the capital offence of violating a young woman in a house where he had been formerly stationed as a keeper. The girl was the daughter of the owner of the house, and it came out that the alleged rape was committed early in the night in the very next room to that in which her father and mother slept. Upon being asked if she screamed, she answered, no. Why not? For fear of wakening my mother.

In the spring of 1848 I had occasion to examine a young woman under circumstances not unlike the above. One night a gentleman had occasion to go to his bedroom at an earlier hour than usual, when, on opening the door of his apartment in the dark, he was startled by hearing stifled moans from the bed, and some one slipped past him and escaped. On groping his way forward, his hand came in contact with the genitals of a female servant, who lay across the bed with her clothes up. The girl, when she had taken time to come to herself, which she did slowly and deliberately, stated to her master that she had been in the room arranging his bed when the footman came upon her, forced her into it, and would have succeeded in violating her had he not been disturbed.

On examining this woman shortly afterwards, no room was left for doubt that the case was a sham one altogether, and that the charge of violence was one got up, on the spur of the moment, to cover the shame of detection; the signs of distress having only commenced when she saw that her situation did not admit of concealment. The house was full of servants, and the only excuse for not raising an outcry which she could allege was that her mistress, an invalid old lady, would have been alarmed.

Decided differences in the age and strength of the two parties may throw some light on the case. "I have seen," says Mr Amos, "an instance of the charge of rape, brought by a stout full-grown woman against a slight lad of seventeen, break down on a sight of the parties." In the same way a like charge by a vigorous young woman against a feeble person of advanced age would, as a general rule, be rejected.

Improbabilities or inconsistencies in the narrative of the complainant, if duly noticed, may of themselves occasionally suffice to negative the possibility of an alleged forced intercourse. Instances of this sort have come within my own knowledge.

In one, in order to gratify personal pique, a woman who had been in the habit of receiving the visits of a gentleman, was persuaded after one of these visits to allege that the intercourse, which was admitted to have taken place, was a forced one.

In the other instance a young farmer had a voluntary intercourse with a young woman in his neighbourhood. Next day the woman charged him before a magistrate with having ravished her. On the precognition, however, it came out, from the woman's own account, that she had discovered and pointed out to the farmer, before his leaving the house, that his trousers had been torn somehow, and that she had been considerate enough, notwithstanding the awful situation he had placed her in, to sit down quietly and repair the damage to the garment in question. On seeing this statement in the indictment Crown Counsel at once abandoned the prosecution.

In the preceding remarks it has been assumed that the investigation into the charge of rape on the virgin female has to be followed out in the living victim. It may happen, however, though much more rarely, that the unfortunate party has perished from the accompanying violence, and that the investigation has to be undertaken on the dead body. The task here may be either a very easy one, or it may be attended with extreme difficulty according to circumstances. Thus the amount of violence may of itself suffice to account for death, and the genital injuries may be of such a marked kind as to leave no reasonable doubt that a rape has been committed during life. On the other hand, it will sometimes happen that the immediate cause of death may not be very obvious, nor the proofs of defloration very distinct. This was the case in the instance of the woman Smith, previously adverted to. On such occasions it will be for the medical jurist to consider whether the marks of violence on the person, and about the genitals, are sufficiently marked to enable him to infer with certainty that the woman had been violated during life; while it will be for him to prove the mode in which she had come by her death, as in ordinary cases of homicide. On the other hand there may be traces of violence on the genitals in the dead body, which have been purposely caused to divert attention from the real murderer, and to suggest the idea that a rape had been committed on the female during life. Unlikely as such an occurrence may appear, an instance of this kind was met with in the case of a murder at Cults some years ago. There were two wounds, one superficial on the left labium, the other deep, and passing through the nympha on the right side, from which merely a bloody serum had oozed, showing that these had been inflicted after the death of the woman from a deep wound in the throat. It was conjectured that the murderer in this case wished it to be thought that his victim had been violated, and that such an impression would divert suspicion from him, as she was well known to have for some time cohabited with him, and he would not be thought likely to need to have recourse to force upon his own concubine. In this case, however, all this is merely inferential, as the suspected murderer, though tried for the crime, escaped under a verdict of not proven.

III. The third and last division of our subject embraces the consideration of the question of violation after puberty, where the female is known to have been accustomed to sexual connection.

This division will not detain us long after the full consideration of the one last discussed.

A rape, I again repeat, may be committed on any female, whether maid, wife, or widow, or even on a common prostitute, provided clear and decisive evidence be adduced of the act having been committed by violence or without the woman's consent.

The proof in all these cases must obviously rest mainly on the evidence from facts other than the physical violence sustained by the parties at the time of the assault. With these, however, we have but little concern. Let us attend only to those which properly come within the province of the medical jurist, namely—the Physical Proofs. The signs of virginity and of defloration of course do not enter as elements into the inquiry. All we have to attend to are the proofs of a sexual intercourse of a compulsory kind at the time alleged. In the great majority of cases of rape perpetrated on either a wife, widow, prostitute, or unchaste female, the physical injuries to the organs of generation, consequent on a first concubitus with a male, are not to be looked for, for obvious reasons; but it should not be lost sight of that local injuries very similar to some of these may occur even in the circumstances we are considering.

In some women the vagina is naturally small even after frequent connection under ordinary circumstances, and should the rape be committed on such a person by one whose male organ is unusually large, local injuries might be produced on the female genitals. The same thing might happen where the intercourse was effected with brutality, or where several men in succession had forced connection with the same woman. We are not, however, entitled to look for these signs of connection in the generality of instances, particularly where the female has borne children, or is past the prime of life.

The marks of bruises, scratches, or other injuries on the other parts of the person will be as often met with in this class of females as in virgins.

Blood stains, in women who have had frequent intercourse, are not to be expected, unless under the circumstances of brutality just adverted to.

Seminal stains should, however, be frequently found in them, as well as in virgins, and may be submitted to the same investigations. Their evidence of the connection condescended upon, however, is ambiguous, as they may have arisen from the woman's connection with another than her ravisher.

Venereal disorders following the alleged forcible involuntary intercourse are even less trustworthy here than in the case of previously chaste women.

Lastly, the occurrence of pregnancy, dating from the day of the supposed rape, will be of no service to us in the case of women living in adultery or cohabiting with their husbands. In widows, and in women previously prostitutes or unchaste, proof would require to be had of the widowhood and of the other parties having left off their loose habits, before pregnancy could be traced to the embrace of the ravisher.

This completes what I had to say on the subject of rape. After the complicated details, however, into which I have of necessity been led, it may be useful to conclude with a summary of the duties of the medical jurist, when called to the investigation of these criminal charges

1. The examiner should attentively examine the form and disposition of the genitals, taking careful note of any tumefaction, unusual redness, bruises, wounds, or discharges, which may be found there. He should observe whether there be any dried matter adhering to any part of the vulva, or any stains on the linen. Marks of recent contusions should be looked for in the vicinity of the vulva, or on other parts of the person. The visit should be as soon after the alleged rape as possible, not later, to be of much service, than the *third* day.

2. The examiner should be careful not to attribute the marks which he finds on the genitals necessarily to a forced or involuntary connection, or to sexual intercourse at all. He should make it distinctly understood that these may be all produced by other causes.

3. The marks of recent defloration being discovered in a young female, and in addition to this, marks of injuries which may have been inflicted at the same date on the thighs, arms, breasts, etc, and those not such as could have been self-inflicted the examiner is then in a condition to state the probability that the female has been violated. These injuries on the genitals and person point to the commission of rape; but in a less positive manner in the case of females who have had frequent connection than in virgins.

4. The absence of the local genital injuries does not necessarily imply that there has been no rape committed, even in the case of virgins past puberty.

5. The marks of recent defloration in children below puberty, when it can be shown that these have not been produced by a local catarrh or other genital disease, establish the probability of rape—a probability which may be much strengthened by the concurrence of injuries in the neighbourhood of the vagina, and on the person generally.

6. To the marks of recent defloration, and injuries to the person generally, the addition of venereal symptoms is only to be reckoned an accessory proof, and that only when their occurrence follows at a fixed date, and it can be ascertained that the woman has not otherwise been exposed to the specific infection:

7. Conception following the occurrence of a supposed rape only proves sexual connection with some one, and its non-supervention cannot negative the possibility of violation.

8. If a woman, supposed to have been ravished, should die from the effects of the violence sustained, a scrupulous examination of *all parts* of the body should be set on foot. Traces of blows on the surface, and of fractures and dislocations, should be looked for; the mouth should be examined, as foreign bodies may have been forced into it to stifle her cries; the signs of recent defloration about the external genitals may be expected, as also possibly spots of semen in the vulva, within the vagina, or on the linen. The cause of death may be other than the lesions of the genitals.

9. The examination of the party charged with the rape may, with considerable probability, connect him with the violence inflicted on the female, from corresponding marks of the struggle being found on his person. In general, however, we can only obtain evidence, in cases of rape, that the female has been ravished, but not to enable us to fix upon the individual ravisher. From an examination of the prisoner we may sometimes be able to pronounce that he was not in a state to commit the rape, as when we find him impotent from any cause.

Lastly. Cases are apt to occur—as in females who have borne children, or in old and profligate women—where the medical jurist will be unable to furnish any testimony to the courts which can be relied on. Such an occurrence, moreover, as the following, is not, by any means impossible—viz., a stranger taking the place of the husband in the bed of the married female without immediate discovery. Here there would be a rape, to all intents and purposes, where there would be no physical appearances to afford grounds for a medical opinion to that effect. We have the authority, however, of Mr. Chitty for stating that the criminal courts would not take adequate cognisance of such a crime, because here there would be the absence of that actual criminal force in general essential to support an indictment for rape.

One or two words on the subject of *rape by females on males.* This offence is classed with sodomy by the English law, though, as ordinarily understood, a different offence. Fortunately, it is but little known in this country as a crime, though such cases have been tried both in France and in Germany, and the parties, on conviction, sentenced to lengthened and severe punishments. In the instances on record abroad, what constituted the crime was the forcing boys under puberty to attempt sexual intercourse, or what alone could approach to it, by females beyond the age of puberty. What gives some colour to the presumed existence of such a practice, in some, at least, of our large towns, is the occasional encounter in hospitals of venereal diseases in impuberant boys One such case, though no disease was communicated, was known to me in a respectable family some years ago, the ages of the woman and the boy being respectively 17 and 7 years

The only available proof of the perpetration of such an offence open to the medical jurist would be the transmission of syphilis, or gonorrhœa, from the woman to the child

Sodomy

Up almost to this time I have been but too well pleased to pass, *sub silentio*, a subject allied to the last which I would scarcely be justified in longer ignoring, as it is now forcing itself on the unwilling attention of medical jurists in this and other countries The crime which brought down the Divine vengeance on the luxurious and corrupt cities of the Plain of Sodom, and which rose into such notoriety in the worst periods of the degeneracy of ancient Greece and Rome, is now, unfortunately, becoming too well known to the law authorities in our large towns, and familiar, in all its hideous details, to not a few of our medical practitioners So much is this the case that one expert (Tardieu) in Paris has had no fewer than sixty cases within a single year in his own practice, and speaks of as many as ninety-seven known to him during a like period, in all the plenitude of their enormity as involving both sexes alike and various ages, and serving as a step to crimes of, if possible, a still deeper dye— murder not excepted

There is no necessity, however, for entering into particulars regarding such obscene acts for the varied forms of which we have to go back to early pagan times to find characteristic names, enough to state that, in one or other of their forms, in certain European capitals, the demand has created a supply of prostitutes of this new class, not only from the ordinary ranks of prostitution as usually understood, but also from that of boys above and below puberty, who, with this view, dress themselves as females and ply their trade not unfrequently with informers, robbers, and assassins, and if in this country we have not quite sunk so low as this, there is some reason to believe that the first step to this degradation has been already taken even here, while in London the police records show that Paris and Berlin, if all were known, do not, perhaps, stand altogether alone in their bad pre-eminence in this respect

Having said so much, I shall now confine myself to the notice of the effects of this vice when practised or committed—1st, on the parties who are active, and 2d on those who are passive in the matter, which embraces nearly all that the medical practitioner need concern himself with in his professional capacity

The effects of this practice, if we are to trust to Tardieu, are sufficiently marked and permanent to serve as characteristic and undoubted evidence of its having existed or having been persevered in, in either of its two forms According to this eminent Parisian expert, who tells us that he founded his statements on the results of 206 actual cases—

In those who lay themselves out as prostitutes in this form the more recent signs vary with circumstances, such as the degree of violence employed, the volume of the male parts, the youth of the victim, and the absence of previous vice, from simple excoriation, heat about the anus, and difficulty in walking, to rhagades, deep rents, extravasation of blood, and inflammation of the mucous membrane and the subjacent areolar tissue

The habitués of this form of the vice are known to present an unnatural development of the nates, a funnel-shaped deformity of the anus, relaxation of its sphincter, the disappearance of the usual folds around the exterior of this aperture, hardened ridges and carunculæ in the same situation, extreme dilatation of the anal orifice, incontinence of the contents of the bowels, ulcerations, rhagades, piles, fistulæ, rectal mucous discharges, and syphilis After a time, too, this miserable trade tells on the general appearance, imparting a hue of ill health to the countenance and causing emaciation of the limbs, which may, in part, be traceable to the habits of life of the parties

Nor, in the second place, does the active addiction to this vice fail to leave its traces at length on the person of its frequent perpetrator Thus, according to Tardieu, of 205 individuals of this class examined by him, 88 exhibited the signs which he has fixed on as characteristic of their condition Amongst these, he places foremost the shape of the penis as generally though not invariably diminutive, tapering from its root to the point, with the meatus urinarius dependent from a twisting of the organ, with occasionally a degree of thickening and flattening of the point of the glans, and the existence of paraphymosis to a marked extent

Such then, according to this authority, are the indications which may be looked for in a large number of such parties, whether prostitutes or their encouragers It must be added, however, that, as already hinted at, notwithstanding the thorough examination of this subject by Tardieu, the signs both of the active and passive forms of this vice have been, to a large extent, contested by Caspar, first in his *Gerichtliche Medicin*, and more fully in his subsequently published *Novellen.* While he denies altogether the validity of Tardieu's test of the active form of this vice, his conclusions as to the indications of its passive form are as follows:— 1. That the diagnostic appearances laid down by Tardieu and others may all be absent, and generally are so; 2. That the trumpet-like depression is worthy of attention; and 3. That the smoothness of the skin in the vicinity of the anus is the most certain of all the uncertain signs of pæderastia.

I need scarcely add, in conclusion, that the conflicting opinions of these two eminent and experienced medical jurists strongly point out the necessity of extreme caution in drawing inferences from physical appearances in cases of the sort we have been considering.

LECTURE X.

PREGNANCY

PRELIMINARY REMARKS.—Legal Relations of the Subject—Occasions for Inquiry into its Existence. TRUE PREGNANCY—Natural Pregnancy—Signs of Natural Pregnancy—Cessation of the Menses—Sympathetic Disorders of the System—Changes in the Manner—Deposition of Pigmentum Nigrum on the Abdomen, Mammæ, and other parts of the Surface—State of the Urine—Appearance of the Vagina—Condition of the Os and Cervix Uteri—Changes in the Uterus—The Active Movements of the Fœtus—The Passive Movements of the Fœtus (Ballotement)—The Stethoscopic Indications—Signs of Extra-Uterine Pregnancy—Signs of Compound Pregnancy—Signs of Complicated Pregnancy. FALSE PREGNANCY—Spasmodic or Nervous Pregnancy—Retained Menses simulating Pregnancy—Moles or False Conceptions—The Disorganised Embryo—The Fleshy Mole—The Vesicular Mole (Hydatid). SIMULATED PREGNANCY.

The subject of pregnancy, to which I now proceed, while common ground to the medical jurist and to the accoucheur, presents itself under circumstances of greater difficulty to the former than to the latter, at the same time embracing fewer points of inquiry. Thus, while both have to determine the existence of pregnancy, and to discriminate betwixt pregnancy and the morbid states which are apt to counterfeit it, the medical jurist is shut out from the data—available to the accoucheur—deducible from the statements of the mother, on which, unlike the midwifery practitioner, the expert cannot rely, but on the contrary must be prepared for every species of falsehood and misrepresentation on her part.

The chief points which are apt to rise in courts of law regarding pregnancy are—1st, The determination of its existence in particular instances; and 2d, If existent, the ascertainment of the period at which it has arrived.

The occasions for such inquiries in law originate in some one or other of the following categories:—

1st. An unmarried female yields to her seducer, and the proof of her subsequent pregnancy must be produced in order to compel a marriage or to obtain damages.

2d. An attempt may be made to conceal pregnancy by the unmarried, or even by the married, under certain circumstances—

as in the case of a wife's separation from her husband, or his casual absence, in order to avoid disgrace in society, or to enable her with impunity to destroy her offspring.

3d. Pregnancy may be feigned in order to gratify the wishes of a husband or relations, to deprive the lawful heir of his just rights of succession, to delay the execution of the sentence of death, or to obtain more indulgent treatment.

In the case of a widow suspected of feigning herself with child in order to produce a supposititious heir to an estate, the heir presumptive may have a writ *de ventre inspiciendo*, as it is called, to examine if she be with child or not.

When pregnancy is pleaded by a criminal in bar of execution, the English law requires that the woman be decided to be *quick with child* before she can have the sentence of death postponed till after delivery, the law of Scotland only requires that the pregnancy be established, without any reference to quickening. There is another enactment in relation to such case in England which has no place in Scotch practice. Before the plea of pregnancy can be admitted, it must be made good by the verdict of a jury of twelve matrons, or discreet women, impanelled from amongst those who may happen to be present in court. The serious mistakes to which this practice has been found to give rise, though they have not led to its abandonment, have so far induced the courts to modify it by conjoining with the female jury some skilled medical witness.

There is another case where the courts have interfered on proof of actual pregnancy being brought before them; that is, where a female in this situation is imprisoned. If it can be shown that she is pregnant, and that the woman's life is endangered, or the infant's safety hazarded, the prisoner may be admitted to bail till after delivery.

It has been recently decided that a female in the pregnant state cannot be compelled to appear and give evidence in a trial, provided it can be shown by the affidavits of competent persons that the delivery will probably happen about the time fixed for the trial.

I need scarcely warn you of the importance of a correct decision in cases of this sort, in which mistakes have been fallen into by medical men and accoucheurs. Thus, both Riolan and Mauriceau have adduced instances in which pregnant women were actually executed after formal examination by surgeons and midwives.

The observations which fall to be made on the subject of

pregnancy refer chiefly to its natural forms, which will consequently first call for our attention, reserving the few remarks bearing on the other forms of it laid down by authors till these have been discussed

The main question which has to come before the medical jurist as regards pregnancy in any one of its forms, is that of its actual existence under any of the circumstances already noticed

The signs of pregnancy, where the foetus is enclosed in the ordinary manner within the uterus, have been variously classed by authors. Thus, we may adopt the twofold division of them into *certain* and *uncertain* signs, the former—the certain signs—being those on which undoubting reliance may be placed in deciding on the existence of the pregnant state; the latter—the uncertain signs—being those which, though taken in connection with the certain signs they may enable us to speak to the probability of pregnancy, cannot be entirely relied on for the determination of this point

In place of this division, some authors have employed the terms *rational* or *subjective*, and *sensible* or *objective* as applicable to the two sets of signs by which pregnancy may be determined. The *rational* signs of these writers, as the term implies, are those of which we can have no evidence beyond the woman's testimony; the *sensible* signs, those of which we can take cognisance from the evidence of our own senses

The rational signs of the latter authorities, it may be here remarked, correspond generally with the uncertain signs of the former, and the sensible to the certain, though not without some important exceptions; for though all the certain signs are sensible ones, the reverse of this does not hold good, all the sensible signs are not certain ones

These distinctions it is of importance to keep in view, for although the medical jurist can only safely rely on those signs of pregnancy which are appreciable by his own senses, and can in no case trust to the woman's testimony, yet he may have his judgment strengthened in many instances by finding the sensible signs corroborated by the rational ones

The signs of an existing state of pregnancy in its earlier period are more equivocal than those which are available in its more advanced stages. Previous to the end of the fifth or the beginning of the sixth month the more important of the sensible signs are not available for our guidance; prior to this date we have mainly the unreliable data afforded by the rational signs. This, however, is of less consequence to the jurist, as few occasions present themselves in practice for such inquiries, and these occasions are but of secondary importance

Keeping this in view, we proceed to consider the uncertain signs of this form of pregnancy, which I shall take as nearly as may be in the order of their occurrence in point of time. By following these signs in the order of their natural succession, we shall fulfil the twofold indication (1) of considering them as signs of an existing pregnancy, and (2), as indicating, so far as they go, the period at which the pregnancy has arrived in any given case.

First in order then, we have the cessation of the menses. This is commonly the first indication which the woman has of having conceived, but difficulties attach to the appreciation of this sign. Thus women have conceived in whom the menses have never appeared at all, while others have had a discharge throughout the greater part, if not the whole duration, of their pregnancies, so closely resembling the menses as not to be readily distinguishable from them. Of such persistent menstruation, or what appears to be menstruation, Elsasser has furnished several authentic instances, while, on the other hand, uterine disorders are known to be occasionally attended with suppression of the menses.

Second, The various sympathetic disorders which have been observed in the earlier stages of pregnancy, such as nausea, vomitings, anorexia, depraved or vitiated appetite, salivation, headache, and toothache, are but equivocal signs, as they may or may not be present, or may arise from other causes than pregnancy.

Third, The changes which occur in the mammæ attest the existence of pregnancy. At an early period the breasts begin to enlarge, their superficial veins become more distinct than usual, and a thin milky fluid may be expressed from them. These changes, however, are not constant in pregnancy, while they have all been known to arise from uterine irritation in non-pregnant females. The milk has been secreted in virgins and old women past the age of childbearing, and even in males; while some females continue to suckle from one pregnancy to another, at a distance of several years. An instance of this last kind came under my notice where lactation had continued for *five* years. On another occasion, when sent to examine a woman charged with the murder of an infant *eleven* days after her delivery, I found her suckling a former child of *three* years which had not been weaned.

Fourth, More importance has been attached to certain changes in and around the nipple, which begin to be marked as early as the commencement of the third month of pregnancy, but which become most distinct about the fourth or fifth month. These appearances were noticed by some of the earlier writers, but the attention of the profession was not drawn to them particularly till their value as signs of pregnancy was advocated by Dr Montgomery.

The changes in question are thus described by that author — A dark circle begins to show itself round the nipple, varying from one to one and a half inches in breadth, increasing in size as the pregnancy advances, and differing in depth of colour according to the complexion of the individual, being generally much darker in persons with black hair, dark eyes, and sallow skins, than in those with fair hair, light coloured eyes, and delicate complexions

The nipple comes to partake of the altered colour of the areola, and appears turgid and prominent.

The part of the areola immediately around the base of the nipple has its surface rendered uneven by the prominence of the glandular follicles, which, varying in number from twelve to twenty, project from the sixteenth to the eighth of an inch

The integument covering the part is softer and moister than that which surrounds it, and the breasts themselves are at the same time full and firm, at least more so than was natural to them previously

When the areola is found possessing these distinctive marks its diagnostic value has been strongly argued for by Montgomery, Hamilton, Rœderer, Dubois, Blundel, Merriman, and Gooch Various circumstances, however, are now generally admitted as sufficient to limit both its value and applicability

Thus, the test can only properly apply to a first pregnancy; the areola being apt to retain its colour and breadth in women who have borne one or more children

It has been shown that pregnancy may exist without the colour of the areola being altered; that all the true characteristics of the areola of pregnancy may be detected after a recent miscarriage, and that the characteristic appearances of the areola have been known to be wanting at the period of labour

Thus, not to quote authorities, I may mention that in my own practice, in one female the areola was not developed in her first and only pregnancy, that, in a second, it was fully developed at the time of the expulsion of a mole and that in a third it presented all the virgin characters at the delivery of a fourth or fifth child

Denman, Dubois, Ley, Laycock, Hohl, Simpson, and Cooper, have witnessed the change of colour of the areola in unimpregnated females as a consequence of uterine disease, and even as the effect of menstruation

While freely admitting the serious drawbacks to the value and applicability of this test of pregnancy, there is one combination of circumstances which has led me to look upon its use as of some importance. The facility with which it can be made available, without necessarily awakening suspicion or shocking the modesty of the female, recommends it strongly in a class of cases which often present themselves in practice, and are not a little embarrassing to professional men. I allude to instances of young women in respectable families, on whom, with or without good grounds, suspicion has arisen of their being pregnant. On occasions of this sort, I have been able to give a pretty strong opinion both for and against the suspected impregnation. One or two instances may be noticed, where this sign has enabled me at once to banish groundless suspicions against virtuous females. One was a young woman of 17. She had morning sickness, suppressed menses, and a degree of abdominal tumefaction corresponding to the sixth month of utero-gestation. The breasts, however, exhibited all the characters of the virgin mammæ. In another, the suspicion originated in some scandalous stories, which had no foundation in fact. In a medico-legal case it was had recourse to with the same effect. At the Aberdeen Spring Circuit of 1839, a female pled her advanced pregnancy to obtain the postponement of her trial. On giving an opinion adverse to her statement, the court proceeded to try the case. Of course in all these instances, nothing farther was affirmed than the high improbability of the impregnation.

A deposition of dark pigment cells has been noticed to occur during the pregnant state, in other situations than in and around the areola, as in the mesial line of the abdominal wall, and on the face and other parts of the general surface.

The discoloration of the belly shows itself in the form of a narrow brown line extending from the pubes to the umbilicus or to the sternum, with a dark, but not raised areola, about a quarter of an inch in breadth, around the navel, most marked in dark complexioned females.

Elsasser says that he found this line in 400 pregnant women examined by him. In 377 of these it extended from the pit of the stomach to the pubes; in 22, only from the navel to the pubes; in the remaining instance, it was wanting below but present above the navel. On the other hand, this observer could not discover the line in certain pregnant women examined by him. Though he has not distinctly stated the number of these exceptional cases, he calculated the proportion in which this sign was found to those in which it was not as 4 to 1. Moreover, he detected the brown line though narrow or faintly coloured, in unimpregnated females. I may add that I have thrice observed the same thing in females, and, what is still more remarkable, in a male, at the Aberdeen deadhouse, in the winter of 1868-9.

The brown discolorations on other parts of the surface of the body, besides the abdomen, in pregnant women, are the small discrete maculæ or freckles, known as liver spots, chloasmata uterina, or pityriasis gravidarum, which develope themselves on the face, neck, breasts, and arms during utero-gestation.

In fifty-eight pregnant women examined by Elsasser, he found these maculæ present in all. In four of them they appeared during the first three months, in twelve at the middle of their pregnancies, in fourteen during the last six or eight weeks. In the remaining cases, the date of the eruption was not ascertained.

The increased development of the pigment cells on various parts of the surface in pregnant women is occasionally witnessed to a still greater extent. Thus moles and warts are at this time liable to become turgid and dark, while brunettes and even blondes occasionally take on a darker hue, and certain cutaneous eruptions become more distinct. I was consulted by a young and healthy brunette, a few weeks after her delivery, in whom the skin of the lower half of the abdomen and of the fronts of both thighs had taken on a hue like that of a mulatto; the persistence of the discoloration from the later months of her pregnancy up to the time of her visit to me had caused her no small alarm.

The value of these liver spots on the various parts of the general surface, as signs of an existing pregnancy, is much lessened, from the difficulty of discriminating betwixt the maculæ of utero-gestation and forms of *ephelis* and *pityriasis versicolor*, while, again, the former, as is well known, may be caused not only by exposure to sunlight, but also by irritation of internal organs, uterine and otherwise.

Fifth, Since 1831 the state of the urine during pregnancy has attracted the attention of practitioners in this and other countries. On standing for some time, the urine of pregnant women after the first month has been observed, though with some exceptions, to become turbid, by the formation, of a fatty pellicle on its surface, followed by the fall of a flaky precipitate. As to the character of this foreign matter, however, accoucheurs and chemists are not agreed, while as to its value as a sign of pregnancy, experts are by no means at one. The deposit, known as kiestine, or gravidine, has been variously characterised as casein (Bird), as a protein compound closely connected with the lacteal secretion (Simon), and as a collection of crystals of triple phosphate, vibriones, and fungi (Lehmann). While several of its earlier observers (Kane, Bird, Eguisei), considered this substance in the urine, when present, as a certain, or all but certain test of utero-gestation, other and later writers have ranked it as nearly or wholly valueless. This unfavourable opinion of the test they rest on the following considerations, which scarcely now admit of dispute:—

That the kiestine shows some diversities in the date of its appearance in the urine of pregnant females.

That it is not invariably to be met with at any one stage of utero-gestation.

That it may occur in the urine of females soon after their delivery, either during or in the absence of lactation.

That it may be found in the urine of virgin females in diseased states of the uterine organs.

Its existence is not altogether unknown in the urine of males and infants.

This, with the acknowledged difficulty in distinguishing with certainty between the kiestine pellicle and a similar appearance occasionally to be witnessed in healthy urine, exceedingly lessens the value of this indication of pregnancy; though it does not authorise us to throw it aside altogether as an auxiliary test in doubtful cases in the earlier months.

In once instance I found this test useful in ordinary practice. In consultation with the late Dr Jamieson, Lecturer on Midwifery in the Aberdeen University, we could not with confidence distinguish, in the case of a lady, whether there was ovarian disease or gravid uterus at the fourth month, when our patient pronounced decidedly for the former, from the absence of kiestine in her urine, which had attracted her notice in her pregnancies previously. A short time showed that she was right in this.

Sixth, No reliance is now placed on the character of the blood, or the state of the pulse, as indications of pregnancy.

Seventh, The tint which the vagina has been observed to assume in the earlier months of pregnancy, varying from that of wine-lees to a violet, or blackish blue, has been relied on as an indication of this state. This appearance, however, may be induced in the vagina by hæmorrhoids in the rectum; while, according to Dubois, it may be witnessed at the time of the cessation of the menses, or after any unusual flow of blood to the external genitals. Moreover, we have the authority of Dr Montgomery for the statement that this state of the vagina is not invariably to be met with in pregnant women.

Passing from these indications of pregnancy, all of them attended in their application with more or less of uncertainty, we come to those which are founded on the expansion of the uterus, and the growth within it of the product of conception. As these advance gradually, the discrimination of the pregnant state becomes more and more easy, so that by the time the utero-gestation has reached from the fourth to the sixth month, all uncertainty has ceased, and we can rest our decision on evidence which is not liable to mislead us. Previously, however to this period the changes taking place in the uterus and its contents are but partially available as tests of an existing pregnancy.

The indications of pregnancy derivable from these sources are drawn from—1st, The state of the os and cervix uteri; 2d, The growth of the uterus; and 3d, The development of the fœtus; the value and certainty of these indications being in the order in which they have been enumerated.

The state of the os and cervix uteri is not only different in pregnant from what it is in non-pregnant females, but it also varies at different stages of the utero-gestation. With the condition of the os and cervix uteri in the unimpregnated female you must be familiar. Soon after conception, on making the usual examination *per vaginam*, the *cervix* is felt to be fuller, rounder, and more spongy or elastic than in its virgin state; while its orifice has lost its transverse shape and well-defined edge, and is rounder and thicker. Gradually as the period of pregnancy advances it not only becomes less prominent, but its position is altered. From and after the sixth month it becomes more and more flattened, till about the period of delivery it can no longer be felt. For the first three months it is easily reached, being low down in the vagina. About the fifth month, or a little earlier, its place is higher, from the ascent of the uterus into the abdomen, and the direction of the os is more towards the back wall of the vagina. After this period it recedes farther from the external parts, and ceases to be distinguishable as a projecting body

The absence of these changes in the os and cervix uteri is of more value than their presence. Thus it may be concluded with certainty that the woman is not with child, especially if the suspected pregnancy have been of some months' duration, should the os uteri be found retaining the character of the unimpregnated state. On the other hand it is known that in some married women the os and cervix uteri never recover their virgin state, while again certain uterine diseases may cause these parts to assume almost exactly the characters which attend the earlier stages of utero-gestation.

The changes in the *body of the uterus* are important to be noted in connection with suspected pregnancy. During the first three months the degree of its development is ascertained with difficulty; but it becomes more easy of detection as pregnancy proceeds. In general, by the end of the *fourth* month, the fundus of the uterus may be felt, especially in a thin person, above the anterior wall of the pelvis. During the *fifth* month it has usually risen to between the pubes and the umbilicus, and the enlargement may be ascertained on examination, per vaginam, if the finger is placed on the forepart of the cervix uteri. In the *sixth* month the fundus uteri has risen as high as the umbilicus. In the *seventh* month it is on a level with a point midway between the umbilicus and the lower end of the sternum. By the end of the *eighth* month it has reached the ensiform cartilage, beyond which it does not subsequently advance.

Even in the earlier periods of pregnancy, but especially towards its natural termination, an important indication not unfrequently comes into play, according to some later observers, namely, the alternate relaxation and contraction of the uterus. This, when present, could only be imitated in certain cases of menorrhagia, from which it could be readily distinguished by the absence of hemorrhage.

The expansion of the uterus is attended with two subsidiary phenomena, which have been laid hold of as indications of pregnancy, namely, the states of the navel and of the linea alba.

It is well known that about the sixth month of pregnancy the increase in bulk of the abdominal contents causes the obliteration of the umbilical pit, after which this part begins to protrude; while again, after the uterus has passed the umbilicus, the pressure on the abdominal wall causes a separation of the recti muscles, so as to give an increase of breadth to the linea alba. I need hardly remind you that both these changes may originate in dropsy or other chronic enlargement of the abdominal contents.

To return to the uterus. The growth of this organ, as discovered from its position in the abdomen and pelvis, it must be borne in mind, may arise from other causes than pregnancy, such as, hydatids, polypus, dropsy, or accumulation within it of the menses, or even from scirrhous thickening of its walls. At the same time the co-existence of other signs of pregnancy would afford a strong conviction of the existence of that condition. A negative opinion, on the other hand, might more safely be formed from the want of correspondence between the state of the uterus and other signs apparently indicating a certain period of pregnancy.

I now come to advert to the last source from which we can draw our indications of pregnancy, namely, from the growth within the uterus of the product of conception. Here we reach a source of evidence of a most satisfactory kind, where we are no longer in danger of falling into those sources of fallacy which attend the practical application of most of the tests which we have hitherto been considering.

The indications derivable from this source are three in number. The discovery of (1.) The *active* movements of the fœtus; (2.) Its *passive* movements; and (3.) The indications of its vitality afforded by the stethoscope. These are the so-called *certain signs*.

The *active* movements of the fœtus. The first sensation to the mother of the living being within her is the cause usually now assigned of these peculiar sensations, sometimes attended with disturbances of the system, experienced by the pregnant female between the twelfth and sixteenth weeks, to which the term *quickening* has been applied. As a test of utero-gestation it is almost useless to the medical jurist, for, not to speak of its occasional absence, and its being sometimes believed by the female to be felt where other sensations have been mistaken for it by her, it cannot, where it has actually been experienced, be verified by the practitioner. It is altogether different, however, when this period is past, and the motions of the fœtus are sufficiently active to be capable of being ascertained by the medical examiner.

The active movements of the fœtus are manifested by an impulse communicated to the walls of the uterus by the body of the child, which first becomes sensible to the mother about the end of the *third* or the beginning of the *fourth* month, though not unfrequently not till the middle of the fifth month. The fœtal movements are described as being at first a *sharp pricking* sensation, or as a sort of *titillation* in some part of the uterus. This is afterwards succeeded by a *stroke* or *distinct percussion*, sensible to the hand placed over the lower part of the abdominal wall, and which, even at this early period, may be sufficiently strong sensibly to displace the uterine walls, and through them to communicate an impulse to those of the abdomen, rendering the elevation thus produced visible to the eye.

Where the woman is thin and the fœtus vigorous and lively this sign may be available to the practitioner as early as the fourth month. In other circumstances it is only in the fifth month, or even later, that this can be accomplished.

To succeed in feeling or exciting the active movements of the fœtus, the examiner should grasp the uterine mass with his spread hand, as if examining the abdomen for an ordinary tumour, pressing it backwards towards the spine with his fingers, or from each side towards the centre, or he may succeed in his object equally well by applying a hand firmly against one side of the uterine tumour, and impressing the opposite side quickly with the fingers of the other hand. These manœuvres are facilitated by placing the woman on her back in bed, with the shoulders and pelvis somewhat elevated, and the lower extremities drawn up in the state of flexion.

Sometimes, however, the application of the spread hand over the front of the abdomen is sufficient for our purpose; at other times we shall best succeed by the sudden application of the hand, previously cooled by immersion in water, which frequently has the effect of making the fœtus, as it were, to start, and thus to communicate a very distinct sensation of its movements.

It is necessary to warn you against mistakes in the appreciation of this sign. Diseased conditions of the uterus or its contents can never mislead the examiner, provided he be sufficiently careful to distinguish the mere changes of place of a part of the uterine mass, or of a dead fœtus, from the independent muscular motions of a living child. He would be a very careless examiner who could confound, as has, however, been done, the movements of flatus in the intestines, or convulsive motions of the uterine walls with the active movements of the fœtus. Such mistakes have often been committed by females themselves, even those who had previously borne children, and they have thus been induced to declare themselves pregnant when they were not so.

There is still one other source of fallacy to which it is proper here to allude, namely, the power which it has been asserted that some women possess of simulating the motions of the child by certain actions of the abdominal muscles. Thus Dr. Blundell, who has called our attention to this fact, mentions the case of a woman seen by the late Dr. Lowder and other eminent accoucheurs, who simulated these movements so exactly, that had they judged from this sign alone they would have pronounced her pregnant.

When the active movements of the fœtus can be felt, it is, of of course, certain that pregnancy exists. Cases, however, have occurred in which this sign was either very late of being appreciable, or where it has not been so, either by the accoucheur or by the mother, up to the termination of the pregnancy. Such occurrences, though extremely rare, require to be kept in view. Of this Dr. Montgomery has met with two instances in his own practice, where he and others failed to make out pregnancy, though in one case of the sixth and in the other of the seventh month. Similar occurrences are recorded in the practice of Desormeaux, Capuron, Baudeloque, Gooch, and Kennedy of Dublin.

I mention such occurrences the more particularly as it has been tempted to throw doubts on them by some teachers of midwifery, who are never willing to admit that they can fail in anything they undertake.

A case in point came before a Court in Aberdeen in 1848. A practitioner in the country attempted to cause the abortion of a woman at the end of the fifth or the beginning of the sixth month of her pregnancy. Two accoucheurs examined the woman shortly afterwards, and gave it as their opinion that the abortion had been effected; the woman, however, was delivered of a healthy infant at the full time.

An instance previously referred to in another connection (Sterility, p. 86) came under my own notice in private practice. The pregnancy was complicated with ascites and a broken constitution, to which the female fell a victim shortly after her delivery. At the date of my first visit she had been seven years married without family, and all that time she had suffered from irritable uterus, which rendered her miserable, and made coition very painful. On the removal of the dropsy, of some months standing, a tumour was detected in the abdomen, about the bulk of the pregnant uterus at the end of the sixth or the beginning of the seventh month; otherwise there was nothing to indicate pregnancy, the possibility of which was denied by the woman herself. The mammæ were natural, the active movements of the foetus could not be felt, the foetal sounds were indistinguishable and it was impossible to reach the cervix uteri for the purpose of attempting ballotement

The *passive* movements of the foetus are so termed to distinguish this sign of pregnancy from the one we have been considering (its active movements) To this sign the appellation "Ballotement" has been given by the French and some British writers.

As the foetus is known to float loosely in the liquor amnii, it is easily conceivable that it may be made to change its place, independently altogether of its own vital movements—just as any other body placed in similar circumstances could be made to move by an impulse communicated to it from without Further, the head of the foetus, as it lies naturally in the uterus resting on the top of the vagina when the mother is in the erect position, can be reached by the fingers of one hand, so as to communicate such an impulse to its whole body as can be perceived by the other hand placed on the abdomen over the most prominent part of the uterine tumour, before it has had time to drop down into its place again and the head comes once more in contact with the examiner's fingers placed in contact with the cervix

The sign thus afforded to us is one which is scarcely inferior in value to that last considered, and it has this advantage over it, that it can be made available whether the foetus be dead or alive at the time of the examination It affords a positive proof of the existence of a foetus in utero there being no other condition or disease of the organ in which a solid body can be felt floating in its cavity

The examiner may not always be able to satisfy himself of the presence of the foetus in this way This may be due to several causes, either from the foetus being unusually small, the cervix being uncommonly long, or from the uterus lying too much beyond the reach of the finger at the time that the examination is instituted It is seldom satisfactorily ascertained either earlier than about the end of the fourth, or later than about the end of the sixth, month of utero-gestation Previous to the first-named period, the foetus is too light to be distinguished by the touch, while, after the last-named period, its bulk hinders it from floating freely enough in the liquor amnii

In making the examination, the practitioner should previously have had the bladder and rectum emptied, in order that the uterus may have as much space as possible for its descent into the pelvis, so as to bring it, as far as can be done, within reach of the examiner's fingers. The woman should be placed in the upright position, or lying with the shoulders much raised. One or two fingers are then to be introduced into the vagina, and carried upwards until their points are applied to the front of the cervix uteri, and as high up on that part as they can be conveniently made to reach without using force, when they must be carefully kept in contact with the part to which they have been thus applied. The other hand of the examiner is then to be placed on the abdomen, over the uterine tumour, which should be pressed downwards towards the cavity of the pelvis; the fingers which have been kept applied to the cervix should then be impressed against it with a quick or slightly jerking motion upwards, when instantly something will be felt to bound away from the fingers, upon which it will, in the course of three or four seconds, be felt to drop again with a gentle pat.

The examiner should be careful not to mistake the movement of the uterus itself for that of the fœtus within it, an error which may very easily be fallen into if the fingers are removed from their contact with the cervix while the examination is being made. Dr. Montgomery has alluded to one instance of a mistake of another kind which could only have occurred in the hands of a very careless examiner,—that of confounding the pulsation of one of the uterine arteries with the drop of the fœtus on the finger.

We now come to the last of the indications of pregnancy which we have to consider, namely,

The *stethoscopic* signs. On applying the stethoscope to the uterine region of the abdomen two distinct and independent sounds are elicited in pregnant women, the one derived from the pulsation of the fœtal heart, and the other from the activity of the circulation either in the vessels of the placenta or in the walls of the uterus. The latter of these sounds indicates the existence of a placenta, or an enlarged uterus, the former the existence of a living fœtus.

The *uterine or placental souffle* is first perceptible in the fourth month, and continues throughout the pregnancy. It is described as a low murmuring or somewhat cooing sound, bearing a resemblance to that made by blowing gently over the mouth of a widemouthed phial, at the same time accompanied by a slight rushing noise, but unattended by any distinct impulse. It is always synchronous with the pulse of the mother. Its detection is usually most easily accomplished by placing the stethoscope upon the sides of the uterine mass. The instrument should be pressed pretty firmly against the part, so as to displace at the same time any air in the interposed intestines, and as much of the liquor amnii as possible, in order to obtain a solid medium for the transmission of the sound. It may not be always possible to discover this sign, as it is liable to occasional interruptions, while it is likewise known to vary with the state of the maternal pulse. Moreover, it is not possible in all cases to distinguish it from sounds caused by other states of the uterus than pregnancy. Thus Dr Montgomery has recorded a case of vascular sarcoma of the uterus which was accompanied by this phenomenon in its most perfect condition, as well as an instance of tumour of the abdomen pressing on the aorta, where this sound was equally distinct. Besides, the murmur may undoubtedly be produced artificially by pressing the end of the stethoscope over the site of the iliac vessels. Some writers consider it quite possible, too, that the placental murmur may remain altogether inappreciable during the whole course of pregnancy in those instances where the placenta has its place of insertion on the posterior wall of the uterus.

The *sound of the fœtal heart* is a much more important sign than that of the placenta, as it is constant, and is not liable to be mistaken for any other. It resembles the ticking of a watch under a pillow, is double like that of the adult heart, and varies in frequency from 120 to 160 beats in the minute. These circumstances serve to distinguish this sound from any merely maternal one with which it could be confounded. It is seldom that it can be made out distinctly earlier than the end of the fifth month. As the pregnancy advances it becomes more and more clear and determined. The period of its appearance, however, is liable to some variation. Thus when the fœtus is so placed in the uterus that its back corresponds to the back of the mother, the sign may be late of being perceived, while in the reverse circumstances it may be made out earlier than usual. In the advanced stages of utero-gestation the fœtus frequently changes its position, but this throws no difficulty in the way of the examiner, as by changing the place of the stethoscope he can always succeed in eliciting the sound, wherever the fœtal heart may be placed at the moment of the examination. It is, however, most frequently and most readily heard, at whatever period the examination is made, by placing the stethoscope on either side of the uterine tumour at a point midway between the navel and the anterior superior spinous process of the ilium, but preferably on the left side.

I am only aware of one case in which a competent practitioner has failed to discover the fœtal pulsation in the course of pregnancy. It is one mentioned by Dr Montgomery, and occurred in his own practice. The woman, however, was at the time labouring under an attack of ascites.

The value of the stethoscopic signs of pregnancy will, from what I have said, be obvious to you. The placental murmur is less trustworthy than the fœtal sound, independently altogether of its liability to be confounded with sounds naturally arising, though it occurs earlier than the other. When both are distinctly made out in the same case, their combined evidence cannot possibly lead us into error. Of course it is only in the event of the fœtus being alive that either of them is available, and on this account they yield in importance to ballotement.

To sum up our estimate of these three *certain* signs of pregnancy, of which we have now completed the consideration,—

We have seen that the first of these,—the *active* movements of the fœtus in utero,—is only available when the fœtus is alive and vigorous, and thus its value is so far limited. The second,—or *ballotement*,—is equally applicable to the appreciation of both the living and dead fœtus, but it is incapable of enabling us to distinguish between a true and a false conception. The third sign, or set of signs,—the *stethoscopic*,—can only be produced by a living child, and one of them at least is not always to be discovered, even in these circumstances.

It is to the combination of these signs, then, that we ought mainly to trust; and, with due precautions, the medical jurist, when these are present, is furnished with data of the most positive kind, and is then enabled to speak with a degree of certainty which is very satisfactory in the difficult and responsible situation which he is liable to have to occupy when called on to speak as to the existence of a suspected pregnancy. It is not meant by this that we are not to avail ourselves, in every such inquiry, of all the indications of the pregnant state. On the contrary, even the less certain signs should be made to bear upon the decision with the weight to which they are respectively entitled.

The points hitherto discussed refer chiefly to the natural form of pregnancy. I have now to advert to certain specialities attaching to the other forms, as laid down by authors, beginning with *extra-uterine pregnancy*. In such pregnancies, or those cases in which the germ, in place of being developed in the uterus, is found outside of it, or in one of its appendages,—in the ovaries, the vagina, or the fallopian tubes—the proofs of the existence of the gravid condition come to be attended with greater difficulties in general than in the former class of cases. For although the signs of pregnancy are here the same as before, the number of them available for our purpose is more restricted than in cases of natural pregnancy.

In the earlier months the symptoms of extra-uterine pregnancy are usually very anomalous, and though in this case the uterus is known to enlarge with the growth of the foetus as in natural pregnancy, it is seldom found to reach to more than twice or thrice the bulk of the virgin womb. Ballotement again, cannot be had recourse to in any of the forms of extra-uterine pregnancy, and it is still an undetermined point whether in these the souffle placentaire should be heard or not. On the other hand the active movements of the foetus, and the pulsation of its heart, can be made out in both ventral and ovarian pregnancies; in the former of these, indeed, more distinctly than in natural pregnancy, from the abdominal parietes only being interposed.

It should be borne in mind in all such cases, that owing to the degree of local disturbance which they usually excite, these forms of pregnancy are liable to be, and have been, mistaken in practice for ordinary disease of the abdomen or pelvis.

The term *complicated pregnancy* has been applied by accoucheurs to the co-existence of pregnancy in any one of its forms with ordinary disease. With this form of pregnancy, however, the medical jurist has little to do, unless so far as it may tend to obscure the proofs of the gravid condition itself, and thus come to demand a little extra attention on his part to determine its existence in the case in hand.

In the so called *false pregnancies*, of midwifery writers, there exist certain abnormal states of the system, which may be confounded with the gravid state of the female where there is no pregnancy present. Here the difficulty arises from the occurrence of morbid symptoms capable of simulating the usual signs of actual pregnancy.

The abnormal states most likely to be confounded with utero-gestation are:—*First*, The so-termed spasmodic or nervous pregnancy; *Second*, Retention of the menses; and *Third*, Moles, or false conceptions.

In the first of these, the spasmodic or nervous pregnancy, the following symptoms have been encountered giving rise, in the mind of the accoucheur, and of the woman herself, to a belief of her actually being with child, namely, enlargement of the uterus and of the breasts, hardness and weight of the uterus, sanguineous and serous discharges, augmentation of the abdomen more or less rapid, milk, or fluid resembling it, in the breasts, and sometimes even pains not unlike those of labour

Cases of this sort are mentioned by Maunceau, Devergie, and others, in which the spasmodic action of the uterus, or the movement of flatus in the intestines, had been mistaken for the active movements of the child

In the second place, in cases of retention of the menses from any cause, either at or subsequently to their first appearance, the uterus may enlarge and rise out of the pelvis, the breasts may become bulky, hard, and tense, and intermitting pains occur, simulating those of labour

One case of this sort w   'ely seen by me, in which a practitioner declared the woman   e eight months gone with child, and the child dead six weeks

Once more, similar symptoms may attend the existence of moles or false conceptions. But neither in these, nor in the so-called spasmodic pregnancy, nor in retention of the menses, have we the certain signs, the absence of which suffices to guide us to the negative conclusion in all these cases

The same criterion, the absence of the certain signs, serves to distinguish real from feigned pregnancy, where the plea of gravidity is set up in any of the instances previously referred to

The question has frequently been discussed in connection with the subject we are treating of, whether it is possible that a woman can have had sexual connection and subsequently have conceived without knowing of it? The answer usually given to this inquiry is that this may happen during states of coma, syncope, or apoplexy, or while under the influence of narcotics, anaes' tics, or deep intoxication, but that its possibility during natural sleep has not been proved

To the analogous question, Whether a woman at a later period can be ignorant of her actual pregnancy? the affirmative answer may be given in the case of a woman living with a husband, as instances of this sort have been recorded. This, however, does not call on us to admit its likelihood or probability in other circumstances, as alleged by some writers

Another question connected with the subject of pregnancy is Whether a woman in the pregnant state is always to be accounted a responsible agent? whether, in fact, these longings and peculiar states of mind which are known to be common in pregnant women should form an excuse for an otherwise undoubtedly criminal action?

That the imagination may obtain such an undue control, and the will become so depraved, in these circumstances, as to compel occasionally the commission of certain crimes, especially theft, is an admission which in some cases is unavoidable, but it would be a dangerous precedent to admit it generally. Social order might suffer seriously from such an indulgence. A woman with a propensity to thieving in all states of her system would have a dangerous latitude allowed her if she were protected by pregnancy. If, however, the disturbance of mind be extraordinary, the medical jurist, who is consulted, will not have much reason to hesitate in excusing the woman, but, if otherwise, it will be his duty to refer the legal authorities to some other quarter for the elucidation of the question, for it does not properly belong to medicine.

In conclusion, I am anxious to say a few words in regard to the legal responsibility of the accoucheur while attending a delivery, as the subject has been unaccountably overlooked in our works on medical jurisprudence.

The view which has been taken of the position of the accoucheur by Mr Chitty is, that since his duty, in the great majority of labours, is not so much to aid or regulate the process as to perform the necessary services towards the child, it should be an invariable rule with him never even to propose an examination, *per vaginam*, still less any operation or interference, except as a matter of absolute necessity, nor then unless in the presence of some attending person. If it should be essential to perform an operation not of frequent use, or of the slightest risk, he advises that medical attendant should, in prudence, obtain the presence and concurrence of one or more professional friends, in order to protect himself from personal imputation and responsibility; "for," he adds, "an indictment may be sustainable against an accoucheur for so unskilfully delivering a woman that she died." One instance of this kind has been referred to by that author as having been tried in England. I would only further add, on this subject, that it has been recently decided in the same country, that if by the undue use of the forceps or other instrument an accoucheur should give a child, while in the act of being born, a mortal wound in the head, although before the child has breathed, and the child be afterwards born alive, but die in consequence of the wound, the medical attendant may be convicted at least of manslaughter

A trial of this kind took place at Stockport in 1842, where a regular practitioner of midwifery was charged with the crime of manslaughter. A conviction was obtained, and he was sentenced in consequence to a twelvemonth's imprisonment. In the trial it came out that the infant had its skull fractured, so as to cause its death immediately after its birth, and that gross ignorance had been displayed by the accoucheur.

This last feature of the case was the one which led to the conviction, for it has been laid down in another reported case, that an error in judgment merely, although occasioning the death of a patient, will not, if the accoucheur be an established practitioner, subject him to criminal responsibility.

Under abortion, we shall advert to the legal position of the midwifery practitioner, in the case of his finding it advisable to have recourse to the induction of premature labour.

LECTURE XI

DELIVERY

OCCASIONS FOR THE INQUIRY—Pretended or Feigned Delivery—Concealed Delivery (Concealment of the Birth) PROOFS OF DELIVERY IN THE LIVING FEMALE—Signs of Delivery at the Full Time—From the Birth to the approach of the Milk Fever—During the Period of the Milk Fever—During the Persistence of the Lochial Discharge—Fallacies attending the application of these Signs—Signs of delivery before the Full Time—Signs deducible from the Pregnancy—Signs deducible from the Delivery—Signs of Delivery at Remote Periods. PROOFS OF DELIVERY IN THE DEAD FEMALE—Characters of the Corpora Lutea—Characters of the Virgin and the Multiparous Uterus. MEDICO-LEGAL QUESTIONS ARISING IN CONNECTION WITH DELIVERY—Delivery without the Woman's Consciousness—Possibility of Super-fœtation—Pregnancy without Delivery.

THE act of parturition, real or supposed, becomes in certain cases a point for the consideration of the medical jurist, and he may be called upon to prove that it has taken place, either recently, or at a more remote period, in the living or newly dead female. The proof of delivery at a more remote period is chiefly called for in certain civil cases of but rare occurrence; that of recent delivery enters as an essential element into every instance of criminal abortion or of infanticide, as well as into certain inquiries connected with the birth of children, some of which will fall to be noticed here, while others will come in better afterwards.

Of Pretended Delivery. It is known that the state of pregnancy has been feigned, and a subsequent delivery equally feigned, with the view of introducing a supposititious child as the heir to a property; with the object of fastening on a putative claim to marriage or pecuniary compensation; or of satisfying an unreasonable husband. It was for the purpose of frustrating attempts of the first kind that the law, *de custodiendo partu*, still in existence, was framed. To obviate the same danger, the caution continues to be observed of calling in some of the cabinet ministers at the birth of princes, and thus securing their legitimacy. Dr Male mentions an instance of pretended delivery, in which a woman presented a dead child to a surgeon as newly born to her, but confessed the deceit on his proceeding to examine her, and finding no placenta, and the parts of generation in their natural state

A similar case is given in the nineteenth volume of the *Lancet*, in which a bundle of rags had been enclosed in a coffin to pass for the child

Capuron gives an instance in which a young woman pretended pregnancy, confined herself to bed, stained her linen with bullock's blood, and assured her lover that she had sent out her child to nurse Two years afterwards, on his demanding his supposed child, she had to confess the deceit, to escape a charge of infanticide brought against her by the law authorities

Dr Paris refers to a case where a woman stole a child to pass off for her own under similar circumstances, and the woman who had lost her child was in consequence subjected to a charge of infanticide

The crime of concealing the birth is in England specially denounced by the Lansdowne Act (9 Geo IV cap 31 § 14), but punishment is not enforced where the presumption can be raised that the woman expected her child to live, as where preparation had been made by her for its birth, and clothes provided for it In a charge of this sort the child's body must be found to authorise a criminal prosecution, though the proof of its having been alive at or after birth does not require to be established It must be shown, however, that the pregnancy had lasted long enough to render the birth of a living child possible

With all this agrees the Scottish practice

To bring the case under the statute, the concealment must have continued during the whole course of the pregnancy, and down to the death or disappearance of the child, without disclosure to a single individual, and the panel must not have called for help or assistance at the birth

It deserves to be noticed here that women in the lower ranks of life show on occasions of this sort a strength and capability of endurance scarcely to have been expected, giving birth unaided to her children, and resuming their work, or travelling a considerable distance, like the American Indians, as if nothing unusual had happened Numerous illustrations of this are to be met with in criminal records, and I have met with such cases in my practice

The proof of delivery in criminal cases fall to be investigated by the medical practitioner Those of them which bear upon the recent delivery of the woman are deducible partly from the examination of the mother, and partly from the inspection of the infant or ovum. In the verification of a delivery at some remote period the proofs must of course be drawn from the mother alone. To the same source we only require to turn for the proof of the mere delivery in either case.

As the proofs derivable from the examination of the infant come in on questions connected with the subjects of birth, abortion, and infanticide, it will be better to confine ourselves at present to the proofs of delivery derivable from the mother.

These may have to be investigated after the recent delivery of the woman, 1*st*, While alive; 2*d*, After her death; and 3*d*, In the living or dead at later periods.

The occurrence of pregnancy and subsequent delivery necessarily implies a series of changes in the animal economy, both functional and organic, which imprint on it traces of a more or less durable character. These changes are best marked where the usual term of utero-gestation has been reached, and before the system has had time to recover from the shock given to it, and the functions performed, at and soon after the abrupt and sudden termination of the puerperal state. In cases of premature labour or abortion, on the other hand, where the system has had time allowed for restoration, the marked character of the changes in question cannot be expected to be observable.

This, it will be observed, leads us to consider the signs of recent delivery at or near the full time. This we may do in the living mother, in the order of their usual occurrence, as in this way we may also obtain some assistance in determining the date of the event in any particular instance.

The *first* period, then, to which an average duration of forty-eight hours has been assigned, embraces the time which elapses from the moment of delivery up to the approach of the milk fever. If the woman be examined at this period the vulva will be found gaping, the labia and nymphæ rent and tumified, the fourchette, if the delivery has been a first one, presents usually a recent laceration, and the perinæum even may be involved occasionally; the vagina will be dilated, and more or less bathed in mucus; the mouth of the uterus is very much dilated and soft, permitting readily of the introduction of two or three fingers, or even of the whole hand, into its cavity, while its lips are thickened, firm, and cleft. The bulky uterus may be felt above the pubes by the hand placed upon the abdomen, and if the pressure be continued for a short time, the soft rounded tumour thus felt may be observed to alter its bulk and consistence from the regular and alternate contraction and relaxation of its parietes under the action of the uterine pains, which may continue for two or three days. The abdominal parietes are relaxed and thrown into folds; the brown line, noticed as a sign of pregnancy, may be observed on them reaching from the pubes to the umbilicus or sternum, and minute clefts crossing each other in all directions may be seen at first pink, and afterwards white and glistening like ordinary cicatrices, the so-termed lineæ albicantes.

Usually, on the completion of the labour, there is no further discharge from the vulva, but at the end of some hours the lochia commence, consisting at this period of pure blood, without any particular odour. Towards the end of the second day the lochia become pale and watery. About the third or fourth day after delivery they have become almost wholly suppressed, under the influence of the milk fever.

The *second* period, lasting usually from thirty-six to forty-eight hours, includes the duration of the milk fever and of the swelling of the breasts. The milk fever generally commences on the *third* day after delivery. Sometimes, however, it begins on the first or second day, or even so late as the fourth or fifth. It is best marked in women who do not nurse their infants. It is preceded by headache, and heat and dryness of the skin; the pulse is at first small and hard, then becomes fuller, and the breasts in a few hours swell; to this succeed moisture of the surface, and an abundant acrid sweat. In from six to twenty-four hours the fever gives way, and a watery milk flows from the nipples, lessening the swelling, tension, and tenderness of the breasts, which, however, go off but slowly.

The *third* period, of from four to five days, is indicated by the characteristic discharge of the lochia. About the *fourth* or *fifth* day, as the milk fever subsides, the lochial discharge reappears in the form of a *yellowish white*, more or less consistent, fluid, having now a peculiar odour, difficult to characterise, but which once felt cannot be mistaken, and which distinguishes it from other genital discharges. It speedily becomes sero-purulent, and in this state may persist from fifteen days to three months, or even to the return of the menses. The flow of the lochia ensures the discharge of the fluids which the uterine walls contain, and the contraction of that organ, which then returns to its proper situation in the pelvis. Five or six weeks usually elapse before it has quite or nearly resumed its former diminished volume in the unimpregnated state, for it never actually does so. About this time, if the woman has not nursed her child, the menses generally reappear.

The marks of contusion and distension about the vulva have generally become entirely effaced within two or three days after delivery.

It is chiefly during the first and second of these periods, which, it should be remembered, are only approximative, that the fact of recent delivery can be properly verified.

The most characteristic sign, during the first period, is the sanguinolent discharge with the odour of the liquor amnii, which odour will often serve to distinguish this discharge from that attendant on the menses, diseases of the uterus, polypus, fibrous tumours, hydatids, and the evacuation of a mole.

The milk fever in the second stage is not always found to occur, or it may be so slight as with difficulty to be made out.

The lochia proper, the flow of which characterises the third period, is a sign of considerable value, and when it continues for some time it becomes still more conclusive; but if the visit be long delayed there is danger of confounding the lochia with the leucorrhœal discharge into which it sometimes degenerates.

Such, then, are the phenomena which usually succeed immediately to delivery—phenomena characteristic enough when sufficiently made out, and when taken in conjunction, but which, taken singly, are not much to be trusted.

The examiner, before proceeding to the inspection of the woman, should observe her general appearance—that is, the look and figure of the woman generally. Soon after delivery the countenance is pallid, the eyes sunken, and not unfrequently surrounded with a dark or purplish ring; there is an appearance of recent exhaustion; the skin is warm and moist, and the perspiration during the third period is remarkable for the peculiar odour which it emits, characterised by the older accoucheurs as the *gravis odor puerperii*, and no doubt connected with the lochial discharge, the smell of both having a close resemblance.

These superficial appearances are, however, more liable to mislead than those which I have noticed as occurring from the changes in and around the genital organs.

The examiner ought to be aware that, besides some variations in the indications from the superficial appearances, the period of the appearance and disappearance of the more important and fixed of the indications of recent pregnancy will often be found to vary

To these a duration of *ten days* is usually assigned, beyond which an examination of the woman can hardly be expected to lead to satisfactory results. But while, on the one hand, it would be unwise to postpone the inspection to the end of this period when it can be done sooner, on the other hand we are not to neglect the examination in any instance simply because more than ten days have elapsed since the suspected delivery. It ought always to be kept in view that there is a remarkable difference in the effects produced by parturition on the system of different individuals, as well as in the merely physical changes made on the condition of the parts more immediately concerned in that process.

In a young, vigorous, and healthy woman, eight days after delivery of a first child, her appearance and the state of the genitals will be such as to leave no trace of recent delivery; while in women of relaxed constitutions, advanced in years, and who have borne numerous children, a longer period than ten days may pass over without effacing the signs we have considered. I have no doubt whatever, from what I have myself observed, that other causes which are not so apparent give rise to differences in this respect between women placed, so far as we can perceive in circumstances precisely alike.

Dr. Montgomery, of Dublin, states that he was called on to examine a woman *five* days after delivery at the full time, and was particularly struck with the degree in which the parts had restored themselves to their natural condition, especially the os and cervix uteri, which hardly differed from their normal unimpregnated size and form.

In 1835, and again in 1839, I examined two different women, both of whom had died from post-partum hemorrhage—one the mother of five children. In the first, the death on the eighth day succeeded a tedious delivery with the forceps; in the other, the death was on the tenth day; yet in each of these cases the vagina and uterus had almost resumed their usual appearance, the abdominal parietes were not relaxed or pendulous, and little or nothing existed calculated to indicate the suspicion of recent parturition.

Instances, again, of the unusually slow disappearance of the indications of pregnancy are occasionally encountered.

On the 4th of June 1840, I examined a woman in custody on a charge of infanticide, who had been delivered of a child *eleven* days before; yet in her the face and surface generally presented the characteristic appearances, the puerperal odour was distinct in the perspiration and in the lochia, and the vagina and uterus were relaxed and ample. This woman was in the prime of life, but had previously borne children.

On the 28th of March 1831, along with another medical man I examined Barbara Craig, who was tried at the Aberdeen Spring Circuit of that year on an alternative charge of child-murder or concealment of pregnancy, and convicted, on her own confession, of the latter crime. This woman was about 50 years of age, and had previously given birth to several illegitimate children. The one for the concealment of whose birth she was tried, it came out in the precognition, was born in the Christmas week preceding, just three months before our examination; yet such was the state of the vagina and uterus, that though some of the indications of recent delivery were wanting, we had considerable hesitation in coming to the conclusion that the proofs of more recent parturition were not sufficiently strong to warrant us in reporting that effect.

But not only ought the examiner to be prepared occasionally to encounter some irregularities in the periods usually assigned to the appearances of the various indications of recent delivery, he must also be prepared to encounter at times more or less imperfect development, or even total absence of some of the more or less important of these; while some of them, when present, may be capable of explanation by other causes than parturition. The air of languor and exhaustion, with the warm moist skin and the pallid countenance and sunken eyes, it is obvious, may exist in certain chronic internal diseases, independently altogether of pregnancy; while again, these marks will not be so likely to be noticed after a first delivery in a young healthy female of rigid fibre, as in one who is past the prime of life, the mother of children, and of a relaxed habit of body.

Again, the puerperal odour in the sweat is not liable to any fallacy when distinctly perceived; but it is not always so strong in women in childbed as to be remarked in every case, if it exist at all.

The lochial discharge, with its characteristic odour, is undoubtedly the most important sign; but the lochia have been known not to appear at all in some instances, in others they appear earlier or later than usual, or speedily disappear without obvious cause, or they may be suppressed from constitutional disturbances. Besides, it may happen that the lochial odour may be naturally indistinct, or this may arise from dilution of the lochia by admixture with leucorrhœal discharges, when these last are very abundant.

The presence of milk in the mammæ, though taken as an

isolated sign, it is not worth much, while it is also calculated to mislead, is yet of considerable importance when noticed in conjunction with other appearances. The fallacies to which it may lead are of two kinds. In the first place, milk may be naturally found in the breasts of females at all ages, without any dependence on or connection with utero-gestation or parturition, as we have seen under "Pregnancy," or it may arise from certain diseased states of the uterus, or from suppression of the menses. In the second place, there may be no secretion of milk after a natural delivery.

Some years ago I visited a lady five days after her delivery of a small child at the full time, on account of symptoms of puerperal fever. She had previously borne two children at the regular period, besides having had two or three premature labours; but she had never nursed her living children on account of a total absence of milk. Her breasts were not at all more developed than those of a girl before puberty; there was no brown areola round the nipples, which were not bigger than those of a girl of ten years. To my surprise, I found on examining the abdomen that it was not at all pendulous or more relaxed than in the virgin state. Such a case must have been a most puzzling one had it been connected with a charge of concealment of birth or of infanticide.

Dr Montgomery states a case almost identical, where the breasts were nearly in the virgin state, and the abdominal parietes and the genitals nearly natural, though the woman had borne eight children, usually in the eighth month, however.

Notwithstanding these deductions from the value of this sign, cases occasionally occur in which its aid may be made available without much risk of its misleading us. Thus the manner in which the secretion takes place after delivery, the attendant warmth of the skin, the turgescence of the glandular structure of the breast, with a certain amount of constitutional sympathy, can rarely, especially during the first few days, allow the examiner to be in doubt of its cause. Again, a microscopic examination of the milk, when present, may sometimes contribute to prove the recent occurrence of parturition. This solved all doubt in a case reported by Mr Mercer Adam. The body of a new-born child, much decomposed, was found in a moor in the south of Scotland. It appeared to have been dead four or five weeks. Suspicion having fallen upon a young woman who was supposed to have been delivered secretly about that time, she was arrested, and acknowledged that she had borne a child about a year and a half before, which she had nursed until within three months of her apprehension, but she firmly denied having been recently delivered. No feasible plan of deciding the question appearing, some one suggested that her breasts should be examined by the microscope. This was accordingly done, and it was found to abound in colostrum globules, showing that parturition had lately occurred. The girl on this confessed that she had recently given birth to a still-born child.

It should be remembered, however, that colostrum has been met with in the milk of the human female so late as the seventh month after delivery.

The dilatation, contusion, and swelling of the vulva, the vagina, and the neck of the uterus do not prove positively that the woman has given birth to a child, for a large polypus or other morbid production expelled from the uterus may produce similar lesions, though from their smaller bulk, in a less marked degree than a full-grown foetus. These appearances will also be found the more distinct the greater the difficulty attending the labour, and the longer the infant in proportion to the size of the maternal passages. They will likewise be better marked in a first than in a subsequent delivery.

Once more, it must be borne in mind that the *bulk* and *position* of the uterus in the hypogastrium may arise from diseased state of that organ, or from the presence in it of a fibrous tumour, hydatids, scirrhus, etc.

Having thus passed in review the signs of recent delivery at or near the full time, the indications which they usually afford us both as to the fact of its having taken place and approximately as to the date of the event, and the fallacies which may arise in both these directions from their unguarded application in particular instances, the following are the conclusions to which this review would lead us:—

1st, That the proof of recent parturition at the full time in the living female can only be safely based upon the presence of most if not all the signs I have enumerated.

2d, That these signs are found to be more or less marked and durable, according to the greater or less severity of the previous labour, and the greater or less vigour of the woman's constitution.

3d, In general these signs cease to be distinguishable after the eighth or tenth day.

4th, The fact of actual delivery may be considered as demonstrated, or the time at which it had taken place fixed at two or three days preceding the examination, if the breasts are found enlarged; if the superficial mammary veins are prominent; if milk of a yellowish color, resembling serum, and of a disagreeable taste (goat-like), can be pressed out of the nipples; if the abdominal parietes are relaxed and covered with minute *pink* cracks; if the recti abdominales be widely separated; if the vulva be gaping, bruised, and swollen, if the fourchette be recently ruptured, if the vagina be loose, with its rugæ obliterated; if the os uteri be open and its lips pendent and thickened; if the uterus form a hard tumour in the hypogastrium; and finally, if a sero-sanguinolent discharge be issuing from the vulva.

5th, The delivery may be assumed to have taken place three or four days previous to the examination, if the traces of contusion and distension of the external genitals though still distinguishable be less evident; if the sero-sanguinolent discharge have ceased, or is very slight; if there be feverish symptoms; if the sweat have the odour already noticed; and if a milky serum be found in the breasts, indicating that the milk fever is at its height, or beginning to decline.

6th, The delivery dates from at least five or six days back to at most eight or ten days, when the contusions and distension are no longer distinctly perceptible; when the uterus has shrunk in the hypogastrium, and can still be felt as a small rounded tumour; and when we find the lochial discharge thick, yellow, and very fetid.

7th and *lastly,* If there be no trace of contusion or distension; if the lochia are watery and nearly inodorous; and if the uterus is scarcely to be felt, it may be assumed with some probability that the period of the delivery has preceded that of the examination by about fifteen days.

The signs of recent delivery in the living mother before the full time will not detain us long. They are the same in kind as those of parturition at the full time, though less in degree, and are consequently still more liable to mislead in this case than in the other. In premature births and *a fortiori* in abortions, the signs of delivery, at whatever time investigated, will be found indistinct in proportion to the immaturity of the ovum.

After abortion at an early period so little change is made in the condition of the uterus and other parts, and the woman may exhibit otherwise so few of the signs of pregnancy, even when examined a day or two after the occurrence, that it may be found impossible to form anything approaching to a decided opinion excepting on careful examination of whatever substance may have been expelled from the uterus, should that be within our reach. If the structure of the ovum be satisfactorily detected and we have sufficient proof that such body was expelled from the woman, there can of course be no longer any doubt.

In premature labour, on the other hand, in the later months, the signs of delivery will be nearly as distinct as after parturition at the full time.

The signs of delivery at remote periods are of some consequence in cases of pretended pregnancy and subsequent pretended delivery. The determination of the fact of delivery, we have seen, is sometimes difficult where the woman is examined shortly after parturition, of course it must be still more so when a period of some length as of months or years, has been suffered to elapse before the examination is instituted. Still, as I have had occasion already to remark, the processes of pregnancy and of delivery leave behind them marks in every female which are more or less indelible. These indications are of two kinds—those which are dependent upon the act of utero-gestation, and those which are the effect of the act of parturition.

Amongst the signs of pregnancy at some former period are—*first*, the brown hue along the linea alba, which, once formed is to a considerable extent persistent; *second*, the flaccidity of the abdominal parietes, which, though often absent in young women of vigorous constitutions, is sometimes very marked and permanent, as in women advanced in life before ceasing to bear; *third*, the lineæ albicantes on the abdomen, which are pretty constant; *fourth*, the silvery streaks on the mammæ left on the subsidence of the swollen state of these organs during their active condition; and, *lastly*, the altered form of the os uteri, previously adverted to under the survey, this opening never regaining its oval shape after pregnancy and delivery. As to this last sign, however, it is to be borne in mind that the same effect has been observed to follow hydrometra and other diseases in the unimpregnated female.

To the third and fourth of these signs more importance is usually attached, though objections have been made to the reception of them both. Thus it has been said of the lineæ albicantes, that, as they arise from a purely mechanical cause, they may have been produced by dropsy or abdominal tumours, as well as by the pregnant uterus. It may be enough, nevertheless, to state that this appearance has never as yet been witnessed as the consequence of any other cause than previous pregnancy, a fact which is at least deserving of being borne in mind by us. Again, as regards the silvery lines on the breasts, there is the same absence of proof of their production in the *** gin from *** causes independently of pregnancy.

The marks left on the person by the delivery *** fewer in the living female than those which originate with the pregnancy, and they are of the most uncertain kind. These are enumerated as follows:—*First*, the absence of the fourchette; *second*, the perineal cicatrix; *third*, the irregularity of the cervix uteri previously referred to; and *fourth*, the milk in the breasts.

The first of these, the absence of the fourchette, may occur from frequent coition, especially where the genitals are but little developed. The cicatrix in the perineum, again, is very often absent in women who have borne children. As to the altered shape of the os uteri, we have seen that it may originate independently of pregnancy. Once more, the presence of milk in the breast of course, can only be looked for during the period in which the woman has continued to nurse her child. Besides, as formerly noticed, milk has been found in the breasts of virgins, of old women and even of men.

To sum *** the question of remote delivery seldom admits of *** the *** unimpeachable proof. None of the characters which I have *** warrant us with any strong confidence in doing more than presuming that the woman has been delivered; we cannot positively affirm anything from their presence, while their absence is conclusive that she has never been a mother.

If from the examination of the living female with which hitherto we have solely been occupied, we turn to the signs of *** ery as they come under our notice in the dead body, we find, in addition to those already noticed, certain appearances about the uterus and its appendages corroborative *** these, where the delivery has been a recent one.

Thus, shortly after delivery the articulations of the pelvis are found to be more moveable than ordinary; the shape of the uterus is seen to be more globular than in the virgin state; its walls are thicker, more spongy and vascular, and its dimensions increased. The remains of the decidua will be found lining the interior of the uterus, except where the placenta had been attached, at which part the uterine surface will either present a raw and bloody appearance, with openings into the uterine sinuses, or will be covered with mammilliform albuminous deposits, and the fallopian tubes and the ovaries will appear turgid and vascular. These appearances fade very gradually, and the organ has not entirely resumed its usual condition till towards the middle or end of the second month. But it is pretty generally conceded that nothing satisfactory will be learned if the examination be postponed beyond the tenth day, and even this period will sometimes be found too late for the verification of the delivery.

In rare instances, the placenta or some portion of it, may be met with in the uterus after death, and the presence of this master sign, as it has been termed, would, of course, leave no doubt of the delivery. If fresh the date of the labour might be estimated at from a few minutes up to a day or two; if putrid, the date of the parturition, if the dead body were fresh, would be further back.

When the placenta is found in cases of this sort, either within the maternal organs or previously expelled, the portion of the cord remaining attached to it should be compared with the portion of the cord remaining adherent to the body of the infant when at hand.

A case in point occurred to me in March 1875. The body of a new-born infant was found in a cellar, and after a recent placenta in a dunghill in the same street. The cord had been torn across, and the two torn ends—the fœtal and placental— when compared were seen accurately to correspond.

There are two other post-mortem signs of recent delivery, which, as affording grounds for difference of opinion, I have reserved for separate notice.

The more important of these is the *corpus luteum*. This being a post-mortem sign both of pregnancy and delivery, its full consideration will carry us back from the earlier stages of utero-gestation to a period a short way beyond its termination after the delivery of the woman.

If the ovary of the healthy virgin female during the child-bearing period be carefully examined, there will usually be found imbedded in it a number of small cavities or vesicles, varying in size from the minutest pin's head to that of a large shot, the least being within, the larger more towards the surface. From twelve to fifteen of such vesicles may commonly be counted in each ovary. They are designated by the term *Graafian vesicles*, from their discoverer De Graaf, or simply by that of *ova*. Later physiologists have asserted that at each menstrual period, one if not two or three of these Graafian vesicles or ova are ripened and thrown off from the ovary, the discharge of ova and their passage along the fallopian tubes being altogether independent of impregnation.

DELIVERY. 165

In the ovary of the impregnated female, besides these vesicles, a vascular spot will be met with, about the size of a large pea or small bean, containing a central cavity, sometimes empty, at other times filled with coagulated blood. In the early weeks of impregnation the ovary at this point presents a distinct protuberance and vascular injection. On making an incision into the ovary at this point, the central cavity—of a round or oval shape—is seen, around which is deposited the peculiar substance which has given the name to this new production, the *corpus luteum* or *glandulosum*, and which has a glandular feeling and a reddish-yellow colour, while blood-vessels are seen to pass into it. As gestation advances, the cavity loses its regular form and diminishes in size, till it is at length obliterated, leaving in its place a white radiated cicatrix in the centre of the yellow substance. By this time the external protuberance on the surface of the ovary has disappeared, and the whole has lost its vascular or injected appearance. Soon after delivery, at latest the fourth or fifth month, the ovary has lost all trace of this production.

So far we have the concurrence of authors as to the state of the ovary in the impregnated female, but here this unanimity ceases, some contending that corpora lutea, such as I have described, are only to be met with as the effect of impregnation, while others as tenaciously urge on the contrary that such corpora lutea, or bodies analogous in appearance, may be found in the ovaries of virgins.

Dr Montgomery attempts to reconcile the conflicting views on this point, by distinguishing between such bodies as I have described, which he contends are the product of conception alone, and the analogous appearance to be encountered in the virgin ovary. The latter he terms *spurious* corpora lutea, and these, he asserts, differ from the *true* corpus luteum in the following particulars:—

First, There is no prominence or enlargement of the ovary over them; *Second*, The cicatrix on the surface is wanting; *Third*, There are often several of them in both ovaries, especially in patients who have died from tubercular diseases; *Fourth*, They are not vascular and cannot be injected; *Fifth*, Their texture is so minute that they seem to consist merely of the remains of a coagulum, and at others appear fibro-cellular, but in no instance presenting the soft, rich, and regularly glandular appearance of the true corpus luteum; and *Lastly*, They have neither the central cavity nor the radiated cicatrix which results from its closure.

These distinctions betwixt true and false corpora lutea, though substantially adopted by several writers, such as Paterson, Ramsbetham, Lee, and Berry, have not been borne out by the researches and experience of other and independent observers.

Thus, both Bischoff and Raciborski state as the result of their researches, that the discharge of the ovum at the ordinary menstrual period is followed by the formation of a corpus luteum similar to that which is formed when the ovum is impregnated and developed.

The same opinion had previously been held by Home, Gouth, Meckel, and Blumenbach, and has been recently reiterated by other writers, though in a more or less qualified form.

Thus, according to Longet the regular *corpora menstrualia*—as for distinction' sake we may term the bodies which appear in the ovaries independently of impregnation—though others indistinguishable from corpora lutea so-called, pass rapidly through their different stages, never attain a high degree of development, are much inferior to the others in size, rapidly assume the yellow coloration, fade again in a few days, and in the course of one or two months become retracted and completely concealed in the ovarian tissue. With this agree substantially the results obtained by Dalton, Ritchie, and Costé, and those of Bischoff, on his returning for a second time to this subject.

It is also of importance to state that two experienced observers, Dr Lee, and Mr Wharton Jones, on one occasion differed as to whether a body shown to them was a corpus luteum or not, while, again, in one authentic case *two* distinct and well-marked corpora lutea were found in the body of a woman seven months pregnant with *one* child, and in another and unimpregnated female two corpora lutea were encountered after death a day or two before the expected menstrual period.

This last instance agrees with the result of the inspection of a woman in the spring of 1864, in whom, though the state of the genitals was such as to negative the possibility of impregnation, two corpora lutea, or rather corpora menstrualia, were found in one ovary, and one in the other. In one of these the corpus luteum was pretty well formed, the others were in different stages of retrocession.

From this brief review of the opinions held by different parties on this disputed topic, we are brought to adopt the following conclusions as pretty near the truth:—

First, That a small imperfectly developed corpus luteum affords no proof of impregnation having taken place.

Second, That in proportion as the corpus luteum approaches its full … and development, so does the proof of impregnation, followed by a somewhat advanced pregnancy, approach to anything like certainty.

Third, That the absence of a corpus luteum from the ovary would not be sufficient to negative the possibility at least of impregnation having taken place.

Fourth, That the differences on which the distinction between spurious and true corpora lutea is based do not refer to separate bodies so much as to different states of the same body.

One other post-mortem sign of previous delivery remains to be noticed as insisted on by Dubois. In the multiparous uterus the anterior and posterior surfaces are more rounded than in the nulliparous uterus. The fundus, instead of being flat is convex, so that there is a considerable protuberance above a line drawn from tube to tube. The vaginal portion of the neck is altered, being more conical and elongated. The os uteri, instead of presenting a transverse fissure, is rounded or puckered; the depression felt by the finger is more evident, and the orifice is considerably larger. According to Meckel the weight exceeds in general that of the virgin uterus by four or five drachms, the average respectively being seven or eight drachms and an ounce and a half.

The interior of the uterus too according to the same authority, offers some remarkable differences in the two states of the organ. The cavity of the body of the multiparous womb is considerably enlarged, the os uteri internum is less distinct, the canal of the cervix shorter, and the rugæ to some extent obliterated. The cavity of the body likewise, instead of being distinctly triangular or oval in shape, the angles into which the fallopian tubes enter having entirely disappeared.

Of the occasional use of attending to such changes of the organ we have an illustration from Dr. Tyler Smith's lectures in the *Lancet* of 1869, p. 58.

"A few years ago, we are told, a lady of family and her maid were burned to death together in a hotel at the west end of London. The bodies were so mutilated as to render any recognition by external signs impossible, but the lady had borne a numerous family, and the identity of her body was ascertained from the condition of the uterus."

These changes, however, it must be remembered, are most evident in women who have borne many children, while they are liable to be imitated, to a certain extent in nulliparous women who have suffered from inflammatory conditions of the uterus.

dysmenorrhœa, polypus, or any of the conditions which excite the growth of the organ, an instance of which I lately encountered. I may also add that in the body of a woman who had borne several children I failed to make out the characters of the multiparous uterus.

Under the subject of delivery certain medico-legal questions are usually treated, some of which I think it better to reserve for notice with those of *birth* and *infanticide*. The others we may discuss here in conclusion.

I. The possibility of delivery without the woman's consciousness.

This question is obviously one which can only be settled by actual facts. That a woman may be delivered without being sensible of it, she having been at the time labouring under cerebral oppression or derangement, as in ordinary coma or delirium, in puerperal convulsions, or while stupified by narcotics, ardent spirits, or anæsthetics, is a fact of repeated observation. But it will not be pretended that under such circumstances the woman could be afterwards ignorant that she had been delivered unless the morbid action had been permanent, or the memory of past events interfered with, as is said to have actually happened in the case of a celebrated literary lady.

II. The possibility of unconscious delivery during natural sleep, unlikely as it might appear, has been attested on sufficient authority.

"Dr Douglas of Dublin," says Dr Montgomery, "was called in haste to a lady who informed him that half-an-hour previously she had been awakened from a natural sleep by the alarm of a daughter about five years of age, who had slept with her, at hearing a child cry in the bed. The mother was only then conscious of the fact of her actual delivery of this infant."

A lady of great respectability, the wife of a peer of the realm, was once actually delivered in her sleep. She immediately awakened her husband, being a little alarmed at finding one more in bed than there was before.

Two further instances of the same sort are referred to by Dr Taylor.

In all these cases it should be noticed, however, that the women had previously borne children. That such an occurrence could happen at the birth of a first child appears very unlikely, and would require undoubted proof.

III. The occurrence of delivery after the life of the mother had become extinct, and consequently the birth having been effected by the independent contractile power of the uterus is a fact which has been attested by so many authors of established credit that we are not entitled to refuse it our belief, though some physiologists have lately attempted to explain away these published cases, and deny the possibility of the occurrence altogether

IV. The remaining question to be noticed here refers to the possibility of pregnancy not followed by delivery in the ordinary sense of the term.

This, it is now known, may happen under different circumstances, as where a blighted ovum is retained for an indefinite time in the uterus, or where a full-grown foetus is detained in the same cavity long beyond the ninth month. The former of these occurrences is so common as to need no illustration. Of the latter and more unusual event we have instances related by Montgomery and Morgagni. In Montgomery's case the foetus perished in the seventh month, and at the usual period the membranes ruptured, giving exit to offensive fluid and gas; the placenta and cord were next discharged some days afterwards, but the infant, in the state of a skeleton, only came away piecemeal during the two years for which the patient survived. Morgagni's case strikingly resembles the above.

During the summer of 1862 a case of this kind occurred in Aberdeenshire. A dead child was retained for many months after the usual term of utero-gestation, and came away in an offensive state.

LECTURE XII.

BIRTH

OCCASIONS FOR THE INQUIRIES REGARDING BIRTHS —Mature and Immature Births—Distinction betwixt Maturity and Prematurity of Birth—Proofs of Maturity and Immaturity—In the Living—In the Dead Infant—Premature and Retarded Births—Proofs of Premature Birth—From the Examination of the Infant—From the Examination of the Mother—Several Modes of Calculating the Duration of Pregnancy—From the Mother's Sensations at the Period of Conception—From the Cessation of the Catamenia—From the Quickening—From Pregnancy following a Single Coitus—Retarded Birth—Natural and Monstrous Births —Classification of Monsters—Single and Plural Births—Superfœtation—Live and Still Births—Viability of the New-born Infant—Legitimate and Illegitimate Births—Earliest Period of Viable Birth—Latest Protraction of Pregnancy

UNDER "Delivery," we have considered the act of parturition in so far as the mother is concerned; we now come to consider a few medico-legal inquiries which bear reference chiefly to the product of conception, or to the fœtus or infant which comes to be born. The information to be derived from the examination of the infant comes in aid of several points already discussed. Thus, in the case of a woman dying undelivered, the development of the fœtus will afford more precise data for fixing the period of the utero-gestation reached than the examination of the mother could furnish. Again, the body of the child after birth, compared with the state of the woman, would enable the medical jurist to fix with more precision than would otherwise be attainable the date of her delivery.

Reserving some other applications of the value of the information derivable from the infant after birth for subsequent notice, the points which I propose to discuss at present under "Birth" regard primarily the infant itself, and the mother only secondarily. Thus, births are either mature or immature, premature or retarded, natural or monstrous, single or plural, live or still, legitimate or illegitimate—facts the determination of which will chiefly be found to rest on medical evidence, while at the same time they are such as may importantly affect the peace and welfare of families, and the safety and honour of individuals.

I. **Mature and immature births**. Maturity in the new-born infant must not be confounded with prematurity. A child born at the full time, and with the usual development of the system proper to that period, is said to be mature; a child, whether equally fully developed as the former, or otherwise, if brought forth before the usual period, say at the seventh or eighth month, is termed premature.

The means of determining the maturity of an infant at birth are those given under "Age" (pp. 39-43) for fixing the period of life in the fœtus at the end of the ninth month. Anything short of that degree of development must be set down as a proof of immaturity.

The examinator, when called upon to determine the maturity or immaturity of a new-born infant, should direct his attention chiefly to the following points:—

1. The *length* and *weight* of the body. 2. The point of the trunk which corresponds to the *middle of its length*. 3. The *measurements of the head* in different directions. 4. The state of the *surface*, as to its colour, the firmness of the cuticle, and the sebaceous secretion. 5. The quantity, length, and colour of the *hairs*. 6. The degree of *consolidation of the cranium*, and the state of the sutures and fontanelles. 7. The *pupil*, whether closed by the pupillary membrane, or open from its disappearance. 8. The consistence, length, and breadth of the *nails*.

By comparing the information thus obtained with the appreciation of the separate data previously pointed out under "Age," it will be perceived that the degree of maturity or immaturity will in most instances be readily ascertained.

If the child be still *alive*, further assistance will be derived from the application of the stethoscope to the chest, and from the observation of the movements of the child. If the air has penetrated into the whole of the air-cells of the lungs, if the beatings of the heart are full and regular, and if the breathing is regularly performed, it is a presumption in favour of the maturity of the infant, and *vice versa*. The same remark holds good with regard to the movements of the child, whether lively and vigorous, or the reverse; to its cries, whether loud and continuous, or weak and incontinuous; to its being able, or otherwise, to seize hold of and to retain the nipple or the finger introduced into the mouth.

If the child is *dead*, the state of the osseous system will afford valuable indications of its maturity or immaturity, and further assistance will be derived from the examination of the brain, the intestinal canal, the situation of the meconium, and the state of the lungs

In all inquiries of this sort the chances of arriving at a correct decision will depend more upon the concurrence of as many data as can be obtained, than on an appreciation of a few of the more prominent of these

Thus I have met with premature infants of the length and weight of mature infants, and *vice versa*.

In a case of infanticide some years ago, an eight months' child rather surpassed the average length and weight of one born at the full time, and in this instance the correction was made by means of the other data.

Closely connected with the inquiry I have been alluding to is the one I shall consider next, namely

II Premature and retarded births. I shall first advert to the question of premature, and secondly to that of retarded birth

Premature birth The problem of prematurity, like that of retardation of birth, is one of more difficult solution than that which we have just considered. It does not rest, like the question of maturity or immaturity, solely on the data derivable from the infant, but is dependent upon information deduced from the inspection and examination of both parent and child.

The information afforded by the examination of the child is precisely of the same kind as we considered under maturity and immaturity If the child exhibits the marks of immaturity already considered, the supposed prematurity of its birth is rendered highly probable ; if, on the contrary, it exhibits no signs of immaturity, the fact of its prematurity is rendered extremely doubtful. Where the degree of immaturity is in exact correspondence with the period of prematurity of the birth alleged by the mother, the proofs derivable from the parent are much strengthened, and *vice versa*.

A premature child, therefore, I repeat, should exhibit all the signs of immaturity, and these should correspond very closely with those which indicate the period of intra-uterine life which it is alleged to have reached at the time of the supposed delivery prior to the natural period of the termination of utero-gestation. It is not meant to be stated that the degree of development at any fixed age is precisely the same in every circumstance, but what I would insist on is that, though there are undoubtedly occurrences affecting chiefly the system of the mother which may have an indirect effect on the fœtus in utero, either in hastening or retarding its progressive increase, and although the same thing may happen from defects confined to the fœtus itself, still these will only be found to operate so far as to modify some of the indications of the fœtal age and never the whole of them. The growth of the ovum may be retarded, for instance, by causes acting injuriously on the ..., so that its bulk or weight may be below that which is considered as the average, still the chance of a mistake thus originating will be obviated by a careful comparison of these with the other indications of its maturity or immaturity.

I now come to the information deducible from the examination of the mother as to the prematurity of the infant. So much depends on the good faith of the female, and so vague and inaccurate are the observations she can be expected to make in regard to the succession of changes taking place in her system from the commencement up to the conclusion of the process of utero-gestation, that it is not surprising that this subject should present unusual difficulties to the medical jurist, or that great difference of opinion should be found in the profession in respect to it. These difficulties and discrepancies have almost all originated in the uncertainty which exists as to the time when impregnation really happens, and consequently when utero-gestation naturally terminates.

In treating of pregnancy I noticed the signs from which the medical jurist is enabled, altogether independently of the testimony of the woman, to judge of the existence of utero-gestation, following as far as I could the order in which they successively appear, and noting the periods of their respective appearances. Such data, however, would be too loose and indeterminate for the settlement of disputed cases of prematurity or retardation. Besides, were they more close and accurate than they are, they would be inapplicable to the question in hand, which seldom arises, though it may occasionally do so, till some time after the woman has been delivered, and we are thus thrown back on the testimony of the mother. Let us then see how far we can depend upon it, supposing, which will seldom be the case, that she has no interest in endeavouring to mislead us.

The accoucheur in private practice, and the female herself in common circumstances, calculate the duration of pregnancy by one or more of four different methods, which I shall notice in succession, in order to determine whether from any or all of them we can obtain any sure data to assist us in our present inquiry.

The *first* of these indications of pregnancy is derived from the occurrence of certain peculiar sensations at the time of the conception.

It is generally agreed that women are sometimes conscious of a peculiar sensation about the period of conception, to whatever cause it may be owing, and that in some few cases its occurrence marks pretty accurately the time they have conceived; but it is nearly as generally agreed on amongst writers on midwifery that all women do not feel these sensations, and, again, that many feel them at times when no conception has taken place. Besides, it is seldom that a woman in her first pregnancy takes any notice of them, from ignorance of their real nature.

The *second* of the indications to which I have referred is the cessation of the catamenia.

The most common way of calculating the time of conception with many practitioners, and by the females themselves, is from the time of the disappearance of the catamenia, with this important difference, however, that the female dates her conception from the last appearance of this discharge, and the practitioner from a period midway between the cessation of the last and the date at which the next menstruation should have occurred, had not impregnation happened during the interval. The latter mode of reckoning, it should be noted, proceeds on the supposition that in the female who is living in social habits with a male, impregnation may take place on any one of the days which intervene between the cessation of the last menstruation and the expected return of the next menstrual period. This, in ordinary circumstances, would give a latitude to the date of the actual conception of about four weeks, which, by the mode of reckoning adopted by the practitioner, is reduced in practice to two. It is well known, however, that some women naturally menstruate at periods different from the usual one, as at the second, third, fifth, or sixth week, and that these modifications of the process are not at all incompatible with impregnation. In a female, therefore, who only menstruated on every fifth or sixth week, on the assumption already stated, it is clear that there would be a wider range of indefinite time for the occurrence of the actual conception than a lunar month, a range in fact of thirty-five or forty-two days, in either of which conception may have followed coition.

The period estimated by the practitioner, though not liable to such a latitude, would still be extended considerably in this case, that is, it would be short of or beyond the usual period of uterogestation by seventeen and a half to twenty-one days.

The state of the question we are considering is not much affected by the disputes which have of late arisen amongst physiologists and accoucheurs as to the periods of greatest susceptibility of the female to impregnation; Bischoff and Raciborski contending that impregnation cannot take place, as usually assumed, at any time between the regular monthly periods but only immediately before or after menstruation, that is within a range of at most ten days, and Oldham, while admitting a greater disposition to impregnation shortly after than before a menstrual period, holds to the general belief that the human female is susceptible of impregnation at any time between the two monthly periods.

Though we were assured that the impregnation could not take place, as contended for by the German physiologists, in the interval between the regular menstrual periods, we would still be as far as ever from being in a position to predicate whether it had occurred immediately after the last appearance of the menses, or immediately before the next expected period.

Further and more important deductions must, in practice, be made from the value of this mode of estimating the duration of pregnancy. Thus many women are very loose and inaccurate in the observation of their menstruating periods, and their statements, even when they do not intentionally deceive, are not to be strictly relied on.

Again, it is well known that the menses not uncommonly appear once or twice subsequently to conception, and that in some women there is a regular monthly discharge, not always easy to be distinguished from the catamenia, which may continue through the whole period of their pregnancy. Once more, some very anomalous cases are recorded, in which the catamenia have never appeared at any other time than during pregnancy, and were then regular in their recurrence.

The *third* source from which the duration of pregnancy has been dated is the occurrence of the phenomena termed the *quickening*.

The first sensation of the active movements of the fœtus by the mother is termed the quickening, because it was long supposed that the fœtus then for the first time became endowed with vitality, or quick.

Considerable variety occurs as to the time of quickening. Dr Denman fixes upon the sixteenth week as the most common period, Pugos on the eighteenth week, Montgomery from the end of the twelfth to the sixteenth week, while all writers allow that it not unfrequently happens earlier or later than these periods. It ought, nevertheless, to be remarked that in a few cases women never quicken, and that in some still more rare instances, they have failed to quicken only in one or two pregnancies, though they have always brought forth living children. It is also of importance to add that both women and accoucheurs have been misled by this sign into the belief that pregnancy existed where the woman had never conceived at all, and that, too, in the case of women who had previously been mothers

From the uncertainty of its appearance, it is obvious that the quickening could not be expected to be of any service to us in a first pregnancy. On the other hand, it appears to be generally admitted that, where it is unequivocally felt, most women experience this sensation about the same period in their different pregnancies

The *last* indication I alluded to for enabling us to fix upon the duration of pregnancy is the occurrence, which occasionally happens, of utero-gestation after not more than a single coitus. There can be no doubt that, as the records of authentic instances of this sort are accumulated, data will be obtained for the solution of the problem as to the exact duration of pregnancy, which will come nearer to the truth than we have as yet arrived in this difficult and unsettled subject. Still, even then, room might be left for some uncertainty on the point in question. Besides the acknowledged infrequency of cases of pregnancy dating from a single coitus, the security for the good faith of the woman would require to be of more undoubted kind than could generally be expected in practice. Again, it is by no means certain that, in the undoubted case of impregnation following a single coitus, the development of the ovum could be correctly calculated from this date. There is now a pretty general agreement among modern physiologists that impregnation only happens on the accidental meeting of the semen with the ovum after its periodical discharge from the ovary at the menstrual period; while it would seem, if we may judge from observations on the lower animals, that the lapse of time between the escape of the ova and their fructification varies on different occasions. From this it is evident that the customary mode of calculating the date of the escape of the ovum from the ovary from the period of the sexual congress does not give the precise commencement of the impregnation, and that it can, at the most, present an approximation to the real results.

Having thus passed under review the twofold source of evidence available for determining the prematurity of a new-born infant—namely, the examination of the infant, and the testimony of the mother—it will be seen that it is only in the event of their agreement that any reliance can be attached to them, and even here much caution is requisite in coming to a positive decision. Approximations to the truth are in fact the most that we are entitled to expect in medico-legal questions of this nature.

The subject of retarded birth presents even greater difficulties than that of premature birth, and its verification is attended with more uncertainty.

Here, the examination of the infant is only capable of yielding negative proof. If the child is immature we may safely affirm that the birth has not been retarded. Some have even gone farther than this, and asserted that in a case of retardation there should be physical appearances on the child to indicate this, and that it ought to exhibit a more than usual degree of development, in consequence of its lengthened residence in the uterus. Experience, however, affords no warrant for any such assumption.

Resting then chiefly, if not entirely, on the evidence derivable from the examination of the mother, and the credibility of her unsupported testimony, it is not to be wondered at that the question of retarded birth, in individual instances, should be one of the least satisfactory in the whole range of medical jurisprudence.

III. The subject which comes next in order is one with which, as medical jurists, we are not likely to have much concern, and it therefore will not long detain us. I refer to the discrimination between natural and monstrous births.

Monstrosity is chiefly of interest to the medical jurist in so far as the evidence which he may be able to afford, as to the actual condition of a being of this sort, is capable of influencing the results of certain civil and criminal proceedings.

The law of Scotland, it is believed, is the same in respect to monsters as the law of England, which holds that "a child which hath not the shape of mankind cannot be heir to or inherit any land, albeit it be brought forth within marriage;" but no definition is given as to what goes to constitute monstrosity. It is doubtful, however, if the greater number of these beings, which are included by medical men in the list of monsters, would be so regarded in law.

Contrary to what is generally believed, it is distinctly laid down in the English law, that the destruction of these beings is illegal; and a case in point has been given by Dr Paris. Two women were tried at York in 1812 for drowning a child with a malformed head. There did not appear to have been any concealment on the part of the prisoners, who were not aware of the illegality of the act. The decision of the court is not given. On the other hand, in France, the procuring abortion in a case of monstrosity seems to be scarcely regarded as a criminal act, for, in the instance of a woman tried at Drôme in 1841 for procuring the birth of an acephalous monster, about the sixth month, an acquittal followed on proof of the monstrosity, notwithstanding the presence on its body of a wound sufficient to have caused its death.

The best classification of monsters is that of Breschet, which I subjoin:—

CLASSIFICATION OF MONSTERS.

ORDER I.—AGENETOUS (Agenesis)	**GENUS I AGENESIA**	Acephalia		Not viable
		Anencephalia		Some have lived 20 days
		Congenital Dropsy	1 Of the ventricles of the brain, with deficiency of some of its parts	Death before or at birth
			2 Of the ventricles of the brain, but with complete development of that organ	Life more or less prolonged
			3 Of the exterior of the fully developed brain	Viable
		Apropsia		Not viable
		Atelopropsia		Not viable
		Absence	1 Of the eyes, eyelids, or iris	Viable
			Of the mouth	Not viable
			Of the lips, tongue, or outer ear	Viable
			2 Of the epiglottis, penis, scrotum, testes, of a member, hand, the bladder, vesiculæ seminales, uterus, vagina, some ribs, vertebræ	Viable
			3 Œsophagus, stomach, heart, liver, or lungs	Not viable
			Septum between the ventricles or auricles of the heart, the diaphragm	Viable
	GENUS II DIEDTENABIA	Fissures on the median line of the cranium, with large encephalocele		Not viable
		Encephalocele less voluminous		Viable
		Spina bifida, with hydrorachis in the upper part of the spinal column		Life for a few days
		Lower down the spinal column		Life for some months, or for a year or two
		Fissures of the lips, jaw-bone, tongue, palate, bladder, penis, urethra, womb, vagina		Viable
		Division of the mesial line of the abdomen, with considerable hernia of the viscera		Viable
		Exomphalla, with hernia of abdominal or thoracic organs		Not viable
		Both proceeding in a less exaggerated form		Viable
		Extrophia		Viable
	GENUS III ATRESIA	Imperforations of the urethra, vagina, uterus, mouth, anus, eyelids, membrana pupillaris		Viable
		" of the œsophagus and intestines		Not viable
	GENUS IV SYMPHISIA	Fusion of the eyes—monopsia		Not viable
		" of other parts of the body		Viable
ORDER II HYPERGENETOUS		Giants		Viable
		Persons with supernumerary organs		
ORDER III DIPLOGENETOUS	**GENUS I FUSION**	Fused or united by some parts of the body		Viable
		United with fusion of parts		
		United in the upper parts and separated in the lower		
		United below and separated above		
	GENUS II PENETRATION	One fœtus containing another, partially or wholly		Viable
ORDER IV HETEROGENETOUS		Extra-uterine fœtus, or more than three fœtuses at a birth		Not viable
		Albinos or chacrelates		Viable
		Fœtus with displacement of organs all		Viable
		except displacement (ectropia) of the heart		
		(thoracic) with fissure of the sternum and hernia of the heart		Not viable
		displacement of the heart (cephalic) or towards the head		

IV. The subject of single and plural births has in itself but an indirect bearing on medical jurisprudence. In twin births the practitioner ought to notice the order of precedence on every occasion, as this may obviate the necessity of a long and expensive litigation to settle the proof of primogeniture, whee the first-born comes to succeed to property or to civil immunities.

The question of plural births is connected with another which has given rise to a good deal of discussion, and to no little difference of opinion in the profession; namely, the possibility or the reverse of what has been termed *superfœtation* or *superconception;* that is, a woman having two separate conceptions, and bearing two separate children, at periods of from a few weeks to some months' distance from one another That a female may give birth to two separate children at periods thus distant, is admitted by all. The point in dispute is whether, in such instances, the dates of the separate conceptions were as far apart from one another as those of the births; the settlement of which question, in one way or the other, may fix the chastity or unchastity of the mother, and the legitimacy or illegitimacy of the child last born Again, it is agreed on all hands that such separate conceptions do in fact occasionally happen in some of the lower animals, though the bearing of this fact on the case in point is disputed, from the circumstance of such animals having a double uterus—a confessedly rare occurrence in the human female, although one such case of double uterus and twin birth has been recorded

The arguments for or against the possibility of superfœtation in women are chiefly physiological. Thus, while it is contended on one side that the closing of the os uteri, and the formation of the decidua, which precede the arrival of the ovum in the uterus, must necessarily render a second conception impossible, by barring the entrance of the seminal fluid; the party taking the opposite side deny that the plug of viscid mucus in the cervix uteri, in the early stage of pregnancy, would actually prove a sufficient barrier against a second impregnation; while it is also affirmed that sufficient space exists between the decidua vera and reflexa, for some time after impregnation, to permit the approach of semen to the Fallopian tubes

Again, while it is affirmed on the one side that the mucus secreted from the vagina of pregnant females, first noticed by Donné, would prove completely destructive to the existence of zoosperms, by reason of its great acidity, and consequently would render the spermatic fluid unprolific; it is contended on the other side, that the period of impregnation at which the vaginal mucus begins to act obstructively to the zoosperms, has not yet been determined.

Once more, it has been contended by the opponents of superfœtation, that as in twin cases the children at birth differ not unfrequently in size, vigour, and apparent age, in the reported cases of superfœtation the blighted ovum may have been retained in the uterus, and after the birth of the mature fœtus have recommenced its growth, and only been expelled after this tardy arrival at maturity. This argument is met by the supporters of superfœtation by a challenge to their opponents to prove that a retarded or blighted ovum can be retained in the uterus after its more vigorous fellow is expelled, long enough to give grounds for an apparent case of superfœtation; or, what they argue is more improbable, that the growth of the former should recommence after the expulsion of the latter.

Such is an impartial statement of the controversy between the parties who take opposite views of this difficult problem. If the weight of authority were to be admitted to decide the question, it would undoubtedly be with the opponents of superfœtation, the writers of most note on midwifery and physiology almost all ranging themselves on this side; nor are their arguments without weight. Some of the cases of alleged superfœtation were undoubtedly instances of double conception and twin births, in which the development of one fœtus was kept back till after the birth of the first delivered of the two. Again, except in one case (Eisenmann's), it does not appear that in any of the instances of alleged superfœtation which have been adduced, any attempt was made to ascertain if a double uterus existed; while, in regard to this exceptional case, where there was but one uterus, its reporter admits that the first infant, which only survived two and a half months, was neither so large nor so lusty as the second born.

V. The subject which comes next in order is that of live and still birth.

The proof of the live birth of an infant forms an essential element in certain inquiries, both in civil and criminal law.

The law of this country has not defined the meaning of the term birth in reference to civil jurisprudence; but if we are to be guided by the numerous decisions which have been given on trials for infanticide, it must be regarded as signifying the *entire delivery of a child* with or without separation from the body of the mother. So long as the infant remains in the uterus, it is said in law to be '*en ventre sa mère,*" but it is legally supposed to be born for many purposes. A child in the womb may have a legacy or an estate made over to it, and may have a guardian assigned to it, but none of these conditions can take effect unless the child is born alive. So the fœtus may be made an executor, but an infant cannot act as such till it has attained the age of seventeen years.

It has been stated by a late authority that vagitus uterinus or vaginalis—that is, the crying of the child before it has left the uterus or maternal passages, would not amount to legal proof of live birth in the Scottish or English law if the child was dead previous to the completion of the act of birth.

In civil practice there are two cases in which the determination of the momentary existence of the new-born infant becomes of importance in a legal point of view. These are the cases involving the questions of *possessio fratris* and *tenancy by the courtesy*.

The first of these,—*possessio fratris*,—is thus explained by Mr. Amos:—" In the event of a man twice married dying and leaving a daughter by each marriage, his estate would be equally shared by the daughters of the two marriages; but if we suppose that there is also a son by the second marriage born in a doubtful state, the legal effect of his momentarily surviving birth would be to disinherit the daughter of the first marriage entirely, and transfer the whole of the estate to the daughter of the second marriage, she being sister to the male heir, while the daughter of the first marriage is only half-blood."

I have already explained the nature of the tenancy by the courtesy. This is generally established or disproved by medical testimony, and the following are the conditions which the law requires in order that the right should exist:—*First*, the child must be born alive; and, *second*, the child must be born while the mother is living. Hence if a child were removed from the uterus or from the passages by the cæsarian section after the death of the mother, or if, as has been known to happen, the child were born after the death of its mother and survived, the husband could not become entitled to his wife's estate.

The most important medico-legal questions connected with this subject are those which arise in contested suits relative to succession or the inheritance of property. A child which is born alive, or has come entirely into the world in a living state, may, by the English law, inherit and transmit property to its heirs, even though its death has immediately and, perhaps from morbid causes, necessarily followed its birth. Should the child be born dead, whether it died in utero or during the act of birth, it does not acquire any civil rights, for it is not regarded as a living being unless it manifests signs of life after it is entirely born

The signs of life fixed upon by the law in Scotland to entitle a child to civil privileges in these circumstances differ from those which are considered sufficient by the English law. The test of life in Scotland is the commencement or establishment of respiration In England, on the other hand, a child may acquire its civil rights although it may be neither seen to breathe nor heard to cry. The pulsation of the child's heart, or even the spasmodic twitching of any of the muscles of its body, is regarded as a satisfactory proof of live birth The motion of a limb, therefore, will be considered good evidence in an English court of law of life after birth. The length of time for which these signs continue after the child is born is wholly immaterial; all that is required to be established is that they were positively manifested A child which survives entire birth for a single instant acquires the same civil rights as if it had continued to live for a month, or longer.

In criminal practice, the proofs of the live or still birth of an infant are of a much more complicated and difficult kind than those requiring to be established in civil cases, and are to be settled on data altogether different, as will be seen when we come to the subject of infanticide.

VI. The subject of the viability or non-viability of the infant at birth will not detain us long.

In France and Germany it is often absolutely essential not only to determine whether a child has been born alive, but also whether it had a capacity for continuing to live This is what is called its *viabilité* in the former country; and an infant is pronounced to be viable when it is considered capable of proceeding on the journey of life under ordinary circumstances According to the "Code Civile," the child which is not born viable, as regards right to inherit, is placed in the same category as if it had not been begotten With reference to legitimacy, if a child born within 180 days after marriage be declared viable, it may be disclaimed by the husband, provided he was neither cognisant of his wife's pregnancy at the time of marriage, nor assisted in registering the infant's birth In Germany, again, though not in France, it is necessary to establish the viability of the infant in a charge of infanticide.

In this country the question of the new born infant's viability is only liable to arise in connection with the presumed maturity or immaturity of its birth

Hitherto it has been usual to consider all infants born previously to the commencement of the *seventh* month as necessarily non-viable. A distinction of so narrow a kind would not now be tenable, overlooking, as it does, a large list of non-viable children

Two classes of cases of this sort present themselves in practice—in one, the cause of the incapacity for living being obvious and apparent; in the other, being less apparent or occult. In the former of these we find the presence of certain malformations, defects, or diseases which are more or less readily detectable, and which when ascertained by us are seen at once to be incompatible with the continuance of the infant's life Breschet, as you will see by the above table (p 178), has distinguished the monsters which are set down as necessarily non-viable, as well as certain malformations, more limited in number, which, according to their character and extent, may bring the infant into the same category, or the reverse Thus he does not consider children with deficient palate as non-viable, admitting, as such cases do, of relief by artificial means. To this, however, there may be exceptions, as in a case which occurred in my own practice In April 1869 it was discovered, after the birth of a fine child, that the palate plate of the superior maxillary bone, the palate bone, the turbinated bones, and part of the vomer, were wanting, rendering the supply of an artificial palate impracticable The child consequently died on the fifth day of starvation, being incapable of swallowing liquids offered to it, or of drawing the nipple of its mother In this instance the infant presented nothing unusual externally

Scleroma, or *skinbound*, is always set down as a morbid state incompatible with the survival of the infant after birth, though here life usually continues for a short time, as in a case which I examined, where the child lived for sixteen weeks

In the class of cases, and these are the ordinary ones, in which defects or morbid states exist, which from their hidden or non-obvious character cannot be made out at the birth, we can only judge of the viability or non-viability of the infant from the extent of its development, and the degree of the establishment of certain of its functions.

Thus we may assume in general that the child is viable if at birth it breathes freely and cries lustily, if it seizes firmly the mother's nipple or a finger introduced into its mouth, if it passes the urine and meconium with facility, if the bones of the cranium are consolidated, the sutures not too wide or the fontanelles too open, if the hairs and the nails are well formed and the skin rosy, if the head and limbs are duly proportioned, and the insertion of the cord not very far from the middle of its length The nearer the length and weight of the infant approach to that of the average at full time, the greater will be the likelihood of our conclusions as to its viability from the above marks being verified by the event

On the other hand, an infant may in general be considered as not likely to live when it is observed to move its limbs feebly, to utter only weak plaints, and that with little intermission when awake, when it cannot grasp the nipple or finger, when the urine and fæces are passed with difficulty or not at all, when it sleeps almost constantly, when the bones of the head are so soft as to yield to slight pressure, when the sutures are broad and the fontanelles very large, the hairs few, white, and short, when there are only membranes in place of nails, when the skin is purplish or has a marbled appearance, when the head is disproportionately large, the lower extremities much shorter than the upper, and the insertion of the cord close to the pubes when the eyelids are agglutinated, and the iris closed by the pupillary membrane, in short, when the child is so puny that all the most important functions are with difficulty performed If to these characters are added a length and weight much below the average of a mature child, it may be pretty safely assumed to be non-viable

Without a concurrence of all these signs, however, the medical jurist should be cautious in pronouncing a new-born and living child non-viable. If he has any doubts he should delay coming to any positive conclusion for a few days or weeks, as it is surprising what a change for the better in the state of the child a good nurse and great care will sometimes effect.

I have lately seen a child born in the seventh month, and whose life was with difficulty preserved for the first few hours, become surprisingly improved in the course of a month, from the combined influence of great attention and good nursing

That cautions of this nature, casually thrown out, are not always thrown away, but are occasionally treasured up for future service, I had a curious illustration a few years ago.

A gentleman who attended my class in a former session, soon

afterwards settled in practice and married. Within little more than four months after his marriage his wife presented him with a fine girl. A month or two after his child was born, a strict religious body to which he belonged held out to him a threat of expulsion from their communion, considering that he must have been guilty of ante-nuptial fornication. In this dilemma he called upon me, as he thought I must be able to satisfy his accusers that the child was a premature birth, reminding me of the remark I had made as to the wonders occasionally effected in the appearance of a puny immature infant by a few weeks good nursing. In this case it had certainly done wonders, for on examining the infant in question it might have passed for a child three or four months of age, in place of one six months after the date of its conception. I forgot to inquire afterwards how he had settled the point with his church session.

VII. The next inquiry connected with the birth of children which demands our attention is that of their legitimacy or illegitimacy, an inquiry which occasionally involves the greater number of the principles discussed in the previous divisions.

The proof in law of the legitimacy or illegitimacy of an infant at birth is most frequently deduced from circumstances alone. Where the medical comes in corroboration of the moral evidence, the points usually calling for proof are, first, as to the earliest period at which a viable child may be born, and, second, as to the latest period to which in such circumstances the gestation may have been protracted.

On these two points the laws of different countries vary not a little, nor has there been much more of agreement in reference to them amongst medical men.

By the law of Scotland, a child born *six* months after the marriage of the mother, or *ten* months after the death of the father, is considered legitimate. (Chitty.)

In England the calculation rests solely on received opinions and a few decisions.

In France the civil code has placed a limit to credulity respecting retarded births, and decrees 300 days, or ten calendar months, to be the most distant period at which the legitimacy of births shall be allowed.

The Prussian code, without absolutely declaring children born in the eleventh month illegitimate, attaches such conditions to the proof of their legitimacy as make it almost unattainable.

Amongst medical authors there is a pretty general agreement

that few children born previously to the commencement of the *seventh* month are able to maintain a separate existence. There is considerable difference of opinion, however, as to the natural limitation of pregnancy, some arguing for a fixed period, others as strenuously contending for an occasional protraction of the gestation. These points will be best discussed separately. We shall therefore consider—

1*st* The earliest period at which a child may be born viable. This is a question obviously of a kind which can only be settled satisfactorily on the basis of authentic facts; nor are these altogether wanting, although their number is still limited, and their value considerably diminished by the difficulties necessarily attendant on their exact verification. Under maturity and prematurity of birth, we have seen the uncertainty of the data to which we are restricted in attempting to fix with precision the date of conception, and consequently the duration of the pregnancy in any case; and on the present occasion, when the natural period of delivery is anticipated, we have only these to rely upon. You will therefore perceive the necessity for the strictest caution in availing yourselves of the evidence in alleged cases of premature birth of viable infants at early periods.

At and after the commencement of the *seventh* month there is no doubt as to the child's being capable of maintaining a separate existence, but prior to this the question of a viable infant being born has been by many disputed. The affirmative here is based upon the following instances of such occurrences by writers of credit.

First, we have the case related by Belloc, in his *Cours de Médecine légale*. The infant, a female, at birth was immature, and considered by Belloc to have reached only *six* months at the utmost, but when last seen by him she was in her seventeenth year, clever, amiable, and graceful, and above the middle stature.

Dr Rodman's case is less satisfactory. The child was reared, though, in the writer's opinion, born at the end of the *nineteenth* week of its mother's pregnancy. But from the data he has adduced in proof of this, it has been assumed that it must have been born about the close of the sixth lunar month, or a little later.

A case recorded by Dr Outrepont, of Bamberg, has been generally admitted as an unequivocal instance of the rearing of a *six* months' child. From the data derived from the mother, and the development of the infant, there was the strongest reason to believe that gestation could not have exceeded *twenty-seven* weeks. When Dr Outrepont last saw the child, in 1816, he was eleven years old, was as big as a boy of seven or eight, and had just begun to read and write

In the same work from which I have taken the last case there is narrated the case of twin children born at the *sixth* month, who, when seen by the reporter, Dr Ruttel, a year after their birth, were both of them healthy and vigorous

Lastly, in a case reported by Dr Barker in the *Medical Times and Gazette*, the child born in the middle of the sixth month was, three years afterwards, though small thriving and healthy

These cases then seem to decide as to the possibility of rearing children born in the sixth month, and when we add to these other cases which have been adduced in evidence less completely satisfactory, but which supply presumptive evidence to the same effect, we must, I think, admit that such incidents happen often enough to deserve to be kept in view in legislative enactments

This decision, which I have purposely rested on independent evidence, receives some collateral support from the record of living births at early periods of pregnancy, of infants who, though not reared to maturity, yet survived their birth to periods which, in the case of some of them, rendered it probable that they might, but for circumstances unconnected with their original immaturity, have reached adult age

2d The other point which I have to notice in respect to the question of legitimacy or illegitimacy is the latest period to which utero-gestation is liable to be protracted in any given instance

I have already had occasion to observe that by the laws of different countries a variable latitude has been assigned to the possible duration of pregnancy, and also that medical men are divided in their opinions on this point, some arguing for a fixed period, beyond which it is never protracted, and others contending for a certain amount of extension beyond the average duration of this state.

It would be mere waste of time to attempt to pass in review the host of authors in ancient and modern times who have ranged themselves on opposite sides in this controversy, as the dispute is one which obviously does not admit of being settled by an appeal to authorities. I shall also disregard wholly such of these alleged cases of protracted gestation as clearly rest upon uncertain and insufficient data. This will confine us to the evidence deducible from the three following sources —1st, The state of the infant,

2d, the information derivable from the mother; and 3d, the argument from analogy with the lower animals

First, The evidence derivable from the state of the infant. From what has been already stated under a previous division, it will be evident that in a case of presumed retardation of birth only indirect evidence can be supplied us from this source. We have seen that a stay in the uterus beyond the average period will not lead to a further development than that usual in a mature child at the natural period. We may, however, decide with reasonable assurance, that if the infant be immature, there has been no protraction of the gestation.

Second, The information derivable from the mother enables us to calculate the duration of pregnancy. It is on this alone that the accoucheur, in private practice, founds his decision; and on the same basis it is that it has been proposed to fix with accuracy the point in dispute for medico-legal purposes. We have already seen the difficulties necessarily attendant on the application of the data derivable from this source, when we passed them under review in succession. After what was stated previously, I need only remind you that those of them which are least liable to lead us into mistake are the calculations reckoned from the cessation of the catamenia, and the pregnancies dating from the occurrence of a single coitus.

Of cases of protracted pregnancies, or those extending beyond the *fortieth* week, as calculated from the cessation of the catamenia, accoucheurs have now furnished us with numerous instances, advanced on the authority of Hunter, Lee, Montgomery, Power, and Murphy. Reducing these into the form of a table, they give us of

PREGNANCIES PROTRACTED

To the 41st week = 287 days,   55 cases
„   42d   „   = 294   „   42 „
„   43d   „   = 301   „   30 „
„   44th „   = 308   „   13 „
„   45th „   = 315   „   12 „
„   47th ,   = 322 to 325   3 „

Thus, it will be seen, affords us in all 155 instances of pregnancies protracted beyond the fortieth week, from the 41st to the 47th week of utero-gestation.

A similar result is brought out by Dr. Simpson, from the tabulation by him of the observations of Merriman, Murphy, and

Reid, where, out of no fewer than 782 cases, 355, or nearly one half, went beyond the 280th day up to the 326th

With these results, derived from the calculation of the pregnancy from the cessation of the catamenia, agree on the whole the observations deduced from the study of the recorded cases of pregnancies, dating from a single coitus. Of these we have now 55 cases, recorded on the authority of Raciborski, Rigby, Merriman, Dewees, and others. Omitting 37 of these, in which the delivery took place on or prior to the 280th day, this leaves us 18 cases of

PREGNANCIES PROTRACTED

In 2 to 281 days = 40 weeks and 1 day
„ 2 „ 283   „   = 40   „   3 days
„ 2 „ 284   „   = 40   „   4   „
„ 2 „ 286   „   = 40   „   6   „
„ 4 „ 287   „   = 41   „
„ 1 „ 288   „   = 41   „   1 day
„ 1 „ 289   „   = 41   „   2 days
„ 1 „ 291   „   = 41   „   4   „
„ 3 „ 293   „   = 41   „   6   „

or, to state it otherwise,

8 were protracted into the 41st week.
7   „   „   42d   „
3 had almost reached the 43d   „

Thirdly, In further support of the conclusion thus arrived at from the evidence derivable from the mother, we have the concurrent testimony of the only other source of evidence within our reach—namely, the argument from analogy with the lower animals. These, it is known, admit of some deviation from the average time of carrying their young. According to Tessier, there is a difference in this period in cows of 67 days, in mares of 83 days, with proportionate periods in sheep, rabbits, and other animals.

Such is the evidence we possess in favour of the possibility of pregnancy being occasionally protracted beyond its average duration of thirty-eight to forty weeks in the human female, and it appears to me to confirm the decision now arrived at by most accoucheurs, that utero-gestation may in a few instances be extended to the forty-fourth, or even to the forty-sixth week

The difficulties attendant on the application of the principles of medical science to the question of the legitimacy or illegitimacy of children in certain circumstances are well illustrated by the proceedings in the celebrated "Gardiner Peerage" cause, which is given in all our works on medical jurisprudence; and although the medical opinions given by the majority of the best witnesses would not now be relied on, the case is deserving of careful study

The evidence in the case of the Rev Fergus Jardine, which went the round of the Church Courts in Scotland in 1856, and which was published afterwards, was of the same unsatisfactory character as that in the Gardiner peerage case. The case was that of a female infant born 174 days, or rather less than six months, after the marriage of the parents, which survived seven months The testimony of several accoucheurs and medical jurists at the trial proved to be so opposite and contradictory that the judges allowed the charge to drop as not proven. But what was least creditable in this instance was that three accoucheurs who had seen the infant at or soon after its birth, had neither weighed nor measured it, and that the evidence adduced as to its immaturity was furnished, not by the medical, but by the non-medical witnesses, while the post-mortem examination was too incomplete to be of any service whatever

In concluding the consideration of the subject of legitimacy, it is necessary to advert shortly to one or two other circumstances besides the points I have noticed, on which the legal decision of cases of this sort may rest Thus, besides or altogether independently of the actual length of the period of gestation, medical evidence may be called for in relation to the two following points *first*, the proof of physical incapacity in the husband from his being, for instance, too young or too old, or from his being known to labour under some bodily defect, rendering it impossible that he could be the father; and, *second*, the proof of sterility or incapacity in the female, making it impossible that the child could be the offspring of a particular woman,—in other words, that it has been a supposititious child.

The data for the determination of these questions have already occupied our attention under Impotence and Sterility, and will not require to be again gone into. It may be of use, however, to notice here that there are few cases of disputed legitimacy, into which other elements than those which concern the medical jurist do not enter, such as the morality or immorality of the female, or the possibility of access or non-access of the husband to the wife. With these, however, the medical witness has no concern.

In connection with the subject of birth there only remain two subjects for notice,—*first*, the maternity of the infant, and, *second*, the question of paternity or affiliation.

The former of these inquiries it will be better to reserve till we come to the subject of Infanticide; the latter will here conclude the series of questions bearing upon the birth of the infant, with which we have been occupied.

The law does not pretend to determine who begot the child when it is born during wedlock, and when from circumstances it might be the child either of the husband or of an adulterer; but it is believed by medical jurists that when the question of paternity is mooted, which is but rarely, corroborative proof might be derived from noting the likeness to the presumed father in features, gestures, or other personal peculiarities. Such evidence, in fact, has been admitted in law; but it is obvious that the friends and relatives of the party, and not the medical jurist, are those who would be best able to supply it.

Affiliation is settled in this country by the oath of the mother, and not by ordinary evidence. The paternity might no doubt be attempted to be repelled by proof of incapacity or other positive causes on the part of the alleged father.

LECTURE XIII.

CRIMINAL ABORTION.

LEGAL MEANING OF THE TERM ABORTION. CAUSES OF ABORTION GENERALLY.—Natural Causes—Traceable to the Mother—Traceable to the Infant. Criminal Causes—Remedies and Drugs—Blood-letting—Emetics and Purgatives—Diuretics—Emmenagogues—Mechanical Agents—Local Genital Irritants. PROOFS OF RECENT ABORTION.—From the Woman's Previous History—From the Examination of her Person—During Life—After Death—From the Inspection of the Child.

In legal medicine, the ordinary distinction between what the accoucheur terms abortion and premature labour respectively does not hold good, the term abortion being applied to labour brought on at any stage of pregnancy. To render such an act criminal, and thus to bring it within the province of the medical jurist, such abortion or fœticide, as it is also termed, must have been effected by the intentional employment of means, unlawfully used with the intention of causing the premature expulsion of the fœtus. It is not necessary, however, in law, in order to bring home the criminal act to an individual, that the means employed to procure abortion on such occasions should have actually succeeded in doing so. It is sufficient that such attempts have been made with evil intentions, and that now, though not formerly, whether prior or posteriorly to the quickening of the fœtus.

By the terms of the law, as it now stands, it is doubtful whether a woman could at present, as was formerly the case, be tried for abortion attempted on herself. In the case of its being done by another the offender is not excused by the consent, or even the solicitation of the female herself, the commission of the crime necessarily implying consent at least on her part.

By the terms of the statute, no discretion is allowed to the medical practitioner, who, in order to save the life of the mother, may deem it advisable to induce premature labour. You are aware that in this country the best practitioners are unanimous in their opinion that, in cases of such deformity of the pelvis as would not permit the passage of the head of a full grown fœtus, the accoucheur is not only warranted, but is required, by a sense of duty to his patient, to bring premature delivery on artificially, with the view of thereby saving the life of both mother and child, or at least that of the former

There can be no doubt, however, that by the strict terms of the law against procuring abortion, no discretionary power is allowed to the medical practitioner to dispense with its operation in any case. The necessity of the occurrence, in fact, never seems to have been contemplated by the framers of the law. Hence it has been argued that, although the law makes no exception in favour of medical men who adopt this practice, neither does it in the statute on wounding make any exception in favour of surgical operations, so that what would be resorted to by the practitioner, not only without evil intention, but, on the contrary, with the very best intentions, would not be held unlawful.

This is undoubtedly a correct and reasonable assumption to a certain extent. No prudent practitioner should, however, decide on performing an operation of this sort without the sanction of the relatives, and the co-incident opinion of a professional friend, and, further, without the conviction in his own mind that, by allowing the woman to go to the full time, he was incurring a greater hazard of evil consequences to her than by at once having recourse to it. The non-observance of these rules in practice is necessarily attended with risk to the practitioner. In the event of the death of the mother and child, there can be no doubt that the practitioner exposes himself to prosecution for a criminal offence, from the imputation of which even an acquittal will not always clear him in the eyes of the public. Within the space of four years several practitioners were tried in England upon charges of this kind, where it came out that, had they attended to the precautions I have pointed out, the possibility of preferring against them a criminal charge would have been avoided.

It will be observed that, in the remarks I have made on this point, I have avoided entering into the disputes between the British and foreign accoucheurs as to whether this procedure is ever to be justified in practice, a question which it is not my province to decide. Perhaps it may not be presumptuous, however, to state as my opinion, that though several of the French accoucheurs may be wrong in deciding against the adoption of premature labour in any case, yet that our own countrymen have recommended its adoption in instances where, perhaps, the case had better been left to nature. We are not without instances of the delivery of females at the full time, who laboured under great deformity of the pelvis, where even the child survived, while, on the other hand, the operation itself is not without risk both to the child and to the mother

But if some risk to the mother may be incurred in bringing on abortion or premature labour even in the hands of the skilled and experienced accoucheur in private practice, how much more serious may the operation prove in the case of the non-professional parties when it is undertaken by them. Here, in place of the time being properly chosen, the best preparations made, and the most watchful care subsequently bestowed, the criminal ruffian operates clandestinely, hurriedly, unassisted, without due preparation, without the requisite skill for his task, and without opportunity, even if competent, for the requisite after-treatment of his victim. In these unfavourable circumstances it is not surprising that many women should perish, when even in the hands of the accoucheur serious consequences, immediate or remote, are not unfrequently encountered, as admitted by Devilliers, De la Motte, Zacchius, Fodéré, and others, such as hypercatharsis, peritonitis, enteritis, uterine hemorrhage, convulsions, shattered frames, and inability to contend with ordinary diseases. On some of these occasions the child has been found to be born alive, where the mother had perished in giving it birth.

The period of pregnancy at which such attempts are made usually dates between the *third* and the *sixth* month, as, earlier than the one period, gestation, though it may be suspected, cannot be known with certainty, and, later than the other, fears of the consequences come to be seriously entertained by the mother

In charges of criminal abortion, medical evidence is called for to determine the two following points, namely,—

Whether the woman has been recently delivered? And by what means the abortion has been brought about?

It will, however, be more convenient for us to discuss these questions in the reverse order

I. The mode in which the abortion, when proved to have taken place, has been brought about. This resolves itself into the inquiry, whether it has been the effect of natural causes, or has been effected by artificial means; in other words, whether the abortion has been natural or criminal.

The causes of abortion among females in civilised life are admitted to be numerous The whole of these may conveniently be included under some one of the three following classes, *first*, the strictly natural or accidental causes; *secondly*, the use of remedies or drugs, and *thirdly*, the effects of mechanical violence, whether employed intentionally or otherwise

The disposition to abort is in some females so strong that the slightest exciting cause will produce it; in other females, on the contrary, the most serious injuries, and the most violent mental and moral impressions are insufficient to occasion abortion. This remark it is of consequence to keep in view when estimating the natural causes which may have been assigned in order to account for its occurrence, as well as in our judgment of the effects of those means usually resorted to for criminal purposes, as it will frequently serve to reconcile the conflicting testimony of authors on this important and often difficult subject. While in private practice, particularly in large towns, we occasionally find abortion taking place from very slight exciting causes, or even from such as escape our notice entirely, criminal cases are constantly happening where the most powerful remedies have been employed, and the use of means resorted to, sufficient to endanger, or even in some instances to destroy life altogether, without having effected the object in view.

In one case with which I am acquainted, drastic purges, very rough exercise, blows on the belly, bloodletting, and strong doses of savine, were employed to destroy an illegitimate child, but without effect, for a fine boy was born at the full time, and still survives. The parents were afterwards married, and have lived together for several years; but such was the effect of the means thus resorted to, on the mother's constitution, that she has never since been able to pass the first four months of several pregnancies without abortion happening, followed by frightful hemorrhages, which have more than once threatened to destroy her life.

One of the finest and largest children I have ever seen was brought forth at the full term to a midwife, who employed perseveringly on herself, for months, every means she could think of for bringing on premature labour.

Amongst the most frequent of the predisposing causes of abortion, naturally occurring, may be mentioned the following, peculiar to the mother—namely, excessive irritability and excitability of the uterus, rigidity of its fibres; unnatural laxity of its muscular coat; flaccidity of its cervix; permanent debility and habitual ill health; many acute or chronic diseases, as fevers, inflammation of vital organs, hysteria; and certain local diseases, such as metritis, scirrhus, polypi, dropsy of the womb, fluor albus, floodings, etc. Amongst the predisposing causes may also be reckoned the local excitement and plethora which occur in certain women at the periods answering to the usual monthly return of the menses in their unimpregnated state; and likewise that where there has been an abortion previously, there is a disposition to throw off the ovum at the same stage of the utero-gestation as was reached on the first occasion.

As occasional causes of abortion, I may add strong or disagreeable impressions on the senses, as from disgusting odours, loud thunder, or discharges of artillery, etc.; powerful mental emotions, as fear, joy, etc., the abuse of food and drink; prolonged and violent bodily exertion; severe jolting, as in a carriage on rough roads; shocks, as from a fall or blow; tight compression, as from stays or other parts of the dress worn too close; immoderate laughter; excessive venery; obstinate constipation, etc.

It is now generally admitted that certain states of the fœtus itself, and of its appendages, are capable of giving rise to abortion, independently altogether of the condition of the female as to health, etc. These are chiefly defects of conformation; original delicacy of its frame, spontaneous diseases, or arrested development, all of which are known to occur in the fœtus during its sojourn in the uterus. The same effect is produced occasionally by detachment of the placenta, by its being attached to the cervix, or over the mouth of the uterus; by varicose enlargement of the placental veins, or by its becoming hypertrophied or scirrhous.

Independently of the above mentioned causes of abortion, whose operation is in some measure obvious to us, there are instances occasionally happening for which we can assign no adequate cause, or to account for which we are compelled to have recourse to mere conjectures. Thus, we find such agencies as changes of temperature, changes in the hygrometric state of the atmosphere, alteration in the electric tension of the surrounding media, etc., called into the service of the accoucheur on such occasions.

Passing now from the so-called natural causes, I come to notice, in the second place, those remedies or drugs which are believed to be capable of producing abortion. That such means are largely employed for this purpose, with criminal intent, there can be no doubt, though as respects their efficacy no little discrepancy exists, especially betwixt the earlier and later writers on medical jurisprudence. Much of this discrepancy will, however, be found to disappear, or at least to be largely diminished, if we consider the very different modes in which all or most of them admit of being employed in the hands of the various parties having recourse to them. Thus, there are perhaps none of the so-called abortives which the physician may not and does not employ in medicinal doses for therapeutic purposes, and where their curative effects alone are desired, and this not only with benefit to the sick pregnant woman, but also without risking the occurrence of abortion; while, on the other hand, there are few of the more active and powerful of these so-called abortives which in unskilful hands, when administered recklessly, in immoderate doses, and without any other indication than to accomplish the desired end, will not be found fitted, with more or less certainty, and in an indirect if not direct way, to secure the object in question.

Of these reputed abortive means, *bloodletting*, especially in the form of leeches to the feet, insides of the thighs, perineum, and groins, has enjoyed a wide reputation from the time of Hippocrates, to whom it was known.

A like efficacy in popular estimation is attributed to *emetics* and *purgatives*. Of these, the parties who have recourse to such substances select those distinguished by the violence of their action, the efficacy attributed to them depending on the irritation they excite in the system being propagated from the intestinal tube to the hypogastric organs. Such emetics as tartar emetic and sulphate of copper are less likely to be efficacious for the desired end than such drastic purgatives as jalap, aloes, colocynth, gamboge, croton oil, and elaterium, whose action is chiefly on the colon and rectum.

A few cases are recorded of the employment of *diuretics* in the hands of those who attempt to procure abortion. Those which are known to have been used for this purpose are cantharides, turpentine, nitrate of potash, and the decoctions of the male fern and the broom, the irritant action of most of these being on the bladder.

Several *emmenagogues*, or supposed emmenagogues, enjoy a popular reputation as abortives. The efficacy of several of these, such as juniper, tansy, rue, pennyroyal, yew, and senega, has been properly doubted, though the dangerous or even fatal effects of some of them are sufficiently established. The evidence in favour of two other substances in this class, as pure abortives, is of a less doubtful sort, although on this point even professional men are not at one. I refer to the ergot of rye (*Secale cornu-*

tum), and the squaw-root (*Actea racemosa*). As regards the first of these, the secale cornutum, some authors deny its power of producing its well-known specific action on the uterus prior to the period of the approach of labour at the full time, while undoubted evidence has been adduced of its having failed on several occasions when administered both by practitioners and criminals with the intention of bringing on abortion. Again, all that we know of the actea racemosa, is that American practitioners regard it as being nearly as powerful as the ergot in inducing uterine action at the full term of pregnancy.

I have purposely excluded some medicaments which have been classed as abortives by medico-legal writers, as it does not seem to me to be enough that a remedy has been followed, on rare occasions, by abortion, to prove its capability in ordinary cases of leading to that result. If this were sufficient to establish a claim to that character, there are few substances in the materia medica which might not be ranked with equal reason in the class of abortives. At the same time there is but little room to doubt that the popular belief in the efficacy of certain vegetable remedies as abortives, although deemed unworthy of notice by medico-legal writers, is not without foundation in fact. Thus, though not now encountered in our pharmacopœias, the old herbals contain lists of plants, mostly bitter, aromatic, and stimulant, which by their harsh action on the stomach and nervous system generally are not unlikely on occasion to produce the effect attributed to them by the vulgar, among whom they are handed down by tradition. Thus, I was assured by the late Professor Dyce that the common *lignum vitæ* of the garden bears the character of a sure abortive in the country districts around Aberdeen. Again, in 1861, a young pregnant woman died suddenly after the exhibition of some vegetable decoction or infusion by a *skilly woman* near Tarves, which had acted in this case as an acrid poison, though its character evaded detection; one or two minute leafy particles under the microscope showing none of the usual appearances of any of our known acrid poisons or garden plants.

The effect of *mechanical violence* in procuring abortion is well known to the regular practitioner, and what is to be lamented equally so, both to the professional ruffian and the ordinary criminal in this line. Further, it is believed, on pretty good grounds, that those who lay themselves out for this nefarious trade trust chiefly to mechanical means for bringing on abortion, though they may, in the first instance, have recourse to such drugs as enjoy a reputation as abortives. Again, the non-professional differs so far from the professional scoundrel that the latter may practise such mechanical means as have an indirect action on the uterus, while the former has recourse at once to such of these as are fitted directly to secure his object. The distinction betwixt those two sets of cases deserves to be kept in view. In the first case certain mechanical agents exert their injurious influence on the gravid uterus in an indirect way, and in a degree exactly proportioned to the amount of the concussion or shock which is given to the system. Such are leaping, reiterated racing, exercise on horseback, smart pressure on the abdomen, continued pressure on the same part, blows on various parts of the trunk, falls, etc. In all these instances the violence may have been unintentional, and accordingly some of them have been already alluded to as amongst the accidental causes of abortion. There are other mechanical means acting more directly on the uterus and its contents which can leave no doubt in our minds as to the object of their employment. Such are some of the following:—Injecting irritant fluids into the vagina, dilatation of the cervix uteri, rupture or separation of the membranes, injecting plain or medicated fluids into the uterine cavity, puncturing the head of the child through the membranes with a stilette.

The dangers attending the use of means of this sort are greater than those consequent on the employment of irritant drugs in exact proportion to their efficacy and certainty, both from the shock imparted to the woman's system and the risk of being followed by violent floodings, fainting fits, or subsequent attacks of peritonitis or metritis, even when the uterus has escaped injury from the awkwardness or recklessness of the operator; effects which may follow at varying periods of from a few minutes or hours to some days.

Tardieu, who has bestowed much pains on the elucidation of this subject, tells us that some women, during attempts of this sort, experience little or no sensation beyond, it may be, a poke (*farfouillement*) or prick, others moderate pain, while in the greater number the operation gives rise to immediate and severe pain, a tearing sensation in the hypogastrium or epigastrium, nervous attacks, faintings, or complete and sudden syncope. A little blood almost always escapes at once, and, though but rarely, liquor amnii. From this time, if the attempt has not been a failure, while the hemorrhage increases, the woman is advised to take violent exercise, prolonged baths, and ergot of rye, unless previously disabled by serious illness. When the manœuvres of the operator have completely succeeded, the expulsion of the fœtus follows within four hours, or sometimes immediately, while in other cases it may not happen for six, seven, eight, or eleven days.

While the efficacy and certainty of such of the mechanical means as act directly on the uterus are, as a general rule, pretty well assured, this does not hold good to anything like the same extent of the means which act more or less indirectly. I have known rapid horse exercise, and riding in a cart over rough roads, used purposely by a pregnant female, without her having in consequence aborted. I have also known tight-laced stays worn with the same object up to the period of delivery at the full time, or shortly before it. In the course of practice, I have met with several cases at the Aberdeen Police Office, in which blows, varying in the degree of their severity, were sustained on various parts of the trunk by pregnant women, and out of forty-seven such instances, though there was moderate flooding, the child escaped unhurt in all, and only once did labour come on immediately, the woman in this case being at the full time. In the whole of them, however, there were premonitory symptoms of labour, which yielded to the free use of anodynes.

Dr Guy has brought forward two illustrative cases of a very striking kind. The first of these, borrowed from Madame Chapelle, was that of a young midwife who was pregnant, and had a narrow pelvis, who, with a view to procure abortion, and avoid the cæsarian operation, threw herself from a height. She died in consequence of the injuries thus produced, but did not miscarry.

The other is related by Velpeau, on the authority of Mauriceau. A female seven months gone with child, to escape from a fire in her room, slid down from the third floor, but, losing her hold from fright, fell upon the stones and fractured her forearm. No abortion followed.

I cannot avoid quoting one additional case of even a stronger kind, from the practice of Wagner, of Berlin, as showing that even the direct coming in aid of the indirect mechanical means may not be certain of producing abortion. In this instance a young woman, seven months with child, had employed savine, and other drugs, with a view to produce miscarriage. As these had no effect, a strong leathern strap was tightly bound round her body. This too availing nothing, her paramour, according to his own confession, knelt upon and compressed the abdomen with all his strength, yet neither did this effect the desired object. The man now trampled on the girl's person, while she lay on her back, and as this also failed, he took a sharp pointed pair of scissors and proceeded to perforate the uterus through the vagina. Much pain and hemorrhage ensued, but did not last long. The woman's health did not suffer in the least, and about the regular time a living child was born, with no external marks of injury on it.

The illustrations I have given are, however, to be regarded as exceptional, and as showing what some robust and hardy women may bear with comparative impunity.

II. We now come to consider the means we possess for determining whether the abortion has actually taken place in any given instance. This, as we have seen, is not necessary to be established to constitute the crime, and only forms an element in the proof when the abortion has been brought about, which is, however, the most usual result. The data for the solution of this point are derived —*first*, from the woman's history; *secondly*, from the examination of her person after the alleged delivery; and, *thirdly*, from the inspection of the child when the child of the prisoner has been found.

First. We have to consider the evidence deducible from the woman's previous history. This is mainly the province of the lawyer, though the facts to be acquired and the inferences to be drawn from them are best elucidated and decided on by the medical jurist.

The previous history of the woman will, however seldom afford us more than presumptive or moral proof of her guilt in attempting or using means to hasten her delivery before the full time. The evidence of criminal intention derivable from this source will be stronger or weaker, according to the nature of the cause of abortion which has been called into operation. When the abortion has arisen from purely natural causes the idea of culpability on her part will be altogether excluded. When it has been brought on by the use of drugs it will be of importance to ascertain, before coming to any decision, whether these drugs were exhibited in medicinal doses, and whether there was any disease present which could call for or justify their employment, and also under whose advice they were had recourse to. The nature of the drug itself is likewise to be taken into account. If the woman cannot satisfy the practitioner on all these points the suspicion against her will be strong, particularly where the medicine is such as is known to have a decided action on the uterus, and to be one which is seldom employed for other than nefarious purposes

In drawing inferences from the circumstances preceding the premature labour, when this has arisen from mechanical causes, it will be advisable to distinguish those which act by the shock to the system from those whose operation is directly on the uterus or its contents The former may or may not have been accidental; they may or may not have been intentional. It is altogether different with the latter. Unless in the exceptional case of the practitioner, who is occasionally compelled to have recourse to the premature expulsion of the ovum to save the life of the mother, the intention of the party who employs instruments to the genitals, or of her who permits this, cannot be misunderstood. This is too obvious to need to be insisted on, and the proof of criminal intent is, if possible, strengthened where the uterus itself has suffered, or where punctures or other similar injuries are observable on the head or body of the infant

The *second* source referred to as evidence of criminal abortion was the examination of the mother after her delivery. In these circumstances the medical jurist may be called on to determine the fact of abortion under two different bearings — the woman may be alive at the time, or she may have fallen a victim to the criminal attempt.

In the former case, where the woman is alive, the attention of the medical examiner must be directed to the state of the system generally, and to that of certain organs in particular in other words, he is to seek in both these directions for the signs of the woman's delivery As, however, these have been already discussed under the subject of Delivery, I need not again recur to them A few remarks are called for, notwithstanding, in this place, from the circumstance that in cases of abortion the delivery has usually taken place, not at the full term of utero-gestation, but in some of the earlier months

I have already referred to the fact, founded on statistics, that criminal abortion is usually practised betwixt the third and fifth months. This circumstance shows the necessity for the examination being conducted with as little delay as possible, as at those stages of pregnancy the indications of recent delivery on the mother will be but slight, and their disappearance proportionately rapid Few of the signs previously laid down as applicable to delivery at the full time will avail us in cases of abortion previously to the eighth month. The fœtus in such instances has not attained sufficient size to distend the abdominal parietes to any great extent, or at all previously to the third month. The marks on the skin are consequently not to be expected any more than the separation of the recti muscles, or the projection of the navel. In general, milk is not to be expected in the breasts when the abortion has taken place early in the pregnancy, though exceptions do occasionally occur. Thus, in two instances I have met with milk in the mammæ in considerable quantity before quickening, and in one case where a false conception came away about the end of the fourth month.

In ordinary cases of abortion the absence of the milk fever also tends to produce uncertainty in the examination, and if, in addition to the above, there has been little or no hemorrhage, the proof of abortion from the signs of recent delivery in the mother will be difficult, if not sometimes impossible.

There is one circumstance, however, which may assist the examiner in cases of abortion, and which does not usually happen in ordinary delivery at the full time. The quality of violence in the former case may have left consequences on the person of the female which may assist the proof of the delivery. Thus, if there has been, as is not unusual, severe flooding, the hemorrhage may still continue, or it may have left the woman in a state of anæmia. There may be fever from the effects of the drugs in the intestinal canal. There may also at times be metritis, peritonitis, or metro-peritonitis, or inflammation of the external genitals, from the use of rough instruments, or wounds inflicted by them, either externally or internally. There may now and then be a fetid discharge, from the dead fœtus having been killed some days before it has come away, or from the whole of the fœtal envelopes not having come off together. Much caution is requisite, however, in judging from such appearances, as they are all more or less fallacious, particularly if taken singly.

I have hitherto supposed the woman to be alive when the examination is conducted with a view of eliciting the proofs of abortion. When the woman, as happens not unfrequently, has fallen a victim to the methods adopted to procure the expulsion of the fœtus, the evidence may be expected to be stronger than where the examination is made in opposite circumstances. When death has taken place during the first three days following abortion, powerful indications are left upon the body, provided the ovum is a few months advanced. Where abortion has taken place after the third month of pregnancy the place of insertion of the placenta may be detected by a rugous, unequal, and suppurating point on the inner wall of the uterus, and the presence of this mark, with, in addition, the corpus luteum in the ovary, are signs of the most satisfactory kind, since the objections which attach to most of the other indications of recent delivery observable in the dead body do not attach to these.

Great assistance may be afforded to the medical jurist in his examination when instruments have been used to effect the premature delivery. In such cases perforations of the neck and body of the uterus have been detected, and consequent effusion of blood, or of the liquor amnii, into the peritoneal cavity, giving rise to inflammation in that quarter. The attention of the examiner ought also to be directed to the state of the stomach and bowels, where traces of irritation or of inflammation to a greater or less extent may be met with, throwing some light upon the use which may have been made of abortive substances, nor should the state of the kidneys and bladder be overlooked, from the known effects of certain abortives on the urinary organs. It is to be borne in mind, however, that some reserve is necessary to be maintained in deciding upon the source of inflammatory appearances in any of the cases supposed, as these, when present, may have arisen from very different causes.

III. In order to determine the fact of abortion in any given case, we have only to consider further the information to be deduced from the inspection of the child, when this has been found.

In the examination of the infant the medical jurist has to attend to the following circumstances:—

First, its *age*; and this is to be done by means of the date furnished by the table of the development of the fœtus, given at page 43.

Second, the fœtus is to be inspected for the purpose of ascertaining, if possible, whether or not it had been *alive* at the time of its expulsion. This, however, is but a secondary point in investigations of this sort, though it should not be overlooked in practice, as it may throw some light on the case in certain instances.

Third, the child may require to be carefully examined in cases of abortion where it is found to have been born alive, in order to discover, if possible, to what cause death has been owing. This inquiry, however, like the last, I reserve for notice afterwards.

Lastly, the inspection of the infant may assist us occasionally in deciding on the criminality of the abortion. Here the examiner should carefully search whether or not the surface of the infant exhibits any traces of punctures, wounds, or other injuries resulting from the employment of penetrating instruments introduced into the uterus. It is not essential that these injuries should be such as to account for the death of the fœtus. The slightest puncture is often a valuable indication on a trial, as it points to the employment of criminal attempts on the fœtal envelopes. It is necessary, however, in such cases to be certain that these injuries were inflicted during the life of the fœtus, otherwise the assertion might be hazarded by the criminal that they had been done after the birth of a still-born infant. The means of discrimination between injuries inflicted before and after death will be discussed when we come to treat of wounds.

In conclusion, I would only further remind you that there is no necessity for the production of the child in charges of criminal abortion to complete the proof of the crime, or that abortion should have followed, or even that any specific injury should have been done to the woman under the circumstances. Cases of this sort, however, rest not upon purely medical, but on mixed general and medical evidence.

LECTURE XIV.

INFANTICIDE.

LEGAL RELATIONS OF THE SUBJECT—Nature of the Proof required to establish the Crime—Crime of Concealment of the Birth—Crime of Exposure of the Child. MEDICO-LEGAL QUESTIONS IN TRIALS FOR INFANTICIDE—Has the Prisoner been recently delivered?—Was the child Mature?—Was it the child of the Prisoner?—Determination of the Maternity—From the Moral Evidence—From the Inspection of the Infant—Determination of the Date of its Birth—Death of the Child in Utero—Death of the Child in the Maternal Passages—Death of the Child immediately after Birth—Determination of the Date of its Death—Changes in the Living Child from Birth to the forty-fifth Day of Extra-uterine Life—Expulsion of the Meconium—The Fall of the Umbilical Cord—The Obliteration of the Fœtal Vessels—The Desquamation of the Cuticle.

THERE is perhaps no subject within the range of medical or economical science which has attracted to itself more discussion, or given rise to more controversy, than that of infanticide, both in its medical and legal aspects. The consequence has been that, on the part of the profession at least, an amount of attention has been bestowed on the evidence presented in this form of violent death, and the means placed within the reach of the medical examiner for the satisfactory reconciliation of apparently contradictory facts by examining into their collateral circumstances, or of rendering these nugatory by showing how they may be foreseen and avoided, or allowance made for them.

This satisfactory result, the fruit of much and persevering research and investigation on the part of the medical jurist, has not as yet been accompanied by corresponding success on that of the legislators and administrators of the law, and strenuous efforts have been made from time to time, though hitherto unsuccessfully, by these parties to secure the efficiency of the legal proofs of child-murder in all cases, and to decide as to the proper punishment which should follow conviction for the crime.

To perceive what has to be done before this can be accomplished, we have to take into account the difficulties which stand in the way of the legal reformer. The proof in cases of this sort is always necessarily of a purely circumstantial character, since secrecy is an essential element in the crime in almost every instance of its perpetration. The peculiar position, too, of the female at the time throws a softening influence over the judgment in estimating the moral guilt of the action, and is considered sufficiently distinctive to remove this crime from its place by the side of an ordinary murder committed in cold blood under the influence of purely vindictive or mercenary feelings. It has been deemed unfair, if not unjust, to doom to the same infamy and the same punishment the hardened and atrocious criminal and the young female of character and reputable connections who, betrayed by the arts of the base seducer, to avoid shame and disgrace and the ruin of all her earthly prospects, is driven by a momentary impulse either to stifle her new-born infant, or to imbue her hands in its blood on its birth.

As hitherto administered, the law has not been at all adverse to the recognition of temporary insanity as an excuse for the destruction of the infant by the then supposed unconscious female. It has even gone a step farther, in admitting that the destruction of the infant by the mother may be effected without the intention having been conceived, thus removing the act altogether out of the category of murder. "In cases of illegitimate birth," says Sheriff Alison, "the mother, in the agonies of pain or despair, is sometimes the cause of the death of her offspring, without any intention of committing such a crime," and he adds, in substance, that allowance is made in law for the neglect of the care necessary for the preservation of the infant's life in such unusual circumstances, as well as for the various accidents attending such a delivery, which may give the appearance of premeditated violence where none such has really been used.

Again, although it was formerly held by our law to be child-murder where the infant had suffered fatal injury in the uterus or passages by the criminal practices of the mother or others, as is still the case abroad, the more ordinary charge of infanticide is now usually here restricted to cases where the mother is supposed to be guilty of the murder of the child after it is born. It has been decided in fact that, in order to substantiate this charge, the *whole* body of the child must have been brought into the world prior to the extinction of life.

It is not for me to dwell on the flimsy character of the pleas set up, in our courts of law, in mitigation of the offence in many of the charges of infanticide, particularly as these are beginning to be acknowledged on the part of legislators and by the administrators of the law themselves, though it is not easy to find out the proper remedy for the existing state of matters. There is a general agreement, however, amongst these parties that the best means to secure the certainty of punishment, is to lessen the stringency and severity of the penal enactments bearing upon it, and so to secure against impunity, or what almost amounts to impunity, on the commission of the crime now become fearfully prevalent among the lower orders.

Up to the year 1809, all that went to constitute the crime of child-murder was the proof of mere neglect on the part of the woman to call in aid during her delivery, and of the subsequent death or disappearance of the child. Since that date more positive proof of homicide has been required, the concealment of the birth being held as a separate and subsidiary offence, punishable by imprisonment for a period not exceeding two years, while to convict a woman of child-murder, the same direct proof of wilful violence has been required as in charges of ordinary homicide

In connection with these two forms of criminal procedure, a few qualifying circumstances call for notice here. In the first place, although, to convict a woman of the crime of infanticide, as I have said, there is required the same direct proof of wilful violence as in charges of ordinary homicide, it is held in law that mere appearances of violence on the child's body are not *per se* sufficient unless some circumstances of evidence exist to indicate that the violence was knowingly and intentionally committed, or that it was of such a kind as of itself to indicate intentional murder

Again, although to a charge of this kind the production of the child's body is not held in law to be essential any more than in other cases of murder, the medical evidence is commonly founded in its production and examination.

Further, on the discovery of the body of the infant the prosecutor is bound to prove that the child had survived its birth, and was actually living when the violence had been offered to it

In cases of child-murder it is usually the case that, at the time of its birth, the child is at or near the full period of its mother's pregnancy, and proof of this is expected of the medical jurist, since its immaturity would transfer the charge to that of abortion. At what stage of the infant's development this distinction would be drawn in law does not appear to be settled

In charges of infanticide medical evidence is called for likewise in proof of the mother's delivery at or near her full time, though how far short of this the birth must have happened to change the designation of the crime is equally unsettled.

To establish the crime of concealment of the pregnancy, whether in connection with the charge of child-murder, or as a separate offence, it is assumed that the mother had arrived at or near the full term of her pregnancy, and that the child had been born at or near the full time, though the proof of this latter does not fall to the public prosecutor, the burden of proving its immaturity being thrown on the accused. It has not been determined in cases of this sort whether the charge of concealment of pregnancy may be repelled by proving that the child was still-born. The crime is, however, rarely made the subject of prosecution, and is never punished to the full extent of the statute, unless in those cases in which murder is also suspected, but cannot be proved.

The exposure of children is a crime which varies in its estimated guilt. When not followed by fatal consequences, the punishment is light. When the child dies, though only by accident, if the accident be connected with the exposure, the charge is that of culpable homicide; and when the death was the inevitable consequence of the exposure, the crime amounts to murder.

On considering the statutes regarding child-murder and concealment of the birth, it will be obvious, from what has been said above, that the following are the fundamental questions which may be laid before a medical witness for his opinion :—

1*st*, Has the prisoner been recently delivered?

2*d*, Was the child mature?

3*d*, Was it the child of the prisoner?

4*th*, Was it dead or alive at its birth?

5*th*, If alive, what was the cause of its death?

Of these questions, the first three may occur on trials for concealment of pregnancy, and all of them may enter into prosecutions for child murder.

The *first* of the above inquiries, Has the prisoner been recently delivered? has been already considered when discussing the signs of delivery, its solution resting upon the presence or absence of these.

The *second* inquiry, Was the child mature? has also been disposed of under the subjects of age, and of premature and immature births.

The *third* inquiry, Was it the child of the prisoner? is that usually termed the determination of the maternity of the child, or the proof of its identity.

The inquiry, Whether the child found really belongs to the prisoner? while one of greater importance than medical witnesses generally imagine, may require a reference to several possible sources of information independently of the moral evidence which will occasionally serve for its settlement. As regards the mother, we have seen that the element of secrecy in every instance necessarily enters into the perpetration of the crime. To counteract, however, this chance of her escaping observation at the time of the commission of the criminal act, she can rarely be in circumstances to escape the notice of others subsequently, the act of parturition giving rise to changes in her appearance and conduct which readily attract the attention of those, especially of her own sex, with whom she must of necessity soon come into contact. Besides, if living in society, it is all but impossible for her to conceal or put away clandestinely the fluid and other discharges attendant on her delivery, however much she may attempt to explain their character when discovered.

But though it may often be comparatively easy to awaken suspicion against the mother, it may occasionally be a more difficult task to connect her subsequently with the infant found. It does not necessarily happen that it is discovered in her possession. She may have had opportunities of removing it to some place of concealment at a distance, of burying it, of throwing it into a river or the sea, where it may not have been found for some time, when all traces of her previous confinement have had time to become obliterated.

A case in point occurred in a neighbouring county (Kincardineshire) in the autumn of 1875. A well-formed infant was found at the sea-shore, which had been born alive, but though the suspected mother was examined at Stonehaven subsequently, the law authorities failed to connect her with the child.

On the other hand, it has been said that medical men have assumed the maternity of the infant where a little attention to circumstances might have obviated serious mistakes. Thus, Fodéré informs us, that he has known instances of women who had miscarried at an early period of pregnancy, yet were declared to be the mothers of children born at the full time, and actually suffered death in consequence.

The question of maternity in all cases is to be answered when it can be done, from a comparison of the state of the child with that of the supposed mother. From such an examination of the prisoner as I have already pointed out under Delivery, the examiner will be able to form an approximation to the period at which she has been delivered. In addition he may, from such an examination, assisted in some instances by the moral evidence, be enabled to determine what had been the nature of the labour, whether easy or difficult, rapid or tedious. By comparing the results thus arrived at with the deductions derivable from the inspection of the infant he may be enabled from their correspondence to draw tolerably sure inferences in regard to the maternity.

In questions of this kind, the chief thing to attend to in respect to the infant is the fixing of its age, or the time it may have survived birth. The date of the child's birth is to be settled, first, by determining the date of its death; that is, whether it died in the uterus, in the maternal passages, or after birth, and how long afterwards; secondly, by ascertaining what period has elapsed after its death.

The marks of the death of the infant in utero will be considered presently when we come to the question of live and still birth in connection with criminal charges. The indications of its death in the maternal passages, and at or immediately after birth, will all come to be determined in another connection before the conclusion of the subject of infanticide.

The period which has elapsed from the death of the infant to the time of the examination must be learned mainly from the law authorities, though there are data, to be noticed when I come to advert to the changes which the human body undergoes after death, which may assist us in this inquiry.

This leaves for notice here the only other point adverted to as requisite for the determination of the maternity, namely, the time the infant, supposing it to have been born alive, has survived its birth. This subject you may remember, when treating of age, I reserved for this part of the course.

The inquiry does not require to extend farther than the fifteenth day of extra-uterine life, which is in fact more than a sufficient period, as a child which had survived even a few hours could but rarely be destroyed without leaving ample general testimony to its previous existence. Indeed, the German jurists limit their inquiries to the first three days of life, after which a child, in their estimation, ceases, legally at least, to be termed a new-born one.

The determination, then, of the age of the child during the

period I have fixed on, rests upon the succession of changes in its body following birth, necessitated by the new physiological position in which it finds itself placed after leaving the uterus. These changes are invariable in their occurrence, and when time has been allowed for their appearance they are sure indications of the child's having survived birth. Their presence, therefore, affords the best proof of this fact, conjoined, as they ought in every case to be, with the indications previously discussed (under age) of the child's maturity.

The changes to which I refer at present are,—

1st, The expulsion of the meconium. 2d, The fall of the umbilical cord; 3d, The obliteration of the fœtal vessels; 4th, The desquamation of the cuticle.

First, The expulsion of the meconium. The meconium is a dark green or olive-coloured matter, of a pulpy consistence, which accumulates in the intestines of the fœtus in the later months of intra-uterine life, and is discharged by the infant after birth at periods varying from a few hours up to a day or even more. Occasionally it is discharged instantly after birth. I cannot, however, admit, with some authors (Devergie) that the discharge of a portion of this matter necessarily indicates that the infant must have been alive at the moment of its expulsion, as, not to insist on its occasional presence in the liquor amnii, it is well known that in breech presentations it is sometimes expelled before the delivery of the head, and it is not unusual to find a small quantity of meconium at the nates in infants who had been still born, and where there was no indication of the labour having been other than natural. But when any considerable portion of the intestines have been thus unloaded, we can have no hesitation in asserting that this could have happened only in a child born alive, and after its birth.

The meconium makes its appearance in the intestines at the sixth month of fœtal life, or even earlier; at first it is rather grey than green, from admixture at this period with epithelial cells shed by the villi. It is mainly made up of a transparent mucus, containing numerous minute indeterminate greyish granules, and fatty granules of a bright yellow colour with a deep dark border, and in the earlier months, greenish yellow cylindrical epithelial cells. From the seventh month onwards crystals of cholesterine are frequent in the meconium, either in clusters of a lozenge shape, or in globular or polyhedral masses, of a rich green colour under the microscope by transmitted light, and yielding with nitric acid the play of colours characteristic of biliverdine, the colouring matter of the bile. These bodies may be found in the infant's discharges from twelve to twenty-four hours after birth, but in sparing numbers.

Subsequently to the discharge of the meconium, according to Billard, from at least one to four days after birth, the intestines discharge a greenish mucus, thrown off from their interior, which might be mistaken for the meconium proper.

A second criterion towards the determination of the child's age is derivable from the study of the series of changes which precede and follow the fall or dropping off of the umbilical cord.

In the infant after its birth, whether live or still born, if the death has not long preceded the birth, the cord is seen to be fresh, firm, bluish, rounded, more or less spiral, and more or less plump according to the abundance or deficiency of the gelatine of Wharton.

In the living infant, after the usual division of the cord, the first change which commonly occurs in the portion attached to the child is a shrivelling of this part, commencing at its cut extremity, and proceeding to its base or point of attachment to the abdomen. This portion of the cord then softens, while around its point of attachment there may be found a sufficiently marked reddening or injection of the abdominal integuments. The cord next dries up, simultaneously with which change it becomes brownish from its summit to its base, and more or less translucent. In this way, in place of its previous rounded form and polished appearance, it now presents a flattened or riband-shaped band, while through its diaphanous or parchment-like walls the contracted blood-vessels within may be perceived.

This dessication of the cord usually begins on the first or second day after birth, and is completed by the end of the fifth day.

In the dead child the cord, instead of a brownish, generally assumes a greyish hue; its investing membrane forms a pulpy pellicle, it loses its previously spiral form, and its vessels have not sensibly diminished in size.

Too much stress should not, however, be laid on these distinctions, as some of the usual changes in the living cord may be artificially produced in the dead child, or what is more to the point to know, they may be produced by purely accidental causes. Thus, in the experiments of Maschka, Caspar, and others, the mummification or parchment-like state of portions of the cord, after its separation by the accoucheur, has been imitated by drying or submitting them to pressure.

The readiness with which the same condition of the cord may be produced accidentally was shown in the case of a child which I had occasion to examine in 1865. The greater part of the cord was in the usual fresh and plump state seen shortly after birth, while a portion of it, which had lain under the nates, and thus suffered compression, was flattened, dried, and mummified or parchment-like. The placenta in this instance had remained attached to the infant.

Again, Maschka has shown that the spiral state of the cord is not invariably to be met with in the child which has survived its birth for a few days. Pressure has also been shown to be sufficient to prevent the puffiness of the cord in the dead child.

The separation or fall of the cord usually takes place at the fifth or sixth day, though occasionally a little earlier or later. Thus, in 130 cases in which this phenomenon was observed by Elsasser, the fall of the cord happened—

On the 4th day in 10 cases.
,, 5th ,, 40 ,,
,, 6th ,, 56 ,,
,, 7th ,, 16 ,,
,, 8th ,, 5 ,,
,, 9th ,, 3 ,,

During this process the base of the cord slowly ulcerates, the umbilical arteries being first divided, and the vein somewhat later.

When the detachment of the cord is attended with ulceration of the integuments around the navel, with oozing out of sero-purulent matter at its base, and when the inflammatory appearances remain after its fall—*i e*, up to the tenth or fourteenth day, the period at which cicatrisation occurs—the value of this sign is, of course, indisputable.

In the natural fall of the cord the membranes are divided circularly and cleanly, without having any detached fibres, which seldom happens when the cord has been forcibly torn away. In addition, it may be seen that the separation of the membranes precedes in the natural process the division of the vessels, so that the cord may be found occasionally adherent to the navel by these, even after the entire separation of the membranes.

Where the cord has been violently torn out of the umbilical

ring the raw and bloody edges of the part sufficiently distinguish this from the cicatrisation of the part after its natural separation

In the dried cord, or when its decomposition has made some progress, it is not always easy to distinguish betwixt its division by a sharp and by a blunt instrument.

The third source from which information may be drawn as to the time the new-born infant may have survived its birth, is the obliteration of the internal vessels peculiar to the fœtus, these are the umbilical arteries, the umbilical vein, the ductus venosus, and the ductus arteriosus or botalli, to which may be added the closure of the foramen ovale

Following Billard and Bernt, it has been laid down by the older writers on medical jurisprudence, that the obliteration of these vessels, and of the foramen ovale, takes place progressively in a particular order, and at stated times after birth, the umbilical arteries first closing in from twenty-four hours to three days, the umbilical vein a little later, the ductus arteriosus requiring about a week for the completion of the process, and the foramen ovale last of all.

In opposition to all this, however, it has been found by the researches of Elsasser, that the obliteration of the fœtal vessels occurs in a very indeterminate manner, both as to time and order of completion In forty-eight out of fifty-two mature still-born children they were all open except the foramen ovale, which was closed in four In ninety-two who died in the first month, they remained open in two-thirds of the whole

Later researches on a still more extensive scale, by the same indefatigable author, prove, from the result of the examination of 370 cases, the little reliance that can be placed on so variable a test In illustration, I may remark that in one still-born child the ductus venosus was found closed, and, in a child which had lived only a quarter of an hour, the foramen ovale and ductus arteriosus were both closed; while, on the other hand, in a child of thirty-nine days old he found all the fœtal channels remaining open Dr Norman Chevers substantiates this statement by the facts which he has collected respecting the frequent contraction and obliteration of the foramen ovale and the ductus arteriosus before birth, and by the fact of their remaining open in certain cases in adult life

In these circumstances you will perceive the futility of relying on such a test, as is presented by the state of the fœtal vessels, as to the period of the birth, or even as to its being a live one or otherwise An error with regard to the latter point was fallen into in a case which was tried at the Ayr Circuit Court in the autumn of 1846, on which occasion two women were brought up charged with the crime of child murder, on no better evidence of live birth than the discovery of an impervious state of the ductus arteriosus, and partial obliteration of the ductus venosus, and this twenty days after its supposed birth, while, on the other hand, the lungs were in the fœtal state.

The last of the available signs of the child's age is the desquamation of the cuticle This appearance should not be confounded with the peeling off of the epidermis from putrefaction after death The desquamation properly so called has not been observed to take place sooner than twenty-four hours after birth. This natural process commences usually at the child's abdomen, and extends successively to the chest, arm-pits, groins, the back, the extremities, the feet, and the hands The shedding is usually in the shape of scales, and in rare cases of powdery dust It may be expected to be completed in healthy infants in from thirty to sixty days, but in weakly or diseased children it occasionally goes on for uncertain periods I have encountered it in a strumous infant still taking place in the fourth month. In every case, however, where it is witnessed at all, the child must have lived at least one day.

The series of changes we have been considering, after the deductions from their value we have found it necessary to make, I need scarcely remind you, are only to be regarded as approximative, and not as closely and rigidly exact in the general case Some jurists add to these the changes on the general surface of the infant's body which follow live birth from the moment of birth to the fourth day, the redness of the skin diminishing after twenty-four hours, its yellowish tinge from the second to the third day, and its more decided yellowness from the third to the fourth day Such changes, though real, scarcely admit of accurate appreciation, besides not being constant in every child

The same remark applies to other proposed indications of the period of survival of the new-born child deducible from the length and ossification of the bones, and the weight of the principal viscera at and soon after birth. These, it is obvious, could only yield rude approximations

LECTURE XV.

INFANTICIDE—(*Continued*)

Was the Infant Live or Still-Born? Proofs of Still-Birth—From its Immaturity—From existing Malformations—From Intra uterine Disease—Indications of its Death in Utero Proofs of Live Birth—From the Shape of the Chest—From the Examination of the Lungs—Their Size, Situation, Tissue, Consistence, Feel, and Colour—Their Weight—Ploucquet's Test—Schmidt's Test—Specific Gravity—Hydrostatic Test—Positive Inference (Respiration)—Objections to the Positive Inference—That Putrefaction may render the Lungs of Still-Born Children buoyant—That Emphysema may do so—That Artificial Respiration may have been practised in a Still Born Child.

Having now disposed of three out of the five leading questions which may arise in the investigation by the medical jurist of charges of infanticide or concealment of birth, I come to the fourth and most important of all—namely, Was the child dead or alive at its birth?

This may be set down as the fundamental inquiry in all cases of infanticide, since there is not a more effectual way of repelling the charge, or a more frequent mode in which it is attempted, than by seeking to prove that the child was still-born. This has long been considered, indeed, as the chief point to be settled by a professional witness, and, in consequence, it has been till recently almost the only subject of serious attention amongst medico-legal authors.

Though not, however, the only inquiry which originates in cases of suspected infanticide, the question of live and still birth holds a principal place in such investigations; and, as experience has shown that the necessity of concealment requires the destruction of the infant on the part of the mother or her accomplices as speedily as possible, the signs of live birth have here to be sought in these changes which follow birth at the shortest appreciable interval, not, as under the last head, in changes requiring a few days for their evolution.

The question we are approaching naturally divides itself into two parts, each of these demanding a separate consideration. The one of these is the means we possess for determining that the child had been dead born, and the other that, on the contrary, it had been live born

I Of the proofs of still-birth The signs which indicate that the child had been still-born are those which go to prove— 1*st*, that it was immature, 2*d*, that it was born with organs in such a state either of congenital malformation, or 3*d*, of intra-uterine disease as negatived the possibility of its surviving birth; or 4*th*, that it must have died from causes unknown, or otherwise in the uterus, or in the passages before time had been afforded for respiration being begun, or for the occurrence of any of the other vital changes which take place immediately after birth.

1*st*. The signs of immaturity to be discovered on the body of the child have been already considered under Immature Birth

2*d*. The congenital malformations, which are incompatible with the existence of extra-uterine life, have also been considered under Birth (*Vide* table at p 178)

3*d* The subject of intra-uterine disease is one which has only lately occupied the attention of the profession, and our acquaintance with it is as yet but very limited Nevertheless, we are not without facts which may be made available for the purposes of the medical jurist. The consideration of this topic, however, will be reserved till we enter upon our last question, where it will come in more naturally

4*th* The marks of the child's death in utero may of themselves decide the question we are considering, independently altogether of the causes which may have led to it To do this, however, a distinction must be made betwixt the effects of putrefaction on the child's body after birth, and the changes which result from its stay in the uterus after its death to which the term *intra-uterine maceration* has been properly applied These are quite distinguishable from the effects of putrefaction, whether in air or water, from the putrid odour being entirely wanting, hence a competent observer will have no difficulty in distinguishing the two An infant which has died in the uterus prior to the approach of labour generally remains there for five to twenty days, and hence the alterations referred to are more or less marked before its expulsion

Though these are sufficiently characteristic, it is not easy to convey a correct idea of them in words :—

Suppose the dead infant laid upon the table, the inspector is struck with the unusual flaccidity of the soft parts; the head is flattened under the influence of gravitation, the ribs are prominent from the yielding of the soft parts of the child to the same influence, the sternum is depressed; the belly is sunk in front, and bulges at the sides, particularly at the groins, and the limbs are flaccid and flattened laterally. The surface of the body has a dark red colour, deepest over the trunk, and without any green tinge at the belly or sides of the chest. The chest is cylindrical, fleshy, soft, reddish, and impregnated with a brownish fluid. The cuticle is in part detached from the cutis vera, and where it continues to adhere, separates readily on handling the body, leaving the true skin smooth, lubricated, glutinous, and of a bright rose hue. Over the hands and feet the epidermis is thickened, blanched, and plaited, as in the hands of washerwomen, or where a poultice has been long applied. The subcutaneous and intermuscular connective tissues, and sometimes the muscles, are infiltrated with reddish serum. Under the scalp, and sometimes under the skin of the groins and arm-pits, an effusion of a gelatinous matter, resembling red currant jelly, is found. Serosanguinolent fluid is effused into the joint cavities, and the viscera are more or less coloured of a reddish brown. The bones of the head are unusually mobile.

Such, as admirably described by Devergie, are the appearances of the child's body after a stay of some days in the uterus after its death.

It should be known, however, that in very rare instances, in place of thus macerating and being thrown off in a few days, the body saponifies, becomes incrusted with phosphate of lime, acquires considerable solidity, and remains for years in the uterus.

Besides ascertaining the state of the dead infant, the medical jurist, where it can be done in a case of this sort, should examine the woman, though the evidence from this source may not be very reliable, resting mainly, as it must do, on her unsupported testimony. The account the mother may be expected to give will be that before her delivery she was seriously ill; that she had had convulsions, floodings, or a fall, or strokes on the belly; that she had been imprudent in lifting a heavy burden, or in taking immoderate exercise, or that she had been in drink, etc. She may further declare that she has felt some of the indications of the death of the child, such as cessation of its active movements, the feeling of its rolling to the dependent side on moving in bed, a sensation of weight about the rectum, general uneasiness, sickness, anorexia, etc.

In addition, the examiner may verify for himself the presence of the fetid vaginal discharge which usually follows delivery in such cases, and which may persist for some days, bearing in mind, however, that besides originating from the expulsion of a putrid infant, such discharges may have been the consequences of other causes, such as retained placenta, or the retention of portions of the membranes in the uterus after an ordinary delivery, as well as from natural diseases of the vagina and uterus

The only other point calling for notice here is the duty of the examiner to determine the absence of any traces of fatal violence on the child's body which might throw light on the cause of its death and expulsion, a subject which will come before us in the sequel.

The sources of evidence of still-birth just passed under review, though not without their value, yield in importance to the means we possess for the settlement of the point in question, derivable from the absence of the proofs of live-birth in the child

II The proof of the child's having been born alive, as I have previously remarked, is usually the main point to be decided in the investigation of this subject, and both in civil and criminal cases its determination must rest almost entirely on medical evidence

I have had occasion already to point out the almost impracticable clog to the efficient prosecution of such an inquiry, caused by the demand for evidence on the part of the medical witness that the *whole* body of the child must have been brought into the world prior to the extinction of its life With this, however, we have no direct concern in our professional capacity It is for the legislator or legal interpreter to get rid of a difficulty entirely of his own raising The medical practitioner can only be expected to prove that the infant died, and died by violence or from wilful neglect, at the time of or subsequently to the period of its leaving the uterus, and that, but for the violence or wilful neglect, there was nothing to have hindered it from continuing to live out of, as it had done in, its mother's womb

The proofs of life in the infant, as a physiological if not a legal question, may have to be gathered under two very different circumstances, namely, where the child has not, and where it has lived to respire

The proof of the child which has not respired having been

born alive is not called for in cases of suspected infanticide. This is so far fortunate, as, with the exception of those instances in which injuries of such a character as would suffice to destroy life, and could only be inflicted out of the uterus, are found on the child's body, the proof would be difficult, if not impossible. The entire absence of these changes in the organs of respiration and circulation, which distinguish extra-uterine from intra-uterine life would put it out of our power to decide whether or not the child had been born alive. I need not point out to you how wide a door is thus opened for the commission of crime, in circumstances which no legal enactment, short of the harshness of the older statutes, could well be made to reach.

The proof of the child's having been born alive, therefore, only arises in criminal practice on those occasions in which the respiration has been established prior to its destruction. The proof in this case is based upon one or more of the three following series of changes in the body of the infant, namely, those which take place after birth—in the respiratory organs; in the organs of circulation; and in the digestive organs. Some further tests have lately been added which are of less value, even if admitted as sufficiently characteristic and of established worth and importance.

Of the series of changes in the respiratory organs.—On these the weight of the proof is necessarily made to rest in the vast majority of cases of alleged infanticide; and, though correctly speaking the proof of respiration is not the proof of live birth, if by birth is meant the entire delivery of the body and the establishment of the independent circulation of the infant, there can be no doubt that it is amply sufficient to decide the point of live birth, physiologically speaking, and furnishes the best and strongest evidence of the child's having been alive at or about the time of its birth, even legally considered.

The points which fall to be investigated under this head are, *first*, the configuration of the chest; and, *second*, the state of the lungs.

First. The configuration of the chest.—As respiration cannot take place without the expansion of the chest, it has been thought that this change in its shape ought to be available for distinguishing between a child that has, and one that has not, lived to respire; and as the sight alone would obviously be too inexact and vague to be depended on in these circumstances, it has been proposed to have recourse to exact measurement, either by determining the circumference, height, and depth of the chest externally, or by estimating the size of the chest by the resulting elevation of the diaphragm, to be ascertained by opening the abdomen. These proposals, originating with Daniel and Ploucquet respectively, have not on trial led to any practical results, and their futility has been established on purely theoretical grounds.

Second. The state of the lungs, and the series of changes which they undergo on the establishment of respiration, yield proofs of live birth which are not liable to the objections urged against the former test. In order to their correct appreciation, however, we must be well acquainted with the physiological functions of these organs both in the fœtal and post-fœtal state. With this view it is of importance to keep in mind that the lungs in the fœtus have no specific office to perform in the animal economy, and that the blood they receive in common with other organs is merely that required for their own growth. Immediately after birth, on the contrary, they not only require the full supply of blood which all the vital organs demand in order to keep up the efficient performance of the important functions they have to fulfil without intermission, but through them the whole blood of the body regularly passes, and, when life is extinguished, in two out of the three modes by which life suddenly ceases, the blood is accumulated in these viscera in greater quantity than in any other part of the system. Not only has the whole blood of the body to pass through the lungs as soon as respiration has been established, but atmospheric air from without has to be introduced in great quantity within their substance, and to permeate into their remotest cells, for the purpose of effecting those changes in the vital fluid for which it is brought there.

Keeping these facts steadily in view, we are prepared for expecting that the appearances presented by the lungs before respiration has begun in them should be different in many respects from those of the same organs after the establishment of this function.

The time required for effecting these changes in the lungs of the mature, healthy, and vigorous new-born infant is undoubtedly extremely short, not exceeding, under favourable circumstances, a few minutes. When the infant, on the other hand, is premature, weakly, or diseased, or has sustained during the progress of the labour any hurt injurious to its viability, a longer period is required for their completion. I have known nearly two hours to elapse before the child was able fully to expand its lungs; and some cases have been adduced by Billard to show that the infant may survive for some days, and afterwards perish, without the lungs having been more than partially distended with air. These cases, to which I shall have occasion to return, are confessedly rare and exceptional, nevertheless the possibility of their occurrence should not be lost sight of.

Whether the arrival of air in the cells of the lungs precedes or follows the afflux of blood to these organs, or whether these changes occur simultaneously, we have no means of knowing. The effects of both occurrences are, however, satisfactorily ascertained. The arrival of air in the cells of the lungs distends these cells, the walls of which were before in close apposition, and thus the aspect of the lungs is entirely changed and their specific gravity diminished. From the same cause their volume is augmented. The afflux of blood injects a crowd of capillary vessels, which terminate at the pulmonary surface, and hence a change in their colour. The quantity of blood being considerable, it follows necessarily that an augmentation of the weight should further result from this occurrence.

If we can establish on satisfactory grounds the mere fact of the existence of these alterations in the lungs after birth—namely, *first*, the arrival of air in them; *second*, the arrival of blood in considerable quantity; *third*, the change of their figure; *fourth*, the change in their specific gravity; *fifth*, the change in their volume; *sixth*, the alteration of their colour; and *seventh*, the augmentation of their weight—we shall have gone far towards the solution of the problem with which we are engaged; still, when we had effected all this, the obstacles in the way of a correct conclusion would yet be formidable.

It might be objected, for instance, that the air in the cells of the lungs had been introduced from without into a dead child by artificial respiration, and not drawn in by a living infant in the natural way, and hence the alteration in the shape, volume, specific gravity, and colour of the lungs.

Again, it might be urged that the afflux of blood to the lungs might be the consequence, not of the establishment of respiration, but the effect of disease, and hence a further explanation of the altered colour as well as of the augmented weight.

Further, putrefaction, by developing gases in organs undergoing decomposition, is capable of explaining the change of figure, specific gravity, and the augmentation of volume in the lungs of the dead child, without the necessity of calling in the aid of natural breathing to explain such occurrences.

These and some other objections, then, have to be obviated before we are entitled to draw any correct inferences from the presence of the alterations which we have assumed to follow the establishment of breathing in the lungs of the new-born and live infant. You will easily perceive, therefore, that nothing short of a carefully-conducted examination of the lungs, and a comparison between their state before and after respiration, can serve the purposes of the medical jurist.

To this we proceed,—

The size and situation of the lungs are the first things to be attended to by the medical examiner. Previous to the entrance of air into the lungs, on opening the chest the viscera do not appear to fill the thoracic cavity. This appearance of vacuity is produced by the operation itself, as has been shown by Billard, and arises from the circumstance that when the chest is opened the abdominal viscera sink down by their own weight, thus enlarging the cavity inferiorly, while the ribs, by virtue of their elasticity, produce an analogous transverse effect. In the infant which has not breathed the lungs appear little voluminous, they seem to occupy but a comparatively small portion of the chest. The pericardium holds a prominent place in front, and the heart is quite uncovered by the lungs, which are placed altogether laterally and posteriorly. On the other hand, the change effected in the volume and situation of the lungs by the admission of air is considerable. The pericardium is nearly covered by the expanded lungs, and the convexity of the diaphragm is lessened. Daniel and Bernt have proposed to measure accurately this increase of volume in the lungs caused by the entrance of air into them, by comparing the amount of water displaced by lungs which have not and those which have been dilated when these organs are sunk in water, but their proposals have not met with any favour from the profession.

The volume of the lungs, which can usually be sufficiently well judged by the eye, is not, however, of itself a satisfactory test of inspiration or non-inspiration. Thus there can be no doubt of the fact adduced by several authors of credit, that very small lungs buried deep in the chest may belong to infants who have breathed. On the other hand, the presence of disease in certain cases may materially interfere in preventing a correct diagnosis. Thus the lungs of still-born children may be filled with serous fluid, which considerably increases their volume, and this might lead an inexpert observer to fancy, without further examination, that they were filled with air. Besides, the increased volume of the lungs, even when it is found to be caused by air in their air-cells, may have been caused by artificial inflation, or the air may have been generated by putrefaction. It is only, therefore, when these alleged fallacies have been respectively eliminated that we can place any confidence on the observation of this change as a positive, though it is invaluable as a negative, test of respiration.

The tissue, consistence, feeling, and colour of the lungs are next to be attended to. When we examine with care lungs not penetrated by the air, we find that they are composed of several hundred lobules; that their margins are sharp, well-defined, and curve inwards, this incurvation being most characteristic in premature infants; that their colour is one varying from a chocolate hue to that of the healthy adult liver; that they are dense and fleshy; that they do not crepitate when handled and cut, that no air can be expressed from their cut surfaces under water; that little or no blood is contained in their tissues; and that their cut surfaces do not exhibit any injected blood-vessels between the lobules. Lungs, on the contrary, which have been inflated with air, naturally or artificially, crepitate on being cut or handled, and feel spongy and light. Their margins, though still appearing sharp, when closely examined are seen to be really rounded, or projecting in tongue-like processes. They appear vesicular, and, when the inspiration has been natural, blood may be squeezed out of them. Devergie first directed attention to the presence of a minute injection of the walls of the air-cells after natural breathing, which may be best observed by the aid of a good lens. Hassal lays great stress on a similar injection of the interstices of the lobules, and asserts that this is never met with in lungs artificially inflated. He further affirms confidently that the air-cells of lungs artificially inflated collapse from the escape of the air when cut into, contrasting in this with the lung after natural breathing. In order to distinguish the interstitial injection, he states that the aid of the microscope is requisite. This test of Hassal is, however, I think, scarcely practicable.

The entrance of air into the fœtal lung on the establishment of natural breathing alters its colour from its previous liver or chocolate hue to a more or less lively rose-red. It should be observed, however, that mere exposure to the air affects in some degree the fœtal colour of the lungs. Again, it has been stated by Dr Taylor that this change in the colour of the lungs from a darker to a lighter hue is not an invariable consequence of a child's having lived after its birth, and he adds that he has known a child to live twenty-four hours respiring feebly, and on examining the body has found the colour of the lungs identical with that of the organs in the fœtal state

I am satisfied, however, that this could only happen after very imperfect respiration, and would not hold good in the ordinary case

It has been stated by Bernt and others that on inflating artificially the lungs of a still-born child the change of colour does not take place as in the child that has respired naturally. That this is incorrect I have no hesitation, with Dr Taylor and Caspar, in positively asserting. In several trials I have found, on inflating the lungs of still-born children, whether fresh or putrid, that they change to a fine rose hue, generally pretty bright, and not at all, as to the mere shade of colour, to be distinguished from the effects of natural breathing

Lungs, whether they have inspired air naturally or not, very generally exhibit near their margins bright red stripes or patches, imparting to the surface of the organs a colour like that of a mixture of wine-lees and chocolate. But in the lungs of children which have breathed naturally there is further visible on their surface defined patches of bright-red, relieved by the dark purplish intervening insular spots which form the ground tone of the whole

This last appearance, imparting to the pulmonic surface a mottled or marbled aspect, was first distinctly pointed out by Devergie, and is relied on by Caspar and other continental authorities as an infallible test of natural breathing, though its absence, Caspar thinks, does not authorise the opposite conclusion

The marbling of the lungs of children who have lived to breathe should not be confounded with a closely corresponding change of colour, chiefly near the margins of the lungs, in their purely fœtal condition, already adverted to. It is by no means rare, as stated by Caspar, to find upon the lobes several bright-red streaks or diffuse patches, whereby they come somewhat to resemble the lungs of those born alive. I am satisfied, however, with this author, from experimental tests, that the insular marbling from natural breathing cannot be imitated by the inflation of the fœtal lungs, the effect of which is to impart to them, not the mottling in question, but an uniform bright-red

It is important to notice in such observations as those in

question that the consistence and colour of the lungs may be more or less influenced by diseases which occasionally affect the new-born infant, such as pulmonary oedema, the red and grey hepatization, and tubercles.

Lungs affected with the red hepatization are violet-hued, are with difficulty inflated, sink when thrown into water, and it is not easy by compression to restore their buoyancy. It is not unfrequently the consequence of a tedious labour, and may thus have preceded as well as followed the birth. It is a mere sanguineous engorgement, and is only the first stage of the ordinary red hepatization.

Crude or suppurating tubercles are often found disseminated through the whole of the lungs in isolated nodules, of a rounded form, and large in proportion to the size of the viscera at this age.

The ordinary effects of putrefaction can never be mistaken by a competent observer for the consequences of natural breathing or artificial inflation of the lungs. These organs may be bulky, more or less spongy, and pervaded by air vesicles; but the vesicles in this case are large, irregular, and generally confined to the surface, being contained not in the air-cells, but in the cellular tissue beneath the pleural lining, or in that of the interstices of the lobes; and, moreover, the gaseous product of putrefaction may be totally expelled by pressure, while air in the air-cells cannot.

The following test I have found sufficiently characteristic of the effects respectively of putrefaction and natural breathing. On cutting a fragment off the lungs and compressing it firmly under water, the air-bubbles which rise from the putrid lung are few in number, large, and it may be of a fœtid odour, while those from the naturally inflated lung are numerous and of minute size.

The weight of the Lungs—the *Static* test.—As the afflux of blood to the fœtal lungs on the establishment of respiration must necessarily add to their weight either relatively or absolutely, it has been proposed to obtain from this source the means of discriminating betwixt the still and live birth of the infant. This proposal has taken the two different forms of the so-called static test. The first of these, known as Ploucquet's test, dates as far back as 1774.

Ploucquet's device was to compare the absolute weight of the lungs with that of the body of the infant. In his observations he found, that where respiration had not taken place, the ratio of the weight of the lungs to that of the body was but as 1 to 70, while on the other hand, where respiration had taken place, it was as 1 to 35, that is, the relative weight of the lu[ng] to that of the body was doubled in consequence of respiration. These ratios were, however, founded on too few observations to be relied on, and subsequent observers have reduced them considerably. Schmidt has made the weight of the lungs before respiration as 1 to 52, and after respiration as 1 to 42; Chaussier, as 1 to 49, and 1 to 39; Devergie, as 1 to 60, and 1 to 45; and Dr John Beck, as 1 to 47 and 1 to 40; Dr Taylor, as 1 to 67.5, and 1 to 46.66; Dr Guy as 1 to 60 and 1 to 50 respectively. The average of these ratios would make the proportion of the weight of the lungs to that of the body not to be doubled in consequence of respiration, as assumed by Ploucquet, but to be only, omitting decimals, as 1 to 55 before, and 1 to 43 after respiration.

But even these averages require to be brought still nearer to each other. Thus, out of a total of 143 children inspected prior to 1868, excluding a few cases in which the test was not employed, as also the bodies of premature infants, and those in which decomposition had made some progress, I found that the remaining 66 gave averages respectively of 1 in 56.4, to 1 in 53.6; while Caspar's ratios in 52 children, brought out these as 1 in 61, to 1 in 59.

The propriety of excluding bodies undergoing decay, in such investigations, must be obvious. My former assistant (Dr Alexander Ogston), in 1868, taking 61 of my cases without selection, found, as a result, that the average weight of the bodies of these children was even greater in still than in live births.

The remaining form of the static test is that which, for distinction's sake, may be termed Schmidt's test, from the name of the person who first urged its claims for adoption.

This author's proposal is that we should compare the actual weight of the lungs of live and still-born children, absolutely, not relatively, confining the application of the static test in this form to those cases in which the weight is such as is never attained by the natural and healthy fœtal lungs. Basing his deductions on the results of the examination by Bernt of 24 still-born children, in which the greatest weight of the healthy lungs was 993 grains, and the medium weight about 550 grains, it is argued by Schmidt, that when the fœtal lungs, being naturally formed and of healthy structure, exceed 1000 grains, such weight may be considered as presumptive proof that the child has breathed; and that, even if the weight exceed in any considerable degree 550 grains, the same conclusion is thus pointed at.

With regard to this statement, later observations have shown that the difference between the weights of the lungs in children who have and have not breathed, is not so great as Schmidt has assumed. Passing by Chaussier's experiments, as he took no pains to select the proper cases for trial, and Dr John Beck's, which are vitiated by the fewness of his cases, three in number, of still birth, we find that Dr Taylor gives, as the result arrived at by him, the average weight of the infants' lungs before respiration at 649, and after it at 927 grains. In my own trials the results were respectively 476.17, and 824.8 grains. Dr Guy's were as follows:—

Still born	. .	874 grains
Imperfect respiration	.	988 ,,
Perfect do.	.	1195 ,,

The averages obtained by Dr Alexander Ogston in 1868 were:—

Still-born	. . .	562.6 grains
Live-born (decomposed)		744.1
,, (fresh)	.	850.1
All live-born		833.6

This, you will observe, raises the average weight of the lungs of still-born children considerably above Schmidt's estimate, while it confirms the truth of the statement advanced by him, that, as a general rule, respiration has the effect of increasing the actual weight of the lungs at birth. But here its value ceases, for there can be no doubt of the truth of the objection first advanced by Chaussier, and supported by Beck, that the lungs of still-born children occasionally exceed in weight the average of those of children who have breathed fully. In three of my own cases the lungs in still-born children were above the average of the live births, in one being 958, in a second 1180, and in a third 1315 grains, while in one case of live birth they weighed only 420 grains.

Here, then, as in the case of Ploucquet's test, we are brought to the conclusion, that though in the general case the establishment of respiration, by the afflux of blood to the lungs, adds to their weight, and alters their weight relatively to that of the whole body, any valuation of the effects of this change, though it may be relatively estimable in the case of averages, cannot be relied on in individual instances of either live or still births.

The Specific Gravity of the Lungs—the *Hydrostatic* test—There can be no doubt that the entrance of air into the fœtal lungs in respiration must diminish their specific gravity. It has accordingly been found that though the lungs previous to their inflation are heavier than water, and consequently sink in that medium, when, on the contrary, their air-cells have received air, their specific gravity is so much lessened as to cause them to float readily in water. On this distinction the hydrostatic test is based.

Raygat is undoubtedly entitled to be considered as the author of this test, it having been employed by him in 1682. In order to employ this test properly, it is usual, after removing in connection the heart, lungs, and thymus gland from the chest, securing the large vessels prior to their division, to introduce the whole into a cylindrical vessel large enough to permit them freely to float or sink in water. For this purpose rain or river water is to be preferred when it can be had, the temperature of which should neither exceed nor fall below the medium, say 60° Fahrenheit.

The examiner should then observe whether the parts thus collectively introduced into the cylinder swim or sink in the water. If the latter, it is to be noticed whether the viscera reach the bottom quickly or slowly. The lungs should then be detached from the heart and thymus gland, and tried in the same way, one after the other. They should afterwards be cut into fragments, and examined in detail as to their gravitating properties; and ultimately the fragments should be compressed so as to expel the air as far as possible, and once more thrown into water.

The general conclusions deducible from the hydrostatic test are, that if the lungs swim the infant has breathed; and that, if they sink, the infant has not breathed.

To these inferences, however, several objections have been offered, which it will be necessary to consider in order.

First, The positive inference deducible from the hydrostatic test is that if the lungs swim in water the infant must have breathed.

It has been objected to this inference, that putrefaction may cause the lungs of the still-born to float in water. It has been shown by the experiments of Mayes and Gross that, out of the body, the lungs of a still-born infant may, under favourable circumstances, generate putrid gases to such an extent as to render them buoyant. Admitting this, the fact undoubtedly is, that, as a general rule, putrefaction does not take place in the infant's lungs before the chest has been laid open to such an extent as would cause them to float in water.

I have had occasion to examine the lungs in 52 still-born

children, at various stages of decay, from a few days up to several weeks (one 5 months) of exposure, but have not encountered an instance of such buoyancy. Some of these bodies had undergone maceration in utero. It is a matter of notoriety, indeed, that in the infant, after birth, the lungs are amongst the last parts of the body to yield to decomposition, and that they may be met with in a comparatively fresh condition when the contents of the head and abdomen are reduced to the state of a fetid pulp. But, as one exception to this has been recorded by Albert in a child which had died in utero, and as the lungs will yield to putrefaction out of the body, and in this state will float, it may be observed that this buoyancy from putrefaction may be readily discriminated from that arising from respiration.

We have seen already, that such air as results from putrefaction collects in large bubbles under the pleural investment, and not in the air-cells of the lungs. Besides, when the air is expelled by pressure, which can be easily done, such lungs sink readily in water, whereas no degree of compression short of that which will entirely break up their tissue, will cause lungs which have been permeated by air naturally, to sink in that medium. Other modes of discrimination have been suggested, such as taking a portion from the centre of the lung, and trying if it will float, ascertaining if the lungs crepitate or not, comparing them with other parts of the body, to ascertain if these be fresh, in which case the freedom of the lungs from putrefaction may safely be assumed.

The proposal of Bouchut would subserve the purpose even more effectually. It consists in examining the surface of the lungs with a magnifying glass, and the central parts of these organs with the microscope, when the presence of minute globules of air is seen in the air cells of the lungs of infants which have breathed, which contrast with the putrid gases whose seat is not in the air cells, but in the interlobular areolar tissue.

It is but fair, however, to admit that a case might occur in which such tests as these might fail to carry complete conviction with them, as where not only the body of the infant generally, but also the lungs, were very far advanced in putrefaction, and could not be readily handled,—a case which removes the inquiry from the medical jurist, for here it would be necessary to concede at once that the proof of live birth could not be obtained, precisely as in other instances where the decomposition of the body cuts us out of evidence of death, as in cases of violence or poisoning.

It has been objected that emphysema may cause the lungs to float in still-born children.

The appearance of the lungs in new-born children, to which the term emphysema has been applied, is a disengagement of air under the pleura, where the child has suffered compression from a narrow pelvis in footling cases, to which the attention of the profession was first called by Chaussier. The fact, however, that such an effect could be produced in the way thus assumed has been doubted, and it has been suggested that such cases as Chaussier has described were nothing more than instances of partial or imperfect respiration during delivery. The fact is, that neither these nor the cases which have been subsequently brought forward in illustration, will bear criticism, as has been shown by Caspar, who contends, with tice, that a single good example has not yet been advance proof of such spontaneous emphysema of the foetal lungs, or the swimming of the lungs from this cause, though this objection to the hydrostatic test continues to be reproduced in medical writings. But not to insist upon this, it may be sufficient to say, that should such an occurrence be met with, no serious difficulty could arise in the application of the hydrostatic test, as the superficial air could as easily be expelled from such a lung, as in the case of the putrid gases.

It has been objected that the lungs of a still-born infant might have been artificially inflated, causing them to float independently of natural breathing.

Out of the body, or in the body, where the chest has previously been laid open, it is easy to inflate the lungs of a new-born child, so as to imitate the lightness and sponginess which characterise the appearance of these organs in the live born. In this process, too, the artificial inflation changes the previous liver or chocolate hue of the foetal lungs to an uniform bright red, without, however, any trace of mottling or marbling being produced. This negative result, so strongly insisted on by Caspar, I had repeatedly observed before I met with the statement in his writings.

It is a very different question, however, as to whether it is possible to inflate the lungs in the entire body, and by the air passages, mediately or immediately, to the same extent as is effected by the natural entrance of the air in ordinary respiration. To give the objection I have just stated its full force, this would require to be proved,---a point which has not yet been attempted. All that has hitherto been asserted is, that artificial respiration has been so far effected in the usual way as to cause some portions of the lungs to float in water on their removal from the chest; but even the possibility of this partial success in artificial respiration has been disputed in the case of the new-born infant, and from the host of authorities *pro* and *con*, this inference at least may be securely drawn, that it is not so easy a matter to inflate even a portion of the lungs, as the objectors to the hydrostatic test so confidently assume in regard to the whole of these organs.

That anything approaching to complete expansion of the lungs can be effected by artificial inflation, I repeat, has never been proved. On the contrary, every attempt purposely made to do so has hitherto failed. Albert, in his experiments by the mouth, and by a tube, did not succeed in forcing any air at all into the lungs in still-born children. Depaul, who has written a very elaborate paper on the subject of artificial respiration, instituted a series of experiments on the dead subject, the result of which showed that even after the lungs were removed from the body great force was needed thoroughly to inflate the lungs, while their resiliancy was sufficient, in these circumstances, to expel again the greater part of the air thus forced into them, and that, as usually performed, it does not effect even the partial inflation necessary to secure its beneficial effect as a means of restoration of the suspended animation of new-born infants.

In his attempts to inflate the lungs of still-born infants, Dr. Taylor uniformly found that the quantity of air which they received under these circumstances was inconsiderable. On examining the bodies of five infants in which inflation had been resorted to, not for the express purpose of creating an objection to the hydrostatic test, but with the *bona fide* intention of resuscitating them, it was found that in three not a particle of air had entered the lungs, while in one, only about a thirteenth part of the structure of the lungs had received air, and in the other case although a small amount of air had penetrated into these organs, it was readily forced out by compression.

Similar results have followed the trials of Caspar and Elsasser. The latter, in experiments on 45 still-born children, with every advantage of posture and science, totally failed to force any air whatever into the lungs of 10, and but partially succeed in 34, while in only 1 was there anything approaching to dilatation of the whole of the lungs, and that was produced by introducing a tube into the trachea in an infant which had made no fewer than six distinct efforts to respire.

But not to insist on the proved impossibility of a person

ignorant of anatomy, and unprovided with the proper instrument and the skill to use it, inflating the lungs of a still-born child to an extent at all likely to interfere with the application of the hydrostatic test, we have seen that after such inflation as could be effected in the entire body of the infant, the air can be readily expelled from the lungs by pressure. Some writers have gone farther than this, which has been the occasion of no little controversy. Some attention to circumstances, therefore, is needed to reconcile the conflicting statements of medico-legal authors on this subject. Thus, Dr. John Beck, in the earlier work of his brother, adopts, without limitation, the dictum of Wildberg, inaccurately ascribed by him to Béclard, that the lungs of a child which has not respired, but which float in consequence of artificial respiration, may by pressure have the air expelled from them, so as to sink in water; while, on the contrary, in a child which has respired naturally, it is impossible, by any pressure, to force out the air so completely from the lungs as to make them sink in water.

Now, in opposition to this it has been asserted, on the authority of Mendel, Bernt, and others, that lungs distended with air, whether artificially or naturally, cannot be made to sink by pressure. That this holds true of lungs fully inflated, which can only be effected after the chest is laid open, I am fully satisfied. In a series of experiments undertaken some years ago with the view of determining the point in question, I invariably found that it was as difficult to express the air from the lungs of still-born children inflated out of the body, as from the lungs of children which had breathed naturally; that, in fact, no amount of pressure short of that which was required to break up their texture into a pulp, sufficed in either case to expel the air from them to such an extent as to make them sink in water.

If, however, we restrict the test of pressure to the discrimination betwixt lungs which have been perfectly expanded with air by the full establishment of natural inspiration, and lungs which have been only partially filled, whether by attempts at artificial inflation in the usual way, or by feeble and incomplete respiration, its value remains unaffected by the opposition it has encountered. The experiment of compression, Dr. Taylor affirms repeatedly, will, when properly applied, enable us to distinguish cases of complete respiration from those of artificial inflation of the lungs in situ. In this he is joined by Beck and Jennings, Wharton and Stillé, and others,—an opinion which has hitherto borne the test of experiment.

I have dwelt on this point the longer, because we find the subject involved in much obscurity in several of our standard medico-legal works, and because it is in truth the most formidable objection which has as yet been advanced against the hydrostatic test. But, in fact, independently altogether of the invalidity of the arguments and assumptions which I have confuted, the circumstances under which it could ever be advanced in practice with any show of probability, are of a very problematical sort. These, to present any appearance of feasibility, must be in the form of one or other of the following combinations of circumstances:— *First*, where it might be suggested that possibly a practitioner or the attendants might have attempted to inflate the lungs of a still-born child in order to establish respiration; *secondly*, that the mother delivered of a still-born child might have attempted the same thing with the view of saving the life of her child; or, *thirdly*, that inflation might have been practised by some malicious person to get up a charge of infanticide against the mother.

To all this the reply is easy. In the first instance, not to recur to what I have already advanced of the partial success of artificial respiration and the means of detecting it, a charge of infanticide could never arise in the circumstances, for the practitioner or attendants would at once be able to negative it by showing that the child had been still-born.

In the second instance, the female who would endeavour to save her child by inflating its lungs should have given other proofs besides this of her natural tenderness. She should not have concealed, at least from intimate friends, the fact of her pregnancy; her delivery should not have been secret; she should have prepared for the birth, the living birth, of her infant; there should be no marks of violence on the body; in short, it would be easy to judge from the history of any given case whether the accused wished the life or death of the child, and therefore whether it was likely that she would, even allowing that with sufficient strength and self-possession she could inflate the infant's lungs.

In the third instance, we have only to consider all that would be required to make it possible for a malicious person to trump up a charge of infanticide against the mother by inflating her infant's lungs. The perpetrator of such a deed should have some medical and medico-legal knowledge. His interference, too, could hardly have been premeditated; at least it must be contingent on the infant's being born dead. In this case also there should be no collusion or semblance of guilt about the mother; no secrecy, no feigning or dissembling; in fine, no violence on the body of the child; or, should there be marks of violence, they should be such as were probably inflicted after death, not before it, as the infant is presumed to have been still-born. So that, after a little reflection, it must be seen how nearly impossible it would be to substantiate a plea of this kind were it set up on a trial for infanticide.

Having said so much on this subject, it is perhaps a work of supererogation to add that in all the attempts which have been purposely made by accoucheurs and jurists to force air into the lungs of still-born infants without opening the thorax it has been found (1) that the air forced in found its way into the stomach and intestines chiefly rather than into the chest; (2) that the lungs in these instances contained little or no blood or mucus; (3) that their cells were usually ruptured at parts of the surface of the lungs; and (4) that as insisted on above, they exhibited an uniform red colour, and never the mottled appearance pointed out by Devergie and Caspar.

LECTURE XVI.

INFANTICIDE—(Continued).

Proofs of Live Birth (*Continued*)—Negative Inference from the Hydrostatic Test (Still birth)—Objections to the Negative Inference, that the Lungs of a still born Infant may swim from disease, that such Lungs may float after Imperfect Respiration—From Life without Respiration after Birth—From the Organs of Circulation—Closure of the Foramen Ovale—Closure of the Ductus Arteriosus—Closure of the Ductus Venosus—Closure of the Umbilical Vessels—From the Digestive Organs—From the Urinary Organs—General Conclusions—Vagitus Uterinus—Vagitus Vaginalis—Respiration before the Completion of the Labour

Having in the last Lecture disposed of the first or positive inference to be drawn from the hydrostatic test, namely the indication, furnished by the floating of the lungs, of the child at birth having breathed, I come to advert to the second or negative inference from the test, namely, that when the lungs are found to sink wholly in water the child could not have breathed.

The sinking of the lungs wholly in water proves that the child had never respired, provided that the following doubts or objections cannot reasonably be entertained:—

First, that the lungs may sink from disease though the child has been live-born. No doubt there are diseases or diseased states which occur, though rarely, in the fœtal lungs about the time of birth—such as tubercles, scirrhus, sanguineous congestion, and pulmonary œdema—which, as we have seen, may cause them to sink in water, even though respiration has taken place to a certain extent. But the existence of disease in the lungs to such a degree would be at once obvious to the examiner, and, besides, they can never be so wholly diseased as that the whole of them should sink in water, for in that case the child, it is obvious, could never have breathed at all. The sanguineous or serous engorgement, moreover, in a child which had once breathed, could be got rid of by pressure, when the lungs would float in water. But, in truth, the assertion that such lungs sink is a purely hypothetical one, and, in the case of congestion of the lungs, at least, has been clearly disproved by Schmidt.

The second objection to the above inference is that the lungs may sink in water where the breathing has been very imperfect.

Some authors, as Drs. Cumming and Beck, have affirmed that it is impossible that the lungs should sink in whole and in part if they have received air. I have, however, already quoted one case from Billard where an infant lived for eleven hours after birth, and yet the lungs in whole and in every part sunk in water. Bernt has related a second case where the same thing happened, though the child survived birth for two hours. Heister gives a third instance precisely similar, where the child lived nine hours. Similar instances have been adduced by Orfila, Taylor, and several German authors. In cases of this nature which have been studied by Jorg and Legendre, the lungs on examination were found to be partly in the fœtal condition, partly hepatized or otherwise diseased, and such instances were encountered in rapid deliveries, where the infants were premature, unhealthy, weak, and puny, and where the attempts at respiration after birth were feeble and imperfect. The condition of the lungs however, in such exceptional cases would at once satisfy the medical examiner both as to the imperfect character of the respiration and the cause of the child's death.

Lastly, the lungs may, it is said, sink in water, though the child has survived birth, because it may have lived for some time without breathing.

Cases bearing out this confessedly rare and difficult to be explained occurrence have been adduced by Hofmann on the authority of Mende, Maschka, and Voltava,—the proof of the child's life having been the continuance of the pulsation of its heart. The most remarkable of these was Maschka's case that of a still-born infant, born at noon, which, after attempts at resuscitation, was left for dead in a cold room, but in which, when visited at eleven o'clock on the following day, weak pulsations of the heart were detected by the stethoscope, while renewed attempts at resuscitation proved abortive. On inspection the lungs, in whole and in fragments, sunk in water.

This, however, as will be seen, is no objection to the hydrostatic test, correctly speaking, for this test is one of respiration, not of life.

In considering the evidence derivable from the hydrostatic test we have limited ourselves to two of the inferences which it is capable of affording us; namely, first, that if the lungs swim in water, the infant has breathed, and secondly, that if they sink in that medium the child has not breathed. There is one other inference, however, which you will find deduced from the same test in works which treat of this subject, namely, that if the lungs swim, but only in part, respiration has partly taken place. To discuss this inference, however, would be a pure work of supererogation, as neither in this country, nor in England I presume, would a charge of infanticide be taken up where it could only be shown that the child had but partially or imperfectly respired. This is the more fortunate for the medical jurist, because, as you must have noticed, it is to such cases of partial breathing that the objections to the hydrostatic test which we have just been considering can, with any show of probability, be made to apply. To admit the force of this inference, therefore, would open a wide door to professional disputes, which, in the present state of our knowledge, scarcely admit of satisfactory settlement, disputes which would perhaps never have arisen had this concession been always made by the medical jurist.

That such an admission as this may, in a few instances, allow of crime being permitted to take place with impunity, there is little room for doubt; but not to confine ourselves here to adducing the legal dictum, that it is better to allow the guilty to escape than to run the risk of punishing the innocent, it appears to me to be very evident, that more good would be done by the vigorous prosecution of those many cases where clear proof of the crime can be brought forward, than by dragging to light a few instances of doubtful culpability, most of which, if properly sifted, would at once slip through the meshes of the law.

The signs of extra-uterine life deducible from the condition of the organs of circulation, are drawn from the series of changes already considered as undergone immediately after birth by the cessation of the functions and obliteration of the ductus arteriosus, the ductus venosus, the umbilical vessels, and the foramen ovale, in consequence of the new course taken by the blood on the establishment of respiration. To these, therefore, we need not recur.

The indications of extra-uterine life, deducible from the examination of the alimentary tube, fall next to be considered.

In some cases the inspection of the stomach may afford evidence of the child's having lived after birth. Thus, traces of food or medicine may be found in it; of the former, the most likely to be encountered will be portions of milk, sugar, or farinaceous articles given before death. Such substances, as might be anticipated, are but rarely met with from the circumstance that the infant is usually despatched with all speed, and neither sought to be fed nor drugged in the interim. In two instances, however, I have found milk curd in the stomach in cases of suspected infanticide.

In a case which led to a trial in Aberdeen in 1836, the odour of opium was perceptible in the stomach, the mother having given her child syrup of poppies to still its cries till she could get an opportunity, in the absence of persons in the next room, of getting rid of it by exposure, from which it perished.

In instances of drowning and smothering, respectively, the fluid in which the child has been immersed if characteristic, may be found in the stomach, in the one case, or pulverulent matters in the other.

Tardieu has called attention to an indication of live birth deducible from the examination of the stomach in the new-born infant. He believes that the presence of air-bubbles in the glairy mucus usually found in this organ can only have arisen from the swallowing of saliva and mucus collected in the mouth and throat, and aerated on the establishment of respiration,—a process which Tardieu considers may require for its production a period of from a few minutes to ten or fifteen minutes at most.

The inference to be drawn from the state of the intestinal canal, previously referred to in another connection (page 38), the presence, namely, of meconium there, is chiefly of use as assisting us in determining the period of survival of the infant after birth. Its presence, however, in any considerable quantity in the large and in a portion of the small intestines, affords a presumption of recent birth, and *vice versa*.

Breslau of Prague has made some original observations as to the condition of the intestinal canal in the fœtus, which, if confirmed, will assist in the determination of the question of live or still birth. His conclusions are as follows:—

1. In children born dead, whether they have died during birth or have been long in a state of decomposition within the uterus, there is never any accumulation of gas either in the stomach or in any part of the intestinal canal.

2. The intestinal canal of newly-born infants never, therefore, floats in water, either as a whole or in small portions; but at once sinks to the bottom of the fluid.

3. The presence of gas in the alimentary canal begins with the respiration. It occurs in the stomach first, passing downwards from this organ. It is independent of the ingestion of food.

4 The swallowing of air from without is probably the first thing which leads to the accumulation of gas in the stomach and intestines

5. Gas may be present in these cavities as soon as the first respiratory movement has been made.

6 As respiration becomes more complete, and has been longer established, the different coils of intestine become more and more distended

This, it will be seen, is an extension of Tardieu's test, last alluded to

The tests of extra-uterine life derived from the state of the urinary organs will not detain us long. The inferences which have been drawn by medical jurists from the state of the bladder as regards its vacuity or fulness are not borne out by experience The absence of urine at this period is certainly no test of the child's having survived birth, as I have repeatedly failed to   d urine in the bladders of still-born infants

The attention of the profession in Germany was a few years ago called to the state of the kidneys as a test of live birth respectively in infants who have and those who have not lived to respire, consisting, in the former case, of a deposit of uric acid crystals in the papillæ, sometimes also in the pelvis of the kidneys, or even in the bladder. This uric acid infarction, as it is termed, is usually encountered in infants who have lived from two to ten days. What exceedingly lessens its value, however, is that besides being limited almost entirely to this period, in which cases of infanticide are very rare, it has not been always found even in these, and has been met with in bodies which gave evidence of their having perished in utero or during labour

A further test of live birth was suggested some years ago by Dr Wreden of St Petersburg It is well known that in the infant before birth the middle ear is filled with a gelatinous substance, which gradually disappears and is replaced by air, subsequently to the establishment of respiration, when the child survives its birth This substance, according to Wreden, is never encountered in the child which has lived for twenty-four hours, though it does not entirely disappear during the first twelve hours This proposed test of the survival of birth for a few hours has been examined by Wendt of Leipzig, and as the result of 300 inspections of the ear in the fœtus and new-born infant, he has come to the conclusion that the gelatinous substance can only be expelled by the establishment of full respiration

In about thirty medico-legal inspections Dr. F Ogston jun. found that the time of the disappearance of the fluid varied within pretty wide limits, from a few hours to two or three weeks, but that its absence was a pretty sure test of the establishment of respiration

For obvious reasons I have taken no notice of the existence on the child's body of injuries of such a character as could only have been produced during life or during the delivery of the infant, which some foreign writers class among proofs of live birth These of themselves would not indicate that the child had lived to respire

Having thus concluded our notice of the various researches, undertaken with the view of ascertaining whether the child had or had not breathed at or after delivery, it may now be well to sum up in a few words the results arrived at

You will have seen that with perhaps one exception there are none of the tests, taken singly, which ought to be relied on for the determination of the point in question Taken together, however, I am of opinion that they will authorise us to draw from them the following deductions —

In the first place, we may conclude that the infant has *not* breathed—

1. When the lungs are little voluminous; when their colour is uniform, and like that of the adult liver, when their tissue is dense, compact, and lobulated, when their margins are sharp and incurved, when on handling or cutting them they do not give the sensation of sponginess or crepitation, and when their cut surfaces on pressure under water give out little blood and no air

2 When the lungs, in a fresh state and in a healthy condition, when thrown into water, both in whole and in fragments, sink in that medium, or if when putrid or emphysematous, but otherwise sound, though floating at first, they sink in water in whole and in parts after being submitted to firm compression

3. When the umbilical vessels, the ductus venosus, and ductus arteriosus, are open and uncontracted, when the foramen ovale is not closed; when the stomach contains no traces of alimentary matter or of drugs, frothy mucus, air, or saliva, and when the meconium is still found over the whole tract of the large intestine

On the other hand we may conclude that the infant has breathed—

1 When the lungs are voluminous and covering the greater part of the pericardium, especially if fresh, sound, and free from

emphysema; when they are distinctly mottled or marbled over the whole of their exterior by slightly-raised rose-red islets in patches, contrasting with the reddish-brown or chocolate hued ground tone of the rest of the surface of the lungs, when their margins are rounded; when they feel spongy and soft, crepitate on being cut or handled; and give out blood in some quantity, and froth with *minute* air-bubbles on compressing their cut surfaces under water.

2. When the lungs on their removal from the chest float buoyantly in water in whole and in fragments, both before and after compression.

3. When traces of milk or other alimentary matter, of drugs, or of frothy mucus, air, or saliva, are found in the stomach.

4. When there is no meconium in the intestines.

5. When the fœtal vessels are contracted and altogether or almost empty of blood.

The case would be still more conclusive where the fœtal vessels were flattened and empty, and the umbilical cord had lost its plumpness. Inflammatory redness around the root of the cord, or the commencement of ulceration at the same part, or the presence of milk, farinaceous or saccharine matters or drugs in the stomach, would, taken alone, except perhaps the first two, prove to demonstration that the infant had survived birth. Almost equally conclusive would be the circumstance of the desiccation of the cord, or of the thickening of the coats, with capillary contraction, of the umbilical vessels and of the ductus venosus and arteriosus over the whole or any considerable part of their course.

Resting upon the basis of such facts and circumstances as these in combination, I cannot see that the inferences I have drawn from them can be seriously attacked; and no one who had given proper attention to the whole aspect of this difficult inquiry could with any show of reason attempt to weaken their force. That they are not fitted to meet the circumstances of every case which may present itself in practice, however, I most readily concede; and in what inquiry within the whole circle of the medical sciences would not a like concession be called for? But, not to dwell upon this obvious line of argument, let us rather look for a moment to the class of cases in which the proofs of respiration might be expected to be of such a kind as would justify only a very guarded opinion, and those in which they would place the medical jurist under the necessity of admitting that he was unable to decide the point at all.

The most important of this class of cases is that where, from the immaturity of the infant at birth, or from its feebleness or puniness, respiration has been but partially established. In these cases only a portion of the lungs may exhibit the changes peculiar to them after respiration, and only portions of them may float in water, and the vessels of uterine life may have undergone no alteration. Here, it is obvious, we would only be entitled to infer that the infant had partially or imperfectly breathed, and this, too, where we had assurance that artificial inflation could not have been practised.

The same conclusion would be arrived at in precisely the same circumstances where the child had been destroyed before it had time allowed it fully to inflate its lungs.

On evidence of this sort a criminal prosecution would not be taken up in this country, except where the suspicion of criminal violence was strong, and where it was expected that the minor charge of concealment of pregnancy could be established.

In such circumstances as the above, the tests of respiration accomplish all that can in fairness be expected of them.

I have now to notice a few rare occasions in which these tests cannot be at all applied. I have already adverted to the fact that immature and puny infants, and those which have been long detained in the pelvis in an otherwise natural labour, may occasionally survive their birth from a few hours up to one or two days, and yet in them the lungs may be found unexpanded, and may sink wholly in water. In instances of this sort, where time had not been afforded for the usual changes in the cord and fœtal vessels, and where no alimentary matters were discernible in the stomach, no indication would be afforded us of the child's having survived birth. Here, however, a charge of infanticide could not originate.

It must also be admitted that there are various methods by which a woman may stifle the life of her infant at or immediately before the moment of its entire birth, and before the commencement of respiration, without leaving obvious traces of violence on its body. If, however, we may judge from the history of infanticide, this is rather to be considered as a possible than as a probable occurrence, requiring, as it would do, a degree of forethought, knowledge, presence of mind, and decision of character scarcely to be expected in a female under the peculiar circumstances of the case. This is so far fortunate, for assuredly the resources of the medical jurist would not be equal to the occasion should it arise, and the crime might thus be perpetrated with impunity, as in this case even the minor charge of concealment of pregnancy could not be sustained

In conclusion, I need scarcely remark that the advance of putridity in the body will obliterate the indications of respiration after birth, as it will obliterate the traces of disease or injury in any corpse under most circumstances. It may be of more use to offer you the advice not to conclude, without examination, as is too often done, that any search for these must necessarily in the state of the case be given up as useless. Early in my practice I met with an instance of this kind where a practitioner of eminence had declined the investigation as hopeless, though, when it was undertaken subsequently, evidence enough was obtained to authorise a trial and lead to conviction. In another instance a conviction was obtained against the party tried, though the child's remains were found, in a mutilated state, some months after its exposure.

In discussing the signs of live birth in the new-born infant deduced from the examination of the respiratory organs, you will not have failed to observe that I have hitherto omitted all notice of a class of cases, to which your attention was drawn at the outset, as presenting almost insuperable difficulties in the proof of live birth, namely—

Cases of respiration before the *entire* birth of the child.—I have omitted these for two reasons. The first of those is that the admission of the possibility of such an occurrence does not militate against the correctness of the inferences I have drawn from the tests of respiration, and does not constitute the smallest objection to their employment. When the proof of respiration having taken place is once established, nothing further can reasonably be demanded of these tests; the when and where the child has lived to breathe must be ascertained from other sources. If the law raises the question as to whether the respiration of the child had occurred prior or posterior to its complete separation from the mother, either before or after its entire birth and the establishment of an independent circulation previous to or after the division of the cord, it must be prepared to say in what light it regards the previous destruction of the life of the infant by the guilty practices of the mother—a point to which I have previously adverted. In the professional mind at least, it is clearly settled that the mother who deliberately takes away the life of her child has otherwise, from natural circumstances, a sufficient chance of escaping with impunity without the law stepping in to multiply artificially these chances by laying down the necessity for proofs of crime of a kind which it is difficult or impossible to obtain from medical sources. I have no wish, however, to escape from the consideration of this subject. The case is altogether different when we are called upon to complicate by it and to confuse an otherwise sufficiently difficult subject with which it has no legitimate connection.

But to proceed. Considering it as a settled point, in English practice at least, that, if it cannot be shown satisfactorily that the breathing of the infant had been performed after its entire separation from the mother at birth, the crime of infanticide cannot be sustained, let us proceed to inquire into the circumstances in which it is likely or possible for the child to breathe before it has been fully born, and yet perish from natural causes prior to the entire birth.

First, we have it stated that the child has been heard to cry in the uterus prior to the rupture of the membranes, and even days before the commencement of the labour.

Second, it has been stated that the child has been known to cry while still wholly in the uterus, but after the commencement of the labour, and subsequently to the rupture of the membranes, the escape of the waters, and the expansion of the os internum, the mouth of the infant being at the time at or close to the os uteri.

These are the two forms of the phenomenon which has been termed *vagitus uterinus*.

Third, it has been stated that the infant has been known to breathe and cry lustily while its head was in the vagina, either in breech presentations after the escape of the trunk, or in head presentations, while the body still remained in the uterus.

This is what is properly to be regarded as *vagitus vaginalis*.

Fourth, It has been argued that the child may breathe on the delivery of the head, before the escape of the shoulders, and perish from natural causes, before the completion of the labour.

These alleged occurrences require to be considered separately, as the confounding of more or fewer of them has led to not a little confusion.

The first form of vagitus uterinus may at once be set aside as fabulous. No evidence can, it is obvious, be received in proof of an occurrence which is physically impossible. In enunciating this opinion, I have no intention of calling in question the facts or experiments which have been adduced to show that, under certain circumstances, the infant, even before the discharge of the liquor amnii, may attempt to expand its lungs, and thus draw in the fluid in which it swims, a point to which I shall return by and by, but this, it will be seen, has nothing to do with the matter in question.

The second form of vagitus uterinus has actually been met with in a few instances, of which the following have been pretty well authenticated.

In 1828 Dr. Holmes of Montreal was called to a lady in labour of her sixth child. The fontanelle presented, and no attempt was made to change the position. The head continuing to descend, the mouth of the child lay on the pubes, and the examining finger could be easily introduced into it. The occiput did not yet fully occupy the cavity of the sacrum. At this time Dr Holmes heard sounds like the cries of a child whose mouth is muffled by some covering, but as they were not very distinct, and not being prepared for them, he thought, when they ceased, that they must have been produced by flatus in the intestines of the mother. In the course of a short time, however, the cries were repeated, and with the greatest distinctness, so as not to admit of a doubt that they proceeded from the child. The pains being very brisk, the head was soon forced down and expelled. The child was a female, and in 1829 was alive and thriving.

In 1834 Dr Jobert was called to assist in the delivery of a woman with deformed pelvis, who had had two abortions previously. After strong pains the membranes had ruptured forty-eight hours before his visit. On examining the woman he found the head of the child above the brim of the pelvis, the occiput and face towards the right and left iliac fossae. The parietal bones had alone entered the brim of the pelvis. The os uteri was dilated to about two inches. As the narrowness of the antero-posterior diameter of the pelvis proved an obstacle to the descent of the head, the forceps was applied to it, when, at the moment the operator commenced his attempts at extraction, the fœtus, during some seconds, uttered repeated and distinct cries, which were heard by all in the room. After this, while considering whether it would be advisable to bring down the feet, from the little effect produced by the forceps, the cries were renewed as distinctly as before, as from the effect of repeated inspirations. Finally, when introducing his hand in order to lay hold of the feet, the moment it passed over the left shoulder, the fœtus for the third time uttered cries, less prolonged than before, yet sufficiently loud to be heard by all who were present. The labour was completed with much difficulty, and the child did not breathe, artificial respiration failing to reanimate the infant, though the heart pulsated strongly after the birth. The lungs were not examined.

The next case is thus related by Dr Collins of Dublin, in his *Practice of Midwifery*. "The most extraordinary occurrence in this case (related by him for another purpose) was the respiration and crying of the child in utero, both of which were heard, as distinctly as possible, four hours before delivery, the latter at a distance of some yards from the couch on which the patient was lying. These facts were witnessed by myself and the assistants, besides several of the pupils (at the Maternity?), both by stethoscopic examination and otherwise. The head was at this time high in the pelvis, the soft parts partly dilated, and the waters but a short time discharged. The cry was so distinct that I imagined the child was placed merely under the bed-clothes. When called to witness this truly singular phenomenon, I little credited the truth of what I was told, and confess, had I not been present, I should have remained sceptical."

It does not appear that the child was otherwise than safely delivered, though version was had recourse to.

A fourth case of vagitus uterinus is one published in *Guy's Hospital Reports*, by Dr Taylor, on the authority of Dr Crothers of Moy.

In March 1841 Dr Crothers was called to a woman in labour of her sixth child. The pains were pretty strong, and the membranes protruding through the os uteri. On rupturing the membranes he found the face presenting, and apparently arrested at the brim of the pelvis. On introducing his finger into the child's mouth he was surprised to hear a distinct cry, which was repeated two or three times, and so loudly as to alarm the mother and attendants. He was obliged to complete the delivery by the forceps. The child was a fine healthy boy.

In a case by Ketteller, of a third pregnancy, the membranes had ruptured and one arm presented. After replacing the arm and attempting to apply the forceps in order to bring down the head, the child was heard to cry repeatedly. On the failure of this operation, he laid hold of the feet of the child in order to turn, and the cry was again heard more than once. Though, on being born, the circulation had ceased, the child recovered.

Up to the present time we have four additional cases of vagitus uterinus, two of which are of more interest to the medical jurist than any of the other recorded instances, from the employment in them, for the first time, of the hydrostatic test.

One of these occurred in the practice of Dr. Falkenbech, who, during the operation of turning, for a cross birth, while the child was undoubtedly within the uterus, heard it several times cry loudly, as did other persons in the room.

In a second case by Landsberg, during a protracted labour with a head presentation, the repeated cries of the child were heard, as if covered by the bedclothes, on the rupture of the membranes, the child surviving, though at first in an insensible state.

In two other cases both narrated by German accoucheurs, the one a cross birth and the other a shoulder presentation, while version was being practised, vagitus was heard distinctly, though muffled. In the one the lungs did not entirely cover the pericardium, though they floated in whole and in part, in the other the lungs completely filled the chest, crepitated on incision, and swam in water.

Had we been authorised to doubt the accuracy of these statements, and others less fully authenticated, as at first was done by medical jurists and accoucheurs, any scepticism on the point would be removed by the authentic details, now being accumulated in medical writings, of instances, if not of vagitus uterinus, of respiration of the child within the uterus.

Hecker gives a case, which he attended, of presentation of the cord, where, finding it impossible to replace it, he proceeded, after the full dilatation of the os uteri, to turn the child. As he had some difficulty in bringing down the head, from one hand of the infant remaining with it in the uterus, he introduced his hand into the vagina to relieve it, when he felt the chest expand as from a deep inspiration. The child was still-born in an apoplectic state, but the examination of the body showed that the lungs had been expanded, and that it had died from smothering, all the usual signs of which were detected by him.

In two similar cases by Hohl, the chest was felt by the accoucheur to expand fully, twice or thrice, while the head was in the uterus. In these, too, the children were still-born, in neither of them, however, was there the slightest trace of air in the lungs.

Bratsky gives the case of a still-born child delivered in the Maternity Hospital of Prague after a labour of twenty hours, in which meconium was found in the air passages, and a few cells distended with air at the borders of the right lower and left upper lobes of the lungs.

In Müller's Clinique at Marburg, a woman gave birth to a dead child after her labour had lasted five hours, the attempt to replace the cord which presented having failed. Here, besides atelectasis of the left lung and indications of death by smothering, patches of expanded air-cells were found in the upper and middle lobes of the right lung.

Two further cases have been recently reported by Hofmann. In one case, the woman, after a lingering labour lasting two days, was delivered eleven hours after the rupture of the membranes, of a still-born child, presenting the usual appearances of death by smothering. The lungs were partly atelectatic, but some fragments of them floated in water. In the remaining case, a cross presentation, the woman gave birth to a still-born child twenty-two hours after the rupture of the membranes. In this instance, besides indications of death by smothering, the right lung was found to be partially inflated, and floated in water.

In an instance in which I assisted at the delivery, in May 1871, where from want of room in the pelvis, which was largely occupied by an ovarian tumour, version was had recourse to, my colleague, Dr. Dyce-Brown, in introducing his hand into the uterus to turn the child (a six months' fœtus), felt its chest expanding as in ordinary breathing, as in Hohl's cases previously adduced. The child was still-born, and the lungs in a fœtal state, with the exception of parts of their margins, from which a few bubbles of air could be expressed.

In none of the above cases, whether of intra-uterine respiration alone, or of such respiration with, in addition, vagitus uterinus, was there anything having a direct bearing on the subject of infanticide. None of them were instances of unassisted or solitary labour, and consequently in all the attendance of the practitioner would have negatived the possibility of a criminal charge originating under the circumstances. In the four best authenticated cases of vagitus, the crying happened where the children had to be turned to effect the delivery; in two others the forceps was required for the completion of the birth, and the two remaining cases were difficult labours assisted by an accoucheur. Moreover, in the whole of these instances either instruments or the hand had been introduced, which would permit the entrance of air into the uterus.

The same remarks apply in substance, even *a fortiori*, to the cases related of respiration without vagitus in the uterus before birth. All were assisted labours. One was a cross and two were cord presentations; turning was had recourse to in four, and all were more or less tedious. In only one were the lungs more than very slightly expanded. It may not be superfluous to add that in five of the cases of expanded lung the cause of death prior to delivery in the still-born children was abundantly evident without the supposition of personal violence. This point will come before us in detail under "Death by Smothering."

The subject of vagitus vaginalis is equally important to the medical jurist with that of vagitus uterinus, with which it has been confounded. The two cases which follow—amongst the best authenticated of those in which the details are given—are of this sort, both having been adduced as instances of vagitus uterinus.

The first is by Mr Thompkins of Preston, from *The Lancet* of July 1834. On examining a woman in labour with her tenth child, he found the face presenting, the chin resting on the pubes. After a few strong pains the face was pressing on the perineum, and the finger of the examiner passed freely into the child's mouth, when it immediately gave a convulsive sob and cried aloud, to the great terror of the mother and bystanders. The fright arrested the pains for an hour, but a dose of ergot of rye brought back the uterine action, and after two more pains the child was expelled alive and well, at least an hour after the crying and respiration in the vagina.

The second case is from the *Gazette Médicale*. In November 1845, M. Tourtois was called to attend a female in labour who had already borne several children. The membranes had been ruptured and the waters discharged about an hour before his arrival. The head was descending into the pelvis; and in attempting to give it a better direction, M. Tourtois introduced two fingers into the child's mouth, when to his surprise he felt them sucked or drawn in with some force. At intervals, for more than half-an-hour, the child continued to suck the finger of the accoucheur with great energy. The woman, after some hours, was delivered of a lively female child, which sucked the breast vigorously an hour after its birth.

The remarks which I have applied to the occurrence of vagitus uterinus are equally applicable to that of vagitus vaginalis. The exceeding rarity of such cases independently of facts, must be apparent. For their production they require that the presentation be a face one, that the child be unusually vigorous, the passages unusually roomy, and after all they demand some medium of conduction betwixt the external air and the mouth of the child, such as hitherto has only been furnished by the manipulations of the accoucheur, which would in any case take them out of the possibility of connection with a charge of infanticide under any conceivable circumstances.

The remaining objection to the validity of the proofs of respiration after birth which we have to consider is of a different sort from the last two—namely, that the child may breathe on the delivery of the head, and perish from natural causes before the completion of the labour. Of this three instances have been given, one on the authority of Dr. Hossack, of New York, and two on that of Dr. Campbell, of Edinburgh. Of other cases said to have happened we have no details. In none of these were the lungs examined after death, so far as is known, and all of them occurred where an accoucheur was in attendance. I am not, however, disposed to insist upon this. Allowing the possibility of the full expansion of the lungs after the delivery of the head, I can see no distinction morally between the destruction of a child partially and one entirely born; and if the law chooses to make such a distinction, classing the one occurrence as murder and the other as an innocent deed, the practitioner should wash his hands of the affair, and honestly tell the court that he has no resources within his profession for showing how much or how little of the body of the infant was within the maternal passages when its life was sacrificed. All that it entitles him to say is, that at the time the child breathed it was so far liberated from the mother as to enable it to have continued to live had no violent hands been stretched out against its life.

INFANTICIDE 253

LECTURE XVII.

INFANTICIDE—(Continued)

What was the Cause of Death?—Death from Natural Causes—Before Delivery—During Labour—From the Tediousness of the Labour—Cephalhæmatoma—Injury of the Head—From arrest of the Circulation during Labour—From accidental Rupture of the Cord during Labour—From Detachment of the Placenta during Labour—From Constriction of the Neck by the Cord during Labour—After Delivery—From Immaturity—From Congenital Malformations—From Weakness or Fatigue in Tedious Labours—From Intra uterine Diseases—From Occlusion of the Mouth and Nostrils by the Membranes—From Fractures or other Injuries by Falls in Rapid Delivery—From Rupture of the Cord in sudden Expulsion of the Child—From Smothering under the Bedclothes—From Overlaying

The *fifth* and last of the questions which the medical jurist may be called upon to determine on trials for infanticide is the cause of the child's death

This was a point of minor consideration in trials under the old statute, for the guilt of the prisoner was supposed to be sufficiently evident if there were proof of the child having lived; but, according to the present law, however necessary and useful that proof may be as preliminary or presumptive evidence, no person can be convicted of child-murder unless it be clearly shown, as in other trials for homicide, that the child was actually murdered; and further, as I have already stated, in cases of child-murder at common law stronger evidence of intentional violence will be required than in other cases, for reasons formerly pointed out "Accordingly," says Mr Alison, "it is a principle of law that mere appearances of violence on the child's body are not *per se* sufficient, unless some circumstances of evidence exist to indicate that the violence was knowingly and intentionally committed, or that they are of such a kind as themselves to indicate intentional murder" There is this one essential difference, however, between the evidence of child-murder and of ordinary homicide, that in the former the very fact of murder having been committed is in general sufficient to attach strong suspicion of guilt to the mother,

...ce it is highly unlikely that any one else could commit the crime—at least without her acquiescence.

The inquiries which present themselves under the present head, it will be thus seen, are partly special, partly of a more general character, which latter will to be considered more appropriately under homicide in general.

Confining ourselves, therefore, to the special character of the inquiries which originate in deaths by violence or neglect of the new-born infant, I go on to remark that the first point to be determined by us here comes to be,—Has the case been one of infanticide at all? Or, in other words, could the child's death have occurred from natural causes?

The solution of this question rests upon three kinds of data: *first*, upon the signs which denote that the child has died before delivery; *secondly*, upon those which indicate that the child has died during the labour, and *thirdly*, upon facts which go to prove that the infant, though born alive, has nevertheless perished after delivery, from causes independent altogether of the will of the mother.

First, Of the death of the child before the commencement of labour.—The signs indicative of the death of the foetus in utero have been anticipated in the instances in which it has perished some time previously to the termination of the pregnancy. In these the maceration of its body would obviate any chance of a charge of infanticide being set up against the mother.

The various causes which may lead to the death of the foetus in utero are such as are partly dependent on the state of the mother, and partly such as originate with the foetus itself. These may be conveniently referred to some of the following categories,—malformation, arrested development, atrophy, tubercle, hydatids, etc., diseases communicated by infection from the mother's system, either directly scrofula and small-pox, or more remotely from the father through her, as in certain forms of syphilis; affections arising from strong mental impressions on the mother; affection originating in morbid alterations of the envelopes of the ovum, in the placenta and cord, or in the uterus itself; and affections which date their occurrence from the influence of external agents, such as falls, blows, pressure, etc.

These classes of cases are only of secondary importance to us, as bearing but indirectly on medical jurisprudence.

From what we have seen under Abortion, the death of the foetus in utero, from violence inflicted directly on the body of the

INFANTICIDE

... from violent impressions made on it generally is of the rarest occurrence, while nothing is more commo... than the immunity of the child from the roughest usage of its mother, and again, the study of the morbid states o... alterations of the maternal organs ... d accesso..., o... of the ... as it ... belongs ... to the accoucheur t... e to the medical witness. Nevertheless, it should not be overlooked by the latter, that c... have occurred where the child has been killed in utero by such violence, or where its death there may admit of being traced to conditions of the mother, or of the fœtus itself, which are capable of being elucidated with mo... or less clearness. I see the propriety, in doubtful c... of attending to the following points laid down by Caspar:—(1), We must endeavour to find out whether the child has been live or still-born; (2), if the mother is known the relative dimensions of her pelvis must be ascertained; (3), the bo... of the child must be carefully examined for finger-marks, scratches, etc.; (4), the condition of the cranial bones must be scrutinised with reference... defective ossification, fractures, callus, or effused blood; (5) the circumstances of the alleged fall, blow, or other violence must be carefully weighed; (6) the previous condition of the woman, betwixt the infliction of the violence and the delivery, should be ascertained.

Second, Of the death of the child during labour.—This may occur in a variety of ways. Not a few children ... a natural ...bleness of constitution, from imperfect developme... ...om malformations, or ...om prematurity, though living up to ...rth, do not survive delive...y. The same result, in other instances, may be traceable to the mere tediousness of the labour, which may operate injuriously in more ways than one. Thus, the delay in the dilatation ... the os uteri, and the premature discharge of the liquor amn... y lead to undue compression of the child's body generally, to the te... long detention of the child's head at the brim of the pelvis, or to the arrest of the functions of the placenta, or of the circulation of the cord, and thus to its death, before the completion of the delivery. Again, after the head has left the uterus, the feebleness of the expulsive pains may delay the completion of the labour too long for the safety of the infant. Once more, the head of the child may suffer injury, at this stage, from deficiency or narrowness of the maternal pelvis, while, from want of room there, the circulation in the co... ...ay be arrested. Hence, in some one or more of these ways the death of the child may be accounted for, it being traceable to such varied causes as asthenia, apoplexy, asphyxia, fractures of the cranial bones, or injury to the brain, leaving appearances on the body of the infant more or less characteristic of the mode of the fatal occurrence, or which may come short of evidence to this effect of a kind which can safely be acted on.

Of death by asthenia under the circumstances in question, the indications in the child's body will be of a purely negative, and consequently uncertain kind.

Cerebral hyperæmia—apoplexia neo-natorum—is believed to be the most common cause of the death of the child during delivery, where the labour has been difficult and protracted. In these instances the appearances in the child's body, indicative of death in this way, may be of a more or less indefinite or reliable character, according to circumstances.

Thus, as stated by Caspar, we may have congestion of the membranes of the brain and of the cerebral sinuses, and blood extravasated, either fluid or clotted, between the pericranium and occipital aponeurosis, beneath the pericranium, or inside the cranium, and these appearances either sufficiently marked to account the death of the infant, or of so slight and indeterminate a kind as would be compatible with its recovery and ultimate survival. Hence in the necessary absence of injury to the scalp or cranial bones, the amount of the congestion, or effusion, or both must be taken into account in coming to a conclusion as to their being the cause, or otherwise, of the death of the child.

One of the most usual consequences of a tedious labour, whether the infant has survived birth, or not, is what is known as the caput succedaneum, or a sero-sanguinolent effusion under the pericranium, giving rise to a diffused swelling at the seat of the effusion, located at the part of the head which had presented, most frequently over one of the parietal bones. Similar sub-pericranial effusions are occasionally encountered, though not so frequently, as the effect of tedious labours, and these are not limited to the presenting part, but are met with on the upper aspect of the cranium, in isolated patches varying in size from the breadth of a pea to that of a shilling or a little more.

The drawing (Plate V.) is intended to represent this appearance as contrasted with the *punctiform ecchymosis* often met with in the same situation in cases of death by smothering. Fig. I. represents those irregularly-sized effusions, while Fig. II. shows the uniformly-sized ecchymoses found in cases of death from smothering. The darker shading in Fig. I. is intended to represent the intense amount of congestion in the cranial bones generally observed to accompany these effusions, which is not so marked in smothering.

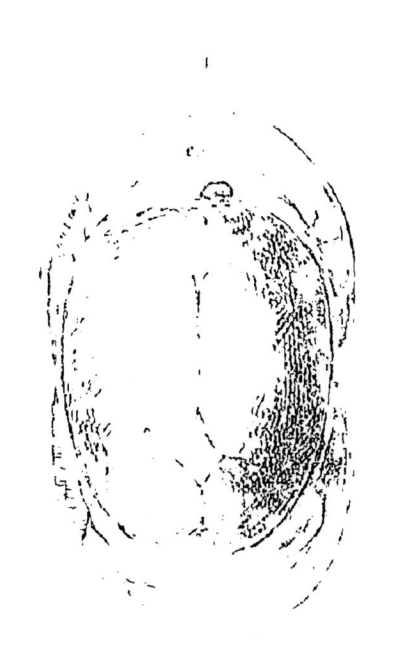

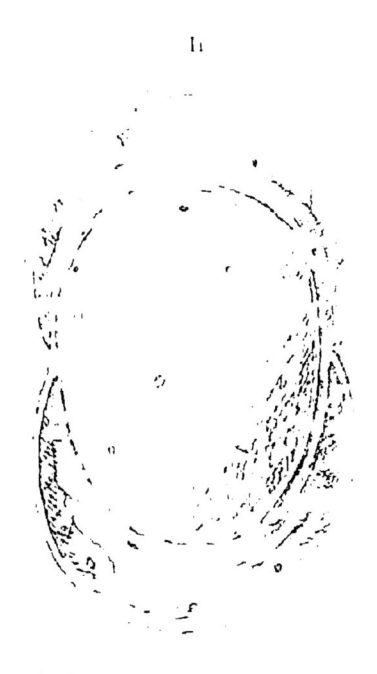

TEDIOUS FOUR CONTRASTED WITH 2 PUNCTIFORM ECCHYMOSIS OF

These irregular effusions should not be confounded with the so-termed capillary or punctiform ecchymoses on which Tardieu lays so much stress, which are usually of uniform size, well-defined rounded outline, and not exceeding the size of small shot, to which I shall have to advert particularly in the sequel.

Light has recently been thrown on those further instances of sub-pericranial effusions of blood met with occasionally in infants, resulting from the tediousness of the labour, and compatible with its survival after birth, to which the term *cephalhæmatoma* has been given. These usually appear after birth, increase in the course of two or three days from the size of half a marble to that of a chestnut or half a hen's egg, remain stationary for a few days, and disappear slowly in from a month to six weeks afterwards, leaving for a time a slight elevation of the skull at the part. But what I have chiefly to direct your attention to are the changes which take place at the seat of the cephalhæmatoma during the process of its spontaneous removal. Prior to the absorption of the clot a fibrinous exudation is poured out around the detached edge of the pericranium, during the subsequent absorption of which a process of ossification is sometimes set up, converting the fibrinous ring into an osseous ridge while that part of the cranium over which the clot has been situated is roughened by the formation of new bone on its surface.

A case of this kind occurred in my practice in 1859 under a rather unusual and puzzling combination of circumstances. The child was an illegitimate one, whose sudden death five weeks after birth gave rise to suspicions against the mother and others. In the course of the inquiry it came out that the infant, immediately after the detachment of the cord, had been allowed to fall off a chair on its head, and at the inspection a clot still unabsorbed was found over one parietal bone and under the other, with, in addition, at the bottom of one of these clots, what appeared to be an old linear fracture. Fortunately for the parties concerned, the fall had been witnessed by a medical man, who, it was found during the inquiry, had been present at the birth, and was able to testify to the purely accidental nature of the occurrence.

The same character of uncertainty which attaches to these marks of congestion and effusion of blood, in connection with the death of the infant during birth or subsequently, originates from the discovery of the more marked and apparently violent appearances which are occasionally encountered at the post-mortem inspection of the body. Even the most serious of these, such as displacement of the bones of the head, an unusual degree of mobility between the separate bones, rupture of their connecting membranes, and fracture of these bones, may occur either from the effects of a difficult labour or from violence inflicted subsequently to birth on the child's head. That appearances of this sort have been encountered after a tedious and difficult labour there can be no doubt, though whether a woman could be delivered in such circumstances without assistance is a different question.

The circumstances under which the most important of these injuries happen deserve consideration. Fractures of the skull, for instance, may undoubtedly occur during labour in consequence of the relative disproportion of the head to the pelvis, or of a deformity of the latter, and the child may survive these injuries for a sufficient time to breathe, as in a case related by Klein, where the infant lived forty-six hours after fracture of the parietal bones, followed by extravasation of blood into the brain and spinal cord; or it may recover from them altogether. Fractures, however, produced in this way are confessedly of very rare occurrence, since the child's head often sustains extreme compression during labour without being seriously injured by it, while from the accompanying circumstances, this usually throws but slight difficulty in the way of the medical jurist in deciding as to the time and mode of their production.

Thus, apart from injuries of this sort caused by the forceps, where, of course, the question of their origin would not originate, light may usually be readily thrown on the mode of their natural production. Some evidence, for instance, would be attainable from the examination of the mother. If her pelvis were free from deformity, and sufficiently roomy as compared with the child's head, the probability of its having thus occurred during the labour might be safely negatived, and the same conclusion would be pointed to in the absence of any proof of the labour having been unusually difficult or protracted. Further, the amount of injury to the child's head would much assist the diagnosis, the amount of violence done to the head by the prolicide being usually much greater than is ever encountered in the circumstances we are considering. Besides, in these cases the cranial bones have been noticed in actual instances to exhibit signs of fragility from defective ossification or unnatural thinness. Such fractures, moreover, are in themselves significant, they are found mostly in the parietal sometimes extending to the frontal and temporal bones, and are never, as far as I know, met with in the occipital bone. Usually they are mere fissures radiating from a central point taking the direction of the fibres, and unattended with laceration of the membranes of the brain or contusions or other injuries of the scalp. Occasionally, however, blood has been found in their vicinity, and cases have been recorded by Landsberg, Danyau, and Ollivier (d'Angers) where the cranium was depressed.

In contrast with this state of the child's head during labour may be noticed the appearances I met with in a case which I examined at Lumsden Village in 1858. Here besides fractures of the parietal and frontal bones, the sides of the head and face were flattened, and impressions of large shoe-nails (tackets) were visible on one cheek. The woman had been delivered secretly in a cowhouse, and the nails in her shoes corresponded with the marks on the child's face, which indicated that she had trampled on and crushed the head of her infant after it had been born alive.

In another case at Rhynie in the winter of 1863-4, besides fractures of the parietal bones, a vertical fracture in the centre of the occipital bone, and unusual mobility of the sutures, there were abrasions on one cheek and temple, the child having been crushed apparently betwixt a meal chest (girnel) and a rough stone wall, against which the chest was placed at a distance of three inches from the wall.

In a third case, which I examined in July 1862, a servant in a family in Aberdeen, to conceal an illegitimate child to which she had given birth in the house of her mistress, had thrust it down the soil-pipe of a privy. Here, besides finding contusions and abrasions on different parts of the surface, and fractures of the lower jaw, left arm, and both legs, and the tongue torn out, I found an angular fracture of the right parietal bone, with effusion of blood under the scalp in its vicinity. Though in this case there could be no room for doubt that the child had died from violence, my colleague was at first inclined to doubt that the fracture of the cranium had its origin in intentional violence, and had not been caused naturally during the labour, though he came at length to the former opinion, to which he subsequently adhered firmly.

Before taking leave of this topic there is a caution I would leave with you, and that is, not to mistake defective ossification of the bones of the fœtal skull at birth for fractures or violence of the cranial tables, as may be done in ignorance of the circumstance that such deficiencies are not unfrequently encountered in cases where intentional or accidental injury is altogether out of the question.

It is well known that children may perish during labour from the premature arrest of the fœtal circulation in various ways—as from detachment of the placenta, and consequent arrest of its functions; prolapse of the cord in head presentations, and compression of it by the head, or by the body or head in foot presentations; and from the cord having been twisted round the child's neck or limbs, and thus suffering compression. Recent researches have incontestably shown that the arrest of the circulation through the cord in these circumstances leads in many instances to instinctive efforts on the part of the child to respire, and that the consequence of this is its death by asphyxia, different in its form as it occurs previously or subsequently to the discharge of the liquor amnii, and necessarily leaving less obvious indications in the dead body than those found in the asphyxia met with after the closure of the foramen ovale and the fœtal blood-vessels. This discovery, I need scarcely add, affords a key to the explanation of the cases of respiration in utero previously adduced. I shall have occasion, however, to return to this point under the subjects of "Death by smothering and drowning."

Accidental rupture of the cord is now believed to lead to death by asphyxia in precisely the same way as has just been stated in compression of the cord (and not, as formerly thought, to death by syncope), the evidence of which would be turgescence and lividity of the features, with a congested state of the contents of the head and the thoracic viscera, and the absence of marks of violence or disease.

The same remark applies to the case of detachment of the placenta during labour.

It has been a moot point whether the twisting of the cord round the child's neck during labour, especially if naturally short, or making several turns around the neck, would lead to death by asphyxia in every case, or to death by coma in the majority of instances. It has also been a disputed point as to whether ecchymoses of the neck of the infant should or should not be expected to be encountered in these circumstances. On the former point facts are wanting to authorise a satisfactory conclusion, while in regard to the latter point we know that, while in the vast majority of instances no mark is left on the child by the cord being coiled round its neck during labour, exceptional cases are recorded in which furrows and discolorations of the skin have been found at the points which have suffered compression.

In the majority of cases, however, the diagnosis betwixt such constriction of the neck of the infant by the navel string and inter-

tional strangulation by a ligature would not be found difficult in actual practice. We have seen that in the greater number of cases the coil of the navel string leaves no mark on the child's neck, as would be the case where hanging or strangulation had been had recourse to; and even in the rarer cases, where the cord had left its traces, these might be readily discriminated. Independently of its circular form, which might occur in strangulation and even in hanging, the broad and soft grooved mark of the cord, free from any trace of excoriation, would contrast with the effects of an ordinary ligature, which are usually the opposite of this.

Tardieu thinks that the presence of the signs of respiration alone would dispose of the plea of strangulation by the umbilical cord during or before birth. He seems, however, to overlook the case of intra-uterine respiration as a possible occurrence here.

Caspar has very properly warned us against the possible error of mistaking for the effects of a ligature the infolding of the skin of the neck of fat infants from the depression of the head after death, an appearance which I have had frequent occasions of noticing after natural death.

Third, The natural causes of the death of the infant subsequently to delivery. Amongst these must be placed—

Immaturity, hindering its surviving birth, which, when distinctly proved, will point out non-viability.

Certain malformations which do not interfere with intra-uterine life are incompatible with extra-uterine life. (See Table of Monsters, p 178.)

Natural feebleness, from which cause the infant, though it may have passed through the labour, especially if that have been a tedious or difficult one, may not be viable.

The infant may perish after delivery from the presence in its system of diseases which have commenced before birth. It is now a fact well established that the foetus in utero is liable to many diseases, both functional and organic, which may lead to its death either before or after its delivery. It is to diseases leading to the death of the infant immediately after delivery that the attention of the medical jurist has to be directed.

Most of these intra-uterine diseases are of too obvious a character to be readily overlooked by the careful examiner. The greater portion of them are distinctly referable to inflammation, especially in the thoracic and abdominal cavities. Tubercles are not unusual in the foetal lungs. Suppuration of the thymus gland is said to be not unusual in the infant at birth. I have encountered two instances of it in practice, and one case of abscess in the anterior mediastinum. Dropsical effusions in several forms take place during fœtal life, sometimes, as in ascites, to such an extent as to interfere with delivery. Induration of the connective tissue, or skin-bound, has been noticed, though rarely at birth; and it would, by impeding the play of the respiratory muscles, prevent the establishment of breathing. Cutaneous eruptions in various forms have been noticed in the new-born infant. Structural and even malignant diseases have been encountered in the mature fœtus in the viscera and blood-vessels, such as hypertrophy of the heart, aneurismal enlargement of the heart and larger arteries; melanosis of the heart, lungs, and thymus gland, jaundice; cirrhosis of the liver; fungus hæmatodes, etc.

In 1869 I was indebted to Dr. Archibald Reith, of Aberdeen, for an opportunity of seeing one of those rare cases of disease of intra-uterine origin to which the attention of the profession in this country was called by Dr. West—namely, occlusion of the gall-duct. As in Dr. West's cases, the child at birth was deeply jaundiced. The navel, on the separation of the cord, exuded small quantities of blood from time to time, and the child sank from exhaustion on the tenth day. The occluded gall-duct was the only morbid change discoverable on inspection after death, which could throw any light on the case. The liver was congested, and the serous surfaces and areolar tissue of a deep yellow tinge.

A case which I visited for Dr. Polson, of Old Aberdeen, in 1875, was very similar to the above, but no *post mortem* examination was allowed.

The child may perish after delivery from occlusion of the mouth and nostrils by the membranes, occurring chiefly when the conception is of a sudden discharged *en masse*. Here, as respiration could not have taken place, no charge of infanticide could hold.

It has been alleged that the infant might perish after delivery in consequence of fractures or other injuries of the head produced by the child falling on the ground in a case of sudden or unexpected delivery. Here as previously noticed in the case of injuries alleged to be producible during the birth, various arguments have been advanced both for and against the likelihood or possibility of such an occurrence. But on this point our appeal must obviously be to facts, though these are of a somewhat conflicting character.

Those who contend for the unlikelihood, to say the least of it, of the child seriously suffering by its sudden expulsion from the

thors, refer, in confirmation of their opinions, to the facts collected by Klein, of Stuttgart. Taking advantage of his situation as a member of the Superior Council of Health, Klein caused a circular to be addressed to the midwifery practitioners of the kingdom of Wurtemberg, requiring reports of the cases of sudden expulsion of the fœtus which might be observed by them. Returns were made in 183 cases. Of these, 155 children were expelled while the mothers were in the upright position, 22 while sitting, and 6 when on the knees; 21 happened in the first labour. Of the whole number not one child died; no fracture of the bones took place, nor any other serious injury; two only suffered from temporary insensibility; and one had an external wound with suggilation over the right parietal bone.

Caspar objects to the loose way in which Klein's returns were collected, as rendering them utterly valueless, resting, as he affirms they did, upon statements not only of midwives but even of clergymen and monthly nurses, ranging over periods of years and tens of years, and adduced from mere memory.

In opposition to the returns of Klein, too, we have some actual cases of serious injury to the child's head from its sudden expulsion. Thus Landsberg gives a case of fracture of the left parietal bone, where the child was shot forth from a woman in labour while attempting to escape from a fire in her house. Dr. Swayne and Caspar have each given instances of the same occurrence. All of these, however, were in women who had previously borne children.

In these circumstances resort has been had to experiment in the case of still-born children after natural delivery. Thus, as reported by Lecieux, Chaussier found that on allowing such children to fall perpendicularly with the head foremost on a paved floor from a height of eighteen inches, a longitudinal or angular fracture was produced in one or both parietal bones in twelve out of fifteen cases; while the effect of a fall of thirty-six inches, out of an equal number of cases, was in twelve fracture of the parietal bones, in a few of these (the number not stated) the fracture extending into the frontal bone.

Similar trials were undertaken by Caspar, who employed fresh bodies for the purpose, which does not seem to have been the case in Chaussier's experiments. The result was that in no fewer than twenty-five new-born infants, dropped from a height of thirty inches, or that of the genitals of a woman in the standing posture, fractures were produced in all but one, and that a premature infant. In these twenty-four cases of fracture, the injury in twenty-two was confined to the temporal bones, in sixteen of them one of the bones being fractured, and in six cases both bones. In one of the remaining two cases both frontal bones, and in the other the occipital bone, were fractured.

These experiments of Chaussier and Caspar, coming in support of actual experience in the several published cases, set at rest the question as to the possibility, or even the likelihood, of fractures of the skull from the sudden expulsion of the fœtus in the standing position of the mother. The attendant circumstances would, however, in such cases point, with at least equal probability, to their purely accidental production, while they come in aid of the tests laid down previously for discriminating betwixt these and the effects of intentional violence. To these I need not recur.

It has been alleged that the infant might perish after delivery, from the rupture of the umbilical cord by the sudden expulsion and the consequent fall of the infant, in a rapid and unexpected delivery. Now, the liability of the cord to suffer in this way has been fully established, cases in point having been adduced by Chamberlayne and Caspar. As to the risk of fatal hemorrhage from the cord in such cases, opinions are divided, such hemorrhage not having been actually witnessed in any of the recorded cases. It should also be known that provision has been made by nature against such risk of hemorrhage after the division of the cord by the circumstance, pointed out by Virchow, that the umbilical arteries, where they leave the child's body, have their muscular coat unusually thick.

The appearance of unusual anæmia in the body, coupled with the absence of indications of death from any other cause, would be our guide to the determination of death in this way did the question arise.

The child after birth may perish by smothering in the bed-clothes; by the face falling into the mother's discharges; by being accidentally dropped into a privy when labour has come on suddenly at stool—a case of which is noticed in the eighth volume of the *Medical and Physical Journal*. The lady being ill with diarrhœa towards the close of pregnancy, was one day seized with labour pains on the night stool, and in a short time brought forth a child before she was able to rise and give the alarm. Such cases are not uncommon. A defence of this nature was set up on a trial for infanticide in Aberdeen some years ago, when the child was found, still in life, in a privy; but in this instance it was proved that the woman had been delivered in bed, and had subsequently thrown the infant into the privy.

In the number of the *Annales d'Hygiène* for April 1857, Robin and Tardieu have related a case of infanticide in which the mother alleged that the infant had fallen suddenly from her into a privy while she was sitting there at stool. The verification by them, however, of certain stains found on the front of her dress showed that the infant had been placed on her lap after its birth.

The most important varieties of suffocation are those occasioned by smothering in the bed-clothes or discharges, for, unlike that last noticed, they may happen after a first labour. Suffocation or drowning in the discharges will be generally recognised by the peculiar contents of the mouth and trachea. As to accidental smothering in the bed-clothes there is no possibility of distinguishing it from the same kind of death produced designedly.

Smothering by being overlaid may, it must be obvious, either be accidental or criminal, and we possess no means of distinguishing the one from the other. The term overlaying, however, of which we so frequently hear, in the case of infants found suddenly dead in bed, is but too often employed by practitioners as a mere cloak for ignorance or neglect of the proper investigation into the real cause of death; and hence in private families the nurse is often unjustly blamed for causing the death of the infant which may have perished from natural causes. I shall have to enter into the details of this subject afterwards. Meantime, I only remark here that in cases of this sort the practitioner should be aware how readily the infant might perish without the mother's complicity. In the supine position the mucus naturally found in the throat of the infant, if not removed, by getting into the trachea, would in some instances suffice to prevent the establishment of respiration, and cause the supervention of asphyxia, and certain positions of the child might produce the like effect.

LECTURE XVIII

INFANTICIDE—(*Concluded*).

DEATH FROM CRIMINAL CAUSES. By Omission—By Smothering—From want of suitable warmth—From want of suitable nourishment—From neglect to Ligature the Cord. Death by Commission. During Labour—By Punctures of the Fontanelles, Orbits, etc.—From Twisting the Neck on the Delivery of the Head—From Detruncation of the head—From Strangulation. After Delivery—From blows on the head and other parts—From Intra uterine Fractures—From Intra-uterine Dislocations—From Wounds of various parts—From Drowning—From Suffocation—From Strangulation—From Hanging—From Poisons. GENERAL REMARKS ON PROOFS OF INFANTICIDE.—POST MORTEM INSPECTION IN CASES OF INFANTICIDE.

HAVING in the last Lecture concluded what I had to say of those cases of death of the viable infant before the commencement of the mother's labour, during the delivery, and after its completion, which admit of explanation from purely natural causes, and which would, if satisfactorily proved or rendered probable, necessarily exclude the charge of infanticide against the mother, I now come to notice the class of cases in which such a charge usually arises—the so termed criminal causes of the infant's death.

We have seen above, and under Abortion, that it is not impossible to endanger the life or insure the death of the fœtus in utero before the commencement of labour. Such cases, however, can but rarely call for the notice of the medical jurist. Little less infrequent are the instances in which the infant has been intentionally destroyed while still in the maternal passages or only partially extruded, though, as we shall notice presently, cases of this sort are recorded. It is found, therefore, that it is at the completion of the labour that such criminal practices against the life of the infant are perpetrated in the great majority of instances.

In discussing the criminal causes of the child's death in charges of infanticide, it will not be very practicable to follow the arrangement of them into those of death by omission and death by commission, as has been done by some writers. It is not always possible in practice to distinguish, for instance, between the criminality or otherwise of the death of the infant from want of suitable warmth or nourishment, the absence or unsuitability of the ligature of the cord, or the failure to remove the infant from under the bed-clothes, or from the maternal discharges.

The means of destroying the child during the labour, which can be properly classed as acts of commission, besides being, as I have stated, few in number, can seldom become the subject of criminal procedure, as for the most part the assistance of a third party would be necessary to put them into execution, while a female, especially in her first labour, would rarely be possessed of the strength or presence of mind requisite to enable her to kill her own child while in the passages. Nevertheless, instances are not wanting of murder committed in this conjuncture by midwives, or even by the mother herself; and, besides, attempts have been made to impute such a crime by inflicting injuries on the body of a still-born child.

The means known to be resorted to for taking away the life of the infant during labour are the following, namely—Puncture of the fontanelles, orbit, or nucha, or even of the chest or belly; twisting of the neck after the delivery of the head; detruncation of the head; and strangulation.

Puncturing the head of the infant as soon as it has presented seems to have been at one time known to midwives and others. In one instance mentioned by Mahon a midwife was executed for the murder of several infants by plunging a needle through the fontanelles into the head while presenting during the labour. Belloc relates a similar case. Fatal injury to the brain is also said to have been caused by the intentional thrusting of needles or other sharp instruments through the nucha, the temples, the inner canthus of the eye, and even through the nostrils. In the same way the spinal cord has been injured and death caused by punctures betwixt the vertebræ. In the *Causes Célèbres* will be found the case of a woman who made a trade of destroying infants by acupuncture through the top of the spinal column and into the brain.

According to Fodéré the death of the infant has been caused by puncture of the heart through the walls of the chest. A sharp instrument has also been run down the throat and up the rectum. A case is recorded in the thirty-fifth volume of the *Edinburgh Medical and Surgical Journal* where the child was evidently destroyed in this way.

In connection with the subject of fatal punctures in the new-born infant, it may be well to point your attention to the possibility of their accidental production. Thus Dr Underwood has related the following interesting fact A gentlewoman informed him that one of her children, after long and incessant crying, fell into strong convulsions, the cause of which was only discovered after its death, when on the cap being taken off, a small pin was discovered sticking up to the head in the large fontanelle.

The points to be attended to in cases of this sort will fall to be discussed when we come to the subject of penetrating wounds.

Twisting the head on the vertebral column, on its first emergence, is a species of violence which kills the infant at once, and yet may elude the observation of the medical jurist unless he be specially on his guard against overlooking it In addition to an unusual degree of mobility of the neck, the distinguishing marks of this mode of death would be the presence of ecchymosis about the upper part of the spine, laceration of the spinal ligaments, displacement or fracture of the higher vertebræ, and injury to the spinal cord.

Proofs of death by detruncation can only be ascertained on the principles which apply to wounds generally The signs will be the more manifest the more tedious the process employed, and the more early begun before dissolution

Death by strangulation may take place during the birth of the infant, on the emergence of the head, or after the completion of the labour. In each case it is of importance to ascertain if the death had preceded or followed the establishment of respiration

The criminal causes of death by commission, after delivery, are as various in the instance of child-murder as in that of ordinary homicide The most usual means, however, are blows or other injuries about the head; incised wounds of the throat, punctures of the fontanelles, nucha, orbits, ear, or heart, drowning; suffocation; smothering; strangulation; hanging, and poisoning

As most of these different modes of death will fall afterwards to be discussed as separate topics, to avoid repetition I shall here only touch upon a few points which have a special and independent bearing upon the subject of infanticide, and to which I shall not have occasion to refer afterwards.

I need not repeat the cautions given under a former head against setting down fractures of the cranial bones as necessarily the effects of intentional violence after birth, cases of such injuries during labour having been adduced by Schmidt, Miessner, and

Siebold, from their practice; in circumstances, however, under which the tests formerly laid down would suffice for their discrimination.

In one of the instances related by Schmidt, the husband, while drunk, in falling struck the belly of his wife, by which the skull of the fœtus was fractured. The child, notwithstanding, was born alive, but soon died.

Another case happened in the lying-in hospital at Friburg. The woman was subject to hysterical fits, and about four weeks before delivery had a fall out of bed during a paroxysm of her illness. The child did not breathe on being born, but its movements showed that it was still alive. It had a large ecchymosis over the right parietal bone, corresponding with a fracture in the bone of about an inch in length.

Dr Montgomery relates two instances similar to the above, one of which occurred in his own practice.

Fractures of the long bones, previous to the commencement of labour, have been sometimes observed as the result of injuries sustained by the mother; but, in other instances, independent of any such cause, and apparently dependent on some defect in their composition.

Dr. Montgomery mentions a patient of his who had a fall from the second story of a house into the street when eight months pregnant. Labour came on that night and the child was born dead, with several of its bones broken.

A case is quoted by Duges, in which a pregnant woman fell on her belly, and caused a fracture of the leg of the child, which was born with the fracture complicated by wounds in the soft parts.

Marc reports a case in which all the bones of the limbs and several others were found fractured, the mother not having met with any accident, and having had an easy and quick labour. The child was born alive, and lived for some days.

Chaussier met with a similar case, in which the child survived for twenty-four hours, where, among a number of fractures, some were consolidated and others recent.

It is but right to warn you that cases which have been brought forward as instances of intra-uterine fractures, have been attributed, with more probability, to injuries sustained during the labour; an objection, however, which could only apply to the case of recent fractures, though it is strongly urged by Caspar.

I have no hesitation, with this author, in rejecting the alleged cases of wounds received by the fœtus in utero through the unwounded abdomen of the mother, though several such narratives have been admitted into works on medical jurisprudence.

We have sufficient evidence, however, of spontaneous dislocations in the fœtus.

Chaussier has related that a young, delicate, and nervous lady, in the ninth month of pregnancy, suddenly felt such violent and rapid movements of her child as nearly caused her to faint. The remainder of her time passed well, and the labour was easy; the child was pale and weak, and had a complete dislocation of the left forearm.

In another instance mentioned by Marc, there was found, in addition to congenital dislocations of both hip-joints, no less than seven other luxations.

Incised wounds of the throat in children present no peculiarities different from injuries of the same sort in adults, which we shall have to consider under homicide.

The special circumstances under which punctures of various parts of the infant's body may occur have been already adverted to.

Drowning has been resorted to as a means of destroying the new-born infant, an instance of which occurred in my practice a few years ago. Unless the child had previously lived to respire, this mode of death would leave no traces on the body. After the establishment of respiration, the plea of the drowning having been accidental will frequently be negatived by the circumstances of the case. Thus, marks of violence on the body would be incompatible with accidental drowning, as would the existence of a ligature on the cord, or its division by a cutting instrument. The nature of the fluid found in the stomach and air-passages might also throw light upon the matter. These and other points will come under our notice under death by drowning.

In cases of death by suffocation the marks of compression about the face, neck, and chest, or the presence of foreign matters, or of a plug in the nostrils, mouth, or throat, would at once indicate the criminal nature of the child's death.

Attention has been drawn by Tardieu and others to the frequency with which suffocation is resorted to with the view of taking away the life of the new-born infant. Thus, Tardieu states that, of 132 new-born infants examined by him in suspicious circumstances, he found that no fewer than 72, or more than one-half, had perished in this way. Fortunately, however, coincidently with the establishment of this fact, new means of discriminating such occurrences have been brought to light. These we must defer considering till an after-part of our course.

In connection with this mode of death the question arises, and is frequently put to the medical witness by the public prosecutor —Could the infant be accidentally smothered from the position it had assumed at the moment of birth if left unassisted? The plea set up in such cases is that the child, in the unconscious state of the mother at the time, had remained under the bed-clothes, its face against the bed, and the mouth and nostrils thus deprived of the access of air, and, it may be, buried in the discharges of liquor amnii or blood

All this, it is needless to say, is possible, and may, as already admitted, render it occasionally difficult to discriminate positively between omission and commission; but to render the hypothesis feasible the child must be assumed to have retained its position for some time, and the instinct of self-preservation further assumed to have been too weak to permit it to turn its head so far as to allow it to cry or respire. If in such a case the mother was too insensible to attend to her infant, the cord should not be found divided so as to interrupt the placental circulation, and no air should be found in the infant's lungs

Strangulation is a not unusual mode of child-murder But in this case, though the proof of the child's having died in this way is not difficult to be obtained, the mothers not unfrequently endeavour to obviate the charge of criminality by one or other of the following pleas. Thus in some German cases lately reported, to explain the marks left on the neck and the indications of asphyxia generally, the mother stated that on the birth of the infant's head she had grasped the neck with her hands to facilitate the subsequent delivery of the body, and thus unintentionally strangled the child.

A plea of this sort was set up in a case tried in the Circuit Court in Aberdeen in April 1873.

For obvious reasons, however, no weight could be properly attached to such an explanation, which would be negatived if the child were found to have respired.

A plea of a more important kind has been occasionally advanced to account for this mode of death. Thus, as formerly noticed, it has happened, though rarely, that in consequence of the umbilical cord being wound round the neck, the child has died during or immediately after birth, and hence the question has arisen whether such a mark could be left by it on the neck as occurs in cases of intentional strangulation, a point already touched upon. The impossibility of this has been argued for Thus Klein states as the result of extensive experience that he has never met with an instance in which ecchymoses or any other marks have been produced by the cord under the circumstances referred to; and with this the experience of midwifery practitioners in general will be found to agree, a result which I have repeatedly verified in actual practice.

On the other hand it must be conceded that Taufheb has recorded some cases in which these appearances were actually observed. Other instances have been collected by Dr Taylor in which ecchymoses have been witnessed on the neck from this cause, though he justly doubts whether the cord in an ordinary labour could produce any but slight and partial injury of this kind on the infant's neck. We have undoubtedly no proof that ruffling or laceration of the skin, severe ecchymoses, or injury of the deep-seated parts of the neck, such as a ligature often causes, could be actually produced by the umbilical cord.

Occasionally the discovery of the ligature still around the neck removes all ambiguity, as was the case in the instance of a woman tried at Aberdeen in 1856, who had strangled her child with a dish-cloth.

The proofs of death by strangulation will come before us afterwards.

Hanging as a form of infanticide is rarely had recourse to, and presents no points requiring special notice in this part of our course.

Poisoning in new-born infants will be noticed in this place only for the purpose of bringing under your view certain appearances which, according to Billard and others, are sometimes found in the oesophagus, stomach, and intestines, which might be mistaken for the effects of certain poisons of the irritant class The internal surface of the oesophagus is often injected in new-born children after death, and it assumes the forms of ramification of vessels or of longitudinal striae.

In the stomach, ulcerations, attended with the collection of a brown or blackish bloody fluid, are sometimes discovered, which might give rise to the suspicion of poisoning The children, too, in whom these ulcerations are found are not unfrequently fat and plump, the ulcers being in all probability of only a few days' standing

Similar appearances have been found in the intestines, giving rise to similar suspicions, while they afford sufficient data to account for the death of the child from natural causes

A case of this kind, to which I shall have occasion to refer afterwards, occurred in my practice some years ago, in which superficial ulcers in the mouth and stomach were observed in an instance of the suspected poisoning of a new-born infant.

I cannot do better now, in concluding the lengthened notice I have been compelled to bestow on the subject of infanticide, than give you a few directions for the systematic conduct of the medico-legal inspection of the infant.

The medical jurist, when called to inspect an infant suspected to have been the victim of foul play, ought at the outset to make himself acquainted with all the particulars of the case—the place where the child was found, the circumstances attending its removal thence, and the facts relative to the suspected party, if suspicion rests upon any one. He should, if possible, visit the place where the infant had been discovered. Information may thus be obtained which may throw important light upon the position of the accused party.

He should then examine the wrappings of the child, if there be any; the marks upon them, if such there are; the thread with which they had been sewed; the character of the ligature, if any, around the cord, etc. In this way the mother is sometimes discovered and brought to trial

Thus in one case tried in Aberdeen, suspicion having fallen upon the mother, the connection betwixt her and the child was established by the correspondence between a piece of brown cloth found around the child and the remainder of the same cloth which was discovered in her apartment

In another case, also tried in Aberdeen, a servant swore to an apron found round the infant as having belonged to her mistress, who had exposed her illegitimate child.

These preliminaries having been attended to, the examiner should proceed to the *external* inspection of the infant's body, noting—

(1) Its general conformation, and especially any defect or vice which might affect its viability.

(2) Its degree of freshness or putridity.

(3) The colour of the skin

(4) The degree of adhesion of the cuticle and of the nails.

(5.) The extent of the saponification, if it has commenced, or of the emphysema, if gases are generated under the skin, etc.

(6.) The natural openings should be examined, as to their being pervious or otherwise, with the discharges which may have proceeded from them

(7.) If any punctures, incised wounds, contusions, or ecchymoses exist, their situation, extent, and depth should be specially noted.

(8) The body should be weighed and measured, observing with what point of the abdomen the centre of its length corresponds

(9) The state of the navel should be particularly attended to, observing, if any part of the cord remains attached to the belly, whether it is fresh, or shrivelled and dry, or free or not from inflammation and vascularity; whether it is spare or plump, whether it has been tied or not; if tied, at what distance from the navel; the degree of torsion of the remains of the cord, its translucence, the volume and course of its vessels, if they contain blood, or if any can be expressed from them; whether it has been cut through or torn, and if the former, whether with a blunt or sharp instrument.

(10) If the placenta is found, the divided points of the cord should be compared, to see if they correspond, and the length of the remains of the cord, both placental and fœtal, should be measured.

An illustration of the importance of these directions presented itself in the case of a woman arraigned for trial in Aberdeen some years ago. The child was found dead with a deep wound across the throat. To account for this, a practitioner interested in the woman's acquittal suggested that the counsel should be instructed to urge that the throat had been cut by her in dividing the cord as it lay across the child's neck. Unfortunately for the validity of this plea, the divided part of the cord would have required to be at seven inches from the navel, whereas in my report it was stated that its free extremity was only three inches from the child's belly.

(11) The sebaceous coating, if present, should be looked for chiefly in the armpits, groins, and hams Its presence shows that no care had been taken, by washing, for the child's preservation

(12) The hairs should be noticed, as to their colour, length, and quantity.

This external general inspection completed, the examiner should proceed to the special inspection, beginning with—

(1.) The head. Ascertaining its form and dimensions in different directions; carefully removing the hairs and examining the scalp; dividing the scalp by a crucial incision, or one from ear to ear; ascertaining the state of the internal surface of the scalp, of the bones and sutures, and the size and appearance of the fontanelles; removing the skull-cap in the usual direction with a stout scissors, examining the brain in situ, and removing it along with the medulla oblongata, in order to inspect the top of the spine and the base of the skull.

(2.) The front of the neck should then be attentively looked at for any grooves caused by ligatures, ecchymoses, or abrasions, after which the larynx and vertebral column may be inspected.

(3) The cavity of the mouth should now be laid open, to ascertain if any plug had been introduced and left there, or if any traces of irritants or corrosives appear.

(4.) To ascertain the state of the chest, the clavicles should be divided with a scissors, avoiding the subclavian vessels, and afterwards the cartilages of the ribs, folding down the sternum and leaving it attached to the abdominal parietes. The situation and volume of the pectoral viscera can now be noted, as well as the state of fulness or vacuity of their vessels. It should now be observed whether the lungs cover the pericardium or be unexpanded and deep in the chest; whether their margins are sharp or rounded; what is their colour and consistence, whether uniform or mottled; whether their capillaries are injected or not; whether they are fresh, emphysematous, or putrid. Their appearance can be compared with that of the thymus gland, and the appearance of that gland noticed. The pericardium should now be opened, and its appearance externally and internally looked at; the thymus gland turned up, the left lung pushed to the right, and the state of the ductus arteriosus ascertained. After the application of double ligatures to the venæ cavæ, the aorta, pulmonary artery, and the trachea, the lungs and thymus gland should be removed from below upwards, and the docimasia pulmonum (Hydrostatic test) practised. The heart should next be opened, to ascertain the quantity and distribution of the blood in its interior, and the state of the foramen ovale; the heart, lungs, and thymus gland should then be separated from each other, after securing their connecting vessels with double ligatures; the lungs weighed and their weight compared with that of the body; note taken whether they float or sink—whether in whole or in part, and whether buoyantly or not—when thrown into water; and, after cutting them into fragments, what portions sink and what float; if the former, whether they are sound or diseased, and what the disease. On handling and cutting the lungs, it should be observed whether they have a spongy or solid feeling, and whether they crepitate or not. By compressing the fragments in air, the amount of blood or other fluid which they may contain can be ascertained, while by doing so under water the presence or absence of air can be discovered; and if they contain air, the size of the air-bubbles given out will assist in the discrimination as to whether it has been contained in the air-cells or in the subpleural or interlobular areolar tissue, and their odour, if fetid, will serve to characterise putrid lungs.

(5) The best mode of opening the abdomen, so as not to interfere with the umbilical vessels, is to remove the sternum at the base of the chest, to carry an incision from the xyphoid cartilage to a point a little above the umbilicus, to prolong the incision downwards and outwards at a little distance from the navel to the anterior superior spinous process of the ilium, and from thence across the pubes to meet the continued incision on the opposite side. The examiner should now search the abdomen for effused blood and sanguinolent serum, or other effused fluids, for marks of putrefaction; for ruptures of the liver, or ecchymoses indicative of effused blood in its interior; for rupture or softening of the spleen. The state of the umbilical vessels should be noted, whether open or contracted, full or empty, the state of the stomach, whether it contains milk or other alimentary matters, or mucus containing air-bubbles; and in what part of the intestines the meconium, if present, is to be found, or if they contain air. The exploration of the bladder, kidneys, and genitals, external and internal, completes this part of the examination.

(6) The spine should be explored throughout.

(7.) To complete the inspection it only remains for the examinator to ascertain whether any ecchymoses exist on the trunk or limbs, for this purpose making free incisions in the latter, and to turn his attention to the bones, in order to learn the state of their development as explained formerly under Age.

LECTURE XIX.

INSANITY

PRELIMINARY REMARKS — Difficulties inherent in the Subject—Difficulties superadded to it—Legal Jealousy of Medical Testimony—Occasions for the Inquiry into the State of the Insane—Duty of the Medical Practitioner in such cases—Failures in the Medical Proof—Classification of Insanity

THE subject of insanity, both in its general and professional aspects, is one of no ordinary difficulty—a difficulty which is enhanced when it comes to be considered medico-legally. When we come to close quarters with the study, we encounter views and opinions which are neither clearly expressed nor consistent with each other, and which, consequently, are neither deserving of, nor likely speedily to receive general assent. While medical inquirers have so far overcome the obstacles in their way as to have made an approach to several points of common agreement, both as to the true place of insanity, as it presents itself to their notice, and as to the more prominent of the phases which they find it to assume, the views regarding these points entertained by the legal profession, and still more by the general public, are to a large extent of a vague and unsettled character. Much has therefore to be accomplished before common ground can be adopted by the educated part of the community, the lawyers, and the medical profession, in order to place the whole subject in a better position than it has yet attained. Some antiquated notions have to be got rid of, the public and the legal authorities must be brought to look upon its problems from a different and wider point of view than they have hitherto done, while the leaders of professional opinion must be prepared on several points to show that the decisions they have arrived at are based on evidence of a more tangible and unchallengeable character than they have yet succeeded in furnishing. It has still to be settled by the medical psychologist whether he is prepared to adopt exclusively the psychical or the somatic theory of insanity, or to fall back on the intermediate one; while the progress of observation of the insane has shown that the older notions as to the purely mental character of the disease cannot be maintained, and professional opinion has been steadily settling towards the corporeal seat of the affection in question. Before adopting this latter hypothesis, fuller proof of its substantial character has to be offered than has as yet been advanced by the psychologist. It is not enough for him to point in evidence to certain morbid appearances presented by the nervous centres in the insane, which he can connect with their previous mental aberrations, morbid changes which he is compelled to admit may, on the one hand, be occasionally absent in the body in cases of undoubted insanity; and, on the other hand, may not unfrequently be present where previous insanity had not been known to exist. To carry out views which, if adopted in their exclusive form, would change the current of opinion, legal and general, and alter the whole face of society, it would be necessary that these should be either admittedly based on evidence without a flaw, and such as were unquestionably entitled to general assent. Meantime we appear to be shut up to the conclusion of those who are disposed to trace the existence of insanity to the mutual action and reaction of the mental and corporeal functions, a conclusion which they believe to be the one most consistent with its observed phenomena, and the best fitted to meet alike the requirements of enlightened opinion, and the interests of this unfortunate class of persons. How far this is to be received as satisfactory in all respects it is not for me to say.

To turn to the more urgent and practical part of the subject as it presents itself to the medical practitioner and to the expert, whose duties in relation to the insane not unfrequently meet and coincide, I go on to remark that, while in not a few of its broader aspects and confirmed shapes, insanity, when present, admits of ready recognition and appreciation, this is not invariably the case in actual practice. Neither the presence of this condition, nor the form the disorder may have assumed, is always found to be distinctly appreciable, or clearly to be traced out. The contrasted conditions of sanity and insanity are sometimes seen to be separated by a line of demarcation of so narrow and intangible a kind, that it may be difficult or impossible satisfactorily to fix their respective boundaries; while again, when we have been able to succeed in recognising the presence of actual insanity, the forms which it may present, however occasionally broadly divergent, at times actually assimilate so closely that their accurate discrimination may puzzle and confuse the most expert enced observer. In the want of such a guide for his direction as would be afforded by some recognised and clear standard of mental capacity, he may fail to detect the disorder in certain of its more obscure forms, or, it may even be, in its more confirmed stages. Hence his acknowledged inability at times to appreciate discriminatively the outward manifestations of insanity where it undoubtedly exists, and to some extent controls the conduct of the individual under examination Even with such a test, were we supplied with it, the disorder might, in some few instances, escape our recognition, from our inability to reach the hidden motives which dominate the conduct and determine the character of an outward manifestation or action

To these difficulties, inherent to a large extent in the subject in the present state of our science, others have to be added which admit of less palliation. Viewing insanity from its practical side, while not insisting on the condition in question being strictly defined, or its position amongst states closely bordering on it being clearly marked off, and though not even at one as to the most reliable tests of its actual existence in every instance, medical men are pretty generally agreed as to the leading forms which it is apt to assume, however differently they may choose to denominate these forms The lawyers, on the contrary, approaching the subject theoretically, assume tests of insanity not only of too limited and narrow a sort to take in all the cases considered by medical authors as instances of the disorder, but also some which are inapplicable to cases admitted to be such by the lawyers themselves This circumstance has led the latter not only to restrict the number of the forms of insanity recognised by medical men, but also to apply different designations from ours to the forms of it which they have themselves admitted

Not only are fewer forms of insanity admitted by the lawyers than are recognised by the profession, and those admitted by them differently denominated, but the tests to which they trust in proof of its actual existence, are not by the medical authorities held to be sufficient to meet these requirements In theory, at least, the legal body professes to regard the testimony of the medical witness on the trial of the insane as of less importance than that of non-professional persons who have had opportunities of taking note of the conduct of the party on trial, holding that the employment of medical men in some such trials is a useless and unnecessary innovation, not originally contemplated, and which ought to be discouraged in practice as much as possible; and the Lunacy Regulation Act of 1862, while modifying the former legal procedure in certain cases, gives the option to courts of law to dispense with medical evidence altogether in some specified instances, at their own discretion. It further appears to be a settled point in legal practice, that in no case are the jury expected to found their decision on the opinions advanced by the medical witness. It is ruled that he can only influence the jury when he can clearly substantiate the facts from which he deduces his opinion, and exhibit to them the reasons for that opinion.

In corroboration of this, at the meeting of the British Medical Association at Sheffield, in August 1876, Dr. Bucknell called attention to a recent charge by Lord Moncreiff, in which it was laid down that soundness or unsoundness of mind was not to be judged of as a matter of science, but by the ordinary rules of daily life; the jury being as good judges as any doctor, whether a man whom they might have met in daily life was sane or not. Dr Bucknell also quoted the opinions of the late Lord Westbury to the same effect.

From all this it will be seen that the opinion of the medical man, in occasions of the sort we have been considering, is not always of so important and indispensable a kind as it has but too frequently been considered by the profession; while it explains to us the circumstance, so often witnessed in the records of our courts of law, of the notorious failures of eminent medical men, familiar with the management of the insane, to influence the bench and the jury. Nor, taking the facts regarding the rules of legal procedure, as I have stated them, is it to be wondered at that evidence tendered by the profession, in accordance with received medical principles, from not being appreciated or understood by the parties in the conduct of the case, should be hesitatingly received, or entirely set aside, and that, even when such evidence cannot be refused—as where it has been duly corroborated, and of a sufficiently weighty sort—there is a *vis inertiæ* to be overcome, on the part of jurors, in cases of life and death, especially when called on to admit the full force of proof, tending not to absolve but to criminate the perpetrators of what in a sane person amounts to a grievous crime. On the other hand, our judges are slow to admit the force of evidence to the opposite effect, and call for tests of irresponsibility, for which we should look in vain in the case of the vast majority of the ordinary inmates of our lunatic asylums All this will come out with sufficient clearness as we proceed.

The question of insanity comes before the law-courts—

I. In criminal causes, where it is pleaded that the prisoner was insane when he committed the crime, and therefore was irresponsible; and that he is insane at the time of the trial, and therefore unfit to give instructions for his defence.

II. In civil causes, when it is sought to set aside some act done or contract entered into by a person alleged to have been insane at the time; and when it is sought to supersede a person in the management of his affairs on the ground of his insanity and consequent incapacity.

III In either civil or criminal causes, when it is objected to a witness that he is insane; that he was insane at the time of the occurrence of the events to which he is to testify; or that he has had a fit of insanity between these events and the trial, which objection is received as valid in Scottish but not in English practice

The decision of the insanity of the party on these occasions is made to rest on different principles in criminal and civil inquiries. In civil inquiries, the tests required and acted on by the legal and medical practitioners are nearly, if not entirely, the same; and hence the two are not so likely to come into collision with each other as in the case of criminal proceedings, where the divergence I have pointed out betwixt the tests relied on by the two professions is apt to occur.

In criminal charges, in law, the *onus probandi* lies upon the panel; and to amount to an exculpation for crime the insanity must be shown to have existed at the time of the act, though it need not be proved to have existed either before or afterwards If, however, there is no direct evidence applicable to this period, the situation of the panel, before or after committing the act, and the general nature of his malady, will form the grounds of determination

In not a few instances the insanity of the prisoner is so evident, and his state so generally known, that the task of the medical jurist will be a very easy one. But cases constantly occur of a very different sort, when the mental disorder, though existing, and directing the actions, will, from its partial development, and less obvious manifestation, require, on the part of the medical examiner, much caution, sagacity, and experience for its successful elucidation

Here, if anywhere, an important duty devolves on the medical witness. Here, if anywhere, he should carefully define, conscientiously feel, and thoroughly understand the testimony he gives, that testimony should be given in a perspicuous manner, be founded on well-established facts which he should be able to detail, and be clear of any hypothetical deductions or ill-established opinions; and he ought to be prepared to explain clearly the reasons which influenced his own mind in coming to the decision at which he may have arrived.

In deciding in court on the state of a criminal believed to be insane, much in actual practice depends on the sagacity of the counsel in instituting the proper inquiries, and still more on the clearness with which the medical evidence is adduced. If the medical witness is able to exhibit, from the conversation, actions, or writings of the prisoner, unequivocal proofs of his derangement, negative evidence will be of little avail either to strengthen or overturn such well-founded illustration. In a question of this sort, however, the most experienced physician, who has seen insanity in all its forms and viewed its more delicate shades, must adapt his testimony to the comprehension and feelings of the parties who are to appreciate his deposition. Their belief of the alleged insanity must be the test by which his scientific opinion is to be established. That which may be deemed by the medical witness clear and unequivocal madness may not hit the sense of the legal gentlemen, nor carry conviction to the jury. To the neglect of such attention to the requirements of our courts of law it has been owing that practitioners who have exclusively devoted their time and skill to patients of this class have not in general, contrary to what might have been expected, made the best appearance in our courts of law in insane cases; while medical jurists have had greater stress laid upon their testimony, from its greater appropriateness to the particular occasion, and its fitting in better with the requirements demanded of them.

The subject of insanity generally does not come within my province—a topic which I must presume to be one which has elsewhere occupied your attention. Without, however, laying down a tolerably full and accurate outline of the different varieties of this disorder—such as forms the basis of the existing classifications—the legal consequences of these varied forms could not be made intelligible. To these, therefore, I now proceed.

Notwithstanding the various views which prevail, both outside and inside the profession, as to the nature of insanity generally, our classifications, whether medical or otherwise, continue to be based on its mental manifestations. Directing our attention to these as furnishing the received classifications of the insane, we find that this disorder manifests its presence, when sufficiently characterised, in the loss of that power which is ordinarily possessed by the individual in his sane state of controlling the chain of associations which arise in his mind. He is no longer able, as before, to call up or dismiss at his pleasure any particular impression he may desire. He cannot now arrest or regulate the succession of his thoughts, as they unfold themselves, one after the other, within him. Consciousness, memory, perception, abstraction, imagination, judgment, are one or all more or less altered from their normal state, whether by excess or defect, and the mind has lost its natural balance.

It would limit our views too much, however, were we to confine insanity entirely to this derangement of the intellectual faculties, as if no other part of the mental constitution could be affected by bodily disorders. The human being is endowed with certain moral powers, comprising the various sentiments, propensities, and affections, which, like the intellect, being connected with the brain, are necessarily affected by pathological conditions of that organ.

This being admitted, it follows that the classification of the insane, founded on these views, fully meets the requirements of the medical practitioner so far as he is at present fitted to judge, recognising, as it does, a distinction amongst the forms of insanity, as the disorder is found to manifest itself mainly, if not entirely, in the intellect in one instance, and the will in another. I have said mainly if not entirely in the intellect in one case, and the will in another; and this I have done for several reasons. In the first place, in our fondness for a purely philosophical classification we must not lose sight of the fact that in practice it is not unfrequently the case that we are not in a very favourable position for discriminating between the play of the one set of faculties and the other, and for saying with certainty to which of these the disorder is confined in every given case, even were we to admit (which we are not prepared to do) that the intellect can be disordered while the moral faculties continue wholly sound, and *vice versa*. Few, I imagine, would be disposed to deny that in the healthy state of the mind the closest connection subsists between the intellectual and the moral powers; the mutual dependence of the tone and vigour of the one on the outward manifestations of the other being well understood in metaphysical science, affording, as it does, a ready clue for the elucidation of much of the diversities of character which are observed to prevail amongst mankind in general; while a careful consideration of them frequently leads us to a just appreciation of the variety of discordant results which are noticeable in the mass, when actuated by motives, outwardly, at least, apparently alike. The same mutual dependence of the two parts of the mental constitution, it is obvious, must hold true in disease as in health, but with this difference, that in the former case the difficulties in the way of our correct observation and accurate appreciation of psychical peculiarities are increased to a very great extent.

This being the case, it is easy to perceive how, in the next place, while it is generally admitted amongst medical writers that there are contrasted and tolerably well-marked forms of insanity, in which the prevailing alienation of mind is pretty clearly traceable in one instance to the intellectual, and in the other to the moral powers, it is certain that some of our highest authorities hold it as equally evident that there can be no serious disorder in the one set of faculties without the other participating in such disorder, to some appreciable extent at least; and that it is usually, if not invariably, the fact that, in those instances in which the disease has assumed the form of the so-termed moral insanity, the intellect, though apparently sound and unaffected, or but little disordered, may in reality be discovered to be the primary seat of the morbid impression, or at least to participate in the disorder to some extent, and *vice versa* Lastly, as one other reason for not pressing the distinction betwixt intellectual and moral disorder too far, or too exclusively, it is to be remembered that such a distinction has, up to the present period, been altogether denied by our law authorities—a point to the consideration of which we shall have to return in the sequel.

Keeping these explanations in view, I now proceed to the classifications of mental diseases adopted by medical and medico-legal authors, which, though varying not a little in form, present but few substantial diversities. In doing so it will, I think, simplify the task if I follow, with some modifications, the arrangement suggested by Dr Ray, based upon that of Pinel as modified by Esquirol. After what I have said, it is scarcely necessary to warn you that this arrangement, though sufficiently accurate for our purpose, is not to be considered as rigorously correct, or that any classification which could be proposed can, in the present state of our knowledge, be reasonably expected to be altogether free from obvious defects

The various diseases usually included in the general term "insanity," or mental derangement, are by Dr Ray arranged under two divisions, founded on two very different conditions of the brain—the first being a want of its ordinary development in the early period of life; the second, some lesion of its structure, or arrest of its functions, subsequent to its ordinary development. In the former of these divisions we have idiocy and imbecility, differing from each other in degree. The various affections embraced in the latter general division are arranged under two subdivisions, mania and dementia, distinguished by the contrast they present in the energy and tone of the mental manifestations. Mania, the first of these subdivisions, is characterised by an exaltation of the faculties, and may be confined to the intellectual or to the moral powers, or it may involve them both, and these powers may be generally or partially deranged. Dementia, the second of these subdivisions, depends on a more or less complete enfeeblement of the faculties, and may be consecutive to injury of the brain, to mania, or to some other disease, or it may be connected with the decay of old age.

This arrangement of mental disorders will be best understood by a glance at the tabular view I have drawn out for your inspection:—

CLASSIFICATION OF INSANITY
(RAY)

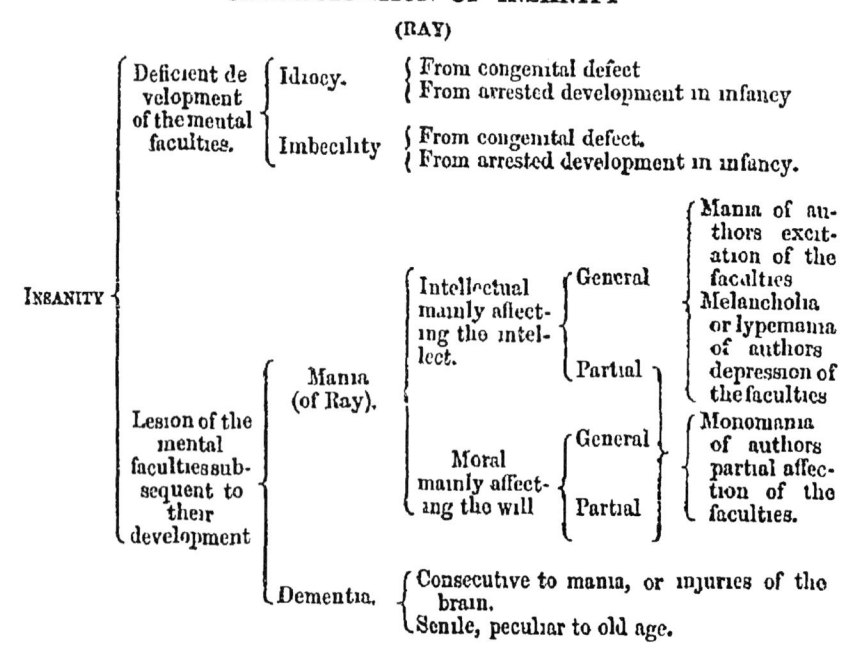

INSANITY
- Deficient development of the mental faculties.
  - Idiocy.
    - From congenital defect.
    - From arrested development in infancy.
  - Imbecility.
    - From congenital defect.
    - From arrested development in infancy.
- Lesion of the mental faculties subsequent to their development.
  - Mania (of Ray).
    - Intellectual mainly affecting the intellect.
      - General
      - Partial
    - Moral mainly affecting the will.
      - General
      - Partial
    - Mania of authors, excitation of the faculties.
    - Melancholia or lypemania of authors, depression of the faculties.
    - Monomania of authors, partial affection of the faculties.
  - Dementia.
    - Consecutive to mania, or injuries of the brain.
    - Senile, peculiar to old age.

The most important defect of Dr. Ray's scheme is the fusing together of the mania and melancholia of other writers. This would be rectified by the division of his general intellectual mania into these two well-established forms of insanity.

I have now to notice the nomenclature in use amongst legal writers

The law of England recognises two states of mental disorder or alienation—dementia naturalis, corresponding to imbecility and idiocy; and dementia adventitia vel accidentalis, or lunacy, embracing the mania, melancholia, and monomania of medical writers Besides the terms idiocy and lunacy, employed by lawyers in the sense we have explained, the term unsound mind (*non compos mentis*) is frequently employed in legal proceedings, not in reference to any particular form of insanity, but to a state of mental incapacity in the person for the management of his affairs, arising from some morbid condition of the intellect

In Scotch law the word "lunacy" was introduced for the first time by modern statutes, and that as a general term, including idiocy. "Physicians," says Mr Bell, " have distinguished, both by their symptoms and effects, many classes of this unhappy malady, but in law they are all reduced to two—namely, idiocy and furiosity.

It will thus be perceived that, while recognising generally the forms of insanity laid down by medical authors, the lawyers refuse to admit the existence of a form of disorder manifested solely, or almost entirely, by defective moral perceptions

LECTURE XX

INSANITY—*(Continued).*

VARIOUS FORMS OF INSANE DISORDERS—Idiocy—Imbecility—Legal Consequences of Idiocy and Imbecility in Criminal Cases—Tests of Mental Incapacity in Civil Cases—Forms of Legal Procedure—Cognition and Inquest—Interdiction—Incapacity for making a Valid Will—Incapacity for entering into a Valid Marriage—Circumstances justifying Personal Restraint.

RETURNING to Dr. Ray's scheme as admitting of being slightly modified by us, and entering on the detailed consideration of the different varieties of mental disorder, it will be seen that his first division includes all those cases in which the faculties of the mind have suffered arrest at birth, or in early life. This takes in idiocy and imbecility, which differ only in degree—the idiot being the more, and the imbecile the less imperfectly rational being.

I. Of idiocy. Idiocy may result either from congenital defect or from arrest of the faculties in infancy or childhood. In every such case, therefore, the powers of the mind are inferior to those of ordinarily endowed persons; but it would be a great mistake to suppose that all idiots are equally defective. It has been asserted with truth that there is even more diversity in the characters of the idiotic and imbecile than in those of the sound in mind, a fact which ought never to be overlooked in judging of the state of such persons. The medical man will often be assisted in judging of the extent to which this mental deficiency actually exists in certain individuals of this class by learning something of their physical history. Thus, when the idiocy is congenital, it is usually more complete than when it is subsequently acquired from the premature arrest of the bodily and mental powers, as yet but little developed. In these circumstances the ideas will have a greater range, and the senses be more perfect, than in congenital idiocy, while the bodily functions will be more perfectly performed. I have lately had a favourable opportunity of studying one of the lowest forms of congenital idiocy. This person (whom I had known from birth up to his ninth year, when he died) had a bodily organisation little superior to that of a vegetable, being destitute of the power of locomotion. He could not lift his own hands, not even his fingers, and remained in the position in which he was laid, which was the horizontal one, for he could not maintain himself erect. The functions of organic life even were imperfectly performed in this being. He was deaf and dumb, and the only manifestation of mind which he was known to possess was just enough of perception to distinguish the person who usually took care of him. In 1841 I had occasion to visit and report to the Crown on the case of an adult at Cairnie (Aberdeenshire), but partially raised above the same condition. The man, about twenty-four years of age, seemed almost insensible to cold; for though in winter, his dress consisted only of a cotton vest with short sleeves, to which was attached a woollen petticoat reaching but a little below the knees. At the visit he was slubbering in a dish of oatmeal porridge, the contents of which he was scattering about him. In a corner he had collected fragments of crockery and glass, to which he appeared to attach not a little value. When a watch was held up before him, he darted across the room to seize it, with an incoherent yell of delight. The use of articulate sounds he had never acquired.

Various grades of mental deficiency, intermediate betwixt idiocy and imbecility, described by Orfila as semi-imbeciles, are encountered in the Cretins and semi-Cretins of Alpine countries.

There is frequently something faulty in the formation of the head and the position of the eyes of idiots, more or less marked in proportion to the grade of deficiency of mind. Their mouth is gaping, and allows the saliva to escape; their lips are thick; their gums are unhealthy, and their teeth soon decay; some, as we have seen, are deaf and dumb or blind; many are incapable of perceiving odours, and swallow indiscriminately whatever kind of food is placed before them; their sensibility, physical and moral, is obtuse, and they are deficient in sensation, perception, and attention. Some are in constant motion; some laugh, others weep, and occasionally they are very prone to mischief.

Idiocy sometimes prevails in families, and is often conjoined with paralysis or epilepsy.

The peculiar physiognomy so frequently characteristic of well-marked idiocy is well brought out in the drawings in Sir Alexander Morrison's work on *Mental Diseases*, and those of Cretins in Orfila's *Atlas*.

II. Imbecility. From the slighter shades of idiocy up to

perfect sanity there are shades of mind which afford ample scope for discussion and litigation. Imbecility, like idiocy, may be congenital or acquired, and, like it, may exist to a greater or less extent in different persons. Imbecility, however, differs from idiocy in this circumstance, that while in the latter there is an utter destitution of everything like reason, the subjects of the former possess some intellectual capacity, though infinitely less than that possessed by the great mass of mankind. Imbeciles are capable of partial education. Their moral and intellectual character is found to vary greatly. While some are fickle and capricious; others show perseverance in the pursuit of a favourite object, while in some it is difficult to engage the attention, in others it is impossible to divert it from their own crotchets. Some imbeciles engage in certain occupations, and manage to take care of themselves and their property, though frequently obliged to others for advice and assistance; they want forethought, and steady and durable attention, and their uneasy and restless disposition unfits them for steady employment. They are subject to violent emotions, a propensity to music or to mimicry is often shown by them; they are likewise frequently given to steal, have occasionally committed murder, and are sometimes made the instruments of crime by others. Houses and stacks of corn have been burned in this way.

The great difficulty attending these cases in medico-legal practice is to trace out the limits whereby persons of this class are distinguished from others who are competent to regulate their social and moral conduct. In criminal trials, there is reason to believe that imbeciles have often been found guilty where they were really not responsible; and in civil suits the decision of the validity of acts done by the imbecile has sometimes turned upon points of which it is difficult to perceive the force or bearing on the question of the capacity of the individual.

This brings us to the next point I proposed to consider— namely, the medico-legal relations of idiocy and imbecility, the two forms of mental deficiency we have just discussed. We shall first consider these states of mind in connection with criminal, and secondly with civil law.

First. Of idiocy and imbecility as a defence against criminal charges. The general principles that determine the legal relations of idiocy are fortunately so obvious, and the fact of its existence —at least in its higher grades—is so easily established, that little occasion has been afforded for doubt or diversity of opinion on these points When, however, this state presents itself in a much less marked degree, and more especially when cases of imbecility come to be the subjects of judicial investigations, ample room is afforded for both. Had it been laid down by the law that the mere existence of idiocy or imbecility exempted the person so affected from punishment, then the task of deciding who were and who were not the proper subjects for punishment would have been comparatively easy This, however, is not the case. Insanity, as such, whatever its form, does not of itself exempt from punishment "To amount to a complete bar to punishment, the insanity, either at the time of committing the crime or of the trial, must," says Mr Alison, "have been of such a kind as entirely deprived him of the use of reason as applied to the act in question, and the knowledge that he was doing wrong in committing it"

Now, if the statements which I have laid before you regarding the mental capacity of the mass of idiots and imbeciles be correct, it is evident that they cannot in strict justice be considered responsible for their actions They evidently want some one or more of the elements which are requisite for judging betwixt right and wrong. To do this, not only must the intellect be developed sufficiently to acquaint the individual with the existence of external objects, and with some of their relations, but the moral powers must be strong enough and sound enough to furnish then specific incentives to pursue that course of conduct of which the intellect has already approved. Crime cannot justly be imputed where there has been neither intention to do nor consciousness of having done any injury The fear of punishment can have no control over the mind of the person whose intellect is incapable of discerning the connection between crime and the punishment attached to it It is not enough to say, that because such an one labours under no delusion, that because he has sufficient intelligence to perform the inferior kinds of employment, observation alone might have made him acquainted with the consequences of criminal acts The error in thus reasoning arises from the habit of estimating the strength and extent of the moral faculties by the ability to go through certain mechanical duties, and to provide for the wants and exigencies of the present moment. Short of this we have a class of beings in whom the mental deficiency is less apparent, and less easily proved to exist, and who are considered by medical authorities to be irresponsible, though they frequently become objects of punishment before the criminal tribunals They are mostly found amongst the lower classes of society, are capable of some easy occupations, are looked upon as simpletons, and often as such subjected to much annoyance. They are often lazy and drunken, are dexterous in thieving, and are thought to be very cunning. They are sometimes violent and passionate, committing homicide or arson upon the least provocation. Those, too, who have strong sexual propensities are easily betrayed into outrages on modesty.

In such cases, though the medical man may not discover that the individual is insane, he may perceive that he is not quite right in his mind. For in most of these cases there is something about the individual which makes him unlike the generality of other people. There seems in all such persons some want of intellect. They do not appear to possess the same composure of mind as common people. They have a great look of cunning, or of vacancy and unsettledness. They will speak rationally, and with consideration, but not with ordinary energy or depth of reflection; and consequently their judgment appears to be impaired.

This state of mind evidently corresponds with that oddity of manner, or half-craziness of disposition, spoken of by Mr. Alison, as not availing the prisoner, unless accompanied by an obscuring of the conscience, or complete alienation of reason.

Thus in the case of Thomas Gray, mentioned by Hume, who was indicted for murder by stabbing, it appeared that he was of a very weak intellect, subject to sudden gusts of passion and excessive drinking, and when in that state half crazy. All this, however, being short of madness, in the sense of the law, he was found guilty of the murder.

In like manner, in the case of Robert Bunthorn, related by the same author, who was charged with having pushed a revenue officer over a precipice into the sea, and thus breaking his thigh, in revenge for the seizure of some contraband goods in his possession, it was found by the jury that the panel's intellects were weak, irregular, and confused, and therefore they recommended him to the leniency of the court. He was sentenced, nevertheless, to the usual punishment.

In the two more recent trials of Barclay and Stirrat, both for murder, the one was sentenced to death and executed, the other sentenced capitally, but the sentence commuted to transportation for life. In both the proof of great weakness of mind was sufficiently brought out.

It is in cases of this sort, in which murder and other serious crimes have been perpetrated by persons more or less evidently of weak mind, and in which the act seems to have been in some measure connected with the usual incentives to crime, that the question of the responsibility of the imbecile usually presents itself to the medical jurist under circumstances of unusual difficulty, and in which the rigorous application of the legal test not unfrequently leads to an erroneous verdict being returned, and a useless punishment inflicted.

The criterion of responsibility drawn from or based on the moral perception of right and wrong is one which can seldom be applied correctly to cases of this nature. It is not right to assume that the moral sense is perfect when we know that the intellect is weak and undeveloped. Besides, we have no means of knowing with certainty that such an individual really has a distinct sense of what is right and what is wrong; although he may acknowledge the distinction in words which he has been taught, he in all likelihood has never felt its influence, and the probability is, that the fear of punishment, and not the sense of right and wrong, alone prevents him from committing those crimes to which his inclinations would lead him. This, no doubt, is just the condition of a real criminal of sound mind, but the difference between the one and the other lies in the respective powers which each possesses of controlling these desires or inclinations, as well as in his knowledge of the criminality of his acts

When an imbecile person commits the crime of murder, or any offence of a heinous nature, the fair inference is, unless the contrary clearly appears, that his moral sense is imperfect, and his control over his propensities very slight. To determine, however, with any degree of precision the responsibility of a person in this condition, our opinion should be formed from personal intercourse with him, from the history of his life, and from the circumstances connected with the commission of the crime, rather than from abstract notions of what his perception of right and wrong may amount to—a point nearly impossible to be satisfactorily determined. We should endeavour to ascertain what education the imbecile has received, of what kind the instruction has been, and what progress he has made in the usual acquirements. We should find out whether or not he has displayed mischievous propensities during the course of his past life, whether or not he has been irascible and sensual, as well as the amount of provocation he may have received. The history of the mode in which the crime was perpetrated is an important element in the inquiry Thus, precautions to ensure secrecy in its commission, or his future safety, the commission of one crime to facilitate the perpetration of another, or the fabrication of an artful story to escape from responsibility or as means of attaching it to some one else, are all circumstances which would infer such a degree of intelligence and of moral perception as should fairly render the individual responsible in the usual manner. They would clearly show that he was aware of the criminal character of his act, and knew its consequences if discovered.

How far extreme punishment, such as that of death, is justifiable in any case in persons of really weak intellect, has been disputed on good grounds.

The above statements and arguments, I believe, embody the conclusions and opinions of the medical profession generally, in instances of the sort we have been considering, however much medical men may differ as to the responsibility of the insane in other forms of insanity.

To some extent the administrators of the law, while not disposed formally to concede the irresponsibility of imbeciles, are willing to depart from the rigour of the law on this point. Thus according to Mr. Bell, in offences inferring arbitrary pains, weakness of intellect is a relevant plea to use in mitigation of punishment. Of this he instances three cases; in one of which the panel, owing to severe wounds on the head, became furious under the influence of intoxicating liquors, and consequently got a short term of imprisonment instead of transportation for life.

Further, while not statedly conceding the irresponsibility of the imbecile, our judges, in dealing with some of the more or less flagrant offences, occasionally bring such persons of weak mind before the Courts with the view, not of obtaining a conviction for crime, but of testing their mental condition, in order to their being transferred to a lunatic asylum.

A very interesting case of this sort was brought before the Circuit Court at Aberdeen in the spring of 1871. The man, 45 years of age, had committed various acts of theft during the previous ten years. He had been five months in an asylum, and two months in the insane wards of the Perth Penitentiary, when at last it was discovered that the delusions on which his two committals had taken place were feigned. Even on the eve of his trial, the two medical men who had originally certified his insanity in order to his being sent to the asylum, again granted a certificate to the same effect, though they subsequently withdrew it, being satisfied that he had imposed on them on the occasion in question. When I visited the man in Stonehaven jail, he pretended to me, as he had done before, that his food was poisoned, that his cell was infested with devils, and so on; but his part was so much overdone that I had no hesitation in certifying, and in giving evidence before the Court that, beyond a certain amount of imbecility, there was nothing unusual in his mental constitution. The non medical witnesses who had known the man spoke of his being peculiar, irascible, cunning, largely given to theft and lying, most of them considering him weak-minded; some sane, others as more rogue than fool—exactly the character usual in this class of imbeciles. The Court took the view of the case, which seemed to me to be the true one.

A similar result followed in the case of a man of the name of Reid, brought up at the Aberdeen Circuit Court in April 1873, on a charge of rape on his own daughter. Though no distinct delusions could be made out, and he was fully aware of the distinction betwixt right and wrong in the crime charged against him, which was clearly brought out in evidence, he was adjudged to be of unsound mind by the Court, and acquitted of the charge on this ground. Reid had been in an asylum five years before, though at the time of apprehension, the medical men who had previously certified his insanity, could find no grounds for again taking the same course. From what I could gather, his condition appeared to have been much the same at both periods, and I had no doubt of his case being one of imbecility.

We have now to consider, in the second place, the legal consequences of mental deficiency in civil cases. The principles which regulate the decision as to the civil consequences of the states of idiocy and imbecility in our courts of law, are not the same by any means as those which determine the responsibility of such persons in criminal cases. In the instances now to be spoken of, the law considers the degree of mental incapacity as that which is to regulate its interference, to a greater or lesser extent, with the freedom of the party. Where, from his not possessing a sufficient degree of understanding, the person is unable to protect himself, the law steps in for this purpose. To this person it gives that guardianship which his incapacity to protect himself renders necessary, it preserves his property inviolable against force or fraud, and as far as practicable, against all other causes of depreciation. The leading provisions of the law of Scotland, which, though different in form, are virtually the same as those of England, for affording relief to those who labour under mental disabilities, are based on a recognition of the obvious and important distinction which subsists between those instances where from an absolute defect of capacity, as in idiocy, the person, as well as the property of the individual, requires protection, and those instances where, from the deficiency being only partial, as in imbecility, personal protection is not called for, and a less stringent remedy will suffice to secure the property of the individual against the craft of others, or his own mischievous exercise of the ordinary powers of administration.

The forms by which the law inquires whether an individual belongs to the former class, termed by them fatuous and naturally idiotic, in order to place him under permanent and unlimited curatory, are those of cognition and inquest

The remedy which the law affords in the latter case, applicable to imbeciles and persons of weak mind, is interdiction, which invalidates all contracts entered into by the party interdicted without the consent of his curators, who are called interdictors.

In Scotland the cognition proceeds on a *brieve* or writ, addressed to the Lord President of the Court of Session, and directs him to inquire "whether the person sought to be cognosced is insane; who is his nearest agnate; and whether such agnate is of lawful age." "And such person shall be deemed insane if he be furious or fatuous, or labours under such unsoundness of mind as to render him incapable of managing his affairs."

The trial is before a judge of the Supreme Court and a special jury. If the insanity of the party be affirmed, the nearest agnate (relation by the father's side) is by law entitled to the guardianship. No one not a near relative can institute proceedings of this kind.

In England, in a like case, a commission is granted by the Court of Chancery, which gives power to dispense with a jury where the property is small By the Act of 1853 the alleged lunatic has still, however, the right to demand a jury, unless the Lord Chancellor shall be satisfied by present examination that he is not mentally competent to form and express a wish for an inquiry before a jury.

These enactments have not been extended to Scotland, where the method by which a jury trial is avoided is that of applying by petition to the Court of Session for the appointment of a judicial factor or *curator bonis* This practice has existed in Scotland for generations In its nature an interim measure, it may be resorted to with a view of guarding the property pending cognition, or where the relatives do not come forward, and it is a recognised remedy in such cases of imbecility as would not warrant cognition. The estate is administered by the factor or curator under the authority of the Court

The petition is usually accompanied by two medical certificates, and if it is opposed the usual procedure is to remit to some competent person to make inquiry, take evidence, and report.

This change, it will be seen, besides remedying the complaints made against the earlier mode of procedure, has so far simplified matters that the commissioner—usually in Scotland the Sheriff—takes the place formerly occupied by the jury, in weighing and balancing the medical and non-medical evidence usually produced on these occasions, of whose superior competency no doubts can be entertained This being the case, I need not stop to rebut the statements by legal writers that the law, properly enough, did not originally contemplate anything beyond this examination by the jury, now superseded, arguing strongly for its intrinsic superiority as a means of proof, and deeming any other evidence superfluous if not often positively mischievous, occasionally enveloping a clear case in doubt, and plunging a doubtful one in still deeper obscurity. It may be that the conduct of the profession in certain trials of this class of cases has furnished grounds in justification of such strictures as these, though this, I contend, has arisen more from the choice of prejudiced and incompetent witnesses than from the defects of medical science, or the insufficiency of properly chosen representatives, on occasions of the sort in question. Of this we had some lamentable illustrations lately in England in the cases of the Windham trial and in that of the convict Townley In both these trials, and in others of a like kind, such obvious defects in the medical testimony were shown by some of the witnesses as would justify, if it did not imperatively demand, no lenient criticism But in order to avoid the disagreeable task of having to comment on living practitioners, the same salutary lesson may be obtained by going back to a case tried in a neighbouring county (Forfarshire) in 1837, of which a full report was published at the time by an able Edinburgh barrister, in which much of the medical evidence for the prosecution was of the loose sort not unfrequently adduced on similar occasions

Yoolow, a farmer's son in Forfarshire, 52 years of age, affected with paralysis from his ninth year upwards, and mostly confined to his room in consequence, though unable to superintend in person his farms, nevertheless took some interest in rustic matters, read his Bible and an occasional newspaper, and went through the ordeal of an examination, by the jury empanelled to try his case, tolerably well, considering his limited opportunities for acquiring information. He was not, besides, without a little dry humour, as was shown by his turning the tables against some of the medical men sent to test his powers. Those on the defence, medical and others, showed that he possessed an intelligent knowledge of the Scriptures, understood money matters well, and that his memory and powers of comparison were good, though his capacity for drawing inferences was, from his habits of life, but limited

One medical witness for the prosecution contended for the great imbecility of Yoolow from his failing to give satisfactory information as to the sale of lambs, the return for wheat sown, and the object of the Corn Bill—matters in which he had shown no interest A second professional witness was of the same opinion, from the man's not knowing whether or not he was entitled to a vote for a member of Parliament under the then recent Reform Bill; though, curiously enough, when told that Yoolow was under trustees, the witness was equally ignorant on the point. More than one witness on this side laid too much stress on the arithmetic test, considering that this person's education had been entirely neglected, and that he had never been entrusted with the care of money or the management of his affairs. What more absurd, for instance, than one of those who had based his opinion of Yoolow's mental incapacity on the circumstance of his not being able to tell how much per cent £20 interest for £12,000 in the bank amounted to, though himself (the witness), when asked to say how much it amounted to, was unable to tell.

Interdiction, the milder remedy to which I have referred, is a system of judicial or voluntary restraint provided for those imbeciles who, from weakness, facility, or profusion, are liable to imposition It is directed at the sight of the judge, by the same forms as in cognition, on proper evidence of the facility of the party, or is voluntarily imposed by the party himself Hence the distinction into voluntary and judicial interdiction Voluntary interdiction is imposed by the sole act of the interdicted party, and is usually executed in the form of a bond, whereby the granter obliges himself to do no deed that may affect his estate, without the consent of certain persons therein named, technically called interdictors Judicial interdiction, with which we have alone to do, is imposed by sentence of the Court of Session, generally proceeding in an action at the instance of a near kinsman of the facile person; but sometimes *ex nobili officio* of the Court, where, during the dependance of a suit, they discover that any of the litigants, by reason of natural infirmity, is subject to imposition.

With respect to the kind and degree of mental impairment which warrants cognition, there prevails the utmost diversity of opinion, both in the legal and medical professions. Mere imbecility, as such, and in its lesser degrees, does not, it is obvious, and cannot warrant the depriving such persons of the management of their property If they have shown no disposition to squander their money on trifles, nor suffered their affairs to be grossly neglected, there can be no reasonable pretence for taking it altogether from their control and enjoyment. Of course there can be no question of its propriety, when it is perfectly obvious that the individual is dissipating his fortune, to the great detriment of himself and of those who are dependent on him.

In such cases the question which arises is not so much as to the exact measure of intellectual capacity requisite to the undisturbed enjoyment of civil rights and privileges as one of capacity in reference to certain ends and duties, and beyond the consideration of these we are not called on to go in our endeavours to settle this question. The speculative opinions of the imbecile person, the little peculiarities of his conduct, his style of living and talking, and his general deportment in society, are points that require but little attention in this inquiry Our business is with the manner in which he has conducted his affairs, and from this chiefly we are to draw our inferences respecting his probable future conduct and capacity. We are not warranted in stripping him of all his possessions and leaving him at the mercy of others the moment we can fix upon a single instance in the course of his life where he has neglected to profit by a happy turn of fortune, has rewarded a service, or bestowed his bounties in a manner altogether opposed to our ideas of forethought and economy Has the individual indulged in repeated acts of extravagance, or of profitless expenditure? Has he engaged in the execution of visionary projects with reckless indifference as to the extent of his means and appliances? Has he squandered his money on favourites, or become an instrument in the hands of designing and profligate associates for advancing their own selfish projects? These are amongst the most prominent questions which require a satisfactory answer, and if they are kept steadily before us there will be little fear of our losing ourselves in the maze of perplexities which the judicial investigation of cases of imbecility frequently creates

These views afford no countenance to the usual practice of

canvassing the whole history of the imbecile person, arraying act against act and speech against speech, and drawing from each an inference for or against his capacity of managing his affairs in his own way. Few of those whose interests become involved in protracted litigation are so destitute of intellect as never to conduct themselves like persons of well-developed minds under similar circumstances. They may write sensible letters, make shrewd bargains, and converse on ordinary topics without betraying any mental deficiency, while yielding to the will of others, and committing acts of folly that can arise from nothing short of unequivocal imbecility. Many also, who, while surrounded by their usual circle of associations, manage their slender means with the utmost economy and prudence, would prove themselves totally inadequate to the management of a large property, and be easily led by the influence of new associates and the excitement of new desires into habits of extravagance and dissipation.

In cases where imbecility is admitted medical men are not unfrequently called in to decide the question, Whether it is such as to incapacitate for making a will? Imbecility of itself forms no bar to the disposal of property by will. It is held that though a person is so imbecile as to be unfitted for the management of his own affairs, and as such may have been cognosced, yet he is capable of executing a testamentary deed. All that is required to establish the wills of persons of weak understanding is that they should have been capable of comprehending their nature and effect—a point entirely independent of the accidental circumstance of cognition. This seems all very rational. Much injustice might be committed by depriving all cognosced imbeciles of the testamentary power, compared with which the temporary inconvenience that would arise from the absence of any statutory provisions on the subject hardly deserves notice. Of course the slightest appearance of interference or improper influence should be closely scrutinised, and the more likely the party is to have been affected by it, so much less the evidence required to substantiate a charge of such interference. These remarks, it should be remembered, however, apply to the slighter degrees of imbecility. Imbeciles in the highest degree are evidently incapable of making a valid will.

Another point which requires to be noticed here is the degree of mental defect which is required to invalidate a marriage contracted under such circumstances. On this subject I may remark that any extent of imbecility which would justify or has already provoked interdiction renders the marriage null and void. When, however, the mental deficiency is less than this, it constitutes no legal impediment to marriage, although on proof of fraud and circumvention such mistakes have been set aside by the courts of law.

With one other point I conclude the subject of imbecility, namely, the circumstances which would justify the medical man in having recourse to personal restraint. The imposition of personal restraint upon these patients is seldom necessary, and would frequently be far from justifiable. It can be necessary only in those cases in which they display vicious propensities, as is sometimes the case; and in those in which it is required, for the safety of others as well as their own comfort. But if imbeciles be perfectly harmless, and if those who are thus partially endowed with intelligence should have any objects of regard, if there be anything upon which they have placed their affections, or in which they take delight—to deprive them of these pleasures, and separate them from the objects of their affections, when we are almost certain that they can form no other attachment, and adopt no new occupations, would be cruel in the highest degree, and without a conceivable object. We can have no expectation of a cure here, as in some other forms of insanity. The imbecile cannot be rendered other than he is by any line of treatment, medical or moral. Of course, where persons do exhibit mischievous propensities—if they be irascible, thieves, or display strong animal appetites, which they not unfrequently do—our obvious duty is to prevent them indulging their vicious inclinations to the injury of others, by having them placed under proper surveillance, or even shut up in a lunatic asylum.

LECTURE XXI.

INSANITY—(*Continued*).

Mania Intellectual Mania. General Intellectual Mania—Partial Intellectual Mania Moral Insanity General Moral Insanity—Partial Moral Insanity—Kleptomania—Erotomania—Pyromania—Homicidal Monomania—Suicidal Monomania—Legal consequences of Intellectual Insanity—In Civil Cases—In Criminal Cases—Legal Tests of Intellectual Insanity—Legal Doctrine of Lucid Intervals—Legal consequences of Moral Insanity—Plea of Moral Insanity in Criminal Trials—Circumstances justifying restraint in Mania

We now come to the second general division of the morbid states included under the term Insanity. It comprehends (as you will perceive from the Table at page 285) all those lesions of the mental faculties which are liable to occur subsequently to the period of their full development; and all the mental affections which are included by the lawyers under the terms dementia adventitia, or lunacy. These are subdivided by Ray into the two species, mania and dementia.

The mania of Ray admits of subdivision, as its manifestations are found to involve principally the intellect or the moral powers; while under either of these two forms, the disorder of the intellect or the will may embrace more or fewer of the mental faculties.

When the disorder is chiefly confined to the intellectual faculties, and when the derangement extends to many, or all of these, we have the forms of insanity termed by Esquirol and others, mania and melancholia, which only differ so far as, that, in the one, the character of the derangement is that of exaltation, and in the other of depression. When the derangement is limited to one, or to a few of the intellectual faculties, we have the one form of the monomania of authors, the partial intellectual mania of Ray. When, again, the derangement is chiefly confined to the moral powers, we have the moral insanity of most writers, the moral mania of Ray. (A glance at the table will make this arrangement more clear and intelligible to you.) I shall adhere to this arrangement, as affording us the most lucid method of discussing the forms of mental disorder at which we have now arrived.

It may be proper at this place to recall to your notice the remark formerly made, that the divisions and subdivisions which we have traced out are not always to be recognised in actual practice. Idiocy and imbecility, for instance, however distinct in general, may pass into mania occasionally, and thus lose their most prominent characters; or, retaining his characteristic features, the idiot or imbecile may exhibit occasional accessions of furious mania. Again, it is not by any means unfrequent that a person becoming insane should at one stage of his disorder exhibit that disorder chiefly, or even entirely, in his moral faculties, and his case would consequently be considered as one of moral insanity, but should, at a later stage of the same attack, have the disorder manifested by the intellectual powers chiefly or entirely and would thus require us to have his case classed as one of mania or monomania, according to the wider or narrower range of his disordered faculties. With these explanations premised, we proceed to consider the mania and melancholia of authors, the general and intellectual mania of Ray, which, for the reasons previously stated, I here class together.

Most of the difficulties arising from every attempt which we make to discriminate between soundness and unsoundness of mind, are got rid of by considering madness as indicated, not so much by any particular extravagance of thought or action, as by a well-marked change of character in the individual, or a departure from his ordinary habits of thinking, feeling, and acting, without any adequate external cause. Such is the diversity of character of different persons, that to compare the suspected maniac with any fixed standard of mind, is sure to lead at times into error. Some men's ordinary habits so closely resemble the behaviour of the maniac, that a stranger would be easily deceived; and, in the opposite case, the confirmed monomaniac, by carefully abstaining from the mention of his hallucinations, has the semblance of a perfectly rational man.

The individual, therefore, supposed insane, is to be compared with himself, not with others; and if there has been no departure from his ordinary manifestations, supposing these not to have been very unusual, he is to be judged sane, although it may be true, nevertheless, that there are peculiarities in his case such as amount to eccentricity, and furnish strong grounds for suspicion of predisposition to madness.

Mania, under whatever form it may appear, is generally preceded, except when produced by injuries or mental shocks, by a change in the natural condition, designated by writers as the period of incubation. This period of incubation of insanity, during which the true state of the patient is generally misunderstood, or not appreciated, may last a long time.

The more prominent symptoms occurring in this incipient state are, neglect of the usual occupations, change of temper and affections, restlesness, indecision, absence of mind, love of solitude, the corporeal health often suffering. The symptoms immediately preceding an attack are, unusually early rising, incessant talking or unusual silence, altered tone of voice, disposition to quarrel—especially with friends and relations, unusual gestures, redness of the eyes, and peculiar sensations in the head or other parts of the body.

In the active or confirmed stage, general intellectual mania is marked by exuberance of ideas expressed with rapidity, and in the utmost confusion and incoherence. The delirium extends to objects of every description; the attention is continually wandering; the efforts of volition are vague and unsteady; the affections are perverted, the muscular power is often much increased; the excitement is expressed by disorderly motions, cries, and threats; the irritability is great, the restlessness incessant, there being little or no sleep. The sensibility is sometimes much increased, sometimes the contrary. The duration of these violent paroxysms or furious fits is very various, from one or more days to several months.

It is not very easy in these cases to analyse the mental manifestations, so as to be able to say what faculties are disordered. Delusions are more rarely dwelt on in this than in the partial form of intellectual insanity, though they undoubtedly exist; the ideas belonging to the imagination alone are confounded with, or mistaken for, real occurrences. The mind, in this state, confounds the images derived from reflection for those of sensation, and mistakes perceptions of the mind for bodily sensations.

It is not to be understood that in this form of insanity the derangement is confined to the intellectual faculties alone. The moral powers are often the first to be perverted. The perversion of these, however, is not so prominent as the intellectual disorders, and differs from those which characterise the moral form of insanity.

This brings us, in the second place, to partial intellectual insanity, or monomania, also frequently termed melancholia, from the predominance, as was incorrectly supposed of depressing and gloomy ideas. The distinction between mania and monomania consists in the alienation being general in the former, and in the latter partial, or confined to a few objects, the difference being more in degree than in kind.

The most simple form of this disorder is that in which the patient has imbibed some single notion contradictory to common sense and to his own experience, and which seems, and no doubt really is, dependent on errors of sensation, whether arising from without, as is supposed by the person, or from morbid feelings experienced within the frame. Thus thousands have believed that their legs were made of glass, or that snakes, fish, or eels had taken up their abode in the stomach or bowels. A young woman, whose case I certified some years ago, in order to her admission to an asylum, firmly believed that she was in the other world, and that it was in my power, if I chose, to bring her back again; going down on her knees and entreating with the greatest urgency that I should do so.

In another class of cases the monomania takes a little wider range, involving a train of morbid ideas, instead of being limited to a single point. The operations of the understanding, even on subjects connected with the insane belief, are sometimes not impaired in any appreciable degree; on the contrary, we are sometimes struck with the acuteness of the reasoning powers displayed by monomaniacs. The dread of ridicule, or regard for their own interests, will sometimes induce these persons to conceal their predominant ideas, though ready enough in general to declare them. Some striking cases of this kind, from Lord Erskine's speech in defence of Hartfield, are given by Beck and others.

In the simplest form of monomania, the understanding appears to be, and probably is, perfectly sound on all subjects but those connected with the hallucination. When, however, the disorder is more complicated, involving a larger train of morbid ideas, the understanding is more extensively deranged than is generally suspected. It is not necessary to insist on the importance of this fact in estimating the degree of criminal responsibility remaining in monomaniacs.

We now come to the more difficult and controverted subject of moral mania or moral insanity. That there is a form of madness, consisting in a morbid perversion of the natural feelings, affections, inclinations, temper, habits, moral dispositions, and natural impulses, without any remarkable disorder or defect of the intellect, or knowing and reasoning faculties, and particularly without any insane delusion or hallucination, and further, that persons thus affected with disorders of the moral powers, without corresponding derangements of the intellect, are really insane, to such a degree as to place them entirely out of the rank of beings who can be justly considered as responsible for their actions, are points which are considered settled, in the affirmative, by such high authorities as Pinel, Esquirol, Georget, Gall, Marc, Rush, Keil, Hoffbauer, Carpenter, Morel, L'Espine, Combe, Conolly, Pritchard, and Ray—who differ, however, as to how far the integrity of the intellectual powers in such cases is to be considered as complete, or only partial. On the other hand, the mass of existing writers on insanity, and of those dating a few years back have ignored the existence of such a limited form of insanity as this, repudiating the entire theory of moral insanity, as advanced by the writers I have named. Amongst these may be mentioned Heinrich, Leubuscher, Gray, Winslow, Moreau, Baillarger, Brodie, Mayo, Griesinger, Liman, and others, while legal authorities, without an exception, refuse to admit that, without complete disorder of the reasoning powers, a plea of insanity can be made good, so as to shelter from the consequences of criminal acts.

Two forms of this so-termed moral insanity are distinguished by such authors as I have named on the affirmative side—the one termed general moral mania, or insanity characterised by the derangement of the greater number of the affective faculties; the other, partial moral mania, or insanity where the disorder is believed to be limited to one or a few of these.

In general moral insanity, Dr. Pritchard states that the leading features are liable to be overlooked at first, and that some time may elapse before its exact character comes to be understood. "Such persons," he adds, "are considered as sane, though a close observation will lead to strong doubts, if nothing more, of their mental soundness. Hereditary predisposition to insanity is discovered, as well as a decided change of temper and disposition; and this change, succeeding a mental shock or severe bodily disorder, has been in some instances gradual and imperceptible, and showing itself as a heightening of previous peculiarities. Individuals labouring under this disorder often reason accurately and argue ingeniously in support of their eccentricities of conduct; but, thinking and acting under the influence of strongly excited feelings, they err both in judgment and conduct. Hence, in some, violent gusts of passion, breaking out without cause, lead to the commission of serious injury to those about them, while in others greater malignity is displayed."

Instances in point are adduced by Pinel, Hoffbauer, Pritchard, and others; and whatever view we take of the mental condition of such parties, whether purely as moral, or as chiefly moral but in part also combined with intellectual disorder, there can be no room for doubt that the affection, such as it is, is far more common in ordinary society than is generally imagined. The singular conduct and whimsical notions displayed by such persons would subject them at once to the imputation of insanity, were there the slightest suspicion in the minds of ordinary observers of aberration of reason in their case. As it is, they are ordinarily set down as eccentric or vicious. The idea of their actions springing from insanity is immediately dispelled by calling to mind the sagacity and general correctness of their conduct in the pursuit of their ordinary avocations; and the most contradictory accounts will be given of their character by those who have come into contact with them on different occasions, and in their varying moods and states of mind.

This affection, from its readiness to pass into some of the forms of intellectual mania, has been relegated by Esquirol and Georget to the initiatory stage, or incubation of the latter disorder. It should be borne in mind, however, that whether this be the case or not, it may continue for an indefinite length of time, and thus become the object of judicial investigation.

Partial moral insanity, we are told, differs from the above—that in this disorder the moral faculties, as a whole, are unaffected, or cannot be observed to be affected, the perversion being, as regards its outward manifestations at least, confined to one or two of the moral powers. In this form of the disease the individual is set down as acting under the influence of a kind of instinctive impulse, which he has not the power to resist or control. With no extraordinary temptation to wrong, but, on the contrary, with every inducement to refrain from it, the party, it is said, commits a crime, the motives which led to it being generally as inexplicable to himself as to others.

This alleged powerlessness of the will, while the reason continues unaffected, has been set down and recognised as a distinct form of insanity, whether general or partial, under some one or other of the following names—namely, homicidal monomania, suicidal monomania, kleptomania, etc., or more generally as mania sine delirio, instinctive monomania, folie raisonnante, etc.

Avoiding unnecessary detail, let us now consider in succession the forms which these alleged cases of insanity are believed to assume in different individuals, beginning with those of them which rest on evidence on whose weight the least stress is laid by their supporters

Of kleptomania, or monomania characterised by an irresistible propensity to theft. The existence of such a form of insanity is contended for by Fodéré, Rush, Gall, Orfila, Pinel, Marc, Pritchard, and others, and is said to have been observed in persons who exhibit an unusual conformation of the head, with weakness of the understanding; in maniacs, during their lucid intervals, as a consequence of diseases and injuries of the brain; and in females, labouring under disordered menstruation, or at the more advanced stages of pregnancy

At the Aberdeen Spring Circuit of 1839, I had an opportunity of investigating a case which, but for the tracing back a short way of a portion of her history which proved the existence of some insane delusions, would have been set down as pure kleptomania. A woman about thirty-eight years of age, was brought from Banff to be tried for various acts of theft. She was of small stature, and had the low forehead and a little of the unsettled manner which characterise many persons of weak mind. With the exception of some very faintly traceable delusions, and a slight degree of mental imbecility, the woman spoke and acted very much as a rational being. She was said, however, to be such an expert thief, that she had been repeatedly committed for that offence to prison in Banff, and so marked was her propensity to theft, that her sole occupation during her last imprisonment, which had lasted five months, was to plan and execute means of possessing herself of anything she could lay her hands on belonging to her fellow-prisoners, whether useful or otherwise. Nothing, it seemed had come amiss to her, and her cell, on her quitting it, was found strewed with rubbish of all sorts.

Pyromania, a form of partial insanity, characterised by an irresistible propensity to set fire to buildings, or other combustibles, has been contended for by Fodéré, Gall, Orfila, Marc, and others. Cases of this sort have frequently come before the French and German tribunals, and the trial of Jonathan Martin, for attempting to set fire to the cathedral at York, is a well-known English case. The existence of such a propensity has been remarked by the German jurists to be not unfrequent in both sexes, about the age of puberty, and particularly in females when the menses are retarded or abnormal, or when there is a tendency to hysteria or epilepsy. The impulse has been united, or has alternated with the desire to commit murder or suicide, and it has been observed that such instinctive impulses are apt to spread by imitation. The parties have confessed that the accomplishment of their desire has relieved them from inexpressible anguish, and has awakened in their minds the greatest possible delight. It is by no means an unfrequent occurrence for insane persons to destroy themselves by fire, setting fire to their beds, and being burned to death, or even going into a heated oven with this intention.

Another criminal propensity has occasionally shown itself, particularly in females at the approach of puberty, in some few instances, it is affirmed, unattended by any other evidence of unsoundness of mind—namely, an irresistible desire to destroy everything they can lay their hands upon, without any malevolent motive being discernible. This tendency, it is well known, is a very common and well-marked feature of intellectual aberration.

A close approach to an instance of this sort occurred here a few years ago. A young woman of respectable appearance but of loose life, was repeatedly convicted and sent to prison for the same crime—that of smashing windows, her first occupation at each period of her relief from confinement being to repeat the offence, and this though she knew that she was followed and watched by the police. I had occasion to examine this person as to her state of mind on more than one of these occasions, but beyond eliciting a motive for her act—revenge against the magistrates and others who conducted or led to the different prosecutions—I could detect no mental peculiarity. Her conduct in jail was marked by great propriety, good temper, industrious habits, and readiness to oblige all about her.

In perhaps the same category might be placed the "Piqueurs" of the French, and the "Madchenschander" of Augsburg, to which Wharton has referred as instances of the passion for setting apart new varieties of monomania, the former being persons who ranged the streets of Paris, cutting the clothes of women, and inflicting other injuries, the latter persons who would rush out from lurking places, inflict a slight stab on young girls with some sharp instrument, and then retreat.

A case like that of the Piqueurs was brought under the notice of the law authorities in Aberdeen a few years ago. A man about fifty-five years of age, who had been a butler in a gentleman's family, but had been for some time out of place, was prior to detection in the habit of frequenting the crowded streets and the public market, and slyly, with a sharp pair of scissors, suddenly snipping ladies' dresses. He was of a taciturn and misanthropic disposition, but beyond a slight degree of imbecility, he showed no other discernible mental alteration

Passing over some other forms of mental disorder classified as instances of partial moral insanity, as having little bearing on our subject, such as erotomania, pseudonomania, oikeiomania, etc, we come to notice the so-called—

Dipsomania, which, of late especially has often been put forward as a bar to criminal responsibility In the wide spread of intemperance amongst the lower orders, and occasionally among those in the higher ranks of modern society, the medical practitioner is not unfrequently placed in a very delicate and embarrassing position He may not only have to decide where drunkenness ends and insanity begins, but what is still more difficult to determine, whether the passion for strong drink has gone so far as to have ended in insanity, or on the contrary, whether the existence of insanity has led to the uncontrollable desire for such an indulgence He may be also called to determine whether the presence of insane delusions, under which criminal acts are committed, originate under the stimulus of drink alone, or are the unqualified offspring of pure insanity To accomplish all this where it can be done, which is not always practicable, the form of monomania known under the names of dipsomania and oinomania, the "Trunksucht" of the Germans, and the "Monomanie de l'ivresse" of the French, must be distinguished from drunkenness, alcoholism, and delirium tremens Unlike these conditions, the insanity in question commences in very temperate people, occurs in paroxysms, has intervals of relief, during which the desire for drink has ceased, or is thought of with dread or horror. The individual has usually suffered previously, or is still suffering, from broken health, lowness of spirits, disordered stomach, loss of bodily strength, and various constitutional or hereditary nervous or muscular disorders, as in some of the other forms of monomania This form of dypsomania has been regarded by such high authorities as Morel, Griesinger, Skae, Forbes-Winslow, and others, not so much as a separate and independent mental disorder, as one of the phases of a more general insane condition. From losing sight of this—

which I believe to be the correct opinion—the decisions of courts of law vary not a little, though in doubtful cases these incline to the side of insanity where the crime involves a serious or extreme punishment

Thus in the case of Dingwall, tried at Aberdeen in September 1857, for the murder of his wife, Lord Deas, in his charge, said that "the prisoner appeared not only to have been peculiar in his mental constitution, but also to have had his mind weakened by successive attacks of disease. . . . Culpable homicide in our law and practice includes what, in some countries, is called murder with extenuating circumstances . . . The state of a prisoner might," his lordship thought, "be an extenuating circumstance, although not such as to warrant an acquittal on the ground of insanity." The verdict accordingly was—guilty of culpable homicide, and the sentence, penal servitude for ten years.

Again, a clergyman in the neighbourhood of Aberdeen was, in 1862, set down by the Ecclesiastical Court as a dipsomaniac, and sent to an asylum, though the insanity was far from being made out. This case was again brought up at the General Assembly of the Church of Scotland of 1873, when, after hearing fresh evidence, the plea of insanity was rebutted, and the case referred back to the court in which the trial had originated, by which, and by the General Assembly in 1875, this decision was confirmed, and the clergyman dismissed from the asylum.

The two remaining forms of this class of mental disorders which call for notice are homicidal and suicidal monomania.

The homicidal form, which insanity in general, especially in its more marked degrees, is apt to assume, has been long known to and acknowledged by the medical profession. It is also agreed on by all our best authorities that the same homicidal tendency may be manifested by those affected with some of the more partial forms of mental disorder, known as instinctive or impulsive monomania —any differences of opinion here having arisen from the different judgments of authors as to the greater or less range of morbid actions actually present in such cases. Those who restrict this class of cases to the morally insane contend that the party in question will perpetrate a murder under the sway of some sudden impulse, independently altogether of his will, impelled to the act by no motive of a criminal kind, and in the absence of any intellectual disorder. It is to the point as to whether the absence of such intellectual disorder, whether obvious or not, is to be taken for granted in such instances that the conflict of opinion has arisen

The chief subjects of this form of monomania whose cases have been narrated, have been found amongst hysterical or nervous women or women recently delivered, hypochondriacal or epileptic patients, and young persons of either sex at the approach of puberty, particularly those of wayward temper and ill-regulated and undisciplined minds. In these subjects the digestive functions are usually disordered, the cerebral circulation disturbed, the heart's action irregular, with some impairment of the senses and of mental activity. The impulse in many cases is resisted for a longer or shorter time, and struggled against in a variety of ways; but in spite of every effort, and with a full consciousness of the horrors in which it would land them, the conflict at last becomes insupportable, and in a state of inconceivable perturbation and anguish—perhaps of despair—the murder is committed, affording for the moment a degree of relief, of satisfaction, or even joy, the very reverse of the previous fury, which could scarcely be expected to arise in the mind had the act been the result of criminal motives instead of disease. The feelings of relief and the mental calm are usually, however, but of short duration, and are succeeded by deep remorse, the party appearing like a person who had awakened out of some horrid dream.

Suicidal monomania, the remaining form of partial moral insanity contended for by several authorities, has many points in common with the homicidal form of the disorder, with which it is said to be sometimes combined. Both, we are told, are usually attended with disorder of the organic structures. This apparently causeless and instinctive act of self-destruction has little in common with the cases of suicide so frequently occurring under the influence of obvious motives, such as mental distraction or depression, bodily pain or privation, and intellectual disorder, the consequence of ordinary disease or maniacal hallucination. Its frequently hereditary character is generally admitted. It is also admitted that it is apt at times to spread by imitation, ill-regulated minds and infirm wills being led to such attempts by the highly-coloured details of some notorious act of self-destruction. As has been remarked, the sight of a weapon, or of a particular spot where a previous suicide has been committed, will often induce a person who may hitherto have been unsuspected of any such disposition at once to destroy himself.

The correct appreciation of the character of these disordered states, and the light in which they are properly to be regarded, will come before us under the second division of the topic to which we have next to proceed—namely, the legal consequences of the two forms of mental disorder just passed under review,—intellectual and moral insanity,—comprising the mania and monomania of medical writers, and which, with dementia, are embraced by lawyers under the term lunacy, or dementia adventitia, vel accidentalis.

The civil consequences of these states will not demand any lengthened notice here. The forms of procedure are laid down by the administrators of the law, and as such merely require to be known by us; while the principles on which they are based are mostly legal ones, and when touching, as they do occasionally, on medical points, come as much within the province of the general practitioner as of the medical jurist.

I have already detailed the mode of legal procedure which is adopted to secure the property of the idiotic and the imbecile. The same steps are followed in the case of the maniac, the brieve being addressed to the President of the Court of Session, directing him to inquire whether the person sought to be cognosced is insane, who is his nearest agnate, and whether such agnate is of lawful age, etc.

In England the trial of the party proceeds on the issue of a writ by the Lord Chancellor, *de lunatico inquirendo*.

The proof demanded in such cases is not made to rest on the insanity of the party in general. It must be demonstrated to the judge and jury that the person has evinced such a weakness of mind as to be incapable of managing his own affairs. It should be borne in mind, however, that though the insanity *per se* is not in common regarded as proof of the incapacity, that incapacity to manage affairs must be shown to be due to some mental defect or disorder, and not merely to want of education or to bodily infirmity.

The civil disabilities which the law thus imposes on this unfortunate class of our fellow-creatures are certainly founded on the most humane and enlightened principles, and have for their object the promotion of their highest welfare: to incapacitate a person from making contracts, bequeathing property, and performing other civil acts, who has lost his natural power of discerning and judging; who mistakes one thing for another, and misapprehends his relations to those around him—is the greatest mercy he could receive, instead of being an arbitrary restriction of his rights. It is only to be regretted that in England the forms of law are so tedious, complicated, and expensive, without being always effective, that justice is not always secured, and that the law, in its care for the property of the insane party, itself not unfrequently wastes the very property which it is seeking to protect from waste. The law of Scotland, it is admitted, has in this respect the advantage of that of England in simplicity and efficiency.

The duty of the medical practitioner is reduced within narrow bounds in cases of general intellectual insanity. A person whose intellectual powers are generally impaired must be seen at once to be in a state that totally unfits him for the management either of himself or of his affairs. All that the medical inquirer has to do is to satisfy himself as to the extent to which the intellectual derangement has spread. Not so, however, when the disorder is confined to one or two of the mental faculties. A person may labour under such a hallucination as renders him to all intents insane, and yet he may be perfectly competent to manage his property. We see some persons managing their affairs with their ordinary shrewdness and discretion, evincing no extraordinary exaltation of feeling and fancy, and on all but a few points in the perfect enjoyment of their reason. Strange as it may appear, it is no less true that, notwithstanding the serious derangement of the reasoning power which a person must have experienced who entertains the strange fancies that sometimes find their way into the mind, it may be exercised on all other subjects, as far as we can see, with no diminution of its natural soundness. The celebrated Pascal believed at times that he was sitting on the brink of a precipice, over which he was in danger of falling. Numberless are the instances of worthy persons who imagine that their heads are turned round, or their limbs made of butter or glass, but who, nevertheless, manage their concerns with their ordinary shrewdness. A young woman whose case I investigated several years ago believed that her brother had cut off her head, which was so loosely replaced on her shoulders that the slightest movement on her part would cause it to fall off.

To deprive such persons as these of the management of their affairs would be to inflict a certain and a serious injury for the purpose of preventing a much smaller one which might never occur. The principle I would inculcate is that monomania invalidates a civil act only when such an act comes within the diseased circle of the mind. No one surely would seriously propose to invalidate such of these men's acts as manifestly have no reference to the crotchets they have imbibed. It should be borne in mind, however, that the delusion, though not connected with the act in question, may be frequently changing, and even if fixed, the mind in respect to other operations may have lost its original soundness to such a degree that it cannot be trusted in the transaction of important affairs. In doubtful instances the general circumstances of the case must decide, a course preferable to that of universal disqualification.

The above principles are in substance applicable to other questions which may arise in cases both of mania and monomania, such as the validity of a will, the validity of a marriage, the propriety or otherwise of personal restraint or seclusion from society.

Thus, in regard to the validity of a will executed by such a person, an individual is in law considered to be of a sane and disposing mind who knows the nature of the act which he has been performing, and is fully aware of its consequences, and that without regard to his mental condition otherwise. Such may be the state of his mind that he may have been cognosced, or even confined in a lunatic asylum, and yet he may not be thereby rendered incompetent to make a valid will unless it can be clearly shown that it has been executed under the existence of some insane delusion which has influenced his mind at the moment.

To invalidate a marriage it must be proved that the insanity existed at or about the time of the contract, because it is considered that there cannot be that rational consent that is necessary to its validity.

One other of the civil relations in which we have to regard the forms of insanity before us occasionally calls for the exercise of some judgment and circumspection on the part of the medical practitioner. I refer to the degree and the character of the disorder which would justify him in advising recourse to personal restraint or seclusion from society. I need scarcely say that no one in the profession should readily be entrapped inadvertently into the serious mistake of favouring the crafty design of some interested relative by committing a merely eccentric person to a lunatic asylum; or, on the other hand, from excess of caution, be a party in affording opportunity to an insane person to squander the means of his family, or to break out into acts of violence on himself or others. It is to be feared, however, that instances occasionally occur in which, on very slight grounds, medical men have facilitated the committal of persons to an asylum in order to screen them or their friends from disgrace, if not from criminal charges

I now come to a more difficult and disputed subject on entering on the legal consequences of the same forms of insanity in criminal cases. Although the plea of insanity, as a ground of exculpation where any crime has been committed, is admissible in law, it is seldom in fact set up, unless in cases liable to be followed by the very severest penalties which can be inflicted. The plea of insanity in bar of trial was set up as recently as 1866 in Glasgow, in a case of lewd practices. It was not successful. The law presumes every man to be in his sound senses, and therefore responsible for his actions, until the contrary be shown. It is stern in its demands, that the ends of justice shall not be evaded by any fictitious plea. The judges of the land always receive the plea of insanity with great caution; and lawyers, accustomed to deal, for the most part, with demonstrative evidence, listen with impatience to medical testimony, which cannot be reduced to the same description of proof which they require to establish ordinary matters of fact. The same witness, who in an ordinary case of homicide would have his evidence received as valid and conclusive, may, when the plea of insanity is at issue, have his testimony listened to with marked disrespect. Much of this unpleasant state of matters is undoubtedly owing to medical witnesses themselves. They are, in many cases, either ignorant or wilfully regardless of the legal tests which are sought, and bring forward, and rest their judgment on others, which, though admitted by their professional brethren as sufficient, are not so received in law. This is so far unreasonable; as however faulty or inapplicable the medical witness may deem the tests which are demanded of him in a court of law, the responsibility for their application does not rest with him, but with those who so apply them. Let us therefore here see what are the tests of insanity which are admissible in criminal cases. These, I must remind you at the outset, are altogether of a different kind from those which we have seen to be applicable to civil cases, and in the application of which medical men and lawyers are substantially agreed.

The test of insanity, which the laws of this country requires to exonerate a person from the consequences of a criminal action, committed by him while in that state, is thus plainly and briefly announced by Mr Chitty.—The question here to be settled is, whether at the time the act was committed, the person was incapable of judging between right and wrong, and did not then know that the particular act was an offence against the laws of God and nature. If he were so capable, i.e., of distinguishing between right and wrong, then, although the mental delusion might be connected with the crime, and stimulated him to commit a murder in revenge for the imaginary injury, yet if he knew that he had no right to revenge himself, he will be criminally responsible.

This decision as to the legal test of insanity, which is as old as the time of Hales, was re-affirmed by the House of Lords in 1843. Prior to this time it was by many judges departed from in cases of monomania; Lord Erskine having laid it down, that though the law regarded the general rule as clear, the application of it was allowed to be often very difficult, and that all that it was necessary to prove, in order to the exculpation of the criminal, in the absence of frenzy or raging madness, was the presence of delusion as the test of insanity, and that the act in question was the unqualified offspring of that delusion. This relaxation in the unbending severity of the old legal test, which had extended to Scotland, was, at the period I have named (1843), replaced by the original enactment. The Lords declared that the jury ought in all cases to be told, that every man should be considered of sound mind until the contrary were clearly proved in evidence; that before a plea of insanity should be allowed, undoubted evidence ought to be adduced that the accused was of unsound mind, and that, at the time he committed the act, he was not conscious of right or wrong. Every person was supposed to know what the law was, and therefore nothing could justify a wrong act, except it was clearly proved that the party did not know right from wrong. If that was not satisfactorily proved, the accused was liable to punishment. If the delusion under which the party laboured were only partial, the party accused was equally liable with a person of sane mind.

The most forcible objection which has been urged against this test of insanity—and in the urging of which the medical profession is unanimous—is its partial applicability to actual practice. The legal test of utter unconsciousness of right and wrong in the performance of acts, it is justly argued, would, in reality, apply only to persons labouring under a furious paroxysm of mania, confirmed idiocy, or active delirium, while it would exclude the greater number of the ordinary inmates of our asylums. While it establishes the legal responsibility for crimes of the majority, perhaps of all general intellectual and a still larger proportion of partial intellectual maniacs, it altogether ignores the existence of the two classes of the morally insane, as laid down by some writers in mental disorders. In legal cases, accordingly, it has been found impossible, in actual practice, in not a few instances, to carry into effect the rigour of the rule formally enunciated in the House of Lords. Even in England, where it has been more strenuously insisted on than in Scotland, it has been departed from by the judges; and parties who upon these rules ought to have been held responsible, have been acquitted, on the legal fiction that they were at the time unconscious, or only insanely conscious, of the wrongfulness of their acts. A more direct infringement of the decisions of the supreme tribunal has of late taken place in Scotland on several occasions. This appears from the charges of two living judges of high repute, the first delivered by the Lord President of the Court of Session (then Lord Justice-Clerk) in the case of Alexander Milne, at Edinburgh in February 1863, and the second by Lord Deas at Aberdeen, in the case of Dingwall previously referred to. These charges were as follows:—

(1.) "If a man knows what he is doing—that is to say, if he knows the act that he is committing, if he knows also the true nature and quality of the act, and apprehends and appreciates its consequences and effects—that man is responsible for what he does. If from the operation of mental disease he does not know what he is doing, or if, although he knows what is the act he is performing he cannot appreciate it, or understand either its nature or quality, its consequences or its effects, then he is not responsible."

(2.) "If the jury believed that the prisoner, when he committed the act, had sufficient mental capacity to know, and did know that the act was contrary to the law, and punishable by the law, it would be their duty to convict him." This his Lordship thought was a safer and more accurate mode of putting the question before the jury than that they should consider whether the accused knew right from wrong.

To the same purport, though less direct, was a part of the charge of the former of these judges in the case of George Stephen, tried at Aberdeen in April 1865, for the murder of a woman near Kintore. After warning the jury that "they must not mistake brain disease, or weakness of mind produced by brain disease, for that kind of insanity which alone exempts from legal responsibility," his Lordship went on to say that, "unless a man is in such a condition from mental disease as to be bereft of reason, and not able to understand what he is doing,—if he does not know what is the act he commits, and is unable to appreciate its nature and quality, or to understand its consequences and effects—if that is true, then, no doubt the person of whom it is proved is insane, and not legally responsible."

I had occasion repeatedly to visit Stephen during the four months of his stay in prison before the trial, but could detect nothing in his mental condition beyond a slight amount of imbecility.

This interpretation of the law of Scotland, it will be seen, goes back to Lord Erskine's decision on the same point, and brings the legal into agreement with the medical view of insanity in connection with criminal acts committed by the parties ranging in the two classes of the generally and partially intellectually insane, without bringing lawyers and the majority of medical writers any nearer to agreement as regards moral insanity. Two things, however, should here be borne in mind. In the first place the criteria brought forwards in proof, by such members of the profession as contend most strenuously for the separate existence of moral insanity, or insanity in the absence of delusion or intellectual disorder, are not such as will endure a very close and searching scrutiny. The marked change of character, and the co-existing disposition to suicide, for instance, characterising the homicidal monomaniac, may be the product of certain morbid conditions of the system, not admitting of alleviation or the hope of cure, or even of mere moral depravity in the habitué of crime, or the confirmed sot. Again, the suddenness of the impulse to which the presumed morally insane person has yielded, the apparently motiveless and inexplicable character of the deed, the openness with which it has been gone about, the neglect by the party of any attempt at escape or concealment subsequently, and the absence of any co-operation with others in effecting the violence in question, though undoubtedly peculiar to recorded cases of this class, and when found in combination, entitled to some weight, may be found to concur to some extent in the mere criminal, or to be absent to a greater or less extent in supposed monomaniacs.

The remaining test advanced, namely, the marked perversion of the will without any concomitant disorder of the intellect, is the characteristic condition of the hardened criminal, as much as that of the so-called morally insane, and the problem would be how to discriminate betwixt the two.

That in these circumstances the lawyers should be unprepared to admit the violent deed itself, or the mode of its commission, and its concomitants, as sufficient evidence of insanity, is not to be wondered at, particularly when not a few medical men of weight and experience, in our own and recent times, concur with them in contending against the existence and distinctive characters of the so-called moral insanity, and the views which would limit the disorder in any one class of monomaniacs to one or two of the moral faculties merely, or to derangement of these without concomitant disturbance of the intellect, contending, on the contrary, that it rarely if ever happens that the mind is clouded with one false notion only. Esquirol, who at first adhered to the side of Pinel on this point, subsequently went so far as to assert that he did not consider it possible that the intellect could be in a state of integrity in moral insanity. To the same purport we have the deliberately expressed opinions of Dr. Mayo and Sir Benjamin Brodie in our own country, and Griesinger, Liman, Falret, and others on the Continent.

From what has been advanced on this side of the question, we can scarcely doubt that there is in every case of true insanity, in whatever form, some latent disorder of the intellectual powers, however difficult we may find it, in some instances, to detect the evidence of any fixed notion, or the existence of any delusive ideas, or, when they have been discovered, correctly to determine the precise extent to which they have gone, or whether or not they have left the faculties clear enough to form an unbiassed judgment of the right or wrong of the action in question, or the legality or illegality of the determination to which it had led. In these circumstances, it is not to be wondered at that, though cases have occurred on the Continent and in America and even in our own country, where the rigid legal test has been departed from, where its inapplicability was at best doubtful, we cannot do otherwise, in fairness than admit that, in the present state of conflicting opinions betwixt lawyers and some medical men holding exclusive views, the truth lies more on the side of the former than of the latter. For, from a careful perusal of many of the controverted cases, especially those of early date, I have come to the conclusion that, while on the one hand the purely medical tests are not always such as will enable us to distinguish the sane from the insane criminal, or the responsible from the irresponsible lunatic, neither are the purely legal tests, on the other hand, of such limited application as the medical practitioner and jurist are apt to represent them in the majority of instances.

I have dwelt the longer on this topic because I have seen with regret that the controversy between the legal and medical bodies has of late been widening instead of narrowing, and that public opinion, as represented by the press, is at present dead against us, and with some show of reason. This has arisen from the circumstance that medical psychologists have shown too much eagerness in seeking to withdraw from responsibility some of the most atrocious criminals, on the ground of their defective organisation, original or acquired, a line of defence which might serve equally well as a shelter from the consequences of any crime whatever. With the theories advanced, however, on occasions of this sort in regard to the nature of insanity in general, and some of its particular forms, which have been unduly multiplied, we have nothing to do.

In order to complete our view of the medico-legal relations of the forms of insanity which we are considering, it will be requisite now to advert to some other points which I have not yet mooted. The first of these is the legal doctrine of lucid intervals. The term lunacy was adopted at the time when it was erroneously supposed that the moon influenced mental disorders, a belief now abandoned by all medical men. "In legal acceptation," says Mr Chitty, "a lucid interval imports any one who has for a time had understanding, but who from grief, disease, or injury, afterwards lost the use of his reason;" and, according to Lord Coke, 'a lunatic at intervals has his understanding, *gaudet lucidis intervallis*, and therefore as distinguishable from an idiot, is only called *non compos mentis*, so long as he has not understanding." Strictly, therefore, lunacy is only a periodical madness, although inaccurately also used to import very permanent adventitious insanity, as distinguished from idiocy, and in the modern statutes, lunacy is used in such comprehensive sense. An insane person is accordingly regarded in law as capable of making a will, entering into the married state, or signing an obligation during a lucid interval, although his property is not restored to him until his final and complete recovery. In criminal cases also, if he exhibit a lucid interval of understanding he may be punished for acts committed during its presence, in the same manner as a sane person is punished.

The burden of the proof, when the existence of a lucid interval is sought to be established, will rest in law on the party who would establish the validity of a particular contract, will, etc, and in a criminal action, on the public or private prosecutor, when the party has been once pronounced insane, and has not been discharged as cured.

Medical men and lawyers differ as to the meaning which should be given to the term lucid interval. The latter speak of it as a temporary cure, and for the moment at least equivalent to the restoration of health, or as an interval in which the mind has thrown off the disease and recovered its general habit, while most of the leading medical authorities deny the existence of such lucid intervals in insanity, or regard these as being only remissions, instead of intermissions, of the disease, abatements of the severity of the symptoms, not temporary cures. They hold that all acts done in such intervals should be cautiously received, seeing that, though no delusions may exist at the time, the mind is left in such a state of weakness and irritability as to be more easily acted on by unprincipled persons than in the ordinary sane state. They contend that it should appear on evidence that the interval of relief was not a limited one, and that the degree of self-possession was not partial but complete.

While the views of these parties in the profession appear to me to have been carried too far in the direction of restriction as regards the civil acts of individuals in the state in question, too great caution cannot, I think, be exercised in admitting the responsibility for crime during the so-called lucid interval, considering how readily a momentary excitement, produced by a returning hallucination and otherwise, may put an end to the intermission, or reproduce the disease

There is another point connected with this subject which it is of importance to notice here A trait which has been greatly relied on as a criterion in doubtful cases of insanity, by legal writers, is the design or contrivance that has been manifested in the commission of the criminal act. In the trial of Bellingham for shooting Mr Percival, the Attorney-general declared that, even if insanity had been manifest in all his other acts, yet the systematic correctness with which the prisoner committed the murder, showed that he possessed a mind at the time capable of distinguishing right from wrong In the trial of a person of the name of Arnold, in 1723, for shooting at Lord Onslow, great stress was laid on the circumstance of his having purchased shot of a much larger size than he usually did when he went out shooting, with the design then formed of committing the murder he afterwards attempted Mr Russel, in his work on crimes, recognises the correctness of the principle, and lays it down as part of the law of the land In this he is followed by Mr Alison.

This criterion, however, I have the best authority for stating, would hardly now be insisted on, if the medical witnesses were unanimous in their opinion of its valuelessness.

If, then, the power of design is really not incompatible with the existence of insanity, this pretended test must be fallacious That it is so, the numerous proofs that we have of ingenuity of contrivance, and adroitness of execution, as characteristic of the plans of the insane, abundantly testify. No one who is not practically acquainted with the habits of those who are insane can readily conceive of the cunning which they will practise when bent on accomplishing a favourite object Indeed, it may be said, without greatly distorting the truth, that the combined cunning of two maniacs, on accomplishing a certain object, is always a match for gacity of a sound individual. Those, for instance, whose madness takes a suicidal direction, are known to display wonderful artfulness in procuring and concealing the means of self-destruction, and in lulling into security the awakened suspicions of their attendants. When desirous of leaving their place of confinement, the consummate tact with which they will set suspicion at rest, the precaution with which they make their preparations for escape, and the sagacity with which they choose the time and place of action, would do infinite credit to the conceptions of the most sound and intelligent minds

LECTURE XXII.

INSANITY (*Concluded*)

DEMENTIA.—Legal consequences of Dementia'—Restraint in Cases of this sort FEIGNED INSANITY CONCEALED INSANITY MEANS OF DETECTING THE EXISTENCE OF INSANITY GENERALLY—The Interrogatory—Continued Observation—The Inquest

DEMENTIA, or the lesion of the mental faculties, subsequently to their development, has less bearing on our subject than the forms of insanity which have preceded It may be the result of mania, of injuries to the brain, or of the pathological or natural changes which occur in that organ in advanced age Its history will usually suffice to distinguish dementia from idiocy and imbecility, with which it is most likely to be confounded, and from mania, with which it has but little in common From the first two of these states it differs in its origin, in idiocy and imbecility the faculties having been arrested prior, not subsequently to their full evolution, as in dementia; while in mania and dementia the contrast is betwixt mental disorder associated with excess or distortion in the one, and with paucity of ideas and feebleness of perception in the other In dementia, however, in addition to loss of mental power, more or less derangement of the faculties is encountered, as in mania; while again, the loss of mental power in the old may be associated with violent mania, or it may appear early in life from causes capable of impairing the activity of the brain and its faculties

The medico-legal points which are apt to arise in connection with dementia refer either to the capacity of such persons for the management of their affairs, or for the disposal of property by will Here much tact and sagacity may be required in coming to a correct decision in this direction. The amount of impairment of the faculties is occasionally less than may at first sight appear, and the judgment when roused may be capable of being directed aright where it seems ordinarily to be incapable of arriving at sound and sensible conclusions; while, on the contrary, the mental disorder and insufficiency may be such as totally to unfit him for conducting himself or his affairs with ordinary prudence or correctness, and to render him the easy prey of designing persons interested in deceiving or misleading him in different ways. Much, here, will depend on the sagacity of the examiner in weighing the evidence of the witnesses who speak to the condition and the conduct of the mentally enfeebled or impaired person, and judging whether these are qualified or not to form and enunciate available testimony; while he should, in addition to this, learn how long the deficiency has existed, what progress it has been making, how far it has advanced; and if any or what amount of control or constraint has been called for or practised in the case. By carefully weighing all, and comparing his own impressions with those of others competent to judge, and likely to be impartial, a correct opinion may be reached without injustice being done in any direction.

In regard to the question of the propriety of restraint in cases of dementia, few difficulties present themselves. In confirmed dementia, as the patient is unable to provide for his own necessities, and absolutely requires that care should be taken to keep him out of the way of harm, it resolves itself into a matter of convenience for the relatives of the party to adopt such measures for that purpose as may best suit themselves.

The patient himself will most probably have no reluctance to be separated from his friends, and may be totally unconscious of the change in his situation; and if it be one of those cases in which a hope of a cure may be entertained, perhaps his treatment will be most effectually conducted in a lunatic establishment. But, in the majority of instances, the sequestration of such patients is not necessary to accomplish the objects which have been already stated to be our warrant for imposing personal restraint upon a patient of unsound mind. The cases which call for confinement are those in which the disease alternates with maniacal paroxysms, where the accessions may be sudden and unexpected, and attended with dangerous violence and fury; or where the disease is the result of sensual indulgences, or of the abuse of intoxicating liquors, when, by withdrawing the cause, a cure or mitigation may be hoped for. When the faculties are not entirely destroyed, and the patient is able to take an interest in any sort of occupation, or in the society of his friends or family, however undignified or childish his pleasures may be, it would be a piece of unnecessary cruelty to consent to his restraint, if these predilections threaten no injury to his person, and if his peculiarity of disposition is not such as would render him an easy prey to the designing. The general object in all such cases is to provide for the safety of the person and property of the patient, as well as that of the community, with the least possible harshness or cruelty to the unfortunate sufferer

The subject of *feigned* insanity is one of some interest to the medical jurist. That insanity can be successfully imitated by a sane person, so as to deceive a competent observer, has been deemed all but impossible by Georget, Conolly, Haslam, and others; but undoubted cases of this kind are known to have occurred. If they have not always been fortunate in their attempts, it is certain that such attempts are not unfrequently made by detected criminals, and by soldiers and seamen wishing to escape from the public service

Several instances of this sort have occurred in my own practice Mr. Marshall has given one instructive instance in which an insane soldier was punished as an impostor, and a second in which an impostor, by not overacting his part, effected his discharge

Two cases of simulated insanity which came under my notice in the prison of Aberdeen, will be reserved for the lecture on feigned diseases A case which occurred in Stonehaven jail was anticipated under idiocy.

The form of insanity which is most frequently assumed is that of general intellectual mania, as the vulgar are apt to consider insanity as being always distinguished by violent action and vociferous and incoherent language The feigning of monomania would be a matter of too much difficulty to be easily sustained, and too easy of detection to serve the purpose of the impostor Dementia is more easily feigned than monomania, but as this form of insanity consists in an entire abolition of all mental power, at least in its higher grades, the discovery of any connected ideas, reasoning or reflection, either by language or gestures, would at once show that the case was not one of real dementia. Idiocy and imbecility could hardly be successfully feigned, as the history of the party would at once betray the deceit

The kindred subject of *concealed* insanity will demand from us a few words Maniacs have occasionally sense enough to conceal their insane notions, in order to escape restraint, or from other causes, and have succeeded in outwitting their friends, or even their medical attendants in some instances In these cases the insane notions have been of such a sort as do not, to all appearance, necessarily influence their general conduct or conversation, or, if they are such, they may profess to have recovered from them. The quietness and apparent sobriety of their speech and manner may assist them in evading scrutiny, from the prevalent idea entertained as to the usual accompaniments of boisterous behaviour and complete disorder of the ideas in the insane.

At the outbreak of the first French Revolution, the mob broke into the hospitals to release those whom they supposed to be unjustly confined, when many of the patients recounted their fancied wrongs so clearly and connectedly as to ensure their liberation—an act the folly of which soon became apparent to their liberators.

Lord Eldon used to relate that, after repeated conferences and much conversation with a lunatic, he was persuaded of the soundness of his understanding, and prevailed on Lord Thurlow to supersede the commission of insanity. The lunatic, calling immediately afterwards on his counsel to thank him for his exertions, convinced him in five minutes that the worst thing he could have done for his client was to get rid of the commission.

There are certain states of mental unsoundness which cannot be included under the term of insanity, though bordering on this state, which it will be requisite for us to notice. The first of these is—

Delirium, in its medico-legal relations. Delirium may be either the effect of disease or the result of intoxication by alcohol or otherwise. In either case, the person so affected is as little master, frequently, of his actions as the furious maniac; but the responsibility of the delirious party for the consequences of his actions in the two cases is differently estimated in law. When the delirium has arisen from natural causes, the patient is regarded, so long as this state exists, as of unsound mind, and even if he should, during the height of the frenzy which sometimes accompanies this state, assault or murder another, he is legally irresponsible for the act.

The same holds good in the case of delirium which has resulted from intoxication by alcohol or otherwise. But it must not be supposed that the state of intoxication itself, voluntarily entered into, can form any defence to a criminal charge of violence.

From what I can gather in regard to delirium tremens, it must be regarded in the same light as an ordinary delirium from drink.

Patients labouring under delirium, in whatever way caused,

are, of course, quite incapable of executing any testamentary deed, unless during the intervals which may occur in its course, or on its cessation, as occasionally happens before death. The law requires that in this affection, as in mania, the occurrence of lucid intervals should be proved beyond a reasonable doubt; but as delirium is merely an adventitious symptom, and not like mania, the habitual state of the patient, it will be satisfied with much less proof in the former than in the latter affection.

In regard to the legal consequences or immunities of *somnambulism* we are in entire ignorance. As the somnambulist does not enjoy the free and rational exercise of his understanding, and is unconscious of his outward relations during the paroxysms, none of his acts can rightfully be imputed to him as crimes. But as the state of somnambulism, particularly in one previously subject to its attacks, might be readily feigned in order to commit a criminal act with impunity, a question of some difficulty in legal medicine might arise.

Another state of mind, analogous to the two last, deserves a moment's attention. I refer to the *Schlaftrunkenheit* of the Germans—i.e., the state of mental confusion sometimes met with betwixt sleeping and waking, on any sudden interruption of a deep sleep, in which the person is scarcely conscious of where he is or what he does, and when he may commit an action which may bring him under a criminal charge.

We have two such cases in the *Zeitschrift fur Gerichtliche Medicin*. In the one a man suddenly wakened, and, seeing his father passing into an adjoining room in a moonlight night, he seized a loaded fowling-piece at his bedside, and shot him dead, under the momentary impression that he was a robber. In the other instance, a peasant, waking suddenly out of a profound sleep, seeing some one standing by his bedside, and thinking it was a murderer, seized an axe and struck a fatal blow over this person's head, whom he then found was his own wife.

On trial, both these men were acquitted of the charge of murder.

Lastly, in regard to the deaf and dumb, it has been averred that the uneducated are altogether irresponsible for any criminal act, but that with the educated this is far from being the case. They are, it is contended, as susceptible of moral culture as of intellectual instruction, and in every moral sense they are amenable to the law for crimes precisely like other men.

Several cases are recorded of the trials of deaf and dumb

prisoners, and it is now quite understood that their trial for crime is a matter of course, unless their mental condition is such as to render them irresponsible for their actions, communication being held with them by writing or by signs, according to their education. A question as to how the law would deal with a deaf and dumb person who was totally uneducated, and supposed to be wholly ignorant of the distinction between right and wrong, is one not likely now to occur, but it may be mentioned that such a case seems to have occurred, and to have been allowed to drop, at the initial difficulty of getting the accused to plead either guilty or not guilty to the indictment.

To complete the subject of insanity in general in its medico-legal bearings, it only now remains for me to advert to the best method to be pursued in the examination of suspected lunatics.

This duty, as we have seen, is no light and unimportant one, and should always be gone about in a cautious and systematic manner. Unless we can satisfy our own minds that the insanity undoubtedly exists, it would be a fearful responsibility for any conscientious person to incur, lightly to decide a point which might involve the life or liberty of a fellow-creature, or, on the other hand, shelter the hardened criminal from the responsibilities which he had deservedly incurred. But on these obvious considerations I need not dwell.

In almost every case of suspected insanity, there are individual features belonging to itself, and to which no general rules will rigidly apply; while again, individual cases will be found to vary in the amount of evidence which they permit us to deduce from them. In one, a single visit, and a few questions and observations, may yield all the evidence we require as to the existing insanity; while another will require, on our part, all the evidence which can be gathered from our own observation and inquiry, coupled with the data derivable from the patient's past history and present condition, so far as it can be deduced from the examination of those about him; while the investigation may, in a few instances, occupy us for a longer or shorter period. This has led to the distinction which we meet with in French writers, into the three different modes of procedure, which they have designated as the interrogatory, continued observation, and the inquest.

These three methods I shall here notice in succession—

First, the interrogatory. Before proceeding to interrogate a patient, the examiner should ascertain from others the form the insanity has assumed, the usual and predominant ideas in his mind, and the questions and conversations which most readily call forth his delusions or bring on his ravings. He should note carefully the deportment of the patient, the expression of his countenance, and the way he presents himself to his visitor.

The method of interrogation suffices in the great majority of cases for the ascertainment of the existence of insanity. It is, however, sometimes useless, or may lead to our pronouncing a person sane whose reason is, nevertheless, deeply affected, and whose will is quite depraved. Thus a person who has lucid intervals, if examined during one of these, may pass muster as sane. Some patients, too, aware of what is going on, are able for a time successfully to control themselves and conceal their predominant ideas. Monomaniacs, besides, from fear of their notions being ridiculed, will at times elude questions which would touch on these, or even deny their belief in them altogether. Again, in the form of insanity first described by Pinel, under the name of *folie raisonnante*, the patient is capable of appearing quite calm in the presence of his visitor, and of explaining away very plausibly his ordinary extravagances. Even parties in dementia, or demi-imbeciles, will sometimes pass muster without their true state being elicited.

To obtain the full benefit of the interrogatory, it should be conducted with caution. Suspicion should not be roused, nor distrust excited. The conversation at first should be of a general kind, leading only, after confidence has been secured, and that by easy transitions, to the peculiar subject which engages the patient's thoughts. If really insane, and unsuspicious, he will probably betray himself. The patient should be led to speak of his relations and friends, particularly of those who have interfered in his affairs, or put restraint upon him, as he will in general require all his self-control to restrain his angry and revengeful feelings towards them. When already in confinement, both Orfila and Georget recommend that the examiner should ask the patient how he likes his situation, and what he thinks of his companions, as many of them are such poor observers, or have so little penetration, that they are ignorant of the nature of their abode, and the character of those around them. Some minor features are not undeserving of notice, such as the desire of talking when once set in motion, unwillingness to listen to others, and the derangement of the digestive organs. A friend who had very large experience of the insane, once informed me that he never met with a clean tongue amongst his patients.

When the interrogatory has failed to elicit the true state of the insane party in a doubtful case, the second method, or that of continued observation, is called for. The examiner here requires that opportunities be afforded him for visiting the patient frequently and freely; for watching him at times when he supposes himself unobserved; and for exercising a general surveillance over his conduct and conversation. He should visit him at times when he is not likely to be expected, examine his attendants; reason with him, and question him as to the motives for treating him as mad. He should encourage him to write to those he considers his friends, and expects will come to his assistance; or to prepare statements of his fancied wrongs and grievances. In this way, if really insane, the examiner will soon be furnished with instances of incoherence and folly, which would never have been brought out by the method of interrogation. As Dr Conolly has remarked, the writings of the insane often betray them, in cases where conversation may be kept up with tolerable correctness and decorum.

Lastly, the inquest differs from the two former methods only that in addition to these a searching inquiry is instituted into the patient's previous history, conduct, and writings; that of his family and connections; and the examination of witnesses who can adduce facts which may assist in elucidating his true state. The means thus indicated, if faithfully and conscientiously followed out, are sufficient to bring out the truth in almost every conceivable case; and should they fail to prove the existence of insanity beyond a doubt, the party is entitled to be considered a sane person, and must be held to be responsible for his actions on the one hand, and entitled to his free agency on the other.

In France and Germany, the method of continued observation is not unfrequently extended over months, or even years, and at the inquest, the medical examiner calls and examines witnesses, and reports to the tribunals, in cases in which his decision may involve matters of life or death—thus exercising a duty which in this country belongs only to the administrators of the law. It does not appear to me, however, that the medical examiner in our own country is shut out from the employment of the methods of continued observation and inquest—methods from which the foreign jurist occasionally derives such invaluable assistance. No obstacle interposes here to his availing himself of the facts he may have learned by watching the state of his patient, from his repeated visits; from the examination of his papers and correspondence; while the information to be derived from tracing the previous history of the patient, and from the testimony of his family and neighbours, may be legitimately turned to the best account, not as in itself enabling him to decide as to the sanity or insanity of the party in question, but in so far as it sets him on the best vantage ground for testing the matter by his own observation and experience. I may add that I have, on more than one occasion, adopted this mode of procedure in cases of a difficult kind, in which there had previously been much difference of opinion, and conflicting evidence on the part of the former examiners.

In one of these cases, in which I had the assistance of my colleague, Dr Macrobin, the question of mental soundness had been left in doubt for about six years. In May 1844, a boy, apparently of sixteen, but said to be of eighteen years, was committed to prison on a charge of theft, to which crime he was known to have been addicted for a considerable time previously. His parents were in comfortable circumstances, and he had been well cared for at home. He had a look of considerable intelligence, though childish in his tastes and habits. He was deaf and dumb, which had led the law authorities to wink at his delinquencies up to the period of his incarceration. After being kept under observation for a month, with the assistance of the governor of the jail, who was able to communicate with the culprit by means of signs mutually understood, we arrived at the conclusion that the boy's mental capacity was defective, and that he laboured under some insane delusions of an innocent character, but deeply fixed. After a stay of some years in an asylum, to which he had been sent by the Crown on our report, it was understood that he had been finally set down as an imbecile, almost an idiot.

Where the task of the examiner does not consist in eliciting proof of the existence of real insanity, but in detecting its assumed character, some excellent directions for our guidance have been adduced by Dr Taylor, which I cannot do better than quote in his own words:—

"In the first place, when feigning is suspected, it will be proper to inquire, whether the person has any motive for pretending to be insane. In reference to persons charged with crime, it is necessary to remember that insanity is rarely assumed until after the commission of the crime, and the actual detection of the criminal. No one feigns insanity merely to avoid suspicion. In general, as in most cases of imposture, the part is overacted, the person does either too much or too little, and he betrays himself by inconsistencies of conduct and language which are never met with in cases of real insanity. There is commonly some probable cause to which insanity may be traced; but, when the malady is feigned, there is no apparent cause; in this case the appearance of the assumed insanity is always sudden; in the real malady the progress of the attack is generally gradual—and when the attack is really sudden, then it will be found to be due to some great mental shock, or other very obvious cause. We should observe whether, for some time previously, there has been any marked change of character in the person, or whether his conduct, when he had no interest to feign, presented any of the usual indications of insanity. Some difficulty may arise when fits of eccentricity or strangeness of character are deposed to by witnesses; but these statements may be inconsistent with each other, and the previous acts of the person may bear no resemblance whatever to those performed by him in the recently assumed condition. A difficulty of this kind rarely presents itself, since, in an impostor no act indicative of insanity can be adduced from any antecedent period of his life. It is *only after the perpetration of a crime and its detection*, that any action approaching to the habits of the insane will be met with. In real insanity the person will not admit that he is insane; in the feigned state all his attempts are directed to make you believe that he is mad; and an impostor may be induced to perform any act, if it be casually observed to another in his hearing, that the performance of such an act will furnish strong evidence of his insanity."

The cases of concealed insanity which I have met with, and on which I have had any difficulty in deciding at the inquest, have been those where the patient had been discharged from one asylum in order to be sent to another, or where the person was aware of the intention of putting him under such restraint—such difficulty in detecting insanity in these instances being, in addition to the acuteness of the patients in concealing their delusions,—the not having been able beforehand to obtain any clue to their previous histories.

One instance of the latter sort I may notice. When called to certify his insanity, in order to have him sent to an asylum, the man, a stout workman, was in an apartment under the charge of three persons, and had been making powerful struggles to obtain his release. On entering the room, he quietly sat down and told me that he had been declared to be insane, and that he knew the purport of my visit, but was ready to submit to any test of his sanity I might consider necessary. When asked as to the reason of his violent and outrageous behaviour, he said that it was quite natural that he should lose his temper under the rough usage to which he had been submitted, and his forcible confinement for a whole day, for which his attendants could assign no reasonable cause. He conversed sensibly and rationally on various topics which had been started, for nearly an hour, and it was only when I was on foot to leave, without having obtained any light on his case, that he asked ruptly if I should like to be in the army. Thinking this might d to something which might farther my object, I at once answered in the affirmative, when he informed me that he was commandant of Leith Fort, that he was raising a regiment, etc. On finding at length that I was leaving him without ordering his liberation, he instantly lost all his self-restraint, recommenced the struggle with his attendants, and before I had left the house had begun to knock about the furniture of the room.

One word in conclusion as to the position of the practitioner in filling up a certificate of insanity to insure his patient's admission into an asylum. He should be careful accurately to fill up all the blanks in the schedule, and give, as clearly and succinctly as he can, the required specification of the facts, both as observed by himself and as acquired from others.

For the usual form of schedules of insanity, *vide* Appendix, No. I.

LECTURE XXIII.

FEIGNED, FACTITIOUS, AND LATENT DISEASES.

FEIGNED DISEASES — FACTITIOUS DISEASES — LATENT DISEASES — Means for their detection.

FEIGNED DISEASES

It is well known that there are individuals who find it for their interest to assume the appearance of illness when they have it not, to aggravate existing ailments; or even to induce disease in themselves, or assist others in doing so. Hence the classification of these impostures into: (1) Feigned diseases, strictly so called, or those which are altogether fictitious; and (2) Factitious diseases, or those which are wholly produced by the patient, or at least with his connivance. To these have been added, by some writers— (3) Exaggerated diseases, or those which, existing in some degree or form, are pretended by the party to exist in a greater degree or different form; and (4) Aggravated diseases, or those which, originating in the first instance without the person's concurrence, are intentionally increased by artificial means.

These distinctions, however, may be carried too far. It is evident, for instance, that a disease which is purely *factitious*, or produced by the party himself, may be aggravated or exaggerated to serve a purpose; while the simulator may be able to convert a feigned into a factitious disease.

Diseases are simulated or artificially brought on from a great variety of motives. To avoid being compelled to engage in the military or naval service, or to obtain a discharge from the public service, or in order to become entitled to a pension, or for other reasons, seamen and soldiers, including their officers, will simulate illnesses which they do not feel. Persons do the same both in public service, and in private life, to escape imprisonment or other punishment. To these may be added all who seek to live in idleness upon the bounty of the public, by exciting their compassion; from the mendicant who covers his limbs with sores, or feigns lameness or mutilation, to the gentleman-beggar, who preys upon the public or his richer relatives, by a less gross but more immoral means of deceit. Lastly, persons not at all in poverty, nor living in a constrained position, will assume the semblance of disease from some inexplicable causes. These are chiefly females; but their number is, on the whole, very small.

The extension given to railway travelling, and the consequent frequency of collisions and other accidents on the rails, have brought out an additional class of simulators now becoming notorious to Boards of Directors and Courts of Law.

The diseases which are best adapted for the purpose of the simulator are those of a chronic kind. The symptoms of these are purely subjective, they produce no sensible disturbance of the system, and consequently the evidence of their existence rests mainly on the veracity of the patient. Other and more obvious diseases, which may also serve his purpose, may be imitated by the effects produced intentionally by the swallowing of certain drugs, by the employment of certain external applications, or by the sustained indulgence in certain deleterious habits.

The extent to which impostures of this kind are not unfrequently carried in the army, and the forms of the diseases assumed or produced by the recruit and the old soldier, will be best seen by a reference to such writings as those of Laurent and Percy in France, and Marshall in our own country. But what has given the widest extension to the attempts at simulation in several European countries, is the conscription now so rigorously enforced by so many of the European military nations.

In our own and other countries it must not be lost sight of, that the prevalence of such deceptive practices is not by any means confined solely to the men in the public services, to the exclusion of their officers. The medical man has sometimes to incur no little odium by refusing certificates of continued ill health to officers on sick leave, or otherwise, for the purpose of obtaining or extending the sick leave, or escaping service in unhealthy or unpopular foreign stations.

Nor has the medical practitioner in civil life less need occasionally to guard against being misled by the artful impostor. Though not so frequently and systematically as in the army and navy, simulators are not rarely encountered in hospital, dispensary, medico-legal, and private practice.

Some years ago a prisoner in the Aberdeen jail was sent to the Royal Infirmary, to be treated for paralysis of his lower extremities. After getting recruited in this institution for a few days, he suddenly recovered the use of his limbs sufficiently to effect his escape

I have known dispensary patients, chiefly elderly women, addicted to opium, pretending to be suffering from colic and other internal pains, in order to obtain laudanum from the institution. In some of these instances, where suspicion was aroused as to the object for such a demand, and when, to test the reality of the statement, the drug was offered in some other form, it was not a little amusing to be told that it was only *in its pure state* that the laudanum gave them any relief

On more than one occasion prisoners in Aberdeen, on being apprehended, have pretended to be insane, in order to escape trial for serious offences. One of these, on being laid hold of, mimicked deafness and dumbness, as well as lypemania, and persisted in maintaining the simulation for some weeks before trial, and for about two months afterwards in the Perth Penitentiary, to which he was sent for a lengthened imprisonment. Another prisoner in the Aberdeen jail pretended to add his soup to the contents of his chamber-pot, and it was only by closely watching him that he was seen, before transferring his food to the vessel, to empty the contents of the latter out of his window, and then carefully to wipe out its interior with the oakum which he had been set to tease out

Amongst mendicants epilepsy is the disease most frequently simulated, and next to that the loss of an arm. An old beggar in Aberdeen mimicked elephantiasis very successfully. The pretended swelling was confined to one leg below the knee, and was produced by padding. To favour the deceit, part of the leg was covered with goldbeaters' leaf, and exposed by drawing down his stocking two or three inches.

I have had occasion already to notice the subjects of feigned pregnancy, delivery, and insanity. Feigned concussions and injuries of the spine will be noticed under Homicide. Feigned poisoning belongs to Toxicology. This leaves for discussion here those forms of disease which are known to be most usually either assumed or affected

Of the former, or purely feigned diseases, the most common on the whole, are deafness, dumbness, or both; and some of the more occult forms of neuroses, such as neuralgia, spinal irritation, muscular debility, spasms, paralysis, contraction of joints, and rheumatism; all of these, complaints which demand but little cunning in the simulator, and no great self-denial on his part

In dumbness, impostors seldom attempt more than ceasing to speak, and in paralysis ceasing to move about. In both cases suspicion should be aroused from the alleged suddenness and the fully formed or confirmed state of the disease from the outset. In a prisoner in Aberdeen jail, who pretended sudden and total deaf-mutism, the imposition was detected by the following test.—While he was walking in the airing-ground a huge bunch of keys was, unseen by him, dropped at his back from a high window without his being at all startled or taking any notice, while, the same thing being done in a case of congenital deaf-mutism, caused the prisoner to start in alarm, and look round in all directions except that from which the sound or impulse had come.

In neuralgia and chronic rheumatism impostors do not admit having any intermission or alleviation of their sufferings like patients so affected, while they are apt to enumerate incompatible symptoms. This last remark applies equally to assumed palsy, so easily affected, and so difficult to be detected.

Contraction and rigidity of the large and small joints are often affected by soldiers and mendicants, and some colour is occasionally given to the imposture by keeping the limb at rest by bandages till some stiffness and wasting of the muscles ensue. That a feigned disease may thus occasionally be converted into a factitious one, appears from a case which came under my notice some years ago. A man, who rode about the streets on a donkey, was brought before the magistrates for begging. Both his knees were bent at right angles and firmly anchylosed, a tourniquet applied to the thigh failing to effect any change in either of the limbs. The muscles of both calves were bulky and firm, the soles of the feet thickened and horny, and it was discovered that a twelvemonth had not elapsed since he had been seen actively at work in the fields in the country. The same conversion of a feigned into a permanent contraction of the joints of one or more fingers, by similar treatment, is said to be occasionally effected by impostors, and the deceit sought to be concealed by burning a portion of the skin over the flexor tendons.

Other diseases of this class call for more ingenuity, and some activity in devising means for securing such of their outward manifestations as will give a colour to the imposture. Hæmoptysis, for instance, which has frequently been pretended, has been mimicked by first swallowing the blood of animals and ejecting it in the presence of witnesses; scurvy has been imitated by irritating and picking the gums. The unhealthy hue of the yellowness of the skin in chronic dyspepsia, jaundice, and hepatitis, has been simulated by the abuse of emetics and purgatives, by overfatigue, by the use of skin dyes, or by taking advantage of a facility, natural or acquired, of ejecting the contents of the stomach at pleasure. The appearance of amaurosis is imitated by the application to the eye of belladonna hyoscyamus, or atropine, to ensure the dilatation and immobility of the pupils. A little watchfulness and attention to circumstances, or a few simple tests, will usually suffice for the detection of such impostures.

To give colour to a feigned attack of epilepsy a ligature round the neck has been applied to induce reddening of the face, soap in the mouth to imitate froth about the lips, and pricking of the gums to give the tongue the appearance of having been bitten by the teeth. The impostor here would find it impossible to imitate the fixing or twitchings of the eyeballs, the insensibility of the pupils, the peculiar perturbation of the heart, the rigidity of the muscles, and the insensibility of the skin and mucous inlets, while the prodromata and the sequelæ of the attack, if ascertainable, would further assist the inspector in determining the nature of the suspected simulation.

Factitious Diseases.

The remaining diseases which call for notice here are the factitious ones, some of which, however, are also partly fictitious. In this category we have scrofulous and other sores, stiffening and contraction of the joints, diseases of the anus, ophthalmia, and cutaneous eruptions.

By the help of caustics and other escharotics, sores have been produced, especially in the neck, in imitation of scrofulous ulcers, and the deceit sought to be strengthened by the application of the juice of euphorbium to favour the swelling and redness of the eyelids, nose, and lips. Ulcers of the legs are frequently said to be excited by mendicants, recruits, and old soldiers, by the application to the parts of corrosives or irritants, or by purely mechanical means. Such ulcers, however, are occasionally only pretended, and for the purpose of deception. In these instances a portion of the spleen or the skin of a frog has, it is said, been glued to the parts; while cancerous sores, we are assured, have been imitated by placing a bit of sponge imbued with blood and water under the dressing.

Fistula in ano has been artificially produced by first making an incision near the anus and then irritating it. Paré mentions a beggar who had introduced a long piece of gut into the rectum in order to imitate prolapsus ani. The bowel, which was that of a bullock, was filled with a mixture of blood and milk, which the impostor had learned to press out in drops at pleasure. A kick with his foot made the gut to tumble out!

A soldier, mentioned by Orfila, by a clever mechanical contrivance, was able to cause a sheep's bladder lodged in the rectum to protrude or disappear at his pleasure. The bladders of rats, or of small fish, partly introduced into the rectum, resemble piles so much as to have deceived superficial observers.

Ophthalmia is produced artificially by the application of various irritant substances to the eye.

Cutaneous affections have been successfully imitated. Herpetic eruptions have been produced by the use of rotten cheese, mussels, oysters, etc., and tinea capitis by nitric acid applied to the scalp, previously guarded by fatty substances. In the *Lancet* for 1850 a case is given where a woman imposed on the surgeons in one of the London hospitals by a series of sloughy sores or superficial discolorations of the skin, which she had produced by hydrochloric acid. The fraud was detected in a provincial hospital which she entered after leaving the Metropolis.

Such are but a few of the impostures not unfrequently practised in various directions. The list might be largely added to. It will be more to the purpose, however, in place of completing their tale, to enforce the necessity for the medical man being in a position to meet and counteract manœuvres of this sort by whomsoever attempted.

To meet this call on him the practitioner ought to be well acquainted with the different classes of diseases most usually simulated, and with the means which are resorted to for producing the appearances of morbid actions or discharges. The history of the person, by showing whether or not he has an interest in seeming ill, may assist the medical man in coming to a decision. He ought also to inquire whether or not his patient has been exposed to the usual exciting cause of his apparent disease. The suspected impostor ought to be drawn into a full account of his illness, its origin, progress, and juvantia and ledentia. In the vast majority of cases it will require more knowledge than is possessed by non-medical persons to give such a narrative as shall be consistent in all its parts; either there will be discrepancies or exaggerations, or the symptoms will be such as are incompatible with the disorder assumed.

I do not think the system of punishment, often adopted in the army and navy, well adapted to obtain confession of the deceit practised; whether that be confined to disagreeable drugs or vexatious restraints, or extended to solitary confinement or personal chastisement. If the imposture is real all this may be borne without attaining the object sought for, while cases have occurred of persons really ill being punished in this way.

Serious diseases are known occasionally to exist in a latent form with little or no outward manifestation during life, and only to be detected on inspection after death. A person labouring under disease in this form, it is obvious, might readily be treated as an impostor. An instance of this sort has been recorded by Mr. Calder of the Life Guards, which deserves to be quoted at length. The soldier whose case he relates had been ten years in the regiment. After his enlistment he deserted, and he lay subsequently in the hospital for a long time feigning deafness, but gave in after a while in despair of thus procuring his discharge. He had next tried, by a course of vicious conduct, to attain his end, knowing that the commanding officers of the regiments of Life Guards have the power of discharging a worthless man at a moment's notice, and that they not unfrequently do so with an incorrigible scoundrel. This, too, failing, he conducted himself well for two years though it was well known that he was very anxious for his discharge. He then came again into hospital complaining of morning sickness and vomiting. There being then no indication of disease about him, no efficient treatment was deemed necessary. He was again discharged, and again admitted, with the same story that he could not get on with his duty in the mornings, that the stables did not agree with him, and so on. In a few days he was again quite well; and, indeed, while in hospital and under the observation of the attendants there, he appeared always so. Circumstances were in this state, when the man's wife stated to the surgeon that she thought his head was affected, and that his movements were sometimes unsteady, even when he had been tasting nothing of a spirituous kind. Still nothing to indicate disease could be detected about this person on a careful inspection, and little more was done than keeping him in hospital and watching him. Shortly after this, says Mr Calder, he was out of afternoon walking with some of the other patients in the yard when I accidentally called. His back was to me as I entered, and from the nature of the place he could not have seen me coming. Just as I caught sight of him I distinctly observed one of his legs give a peculiar twitch as it was moved forwards, and from that moment I felt satisfied that there was something wrong in his head. I now treated him for cerebral disease, and he soon began to show more decidedly that he required it, for his lower limbs became paralytic, and he died less than two months afterwards, with every sign of well-marked disease of the brain.

On inspection after death, besides fulness of the membranes and effusion into the ventricles, a serous cyst was found in the left lobe of the cerebellum containing about two ounces of fluid; and in the same part a vascular tumour of the size of a nut.

Dr Cheyne relates a somewhat similar case to that adduced by Mr Calder.

The subject of latent disease, incidentally brought before us by these two cases, is of sufficient importance to be reserved for a separate notice. Meantime I go on to observe, in conclusion, that though cases of feigned disease present so few points in common that any directions for dealing with them must necessarily be of an indeterminate character, yet that the general principles borrowed from Orfila may not be without some use in practice:—

1. The examiner should compare the pretended cause with the effect ascribed to it. In a great many cases the slightest examination is sufficient to show that no relation exists between them, and that the patient's complaint deserves no consideration.

2. He should have regard to the predisposing causes of the assumed disease. This will often afford proof of the impossibility of the disease being real.

3. He should consider the morals of the individual, the motives he may have for misleading his medical attendant, and the character he bears with others.

4. The character of the prevailing diseases may assist the diagnosis.

Lastly, the juvantia and ledentia may be studied with good effect, as we know the influence which these will have on the assumed disorder.

I have only to add that since Orfila's time the employment of anæsthetics has been had recourse to in certain cases, as in assumed muscular contractions of joints, paralysis, etc.

LECTURE XXIII.

Latent Diseases.

We are indebted to Sir Robert Christison for calling the attention of the profession to this class of diseases. It is a fact, he states, familiar to every physician practically conversant with the features of disease, that many disorders, even those of which the presence is commonly indicated by well-marked symptoms, will in particular cases present throughout the whole, or a great part of their course, a material deficiency or total absence of their usual external characters, and that on this account they are frequently on the one hand confounded with other diseases, on the other entirely concealed from observation. As further stated by Sir Robert, in the practice of medical jurisprudence nothing is more common than for the expert to find his opinion and conduct embarrassed by sudden death arising in the like circumstances, by the discovery of appearances in the dead body adequate apparently to account for death, yet unconnected with any traces of the existence of corresponding disease during life.

In the list of latent diseases Sir Robert Christison enumerates apoplexy, cerebral meningitis, cerebral inflammation, pleuritis, pneumonia, pneumothorax, pulmonary tubercle, diseases of the great vessels within the chest, and affections of the abdomen and spine.

To some of the diseases in the above list the term latent in its stricter sense may, perhaps, with propriety be applied, but to some others of them with considerable latitude. This remark applies with most force to such diseases as cerebral meningitis, softening of the cerebral lobes of the brain, and abscess in its substance, instances of which I have encountered in practice where no complaint of illness was made till within a few hours or days at most of the fatal event. Again, in some cases of the sudden death of persons apparently in ordinary health up to that event, it may have been too much to assume that the morbid changes first disclosed at the *post-mortem* examination had been entirely unconnected with any traces of the existence of disease during life. Had the previous state of these parties been intimately known, it might have been found that some warning, however obscure, had been given of the impending event.

The nearest approach to cases of what may be practically assumed as strictly latent disease, occasionally occurs in certain instances of fatal disease of the heart, aneurisms of large vessels, and apoplexy.

Writers on diseases of the heart and aneurismal ruptures have directed attention to these affections as furnishing the most frequent and marked instances of sudden and unexpected deaths from causes first revealed in dissection.

Next to these, if not so frequently, the profession and the public are apt to fix upon apoplexy as the probable cause of sudden death in persons believed previously to have been in ordinary health

Of such occurrences as these—disease of the heart, aneurism, and apoplexy—works on pathology and the practice of medicine supply sufficiently numerous illustrations to excuse me from entering here into detailed narratives One or two instances may, however, be mentioned

Under " Wounds," I have directed your attention to the case of a carpenter who dropped down dead from rupture of the heart while at work in his own house. A similar case of rupture of the heart, involving also the ascending aorta, which was much dilated and unusually lacerable, occurred at Aberdeen in 1830, in a militia officer who was taken ill in a privy and died by syncope in a very short time In August 1853, an old man in Trinity Street (Aberdeen) was engaged in a quarrel with his daughter, when he dropped down dead His daughter was apprehended for assaulting him, but on investigation the law authorities were satisfied that she had not touched her father, who at the moment of his death was in a furious passion, and swearing at a great rate Dissection disclosed a large soft clot of blood in the left division of the cerebellum

A near approach to the above instances in the suddenness and unexpectedness of the fatal event is furnished by cases of the so-called pulmonary apoplexy, of which I have examined upwards of forty cases The first twenty were recorded in 1866, in the thirty-seventh volume of the *British and Foreign Medico-Chirurgical Review* These cases predominated in females past the middle period of life, and the parties had been unexpectedly found dead in bed From this last circumstance, and in the absence of any clue to the cause of death, the cases in the *Review*, and the subsequent ones, had been considered as calling for judicial investigation So late as the months of January and February last (1877), I have assisted at two such inspections In one of those the dead body of a man of sixty-two years, and of intemperate habits, had been found undressed, partly in and partly out of his bed ; in the other instance a young man of twenty-four years was found dead on the floor of a house into which he had gone, as it was supposed, somewhat the worse of drink.

In some of the diseases in Sir Robert Christison's list latency is not in most instances well made out, some warning, though it may be obscure, being usually to be observed of the existence of disease before death. Of these I may mention cerebral meningitis and cerebral softening. In cases which I have encountered of both diseases, some previous suspicious circumstances, though not a little obscure and undefined, existed for from two to three days before death. One instance of obscure cerebral disease at New Machar (Aberdeenshire), in July 1859, led to a legal investigation. Suspicion had attached to a woman on account of the successive deaths, without any known or assigned cause, within a period of two years, of three step-children all in early life. The case which was investigated was that of the third, a girl of fourteen years. Ten days before her death she had complained of headache, and after two days had taken to bed, without any suspicion of serious illness, or attention being paid to her. The inspection disclosed a flattening of the cerebral convolutions, a marked degree of dryness and firmness of the mass of the brain, and an absence of blood everywhere within the cranium. From what could be gathered of the history of the two previous deaths, it appeared probable that they had also succumbed to hypertrophy of the brain, from the close correspondence of the accounts of their illnesses, with that of their sister.

Of the facility with which latent disease may elude the detection even of competent and experienced medical practitioners, the following case is an illustration:—In June 1876 a patient in the Aberdeen Infirmary, whose case was considered to be one merely of bronchitis, proved so troublesome that it was found necessary to dismiss him from the institution for insubordination. He had not, however, proceeded beyond a few hundred yards from the house when he suddenly dropped down dead. At the inspection next day both surfaces of the pleura (costal and visceral) on the right side were seen to be intensely reddened, the right pleural cavity containing three pints by measure of serum, in which floated numerous loose flakes of lymph.

I have still more recently (January 1877) encountered a case of almost precisely the same sort as the last. A young man's death was so sudden, and his surroundings were of so suspicious a kind, that suspicions of foul play had reached the law authorities. It was known, however, that he had been complaining of illness for some days, though an experienced medical man in one of our public charities did not suspect the presence of any serious disease. The inspection disclosed such a copious effusion of sero-purulent matter in the left pleural cavity as to have compressed the lung on that side and pushed aside the opposite one to some extent.

In cases of latent diseases, Sir Robert Christison warns the medical jurist against the mistake of trusting merely to the discovery in the dead body of appearances sufficient to account for death. He advises that evidence should be taken from a variety of sources, such as derangements of structure incompatible with the continuance of circulation or respiration; the presence of morbid appearances seldom encountered except where death immediately follows, the eliciting of symptoms before death corresponding with the appearances discovered at the inspection; the improbability in the case of previous violence; and from the collateral conditions under which latent diseases are usually observed to prove suddenly fatal. By attending to one or other or several of these criteria, he thinks that an opinion strongly presumptive, if not positive, may be formed on the cause of death in the cases coming under the head of "Latent Disease."

LECTURE XXIV.

DEATH IN ITS MEDICO-LEGAL ASPECTS.

PRELIMINARY REMARKS — Modes of Occurrence (Causes of Death)—Occasions for Inquiry—In Civil Cases—In Criminal Cases—Systemic and Molecular Death—Various modes of its occurrence—Death by Syncope, by Asphyxia (Apnœa), by Coma, by Comato-Asphyxia.

THE inquiries opening up to the medical jurist may be referred to two categories—questions affecting the civil and social rights of individuals, and those arising in connection with injuries against their persons. The inquiries originating in connection with this latter class, on which we are now to enter, include some of the most difficult and important points with which the expert has to deal, and demand a proportionate share of his attention, as on their correct settlement may hinge in a great measure, on not a few occasions, the life or liberty of a fellow-creature.

As all injuries against the person, either immediately or remotely, may, and often do, terminate fatally, in order to our being able to trace the connection between the fatal event and the violence inflicted, it is necessary to have an intimate acquaintance with the various modes of sudden and less sudden death, and with the appearances they respectively leave on the body, and to be able readily to discriminate between these forms of death as brought about by natural causes or the reverse, as furnishing grounds for our decision in cases of violence.

Independently, however, of this relative importance, the subject of death is of interest to the medical jurist, as many questions arise in law which require on the part of the medical man an intimate acquaintance with its phenomena, and with the succession of the changes immediately preceding, or following more or less remotely, the closing scenes of life. The subject, altogether, is one of growing importance as a separate study; for questions of a varied and comprehensive character are now being constantly mooted, in connection more especially with cases of natural and of violent death, not previously adverted to, which are inadequately if at all, discussed in works on medical jurisprudence dating but a few years back, and for the solution of which we mostly to look to later and especially to foreign authors, by whom the subject has been handled with considerable fulness and accuracy

Of the points I have indicated, those which have been laid down with most clearness and precision in our English works have been the subjects of sudden death and the modes of its occurrence. This has been owing chiefly to the circumstance of these topics being considered to belong both to physiology and pathology, thus falling in with the schemes of writers on both of these departments of medical science. It is altogether different, however, with the consideration of the changes which take place in the body after dissolution—a subject which has in a great measure been left to the medical jurist, who has not neglected this important and difficult department of his special duties, though there is still od ɔ˙ɔ left for him to do before he can be said to have m d all its details. In this direction there are three of mo s which stand out most prominently from the rest. The m t of these regards the reality as contradistinguished from the appearance of death; the second, the determination, in the body, of the period of its decease, where nothing is otherwise known of the date of that event; and the third, the ready discrimination, at different stages of its decay, betwixt the usual effects of disease or of violence, and the ordinary progress of its natural decomposition

The importance of the first of these inquiries, it must be owned has been somewhat exaggerated, especially in medico-legal writings dating a few years back, and, accordingly, it has had a disproportionate space devoted in these to its consideration. The settlement of the reality of death owes what interest it possesses for us to the fallacies which have long existed, and still cling to the popular mind, as to the frequency of apparent as contradistinguished from real death, and the consequent dread of premature interment thence arising, of which we have so many fabulous narratives largely received. The importance of the second and third of the inquiries I have mentioned has only been fully realised of late, and belongs almost exclusively to the domain of forensic medicine

In following up the several lines of inquiry thus briefly indicated, I shall trace out the natural order and sequence of events as far as practicable, first considering the immediate causes of death, or, more correctly speaking, the modes of its occurrence; and afterwards the succession of phenomena by which it is followed

The study of the subject of death in reference to its immediate causes, or the modes in which it may be brought about on different occasions, is the key to the series of problems the solution of which falls to the medical jurist in almost every instance of sudden and violent death under unknown or suspicious circumstances.

The fixing with some precision of the period which may have elapsed in any particular instance since the death of the party, on the view of the body, may be a point of great importance both in civil and criminal proceedings. It may, for example, be of the utmost consequence to the surviving relatives of a person found dead that it should be ascertained, at least with tolerable certainty, at what time his death took place, as such information may be necessary to secure to them civil rights, or the succession to property of which otherwise they might be lawfully deprived.

The period of death becomes occasionally of importance in criminal proceedings, as in instances which I shall have occasion to notice presently. But it is not in connection with these applications to practice alone that the subject of the changes undergone by the body after death becomes of interest and importance to the medical jurist. Many of these changes are known to simulate the effects of violence, of poisons, or even natural disease in the living body, and, without careful discrimination, may lead, as they have not unfrequently done, to dangerous and disgraceful mistakes. One of the most interesting practical illustrations of the truth of these remarks is furnished by the successful prosecution of the search for poisons in the body long after burial. In 1824 the successful investigations connected with a body thirty days buried first set Orfila about the inquiry up to what period poisons might be recovered in such cases. Since that time the fact of poisoning has been satisfactorily proved, at the different dates of interment, from a few weeks up to as many as eleven or even thirteen years. It is now known, in fact, that, as a class, the mineral poisons remain in the dead body for an almost indefinite period; and that, although ultimately they enter into new combinations, chiefly from the development of ammonia, yet that their bases may still be recovered from the tissues long after death. The progress of recent research has also shown that the greater number of the most commonly employed of the organic poisons, especially the alkaloids, persist in the tissues unchanged for long periods.

In the case of wounds involving the bones their traces may also be detected; but the question here arises whether the wound has been inflicted during life or after death. The characteristics of a wound of the soft parts, made during life, are not so much the solution of continuity by the cutting instrument as the vital phenomena which have followed his division. These usually are—greater or less hæmorrhage, inflammatory injection of the capillaries, redness and tumefaction of the surrounding parts, etc.—effects which all speedily disappear under the influence of putrefaction, or which soon come to be confounded with the products of it. Nevertheless it may afford a strong presumption in favour of a charge of homicide that such a solution of continuity is found in the dead body. Such investigations are never undertaken without a strong suspicion of violent death; and if traces of wounds are discovered corresponding exactly with the cause assigned, they go far to strengthen the *corpus delicti*. For instance, it often happens that a penetrating wound of the chest will be distinguishable several months after death; while a foreign body left in the wound, such as a bullet etc, or effusions of blood accompanying such wounds, can also be recognised under like circumstances. The same remark applies to ruptures of the larger blood-vessels in consequence of blows or falls, to ruptures of the liver or spleen, the destruction of the eye, gunshot wounds, ruptures of muscles, and some other injuries.

It is different, however, with injuries not leading to a solution of continuity, contusions, for example. Putrefaction not only gives rise to appearances which imitate these, but it also in a short time obliterates all traces of them when actually existing.

In cases of hanging, and still more of strangulation, the disinterment of the body at late periods after death may discover the cord still around the neck.

In cases of infanticide, useful information may be obtained long after death. It has been remarked already, under Infanticide, that the lungs of new-born infants resist the progress of putrefaction longer than the other soft parts, and that it is sometimes possible to determine whether they had been inflated by air or otherwise, months after death. Besides, putrefaction does not seriously hinder us in ascertaining the age of a child in such instances. In 1839 search was made for the remains of a child in Aberdeenshire with the sole object of fixing its age when prematurely expelled, though this object was defeated by the person who had buried it being either unable or unwilling to point out the exact spot of sepulture. The infant had been buried two or three years, and the point sought to be determined was, whether it was a five or a seven months' fœtus.

The examination of the body of the mother at some time after burial may also be useful in cases of abortion, where death has immediately followed delivery. If, for example, a woman has perished from inflammation of the uterus, or from acute metro-peritonitis, in consequence of the not unusual guilty practice of midwives or others who bring on abortion or premature labour, there would be little difficulty in proving that the walls of the uterus had been pierced by the improper use of the instruments which they frequently employ for the purpose, where such puncture has been made.

In the summer of 1841 I and another medical man were directed to attend the disinterment, and to examine the body of a woman who was suspected of having met with foul play in Aberdeen. She had at the time been seven months buried, and if nothing else could have been learned, it would have been an object to have discovered whether she had been delivered, or otherwise, before her death. The investigation, however, was futile in this instance, from the gravedigger having been unable to find the body after several days' search.

Even in those instances in which the body has been already reduced to the state of a mere skeleton, it is sometimes an object—as we have seen under Age, Sex, and Personal Identity—to ascertain the sex to which the individual may have belonged, the height of the individual, etc. But, in rare cases, information less to have been expected has been elicited by such investigations as in the case of Robert and Bastien, tried at Paris in 1833 for the murder of Widow Houet. The assassins had interred the body eleven years previous to the discovery and trial. Though entirely reduced to the state of a skeleton, the third, fourth, fifth, and sixth cervical vertebræ were found, held together by a black matter formed at the expense of the soft parts of the neck, and the whole was still encircled by several turns of the cord with which the woman had been strangled. Not only was the commission of the crime thus proved, but from the length and colour of the hair, state of the teeth, the conformation and length of the bones, and from the discovery of a ring on one of the fingers, no doubt was left of the identity.

Enough, I presume, has thus been said to convince you that the series of inquiries relating to the subject of death and its consequents, as regards the body, both demands and justifies a somewhat extended notice in such a course as this. Without further preface, then, I begin its formal consideration with—

1st, The so-called immediate causes of death, or, as I prefer to say, the modes of its occurrence.

It is now pretty generally agreed—amongst British pathologists at least—that however numerous and diversified may be the abnormal states of the system, and however diverse their modes of operation in leading to the fatal issue, their ultimate effects are all referable to a very limited number of causes, comprising, as these do, the whole of the modes in which life is known to terminate. It is true that we are as yet very far from being able so accurately to trace causes to their effects, as to be able to tell with unerring certainty, what share each of the diseased states which have been discriminated from the others may have in inducing the fatal termination in every individual case of loss of life from the effect of disease or accident. Still less are we yet in a position to distinguish accurately, in every instance, the direct from the indirect action of disease or accident upon those organs of the system, to the arrest, primarily or secondarily, of whose functions death is in all cases to be attributed. Much, however, has been done of late years to enable us to determine, with a surprising degree of accuracy, the precise mode in which the various noxious agents which are arrayed against the life of man are able ultimately to prevail to its extinction.

The subject is one of vast and growing importance to the whole profession; and to none is an intimate knowledge of it more indispensable than to the medical jurist. On the familiarity which he has acquired with the causes of death he must in a great measure rely, in pronouncing on the share which any alleged criminal interference may have had in leading to loss of life, or in discriminating betwixt the result of such interference and that of ordinary or natural causes. The topic, you will thus see, is a very wide one, ranging, as it does, over the whole field of general pathology. In discussing it, however, it will not be necessary for us to follow it beyond the bounds of our own special science. This is the more fortunate for us, as hitherto but little attention has been paid by pathologists to the state of some of the more important organs of the body immediately preceding the arrest of the vital functions, though we are not altogether without information on this obscure point.

Thus, our continental brethren have directed attention to the occurrence of œdema of the lungs generally as the immediate precursor of death in certain diseases of the heart, and œdema of those portions of the lungs which alone had remained in a condition to fulfil their ordinary functions, while the rest of these organs had been for some time too diseased to accomplish this. Again, has been observed, that, where weakened power of the heart to propel the blood from its left side has existed, to whatever disease attributed, inspection has shown that an accumulation of blood had taken place, not only in the right cavities of the heart but in the pulmonary artery and its branches—a state of matters which must have preceded the final stoppage of the arterial current.

Once more, and briefly—for on this point I cannot afford time to dwell—I may be allowed to call your attention to the part which the so-called pulmonary apoplexy sometimes plays in elderly and feeble persons as an immediate precursor of death, and to which my attention was called prior to 1866. But to proceed,—

The actions carried on in the living body in its ordinary relations, and the respective modes in which life is affected by the arrest of the leading functions essential to the continuance of life, are thus clearly and briefly brought before us by Dr Symmonds:—

' Systemic life, as contradistinguished from molecular—or, in other words, the conjoined organism as constituted by the harmonious play of the vital functions, as contrasted with the mere vegetative functions—is constituted by those actions which maintain the material dependence of the several parts of the organic whole. Such are the functions which provide new matter for the blood (digestion and absorption), that which effects a chemical change in the blood (respiration), that which distributes it through the organs and tissues (circulation); that which removes from the blood effete matters (secretion and excretion), and that which is intimately connected with all these functions, though we are ignorant of the mode of its operation, *i.e.*, the function of innervation. The cessation of these actions, and the consequent solution of connection of the various parts of the body, constitute systemic death.'

"Life, in short, cannot continue without the combined integrity of the nervous, circulatory, respiratory, and nutritive and digestive systems, all mutually dependent on each other, and alike indispensable to life. The first three are immediately necessary to life, the last only remotely; so that a severe injury, or the suspension of the functions of any of the former, generally proves quickly fatal or causes sudden death; while injury of the latter commonly proves more slowly fatal, and so causes what is termed lingering death."

Each of the systems I have enumerated may be either directly affected by an injury upon itself, or indirectly, by an injury to some of the others. Thus, first, the nervous system may be either directly affected by an injury of the brain or other parts of the nervous system, or it may be affected indirectly by a severe injury of either of the other systems—as an injury of the heart, lungs, or bowels. Secondly, the circulatory system may be either directly affected by an injury of the heart or some of the blood-vessels, causing hæmorrhage, or indirectly, by lesion of some of the other systems—as by a deficient supply of nervous energy, either from increased or diminished pressure upon the brain; from poison taken into the system; from injury of some part of the nutritive system, or from a want of oxygenised blood caused by injury of the respiratory organs. Thirdly, the respiratory system may be either directly affected by a wound of the chest, by effusion of blood or air into its cavity, by injury of the trachea, or indirectly, by injury of the circulatory or nervous system. And fourthly, the nutritive or digestive system may be affected either directly, by a wound or blow upon some part of the chylopoietic viscera, or indirectly, by injury of the nervous, circulatory, or respiratory systems.

It is generally after violent injuries of the circulatory, respiratory, or nervous systems that we expect to find the fatal event immediately or suddenly succeeding their reception, though even an injury of the digestive system may occasionally cause death in a few hours. In this case, however, the cause of death is usually to be traced to the indirect operation of the injury on the nervous, circulatory, or respiratory systems; hence we may refer the occurrence of sudden death to the failure of the functions of one or other of these three.

When the injurious agent, whatever it may be, has exerted its noxious agency, either directly or indirectly, on the central organ of the nervous system, so as to lead to the arrest of its functions, death is said to have happened by coma; when its operation has been on the respiratory organs, producing the suspension of the changes effected by them on the blood, death is stated to have taken place by asphyxia; and again, when its action, direct or indirect, is on the central organ of the circulation, followed immediately, or after some time, by cessation of its functions, the death is said to occur by syncope.

In proceeding to notice in detail the three different modes of death—namely by coma, by asphyxia, and by syncope—I shall have occasion to advert incidentally to the different arrangements of these adopted by the German jurists, which, as being less simple and lucid, are not well adapted for practical purposes, and are admittedly less defensible on logical grounds. I begin with—

1. Death by *syncope*, or death beginning at the heart. The causes of death by syncope have been classed under four divisions, as these are found to act more especially on (1) the circulatory system, (2) the nervous system, (3) the other organs of the body, or (4) as they are either more general or more obscure in their mode of operation.

To the first of these divisions are referred all cases of extensive hæmorrhage, whether by wounds of the heart itself or of the larger blood-vessels; escape of this fluid from other organs, as the uterus, lungs, etc.; excessive discharges which indirectly lessen the quantity of the circulating fluid, as extensive suppuration, starvation, etc. This division corresponds exactly with the so-called anæmic death of the Germans, and the anæmia of pathologists generally.

To the second division may be referred certain agencies which depress or exhaust the nervous system without interfering with the amount of the circulating fluid within the body,—such as certain poisons, acute peritonitis, low fevers, malignant cholera, severe lesions of the brain, concussions of the spine, severe blows on the præcordia or epigastrium, the entrance of air into the veins, etc. This corresponds pretty closely with the neuro-paralytic death of the Germans, and the asthenia of pathologists.

In the two remaining divisions some of the causes of death are less clearly discernible. Those which stand out most distinctly are the injuries which destroy life with violence—sudden in its character and extreme in its severity—such as being crushed by falling buildings, beams, masts, the wheels of machinery, etc.; being run over by carriages or railway trains, and which come under the designation of mechanical deaths in German medico-legal works. A less clearly marked class of cases in these two divisions is that which the Germans distinguish as dysæmic deaths,—such as are traceable, though obscurely, to the chronic ingestion of arsenic, alcohol, phosphorus, and probably some of the alkaloids; and those cases in which severe injuries followed by illness and operative interference destroy life by pyæmia. The operation of these various causes, and of others of a like kind, is more or less readily understood.

The heart's action coming to be arrested, the brain, the lungs, and consequently all the other organs of the body, cease to receive more blood, leading to the almost instantaneous and simultaneous cessation of circulation, respiration, and innervation. In such cases the examination of the body shows only negative indications of the cause of death.

The absence in most instances of any morbid appearance, coupled with the equality of the distribution of the blood between the right and left sides of the heart, and between the arteries and veins, sufficiently distinguish between death by syncope and death by either coma or asphyxia.

Devergie has contended for a speciality in regard to syncope following wounds of the heart itself, not immediately fatal, as these are found to have their seats on the right or left sides of this organ, when the appearances differ, not only from ordinary cases of syncope, but also according to the side of the heart which has been wounded. Thus he asserts that the wounding of the right side of the heart, by arresting the propulsion of the blood, leads to the accumulation of this fluid in the larger veins, with deficiency of it in the lungs, brain, and left cavities of the heart; and that, on the other hand, in the wounding of the left side of the heart, from the same cause, the lungs will be found gorged with blood, the right cavities of the heart distended with this fluid, and its left cavities empty.

It is doubtful, however, how far these criteria of Devergie are to be trusted. I have failed to realise his distinctions in actual cases of wounds and ruptures of the heart, both prior to the year 1867 and subsequently.

2. I now come to notice the second of the modes of death, enumerated as death beginning at the lungs. To this mode of death the term *asphyxia* is generally applied, though objectionable on some accounts as implying, when correctly interpreted, rather death by syncope than death by the primary arrest of the functions of the lungs—the word asphyxia meaning literally, not breathlessness, but pulselessness. As now understood, however, the necessity of substituting for it the term apnœa, need not be insisted on, as has been done by some writers, it being difficult to get rid of words in such general use as the one in question.

Fatal asphyxia or apnœa may be brought about by causes which act in any of the three following ways, namely—(1) by arresting the action of the muscles of inspiration; (2) by leading to the cessation of the action of the lungs themselves; or (3) by the exclusion of the atmospheric air from the lungs.

First, Arrest of the action of the muscles of inspiration may be due to the exhaustion of the muscles themselves from the sedative effects on them of cold or debility; to loss of nervous influence to them, as from division or compression of the upper part of the spinal cord, or of the phrenic or pneumogastric nerves; to mechanical restraint, as by pressure on the chest or abdomen, or to tonic spasm, as in death from the tetanus caused by nux vomica and one or two other poisons.

Second, Cessation of the action of the lungs may be due to division or compression of the eighth pair of nerves; or a mechanical obstacle, as by the admission of air or of the abdominal viscera into the chest in wounds of the thorax and abdomen.

Third, The partial or complete exclusion of atmospheric air from the lungs may be brought about by its entire absence or extreme rarification; it may be mechanically excluded by a foreign body in the larynx, trachea, or upper part of the œsophagus, by submersion, by suffocation, by strangulation, or by suspension; the place of the atmosphere may be taken by a gas which acts merely by excluding it, or lastly, irritant gases, by producing spasm of the glottis, may effectually bar the admission of the air to the lungs.

The two former of these sets of causes lead up to the fatal result by suspending the mechanical actions of the respiratory organs, the two latter by arresting the chemical changes going on in them. Their ultimate effect, however, is the same, the arrest of the mechanical speedily involving that of the chemical functions of the lungs. The suspension of these, whether directly or indirectly brought about, necessarily involves in a very short period the arrest of the action of the heart, and subsequently of the functions of the brain. The air having ceased to arrive at the lungs, the current of the circulation becomes entirely venous, no longer affording them their necessary stimulus; the heart's action becomes enfeebled, the general circulation is carried on in a languid manner, and, injuriously affecting the brain, its functions cease to be performed. The lungs having now become gorged with blood, the circulation is arrested there, the left cavities of the heart are emptied, and death supervenes.

The most prominent of the morbid appearances after death by asphyxia only will require notice at present, as these are sufficient to distinguish it from death by syncope. They consist in engorgement, to a greater or less extent, of the right cavities of the heart and of all the more important viscera—as the lungs, liver, spleen, kidneys, and brain—with a comparative vacuity of the left side of the heart and the arterial vessels. To this subject, however, I shall have to refer afterwards in greater detail

3. The only mode of death which remains to be adverted to is the third of those enumerated, death by *coma*, or death beginning at the brain. The primary arrest of the functions of the brain may be induced by a variety of causes. Amongst the most common of these is (1) pressure on the brain or medulla oblongata, by effused blood, depressed bone, etc. (2) Another very important and not uncommon cause of coma arises from the effects of blows, falls, etc., on the head and other parts, when of a severe sort—formerly attributed to the mere deficiency of nervous energy of the brain, following the concussion or shock, but now to derangements, more or less distinguishable, of the cerebral structures. (3) The use of certain substances, such as narcotic poisons, etc., may be followed by coma, in consequence of the specific influence which they exert on the brain and nervous system. (4) Lastly, the hæmorrhages or discharges from wounds, when insufficient to induce fatal syncope, may lead to death by coma from their paralysing effects on the nervous centres

When the cause of death is such as to act primarily upon the brain so as to suspend its functions, the first effect which succeeds is the interruption of the mechanical, and, subsequently, of the chemical processes which the respiratory organs perform; which next involves the functions of the heart in precisely the same manner as if the cause had acted primarily on the lungs. From this it will be gathered that the essential appearances after death in either of these two ways are nearly, if not entirely alike, both in coma and asphyxia—an amount of agreement, however, which is usually wholly encountered in those instances in which asphyxia has followed coma.

From what I have said it results,—

1. That if the cause of death acts primarily by the complete suspension of the action of the heart, we should find the lungs, the brain, and the capillary system generally, nearly in their natural state. The arteries should contain blood, as well as both sides of the heart, where it should be found in nearly equal quantities.

2. In death beginning at the lungs; the left heart, the arteries, and the brain are almost deprived of blood, while the capillaries generally, the veins, and the right heart, are full of it.

Finally, in death beginning at the brain, the arteries and the left heart are empty, and this although the suspension of its functions has been the effect of a concussion or otherwise. The right heart, the veins, and the lungs contain, on the contrary, a notable quantity of blood, but much less than when the death has begun at the lungs. There may likewise be congestion or effusion of blood within the head, in consequence less of this mode of death than of cerebral hyperæmia or apoplexy.

Such, then, are the general principles on which we proceed in practice, to the determination in all cases of the immediate causes of death, whether suddenly or consecutively — at more or less distant periods, — and whether from the effects, direct or indirect, of injuries of whatever kind. As will have been seen, the heads to which they have been referred embrace the explanation of all the modes of death, whether occurring naturally or otherwise, and as such yield us the widest generalisations of which the state of the subject will as yet admit. That there are causes of death which do not allow of being distinctly classified or arranged under any one of these divisions, cannot be denied; whether we limit these to instances of violent death, or extend their range so as to include deaths from natural causes. It must be conceded, then, that if we are possessed of no other information than what is deducible from the examination of the dead body, it may happen that we can neither discern the true cause to which the cessation of life is to be properly attributed, nor be in a condition to connect that cause with the agency which may have preceded it. But cases of this puzzling sort, though they may occur, are but rarely encountered in practice, and would almost disappear entirely in the instances in which the previous history was known.

A more important defect attaches, however, to the scheme which I have attempted to elucidate — namely, the difficulty of determining, in every instance, the distinct boundaries which separate death by coma from death from asphyxia, and the reverse. As we have seen, death by coma virtually resolves itself into death by asphyxia, which makes it not unfrequently difficult, if not sometimes really impossible, to deduce, from the view of the dead body, to which site — the brain or the lungs — to ascribe the primary congestion. In these circumstances our German brethren have adopted a fourth form of sudden death, compounded of these two, which we might translate into the synonymous term of comato-asphyxia. But whether we adopt this additional form of death or not, the existence of such a class of cases, in which the predominance of the appearances due to either the one or the other of the two divisions—coma and asphyxia—does not admit of question, and is sometimes encountered under circumstances of no unimportant kind. Some years ago I had occasion to publish an instance of this sort in a female who died under the hands of a person attempting to force her, and in which I, for one, would not undertake, after the most lengthened examination of the body and careful study of all its appearances, to decide positively whether she had died by the one form of death or the other—a caution which the event justified, as her assailant, in his dying declaration, freely and voluntarily emitted, admitted enough to show that the mode of death—namely, by suffocation, as assumed by the court and leaned to by the other medical witnesses—could not have been the real one.

On this point I need only add that the classification of the various forms of sudden and slower death which I have thought it best to follow is the one first sketched out by Bichat, and still adhered to by all our British and American medical jurists, and is more comprehensive than that followed in Germany, which omits most of the causes of natural death, and deals chiefly with those of a violent sort, sets up distinctions without difference, necessitates conclusions based upon purely speculative views, and leaves no key to those mixed cases of apparently violent but really natural death, and *vice versa*, with which the medical jurist has often to deal.

Having thus concluded what had to be said on the modes of its occurrence, I come next to advert to the series of changes which are found to follow the death of the body prior to the commencement in it of the process of decomposition. This, however, must be reserved till next lecture.

LECTURE XXV.

DEATH—(*Continued*).

Changes attending and following the Death of the Body prior to the commencement in it of the Process of Decomposition—Cessation of the Vital Functions—Real as distinguished from Apparent Death—Extinction of the Cerebral Functions—Arrest of the Respiration—Arrest of the Circulation—Extinction of the Organic Functions—Coagulation of the Blood—Loss of Muscular Contractility—Loss of Animal Heat—Apparent Exceptions.

HAVING at last lecture concluded what I had to say on the modes of its occurrence, it now falls to me to notice, in the second place, the series of changes which are found to follow the death of the body. These have been studied by medical jurists from two different points of view; as they bear, *first*, on the distinction betwixt real and apparent death; and *secondly*, on the intimate connection which they are seen to have with many of the most important investigations arising in connection with medico-legal practice. The two sets of inquiries, however, admit of being considered in connection, as the signs which point to the reality of death are merely links in the series of changes naturally following the departure of the life of the body.

Life is the conjoined operation of certain actions peculiar to organised bodies: and according as the organisation is more complicated, so much the higher are the manifestations of vitality. In man and the higher animals we find united both the organs and functions common to them with vegetables and with animals approaching to vegetables in structure. So perfect, however, is the unity of the compound being, Man, and so naturally dependent are the higher on the lower functions, and *vice versa*, that a cessation of one set of actions soon of necessity involves that of all the rest. Nevertheless, this cessation is not simultaneous. Hence the distinction between real and apparent death.

In common with other observers, medical men are accustomed to attach the notion of life to the appearance of those functions classed as vital, which include sensibility, circulation, and respiration. When these are no longer manifested the person is said to be dead; and the period of the cessation of these phenomena is considered as the date of the cessation of life. This, however, is not strictly accurate. It would be more correct were we to limit our notions of apparent—or, as it has been termed, systemic—death, to the consequences of the arrest of the functions of the brain, heart, and lungs; and those of real death to the consequences of the arrest both of the vital functions, and also of those of nutrition and contraction, the cessation of which has been classed as molecular, in contradistinction to systemic death. Some such discrimination is all the more necessary on our part from the circumstance of our not being in possession of means for readily determining with accuracy the precise period of the cessation of the vital or of the organic functions, and consequently for fixing on the precise moment at which systemic has been followed by molecular death. This being the case, it is not surprising that instances have been adduced of persons apparently dead having recovered and lived for longer or shorter periods. This admission, does not bind us, nevertheless, to the reception of all the marvels which we find in authors, the credulity of whom has thrown an air of romance over the whole subject, and imbued the popular mind with a terror of premature interment, which neither reason nor fact is likely speedily to eradicate.

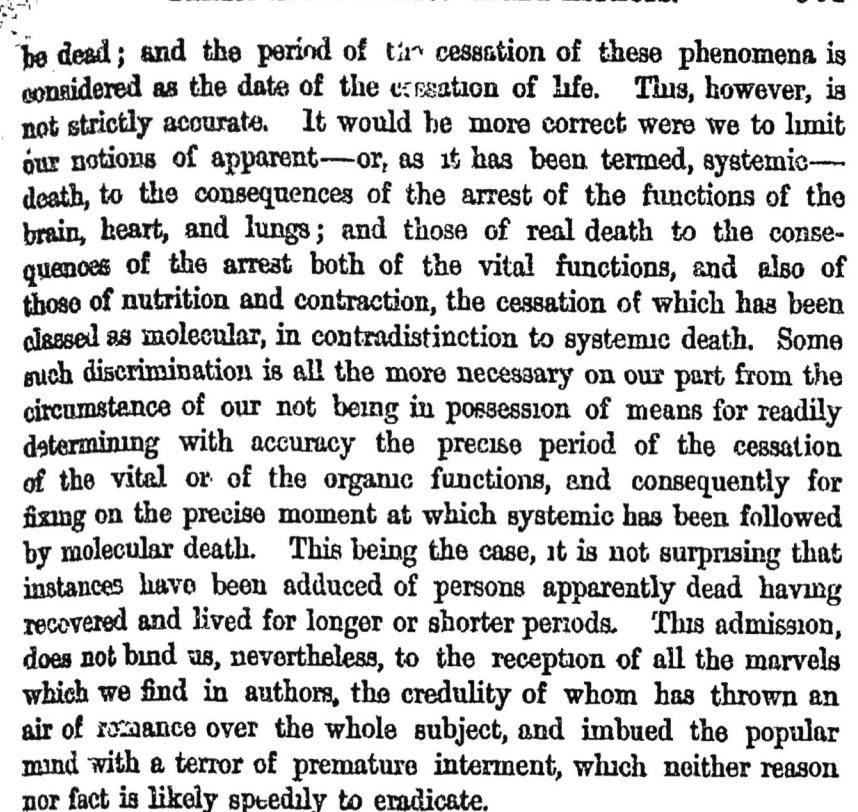

The pros and cons of the subject of the possibility of a person recovering after apparent death have latterly been rather evaded than discussed by medico-legal writers. Let us see how far facts will bear us in this obscure topic.

In the first place, it must be admitted that most, if not all, of the cases which have hitherto been selected as illustrative of the reality of such occurrences are not such as will endure a very close scrutiny. I proceed to notice briefly some of those which bear on their face some marks of authenticity

We are assured by Orfila and others that medical historians have been nearly unanimous in ascribing the flight of Vesalius, the great anatomist, to the unfortunate mistake of laying bare the heart of a nobleman apparently dead, the palpitation of which was the first warning of the true state of matters. The whole story, however, it now turns out, was an idle rumour, which originated after the death of Vesalius, to account for a pilgrimage which he made to Jerusalem, in order to escape from Spain, where he was detained against his will by the bigoted Philip the Second, and enable him to return to his native country, for which he pined.

Next we have the narrative of Louis, the celebrated French writer on medical jurisprudence, to the following effect:—A patient, who was supposed to have died in the Hôpital Salpêtrière, was removed to his dissecting-room. Next morning Louis was informed that moans had been heard in the anatomical theatre, and, on proceeding there he found, to his horror, that the supposed corpse had revived during the night, and had actually died in the struggles to disengage herself from the winding-sheet in which she was enveloped, as was evident, he thought, from the position in which she was found.

Now, apart from the moans heard in this case—of the evidence of which one may reasonably doubt,—there is nothing in the rest of the narration which does not admit of satisfactory explanation on physiological grounds. Thus, it is well known that violent and painful diseases, which prove suddenly fatal, are favourable to the rapid formation of gases, which, by agitating the limbs, give rise to movements in the corpse mimicking those of life "So powerful is this gas in bodies that have lain long in the water," says Devergie, "that, unless secured to the table, they are often observed at the Morgue to be heaved up and thrown to the ground." This explains the reported cases of bodies turning in their coffins, of which we have so many popular tales.

One of the latest of these occurs in a quarter where it was scarcely to be expected—namely, in a report to the French Government on the best means for preventing premature interment, presented by a commission in 1866, where the names of Larrey, Tardieu, Devergie, and others, occur. Here, as in many similar instances of the alleged dangers of premature interment, we have cases advanced on very loose evidence, and with an absence of names, dates, and localities, to say the least of it, very suspicious. One of these cases is very like that of Louis at the Salpêtrière The alleged fact rests on the authority of a person some years dead, and by whom transmitted is not said. This person, four years after the death of his father, wishing once more to look upon his body, after its disinterment, found it resting on its right side, the hands detached from the rosary by which they had been encircled.

Such is a specimen of the kind of proofs offered to us of apparent being taken for real death. We must not, however, go so far as to deny altogether the possibility of such a mistake It is well known that Rigardeaux (in 1745) delivered a child by the feet from a woman supposed to have been seven hours dead, but who subsequently revived, and was, with her child, alive three years after. Again, the young female relative of a late eminent practitioner in Aberdeen, some years ago, while labouring under pericarditis, was left four hours for dead by her relatives, though she revived and lived for twenty-four hours longer. I was in attendance, as assistant, in this case, at the time of its occurrence, and had notice sent me of her death on the occasion referred to.

This, with the cases of Colonel Townshend and others, which I shall have occasion to detail presently, gives a colour of probability to the cases of reported recoveries after one or two hours of apparent death, adduced in the publications of the Royal Humane Society.

Allowing for much of fiction or vague statement mixed up with and encumbering this subject, enough of evidence might be thus adduced to warrant me in directing attention to the means of discriminating between real and apparent death, even if these signs were not important to us as indicative of the order in which several of the characteristics of life leave the body.

The morbid states which might be most readily supposed to simulate death, are syncope, apoplexy, asphyxia, catalepsy, and hysteria. In these and all other cases, the indications of real, as contradistinguished from apparent death, are drawn from various sources — as, first, from the cessation of the vital functions; secondly, from the cessation of the organic functions; thirdly, from the occurrence of certain changes in the tissues incompatible with the maintenance of life; and fourthly, from those peculiar alterations in the body which are due to the commencement in it of the process of decomposition. These I shall consider as nearly as possible in the order just stated, since they derive their importance for us, not so much as indications of death, but as being links in the chain of phenomena exhibited by the body subsequent to the extinction of life.

First, of the extinction of the vital functions. The least important of these is the cessation of the functions of the sensorium, or insensibility. This state not only precedes, in most cases, real death by some hours, but also is so frequently seen without being necessarily followed by dissolution, that no reliance can be placed on it, by itself, as a sign of death. When to this, however, is added the arrest of the respiration, the idea of death is so complete in the minds of ordinary observers, that, in popular language, loss of breath is synonymous with death So close is the connection between respiration and circulation, that the cessation of the breathing, when complete and final, is followed, at an interval of two or three minutes, by the stoppage of the circulation. In these circumstances the failure of the respiration is followed by insensibility, which is even more speedy in its occurrence than the arrest of the circulation. The extinction of the vital functions, which would at first sight appear to afford decisive evidence that the person is no longer alive, is open, however, to the two-fold objection, that we cannot distinguish, with absolute certainty, the minimum action of these functions from their complete annihilation, and that recoveries have taken place after their apparent cessation.

In the case of Colonel Townshend, so often quoted, that individual, in the presence of Dr Cheyne and others, showed that he possessed the singular power of bringing about a gradual diminution of his breathing and circulation, till, in a short time, the action of the heart could be no longer felt; while a mirror held before his mouth was not dimmed in the least degree. So complete, to all appearance, was the extinction of the vital functions, that the observers, thinking that he had carried the experiment too far, were about to leave him for dead when they observed some motion about the body; and, upon examination, found his pulse and the action of his heart gradually returning, when he began to breathe gently and to speak softly.

A similar case was related by the late Dr Duncan of Edinburgh, in his lectures, which he described, if I remember rightly, as having been witnessed by himself and the other medical professors in the University. The subject of it was a medical student, who, like Colonel Townshend, simulated successfully the appearances of death. He died, however, some time afterwards, of disease of the heart. Townshend expired on the evening of the day on which he exhibited his power over the vital functions.

A similar control over these functions was claimed by the late Professor ———, of Aberdeen University. That he had this control, if not directly, at least in an indirect form, and one which admits of explanation, was shown by the following circumstance. As some doubts had been expressed of the alleged fact, on one occasion, without any warning of his intention, he ran once round the table in his room, and threw himself suddenly on a couch. At this moment his face was deadly pale, his breathing could not be perceived, and his pulse could not be felt at the wrist. On moistening his lips with a stimulant, the pulse began to return, at first feebly, and he could be seen to breathe before time was afforded for exposing the chest to apply the stethoscope.

Whether, as in this instance, Townshend and the Edinburgh student brought on the syncope indirectly through the previous stoppage of the respiration, we have no means of knowing. If so, the unnatural character of the occurrence is much lessened, if not sufficiently explained.

Professor —— had suffered for several years before his death from fatty degeneration of the heart, and was liable to faintings after exercise or other exertion. He died about two years after the occurrence just mentioned,—and which I witnessed,—in England, after a very short illness.

In such instances as the above the cessation of the vital functions could only have been apparent; but there can be little doubt that, in some of the cases of reported restoration, after some minutes of submersion in water, the extinction was real, probably in consequence of syncope, or of some state approaching to it, having come on, in place of asphyxia, as usually happens. As to the alleged cases of persons who have been said to have been many hours, and even days, without pulse or breathing, I do not hesitate to affirm, with Dr. Symonds, that the observers were deceived, and that in reality both these functions were performed, though in so low a degree as to escape detection, as in hybernating animals.

It is but proper, however, to add, on this point, the striking circumstance related in his lectures by Professor Maschka of Prague. A mature child, which showed no signs of life, was placed in the anatomical rooms of the University, left there for fourteen hours, and then taken to the physiology class-room. On laying open the chest no blood flowed from the integuments and soft parts in front. When the heart was reached, it was seen pulsating at the rate of twenty beats per minute. The lungs were seen to be in the fœtal condition. The professor stated to his class that the occurrence was witnessed by himself and some of his colleagues.

In actual practice it might often be difficult to determine betwixt the minimum of the vital functions and their entire arrest, none of the usual tests advanced being much to be relied on. Thus, in hybernating animals, who are known to breathe, a mirror is not dimmed by them when in this state—so that this popular test must fail,—though the breathing has not entirely ceased. In the same way we become aware of the fallacy of the Winslow test of placing a vessel full of water over the bottom of the chest. In Dr Marshall Hall's experiments with the bat, a delicate apparatus which he had contrived to detect the slightest motion was not disturbed during the continuance of his experiments with this animal in the torpid state. As to the circulation, it may continue though no pulsation can be felt over the arteries or the cardiac region, and no sound be perceptible by auscultation, as I have once or twice witnessed in profound coma from intoxication, notwithstanding which recovery took place.

Few practitioners would be willing to apply Foubert's test of the cessation of the circulation—namely, cutting through one of the intercostal spaces, and feeling the heart through it with the point of the finger.

Various practical methods of testing the reality of death have, however, been proposed, such as that of Laborde, who states that if a needle be plunged into the muscles of a limb in the dead body, it will be found on removal, after from twenty to sixty minutes, to retain its lustre; while, in the living, a needle, similarly treated, will have become oxidised. or that of Dupont, by dropping atropine into the eye, and observing if it acts on the pupil.

Some still simpler tests of the arrest of the circulation, and consequently of the reality of death, have been suggested—namely, the injection of a few drops of ammonia under the skin, which, in the dead body, gives rise to no surrounding redness, as it does while life continues; or, again, the tying of a ligature round a finger, and noting if redness occurs or not beyond the ligatured part of the finger.

Simultaneously with the arrest of the vital functions the eyes lose their lustre, the surface generally assumes a marked pallor, and the muscles become relaxed. To all of these appearances, which usually mark off very distinctly the moment of the cessation of the vital as contrasted with the mere organic functions, some, at least, apparent exceptions are known occasionally to occur. The eyes, for instance, retain their lustre for some time after death from breathing carbonic acid gas. The pallor of the surface, in certain cases presently to be noticed, may be so slight or evanescent as to be scarcely sufficient to attract attention. The muscular relaxation again, which, in ordinary cases, equally with the pallor of the surface, is, as I have said, a marked feature of the change from life to death, may also fail to take place, as in a class of instances to which I shall have to refer by-and-by.

The phenomena last adverted to, you will have noticed, occur simultaneously with the extinction of the vital functions Those to which I have now to direct your attention, are, secondly, the phenomena which follow the arrest of the vital functions, and indicate the occurrence of molecular death, or the arrest of the organic functions. Their occurrence precedes, in order of time, the subsequent changes originating in physical alterations of the tissues.

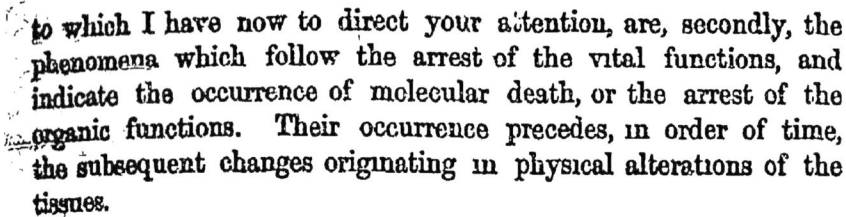

1. The most important phenomenon belonging to this period is the coagulation of the blood in the heart. In this organ the form assumed by the blood is occasionally that of a fibrinous clot, sometimes a soft clot. In some forms of death the blood remains to all appearance fluid, though this is asserted by Hassal to be only apparently the fact in any case. To what extent the coagulation of the blood takes place in the interior of the body, elsewhere than in the heart and large vessels, is a moot point, to which we shall have to return under Wounds. There is no doubt of the fact, however, that blood withdrawn from the body within the first three or four hours after death will, as a general rule, be found to coagulate on exposure.

2. In addition to this sign of death and indication of its reality, we have the further phenomenon, the loss of muscular contractibility,—like the last, a sign of greater value and importance than any of those which have been as yet adverted to. This change is not to be confounded with the mere state of relaxation of the muscles, which, as we have seen, so strikingly marks the cessation of the vital functions. Although the tonicity of the muscles has ceased at the moment of systemic death, these tissues are found to retain their contractibility for some time longer, admitting, as this property does, of being readily elicited by certain stimuli.

The appearance and disappearance of the muscular contractibility in different parts of the body is believed to follow a certain fixed order. Thus, according to Nysten, the parts which first present this change are the neck and trunk, it then appears in the lower extremities, and lastly, in the upper—its departure observing the same order. With this agree substantially the later assertions of Kussmaul.

The duration of this phenomenon in the dead body is shortened by its exposure to warmth and moisture, and to ammoniacal, carbonic, and sulphuretted hydrogen gases; it is unaffected by carburetted hydrogen, chlorine, and sulphurous acid gases, nor is it diminished in cases of asphyxia, strangulation, and drowning.

But, independently of these causes affecting the continuance of this property of the muscular fibre after death, it has been lately discovered that the nature of the disease of which the person has died exerts a considerable influence on this change. Thus, in some experiments on the muscles of the trunk and limbs with the galvanic stimulus, the irritability was found to disappear in peritonitis in about three hours; in phthisis, scirrhus, and cancer, in from three to six hours; in death from profuse hæmorrhage or mortal lesions of the heart, in about nine hours; in apoplexy with paralysis, in about twelve hours; and in adynamic fevers and pneumonia, in from ten to fifteen hours.

The continuance of contractibility in the muscles after the extinction of the vital powers explains some facts already adverted to, as well as some which will come under our notice afterwards—namely, the alleged delivery of the fœtus, and the discharge of the urine and fæces after apparent death; the appearances of wounds at various periods after death, etc. The best method for testing its presence is by galvanism, though it may be shown to exist by simply pricking, or otherwise irritating a nerve of motion leading to the part. As a general principle it may be stated, that the disappearance of the muscular irritability is synchronous with the commencement of cadaveric rigidity.

3. The loss of animal heat which follows the extinction of the vital functions is a more equivocal sign of death than the phenomenon last mentioned. The mean time required for the complete cooling of the corpse has been fixed by Caspar at from eight to twelve hours. The process, however, admits of modification by a great variety of circumstances. As a general rule, the cooling of the dead body is slower of completion after acute than after chronic diseases. It is usually considerably retarded in asphyxial cases, except in the case of submersion. In suddenly fatal apoplexy, accident, or acute disease, the body has often been found to retain its heat for long periods. After death by hanging, suffocation, or breathing carbonic acid gas, it has been observed to retain its heat from twenty-four to forty-eight hours, or even longer, though in some cases of fatal asphyxia it has been known to cool as rapidly as in death from other causes.

It has been observed, on the other hand, that in those who have died from chronic disease, and in whom death has taken place slowly, the bodies have cooled very rapidly. They have been found quite cold on the surface within four or five hours after death; at least as cold as other subjects after the lapse of fifteen or twenty hours who have died under reverse circumstances.

In such cases coldness of the body is commonly manifested, before dissolution, in the parts most exposed, as the hands and feet, the nose and the ears.

The human body, cæteris paribus, will part with its heat in the same way as any other mass of matter placed in a medium cooler than itself, namely, by radiation and conduction. Thus, the fact is easily explained that the body parts with its heat sooner in water than in air, in a current of air than in a tranquil atmosphere, and in a large than in a small room; as also the circumstance that the body of an adult cools more slowly than that of a child or of an old person, a fat than a lean person, a body wrapped in clothes than a naked corpse, etc.

The time the body will take to cool may occasionally form an important element in a case of murder, by the connection which the period of death may have with the act of the accused party.

In the case of a person of the name of Millie, for the manslaughter of whom a man named Bolam was tried in England some years ago, the body, although clothed, is reported to have been found cold about nine hours after death.

In the case of William Spicer, tried for the murder of his wife at Reading, in March, 1846, the facts connected with the rigidity and cooling of the body, and the period of time required for the development of these conditions, formed essential elements in the chain of circumstantial evidence by which guilt was brought home to the panel. Two contused wounds were found on the woman's temples, sufficient to have stunned her, but not to have caused her death. It appeared probable that the prisoner had thrown her down a cellar-stairs, where she was found lying dead with fracture of the skull, and of the second cervical vertebra. The noise of the fall of the deceased was heard about half-past twelve; her body, when discovered at nine o'clock, was quite cold and rigid. The inference which the prosecutor required to establish was that she had been dead for the whole of this period. In proof of the correctness of this assumption, the medical witness declared that at that season rigidity would not come on before at least from eight to ten hours—a period which corresponded with a short visit to his house by the panel at the time the fall was heard, and completely negatived the possibility of a statement made by him that he had seen his wife in life on a subsequent visit at a quarter to five.

There is a curious circumstance connected with the one we have been considering, and forming an apparent exception to the rule regarding the cooling of the body after the cessation of the vital functions, which requires here to be adverted to. I allude to certain alleged instances of the corpse, without any evident cause, maintaining its temperature for many hours after dissolution, or even exhibiting a degree of heat greater than it had done during life. Thus, Dr. Davy has found a temperature of 113° F. in the pericardium after death.

The difficulties which such an occurrence might give rise to are well illustrated by the following case, which appeared in the *Lancet*, and which had evidently been communicated by the reporter in a fit of remorse, occasioned by his precipitancy.

In October 1840, a servant-girl, who had retired to bed in apparently perfect health, was found the following morning, as it appeared, dead. A surgeon who was called pronounced her to be really so, and that she had been dead for some hours. A coroner's inquest was summoned for four o'clock, and the reporter and the surgeon who had been called in to the girl were ordered to inspect the body previous to its sitting. On proceeding to the house for this purpose at two o'clock, the inspectors found the girl lying in bed in an easy posture, her face pallid, but placid and composed, as if she were in a deep sleep, while the heat of the body had not diminished. A vein was opened by them, and various stimuli applied, but without affording any sign of resuscitation. After two hours of hesitation and delay, a message being brought that the jury were waiting for their evidence, they were forced to proceed to the inspection. In moving the body for this purpose the warmth and pliancy of the limbs were such as to give the examiners the idea that they had to do with a living subject! The internal cavities, as they proceeded, were found so warm that a very copious steam issued from them on their exposure. All the viscera were in a healthy state, and nothing was detected which could throw the smallest light on the cause of this person's death.

The explanation of such an occurrence as the above is not difficult. In such instances the body will have parted with its natural heat so slowly, that, before this has had time to disappear, the commencement of putrefaction—which is unusually early in such cases—will have led to the evolution of additional heat, by the occurrence of those chemical changes on which this process depends. One or two facts from my own experience will place this matter in its true light. The cases which follow, allowing for some exaggeration in the *Lancet* case, do not differ from it essentially.

A seaman affected with scorbutus died suddenly from (as was found on dissection) the effusion into the pleural cavities of sixteen ounces of serum. Next day, on proceeding to his house for the inspection, I was informed that the body had retained its heat, and the limbs their flexibility. The heat of the trunk and limbs was little, if at all, below the vital temperature. Next day putrefaction had advanced so far as to leave no doubt of his state, the heat being greatest in the chest, where the decomposition was farthest advanced. I once witnessed the momentary alarm of a student on the removal of the sternum at finding the contents of the chest warm, and steam issuing from its cavity. The following case, however, is more to the point.—

One morning, in the summer of 1840, I was sent for to Littlejohn Street, Aberdeen, to see a lad of seventeen, who had just fallen down in the street, when on his way to a workshop in the neighbourhood. He had immediately before left his parents' house in good health and spirits. The death appeared to have been instantaneous. Finding that nothing could be done I left as soon as I perceived that he was really dead. On the afternoon of the same day I was again sent for by the lad's mother, who stated that she had been deterred from proceeding to dispose of the body by observing that it did not become cold, as might have been expected had he been really dead; that the limbs were still supple; and that within the previous half-hour the colour had returned to his cheeks. In short, she expected that he was about to come to life again. These statements were undoubtedly correct, and it was my painful duty to make the poor woman aware that all this was owing to the very rapid approach of decomposition in this instance, which, by next day, was fully developed in the body, the increased temperature still continuing.

In some rare cases the commencement of putrefaction, with the consequent warmth of the body caused by it, follows dissolution so speedily that the previous rigidity of the limbs which succeeds the cooling of the corpse has escaped notice altogether, from its slightly marked character or brief duration. Instances of this exceptional sort are encountered after the sudden deaths, especially in very warm weather, of persons previously in health, who have fallen victims after brief illness to attacks of acute inflammatory or apoplectic diseases. In all such cases a careful investigation will lead to detection of some of the indications of the commencement of decomposition in the body.

The continuance of secretion, absorption, and nutrition for a short period after death has been contended for, from the exudation of serous fluids in some parts, their disappearance in others, and the alleged growth of the hair after the extinction of the vital functions. These facts—admitting to some extent their reality—are capable of explanation on such merely physical principles as transudation, endosmose, penetration, etc., without supposing the continuance for a time after death of the molecular processes; others of them may be accounted for on chemical principles. Still, it is not impossible that, as in some of the lower grades of organisation, cell-growth, from its comparative independence of the vital functions, may continue for a short period after the cessation of these functions.

From the combination of the signs we have passed in review—namely, *first*, the cessation of the vital functions; *second*, the lustreless eye; *third*, the loss of muscular contractility; *fourth*, the pallor of the surface; *fifth*, the loss of the animal heat; and *sixth*, the relaxation of the muscles—Caspar fixes the period which may have elapsed since the death at from ten to twelve hours at the longest.

LECTURE XXVI.

DEATH—(*Continued*).

PHYSICAL CHANGES IN THE BODY BEFORE PUTREFACTION HAS COMMENCED —Cadaveric Softening—Cadaveric Rigidity—Cadaveric Spasm—Tetanic Spasm —Cadaveric Lividities (Hypostases)—External Hypostases—Internal Hypostases — CHANGES IN THE EXTERNAL ASPECT.—Facies Hippocratica—Flattening of the Soft Parts—Changes in the Eyeball and Pupil—Changes in the State of the Hands.—CHANGES ORIGINATING IN THE PROCESS OF DECOMPOSITION —Conditions capable of retarding or hastening Decomposition—Congelation—Elevated Temperature—Electricity—Various Gases, etc.

SUCCEEDING the phenomena last discussed—namely, coagulation of the blood, loss of muscular contractility, loss of animal heat, and relaxation of the muscles,—I have next to advert to the appearance of a set of signs of death incompatible with the maintenance of life, originating in physical alteration of the soft solids, and preceding, in order of time, the commencement of decomposition. The most prominent of the changes marking off this middle period are, softening of the muscles on the one hand, rigidity of the muscles on the other, and the appearance of lividities on the surface of the body.

The softening of the animal tissues which follows dissolution after a short period, is not to be confounded with the reappearance of the same phenomenon at a later period under the influence of decomposition The latter is the cadaveric softening of authors, and follows the disappearance of rigidity; while the former, on the contrary, is found to precede its advent

The softness or want of elasticity of the textures of the body, which speedily succeeds death, is the first of the alterations in it which are due to the destruction of their physical properties It is doubtless owing partly to differences in the distribution of the fluids present in the tissues, and partly to changes in the tissues themselves The flattening of those parts of the body upon which it rests, in consequence of this loss of its elasticity, has been considered, on good grounds, as a valuable criterion of the reality of death The flexibility of the joints, which is noticeable at the same time, obviously depends on the now relaxed state of the muscles generally; a phenomenon, as we shall presently see, not universally observed in the dead body.

The next sign, which may be regarded as indicative of a further stage—distinguishable, in general, with sufficient accuracy, in the series of evolutions in the dead body,—is that of the appearance of cadaveric rigidity, or that change which occurs in the body after death, when the softening described at last lecture has given place to an opposite state of the limbs and joints. In place of their former flaccidity, the muscles now acquire a brawny firmness, and it requires some force to move the joints from the position, whatever that may be, which they have by this time assumed. This state of the muscles and joints continues till the approach of putrefaction; but it is not equally marked in all cases, nor does the period of its appearance and disappearance correspond in different bodies. In those cases, which I formerly noticed, where the vital heat is succeeded, without any appreciable interval, by the rise of temperature caused by the commencement of decomposition, the rigidity is usually so slight, or has given place so speedily to cadaveric softening, as to have escaped notice entirely. Cadaveric rigidity is considered an important indication of the reality of death. This change is first noticed in the lower jaw, then in the neck and trunk, it next appears in the lower extremities; and, last of all, the upper. Its departure observes the same order, and, once gone, it does not return, but gives place to a state of relaxation of the soft parts, even more marked than before.

The period of the appearance of cadaveric rigidity is liable to vary considerably in different cases. Eight, ten, and twenty hours after death have been fixed on as the date of its occurrence, while an occasional delay has been contended for of even thirty hours. Its mean duration is from twenty-four to thirty-six hours, although it has been known at times to last for six or seven days, or even more. These results are modified by season, temperature, and the nature of the fatal disease or injury. As a general rule, a low temperature favours the rigidity of the body; as does previous vigour of constitution, sudden death from violence or accident, and the middle period of life; though it has been met with well-marked in the very old, and even in still-born infants, of which I have lately met with an example. After diseases of the nervous system, fevers, narcotic poisoning, and death by lightning, the cadaveric rigidity is but little marked, though even in those cases it may usually be observed to occur. That the seat of the rigidity is the muscular system is universally admitted, but what the precise state of the muscular tissues is, has not been determined, notwithstanding the various explanations which have been advanced on the subject by physiologists and medical jurists.

The above remarks apply to rigidity as it manifests itself in the limbs and joints. It should not be overlooked, however, that the same phenomenon is to be met with occasionally in certain internal parts, such as the heart and intestinal tract. In the latter situation, its occurrence can lead to no mistake. In the former, the contraction thus induced has led to the assumption of the heart being hypertrophied, from the close contraction of the left ventricle, which in these instances mimics very closely the so-called concentric hypertrophy. Indeed, so much is this the case, that certain pathologists have set down all such cases, as noticed by authors, to cadaveric rigidity merely, in the absence of actual disease.

Cadaveric Spasm.—It is of importance to be aware of a species of rigidity different from the above, which is liable to occur after death, and which might be easily confounded with cadaveric rigidity. I allude to what has been termed cadaveric spasm. It consists in a sort of spasmodic contraction assumed by the muscles at or before death, which they are found to retain for some hours after death, passing then into true cadaveric rigidity. This so-called spasm has usually been observed in certain cases of sudden death; as after the more violent forms of death in battle; after *apoplexie foudroyante*, and serious cerebro-spinal injuries. I have known it to occur, however, after deaths by pneumonia and pulmonary apoplexy.

That this state of the body after death is not of very rare occurrence, I am inclined to think, from having met with several instances in my practice, having had occasion in 1850 to record three such cases, in a paper in the *Medical Gazette*, and eight more in a review of "Kussmaul on Cadaveric Rigidity," in the *British and Foreign Medico-Chirurgical Review*.

A startling incident at the famous Balaklava charge in the Crimean war belongs apparently to this class of cases. Captain Nolan, while riding in advance of the cavalry, received a wound from a Russian shell, which tore open his chest. The arm which he was waving in the air at the moment remained high uplifted, and he retained his seat on his horse, which wheeled round and retreated; the rider gave a death-shriek, and passed through the ranks in the same position and attitude before dropping from the saddle.

I need scarcely say that it is of importance in medico-legal practice, to be aware of the occasional occurrence of such cases as these. Thus, a weapon grasped in the hand of a corpse points to death by suicide, as such a circumstance could not be produced by a murderer. It has been actually found that the hand of a dead person cannot be made to grasp a weapon in the same way as a hand that has had it firmly held by the contraction of the muscles at or before the extinction of life. At the trial of a person named Saville, in 1844, in England, it came out in evidence that the deceased, his wife, was found dead with her throat cut, and that there was a razor, not grasped, but lying loosely in her hand. There was no blood upon the hand which held the razor, and this, together with the fact of its being loose, rendered it certain that the weapon must have been placed there by some one after the woman's death.

In a case tried in France in 1835, a man narrowly escaped conviction as the murderer of his father. The latter had been found dead in a sitting posture, with a recently discharged pistol grasped in his right hand, the weapon resting upon the thigh in such a way that the slightest motion of the part would apparently have caused it to fall. It was assumed that the son had produced the injury to the face which had been the cause of death, and had afterwards placed the pistol in his father's hand in order to induce the supposition of suicide. The medical evidence, by showing that the grasping of the weapon could not have been simulated after death, led to an acquittal.

The occurrence of the same phenomenon, on the other hand, may by attention to minute circumstances, negative the possibility of suicide.

Thus, in the case of Lord William Russell, murdered by his valet, it was observed that one hand of the deceased firmly grasped the sheet of the bed, as if in a struggle with an assassin.

In a case tried in England the prisoner was charged with the murder of an old woman with whom he cohabited. The body was discovered with injuries about the head, pointing to death by violence. In her right hand was found a considerable quantity of brown hair, and in the other a single grey hair, all grasped evidently in the struggle for life. The morning following the murder the prisoner went to a hairdresser, and desired to have his hair and whiskers cut. This man observed that the hair and whiskers had been recently cut, and evidently by some one unaccustomed to hair-cutting. The whiskers, unlike the hair of the head, had turned grey. The hairdresser was of opinion that the hair found in the hands of the deceased was of the same colour as the prisoner's. This, with other circumstances, led to his conviction.

In some of my own cases the suspicion against the possibility of criminal violence was averted, from attention to the circumstances of the deaths. One or two of these, which called for investigation by the law authorities, I may briefly relate.

In April 1833, a woman, aged thirty-six, was found dead in a house of bad fame in Albion Street, Aberdeen. She had been drinking shortly before with some young men, who were observed to leave the house suddenly, and to take to their heels. The woman lay on her back, her knees drawn up, and her hands grasping the clothes, the body retaining its position in consequence of cadaveric spasm having come on at the moment of death. It was discovered on dissection that this female had died of pneumonia, and it came out in the precognition that one of the young men had been attempting to have connection with her at the moment of death, which the woman was making some effort to prevent. The parties were all in drink at the time.

In the case of rape and murder referred to near the conclusion of Lecture XXIV., p 359, the body of the victim had been fixed at death in much the same position as in the last case: one of the knees and one elbow were half bent, one of the upper extremities being extended at a right angle with the trunk, and the thighs apart.

A woman who kept a brothel in Aberdeen was found in April 1837 in bed, suffocated; her face was buried in the pillow, and her limbs fixed by cadaveric spasm in such a position as to show that she had died in a severe struggle to escape from the prone position in which she was lying at the time of her death As the inmates of the house were of the worst description, and as the woman was known to have had money in her possession, a suspicion arose that she had been murdered It turned out on investigation, however, that the deceased had been thrown carelessly into bed in a state of intoxication with her face downwards, and left there, and that she was believed to have been too drunk to rectify her position, notwithstanding some convulsive efforts to do so, when the weight of her head and bust, by burying her mouth and nostrils in the pillow, had caused suffocation.

It should be known, however, that a similar rigid state of the muscles occurs at or after death by strychnia poisoning, persisting till ordinary cadaveric rigidity comes on, and only disappearing along with it. To distinguish betwixt this rigidity from strychnia and ordinary cadaveric rigidity, we are furnished with a discriminating test in the circumstance, which I have been able to verify, that when the former is forcibly overcome, it returns after some time, which is not the case with the latter.

Other forms of tetanic spasm—such as are occasionally seen in cases of apoplexy, catalepsy, syncope, and asphyxia—it is believed disappear shortly after death.

When to the series of signs in the period taken under review —pallor, lustreless eyes, loss of muscular contractility, and of animal heat, and primary relaxation of the muscles—is added the subsequent appearance of cadaveric rigidity, the body, according to Caspar, may be presumed to be that of a person who has been dead within from two to three days at the longest.

We have now to turn to certain appearances on the surface and internal parts of the dead body, which are referable, though not limited, to the period we are considering, to which the somewhat vague term lividities, and others equally loose, have been applied. In order to avoid the error of confounding the different appearances which have been classed together under the common name of lividities by medico-legal writers, we shall separately consider here—(1), those of them which appear spontaneously on the surface of the body after death, and before the access of putrefaction in it, under the name of cadaveric lividities, the so-termed external hypostases of Caspar; and (2), those internal lividities which follow death and precede decomposition, known simply as the hypostases of most authors, or the internal hypostases of Caspar. This will sufficiently discriminate those external appearances, the effects of natural causes, from ecchymoses, the result of violence during life, and also from certain appearances, whether external or internal, which have been mistaken for the results of increased vascular action or congestion before death.

Cadaveric lividities of the first sort, then, are certain reddish patches which appear on the surface of the body in the act of cooling, giving to the previously pale skin a somewhat mottled appearance. Though at first usually of a pure yet dull red, they commonly soon deepen to a shade of colour varying from a livid or coppery red to a reddish blue. The skin presents no sensible elevation at the part, as in ecchymoses. Their shape, as first noticed, is extremely irregular, appearing as they do in isolated patches, which afterwards coalesce and cover large portions of the surface of the dependent parts of the body. They are rarely wanting in this marked form when the body is examined at from twelve to twenty-four hours after death; though, occasionally, they are either absent or but faintly traced, as after death by copious hæmorrhages or anæmia. They are readily distinguishable from all other discolorations of the skin, by dividing the skin and subcutaneous areolar tissue at the part, as such incisions never yield effused fluid or coagulated blood; or, at the most, exhibit a few bloody points from the division of small veins in the skin or areolar tissue underneath it

In speaking of these cadaveric lividities I have avoided the term occasionally applied to them by medical jurists—suggillations,—as this term is by a few authors restricted to ecchymoses proper, while the mass of writers employ it as synonymous with the appearance we are considering—a clashing of meanings which is rather unfortunate, and which ought if possible to be avoided.

These cadaveric lividities, or external hypostases, it will be seen from what I have said, readily admit of being distinguished from appearances likely to be confounded with them, by a little attention to the following criteria:—First, their seat,—the superficial layer of the true skin; secondly, their extent,—involving large portions of the body, or to be met with in different parts of it at the same time; thirdly, their circumference,—which, though irregular and slashed, terminates abruptly, and not by a gradual fading into the surrounding colourless skin; fourthly, the entire absence of extravasated blood at their site, and, lastly, by the failure in detecting any trace of contusion or ruffling, at the part, of the cuticle or true skin

It is to be feared that a want of attention to these circumstances has led to the fatal mistake of confounding these lividities with the effects of violence during life. Thus, in two cases, for which we are indebted to Sir Robert Christison, criminal responsibility is believed to have attached to innocent individuals.

In one instance of this sort, which occurred in Aberdeen in 1764, two persons were condemned for the murder of a relative, chiefly on the evidence of a broad blue mark observed on the neck of the latter after death, which the witnesses compared to that produced by strangulation, but which there was reason to believe, from their own description of it, must have been due to natural changes taking place after death.

Another case occurred in Edinburgh in 1808. Two persons were tried for the murder of a companion with whom they had been drinking and quarrelling, and who was discovered soon afterwards lying dead in a wood, with marks of what were thought to be numerous contusions all over his body. On the trial the medical witnesses proved that the apparent contusions were nothing else than the livid patches sometimes met with on the body after natural death. The accused parties were consequently acquitted.

These cadaveric lividities, though their importance to the medical jurist must be obvious from what has now been stated, are not much to be trusted as indications of the reality of death, on account of their liability to be confounded with similar marks which may be met with on the body at or before death, and from which it is sometimes difficult to distinguish them without proceeding to divide the integuments. The appearances to which I refer—also sometimes loosely classed as suggillations—can scarcely be fitly characterised as hypostases, as they occur, not on the dependent but on the non-dependent parts of the body; nor can they be called cadaveric lividities, since they are to be encountered occasionally on the living as well as on the dead. Livid patches of this sort are met with on the legs and feet of aged persons, and in the same situation on the bodies of those dying of scurvy, typhus, and other adynamic diseases. In subjects not belonging to either of these categories such patches are not infrequently seen on the face; often on the front of the neck and upper and fore part of the chest; sometimes on the sides of the trunk, and frequently on the fronts and sides of the limbs, as in cases of apoplexy, hanging, suffocation, and especially after death by carbonic acid.

The same remarks apply to those diffused dusky-red patches met with on portions of the surface of the body, known as frost-erythyms, to which I have thought it proper to attach some value as indicative of death by cold, in two articles, one furnished to the sixteenth volume of the *British and Foreign Medico-Chirurgical Review*, page 485, and another (at the request of Caspar) to the first volume, new series, of the *Vierteljahrsschrift fur Gerichtliche Medicin*, page 149.

The discolorations of either of these sorts, however, are but rarely of so extended a character as cadaveric lividities. They have usually a better defined outline, while the blood, whose presence gives rise to them, is diffused in sparing quantity through the areolar tissue—not incorporated with the true skin. Besides, the respective sites of the two appearances may serve sufficiently to discriminate the one from the other. The date of the first appearance of the true cadaveric lividities on the surface of the body has been fixed by Caspar at the period of from twelve to fifteen hours after death.

Turning now from the surface of the dead body to its internal parts, I must direct your attention shortly to hypostases of the more important viscera, originating, like the cadaveric lividities on dependent parts of the surface, in the gravitation of the blood after death. These internal hypostases are met with in their most marked shape in the brain, lungs, intestines, kidneys, and spinal cord. In the brain this phenomenon might be mistaken for the so-called congestive apoplexy. In the lungs this post-mortem appearance sometimes presents no unapt resemblance to pulmonary apoplexy, or to the first stage of pneumonia; as does its existence in the intestinal canal, and in the veins of the spinal meninges, to inflammatory injection of these parts. The position of these several hypostases, especially in the lungs and intestines, will afford the best corrective of this possible error.

A few additional changes in the body, prior to the occurrence of decomposition, call for a short notice at this place. One of the most prominent of these is what has been long known, from its delineation by the Father of Medicine, as *The Facies Hippocratica*. This appearance, characterised by sinking of the eyes, hollowness of the temples, sharpness of the nose, dryness and harshness of the forehead, sallowness of the countenance, and flaccidity and paleness of the lips, precedes death, and continues to be recognisable after dissolution.

The flattening of the soft parts on which the body has rested after death occurs from their loss of elasticity.

Besides the disappearance of the lustre of the cornea this part becomes subsequently opaque and milky; a film of mucus is seen adhering to it; while from the diminution of the aqueous humour, it becomes sensibly flattened. These appearances, however, are known to be absent, as after death by carbonic and hydrocyanic acids, where the eyes continue for some time prominent and glistening.

An appearance almost constant in the dead body is a more or less flexed state of the fingers and thumbs, the latter from this cause being sometimes bent across the palms, and the fingers closed on them. It is best marked where the cadaveric rigidity is strongly developed, as after the sudden deaths of previously healthy adults with muscular limbs.

Caspar lays it down that a body which, in addition to the appearances which characterise the first period after death, exhibits those of the middle period,—softening of the muscles, succeeded by rigidity of these; external and internal hypostases, and coagulation of the blood—may be presumed to be that of a person who has died within from two to three days at the longest.

Having thus passed in review the succession of changes occurring in the body after death, prior to the commencement in it of decomposition, whether looked upon as signs of death or as serving to point out, approximately at least, the period after the extinction of life at which they may have respectively taken place, I have done so in what seemed to me the most natural order, examining first the phenomena derived from the extinction of the vital functions, and second those of the succeeding changes, which, while they precede decomposition, are known to be incompatible with the maintenance of life. I now come to the series of phenomena which appear later, and which date from and take their rise in the putrefactive process in the various fluids and solids of the body. In following out the successive steps of the putrefactive process I have to advert to a series of medico-legal points of considerable interest and importance, as will be seen as we proceed

This further and last stage of the body's change after death commences, as I have said, with the occurrence of putrefaction, and runs on to its entire completion. From particular causes putrefaction may be modified or arrested, such as by the exposure of the corpse to extremes of heat and cold—when in the one case it dries up and mummifies, and in the other the *status quo* may to a certain extent be preserved, but only to a certain extent. Short of this the process may be hastened or delayed, so far, but only so far, as witnessed in interments in certain soils or localities of opposite characters as to moisture and dryness, or of non-absorbent or absorbent qualities. The concealment in a dry stone wall was found in one instance, previously referred to, to have reduced an infant's body to the condition of a dried mummy; and in the year 1875 the body of a new-born infant at the full time was found at Aberdeen in a servant's chest in the same condition In the latter instance the body had been three months shut up; in the former probably from one to two years

Fresh-burnt charcoal has almost unlimited power, when around a corpse in quantity, of resisting decomposition—as have, to some extent, when properly employed, certain antiseptics used for this purpose in anatomical rooms; but with these we have nothing to do.

Certain gases are known to hasten, retard, or modify putrefaction. A temperature of from 60° to 90° Fahrenheit (the heat of our summer) is the most favourable for the process of putrefaction, particularly if to this be added a frequent renewal of the surrounding atmosphere. In ignorance of this we sometimes find medical men directing the relatives of a dead person, when the interment is wished to be delayed as long as possible, to open all the windows, in order thoroughly to ventilate the apartment, while directions precisely the reverse should be given. A small apartment should be chosen; the doors, windows, and fireplace should be kept closely shut, and the body be enclosed in the coffin, with its lid down; of course, before admitting visitors, the air of the apartment should be renewed

The gases present in the atmosphere, both singly and in combination, favour decomposition, but the oxygen is known to have the greater effect in inducing this change, as in nitrogen alone the process advances but slowly. Carbonic acid gas acts like pure nitrogen.

Putrefaction is always slower in water than in the atmosphere.

In water the process is very rapid when the fluid has a temperature of from 64° to 68° Fahrenheit; and, on the contrary, very slow if the temperature of the fluid is lower than this

It is generally admitted that putrefaction takes place more rapidly in stagnant than in running water. The water of privies retards it most of all. In such circumstances saponification is very readily produced.

In the earth the progress of putrefaction varies considerably, as we have seen, according to the character of the soil, temperature and humidity, dryness, etc. The deeper the corpse is buried the slower its decomposition. Experience shows that, *cæteris paribus*, very young infants putrefy sooner than adults or old people, and females than males When the body has been mutilated, or solutions of continuity were present before burial, decomposition is hastened. Contusions, ecchymoses, and effusions of fluid have the same effect. Persons perishing of acute diseases decay sooner than those that had been affected with chronic maladies. Copious hæmorrhages before death retard putrefaction; whilst, on the other hand, eruptive diseases and inflammatory affections hasten it. The delay of the interment hurries on the commencement of decomposition, and *vice versa*. When the body is exposed in summer opportunity is afforded for insects to deposit their ova, which becoming hatched after burial or exposure to the air, the larvæ forward the work of destruction.

The greater the superincumbent pressure the slower the march of decomposition. A corpse interred without a coffin decays faster than a corpse buried in one, and the more numerous and closer the envelopes the more is the process retarded.

The most abundant product of putrefaction is carburetted hydrogen, the evolution of this gas in the decaying body playing an important part in the production of some of the most characteristic appearances in the dead body. This will be seen as we proceed.

LECTURE XXVII

DEATH—(*Concluded*).

Putrefaction of the Body in the Atmosphere—Putrefaction of the Body in the Water—Putrefaction of the Body in the Earth.—Pseudo-Morbid Discoloration—Discrimination from the Effects of Disease—Discrimination from the Effects of Injuries—Discrimination from the Effects of Decomposition—Discrimination from the Results of other Causes —Pseudo-Morbid Softening—Discrimination betwixt Post-Mortem and Vital Softening —Pseudo-Morbid Effusion—Products of Putrefaction—Adipocere—Putrefaction in various Media—Bodily Changes in the Process generally—Maculæ Mortis—General Softening of the Solids and further Liquefaction of the Fluids—Green Discoloration—Evolution of Gases—Vesication of the Surface—Brown Discolorations—Rupture of the great Cavities—Carbonisation of the Soft Parts—Data for estimating the periods of these changes.

In dealing with the medico-legal relations of death at last lecture it fell to me to commence the consideration of the last of the series of changes in the dead body following the departure of life. After having disposed of the external or extraneous influences of various kinds which arrest, modify, or hasten the changes in the corpse characterised as the process of its decomposition, it only remains here to complete the subject of death generally, so far as it bears more or less directly on forensic medicine, by adverting to the remaining points which are of interest to us in our special pursuit.

The leading appearances presented by the human body in its passage through the various stages of its decay, at and subsequently to the commencement in it of putrefaction, have been very closely studied and detailed by Orfila, Lesueur, and Devergie in France, and by Muntz and Caspar in Germany,—by the last author, however, more from their practical than exhaustive side. In following, to a large extent, our guides in this important subject, the remarks which follow will be found to refer chiefly to the body as it is found to decay in the atmosphere, though the differences which such bodies present as contrasted with those decaying in the water, or in the earth, are not of so prominent a kind as to demand a separate consideration, while they admit of being treated in connection.

On the exterior of the body the first sign of commencing putrefaction is the greenish discoloration of the abdominal walls, simultaneously with which the putrid odour is usually first perceptible.

This greenness commonly commences at the centre of the belly, in the form of a small patch, thence extending gradually to the groins, breast, face, neck, and superior and inferior extremities, in succession. This order of succession of the green discoloration, which is all but constant in bodies putrefying in the atmosphere and the earth, is not, however, that which takes place, as a rule, in bodies which have lain in water. Here the coloration makes its first appearance over the sternum, thence extending to the neck, belly, and shoulders, and then coalescing with patches which have commenced in the groins. This difference in the order of succession of these spots is usually so constant that it has been fixed on by Devergie and Caspar as a sufficient test for discriminating bodies which have begun to decay in water, from those which commenced their decay in the two other media. Too much stress, however, should not be laid on this test, as I have met with the green discoloration of the belly in drowned bodies before it had appeared on the chest.

After a few days, the green discoloration has become deeper and spread over the whole of the abdomen and the genitals. In a few days longer the separate patches have coalesced over the trunk, and the front of the face and neck presents a shade of red.

Subsequently the discoloured patches on the surface of the body will have assumed more or less of a brownish hue, in union with the green; ultimately the green patches, where most strongly developed, take a deep brownish-black colour, best seen on the face and upper part of the chest in the bodies of the drowned, after some stay in water.

Simultaneously with these changes of colour on its surface, gases begin to be generated and accumulate under the skin, in the submucous and intermuscular tissues, and in the interior of the hollow organs of the body.

The more or less abundant generation of gases in the corpse explains three distinct series of appearances which mark the progress of its decomposition:—

First, we have, from this cause, distension of the scrotum,

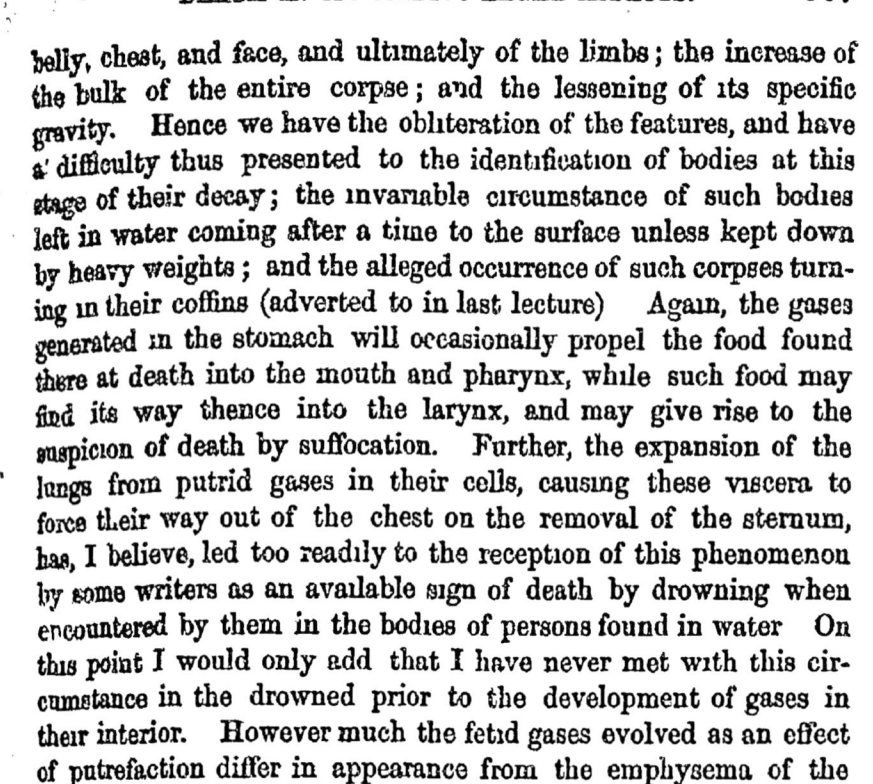

belly, chest, and face, and ultimately of the limbs; the increase of the bulk of the entire corpse; and the lessening of its specific gravity. Hence we have the obliteration of the features, and have a difficulty thus presented to the identification of bodies at this stage of their decay; the invariable circumstance of such bodies left in water coming after a time to the surface unless kept down by heavy weights; and the alleged occurrence of such corpses turning in their coffins (adverted to in last lecture) Again, the gases generated in the stomach will occasionally propel the food found there at death into the mouth and pharynx, while such food may find its way thence into the larynx, and may give rise to the suspicion of death by suffocation. Further, the expansion of the lungs from putrid gases in their cells, causing these viscera to force their way out of the chest on the removal of the sternum, has, I believe, led too readily to the reception of this phenomenon by some writers as an available sign of death by drowning when encountered by them in the bodies of persons found in water On this point I would only add that I have never met with this circumstance in the drowned prior to the development of gases in their interior. However much the fetid gases evolved as an effect of putrefaction differ in appearance from the emphysema of the living, whether in the areolar tissue, the cavities of the body, or the interior of the hollow organs, the line of demarcation between the two may not always very easily be drawn on inspection. This, however, is of the less consequence, as in the latter case no inferences would be drawn from the appearance of emphysema alone, unattended by its usual co-existing organic changes.

Second, a further series of effects arising in the putrid body from gaseous development is traceable to the consequent displacement of the now fluid blood from the places where it is most largely found accumulated—such as the cavities of the heart, and the large blood-vessels connected with them. Hence the empty state of these, the blood which they originally contained having been propelled onwards to the capillaries. Hence, too, the diffused reddening of the skin and the areolar tissue in bodies examined some weeks after death, and the more or less marked redness of the mucous and serous surfaces, and of such of the viscera as are naturally the most largely supplied with blood—changes which, I need scarcely remind you, might readily be mistaken by a careless observer for the consequences of inflammation or of irritant poisons during life

The diffuse redness of the skin to which I have just referred may be almost, if not entirely, absent, unless under the circumstances I have noticed. Different from the ordinary cadaveric lividities, and later in appearing, it may often escape notice till the displacement of the cuticle reveals the depth of coloration of the cutis vera—an appearance best marked in the bodies of the drowned after a prolonged stay in water, in corpses a considerable time buried, and in those of infants perishing and being retained long in the uterus

Coincident with this more developed reddening of the surface of putrid bodies, the cuticle is loose and readily to be detached, the subcutaneous areolar tissue is bathed in reddish serum in such situations as the front of the neck, the groins, and the back part of the scalp, presenting gelatinous-looking effusions of the appearance of red-currant jelly. Independently of the co-existence of fetid gases and the extent of the diffusion of these appearances of the skin and subcutaneous areolar tissue, with perhaps the addition of blisters filled with reddish serum, this effect of putrefaction could scarcely be mistaken for the consequences of morbid agencies during life.

I cannot speak, however, so confidently as to the distinctive character of the reddenings of the mucous and serous surfaces in the interior of the body from the gaseous development. In these circumstances the internal surfaces assume different shades of colour, from the deep rose-red, most frequently encountered, to a brownish or blackish-red—appearances which might be mistaken for the effects of inflammation during life. The chances of mistake here, however, may be generally obviated by attention to the circumstance, that in this form of post-mortem redness, the blood-vessels of the part are either empty or filled with putrid gases; and, what is still more important, that the reddening is not confined to the surfaces of single organs, but involves almost all the naturally colourless membranes and tubes —the parenchymatous viscera, the alimentary and respiratory canals, the bloodvessels, etc. Less stress is to be laid on the circumstance, occasionally relied on as an auxiliary test, that inflammatory redness consists rather in injection of the vessels, striæ, dots, or streaks, than in the mere dyeing of the parts, seen in cadaveric redness (Devergie); actual exceptions to this having been encountered by Yellowly in the dead body; while such so-called inflammatory appearances have been produced artificially by Roget and Trousseau

Orfila and Devergie have both remarked, as peculiar to the

reddening of mucous membranes from the effects of putrefaction, that ecchymoses are never thus produced—an observation of considerable importance if verified by others.

Devergie has also called attention to the circumstance that in general, parts which have been inflamed at the time of death run more rapidly into putrefaction than healthy parts; and that, consequently, the conclusion is authorised that the discovery of one part running into putrefaction, while the rest of the body is free from it, implies the previous existence of inflammation in that part. Too much stress, however, should not be laid on a distinction of this sort, for reasons which must be obvious

Two further distinctive tests proposed by this author are, perhaps, more trustworthy, namely, (1) That in post-mortem redness the colour is limited to the course of the vessels, while in inflammatory redness the parts around the vessels partake more or less of the coloration; and (2) that in inflammatory redness the colour is usually limited to the inflamed membrane, while in redness from putrefaction the colour pervades the whole of the tissues of the part. (The first of these characteristics of putrefaction is very well seen in a drawing of a putrid stomach in Caspar's Atlas.)

I need scarcely add, that in deciding betwixt such post-mortem and certain inflammatory appearances, collateral circumstances must be taken into account In this way the presence or absence of inflammatory changes and products—such as thickening of membranes, false membranes, copious mucous or purulent exudations, consolidation of tissues, etc.—would give the character of certainty to signs, themselves insufficient to yield more than strong presumption In some instances, indeed, the failure of such collateral circumstances would be fatal to the assumption of previous inflammatory disease of the part, as in the case of suspected inflammation of the brain and its membranes, or that of the upper part of the air-passages. As regards the brain, for instance, it is admitted by pathologists that with the exception of such obvious changes as apoplectic clots, abscesses, or tumours presenting themselves, the examination of the organ yields, in general, no means of distinguishing morbid from post-mortem discolorations—a difficulty which is increased when the discrimination has to be applied to the surface, and, above all, to the membranes of the brain Again, Caspar has been at pains to show that post-mortem changes commence at an unusually early period in the air-passages, and especially about the top of the trachea, which, while with difficulty distinguishable from, might be readily mistaken for the effects of laryngitis or death by drowning. To illustrate this he has given two figures in his Atlas, contrasting this pseudo-morbid redness of the larynx and trachea after death from natural causes, with the same parts in a person who had died by hanging. The colour in the latter is higher than that in the former; but this, of course, would depend on the time after death not having allowed of its darkening.

Before leaving this subject, it may be well to direct your attention to some forms of redness of the intestinal tube other than either inflammation or putrefaction are known to occasion.

Thus, Orfila first pointed out the circumstance, that in persons in good health, perishing suddenly while digestion was going on in the stomach, the interior of this organ will usually be found uniformly and distinctly reddened.

Again, in the case of habitual drunkards, after sudden death, as by drowning or hanging, the interior of the stomach, and, to a less extent, of the smaller intestines, though pale at the moment of exposure, speedily assumes a distinct deep-red colour from the action of the air.

Once more, it might happen that substances taken into the stomach might give rise to redness of the interior of this organ. Of this we have an instructive instance adduced by Sir Robert Christison, where the inspector referred the colour to inflammatory action, though it was found to have been caused by a strong infusion of the corn poppy (*Papaver rhœas*).

Nor are these all the changes of colour which may be met with in the alimentary tube from the action of causes operating on the tube itself at or immediately before death, as well as those depending on the state of the neighbouring viscera at or after death, and having no connection with either inflammation or putrefaction. Thus, it is known that the presence of gases is capable of variously affecting the colour of the blood in the intestines, in much the same way as is done by certain of the acids. The transudation of the contents of the gall-bladder through the coats of the duodenum, or even of the stomach, may simulate the effects of nitric acid swallowed during life. The gastric juice, even where not in sufficient quantity to corrode the coats of the stomach, is capable of effecting changes of colour in the interior of the organ. But this is a digression from our subject.

To return. Some other forms of redness encountered in the dead body may present serious obstacles to a ready diagnosis;

but as these have more bearing on general pathology than on forensic medicine, their consideration need not detain us long. We have an example of such a form of redness in the injected state of the dura mater, particularly towards the back parts of the head, from venous fulness, both in fresh and putrid bodies, and, à fortiori, of the coverings of the spinal cord, from the same cause, which makes it sometimes difficult, if not impossible, to decide betwixt the natural appearance of the part and the consequence of disease or decomposition. The same remark applies to the pia mater, and even the substance of the brain at times, where blood is accumulated within its vessels, whether from the mode of natural death, or from the effects of intoxication, narcotics, deaths by hanging, drowning, etc.

Third, a further consequence in the decaying body, besides the evolution of gases, is the effusion of fluid into its cavities. The gaseous fermentation of the masses of blood accumulated at death in the heart and larger bloodvessels not only suffices to propel this fluid onwards to the capillaries, but the *vis a tergo* increasing, ultimately forces it further in the direction where it meets with least resistance. Hence originate those effusions, consisting of serum tinged with the colouring matter of the blood, met with most copiously in the cavities lined with serous membranes. These effusions are most frequently encountered in the pleura and pericardium, and less usually in the peritoneum. The quantity of such fluid may amount to some pints. Its colour is commonly a brownish-red, and it exhales a putrid colour. The effusion is seldom met with in the cavities till some weeks after death; probably never during the first week. It has never been found coagulated.

Both Orfila and Devergie assure us that they have never observed these effusions within the cavities of the hollow organs lined by mucous membranes.

The accumulations of cerebro-spinal fluid at the base of the brain and in the theca vertebralis, though less frequent, are phenomena of a more puzzling kind; and the discrimination between the effects of disease or injury during life, and the results of post-mortem change, may readily elude our grasp.

It would be difficult to confound the post-mortem effusions encountered in the pleura, pericardium, and peritoneum with effusions of blood, serum, or pus of vital origin. The homogeneity of the fluid in putrid bodies, the absence from it of pus or false membranes; the colour, different from that of blood, which becomes quite black when it putrefies—serve as so many tests which would characterise these effusions.

A further characteristic feature in the series of changes undergone by the body after death is the softening of its tissues. The softening, however, occurs equally as an effect of inflammation during life and of decomposition after death. From each of these sources it may be met with on the surface and in all the textures of the body, though most frequently encountered in the brain, spleen, and gastro-intestinal mucous membrane.

Certain deficiencies of the surface of the body encountered in decaying bodies are occasionally of a puzzling character, and their origin may often not admit of being traced successfully, whether to such cadaveric softening or other altogether independent causes. Thus, in bodies which have lain for some time in water, the scalp may be wanting over a great part of the head, but whether from cadaveric softening or the erosive action of water, it may be impossible to decide. It is known that the previous existence at these parts of bruises, lacerations, or contused or other wounds, favours the ready disappearance of the soft parts of the exterior in that medium, from the erosive action of water independently of decomposition. It must be borne in mind, besides, that such breaches of the surface of the body may be traceable in drowned corpses to the ravages of fishes or crustacea.

In the dead body left exposed to the atmosphere for some time, certain breaches of continuity occasionally met with on the surface, simultaneously with advancing putrefaction, would give little room for mistake. For instance, rats and other vermin will attack a corpse, gnawing such exposed parts as the face and fingers. I observed such appearances in the face of an old woman found dead in her room several weeks after her death. Similar erosions were found on the hands and face of a decaying corpse found suspended in a wood at Newe (Aberdeenshire) a few summers ago. The distinctive appearances in this instance were attributed by the gamekeepers on the estate to squirrels.

It may not be out of place to remark here that the effects of voracious animals, either in or out of water, present a different aspect from those traceable either to the erosive action of water, or the progress of putrefaction—the former injuries presenting distinct, well-defined, and sharp margins; the edges of the latter, on the contrary, being usually ill-defined and softened.

The softened brain in the decaying body is sometimes forced along the cerebral and internal jugular veins by the gases evolved within the cranium, giving an appearance which might simulate phlebitis; while, again, the softened gastro-intestinal mucous membrane might suggest the action of irritant poison in the living.

To distinguish cadaveric from inflammatory softening, the following tests have been proposed:—

Firstly. Vital softening is rarely general, but almost always limited in the adult within very narrow bounds. In putrefaction, on the contrary, it invades the whole of an organ, the diminution of consistency being in proportion to the density of its different constituent parts. To take the cerebral mass, for example, the lobes are softer than the cerebral protuberance; the cerebellum than the cerebrum, etc; and the same cause acting at the same time upon all these parts will produce an amount of softening in proportion to their respective densities in the healthy state.

Secondly. Vital softening rarely affects the whole of any one viscus, as is the case with cadaveric softening, particularly in such organs as the spleen, lungs, and liver. Such general vital softening, has, however, been encountered in the brain by Billard. One instance, closely approaching to this—certainly very unusual—occurrence, I have met with in practice, in a young man of seventeen.

Thirdly. When acute inflammation leads to softening, the substance of the inflamed organ is usually infiltrated with serum or pus, and not unfrequently its investing membrane will show traces of vascular injection, adhesions to the walls of or effusion of serum into the cavity in which it lies. Of course, where the softening is the effect of putrefaction, no such appearances are observable.

Lastly. In doubtful cases of softening of portions of the brain, pathologists recommend recourse to be had to the microscope, and insist that vital may readily be distinguished from cadaveric softening by the presence of exudation corpuscles in the one, and not in the other.

With the exception of the last, these tests are equally applicable to softenings encountered in the lungs, kidneys, liver, and heart. In the lungs it would be difficult to confound the cadaveric with the inflammatory softening. The latter follows the red or gray hepatisation, of which two states the former could alone be mistaken for cadaveric engorgement, though there is little analogy between a softened mass, impregnated with fluids, easily tearing in all directions, brownish, diffluent, and putrid, and the hepatised tissue of an inflamed lung, soft, homogeneous, indurated in certain points, and of the consistence of the healthy liver. After putrefaction had advanced some way there would be no means left for knowing whether the softening had been caused by putrefaction or not.

It is not so easy to carry this distinction to the different states of the spleen. This organ is very easily softened by putrefaction. The smell might be of some use, supposing a case where the other organs of the body were sound, while the spleen was softened. In the opposite circumstances nothing positive as to its source could be determined.

The same thing holds true of the heart. When the softening of the heart is attended with the coloration of its tissues, or with the yellow hue of withered leaves, it is said to be a proof of vital softening; but it is when attended with the coloration of its membranes or texture that there are doubts of its source.

The same remark applies to the liver.

Nothing at all resembling the gelatiniform softening of the stomach has been observed to be produced by putrefaction. The solvent action of the gastric juice on this organ after death presents a marked contrast to the change induced by decomposition.

Another phenomenon in the process of decomposition is the appearance of blisters on the surface of the body, containing more or less greenish or reddish fluid. When the putrefaction has taken place under ground, besides these reddish or greenish blisters at certain parts of the surface of the body, at other parts, particularly over the feet, the cuticle is raised into plicæ, and thickened and blanched as from the action of a poultice or soaking in water. Precisely the same appearance is met with in bodies which have lain in water; first in the hands and feet, and subsequently at the knees and elbows—a peculiarity to which we shall have to return under Death by Drowning.

Another product of putrefaction, under certain circumstances, is a saponaceous matter termed adipocere. This change takes place very readily in young subjects; in those who are very fat; in the water of privies; less promptly in stagnant than in running water; readily in moist, rich earths; very rarely in dry soils, and all the more readily if the bodies are piled upon each other, the lowest being the first saponified.

It will not be necessary to pursue into details the further progress of the putrefactive process, as having but little or no bearing upon our subject; suffice it to state generally that the muscles become softened and greenish; the softened brain takes a grayish or ashy tint, the interior of the softened heart a dark-red dye, the flaccid stomach and intestines various shades of red and blue; on the detachment of the cuticle the skin exudes a brownish liquid; larvæ appear about the nose, eyes, and mouth; the surface takes on a brown tint; the abdomen bursts, giving exit to gases and putrid fluids; and the brain escapes by the orbits.

If decomposition is not arrested at this stage, the soft parts of the head, chest, and neck, and subsequently of the limbs, fall into putrilage, leaving the chest and belly fallen in; the lungs collapsed, contracted, slate-blue, and lacerable; the stomach softened, of a whitish-gray, with blue spots; the intestines shrunk into small dimensions, and dry; and the spleen reduced to a black pulp.

At a later stage the soft parts of the face and of the chest have disappeared; the abdominal parietes are seen resting on the spine; the muscles of the limbs are like rotten wood, those of the body absent or adipocerous; the brain like glazed earthenware; the lungs are flat, hard, and glued to the vertebræ; the liver flattened, blackish-brown, and slightly dried; and the stomach a mere hollow cylinder.

Finally, if the body has been buried, the bones are disarticulated, and the remains of the soft parts of the chest and belly are found adherent to the spine, in the form of a black, humid, glossy matter, of less than an inch in thickness.

Notwithstanding the admitted variations which are observable in the periods occupied by the series of changes which I have just traced in the decay of the body after death, attempts have been made to obtain some tolerably sure data for enabling us to approximate at least to the particular period which its decay has reached in individual instances, calculated from the time of the decease.

The earliest of these attempts was made by Devergie, at the Morgue in Paris, from the examination and histories of bodies exposed there on their removal from the water, after a stay of different periods in that medium, as discovered by him on careful inquiry. Devergie arguing that the temperature of the water being more uniform than that, at least, of the atmosphere, if not of the earth, would, if correct approximations could be obtained, be the most likely to yield data that might be useful in practice. Caspar, however, urging that the process of decomposition being essentially the same in the different media, and only modified as to its rate by the qualifying circumstances which I have enumerated, independently of the media in which it may take place, proposes to establish a general ratio for all the three media.

But little reliance is to be placed on the data furnished by either of these authors. Devergie has made the formal attempt to give precision to the point in question, by laying down, in the first volume of his work on Legal Medicine, data for determining the period which a body in winter must have remained in water, and subsequently the modifications these data will have to undergo to adapt them for the other seasons of the year.

In testing these data of Devergie's in 113 observations of drowned bodies (prior to 1851), at different seasons of the year, I found that, judging by them, very large allowances must be made for the not inconsiderable variations in the periods fixed by this author. Caspar's data refer to bodies exposed to the atmosphere, and are as follows—*i.e*, assuming the temperature to be the mean of the two seasons :—

(1) The greenish discoloration of the abdomen and the softening of the eyeballs indicate that the person has been dead from twenty-four to seventy-two hours.

(2) After three to five days, the green discoloration has become deeper, and extended over the whole of the abdomen, including the genitals; while similar patches have begun to appear on other parts, especially the back, lower extremities, the neck, and sides of the chest.

(3) In about eight or ten days, the greenish patches have coalesced, and changed to a reddish-green, gaseous products have become developed in the abdomen; the cornea has become concave; the sphincter ani has relaxed; and the ramifications of the subcutaneous veins can be traced on the neck, breast, and limbs.

(4.) After fourteen or twenty days, blisters have appeared on the skin, and the development of gases has become general, distending the whole body.

(5) Lastly, after this period it is impossible to determine the date of the decease.

To complete this subject, I have only to add that Caspar considers that, as a general rule, at a tolerably similar average temperature, the degree of putrefaction present in a body after lying in the open air for one week (or month) corresponds to that found in a body lying in the water for two weeks (or months), or after lying in the earth, in the usual manner, for eight weeks (or months).

LECTURE XXVIII

MEDICO-LEGAL INSPECTIONS

MEDICO-LEGAL INSPECTIONS —Mode of conducting these —JURIDICAL EXHUMATIONS —Risks attending such Exhumations—Directions for conducting them—Where the Body is entire—Where the Skeleton only remains

THE post-mortem inspection in legal medicine is a more important and difficult matter than it usually is in private practice. It is not enough here to point out in some one or other organ or organs such obvious morbid changes as will suffice to explain the character of the symptoms which marked the closing scenes of life, and will account for the fatal event. The medical jurist must be able from this source to trace, as far as can be done, the chain of connection, whether longer or shorter, betwixt the morbid agency—the injury received, the poison administered—and its ultimate consequences, and carefully and accurately to distinguish the effects of merely natural causes from those which are purely adventitious. In other words, the effect produced must be shown by him to be such as inevitably followed, and could only have resulted from, the causes suspected or assigned on reasonable presumption; and the verification of whose truth, or its original suggestion and consequent establishment, are the tasks which fall to his especial province.

The nature of the duties thus devolving on the expert will have been sufficiently seen from the elucidation of the subjects which have immediately preceded—the points which call for particular attention in all such investigations, the cautions to be kept in view in drawing conclusions from the appearances presenting themselves in the course of the inspection, and the difficulties which the different aspects of the body in its various stages of alteration after death may occasion, in regard to the correct appreciation of the cause, progress, and ultimate termination of previous vital actions within or foreign to the organism. All this, it will be perceived, necessitates here a thoroughness of investigation not called for elsewhere, and one which overlooks no circumstance, however apparently trivial, which may throw light upon the case in hand, or on the previous history of the party.

Still, it may be observed that, although the inspection of the dead body by the medical jurist may, and usually does, embrace more points than are called for in an ordinary post-mortem examination, the mode of procedure otherwise, in either case, is nearly the same in the majority of cases; any differences in this respect regarding rather certain special investigations than those called for in the ordinary run of cases. Thus, I have already had occasion to point out the best mode of procedure in the inspection of the infant in cases of suspected infanticide, and shall afterwards have to notice the best mode of procedure in certain other instances, which present other peculiarities, requiring to be traced out in a prescribed order.

This being the case, and presuming that you are sufficiently familiar with the ordinary mode of procedure in post-mortem inspections, I shall confine myself at present to the notice, in order, of the more obvious directions requiring your attention in the conduct of medico-legal inspections generally

1. Thus, in every autopsy undertaken for forensic purposes, it is desirable that the examiner should be enabled by the legal authorities to undertake the investigation as soon after death as possible, before any of the various post-mortem phenomena, already described, have intervened to obscure facts and appearances, or to render their correct appreciation difficult or impossible. At from twenty-four to forty-eight hours after death the body is in the fittest state for its efficient and satisfactory examination. On the Continent the autopsy is not legally permissible till twenty-four hours have elapsed; and though in this country no legal enactment of the same kind exists, public opinion would be against an inspection much earlier than this.

But as, from various causes, this inspection cannot always be set on foot before the changes which are induced in the body by the progress of decay have had time to commence or proceed, the medical jurist must be ready to undertake the autopsy at any later period at which he may be called on to do so I have had occasion already to direct your attention to the circumstances under which the inspection of the body may be usefully undertaken long after death, and need not here recur to this topic. Several additional illustrations to the same purport will be found in Caspar's *Forensic Medicine* lately translated and published by the New Sydenham Society.

2 It is desirable in every medico-legal autopsy that the body, as respects its position and surroundings, should have been as little

interfered with as possible. This is especially important in all cases of sudden and violent death. Where this precaution has not been attended to on the part of the attendants of the deceased or the law authorities, it may be necessary to procure information on these points from those who have been present at the death, who have been the first to discover the body afterwards, or who have seen it before it had been in any way disturbed. The impossibility of supplying such desiderata, however, either at first or second hand, only renders it the more imperative on the examiner to attend closely to such indications deducible from extraneous sources as may still be available.

3. The medico-legal examiner is not at liberty to decline the investigation as superfluous or useless, even where the body has been further interfered with As remarked by Caspar, cases occasionally occur in which the body, being brought to the medico-legal dissecting-table, has not only had all its cavities, but even all its organs laid open, partly from precipitation, and partly because it was not known at the time of death that the case would come under the cognisance of the law, etc.

I have met with instances of this sort in my own practice, and Caspar has adduced some instructive cases, as, for instance, of fractures at the base of the skull, rupture of the liver, fracture of the ribs, and gunshot wound of the axillary artery, in bodies previously dissected. In one of my own cases I was able to verify fractures of two of the cervical vertebræ after a previous inspection at the Aberdeen Infirmary.

4. In medico-legal cases which are likely to come before any of the courts the inspection should be made by at least two properly qualified medical men. This is necessary, because the testimony of two witnesses is required to substantiate facts in courts of law. Besides, one might overlook things of importance which would not escape two. They should proceed to the duty imposed on them with impartial and unbiased minds, and should be careful to adopt no opinion which they cannot establish on scientific grounds. They should also proceed deliberately, and not allow themselves to be hurried in their examination

5. It not unfrequently happens, in cases which are thought to be instances of suicide, that the authorities only require the report of one medical man to establish the proof of this fact. In such an instance, should any circumstance become apparent which would tend to excite the suspicion that a wrong estimate had been formed—that the case, for example, was one of homicide,

not suicide,—it would be proper to suspend proceedings till another medical man was procured, who would be able to certify to the appearances. I have more than once been under the necessity of doing this.

6. The medical inspectors should not proceed to examine the body without a regular warrant from the properly constituted legal authorities. If the inspectors have not this warrant they are liable to be obstructed and fettered in their examination by the unreasonable and improper interference of the friends of the deceased, who may even have an interest in obstructing the proceedings.

A warrant is necessary, also, to give power to exclude improper persons from being present at the inspection, who may intrude themselves, either from curiosity or otherwise. There can be no objection, however, to one or two of the friends of the deceased being present, if they are neither the suspected parties nor the principal witnesses in the case. Neither could there be any reasonable objection to the presence of one or more medical men on the part of the accused, if desired; for this may be said to be an important part of his trial.

7. It occasionally happens that, notwithstanding the medical examiners are furnished with a legal warrant, the relatives of the deceased, from ignorance or obstinacy, may refuse their permission for the inspection. In this case the examiners should not attempt to proceed by force, but at once where mere persuasion has failed, return to the party who has granted the warrant, who in such cases will direct an officer to take possession of the body, whether the refusing persons give their consent or not.

The warrant in Scotland (technically, the remit) directs the medical jurist to examine the body and report as to the appearances and the cause of death.

8. In addition to the usual instruments required for opening the different cavities of the body and the spinal canal, a measure for fluids, a linear measure, and an apparatus for weighing may also be necessary.

9. In connection with investigations of this sort, a duty of a somewhat extraneous character may have to be undertaken by the medical jurist, and one which will be best discharged before proceeding with the proper work in hand. I refer to those occasions, sometimes arising, in which, in addition to the inspection of the dead body found under suspicious circumstances, the expert may be called on to examine a party presumably connected with the death in question. Here the points which chiefly call

for notice are the physical appearance of the examinee; the state of his dress, any marks of violence on his person; any traces of blood on the surface of his body, or on his clothes, etc.

In an alleged charge of rape, for instance, seminal or bloodstains should be looked for on the shirt of the accused. If he had inflicted a serious wound on the woman, blood should be discovered on his hands or dress, unless previously removed. In the case of rape and murder, referred to in Lecture IX., p 118, soot was detected in the seams of a pair of corduroy trousers, the man having entered the cottage of his victim by descending the wooden chimney (*Scottice*, lum). In a case of murder committed near Kintore, the only suspicious circumstance elicited at the examination of the accused was the detection of slight traces of blood in the seams betwixt the soles and uppers of his shoes. In a man of the name of Fraser, apprehended in Aberdeen some years ago for attempted rape, a linear scratch was detected on the upper surface of the penis. At the apprehension of a factory operative in 1870 the accused was found in possession of several of the drugs used as abortives, and of a uterine sound. Cases of this sort might easily be multiplied.

But to return to the post-mortem examination :—

10. When the body has remained in the spot where it was discovered, and has not been disturbed by the relatives or others, it may be of importance to direct attention to the situation and position of the corpse before it is interfered with, the state of the clothes, whether it is wholly or partially dressed, whether, if dressed, the clothes are disarranged or are decently disposed; whether they have been torn, stained with mud, blood, or other foreign matters. Any blood near the body, or other marks of violence, footprints, indications of a struggle, or running; lethal weapons, etc.,—should be noted. For it often happens that, by attention to such circumstances as these, the guilt or innocence of the accused is established.

11. It is also of consequence to be furnished with an account of the circumstances attending the death of an individual, so far as these can be ascertained; for this often calls attention to important particulars which might otherwise escape notice. The authorities, however, are rarely willing to communicate such information, lest it should bias the examiners; but this unwillingness will usually be got over, if the medical inspectors state explicitly the purpose for which the information is required.

If the clothes, etc., are likely to be produced on the trial, the examiners should see them sealed and labelled on the spot, and should attach their signatures or initials to the label, in order that they may be able to identify them at once when afterwards brought into court.

12 The body is to be stripped, if not previously done, the state of the corpse, the apparent age, the position of the limbs, and the expression of the countenance, are to be particularly observed, if not already identified, its height should be ascertained, and any marks of scars, small-pox, nævi materni, etc., which might serve for identification carefully noticed. If any stains are to be detected about the lips, teeth, or nostrils, or about the fingers, these should be particularly examined; and, also, any vomited matters near the mouth, or any discharges which may have escaped from the outlets of the body,—carefully preserving these.

Any filth or foreign matter on the surface of the body should then be washed away, as such matters may obscure slight discolorations, and may hide minute scratches or abrasions of the skin, nævi, tattooings, or superficial cicatrices Any spots of blood, above all, should be washed off In the case of rape and murder to which I had to refer in this and a previous lecture, two medical men, who had viewed the body previous to the official inspection, certified, in a report drawn up by them for the law authorities, that there were marks of bruises on the upper and inner part of the woman's thighs. The application of a wet sponge to the parts in their presence convinced them of their error on this point.

In every instance of suspected or probable death by violence, it is advisable to cut short the hair, or, better, to shave the head, as contusions, abrasions, and such slight wounds as have not bled may otherwise escape notice at the inspection

13. It is always proper at every medico-legal dissection to write out notes of the points elicited in the course of the examination, as well as of the whole investigation This should be done fully, slowly, and deliberately, indicating all the points inquired into, with the observations made and appearances presented, negative as well as positive, and stating simple facts only, without either generalisations or opinions These notes are best managed where one inspector conducts the examination and the other takes notes of its successive steps, the person dictating taking care that the other practitioner or practitioners present fully concur in what is thus dictated. When finished, the signatures of *all the medical persons present* should be obtained to the

document, particularly if any professional witnesses for the accused are present, as it prevents them from objecting to any of the facts on the trial. These notes should be looked over by all the inspectors before the body is sewed up, so that omissions in the notes or in the inspection itself may be then supplied. A copy of this document should always be preserved by the examiners for future reference, to prevent their forgetting the facts elicited.

14 The examination and dissection of the dead body should, if possible, not be undertaken except with sufficient daylight in prospect to allow the whole inspection to be made without artificial light.

15 After the points already noticed have been attended to, the surface of the body should be inspected with regard to its colour—whether the skin be rosy, blanched, or natural. The state of the eyes should be noted; the eyelids, whether shut or open; the state of the pupils, if dilated, contracted, or natural; the state of the mouth, nose, and ears; the marks of putrefaction, if present; the hands and feet, particularly the state of the nails. The state of the outlets of the body—the anus and the genitals,— also the breasts (in the female) and the abdomen, should be noted.

In order to impress you with the importance that occasionally attaches to the observation of these minute particulars, which are so apt to be overlooked or despised, I may mention that a legal functionary once related to me the particulars of a case that came under his notice, in which a murder was committed, the crime having been brought home to the guilty party chiefly by the apparently trifling circumstance that a few fragments of a white substance, which proved to be cuticle, were found under the nails of the deceased person. These portions of cuticle were preserved, and when afterwards compared with certain abrasions on the face of the guilty person, were found exactly to agree with them; the deceased having, in the struggle which took place, applied his nails to the face of his assailant. I am sorry to say that I am unable to give any reference to where the case is to be found—if, indeed, it ever was recorded,—as the conversation took place many years ago.

16 The inspection proper should never be confined solely to the cavity of the body where the fatal lesion is suspected or discovered. The whole of the great cavities of the body should be opened, and the state of the viscera, whether healthy or morbid, noted down. When there is room for the slightest doubt to be raised whether the diseased appearances found in the inspected parts are sufficient to account for death, the whole length of the spinal

cord ought to be laid bare, which will put it out of the power of the counsel to raise quibbling objections on the trial, as occurred in a case tried in Aberdeen at the Autumn Circuit, 1838 —

Two men were seen to quarrel in a crowd at a cattle market in Banffshire, when one of them, a stout, powerful man, threw the other on his back, sat down cross-legged on his chest, and twisted his victim's cravat till death by strangulation followed. A medical inspection, directed by the law authorities in the case, was not a very full one, and the spine had not been opened This omission was taken advantage of by the counsel for the defence, who set up a theory that the man had died from spinal apoplexy —a plea which, however improbable in the circumstances of the case, could not be satisfactorily refuted by the Crown from the want of any evidence as to the state of the spine.

17. In proceeding to the dissection it has been directed that the cavity in which the cause of death is supposed to be situated should be the first to be opened. But even if this be known, some obvious objections apply to such a procedure It is better, therefore, to proceed in a systematic manner in every instance. For this purpose some such method as the following may be advantageously adopted —

If not previously done, the hairs are to be cut close, to give a complete view of the scalp. The head should be raised with a block as high as can be done without stretching the parts about the nucha. The head is then to be opened in the usual way, and the brain examined *in situ*. The head should be allowed to remain in the same posture till the state of the heart and large vessels in the thorax is ascertained, or, if lowered to its former position, an assistant should be directed to compress the vessels at the base of the skull, and prevent any draining of blood from the carotid or vertebral arteries or jugular veins.

The chest should then be laid open in the usual way, taking care in removing the sternum that the jugular and subclavian veins are not opened. After glancing at the state of the exterior of the lungs, so far as they are exposed, the cavity of the pericardium should be cautiously opened, without moving the parts within it After noting the quantity and appearance of any fluid in this sac, and the aspect and state of apparent fulness of the different compartments of the heart, the left ventricle should be laid open by a longitudinal incision with a scalpel, without displacing it from its original position, noting the state of its interior, and the quantity and appearance of the blood in it.

With a scissors the incision should be extended to the auricle, and the same information obtained regarding its interior, as well as the commencement of the aorta, and the pulmonary veins The blood is then to be gently sponged up, taking care that none of it escapes into the general cavity of the chest, and the right side of the heart is to be examined in precisely the same way It will be convenient then, after applying ligatures to the arteries and veins attached to the heart, to remove this viscus, and examine it as to its healthy or morbid state The lecture on the Modes of Death will have prepared you for appreciating the important information to be derived from this method of procedure in regard to the heart. If death has taken place by coma or asphyxia, you are already aware that a strong confirmation of this is obtained when the right cavities of the heart are found gorged with blood, and the left nearly empty. Or, supposing the person to have died of hæmorrhage, or by syncope from any other cause, you would expect to find the blood in nearly equal proportions in both sides of the heart. I may merely note here, in passing, that in some cases of death by violence the heart's cavities may be met not only free from blood, but their inner walls clean—a state of matters in this viscus which will call for special notice in a future lecture The state of the cavities of the pleura should next be ascertained, but before proceeding to disturb the lungs it is best to inspect the mouth.

For this purpose the usual vertical incision along the front of the chest should be continued upwards, along the front of the neck and over the chin to the lower lip, turning back the flap to ascertain the state of the muscles, vessels, and nerves of the neck The symphysis of the lower jaw, when sawn through, allows the inspector to divide the attachments of the muscles to the rami of the jaw, which can then be turned back and dislocated outwards, thus completely exposing the mouth and the pharynx. By drawing the tongue to one side, the larynx, and the trachea as far as its subdivision, can be exposed The lungs, with the trachea attached, can now be easily examined, either *in situ* or by removal altogether from the chest, taking care, after examining the œsophagus, first to apply a ligature to it and to the aorta and descending cava

The inspection of the abdomen requires little notice The whole of the viscera should be examined, and particularly the stomach and smaller intestines, as also the uterus and vagina in the female, and the rectum in both sexes

18. The notes of the inspection taken as above are not to be produced as part of the evidence at the trial which may follow, but are solely for the guidance of the practitioner, or the law authorities if called for by them. In Scotland official instructions issued for the use of the public prosecutors in 1839 direct that, where no further examination is required, the inspectors must deliver to the authorities, within two days after the post-mortem examination, a written report containing their opinion on the case, with the reasons succinctly but clearly stated. They must understand that they cannot found their opinion on any facts represented to have been ascertained by themselves during the inspection which are not specified in their notes.

This report—which is intended to form part of the written productions on a trial—should be framed with a view to be understood by a jury, and should therefore be free from technicalities.

The official document to which I have just referred was one drawn up at the request of the Crown officers in Scotland by Sir Robert Christison, the late Mr. Syme, and Dr Traill, and sent out by the Lord Advocate. It was republished in 1868, and is now in the hands of all the Scottish Procurators-Fiscal. I have availed myself largely in this lecture of its contents, as the value and importance of the directions for the conduct of the legal inspection in criminal cases by these eminent authorities amply entitle them to your fullest confidence and attention. I have also freely availed myself in what has preceded of the excellent directions in Devergie's work on *Legal Medicine*.

To complete the present subject I have only further here to advert to a kindred topic—medico-legal disinterment, or juridical exhumation. I have already noticed the occasions on which it may be required of the medical jurist to undertake, with any prospect of utility, the examination of bodies which have been already interred.

The dangers attendant on these disinterments have been overestimated on the one hand, and under-estimated on the other, both by the profession and the public. That with due care and attention there is no stage of the body's decay at which it may not be inspected, has been shown by Parent du Chatelet by a copious deduction from facts. The same opinion is advanced by Orfila, Tardieu, and more guardedly by Devergie.

In proof of his position, Parent du Chatelet points to the history of the sanitary state of the dissecting-rooms in Paris, to the results of certain experiments of his own, to the disinterment of from 15,000 to 20,000 bodies in all stages of decomposition, undertaken for the purpose of eradicating the Cimetière des Innocens at Paris in 1789; to the disinterment at all seasons of the year at Père-la-Chaise of about 200 bodies annually, at two, three, four, or more months after death, which have been deposited temporarily in trenches previous to their removal to family grounds or more suitable graves elsewhere; and to the experience of the Commission of the Provisional Government of France in disposing of the victims of the Revolution of 1830.

It must be admitted, however, that this author has underrated the hazards of such inspections, as shown by published cases of serious or fatal results from exposure to the emanations from putrid bodies, particularly during the period at which the evolution of gases is most active, prior and posterior to which period the danger is reduced to a minimum.

The following directions are given by Devergie for conducting the disinterment of bodies some time buried :—

1. Never to proceed to the operation fasting, and to be sure first to take a dram   2. To disinter the body early in the morning, if in summer, as at this time the air is cooler, and the disengagement of gas less free   3. To provide sponges, towels, water, and from three to four pounds of dry chloride of lime; a pound of the chloride is to be diffused through two pailsful of water.   4. To prepare a large table, to be placed on a platform raised above the ground, and, if possible, in a current of air   5. To proceed as speedily as possible with the disinterment of the body, and with a relay of gravediggers   As soon as the coffin is exposed, it is to be copiously sprinkled with the solution of the chloride, to enable the workmen to draw it up without danger, which is to be done with ropes   6. To open the coffin at the side of the grave, remove the body, and to have it exposed to the air for a short time (from fifteen to twenty minutes)   7. To place it on the table, sprinkling around the body (but not on it) dry chloride of lime to at least the amount of half a pound, replacing it by a like quantity three or four times during the examination   8. To proceed to the inspection of the body, during which the examiners' hands are to be repeatedly washed with the solution of the chloride   9. During the course of the inspection the examiner should keep on the windward side of the body.

Where the body interred has had time to be reduced to the state of a skeleton, these precautions for avoiding danger on the part of the examiners are not called for. In this case, that no part of the bones may be lost or destroyed, the following directions from the same author may be followed with advantage:— 1. The suspected spot itself should not be touched in the first instance. 2 A trench ought to be dug, at a distance of twelve or fourteen feet from the suspected spot, of about fifteen or twenty feet in length, by four feet and a half or five feet in breadth; observing, as the bones are approached, whether the soil has been previously disturbed, which can be readily done by comparing it with the earth first dug up. 3. As soon as the workmen come upon the bones they are to stop, and begin their operations on the opposite side. 4. The body is then to be exposed, little by little, and when the point is reached where the first bones were observed, the earth is to be passed through a fine sieve; by this means all the smaller bones may be collected, and even the nails 5. As bone after bone is detected, the directions in which the skeleton's head and feet were placed should be noticed. 6 The respective depths of the different bones from the surface may afford some indications of the manner in which the grave was originally dug. 7. If any remains of a cord are found around the cervical vertebræ, its position is to be carefully noted 8 The bones are to be collected, and their respective lengths ascertained, and whether or not they mutually correspond. By this means, with the aid of Sue and Orfila's tables, or those of Gordon of Edinburgh, the length of the individual during life may be ascertained, adding one inch and a half as an allowance for the thickness of the soft parts, and keeping in view that average results only are attainable in this way, since, as shown by Dr Guy, even such averages are not always to be implicitly trusted, from the occasional want of correspondence in the proportionate lengths of the long bones. Lastly, the points adverted to in the lectures on Age and Sex require to be attended to in the examination of the skeleton procured by disinterment.

At the request of several members of the profession I append several examples of medico-legal reports as required in Scotland, in the form approved of by the Crown-office of Edinburgh (Appendix II)

LECTURE XXIX.

HOMICIDE.

SUBJECTS INCLUDED UNDER THIS TERM. IMPORTANCE OF THE SUBJECT LEGAL CONSEQUENCES ATTACHING TO IT—Murder—Culpable Homicide—Justifiable Homicide—Casual Homicide—CHARACTER OF THE EVIDENCE REQUIRED IN CHARGES OF HOMICIDE—Death must have followed the Injury—Death must have been the usual consequence of it—Determination of the period of the Death—Determination of the previous state of the party—The treatment of the Injury to be taken into account

By strict adherence to the legal sense of the term homicide, we exclude such injuries as are the results of either accident or of suicide, though the injury may be in each of the same character, and involve the same consequences, as in the purely homicidal act. Hence it is that the exigencies of my position require me to depart from the trammels of the legal definition, and to discuss the various forms of violent death, as they present themselves to our notice, without regard to the facts of their being either accidental, suicidal, or homicidal; agreeing, as all of these are usually found to do, in all their more important points. We thus enter on a wide range of subjects;—Wounds, in the widest sense of the term; the different forms of death by Asphyxia, as drowning, hanging, etc.; deaths by Cold, Heat, Starvation, and Lightning, and death by Poisons

Such injuries as the above, when homicidal, are ranged by lawyers under one or other of the following categories—namely, wilful homicide or murder, culpable homicide or manslaughter; casual homicide; and justifiable homicide Murder implies the intentional infliction of a mortal injury, culpable homicide the infliction of such an injury without the intention of killing, but with the design of doing some serious bodily harm, or by culpable negligence; casual homicide where the injury, though not in itself of a fatal character, has indirectly proved so, and justifiable homicide, the effects of such injuries inflicted in self-defence.

In most of the United States of America the crime of murder

is classed under one or other of two forms, murder in the first, and in the second degree; the former being where the crime is intentional, or where it is committed in the perpetration of, or attempt to perpetrate, any burglary, arson, rape, or robbery, or where it is by poison; when not falling under any of these heads, it is murder in the second degree.

These distinctions, however, are more for the guidance of those who administer justice, or who are members of the legal profession, than for the medical jurist. But by the last, however, they should also be kept in view; for the opinion expressed by him as to the nature and extent of the injury may, in many cases, fix the division to which the homicide belongs. Besides, by the facts ascertained by the expert, both the mode employed and the intent of the killer may sometimes be rendered obvious. Moreover, it can only be by the evidence of the medical jurist that the judge and jury can find out whether the injury sustained was of itself of a mortal character, or had proved fatal from subsequent accident or casualty, by previous or acquired disease, infirmity, or improper treatment

This being the case, it will be necessary to direct your attention—First, to the more important of the circumstances which are capable of modifying the legal character of homicidal acts as they come within the province of the medical jurist; and second, to the character of the evidence which he will be expected to adduce for the guidance of the legal authorities in the conduct of the case.

On the circumstances which may modify the legal character of a homicidal act I need not dwell at any length.

The effects of age and sex in qualifying the effects of injuries are sufficiently known and appreciated by the profession, and need not be dwelt on.

The same remark applies to those constitutional peculiarities which render injuries much more serious to some individuals than to others; such as malformations, transpositions of abdominal or thoracic viscera, attenuation of the cranial and other bones, preternaturally phlogistic or hæmorrhagic diathesis, weak and unhealthy constitution, whether from natural causes or intemperance, or from the effects of previous injury or disease.

A more important and difficult class of causes capable of modifying the effect of injuries are those set down, in legal phrase, as *malum regimen*, or misgovernment on the part of the injured party, or his medical attendant This includes the want of assistance or proper medical attendance to the hurt party, either accidental or unavoidable; irregularities on the part of the patient or his attendant; previous intoxication of the patient; his improper conduct subsequently, and ignorance, inattention, or mismanagement on the part of the medical practitioner

Confining ourselves here to the strictly legal aspect of the evidence expected of the expert in the investigation of a case of homicide, in so far as it has come under his notice in his professional character, I need scarcely say that, from the wide range of topics included under the designation of homicide, much of the medical evidence will have to rest upon the nature of the specific injury inquired into. Hence I need only advert here to those points which have a general bearing on the whole, or the greater number, of the injuries of this class.

The opinion of the medical witness may be asked regarding the import of several circumstances which may have come within his cognisance in the course of his professional attendance; such as the general character, temper, and habits both of the deceased and the prisoner, their relation to each other, their relative ages, their relative strength, and the provocation, by expression or otherwise, which the respective characters of the parties might have rendered probable. An opinion on other points belonging legitimately to his province, is more certain, however, to be required of the medical witness; such as the nature and situation of a wound, or other injury, the nature of the weapon employed in its infliction, and the manner in which death was occasioned; points which will call for detailed consideration by and by, under the separate forms of homicide.

The expert should be aware that in addition to evidence of intent, which he may be able occasionally to supply, he may be called on to prove that the person injured had died of the hurt, whatever that may have been, and that directly, or by its usual and probable consequences; points, the establishment of which may involve the answer to not a few nice and difficult questions in the course of the legal investigation. Here it is that the consideration of the circumstances which are capable of influencing the result of homicidal injuries, comes into play. An incised wound of a limb, for instance, or a lacerated wound of the scalp, of a trifling kind, may be inflicted; the person is taken to an hospital, or elsewhere, erysipelas, or a contagious fever supervenes, and death ensues.

In 1834, a girl of sixteen was struck on the head by a

paralytic old woman with a walking-stick, in consequence of some provoking language. The scalp became erysipelatous; the patient was taken to the Aberdeen Infirmary, where she died. At the post-mortem examination a layer of purulent matter was found under the scalp, and the outer table of the skull was carious.

About the same period I saw a case where a blow on the cheek with a bunch of keys was followed by a fatal attack of erysipelas of the head and face.

It should be known to the expert who has to tender evidence in a case of homicide, that if the death of the injured person has been owing to the usual consequences of the injury, it is immaterial to the legal proof that a period of many months has elapsed between the one and the other, or in how feeble or declining a state the deceased may have been when he received the wound, or other violence, or that under more skilful treatment he might have recovered. In cases coming under this description, the following principles are acted on (Alison)—(1) How feeble soever the condition of the sufferer may have been, and how short his tenor of life, it is equally murder, as if the person killed had been in the prime of youth and vigour. (2.) If the death be duly owing to the wound, it signifies not that, under more favourable circumstances, and with more skilful treatment, the fatal result might have been averted. (3.) Though death do not ensue for weeks or months after the injury was received, yet if the wound, or other injury, be severe, and keep in a regular progression from bad to worse, so that the patient continually languishes, and is consumed by it as by a disease, this in reason and law is quite the same as if he had died on the spot. By the English law, however, a limit is fixed to the time of death after injury, that time being a year and a day, beyond which, if the patient survives, a charge of homicide against the assailant will not lie. (4) If a physician or surgeon give his patient a potion or plaster, intending to do him good, but contrary to expectation it kills, this will, in the general case, be considered as misadventure. But if the medicine were administered, or the operation performed by a person not a regular physician or surgeon, the killing would be manslaughter. The same will hold if the pretended remedy be obviously and notoriously perilous and unsuitable for the particular case where it produced fatal consequences.

A case in point occurred at Aberdeen in the summer of 1842. A person who had studied medicine for a short time, hearing that a young woman had fallen down in a fit in a neigh-boarding house, went and volunteered his services, and being ignorant of the real nature of her illness, and unacquainted with the action of remedies, by a sort of hap-hazard sent for 15 grains of muriate of morphia, and exhibited about 10 grains of it, which caused the woman's death within a few hours. For this he was tried at the ensuing circuit, and, being found guilty on his own confession, was sentenced to four months' imprisonment

In another case an unqualified practitioner from Ellon, Aberdeenshire, was sentenced to several months' imprisonment for administering an overdose of Vinum Opii to an infant

Though no limit is fixed by the Scottish law, as in England, to the period a person may survive an injury which may ultimately prove fatal, it were well for the practitioner, that, as in England and in most of the continental nations, such a term should be fixed. It is well known to the profession, that when the fatal result of an injury is long in following its receipt, it becomes increasingly difficult, owing to such long delay, accurately and satisfactorily to trace the connection betwixt the injury and the death   So much is this found to be the case, that even in Scotland no case, I believe, would lie at any lengthened period after the commission of a homicidal act, notwithstanding the unlimited time which the liberal interpretation of the legal rule would admit.

LECTURE XXX.

WOUNDS.

LEGAL DEFINITION OF THE TERM WOUND. — DIAGNOSIS OF WOUNDS — PENETRATING WOUNDS. — Character — Varieties — INCISED WOUNDS — Character — Varieties — Size and Direction — Appearance of Edges — Occasional resemblance to Contused Wounds — Means for the Determination of their Points of Commencement and Termination — Two or more Wounds from One Application of the Instrument — Date of the Wound — Cicatrices — Whether the Wound was inflicted during Life or after Death.

AMONGST the various forms of homicidal violence a prominent place must be assigned to wounds, as understood in legal medicine. In legal medicine the term is made to include all those local alterations of any part of the body which are produced by violent means, whether the cause has been directed against the body, or the body against the wounding cause. Hence such wounds are classed as incisions, lacerations, contusions, concussions, fractures, dislocations, sprains, and burns, whether by fire or by escharotics.

The adoption of this arrangement has been found to be attended with certain obvious advantages in practice, and has caused it to be retained, though it is liable to some objections. Thus, it will be observed, that it comprehends certain injuries which are excluded from the class of wounds, as this term is made use of in surgical language. According to the ordinary acceptation of the term a wound denotes an accidental solution of continuity of the soft parts, more or less recent, generally bloody, and occasioned by a mechanical cause; and as it varies with its cause, it may be that which is termed a scratch, excoriation, puncture, cut, contused wound, gunshot wound, bite, laceration, venomous wound, and the like.

Again, the law interprets the term wound somewhat differently from either the medical jurist or the ordinary surgeon. Whatever the injury done to either the soft or hard parts of the body, or the extent to which the solution of their continuity may have been carried, unless the continuity of the skin be broken, it is not held in law to constitute a wound. It even appears, from several recent decisions, that an abrasion of the cuticle is not to be understood as a breaking of the continuity of the skin; the cutis or true skin must participate in the injury, and probably the connective tissue beneath.

In these circumstances it is not to be wondered at that, owing to the unsettled meaning of the term wound, it has happened, on more than one occasion, that medical witnesses have differed in their evidence, and that some difficulty has arisen in the prosecution of criminal charges

To obviate these inconveniences, to give them the mildest term, different suggestions have been made, the most feasible of these being those of Drs. Taylor and Guy But, to meet the case in hand, not only must the proposed nomenclature be in itself free from reasonable and obvious objections; the terms suggested would also require the support of both our legal authorities and our surgical brethren, in order to be available in medico-legal practice Till this is obtained, all the requirements of our position may be readily met by the adoption of brief descriptions in place of definitions, or by short explanations. For example, we may speak of a division of the soft or hard parts, enumerating the parts divided, or we may speak of a bruise or contusion, shock or concussion, a fracture, burn, dislocation, etc.; or, retaining the term wound in its usual surgical and generic sense, we may couple it with its appropriate specific qualification, and speak of an incised, punctured, lacerated, contused, or gunshot wound

In this way we leave it to the lawyers to settle amongst themselves whether they are to consider a solution of continuity of the soft parts as a wound or otherwise when the true skin has escaped division; or whether the term wound is to be held as applicable to one form, and denied to another form of the same injury, when the only distinction which can be drawn between them is, as in the case of fractures, that the skin has or has not been involved in the separation of the tissues

With these necessary explanations premised, I now proceed to advert to those points connected with the large and important classes of injuries bearing upon legal medicine which have been specified, restricting myself to such of these as are either altogether overlooked in purely surgical works, or whose importance is chiefly or entirely derived from their connection with medico-legal inquiries. This will lead me to speak, *first*, of the distinctive characters, or the diagnosis, of wounds and other allied injuries, with certain inquiries arising out of these; *secondly*, of their prognosis, or their characters as regards the relative importance which their extent, the parts of the body in which they are situated, and the organs which they may have involved, may cause them to assume in particular instances; and, *lastly*, of the post-mortem inspection of fatal cases, which will afford me an opportunity of considering some points common to all or many of these various injuries.

And, first, of the diagnosis of wounds in the medico-legal acceptation of the term. I begin with

I. Penetrating Wounds.—Such wounds—also termed punctured—are usually caused by pointed instruments, such as a sword, bayonet, or a knife thrust in as a wedge, and not used as a saw. Consequently, their depth will be much greater than their superficial extent. In general their margins will be found apart, not in close contact. The gularity and evenness of their edges will be affected by the sharpness or bluntness of the weapon or agent by which they have been produced. Thus, penetrating wounds following thrusts with instruments, properly so called, may usually be distinguished from those caused by glass, crockery, nails, etc., by the sharpness of their edges, their freedom from contusion, and their amount of retraction, or the reverse. Such wounds almost never heal by the first intention. However occasioned, they bleed but sparingly, either outwardly or inwardly, unless about the female genitals; when the larger vessels of the neck are divided, or when they have penetrated the larger cavities—in which case, from the absence of the support of muscles and firm sheaths, as in the limbs, the wounded vessels are apt to bleed copiously. The difficulty, too, in this last case, with which the blood coagulates when out of the reach of the air, adds to the importance of such wounds of arteries within the cavities of the body. Hence it is that trifling wounds of the liver, spleen, lungs, etc., which have involved none of the larger bloodvessels, frequently prove fatal from the resulting hæmorrhage. Some instructive cases of this sort I shall have occasion to bring forward in another connection by and by.

Although a bayonet wound may usually be distinguished from a small sword wound, it is a mistake to suppose that in this class of wounds the solutions of continuity always take the shape of the instruments by which they were produced. This was first pointed out by Dupuytren. From cases and experiments on the dead body, it was proved by him that cylindrical pins produce elongated openings with two very distinct angles, the direction of the wound varying with its situation In the neck, at the armpits, and in the linea alba, the long direction of the wounds was parallel to the axis of the body, transverse on the sides of the chest, and oblique on the sides of the abdomen. When at any part of an otherwise cylindrical instrument there were projecting angles, the wound, he found, took the form of these angles.

It has also been observed that, independently of the region of the body and the shape of the instrument, the appearances of penetrating wounds differ with the tissues divided, the state of tension or relaxation of the skin, and the direction in which the thrust is made. Thus, when the weapon has penetrated in an oblique direction through the tissues, or when the latter are irregularly stretched, the shape of the wound does not correspond with that of the weapon. Thus punctured wounds made by the same instrument may differ in shape, and be either triangular or oval, according to the circumstances just indicated

It is to be remembered that wounds made by penetrating instruments are seldom so large as the instrument which caused them, from the instrument having produced rather a separation of the fibres of the tissue than their division. The bones do not form in every case an exception to this, as has been affirmed. Thus—

Several years ago a young man in Aberdeen, while shooting, had the head of the breech-pin of his gun lodged in the frontal sinus from the bursting of the barrel The opposite extremity or point of the nail projected from the forehead, but, though movable, it could not be withdrawn without previously removing a portion of the outer table of the skull by the trephine

In the case of penetrating wounds the defence is not unfrequently set up, that the injury may have arisen in consequence of the person falling against some projecting body—as the corner of a chair or table, a nail in the wall, a sharp stone, or broken glass or earthenware

A defence of this sort was set up at Aberdeen in 1846, on a trial for the murder of a female at Ellon, by a penetrating wound in the genitals; and again in the case of a woman at Kebbaty, for which her master was tried at Aberdeen for homicide in 1855. To the former of these I shall have to recur in another connection afterwards The latter trial was, in several respects, a curious and instructive one, in which counsel of the first eminence were employed for the defence. The victim, who was of very intemperate habits, had died of hæmorrhage from two minute penetrating wounds involving the frontal branch of the left temporal artery. These wounds, it was argued on the defence, must have been caused by the deceased, while drunk, falling accidentally against the heads of two nails projecting from the front board of a wooden bed, near which the body was discovered. Several objections, however, stood in the way of the adoption of this theory: First, a pair of round-pointed scissors, the points of which were bloody, was found in the apartment Secondly, the distance betwixt the two wounds did not correspond with that between the two nails. Thirdly, the nails were so close to an angle formed between the board in question and a folding-door in front of the bed, that the woman's head could not have come in contact with them without a good deal of manœuvring on her part, while in the recumbent posture. Fourthly, no such nails were observed in the board at the time of the post-mortem examination, though blood upon it had been observed and noted down; while the friends of the accused had had possession of the key of the cottage for some time previous to the trial. Lastly, we (the examiners) had satisfied ourselves at the inspection of the body that the wounds had been inflicted in, not out of the bed—a conclusion founded on our finding abundant traces of blood in the bed, in the passage leading to the kitchen, and on seats in the kitchen, with absence of blood on the floor in front of the bed; the woman, apparently, after the receipt of the wounds, having risen from her bed, wandered along a pretty long passage to the kitchen, seated herself there, and afterwards had found her way to the bed to die

The examiner, then, I repeat, should be careful in such a case to inspect the locality, and thus be in a condition to meet the suggestion which may be set forth on the defence as to the possibility or probability of the purely accidental origin of the lesions causing death. Another lesson taught by the occurrence of such a case as the above is the propriety of noting the distance of wounds from each other when more than one is found in the same position In the Kebbaty case, the distance betwixt the two wounds and the two nails did not correspond In further enforcement of the same lesson, I may be permitted to refer again to the case of a female tried at Aberdeen in 1844 for child murder, by an irregular wound in the neck of her infant. On the defence a medical man suggested that the wound on the front of the child's throat had been of purely accidental origin: that the woman, in dividing the umbilical cord, had allowed the point of the knife to pass into the neck. The measurement of the portion of the cord at the post-mortem examination, however, did not tally at all with this ingenious theory

In instances of the sort we are considering, independently of the absence of any efficient wounding cause—a point of some importance,—a little attention to the appearance of the wound will often suffice to obviate the plea of its accidental and indirect origin. Thus, wounds made by coming against foreign bodies are seen to be more or less contused and lacerated if the body is blunt, while even if sharp their edges will be irregular and uneven —circumstances commonly the reverse of what is known to happen after the entrance of penetrating instruments. Besides, wounds produced in the former way seldom extend far below the surface.

In penetrating wounds, the openings made by the instrument in the clothes before entering the body are, as a rule, usually smaller than the weapon which produced them. In passing through the clothes, such instruments, however, do not invariably leave distinct traces of their course. Thus, when their diameter is small, the instrument may merely separate, without dividing, the threads of the cloth, as in the case of woollen garments, which are possessed of considerable elasticity; or the cloth—as where the wound has but little depth—may have been carried in by the point of the instrument, without injury to it, and drawn out again by the movements of the body. This last circumstance, however, has never, it is believed, been encountered in the case of a sharp-pointed instrument.

Once more, a wound partaking partly of the character of an incised, partly of that of a punctured one, may be met with, appearing externally as one incision, and with two or more internal divisions of the tissues or organs, the whole inflicted at one time by the same weapon. This may be effected by the weapon having been only partially withdrawn after the superficial or incised wound was made, and then plunged farther into the body in another direction, as is often the case in a close struggle. Thus, in a case related by Bayard, the corpse presented a single gaping wound in the breast, out of proportion to the weapon found at the spot where the murder was committed; but the left ventricle of the heart was perforated through and through, and its walls wounded likewise at a different part

I lately met with an instance of the same sort in a different part of the body. The corpse of a man was found in a wood at

Nigg, near Aberdeen, in 1875. Beside it lay one of those triangular knives used by shoemakers for cutting leather. With this weapon it appeared that an irregular superficial wound, two inches in length, and presenting the character of an incised wound, had been made in front of the cricoid cartilage near its middle. From this wound the knife seemed to have been thrust downwards, nearly in a vertical direction, dividing across the thyroid cartilage and the first three rings of the trachea.

One other circumstance in connection with punctured wounds may be noticed here, in conclusion. Such wounds, even when inflicted by a sharp knife, are not invariably characterised by a straight cut, but sometimes are seen to have sent off a spur somewhere in their course, like the two lines of the Greek letter γ. This seems to me to be explicable on the supposition that, in withdrawing the knife, the wrist of the assailant is turned half round to facilitate the removal of the instrument, while the assailed, from shrinking, may change posture. I mention this because, on more than one occasion of this sort, my colleagues at the inspection had some hesitation in deciding that such a gamma-shaped wound admitted of explanation, without the necessity of conceiving that the instrument had been more than once projected into the body. Such appearances occurred at Aberdeen in 1875, in a case where several stabs were given on different parts of the trunk. It may not be without interest to notice, further, the fact that in this instance the woman's dress, loosely worn, exhibited more cuts than the sum of the corresponding wounds, from the knife—a sharp-pointed kitchen one—having passed twice through folds of her dress in order to reach more than one of the wounds.

II. Incised wounds are those made by weapons with cutting edges, more or less sharp, and which are drawn across the surface in the manner of a saw, not used as a wedge as in penetrating wounds. These injuries are known from the circumstance of their superficial extent being usually greater than their depth. Such wounds bleed more largely than all others in the vast majority of instances. When the edge of the weapon by which they are caused is keen, their margins are sharp, straight, and well defined, though there are some exceptions to this, the general rule. Thus it has been observed that, however sharp a cutting instrument may have been, if considerable force has been employed, it will be found not only to have cut, but also to have bruised and lacerated the parts divided. Incised wounds also gape more than others differently produced, though the amount of the retraction of their edges will vary according to circumstances. Hence it is that, except perhaps in the bones, the extent of wounds of this class bears a less close relation to the size of the instruments which have inflicted them than in those last considered. In these cases the state of contraction or relaxation of the muscles at the moment has a considerable influence on the size of the wound, their traction facilitating the infliction and augmenting the extent of the wound, while their relaxation has the opposite effect, so that the same instrument, employed with a similar degree of force, may produce wounds on the same part of the body very different from each other, both in severity and extent Thus, as remarked by Boyer, a stroke with a sabre above the knee in the flexed state of the limb will produce a very large and deep wound, whereas the extent and gaping of the wound will be comparatively trifling when the stroke has been applied to the thigh in an extended state, and in a relaxed state of its muscles.

An incised flesh-wound in the direction of the fibres of the muscles will give rise to little or no gaping of the wound; while in the case of the incision being made in a direction immediately across the muscular fibres the wound will appear deeper and will be found to gape more

In reference to the kind of instrument producing it, it is of importance to attend particularly to the condition of the edges of an incised wound, which can only be satisfactorily done while the wound is quite recent. Where the instrument is sharp, and where, as is usually the case, it has been drawn across the part, the edges of the wound will be found to be quite straight On the other hand, when the instrument is blunt, or where, as sometimes happens, it has been pressed against the part, as in penetrating wounds, on the principle of the wedge, without being drawn along it, the edges of the wound will be found to be more or less serrated and irregular

After the lapse of twenty-four or forty-eight hours, when the wound has not healed by the first intention, it is sometimes difficult, if not impossible, to say very positively whether it has been the effect of a sharp or a blunt instrument By this time, however straight originally, the absorbents may have acted on the edges of the incision, and given it a more or less serrated margin

Again, it should be known that a blunt body, such as a stick, may in certain circumstances inflict a wound which it is not always possible to distinguish from an ordinary cut with a moderately sharp instrument. A blow with a stick or other blunt body—especially if round and smooth—when given with a very considerable degree of force and velocity, to a part such as the scalp or the shin, where no mass of soft parts intervenes betwixt the skin and the bone underneath, will produce a wound so straight-edged as to be with difficulty distinguished from a wound with a cutting instrument, while, if the cutting instrument was not a very sharp one, or had not been drawn across the wounded part, but used as a wedge, no means will be left us of determining the point in question. This has been well illustrated by Dr Taylor in the following cases —

Thus, on the occasion of a trial at Chelmsford, in 1842, a person was convicted of the crime of inflicting a wound on the face with a knife, and a respectable female, who had been charged as an accessory, was sentenced to a severe punishment for aiding in the supposed act of stabbing. The proof in this case rested on the evidence of a surgeon, who swore that the wound on the prosecutrix had been produced by a knife, and not by a blow with the fist, as was alleged by the defence, though the latter opinion, as appears by the circumstances adduced in the general evidence, was by far the more probable one, the grounds for concluding that any knife had been used resting chiefly on the loose statement of the prosecutrix herself

In another case, for which we are indebted to the same author, the person was acquitted of a charge of stabbing on the head with a knife, from the difficulty of deciding, from the appearance of the wound, by what means it had been caused. In this instance it was proved that the prisoner had a knife in his hand when he struck the blow

But, what seems more unlikely, a round body may, in striking the head, produce a wound with straight edges In the summer of 1871, a cricket-ball caused a wound across the forehead of a young lady, immediately above, and of the length of, one of the eyebrows, which I could not have distinguished from a wound by a cutting instrument

In incised wounds three distinct portions may frequently be distinguished pretty accurately —(1) The commencement of the incision; (2) its termination, and (3) its centre Thus, the commencement and the termination of the incision differ, the former having only one point, the latter ending in a bifurcation, or in several points Again, it is not unfrequently to be seen—in cases of cut throat, for instance—that one or two superficial and

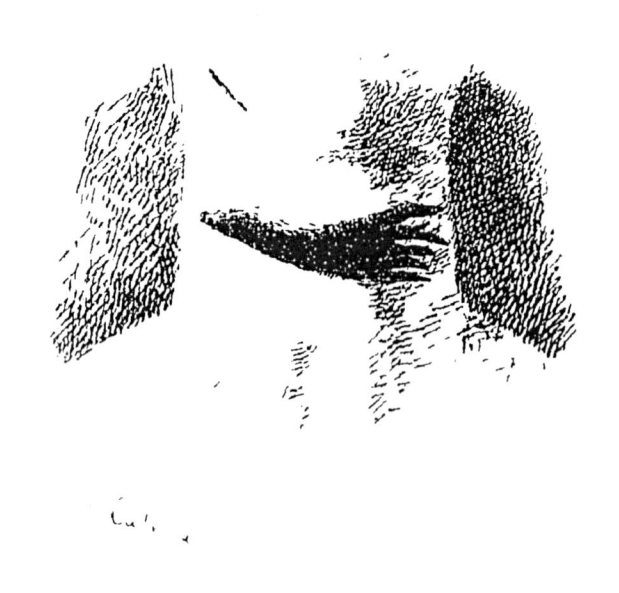

HOMICIDAL CUTTHROAT
SHOWING A TENTATIVE CUT AT THE COMMENCEMENT
& THE SERRATION AT THE TERMINATION OF THE WOUND

SUICIDAL CUTTHROAT

SHOWING THE TENTATIVE CUTS AT THE COMMENCEMENT,
AND THE SERRATION AT THE TERMINATION OF THE WOUND

Pl VIII

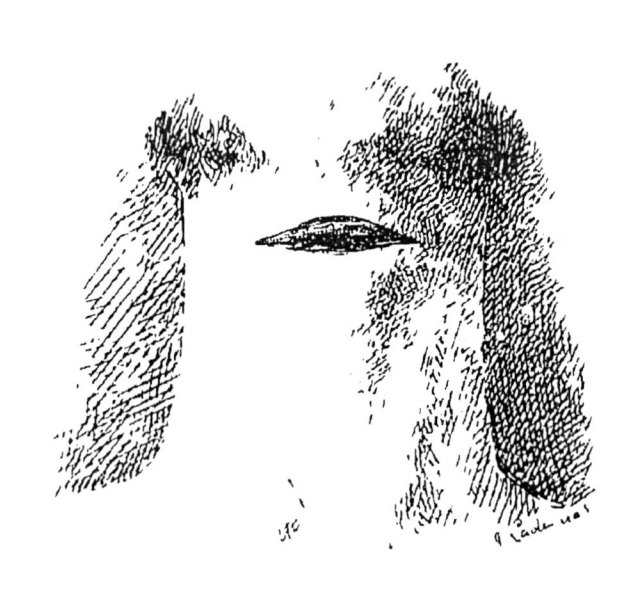

SUICIDAL CUTTHROAT
SHOWING NO INDICATION OF THE COMMENCEMENT & TERMINATION OF THE WOUND

To face Pl IX

Pl IX

SUICIDAL CUTTHROAT
THE WOUNDS INFLICTED BY A RAZOR IN EACH HAND

To face Pl VIII

slight incisions have been made before the person had been able to inflict the principal wound, and these are almost always, though not invariably, found near its commencement. Again, where the parts divided are nearly of uniform consistency, the deepest part of the wound is commonly nearer to the commencement than to the termination of the wound—*i e.* nearer to the single-pointed extremity than to its forked one

Once more, in wounds of this sort, where angular flaps exist in the edges of the incision, the free angles or points will be observed to point towards their commencement

Most of these distinctive characters usually come out best in wounds of the throat, though even in these they are not invariable in their occurrence. They are most apt to fail in suicidal cut throats inflicted with blunt instruments They come out pretty clearly in the accompanying woodcut taken from a cast of the neck of a woman (Harvey) murdered at Cults, near Aberdeen, in 1854 (Fig. VI.) The wound, judging from the above criteria, had commenced on the right side

The characteristics of such wounds, however, come out even better in Fig VII, copied from a cast taken from a male suicide, where the wound was adjudged on the same grounds to have commenced on the left side of the neck

In judging betwixt homicidal and suicidal cut throat from the direction of a wound, I need scarcely warn you that the decision must be reversed in the instances of murder and suicide by left-handed persons Such a suicidal wound was inflicted on herself by an old woman of dissipated habits at Bridge Street, Aberdeen, in 1855.

I have already noticed the indeterminate character that is occasionally shown by wounds of the throat with blunt instruments by determined suicides (of which I have several casts in my museum) Thus, Fig VIII. represents the neck of a man who committed suicide with a razor in the police cells a few years ago The same want of characteristic appearance may be sometimes met with under opposite circumstances

Fig IX shows a case where a female cut her throat with a razor in each hand

I need scarcely insist on the importance of your attention in cases of this sort being carefully directed to such particulars as the above at the post-mortem examination when these characteristics are sufficiently well marked and readily distinguishable In this way the medical jurist may, for instance, be able occasionally to discriminate a case of homicide from one of suicide, or, again, to determine the position of the murderer in reference to his victim while inflicting the fatal injury

A little attention will serve to bring out one other point bearing on the diagnosis of incised wounds. Thus, while an incision in a dead body, made by drawing a sharp cutting instrument across the part, will usually take a straight course from its commencement to its termination without any deviation or complication, this can scarcely be expected to be the case with homicidal or suicidal wounds in the living. In these cases the principal incision is rarely the only one; while the line of the incision will have diverged more or less from the straight course. Here, the instinctive shrinking of the suicide, and still more, the partly voluntary and determined, partly also instinctive, shrinking back from pain of the murderer's victim, may hinder the first touch of the weapon from doing its intended work, and require its reapplication. The writhing of the murderer's victim, and the rotation of the assassin's wrist, usually still more than in the infliction of a punctured wound, insures a change of direction to some extent in the line of incision. From these circumstances an incision of any length will be found to have diverged more or less from the straight course, or, what is more frequently the case, it will show some of those spurs or branches previously adverted to, and shown in some of the woodcuts. (*Vide* Figs VI and VII) Further, from the operation of the same causes it will sometimes happen that in an incised, as in a penetrating wound, though there may be but one incision in the skin, two or more wounds will be seen to have been made underneath by the same propulsion of the weapon. This, as previously explained in the case of a punctured wound, is effected by the weapon having been only partially withdrawn, or having been made to change its direction after the outward wound was made, and then plunged into the deeper parts in a new direction, and with new and added force. Again, as pointed out by Caspar, incised wounds —of the throat especially—though made by one application of the cutting instrument to the part, may leave several distinct superficial incisions. This author adduces an interesting case in illustration, in which the inspectors had made four incised wounds out of the one which really existed; the interruptions which had occurred in this single incision being explicable on the supposition that the head had been bent forward at the moment of its infliction

In penetrating wounds I had occasion to remark that the

incision through articles of clothing made by the instrument in penetrating these is usually smaller than the weapon The reverse of this is commonly observable after incised wounds, as will be readily understood from the direction taken by the weapon

To complete this notice of the medico-legal points arising in connection with incised wounds, some points still remain for consideration. First, it may occasionally be of importance for the medical jurist to be familiar with the appearances put on by incised wounds during the process of healing, the character of the cicatrices left by them, and the probable age to be assigned to the scars. Thus, as a general rule, it has been assumed that such wounds will be bloody during the first twelve hours; that about the end of this period inflammation will have commenced, with secretion of serosity, which will continue during the second day, that on the third day sero-purulent matter will begin to exude; that by the fourth or fifth day, or even later, suppuration will be fully established; that in a simple wound, without loss of substance, suppuration may last from five to eight days; and that from the fifteenth to the eighteenth day the wound will be cicatrised

I need scarcely say, however, that various circumstances may influence the progress towards cure of an incised wound (1) In some healthy persons, for instance, such a wound may heal by the first intention, without going through any of these changes; while in an unhealthy subject, or under unfavourable circumstances, the cure may be long protracted (2) The ages of the parties may influence the result, wounds healing quickly in early life, as a rule, and in aged persons slowly. (3) The depth of the wound and the parts involved may also affect the time of the healing (4) The locality of the incision may have to be taken into account. Wounds, for instance, heal more rapidly in the upper than in the lower extremities, and on the face than on the head (5) While, again, cicatrisation may be facilitated on the one hand, or retarded on the other, by the ease or difficulty of securing rest in the wounded part, as in incisions away from or near large joints, at a distance from and not involving powerful muscles, or the reverse

Beyond a very limited time we have no data to enable us to fix the date of an existing cicatrix At first, indeed, it has a pink hue, and shows little firmness or consistence; but after from forty to fifty days it is found to be white and firm—characters which are from henceforth persistent and unchangeable. But from the careful study of old cicatrices some points regarding their originating causes may be gathered which may be useful, as in cases of disputed identity.

Thus, cicatrices left by incised differ from those which follow contused, lacerated, or gunshot wounds, not to speak of the effects of burns, scrofulous or syphilitic ulcers, scarifications, setons, etc. The shape of the weapon which inflicted them, or their original extent, cannot, however, be accurately judged of, as such wounds contract in healing, and the skin at the part may pucker or otherwise alter to some extent.

Under Identity I anticipated the question of the possibility of a scar once formed ever disappearing, as denied by some authorities, and admitted in a qualified shape by others

Once more, in connection with incised wounds found on the dead body, a question of still more importance may arise in legal medicine—namely, whether these had or had not been inflicted during life. The determination of this point, in practice, will usually be found to hinge on the settlement of the period of the infliction of the wound—whether that had been immediately before or after death, or at a period somewhat more removed from the moment of the extinction of life. Thus, the experiments of Orfila on dogs, and those of Taylor on limbs freshly amputated, showed that the appearances of wounds inflicted immediately after death so closely resemble those of wounds inflicted immediately before death as not to be distinguishable from each other. When, however, the infliction of the respective wounds dates a few hours from the period of the extinction of life, the characters of wounds inflicted before and after death present some marked distinctions which may serve for their ready discrimination in most cases

Thus—(1.) As a general rule, wounds inflicted after death do not indicate that any, or but the most sparing, effusion of blood has taken place; while wounds during life will have bled freely (2.) In wounds inflicted during life, blood in a clotted state will usually be found in the surrounding tissues, or about the lips of the wound, while in wounds inflicted after death this will be almost invariably wanting. (3.) While the edges of a wound inflicted after death will usually be found in pretty close apposition, those of a wound inflicted during life will, on the contrary, be seen to have retracted to a greater or less degree, in proportion to its extent Lastly, a wound inflicted a few hours before death will be found to have its edges more or less swollen and injected, and, if of small extent, its lips may be seen loosely agglutinated while a wound inflicted on the dead body will present nothing at all corresponding to this appearance

A concurrence of the whole of the positive appearances I have noticed—copious hæmorrhage, clotted blood in and around the wound, with retraction, swelling, injection, and partial agglutination of its edges—would undoubtedly indicate that such a wound had been inflicted during life; while the absence of the whole of them, in any instance, would as certainly point to its infliction after death. It must be borne in mind, however, that some of the indications of a wound during life may be met with in wounds inflicted soon after death—i.e., short of ten or twelve hours; while, further, some of the positive signs in the former case may either be entirely wanting, or but slightly pronounced, or they may be present, to some extent in the latter case. Thus the retraction of the divided artery within its sheath may limit the effusion of blood in the living, while a wound of the right side of the heart, or the division of a large vein, may lead to a considerable effusion of blood around a wound in the dead body.

Further, in certain conditions of the blood during life, effused blood does not coagulate very readily, or only imperfectly, though this has been positively denied by Caspar and others; while, if we are to trust this author, blood drawn from or escaped from a body some hours, or even days after death, has been seen to coagulate, and in other cases coagula have formed in the body some time after death. Now, apart from the former of these statements, which requires more confirmation than has yet been adduced, the instances brought forward in proof of the latter statement—namely, the formation of coagula in the dead body at late periods after death—cannot be permitted to rest on data which do not bear out the conclusions drawn from them. It is obviously no proof that the blood in or around a post-mortem wound may coagulate that clotted blood has been met with near a contused or gunshot wound which has proved suddenly fatal, or in the umbilical vein or under the scalp of the still-born child. Nor is the experiment very free from self-contradiction or obscurity, that, after a blow intentionally made with a wooden block on the head of a drowned person three days after death, a coagulum one line in thickness was met with under the pericranium on examination, while all the rest of the blood in the body was remarkably fluid.

Once more, the swelling of the integuments, brought forward as a sign of vital reaction in a wound inflicted during life, may not have had time to appear before the death of the person; while the amount of retraction of the edges of a wound in the living will be more or less marked according to the direction and position of the wound, the retraction in general being greater in wounds of the head and limbs than in those of the trunk, and in those of the wounds which are transverse, the gaping will be greater than when their direction has been parallel with the limb

In the case of incised wounds, then, the following are the positions I would be inclined to lay down as to the period of their production:—

(1) That the concurrence of the whole of the positive signs— free bleeding, clots around the wound, retraction of its edges, with tumefaction and partial agglutination of these—would point with a probability approaching more or less to certainty, according to the degree of their distinctness, to the infliction of the wound found on a dead body having taken place during life

(2) That the precisely opposite set of circumstances would authorise the probability of its having only been made after death; and

(3.) That the only data which would point with certainty to the conclusion that the wound must have been inflicted during life would be the discovery in it of such vital changes as distinct tumefaction, vascular injection, and effusion of lymph or other inflammatory products

LECTURE XXXI.

WOUNDS—(*Continued*).

CONTUSIONS—Effects of Blows or Falls—Concussion of the Nervous System; of the Viscera—Contusion—Local Effects—Contusion without Ecchymosis—Contusion with Ecchymosis—Date of the Bruise—Deep-seated Contusion—Seat of the Bruise—Latent Bruises—Amount of Discoloration—Date of Production—Whether before or after Death—CONTUSED WOUNDS—Character—Disorganisation (Attrition)—Immediate Effects

CONTINUING the subject of Wounds, commenced in last lecture, as understood in legal medicine, I now come to advert to—

III. Contusions and Contused Wounds,—which I class together for obvious reasons. The forcible contact by which these injuries are produced may give rise to effects on the human body of three several kinds, namely (1) Concussion, (2) Contusion, and (3) Disorganisation; and these effects may be coincident with a wound, the extent of which may vary from a simple excoriation up to the most extensive solution of continuity.

These distinctions, however convenient in practice, must not, nevertheless, be pressed too far. Though, for all practical purposes, we may admit the occurrence of concussion apart from contusion, or of contusion apart from disorganisation, these three different effects of the injury are perhaps seldom or never met with singly. Thus it has been forcibly urged, of late especially, that such a concussion or shock as would give rise to serious or alarming symptoms could not be received by the body without contusion or disorganisation, outwardly or inwardly, to some extent, at the same time; and *vice versa*.

(1.) As regards Concussion, it has been held that one effect invariably succeeding the forcible and sudden contact of the body with some hard or resisting external substance, is such a disturbance of the system as is best characterised by this term. The extent of injury thus produced will usually be found to vary with, *first*, the intensity of the impulse, *second*, the consistence of the part impinged against, and *third*, the form of this part. These results manifest themselves in disorder of the functions of the nervous system—the disorder amounting to a mere disturbance of that system when it has been slight, a temporary suspension when it has been more severe, and the complete cessation of its functions when it has been very intense

The results of such strokes will be found to differ according to the part of the nervous system which has been the seat of the concussion, and according to is importance to the system in general Thus, a concussion of the brain may extinguish momentarily the general sensibility and power of motion, or death may supervene A concussion of the spine may produce more or less injury of the mobility and sensibility of the parts supplied with nerves from the spinal cord.

When a stroke has been inflicted, or an impulse received, on parts of the body in the vicinity of the more important of the nerves of organic life, effects analogous to the above are observed in the organs supplied from these sources Thus, a stroke over the epigastrium may prove suddenly fatal, by arresting the heart's action—as is occasionally witnessed in prize fights, or its effect may be to derange the functions of the stomach, liver, or heart, to be followed by a tedious recovery. The same remarks apply to blows on the præcordia

Blows in the vicinity of other organs besides the brain and heart—such as the bladder, intestines, kidneys, and uterus—may equally lead to simple derangement, temporary suspension or the entire arrest of their functions

Of course, where the organ is either a vital one, or one which is, indirectly, of nearly equal, importance to the well-being of the system, the consequence of the final suspension of its functions will be fatal.

These different effects of blows not unfrequently present themselves to the medical jurist under puzzling circumstances Thus, in the case of concussion proving instantly fatal, death takes place by syncope, leaving no traces of the mode of its production in the interior of the dead body, while, except in the case of concussion of the brain, there will be no indication left at the part struck of the previous receipt of the blow I have said except in the case of concussion of the brain, because blows about the head, however suddenly fatal, usually leave some local indications on the scalp This, however, is not always to be expected after fatal blows over the præcordia, epigastrium, or front of the belly generally I have inspected instances of these last forms of sudden death where a careful examination of the parts struck failed to detect any local injuries at or near the surface of the body —cases of which I shall have occasion to adduce afterwards

How far in instances of concussion of the brain of so severe a kind as to have proved instantly fatal, traces of injury of an obvious sort may not be detectable, has been disputed by surgical authorities In the face of recorded cases, these parties challenge the validity of the statements hitherto accepted of instantaneous or very sudden deaths, attributed to concussion of the brain, in which no deviation from the healthy structure of the cranial contents could be detected They contend that, in the instances adduced of such concussion simply, if the examination of the bodies had been sufficiently close, and the condition of the spinal cord and the heart not overlooked or insufficiently taken into account, the conclusion come to as to the immediate cause of death might have been different In cases of this sort Holmes and others, therefore, contend that the effects generally attributed to concussion are due, not to the concussion itself, but to contusion of the brain Though not all exactly agreed as to the precise lesion that ought t be found in instances of this sort, they condescend upon certain indications of disordered structures—such as milletseed-sized extravasations of blood disseminated through the substance of the brain ; circumscribed patches of contusion on the organ; and specks of extravasated blood in the structure of the pons Varolii How far the views of these writers deserve adoption has yet to be determined. All that I need say of them is, that, practically, if found to be in advance of the views of the mass of our surgical and medico-legal authorities, they would only necessitate the transference of the term from concussion to contusion of the brain in cases of severe cerebral shock

In the case of concussions of the spine instantly fatal, the same difficulty is not so apt to arise as after such concussions of the brain From the more solid and immovable character of the bony skeleton in the former instance, the fatal issue of the injury will usually leave traces which can scarcely be overlooked : ruptures of the ligaments, extravasations of blood outside or inside the spinal canal, fractures of the laminæ or bodies of the vertebræ, dislocations or displacements of these, etc On occasions of this sort, in railway accidents, I have seen the spine bent at nearly an acute angle

Where, however, the spinal concussion is less severe, and life is prolonged—it may be almost indefinitely—the position of the medical jurist often comes to be one of great difficulty and responsibility. Witness the conflicting evidence we occasionally meet with in trials for railway damages, where one surgeon will allege that the patient is shamming or merely hysterical, while another will speak as to effects of the most serious sort, having indelible consequences affecting both the bodily and mental powers. And even should the patient sooner or later succumb to the alleged injury, conflicting testimony comes out as to the condition of the spinal cord or its investments.

This brings me to notice certain effects which are occasionally observed to follow shocks to the nervous system from blows over the spine, but more particularly over the præcordia and epigastrium, and which, though severe, are followed by ultimate recovery, the result being here a more or less tedious illness, marked by several of the most proteiform features—at one period, head symptoms predominating; at another, the heart's action being very irregular; at a third, the symptoms indicative of functional disorder of the spine presenting themselves; at a fourth, the train of morbid actions approaching the more marked forms of hysteria, or even of chorea, and all these, at times, interchangeably, in the same case. In these cases it is not always easy to connect the alleged injury with its results. There may, or may not, be local appearances indicative of the blow, and the train of morbid symptoms may, or may not, immediately succeed the stroke, or be such as can be clearly traceable to it. A good instance of this occurred here some years ago in a young man, whose opponent in a street fight took a hammer out of his pocket, and struck him a severe blow with it over the præcordia. Such a train of symptoms followed as I have just described, lasting for three weeks, though there was no trace of the blow at the part struck. A similar train of symptoms occasionally follows strokes about the head, with consequences varying from some weeks of illness of the same ill-defined sort, ending now in ultimate recovery, now in more or less prolonged illness, short of, or actually of, a fatal character. A case of this sort occurred at Mannofield in 1865, and another some years earlier at Methlic, both in Aberdeenshire. In the former a boy of nine was beaten about the head by an older boy with his cap. He was carried home insensible, and put to bed. Though no local injuries could be detected about the head, the boy was ill for six weeks, at one time his case looking like one of hysteria or chorea, at another like an irregular attack of typhus fever. In the other case, a boy of thirteen engaged in a school fight received a trifling abrasion of the scalp. He continued to attend school for a week, he then took to bed, and died after six weeks of anomalous symptoms. At the inspection, the only morbid appearances which I could detect, after a careful examination of the whole body, were a little thickening of the pia mater and some drops of pus over the upper surface of one of the cerebral hemispheres.

In instances of this sort the medical evidence must necessarily be of a somewhat indefinite character. Positive conclusions are with difficulty arrived at. The diagnosis becomes easier, and more definite and satisfactory, where the effect of the injury is not confined to the mere concussion or shock to the organ affected, but involves its mechanical disturbance—rupture of the vessels, and laceration or disorganisation of its tissues.

Before proceeding to notice the more severe consequences of blows, I shall here discuss those more strictly local effects which I mentioned at the outset, as the second of the threefold results of strokes with blunt bodies, namely,—

(2.) Contusion. Such forcible contact may, of course, involve solution of continuity of the surface of the body, though the term contusion is usually restricted to injuries not attended or complicated with such external wounds; and this being the case it may be advisable to limit my observations in the first place to these, reserving what I have to say of the former class of injuries for notice under the head of contused wounds.

First, then, of contusions, strictly so called. The idea of contusion, as thus restricted, involves in it the previous application to the body of sudden pressure, accompanied with concussion or commotion, or of pressure continued for some time. It may be effected without involving the rupture of the capillaries of the part struck, or it may involve injuries of these minute vessels. In the former case the contusion may not manifest itself by any sensible phenomena; the part struck is painful, the meshes of the tissues of the skin have been compressed, and it is only after some minutes that the part swells slightly and reddens, the redness and swelling disappearing in from twenty-four to thirty-six hours, leaving no trace of the injury. But if, at the time of the receipt of such a contusion, death was the immediate consequence of some other cause, the part struck (in which the cellular layers of the skin have momentarily suffered compression, and from which the greater part of the liquids which traverse it have been driven back) undergoes by evaporation a loss of its fluids, which causes its very speedy desiccation, and the dried skin becomes brownish and hard, presenting very much the appearance of parchment. This last effect, however, it must be remembered, may be as readily produced on the dead as on the living, and it may not be possible for the examiner to determine satisfactorily, from the appearances alone on the dead body, whether the parchment-like state of the skin in any given case is to be ranked as a vital or as a cadaveric phenomenon. The pressure, which has sufficed to expel the fluids from the areolar tissue, either shortly before or soon after death, will be followed in the corpse by this state of the skin on its exposure to the air. Thus the parchment-like skin has been observed, on the one hand, where ligatures have been applied to the wrists or other parts of the limbs by the murderer to facilitate his purpose; from the effects of the cord by which a hanged person has been suspended, or from the pressure of the thumbs or fingers on the neck employed to stifle or strangle, while, on the other hand, the same appearance has been equally witnessed where ligatures have been applied to the wrists or ankles in laying out the dead body, or where it has been suspended after the extinction of life.

Of the readiness with which the appearance in question may be imitated in the corpse, we have two illustrative instances represented in Caspar's "Atlas." One exhibits the groove and the parchment-like skin on the front of the neck in the body of a person suspended by a ligature after death. In the other we have the appearance produced artificially on the forearm of a woman's corpse by a flannel roller.

Before leaving these local effects of compression of the surface of the body, it may be useful to notice a mistake unaccountably fallen into by Tardieu, and from which he has drawn an inference which appears to me decidedly erroneous. While clearly admitting that the parchment-like state of the skin is as readily producible in the dead as in the living body, he assumes that, in order to its production, the pressure must have been not only direct and considerable, but kept up persistently for some time, and on this supposed test he founds a distinctive diagnosis betwixt cases of suicidal and homicidal hanging and strangulation. This, however, is entirely at variance with my own experience, as I have met with the parchment-like skin in instances where the pressure had been only momentary, as in the case of the wheel of a cart having passed over the body, producing sudden or instantaneously fatal injury, such as fractures of the bones, or ruptures of viscera.

Where the stroke has involved the rupture of the capillaries the contusion is accompanied by ecchymosis, or infiltration of blood into the areolar tissue of the part. Ecchymosis, then, is one of the phenomena of contusion; but it is not an invariable or necessary one, for as a contusion may be produced without ecchymosis, so likewise ecchymosis may occur without contusion, as is observed after some diseases with lowered vitality, and more especially in scurvy and purpura. The so-called vibices in these two diseases are, in fact, ecchymoses in the living.

As regards the diagnosis of contusions, strictly so called, not a little difficulty and confusion has arisen from the use of the terms ecchymoses, vibices, suggilations, contusions, discolorations, lividities, and hypostases, as purely synonymous terms—which is unfortunate, since, as we have seen under a former subject, discolorations, lividities, and hypostases are cadaveric phenomena, depending on the stagnation or gravitation of the blood in the capillaries, while the tissues themselves are unaffected. Again, the term suggilation is employed in the same loose way as the synonym of both ecchymosis and hypostasis—the one usually a vital, and the other a post-mortem phenomenon.

At the autumn circuit of 1838 I was employed on the defence, in a capital charge where the examiners of the victim's body certified in their report that certain cadaveric lividities or hypostases on its dependent parts must have been the consequence of a heavy fall during life. Nor is this the only case where I have known such serious mistakes to have been made.

Some distinctions have been made in classifying ecchymoses, which are rather fine-drawn, and liable to mislead, though useful to be kept in mind. Thus we have ecchymoses limited to the skin; ecchymoses extending to the subcutaneous areolar tissue without, and ecchymoses in the latter tissue with, rupture of the skin; or, as they are called, ecchymosis simply, ecchymosis by infiltration, and ecchymosis with effusion. In those well-marked forms of ecchymosis with which we have mostly to do, we have the three characters combined.

When such ecchymosis has its seat, as is usual, on or near the surface of the body, the integuments in a short time assume a blackish or deep violet colour. At a later period this violet gives place to a bluish colour, the blue to a green, this last to yellow, the yellow yielding finally to the natural hue of the skin—the succession of these phenomena occupying a space of several days. It is, however, impossible to assign any fixed period to these appearances, because the shades of colour appear sooner or later, according to the depth the ecchymosis extends below the surface. It may be stated generally that the blue colour appears about the second day, the green from the fifth to the sixth day, the yellow from the seventh to the eighth day; and the complete disappearance of the mark occurs from the tenth to the twelfth day, or even later. Though ecchymoses occur, as we have seen, most readily on the surface of the body, it is well to be aware of the fact, that in some cases the ecchymosis may not involve or affect the skin at all. In other words, there may have been contusion, and yet the discoloration may not be visible on the surface of the body. The ecchymosis may be confined to the subcutaneous areolar tissue without the skin participating in it. In this case the coloration of the skin does not appear till from twenty-four to thirty-six hours, or even later. I was much struck with this in a case of assault with intent to commit rape, tried at Aberdeen in 1838, where the marks of pretty severe blows on the limbs were not discovered for the first four days after their infliction.

Again, an ecchymosis may exist among the deeper-seated muscles of a limb, without any trace of it becoming observable on the surface. In such a case, all that can be noticed is that at the end of forty, fifty, or sixty days, yellowish, green, or bluish spots of irregular figure appear over the injured part.

Further, it is important to be aware that age and enfeebled constitution have a remarkable influence upon the time necessary for the complete resolution of ecchymoses. This remark we owe to Mr Watson, who states that he has found the clot distinct when cut into in such a case, though probably much lessened in size, several weeks after the infliction of an injury. In the case of an old man, he adds, I found it distinct five weeks after. In the case of an old woman injured in Aberdeen in 1838, the sloughing of a portion of the skin of the leg first revealed an extensive subcutaneous ecchymosis about three weeks after the receipt of a severe bruise.

Again, the discoloration depending on a contusion may spread to a very considerable extent during the first few days after the accident, giving the idea of a very large bruise, while it is in reality very limited. This is observable after sprains of the ankles, where the lower half of the leg becomes blue or green.

It should also be known to the medical jurist that, in contusions of different parts of the body, the infiltrated blood spreads over portions of the surface in a direction and to an extent not proportionate to the severity of the blow alone, but chiefly to the density of the tissues, and their resistance to the effusion of the blood. In this way, as first pointed out by Velpeau, we explain the fact, frequently verified, that the ecchymosis does not constantly appear in the situation which the seat of the contusion would indicate. In a contusion of the armpit, for instance, the discoloration appears below the injured part; while in the iliac and hypogastric regions, the discoloration, on the contrary, appears above the point struck. This latter arises from the areolar tissue being more closely adherent to the brim of the pelvis than it is either above or below this part. The same remark applies to the knee, the shoulder, the chest, and other parts of the body. Thus, a contusion over the greater trochanter of the femur will be followed by an ecchymosis below the contused spot. When the inner head of the tibia is struck, the ecchymosis makes its appearance higher up the limb. When the blow is received on the calf, the effused blood spreads along the side of the knee-joint. When the contusion is on the inner or outer surface of the leg, the effusion spreads equally upwards or downwards; when on the nates, the ecchymosis is on the outside of the thigh; when on the back, the loins, or sides of the chest, it extends in preference towards the iliac fossæ. When the seat of the contusion is on the sides of the neck, the ecchymosis is more forwards and downwards; when on the forehead, the eyelids are discoloured.

The bearing of these remarks on medical jurisprudence will be readily seen, since it is sometimes of importance to know if the seat of the contusion is that in which the ecchymosis is detected. It may be necessary, for example, to determine whether the position of an assailant in a scuffle was such that a certain blow could have been inflicted by him or otherwise.

Some evidence has been brought forward by Dr Taylor to show that the effect of a blow may manifest itself not at the part struck, but on the opposite side of the limb, for instance; or again, in case of injury of the leg, above the knee. The proof of this is not, however, so clear as could be wished.

It should be kept in view by the medical jurist that ecchymoses may sometimes proceed from causes irrespective of the direct application of violence to the skin, as in certain states of the body, such as scurvy, purpura, etc., from strong muscular efforts, or sudden and severe strains on the tendons. Once more, it is a remarkable fact, but one repeatedly verified, that internal injuries of the most extensive kind are sometimes sustained after blows or falls, without leaving any external mark on the body.

This occurrence is well illustrated by the following instance related by Dupuytren, quoted by Devergie:—

A French soldier, in 1814, was brought to Dupuytren from under the walls of Paris in an ambulance, but, as no marks of violence could be discovered on his body, he might have become the laughing-stock of his companions, if that surgeon, on examining the lumbar region, had not found it fluctuating and disorganised under the integuments to a great extent. The man sank in a few hours. On inspection, the subcutaneous cellular tissue, the abdominal parietes, and the left kidney, were all found reduced to a pulp, the lumbar muscles torn, and the lower ribs, as it were, worm-eaten (*vermoullé*), and the abdominal cavity and the left side of the chest filled with black blood. The skin alone had escaped the action of the bullet.

In a case of homicide from Kincardineshire, tried at Aberdeen in 1832, a man had his bladder ruptured by a kick in the hypogastrium with the toe of a heavy loaded shoe, from a fellow-labourer in the harvest field, where dissection left no indication in the abdominal wall of the precise part struck.

In another case of homicide, to be adverted to more fully afterwards, the liver was ruptured and the gall-bladder detached, from a person having come down with all his weight on the epigastrium of his victim. Here, too, though the death was not immediate, there was left no discoloration, and no effusion of blood immediately under the integuments. It is not, however, only in injuries of this sort applied to the yielding walls of the abdomen that ecchymoses of the skin and muscles may be looked for in vain.

In the case of a man at Insch (Aberdeenshire), in September 1838, pitched from the top of a cart piled high with furniture, several ribs were fractured, and one lung extensively lacerated, without injury to the integuments or muscles.

In March 1832 an old woman's body was found in a court in Upperkirkgate (Aberdeen). Quarrelling had been heard in the house, and, from the legal investigation which took place, it could not be ascertained whether she had fallen from, or been pitched out of, a window on the third floor, below which she was found dead. Here, on inspection, I found the pelvis comminuted, eleven of the ribs and three of the lumbar vertebræ fractured, and the spleen ruptured, but the exterior showing no sign of contusion.

These cases, it should be borne in mind, however, form but

exceptions to the general rule, and the fact that in one of them death must have been immediate, goes far to explain their peculiarities.

Ecchymosis confined to the skin, and, *à fortiori*, when extending to the cellular tissue, is followed by swelling of the part. The resulting tumour is firm and compact in ecchymosis with infiltration; it is soft, fluctuating, and above all elastic, in ecchymosis with effusion. These tumours become denser and firmer in proportion as the absorption of the fluid parts of the blood proceeds, but they subside gradually, and soon disappear, if not followed by inflammation. The size of the tumour is regulated by the vascularity of the part, or by the size of the vessel ruptured, rather than by the extent or severity of the blow. On cutting into one of these tumours, the blood, though it may be found partly fluid, partly coagulated, is most frequently in the latter state.

The same characters belong to contusions with ecchymoses in all the soft parts, only their margins are better defined when they occur in mucous or serous membranes. In the parenchymatous viscera, however, some of these characters are wanting. Thus, in the brain, the blood is mixed with the substance of the organ, in the form of a pulp, particularly when the effusion is extensive, and the contusion severe. In the liver the brown colour and the granular texture of this organ give it a peculiar appearance. In contusions of the kidneys, the tissue, on account of its density, is rarely disorganised.

Ecchymosis is most readily produced in connective tissue, and in soft parts resting on solid bones, particularly the flat bones; less so in the skin and muscles, on account of their elasticity. Hence the readiness of its production in the scalp. In some persons a very slight force is sufficient to produce ecchymosis. The harder and denser the body employed to strike with, the more marked the effects which follow the blow.

Under Identity I had occasion to remark that the assailant had, on one occasion, been discovered by the impression of a key, wherewith, in an attempt at murder in the ___ intended victim had struck him on the face in self-defence. The contusion corresponding with the wards of the key, which was of an unusual form. It may be proper, therefore, to state here, that such correspondence is rarely to be met with, the mark of contusion being almost always larger than the instrument which has inflicted it, while its seat, as we have already seen, does not always indicate the seat of the blow.

In the case of contusions, as in that of incised wounds, a question of considerable interest, in a medico-legal point of view, not unfrequently arises, when such injuries are found on the dead body; namely, whether the contusions had been inflicted during the life, or after the death of the party? In cases of contusions inflicted two or three hours before death, no difficulty is encountered in deciding to that effect in the vast majority of instances. The change of colour in the bruised part cannot be confounded with any post-mortem appearance in the ordinary state of the body. Besides, the effects of a blow on the dead body, at a like distance of time after death, would not be attended with the tumefaction, and the escape of blood into the cellular tissue, which take place in the previous instance, unless in the rare exception of a large vein having been ruptured, and the blood having remained in a fluid state.

The difficulty usually consists in distinguishing a bruise produced immediately or almost immediately before death, from one produced in the body a few minutes, or at most a very few hours, after death. It has been proved, in fact, by the experiments of Sir Robert Christison, that some strokes inflicted shortly after death produce marks which, as far as their colour is concerned, do not differ at all from the effect of blows during the last moments of life. Christison has observed that, in general, the discoloration is produced in this case in the same manner as in certain cadaveric lividities, by the effusion of an excessively thin layer of the fluid part of the blood on the surface of the true skin under the cuticle, and that this coloration cannot be confounded with a true ecchymosis, which is caused by blood extravasated into the subcutaneous cellular tissue. Christison's experiments prove, however, that sometimes, in consequence of blows after death, the effused blood may form a sensibly thick layer within the tissue of the cutis vera; and that occasionally, also, blood may be effused into the subcutaneous connective tissue, so as to discolour it over a limited space. The following, notwithstanding, may be considered as the characteristic marks of blows inflicted during life:—1. Swelling of the part, the consequence of the blood effused. This, he states, is certainly never produced in the dead body. 2. Coagulation of the blood effused into the subjacent cellular tissue, with or without tumefaction. This appearance, says Christison, I have never seen accompanying contusions caused in the dead body; but it may be doubted, he adds, whether clots might not be formed if the injury was inflicted soon after death, and had the effect of lacerating a considerable vessel in the neighbourhood of loose cellular tissue. 3. The most characteristic sign of contusion during life Christison considers to be, incorporation of blood with the whole thickness of the true skin, rendering it black instead of white, and increasing its firmness and resistance. This sign is not always present, as it is well known that a blow may occasion extensive effusion below the skin without affecting the skin itself; but when present Christison considers it decisive.

After the full consideration I have found it necessary to bestow upon contusions proper, it will not be necessary to say much on contused wounds or contusion with laceration or division of the skin and superficial tissues, the remaining branch of this subject.

The co-existence of a wound with a contusion does not much affect the character of the latter injury, most of the characters of a contusion without, continuing the same as a contusion with a solution of continuity. In the latter case, however, though there may be hæmorrhage into the surrounding tissues, there is rarely, if ever, much escape of blood outwardly. The mode in which the blood-vessels are divided favours, in this case, the form of intra and extra-vascular clots, which tend to arrest the flow, while in some instances it is believed to act much like that performed by the surgeon.

The aspect of wounds of this class is too characteristic to require description. Unless over the cranium, as formerly said, then uneven and irregular edges, and less acute angles, sufficiently distinguish them from incised wounds; but, beyond this negative opinion, it is sometimes impossible to go in determining the mode of their production, often due, as they are, to accident, and seldom presenting any peculiarity by which the use of a weapon can be positively inferred, while an opinion can rarely be given, from the mere inspection of the wound, as to the cause of the injury. In such instances it must be borne in mind that a contused wound may be equally the effect of the party coming forcibly against a blunt body, as of the blunt body coming forcibly against the party—i.e. the wound may have been produced by a fall or a blow. In such cases the only safe criterion is deduced from the relative position of the parties at the time of the receipt of the injury, where this had been ascertained. Where an instrument is shown, the medical jurist, in addition, may be enabled, from its character and position, to state the possibility or probability of the wound having been made by a blunt instrument similar to that produced at the trial.

(3.) The last result which was stated to follow a stroke with a blunt body was the disorganisation of the part struck. This is termed attrition, and differs both from contusion and laceration—from contusion because there the structure is preserved, while in attrition it is more or less completely destroyed; from laceration, because in that form of injury the tissues are, as the word implies, torn, while in attrition they are broken down.

Attrition is necessarily followed by ecchymosis, the broken-down tissue forming a pouch or cavity for the effused blood, the consequence of which is—at least as far as the internal soft parts are concerned—a tumour, similar to an ordinary contusion, but with a feeling of fluctuation at the part. Attrition is usually met with in the limbs, in the thicker parts of the walls of the cavities of the body, or in the parenchymatous viscera. The hollow viscera and the membranous parts are in such cases more liable to laceration than to attrition.

Attrition may take place in the deep-seated parts without involving the integuments, in the same way as I have noticed in the case of mere contusions.

Such, then, are the three leading forms which injuries, caused by falls or blows on the surface of the body, may occasion, either singly or in combination, and which I have regarded almost wholly from their more obvious aspects, as local and direct forms of violence. Injuries of this sort, however, are not always confined to the mere concussion or shock; the contusion or disorganisation alone of the part to which the violence has been applied; or the derangement or arrest of the functions of the organs sympathising with the part. Such injuries, in addition, may involve distant parts by the mechanical impulse transmitted to them through the intermediate structures.

The consideration of these, however, must be reserved for my next lecture.

LECTURE XXXII.

WOUNDS—(*Continued*).

CONTUSED WOUNDS (*continued*)—Consecutive Disorders—Rupture of the Liver—Detachment of the Gall-Bladder—Rupture of the Spleen—Laceration of the Lungs—Rupture of the Stomach—Rupture of the Urinary Bladder—Rupture of the Heart—Rupture of the Brain—Rupture of the Blood-vessels—Rupture of the Veins—Rupture of the Muscles—Injuries of Bones. LACERATED WOUNDS.—Character. GUNSHOT WOUNDS.—Character—Typical Character—Occasional Variations—Effects independent of Ball or Wadding—Effects of varying Momentum of the Projectile—Effects of various Projectiles—Effects of the Structural Differences of the parts injured—Effects as influenced by the Direction taken by the Projectile—Effects as influenced by the Distance from which the Weapon was discharged—Effects as influenced by the passage of the Projectile through Articles of Clothing—Effects of the passage of Projectiles through Bones—Latent Injuries from Firearms—Period of the Discharge of the Firearm

AT last Lecture your attention was directed to the three leading effects on the human body of blows or falls, regarded in their obvious aspects as local and direct forms of violence, and the impressions made by them indirectly on the cerebro-spinal system. These effects we have now to follow, beyond the mere local results to the part of the body impinged against, or the arrest of the functions of the organs sympathising with the injured part, to the additional injuries primarily of a mechanical sort which may be inflicted on distant parts, transmitted through the intermediate structures impinged against.

These mediate or consecutive mechanical disorders are sometimes such as may be readily overlooked at the time of the receipt of the injury in question, and their alarming or fatal nature may only become apparent after the lapse of a few hours or days. The more important of these, to which I limit myself, are lacerations of internal organs, and ruptures of blood-vessels, and of other deep-seated parts.

Injuries of this serious character are of the rarest possible occurrence after common assaults with the fists or even with sticks or stones, except in blows about the head rupturing intercranial arteries, or occasionally, though but seldom, lacerating the brain.

Such injuries are more common as effects of falls from a height, the fall of heavy bodies on the person, or what is most likely of all to produce them, the concussion or shock in railway accidents.

Ruptures of viscera are most easily produced when the organs involved are naturally dense, voluminous, and readily displaced. Hence the comparative frequency of these accidents in the liver, kidneys, and spleen, and their greater rarity in the heart, lungs, brain, bladder, and alimentary tube. Internal arteries and veins, from their elasticity, when in a healthy state, enjoy a considerable immunity from untoward shocks, excepting those which lie within the cranium or spinal canal.

The dropping of the dead body from a height of eighteen feet, in Richerand's experiments, gave rise to ruptures of the liver and spleen, with other more or less extensive injuries. In persons killed by falling from the second, third, or fourth floors of houses, besides numerous fractures of bone, Devergie discovered ruptures of the liver, spleen, lungs, stomach, bladder, diaphragm, and thoracic and abdominal aorta.

The amount of mechanical injury occasionally met with after railway accidents may be judged of from the following case, which presents points of interest deserving of being related.

In 1866, the instant death of an old woman was caused by her being caught between the buffers of a railway train which was being shunted at the Waterloo Station in Aberdeen, when the inspection showed several of the dorsal vertebræ dislocated forwards into the chest and abdomen, the lungs torn up into fourteen fragments of various sizes, which lay loose in the chest in a mass of fluid blood, and the heart torn across near its base, the ventricles detached from the auricles, and the large blood-vessels (arterial and venous) of the heart in fragments.

In ruptures of the liver the torn surfaces are usually rough and granular, without retraction or ecchymosis, the blood furnished by them escaping into the abdominal cavity, and gravitating to the loins and pelvis, sometimes partly in the fluid, partly in the clotted state, often almost wholly fluid, and but seldom in any great quantity. The ruptures of the liver in Devergie's inspections were all on the upper or lower surfaces of this organ, and most frequently in the vicinity of its left lobe, consisting of mere clefts, directed from before backwards, or with but slight obliquity. In two cases of this sort which I have had occasion to examine, however, the rents were at the posterior margin of the liver; in a third, the rent, a transverse one, was at the base of the right lobe, while

In a fourth case, both the larger lobes were torn in more than one place, and in a direction from before backwards. An extensive rent of the right lobe of the liver, in a girl of eight years, came under my notice at Fyvie (Aberdeenshire), in July 1838. A boy of sixteen was left by his mother, a tramp, in charge of two younger sisters. The girl in question had been submitted by the boy to rough treatment, having been placed by him on the bare back of a donkey, and driven over a mile or more of uncultivated stony ground. Besides the injury of the liver, a small clot of blood on the anterior surface of the brain, and some severe contusions of the limbs, were encountered at the inspection.

The two following cases of rupture of the liver, in addition to other fatal injuries, from presenting some additional features of novelty, seem to me to be deserving of notice.

In September 1854 a woman lost her life in a railway collision at Kittybrewster, near Aberdeen. The inspection showed a fracture of the left fibula and right ilium, the first lumbar vertebra an inch apart from the last dorsal, and the spinal cord torn across at this part. Besides this, a lacerated wound, extending from above the middle of the crest of the right ilium to the vicinity of the symphysis pubis, laid open the abdominal cavity. Through this wound were found protruding the whole of the smaller, and a large proportion of the larger intestines, the right kidney, fragments of the pancreas, the pyloric portion of the stomach, and about a third of the liver with the gall-bladder attached, the two last detached from their natural connections, and quite clear of the wound.

The remaining case gave rise to a trial for homicide at Aberdeen in 1839, and has been already briefly referred to in another connection at last Lecture. A man of the name of Brown, in a scuffle with the police in North Street (Aberdeen), was thrown on his back, and when in this position a constable came down with his knee on the man's epigastrium. Brown was taken to the police office, and subsequently sent to the Royal Infirmary, in a state of collapse, where, without any reaction, he sank in about forty-eight hours. At the inspection of the body, along with the late Dr. Kilgour, we found a quantity of blood, mostly fluid, in the abdominal cavity, the gall-bladder lying loose in the pelvis, and the lower surface of the liver at the cystic hollow raw and bloody, from the detachment of a thin layer of the organ, found adherent to the gall-bladder.

In the two cases just noticed, the gall-bladder itself had escaped injury, the organ being detached at the cystic duct.

Ruptures of the gall-bladder proper have usually been the effects of emetics given to ensure the expulsion of gall-stones; though one case of this injury is recorded from the fall of an old man from his bed on the floor of his room, where a gall-stone was found impacted in the cystic duct.

Ruptures of the spleen exhibit a clean edge, and occur on the convexity of this viscus, excepting where the injury has been of a very violent character, when part of the substance of the organ has been found reduced to a pulp. I have met with such ruptures after falls from a height, after railway accidents, and from severe blows. One case, in the first of these ways, was noticed in another connection at last Lecture. In a recent case, examined along with Dr. Fiddes in January 1877, where a woman precipitated herself from a window in the third floor of a house, there were not only two lengthened superficial rents of the spleen in a longitudinal direction, and three smaller transverse rents near its outer margin, all in front, but also several superficial ones across the viscus, and one spot about an inch and a half in greatest breadth irregularly reduced to the state of pulp, at the back part of the organ. In 1854 I had occasion to examine the body of a female child of fifteen months, where violent blows had produced rupture, to some depth, of the upper part of the spleen, in addition to fractures of the ribs, and other serious injuries.

Ruptures of the stomach are very rare. They may occur from general concussion of the body, as in falls, or by blows on the epigastrium. Their direction is usually transverse, and they may affect the whole, or be limited to any one of its coats. I met with a case where the stomach ruptured spontaneously in a young lady, while labouring under obscure gastric disturbance.

The smaller size of the intestines, and their freedom of motion in the abdomen, render ruptures of these viscera still rarer than those of the stomach

Rupture of the bladder is usually the effect of a direct blow on the hypogastrium, as in the case of homicide, adduced in the last Lecture, from a kick with a heavily ironed shoe.

In the last case but one, of rupture of the spleen, noticed above, where the woman's death was almost instantaneous, there was also a large irregular rent in the fundus of the bladder, through which a quantity of urine had escaped into the abdominal cavity, along with sixteen ounces of effused blood, mostly fluid, but partly clotted.

The facility with which ruptures of the heart are occasionally produced in certain diseased states of the organ, such as attenuation and aneurism of its walls, is well known to pathologists. Ruptures from shocks have been less noticed in practice. One instance of this of an extreme sort has just been adverted to in connection with a railway accident. A previous case from violence, in a different form, occurred at Aberdeen in June 1855, in a girl of four years. She had been struck with the shaft of a cart, and died in a few seconds. The cause of death was shown at the inspection. by the detection of a rent in the wall of the right auricle, extending into the superior vena cava, accompanied with a large effusion of blood into the pericardium.

Spontaneous ruptures of the heart occasionally occur, which we can neither confidently refer to injury nor disease. A case which I examined in the spring of 1863 appeared to me to belong to this category. The subject, an apparently healthy man, under thirty years of age, after his day's work as a carpenter, was occupying himself sawing a piece of wood at home, when he suddenly dropped down dead. At the inspection the heart was found large for his size, but otherwise presenting nothing unusual, beyond the rent through both ventricles, at the part where they joined the auricles. I have lately examined the body of a woman of sixty, where the anterior wall of the left ventricle had given way in two places, ending in sudden death on the street. In this case the walls of the heart and its valves presented nothing which could be called morbid. The ascending aorta and its arch were, however, very much enlarged, but otherwise exhibiting nothing unusual.

In a case of this sort, then, the diagnosis betwixt the rupture of the heart from violence, and its spontaneous rupture, might occasionally be difficult, from the circumstance that such shocks, as in the girl's case, when instantaneously fatal, rarely leave any traces of the blow on the walls of the chest. In this instance, independently of the extraneous evidence of the violence having been received, the diagnosis was facilitated from the fact of rupture of the heart being so very unlikely at this early age; such disease of the heart as might have led to its spontaneous rupture being all but unknown prior to adult age.

Ruptures of the cerebral mass from violence are believed by Caspar and others to be extremely rare. Caspar says that he has only met with one instance. This comparative immunity appears to be explicable by the form which these injuries usually take, being rather a breaking down of the cerebral tissue than rents, as they present themselves in other organs. In this form these injuries are not unusual in those mixed cases of concussion and contusion, already noticed as being set down by some late authors as contusion of the brain. If I may judge from a few instances I have met with, they are usually encountered at its base. One was in the cerebellum.

Cases of this sort may, or may not, be accompanied by fractures of the skull at some point corresponding with the injured brain.

In a case which I inspected along with the late Dr. Benjamin Williamson, the basilar artery was found ruptured, with effusion of blood at the base of the brain, without fracture or other injury beyond a trifling contused scalp wound on the top of the head. The rupture of the vessel, in this instance, was the result of the fall, on the crown of the head of a small stone, dropped from a height by a mason at work on a house top. The patient, a girl of fourteen, survived the accident, in a deeply comatose state, for ten days.

In drunken squabbles, or passionate quarrels, spontaneous ruptures of the cerebral vessels are not unusual, in circumstances occasionally very puzzling to the medical jurist. These occurrences are, however, usually found to be traceable rather to the direct and immediate effects of the alcoholic stimulus, or the excited passions of the moment, disturbing the balance of the circulation within the head, than to any chance blow which may have been received or been suspected.

Ruptures of the larger blood-vessels within the other cavities of the body are not unusual consequences of heavy falls. The most frequent of these are ruptures of the thoracic and abdominal aorta. Their direction is mostly either transverse or oblique, seldom extending entirely around the vessel, exhibiting either a clean division or one with angular margins, and leading to copious discharges of fluid blood into the thoracic or abdominal cavities.

A case of spontaneous rupture of the ascending aorta occurred here some years ago. A military gentleman in Aberdeen was seized with death-like pallor and faintness in the water-closet, from which he partially rallied, though he died of a faint seven hours after. The aorta, on inspection, was found torn into shreds, with a large effusion into the chest, chiefly of fluid, but partly of clotted blood. The rupture, in the first instance, had probably been partial.

A similar case was lately reported to me by Dr. Barclay, of Banff.

The larger veins may be ruptured from violence, or may burst suddenly in previously diseased conditions, and prove instantly fatal. Such spontaneous ruptures are mostly encountered in the larger veins of the lower extremities. The rents take various directions, leaving angular flaps.

Of the muscles, the one which most frequently suffers from concussion is the diaphragm. Ruptures of this muscle are known to have been caused by falls on the hands and feet, blows on the belly, the passage of a heavy vehicle over the trunk, or trampling on it with a heavy person's knees. The rent, usually of the fibres joining the left side of the central tendon, variable in extent, and with ragged edges, gives rise to but sparing hæmorrhage. In such cases portions of the liver, or of the stomach, the spleen, or parts of the intestines, have been met with protruding into the chest, and compressing the lungs. In one case which I had the opportunity of examining, the rupture of the diaphragm was produced in the dead body. During a night of strong wind, a man, it was supposed, while walking by the edge of the Quay, at Footdee (Aberdeen), had been overpowered by the gale and blown into the water, where he perished. His body was not found for some days, and when it was examined, the greater part of the intestinal canal, and the whole of the liver, were observed to have been forced into the cavity of the chest, through a large rent in the diaphragm. Other injuries were found in the body, all produced after death, in consequence of the corpse having floated under a ship in the harbour, which, at low tide, had crushed it severely.

Amongst the curiosities in medicine, we have an instance of a person surviving a rupture of the diaphragm. A seaman, as related in the Guy's Hospital Reports, whose death followed the amputation of a limb four months after the injury which led to the loss of his leg, was, though unsuspected till inspection disclosed it, found to have had the diaphragm ruptured to such an extent as to have permitted the intrusion into the chest of the stomach, and portions of the colon and omentum.

Ruptures of the muscles generally, and fractures of the bones from concussion, are too well known to need to be spoken of. One effect, however, of serious injuries, leading to extensive fractures of bones, deserves a passing notice. I refer to the fact, occasionally encountered, of injuries of this sort proving instantly fatal by syncope from the extent of the shock, when the total want of blood in the vicinity might lead to their being mistaken for fractures produced, not in the living, but in the dead body.

My attention was first directed to this point in 1839, on the examination of the body of a workman, killed by the chimney of a house which was being pulled down falling on his head. In this instance, although a fissure had traversed both temporal bones, and both middle meningeal arteries had been torn across, not a drop of blood had been effused in the vicinity of these injuries. Nor, though the base of the skull also was extensively fractured, did the quantity of blood effused at this part exceed half a teaspoonful.

A case which occurred in the winter of 1860-1, is interesting as showing how long a person may survive fractures at the base of the skull. A late anatomical porter at the University of Aberdeen, the person referred to, lived for seven weeks after an injury of this kind, with occasional consciousness, notwithstanding the presence of an extensive clot of blood on the surface of the brain, occupying, however, chiefly the upper aspect of the hemisphere.

IV. I come next to speak shortly of Lacerated Wounds.

Bodies which tear, in place of cutting, produce their effects on the resulting solution of continuity in different ways. Such wounds are attended by considerable separation of their edges. This separation, which is purely passive, may be the consequence in part of loss of substance; but it is mainly owing to their connections with the surrounding parts having been destroyed along with more or less destruction of their physical or vital properties. Again, there is always more or less thickening of the margins of such wounds, from the bruising of their edges. In this respect they resemble contused wounds; but from these they may in general be distinguished by the shreddiness and irregularity of their margins. Lastly, such wounds are remarkable for the want of correspondence between the quantity of blood lost and the importance and vascularity of the parts divided. Limbs have even been torn away in this manner, and not a drop of blood has flowed from the wounded surface.

In the case of a person to whom I was called some years ago, who had got entangled with the machinery at a bone-mill in Loch Street, Aberdeen, the wounded surfaces, though raw, would not have wetted a cloth. The muscles in one side of the abdomen were laid bare to a considerable extent; the scrotum, and one of the testes, torn away; the penis had the integuments completely dissected off; and there was so much of the common integument of one thigh carried away as to leave a large surface of the muscles on its front and inside, like those of the side of the belly, completely exposed. This person survived till the fourth day, and still no hæmorrhage took place.

Lacerated wounds are frequently attended with marks of contusion. There may likewise be clotted blood effused into the parts in their vicinity; and it is only when these exceptional appearances are present that we can speak with any confidence as to their having been produced during life, when they are encountered in the dead body.

V. I now come to the important subject of Gunshot Wounds

Injuries of this class, while they differ amongst themselves, have, in the general case, many points in common, which serve, with some exceptions, to distinguish them from those which have been already passed under review.

Injuries produced by firearms partake of the character of contused wounds, with more or less of laceration of the tissues, and occasionally exhibit the appearance of burns. As in the case of contused wounds, they bleed but sparingly, if at all, and, like these, their margins are rounded and thickened, thus contrasting strongly with incised wounds, and wounds with sharp penetrating instruments; while the bottom of the wound is reddish-brown, and the surrounding parts ecchymosed, and occasionally blackened, as in burns. Such wounds, in the living, are usually attended with more or less of numbness or insensibility of the part struck, and if the person survives, the inflammation which succeeds is commonly extensive and severe.

When the projectile has produced more than one wound, as where a ball has traversed the body or a limb, the entrance wound will differ from the exit wound. The entrance opening will be smaller than the exit one. The edges of the former will be depressed and contused, the edges of the latter projecting and torn. The entrance wound will be dry and dark-coloured, the exit one raw and bloody. There will be loss of substance in the former case, but none in the latter. These appearances are well represented in Caspar's Atlas.

When a ball has traversed in succession different tissues of the body, its course may admit of being readily traced by its points of entrance and exit in its course through the various tissues involved; the openings, as they are traced inwards, increasing in size, and becoming more and more irregular as they depart from the surface; while again, at the point where the ball has been arrested in its course, the cavity at the part where it has lodged will be larger than at any part of its traject.

A good instance of this was met with in the examination of the body of a man who was fired at by an assassin, near Kintore, in June 1830. The entrance wound on the right side of the chest was small, clearly defined, and depressed, with characteristic entrance and exit openings, respectively, where the ball had buried itself in the body—namely, in the lower lobe of the right lung, the diaphragm, and the right lobe of the liver, while in the last part the projectile had scooped out a cavity for itself and been arrested there. The same thing was observed in the instance of a man who shot himself through the heart in Marischal Street, Aberdeen, in 1870. The entrance wounds on the skin and on the front of the pericardium, as also the entrance and exit wounds on the front and back of the heart, pointed out the course of the rifle-ball.

The same contrasts, to a certain extent, betwixt the entrance and exit wounds by a ball traversing the soft parts of the body, may also be encountered where such a projectile has traversed the cranium.

Two woodcuts in the second volume of Holmes' *System of Surgery*, pp. 157 and 158, give a very faithful representation of the entrance and exit wounds by pistol-balls in the bones of the skull, with the respective sizes of the two openings, and the bevellings of the outer and inner tables of the skull respectively in each, the bevellings being on the inner table in the entrance and on the outer table in the exit wound. In the first of these woodcuts the ball had traversed the head at point-blank distance; in the other, the momentum being less, the ball, a conical one, had further caused linear fractures of the skull.

These delineations closely correspond with calvaria in my possession.

When the ball has entered the body or a limb and lodged there, instead of traversing either of these, the character of the wound will be that of the entrance wound as described above.

These characteristics of two large classes of gunshot wounds, when distinctly made out, are sufficiently diagnostic to mark them off from the other classes of wounds previously passed under review. They are not, however, to be pressed too far, while they may even fail us altogether; as where injuries caused by gunpowder are not to be distinguished by their effects from those caused by projectiles propelled by cannons, mortars, etc.; cases not likely to come often before the medical jurist, or, should they do so, to cause him much embarrassment.

Short of this, nevertheless, the characteristic marks of such injuries as usually come under the designation of gunshot wounds, may be so modified by circumstances, or be so imperfectly marked, as to diminish their diagnostic value. It is not immaterial, for instance, to the effects produced by firearms, whether a ball has been fired off close to the body, or from a greater distance; whether it has struck a person perpendicularly, or at an acute or obtuse angle; or whether it has impinged on the body while its original momentum was unimpaired, or only after its impetus had been lessened or nearly lost. The character of the tissues traversed by the ball, or by which its force had been modified or interfered with, the material which had served as a projectile, and the kind of firearm from which it had been propelled, will all have had their influence on the result. Hence it need scarcely surprise us to find differences of statements, amongst competent observers, as to the prevalence in such wounds of even the mere mechanical conditions generally assumed as their characteristics. Thus we find it stated that a ball sent by a rifle will leave a semilunar slit, and not a round hole, at its point of entrance; that it will leave no trace of contusion there; and that a spent ball has been known to bruise extensively without causing any or but a slight breach of continuity. Again, as the blackened or scorched appearance of the edges of the entrance wound may be caused in more than one way, its presence or absence has to be accounted for by the history of the case, and is not found to be invariable in its occurrence. Where, as is frequently the fact, the blackening is owing to ecchymosis being produced, the production or non-production of this ecchymosis will account for the extent or absence of the blackening. The blackening, the result of contusion of the edges of the wound, differs, and may be distinguished from that occasionally produced by the gunpowder when the firearm has been discharged close to the body; as in this case, the discoloration appears in patches, studded with grayish-black dots. It is also to be distinguished from the actual burns sometimes known to arise from the clothes being set on fire by the wadding. Of this I met with a well-marked instance a few years ago, where a youth had fired a fowling-piece in jest at the nates of a young woman, not knowing it to be loaded. In a French case the question was raised as to the possibility of the discharge of a firearm close to the body setting fire to the clothes, and the fire extending from this to any distance along the dress of the party On this question the Academy decided, after several experimental trials, that though the clothing may be set on fire in this way, and the fire spread to a limited extent, yet that the burning is usually confined to the borders of the orifice in the dress.

Again, the absence of laceration may not be an invariable characteristic of the entrance wound. From the nature of the projectile itself, or from the force with which it has been propelled, in place of leaving a small well-defined opening, it may lacerate the parts more or less extensively and irregularly, both at its entrance and along its course through the subjacent tissues. The explosion of the powder alone, independently altogether of any ball or wadding, at point-blank distance, is capable of producing very severe injuries of this kind. A pistol, for instance, without ball or wadding, introduced within the lips and fired, will give rise to results little less serious than if charged with a ball. When wadding has been used in like circumstances, it is known to have caused extensive laceration of the soft parts, with fractures of the bones of the face and the base of the skull. In a case of this sort which I examined in 1840, a determined suicide, liberated from the Aberdeen Asylum, had literally blown away the upper part of the face and the top of the head by firing a horse-pistol into his mouth. A striking feature in this case was, that though the pistol had burst at its discharge and lacerated the right thumb and forefinger, its destructive effects on the head and face had been little neutralised in consequence.

The extent of injury which may be caused by firing off a rusty fowling-piece at point-blank distance, without any ball, by a determined suicide, was shown in a body which I examined at New Machar in 1868. The features were almost completely obliterated, and the facial bones extensively comminuted. The stock of the gun had been placed on the ground, and the trigger drawn by the man's foot as he sat on the ground.

Again, as remarked by Dupuytren, a pistol fired off close to the abdomen, without a ball, has produced a fatal wound at this part of the body from the entrance of the wadding alone

In contrast to this, it may not be out of place here to call your attention to the fact, accidentally attested, that a loaded pistol fired off quite close to the body—with its muzzle resting firmly against the breast, for instance—will either burst, or recoil without the ball or wadding having touched the person at whom has been fired; the only result being a contusion or slight contused wound, caused, not by the projectile, but by the compression of the air within the barrel of the weapon.

Thus, we are told that a man was brought to the Hospital St. Louis, in Paris, a few years ago, to be treated for a slight contusion at the region of the heart. He had been engaged in a duel. The muzzle of the pistol, when fired, had been pressed against the chest. The instrument had rebounded back, and the ball fell harmless to the ground.

In judging of the effect of a projectile, regard must be had, not only to its character, but also to its momentum at the time of its striking the body. We have seen that, in certain circumstances, the wadding of a gun may act as a ball does This depends on the circumstance that, at its exit from the instrument, the momentum communicated to it by the charge is not less than that which the ball would have had imparted to it at the same point. Thus, as in the case of paper or cotton wadding, any solid body whatever—a ball of wax or cork equally with one of lead or iron—may produce an equal amount of external violence. The amount of penetration, however, will here be different—bodies of soft substance and loose texture rarely penetrating to any depth. From the same cause a number of small shot may either produce the same effect as a single bullet, or only such as is of the most trifling character. Instances of this last occurrence are not uncommon, from the speedy scattering of the small shot after they have left the weapon.

In this way, then, by inquiry into the history of different cases of gunshot wounds, and the effects of circumstances in leading to the diversified appearances which they are respectively found to present, we may arrive at some clue to their diagnosis, where differences of professional opinion regarding them are not unlikely to be formed, or to be enforced. This clue is not, however, so readily to be seized on, as regards the respective characteristics of the entrance and exit wounds where the ball has traversed the chest, abdomen, or limbs, as is often assumed. Hence the greater or less amount of disagreement on this point to be met with amongst different observers. Thus, both from observations on the living and experiments in the dead body, Olivier and Malle were led to deny the truth of the common belief, that the entrance wound in the body is always smaller than the exit one. Roux, on the same evidence, came to the conclusion that similar traces of the projectile will be left on the two sides of a limb where the weapon has been fired close to the body, and the ball has, in its traject through the tissues, lost but little of its momentum. Founding on what he had seen in Paris during the Revolution of 1848, Huguier came to the following conclusions:—1st, That in gunshot wounds the entrance opening, far from being always smaller than the exit one, is often of equal size; 2d, That Roux's conclusion, just noticed, holds good as to the equal sizes of the two openings when the projectile has not spent its force in its passage through the tissues; 3d, That the entrance wound is only smaller than the exit wound when the ball in its traject has lost much of its force; while, 4th, The entrance wound will be larger than the exit wound where these last circumstances are reversed. Caspar has gone further than this, and affirms, unconditionally, that the exit is always smaller than the entrance wound.

It is not for me to attempt to reconcile these statements of competent observers with the diagnostic marks, generally enunciated by most medico-legal writers, as characteristic respectively of the entrance and exit, where projectiles have passed in, through, and out of the body. Some general considerations, however, may be suggested in explanation of such points of disagreement.

In judging of the effects of projectiles on the human body, sufficient account has not always been taken of the differences of its structure and the combinations of its tissues, as contrasted with the homogeneity and uniformity of structure in the substances with which the comparison of these effects of projectiles has been made; while results deduced from the latter have been applied to the former. Though the laws of physics are uniform and fixed, and the organic and inorganic kingdoms are equally affected by these, it does not necessarily follow that the same results should succeed the penetration of the human body by projectiles, as are observed in the piercing of media differing in mechanical and physical properties, and of more or less homogeneous and uncomplicated textures. In the one case, while the results vary, in the other they show the strictest uniformity. This uniformity, as regards the latter, is seen in experiments with projectiles directed against various inorganic media of a homogeneous kind. Experiments have shown, for instance, that a ball penetrating any such mass, if not very brittle, such as a thick plank of wood, usually makes a small hole, nearly the size of the projectile, with sharp edges; as it proceeds, the canal goes on increasing in diameter; if arrested in its course, the cavity around the ball is larger than the diameter of the rest of the canal; and when it passes through and through the plank, the exit opening is larger than the entrance, and its edges are irregular and splintered. The same results have been obtained from different kinds of projectiles, such as a ball of wax, a few inches of candle, and a ball of moist chopped paper.

This, it will be seen, corresponds with the mere physical or mechanical alterations in the human body, which are laid down as typical characters of gunshot wounds. These results, however, have not in all cases been observed to follow such wounds in the living, or when effected purposely in experiments on the dead body.

Notwithstanding this admission, however, we may safely infer that the long prevalent opinion, based upon ordinary physical principles, as regards the respective characters of the entrance and exit openings—notwithstanding Caspar's dogmatic assertion—requires rather to be modified than abandoned; which is all the length that the other authorities I have quoted demand of us to go. Where, as in ordinary experiments with homogeneous media, the ball has penetrated rapidly and directly, and traversed in a straight line masses of soft parts of nearly equal consistency, the results will be essentially alike, the openings differing but slightly if at all. Again, the obliquity of the direction of the ball, as it enters, and the resistance it may encounter in its traject from tissues of such varied density as the skin and muscles, or the soft viscera, on the one side, and bones, cartilages, and tendons, on the other, will obviously seriously affect the observed results. Here the entrance will be less than the exit wound.

While, therefore, we must be prepared to abandon our exclusive reliance on the criterion of size as regards the openings in question, as certainly distinctive of the entrance and exit of the projectile, we must look to the circumstances of the case, and to the remaining indications, in order to assist us in settling the point, where the requisite data are procurable, which, however, may not always be the case. We may not, for example, be enabled to decide as to the distance at which the firearm has been discharged, or the direction in which it has been pointed.

Again, as regards the other marks, our proofs may be occasionally indistinct or defective. Thus, the depression or elevation of the edges of the two respective wounds may be either altogether wanting, or affected by the absence or excess of subcutaneous fat, or the amount of effused blood. The elasticity of the soft parts of the living body, above all, tends to the speedy restoration of the natural level of the surface after its displacement by the projectile at the moment of its passage. That this is the true explanation of the difference betwixt the appearances respectively of the openings, in experimental trials on dead matter, and on the living body, in most instances, seems to me to be evident from the fact which I have observed from the passage of a ball through such an inelastic mass as the liver, where I have had occasion to observe the depression unusually marked at the point of entrance, though the party had survived the wound for a good many hours

The distance, likewise, at which the firearm has been discharged must be taken into account, as affecting the character of the two openings differently. Thus, when the gun has been fired off at a distance, it has been found that the laceration has usually been confined to the exit wound, and that the size of the entrance has only equalled, or even been less than, that of the exit wound; and that, when fired near at hand, the entrance wound has often presented torn edges.

Any defect of evidence which may be encountered in cases of the kind we have been considering, occasionally admits of being supplemented from a different quarter. Thus, when the projectile has passed through the clothes of the person fired at, it has been generally observed, that at the entrance hole of the ball, the tissue, of whatever kind, exhibits a more or less ragged and irregular opening, along with loss of substance; while the injury to the stuff caused by the exit of the projectile is not so much a hole as a rent, either straight or shreddy, which will admit the tissue to be so replaced as readily to show that there has been no part of its texture destroyed or carried away.

The opening made by the ball in entering is always smaller in the clothes than in the skin.

In general, projectiles buried in or passing through the bones leave injuries of an undefined sort; though, as we saw in the skull, exceptions to this occur. I had occasion to notice previously, in the case of contusions, that deep-seated parts may be severely injured, without leaving any trace of the violence on the surface. In the same way, when projectiles have struck the body obliquely, the viscera of the abdomen have been found ruptured without any observable wound or contusion of its parietes. There has been concussion of the brain without injury of the scalp, and even comminution of bones without wound or appearance of injury of the integuments. These are the cases which were known to older surgeons as "wind contusions," on the mistaken notion that the projectile had passed close to without touching the body.

In connection with gunshot wounds, the question sometimes arises as to the period at which the gun was last fired; and witnesses accustomed to the use of firearms will occasionally speak with much confidence on this point. Observing this fact, medical jurists have attempted to arrive at some data which may assist them in this direction. Accordingly it has been found that when the combustion of the powder has been imperfect, the inside of the barrel of the gun or pistol, near its mouth, is either found blackened by a coating of charcoal and sulphide of potassium, shortly after the discharge; or where the discharge has been perfect, whitened by a crust of sulphate and carbonate of potass; while, after an interval of some days, varying with the amount of moisture in the atmosphere, the mixed residue of charcoal and sulphide of potassium has become converted into sulphate of potass, which after a still longer interval has been found to contain peroxide of iron.

Farther than this the researches of Boutigny, in France, have not led to any conclusions which can be relied on for the settlement of the question.

LECTURE XXXIII.

WOUNDS—(Continued).

POISONED WOUNDS. BURNS.—Death from Burns—Respective Characters of Burns. DISLOCATIONS. FRACTURES.—Fractures independent of External Violence—Respective Characters of Fractures in the Living and Dead Body. BLOOD STAINS.—Character of—Recent Stains—Older Stains—Stains resembling Blood—Stains from Dried Blood—Various Tests for Blood—Teichmann's Test—Polycroic Test—Schoenbein's Test—Spectrum Test—Microscopical Test—Chemical Examination—Stains from Liquid Blood—Stains on Weapons or Instruments—Stains on Wood—Distinction betwixt Blood and Cerebral Stains—Distinction betwixt Menstrual and other Blood—Distinction betwixt Brute and Human Blood.

PROCEEDING with the subject of wounds in their medico-legal relations:

VI. Poisoned wounds should come next. *Quâ* wounds, these, however, do not belong to this part of the course. In themselves, and apart from the varying effects of the foreign matter—the poison—for which they may have served as the channel of introduction into the body, their diagnostic marks are those of some one or other of the injuries previously noticed—punctured, incised, or lacerated wounds, or even mere scratches or contusions

VII. Burns, to which I have now to call your attention, though, in general, sufficiently characteristic to admit of being classed apart from the injuries previously considered, vary amongst themselves to a considerable extent with the producing cause, whether that cause has been an elevated temperature, either in the form of dry heat, or through the medium of liquids, or of incandescent bodies. These varying effects of heat on the body have been differently classified by surgical writers as they rise in severity from the mere reddening of the surface to the destruction of the deep-seated parts.

I purposely here exclude the injurious effects of certain irritant and escharotic substances, which are capable of giving rise to consequences not unlike those of the agencies which owe their injurious or destructive properties to the mere elevation of the temperature, but which are not likely to be readily confounded with burns, strictly so called; unless we take in the sequelæ of both the one and the other, when the diagnosis may become impossible, from the similarity or identity of their effects.

Injuries of this class are only liable to come within the province of the medical jurist when he may be called on to determine (1) whether, when death had followed their production, they had in any particular instance been the cause of death; or (2) whether, when found on the dead body, they had been inflicted during life or only after death

Death following burns may take place in two different ways. Severe and extensive burns, particularly in the young, may destroy life from the depression of the nervous system, owing to the number of cutaneous nerves injuriously affected; or, where the party has escaped this first danger, he may perish, at a later period, from the inflammatory reaction, and its usual consequences —extensive suppuration and hectic fever—even where he has escaped some of the intermediate consequences.

Little difficulty is likely to arise in the inspection of the dead body, as to the connection of certain morbid appearances in its interior, with injuries of this class present on its exterior, dating before the extinction of life. It is where the appearances on the dead body, characteristic of burns, are met with on its exterior, that the inquiry may originate as to whether these could have been produced on it before death? Instances of this sort are referred to by Fodéré, Taylor, Christison, and Caspar, where death had been the result of violence, and fire had been subsequently applied to the corpse to conceal the murderer's deed, and to suggest the idea of accidental death by fire.

The data possessed by us for the satisfactory settlement of the point as to whether certain appearances on the surface of the dead body, of a characteristic sort, ought to be regarded as of vital or only of post-mortem origin, are derived from the researches of Christison and Taylor, the results of which, with some minor differences, are substantially in agreement.

According to Sir Robert Christison, of the effects which follow the application of heat to the living body the most immediate is a blush of redness around the burnt part, removable by gentle pressure, disappearing in no long time, and not permanent after death. Next to this in order, and following almost immediately, is a narrow line of deep redness, separated from the burnt part by a stripe of dead whiteness (bounded towards the white stripe by an abrupt line of demarcation) passing at its outer edge by insensible degrees into the diffused blush, but not capable of being removed, like it, by moderate pressure. This line of redness may be seen, he states, after the application of the actual cautery. The phenomenon which follows these is the appearance of blisters, which, when the agent is a scalding fluid, generally appear in a very few minutes in the living, or may be delayed for hours when the scalds are extensive, as in young children; while, when the agent is an incandescent body, this appearance is not of such invariable occurrence, though often observed very soon after an ordinary burn caused by the clothes catching fire.

A line of redness near the burn, not removable by pressure, and blisters filled with serum, Christison considers as certain signs of a burn inflicted during life. In a series of experiments in bodies dead from ten to thirty minutes, he failed to produce such appearances by boiling water, by a hot poker, or by cauterising irons.

A repetition of the experiments of Christison by Dr Taylor led him to the same results and the same conclusions, though he warns us that the absence of the appearances thus relied on as vital does not point with certainty to the opposite conclusion. Caspar, after repeating and varying Christison's and Taylor's experiments on the dead body, failed to produce redness or serous vesication; and strongly asserts that it is quite impossible to confound a burn inflicted during life with one inflicted after death.

This last author has met and combated the assertion of Leuret, that in anasarcous subjects, vesications filled with serum may be caused by heat in the dead body twenty-four hours after death.

The only qualifications of the above conclusions of Christison and Taylor I would be disposed to make are—*First*, that not only must we take into account the occasional failure, as admitted by Christison, under certain circumstances, of vesication after vital burns, but also the non-occurrence, in some instances, of the redness of the burnt part; and *Second*, that vesication without accompanying redness, on a dead body, would not suffice to authorise the conclusion that the burn had been caused during life, as such blisters are met with from pemphigus in the living, and in the corpse from the progress of putrefaction.

My attention was called to the first of these points by the occurrence in police practice of the following case:—A woman was found at the Links (Aberdeen) in a state of insensibility from cold. Among other means adopted for rousing her, tin flasks filled with boiling water were applied to her feet and sides. On examining her two hours after, the cloths in which the jars were wrapped were found to have slipped aside at the chest, and the cuticle on the insides of both forearms was seen to be shrivelled and loose, but with entire absence of redness and vesication at these parts. She was at the time still insensible, with the pulse at the wrist barely perceptible. It was only next morning, when she had completely recovered from the effects of the cold, that the insides of the forearms were noticed to be largely blistered, and the blisters surrounded with broad patches of redness. It must be seen in this instance, that, had recovery not taken place, the appearance of the arms, as first seen, would have indicated post-mortem, not vital burns.

In connection with the subject of burns, it may not be out of place here to notice the alleged occurrence of what has been termed spontaneous human combustion, and the occasional preternatural combustibility of the human body.

The first of those points may now be safely set aside as inadmissible, notwithstanding the high authority of Orfila and Devergie in its favour, and that some cases had been advanced, previous to their time, in proof, as it was believed, of such spontaneous combustion.

The second point—the occasional preternatural combustibility of the body—is also believed by our best writers on medical jurisprudence to carry with it its own condemnation. The arguments in its favour rest upon the occurrence at times of such cases as the following, which, with a similar one, came under my own notice in 1869. A woman of sixty-six, of intemperate habits, was left in her house alone at 10 A.M. At 11 (an hour after) her body was found on the third step of the stair near the kitchen; the step on which the corpse rested, and one of the spokes of the wooden hand-rail, being charred; as were the seat of a chair and a small portion of the front of a straw mattress on a bed, both in the kitchen on the same floor and adjoining the staircase. Contrasted with this moderate amount of combustion exterior to the woman's body, was the extent of its effects on herself. On the front of the head and face, the absence of the soft parts left the exposed bones blackened and calcined. On the back of the neck and chest, patches of a greasy charcoal were found here and there; and beside them the spinal column and several of the ribs exposed and burned black. The abdominal wall was wanting, the intestines a burned and blackened mass, and the surface of the liver calcined. The upper limbs were distorted, the elbows strongly flexed, and everywhere charred to a great depth; the bones, however, even of the fingers, preserving their position. The right thigh had its deeper muscles still uncharred, but presenting the appearance of roast beef, and very dry. The skin and superficial muscles were totally burnt away. The right leg, only partially attached to the thigh, was entirely converted into a greasy black charred mass, even the bones not escaping. The right foot, totally detached from the leg, had been changed into a soft, black, greasy, and shapeless cinder. The left thigh, leg, and foot in a condition similar to the right. Not a vestige of clothing remained anywhere. This case was published from our notes of the judicial inspection by Dr. Alexander Ogston, in the *British and Foreign Medico-Chirurgical Review*. An elaborate study of the subject proves, in the opinion of the reporter of this case, the occasional preternatural combustibility of the body, a point on which I am disposed to agree with him, notwithstanding the ingenious attempts to explain away such instances as the above. That the combustion in this case had originated from a few smouldering ashes in the kitchen grate can scarcely be questioned, but this appears to me to be insufficient to account for the fact of such extensive destruction of the body from the limited amount of combustible matter *ab extra*, without assuming that the body was in a condition unusually favourable for and predisposed to the feeding at its own fire, particularly when we consider the well-known fact of the difficulty experienced in the destruction of the corpse by combustion.

The question, however, of the occasional preternatural combustibility of the human body, is one which I think should still be considered as *sub judice*.

VIII. Of Dislocations it would be waste of time to speak, as on this subject I have nothing to add to what is to be found in ordinary surgical treatises.

IX. *Lastly*. As regards Fractures, one or two medico-legal points require to be adverted to, arising out of the mode of their production.

In the first place, then, we are not to set down fractures as necessarily in every case the result of external violence alone. On the contrary, they have been known occasionally to arise from muscular action, either ordinary or violent. Under Infanticide I adverted to cases of such injuries occurring spontaneously in the *fœtus in utero*. Nor are such so-called spontaneous fractures unknown in adults; either as the result of violent muscular efforts on healthy bones, or of slighter muscular contractions and insignificant or unknown causes in scorbutic or ricketty subjects.

A case of this last sort occurred in a carter in Aberdeen a few years ago. He got extensive comminuted fractures of both femurs from jumping down from the shaft of his cart, and had on previous occasions fractured his limbs by equally slight causes.

It has been laid down by Caspar, that severe and extensive fractures met with in the dead body afford a presumption that such fractures had taken place during life; and that an amount of force, which, if applied during life, would indubitably have produced fissures, if not fracture or complete smashing of the skull, leaves the dead skull quite uninjured. This, it may be observed, however, is contrary to what is asserted in surgical works.

The presence or absence of effused blood in the vicinity of fractures in the dead body will not assist the medical jurist in determining the date of the injury.

The test which alone can be relied on with undoubting confidence, in proof of the fracture having been caused during life, is the commencement, at the part, of the restorative process. The presence of coagulated blood betwixt the ends of the fractured bones was formerly held to indicate a fracture in the living as distinguished from one in the dead body, but this sign is now only considered to prove that the injury took place recently before or recently after death. Should the evidence establish that the fracture must have been produced either during life, or many hours after death, then the discovery of coagula of blood between the fractured ends of the bone would at once decide the case, for, after the cooling of the body, it is altogether improbable that any blood effused should then coagulate, notwithstanding the strange assertion to that effect by Caspar, formerly adverted to. The fact should be borne in mind, however, that, though rarely, blood has been found effused around fractures produced after death; while, again, as I had occasion to notice formerly, fractures followed by instant death may give rise to little or no effusion of blood.

It occasionally happens that blows or falls of no great severity will cause fractures of a severe or fatal kind, only admitting of explanation by attention to circumstances.

In a case which occurred in 1839, death from diffuse suppuration took place on the seventh day after a blow on the shoulder, producing a comminuted fracture of the head of the humerus which, at the inspection, proved to be made up of cancelli covered with a shell of bone almost as thin as paper. In November 1840, a large effusion of blood under the dura mater led to the death of a man who had in a scuffle either received a slight blow or lost his balance, and had fallen on soft ground (it was not certainly known which) A fissure was found at the inspection commencing at the temple, branching off in different directions at the base of the skull. The skull in this instance was unusually thin and diaphanous.

In January 1857, a man was seen to go into a granary at Ythsie (Aberdeenshire), taking with him a bottle of whisky. An hour after he was found on the stone floor insensible, and died in a few minutes It was conjectured that he had lain down on the drying-floor at one end of the building four feet above the general level, and when attempting to leave it by some steps, had fallen forward on the stone floor. On inspecting the body along with Dr Irvine of Tarves, we detected a comminuted and depressed fracture of the frontal bone; two linear fractures, one running from the left temple across the top of the head, downwards through the right temporal bone, and ending in the foramen lacerum anterius, with branches in different directions, the other from the summit of the head to the base of the skull on the opposite side; a linear rent two and a half inches in length, and averaging a quarter of an inch in depth across the upper and forepart of the left cerebral hemisphere; a transverse fracture of the sternum; and a fracture of one rib. In this instance the man was a thick-set, bulky, and heavy person, which, with probably a considerably added momentum from a run forwards, may explain the extent of the violence from such a short fall. A case almost parallel was examined here in 1854, after a fall over the quay wall of the Aberdeen Harbour; but in this instance the fall had been from nine to ten feet. Occurrences like these present but few difficulties to the medical jurist, though, so far as regards the injuries to the cranium, such effects of falls are not uncommon, even where the height had not been great. In October 1875, I was present at an inspection by my assistant, of a case where a workman had perished from extensive fractures of the base of the skull seven hours after a fall down six steps of a stair.

Further, I may remark on this subject, that though it can only be on the rarest possible occasions that we are in a position to determine, from the appearance of a fracture of bone, independently of its attendant injuries, the amount of violence received, or the character of the instrument by which it has been inflicted, yet

Pl X

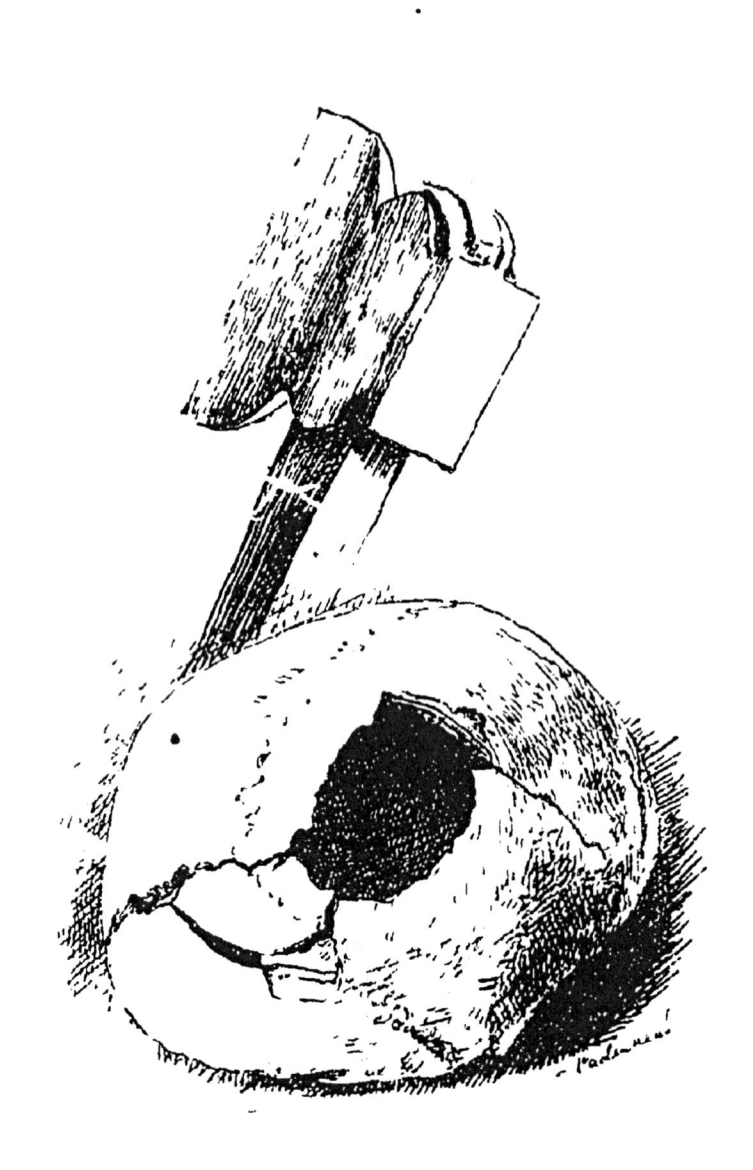

FRACTURE OF THE SKULL BY THE BACK OF AN AXE.
SHOWING THE SHAPE OF THE WEAPON,— SEEN FROM OUTSIDE THE SKULL

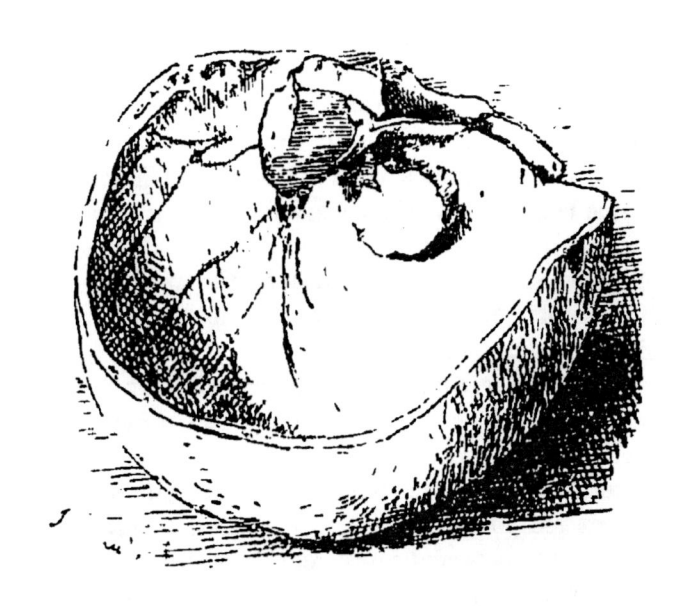

Pl XI

FRACTURE OF THE SKULL BY A HAMMER
SHOWING THE SHAPE OF THE WEAPON — SEEN FROM WITHIN THE SKULL

such exceptional cases may occasionally be encountered. We have seen, for instance, under gunshot wounds, that a ball discharged at point blank distance will traverse the cranium, leaving the entrance and exit openings of regularly rounded forms free from splinters, and, the former especially, nearly of the size of the projectile which had passed through the cranial vault. What is more to the point to observe here, as being still rarer, is, that the size and shape of a fracture inflicted by a blunt body with considerable violence, may sometimes correspond to the size and shape of the striking part of the instrument which has been employed. Thus, in the case of murder at Cairnhall, in 1864—referred to under Identity in connection with the footprints of the murderer—the fatal blow with the back of an axe had penetrated the skull, leaving the fractured and depressed portions of a four-sided shape, and of the length and breadth of the back of the weapon. [Fig. X.] Again, in the case of a young man tried at Aberdeen for the murder of his mother in June 1867, the same correspondence was encountered in two depressed fractures of the left frontal and temporal bones, inflicted with the head of a hammer. [Fig XI]

This brings me to the consideration of a subject rising out of those concluded; namely, blood stains and their verification, a topic of considerable importance to the medical jurist, and one which has of late attracted the attention of chemists and microscopists to a large extent.

The duty of verifying the character of stains suspected to have been caused by blood, falls to the medical jurist on different occasions. Thus, where a person has been found dead from wounds inflicted by another, and where an instrument with red stains on it is detected in the possession of, or which had been known to belong to, the suspected murderer, or where such stains are found on the clothes or person of the accused, it may be of importance to the proof of his guilt, that these stains should be shown to have been actually produced by blood.

The appearance of blood so recently effused as to be still liquid, is so characteristic as to leave but little room for hesitation or doubt as to its nature. But, where the homicide has been effected some time prior to the examination; when the blood with which the clothes or the instrument is stained has had time to dry up, or where the instrument has been partially cleaned, or the clothes attempted to be washed, it must often be a matter of reasonable doubt, on the mere view of the stains, whether they are owing to blood, or to some other red matter

Before proceeding to the more particular examination of suspected blood stains, their general appearance should be carefully noted; attention being directed to their position, number, configuration, size, amount and disposition of colour, and other particulars. By this means it may sometimes be ascertained, whether the blood has flowed continuously or in jets, i.e., from a vein or an artery; whether it has come directly from a wound, or merely from contact with blood previously effused in another situation. Blood, too, which has escaped from an incision at or after death, may thus be occasionally distinguishable from the blood which had escaped earlier from the fatal wound. Further, it is possible at times to determine, in this way, the relative position of the wounded man and his assailant, at the time when the wound was inflicted.

Thus, in an interesting English case, reported in the *London Medical Gazette*, a woman was found dead at the foot of a stair, with fractures of the skull and vertebral bones, and wound of a branch of the temporal artery. That, in this case, the wound of the artery had not been caused by the fall, was clearly brought out by the discovery of jets of blood, such as must have come from an artery during life, on the wall at the top of the stair, four or five feet from the floor.

In a case of murder which I investigated at Glenmillan, in 1869, the locality of the fatal blow was brought out in the same way. The man's body was found in a field about thirty yards from the nearest house. His skull was beaten in, apparently by some ponderous weapon, such as the back of an axe. But though the quantity of blood at the place showed that he had perished at the spot where his body was discovered, yet the finding of jets of blood on the side-posts of the door of the house, and on the plaster of the wall in its vicinity, at the height of four or five feet from the ground, pointed out the house-door as the place where the injury had been inflicted.

In the case of the death of the woman at Cluny, from a wound in the temporal artery, formerly referred to, by following out this line of observation, it came out very clearly that the deceased had been in bed when she received the wound, that after she had bled there for some time she got up, and found her way, through a passage, to the kitchen; that after groping about for a little, she had succeeded in lighting a candle, gone back to the bedroom, and returned to bed.

Again, in a case of murder at Cults, to which I shall have

once more to recur, two wounds in the genitals were found to have been inflicted after a large proportion of the blood in the body had escaped through a deep incision in the throat. This was ascertained from the observation of the circumstance, that the effusion from the genital wounds consisted merely of reddish serum which had gravitated from the wounds directly downwards while she lay on her back, the posture in which the body was found

As regards the mere colour of the blood, too much stress should not be laid on the distinction betwixt blood recently effused and that which is older, as sometimes deduced from the respective appearances of different stains or blood-spots. For, while it holds good generally that recent stains are red, and older stains brown, the change of colour is influenced by other circumstances than age alone. Thus, this change is more speedily induced by warm than by cold weather. Thus, too, the colour will more speedily darken where the layer of blood is thick than where it is thinner. The nature of the stuff, and that of its surface, will further influence the shade of colour of the stain. Thus, from their relative porosity, or the reverse, as well as from contrast, marks of blood upon white stuffs, and upon light wood, are paler and duller than those on articles of greater density, as varnished or painted wood, iron, and stone.

To Ollivier (d'Angers) we owe the notice of the important fact, that on coloured stuffs, especially on those which are brown, blue, or black, the spot is more easily recognised by candle-light than by daylight. He had been directed to re-examine the room of a person accused of murder. Having already visited it in the daytime his second examination was conducted at night, and he then discovered, by holding a lighted candle near the paper hangings, which were of a pale blue colour, a number of drops of an obscure dirty red, which by day had the aspect of small black specks, and were lost in the general pattern of the paper. On a further examination other spots of the same kind were found on the furniture. On the chimney jamb, which was painted blue, there was a large stain of blood, which appeared red by the light of the candle. The next day, by daylight, Barruel and Lesueur could not find these spots, and were obliged to make use of artificial light to discover them. The same remarks will, of course, apply to spots of blood upon dark woollen cloth.

It is necessary, however, here to suggest to you, that broad daylight should, in the general case, be preferred to artificial light in the search for obscure traces of blood. I have failed to detect some of these stains at night which came out distinctly on the following day. Once more, it may not be useless to warn the medical jurist to search for traces of blood in places where it would be apt to escape the notice of a person wishing to obliterate all traces of it; such as in the seams of clothes, the soles and seams of shoes, etc.

Every such stain, or appreciable trace of blood, unless washing or friction has been previously had recourse to, will present some sensible characters which may be deserving of being attended to. Thus, as remarked by Dr Taylor, the crimson stain of blood is unlike that of any other colouring matter, and when the stained portion presents the character of a dry coagulum, the stain cannot be easily mistaken by a practised eye for that caused by other red colours. To bring this out, where it is of minute size, recourse may require to be had to a strong light, under the low power of the microscope. In this case, on the stained part, or at least on the fibres, if on cloth, either a shining glossy film will be detected, or a dried jelly-like clot will be seen investing the cloth or its fibres, these having a more or less deep shade of redness.

Other stains, however, approach, on some points, to those of blood :—

Thus, as pointed out by Lassaigne, the dejections of fleas, bugs, and flies, on undyed stuffs, correspond pretty closely with the stains produced on these by small drops of blood, as far as their ground tints are concerned :—

The stains from the flea and the bug agree with those from blood, in yielding to water a rich colouring matter and traces of albumen. The respective shades of colour differ somewhat, however; that from the parasites being a currant-red, while that from blood verges more or less to a brownish or greenish-red. A better distinctive mark is afforded, according to Lassaigne, by the characteristic odour of the two insects, which is brought out readily by merely moistening the stain with water.

The reddish stain produced by crushing the common fly between folds of cloth, Lassaigne found to be caused by the escape of the red-coloured aqueous humour from their large compound eyes. From its appearance alone, he found that this could not be distinguished from the stain caused by a drop of blood. On macerating it in water, however, the water took an orange-yellow tint, and was found to contain no albumen, leaving the original stain of a yellowish-brown. The colour of the fluid thus obtained was discharged by chlorine without affording any precipitate. On touching the fly-stains with various reagents, this observer also obtained characteristic results, and such as a deep violet with sulphuric acid, and a bright red with nitric acid.

When due care has been taken to obviate the chance of mistaking the sources of such reddish stains as the above, and where the quantity of blood has been such as to present its more obvious characters, nothing further than a mere inspection may be required It will often happen in practice, however, that from either the minuteness or indistinctness of the stains, or their having been interfered with by wetting, rubbing, or otherwise, more rigid methods will be required for their discrimination and verification

For the ready verification of doubtful blood stains on articles of dress, the following steps may, in the first instance, be taken. The stained portion of the stuff should be cut out and suspended by a thread in a small test tube containing as much distilled water as will cover the stain. On standing, if the stain is from blood, the colouring matter speedily detaches itself from the cloth and gravitates to the bottom of the tube, the supernatant fluid remaining nearly clear, leaving any fibrine which may have been present on the cloth still adherent to it in the form of a soft grayish or slightly reddish film The reddish fluid at the bottom of the tube on being now heated becomes milky, if a mere trace of albumen is present in it, but if albumen is more abundant in it, will yield a coagulum of a dirty grayish or greenish colour, all trace of redness in the fluid having by this time disappeared. This clot re-dissolves on the addition of caustic potass, the solution having a reddish-yellow hue by reflected, and a green colour by transmitted, light

In order to strengthen the proof that the colour of the stain is from blood, other processes supplementary to or in lieu of the above procedure have been advised. Of these, writers on chemistry and physics have spoken with most confidence of—

Teichmann's test, which, as modified by Buchner and Simon, is substantially as follows.—The stained portion of the stuff is to be cut away from the rest, macerated if recent, and if old boiled with an excess of glacial acetic acid, till the acid is coloured, when it is to be evaporated to dryness on a watch-glass When now placed in the field of the microscope the matter in the watch-glass will be found to present hæmine, in the form of rhomboidal tabular, or needle-shaped crystals which lie across one another in star-shaped masses, varying in colour from a faint yellowish-red to a deep blood-red As the presence of the saline matter of the blood is requisite to the success of this process, and as this may have been previously all washed away, the advice has been given to add a *very small* particle of common salt to the acetic acid before the maceration or boiling, in order to insure the appearance of the crystals. Dr Taylor and others have dispensed with the common salt in this process, as unnecessary, and as liable to encumber the field of view with crystals of chloride of sodium. These, however, can easily be dissolved out by water, which leaves the hæmine crystals untouched.

In 1861 Schonbein announced a new test for blood. He found that peroxide of hydrogen or antozone had no action on tincture of guaiacum, but that when blood was present in the fluid a blue colour was produced. Hence he concluded that there could be no blood present when there was no blue reaction, and that the production of a blue colour, though it might not lead to a positive conclusion as to the presence of blood, yet was a sufficient corroboration of other tests for blood. Dr. Taylor goes further than this, and adopts Schonbein's conclusion without any qualification. He employs an etherial solution of the peroxide of hydrogen, and takes up the blue precipitate with an excess of alcohol or ether, when he obtains a deep sapphire blue solution

Once more: it has been proposed to apply the process of spectrum analysis to the detection of the blood in suspected stains. Fresh blood produces two dark absorption bands in the spectrum; one in the middle of the green, and the other at the junction of the yellow and the green. These, however, may be modified by various causes.

Now, to all these tests it has been shown that serious, if not fatal, objections admit of being urged. To bring out their expected results, the quantity of colouring matter on the stains falling to be examined would require to be more considerable than is usually to be found present on those stains submitted to the medical examiner. Nor is this the sole objection to their use on such occasions. Teichmann's test, for instance, has been shown by Roussin and Kunze to be liable to much uncertainty. Both these persons have come to the conclusion that spots of human blood, or even the fluid itself, in appreciable quantity, may fail to yield any hæmine crystals whatever, or only such as are of so indefinite a character as to be utterly worthless for diagnosis. Similar failures have been found to follow the attempts at bringing out the polychroism of the blood, even in the hands of competent experimentalists In the hands of Liman and others, Schonbein's test yielded very doubtful results; while they found that many substances belonging to the three kingdoms of nature yielded the blue reaction with guaiacum. The whole question has recently been examined by Pinard in France with substantially the same results *

As regards the spectrum analysis, it has been admitted by those who have examined it in connection with blood stains, that they found it difficult to extract the cruorine—the colouring matter in which the process hinges—from stuffs of various kinds; and further, that with the cruorine—even when successfully extracted—foreign matters are usually found mixed, whose presence either hinders the production of the spectrum altogether, or renders the fluid so turbid as to interfere with its distinctness

All this being admitted, it has been proposed by Roussin, who has carefully investigated the subject, to dispense altogether with the chemical proof of doubtful blood stains, and to trust entirely to the microscopical examination. For this purpose, this expert advises that the stained stuff should be carefully examined; that a separate, distinct, and well-defined spot should be selected, choosing one which has escaped traction and friction; that from this a portion not exceeding the breadth of a threepenny-piece be cut out with blunt-pointed scissors, or the point of a scalpel, and spread out on a glass slide. On this from a pipette is to be dropped a few drops of a fluid composed of three parts by weight of glycerine, one part of concentrated sulphuric acid, and as much distilled water as will bring the compound to the specific gravity of 1028, leaving the stuff to imbibe the fluid for about three hours. At the end of that time two glass rods drawn out to fine points are to be used to press the stuff and move it about, and afterwards to disentangle its separate threads; the threads are then to be collected and withdrawn from the fluid, and the fluid immediately covered with a cover glass, when it is ready for placing in the field of the microscope.

By this process, the blood globules will be easily recognised, of their natural size and shape, with a stain of even a smaller size, than that prescribed by Roussin, provided the stain is recent and tolerably distinct As admitted by its author, its success, however, will be interfered with where the stuff has been previously submitted to traction or friction. I have found also that it succeeds best with recent stains. In practice, on some occasions I

* I have also obtained the blue colour, with the guaiacum and peroxide of hydrogen, from sweat stains.—*Ed*

have attempted to combine the whole or the greater number of the above tests as follows:—

The stained portion of the cloth is to be cut out, and suspended by a fine thread in a test tube containing distilled water. If the stain has been from rust or red paint—the peroxide of iron—the cloth will yield no colour to the water, and the addition to the contents of the tube of hydrochloric acid will destroy the colour of the stain; will render the fluid yellowish; and the yellow fluid on the further addition to it of ferro-cyanide of potassium will indicate the presence of protochloride of iron.

If the stain has been from blood, the colouring matter will detach itself from the cloth in the form of reddish striæ and collect at the bottom of the tube, while the water will there assume a red colour more or less pronounced.

(1.) A portion of the contents of the tube may now be used for the spectroscope. (2.) Two or three drops of the fluid from the bottom of the tube may be cautiously withdrawn by a pipette and placed in the field of the microscope, and the slide examined for blood disks, epithelial scales, or fragments of capillary tubes. (3.) Two or three more drops similarly withdrawn from the bottom of the tube may be placed on a glass slide, glacial acetic acid and a *very* minute crystal of common salt added, left to spontaneous evaporation, or gently heated, and when dried looked at by the microscope for blood crystals. (4.) A little of the fluid may be dropped on bibulous paper, and submitted to the guaiacum test. (5.) A little more of the fluid, after the addition of ammonia, may be watched for any change other than a heightening of its colour. If the red colour proceeds from vegetable matters, it will be changed to blue, green, etc. (6) The remainder of the fluid in the tube may now be heated without or with nitric acid, for albumen, which if present will render it milky or throw down a coagulum from it, of a dirty gray colour, leaving the water without any trace of red. (7) The turbidity or coagulum, if from albumen, will disappear or be re-dissolved on the addition of caustic potash, and assume a brownish red by reflected, and a green colour by transmitted, light. (8) When the stain has arisen from a layer of blood of perceptible thickness, the cloth, after the maceration, may exhibit a soft, white, grayish, or rosy adherent matter, which, when removed and placed under the microscope, will prove to be the fibrine of the blood.

If, in place of stains on clothes, a liquid, supposed to be blood, has to be submitted to examination, by adding a drop or two of the suspected fluid to distilled water in a tube, the various steps of the above method will give the same results, with, of course, the exception of the last—the discovery of the fibrine.

To ensure the success of the above method, several precautions require to be taken, and allowance made for some modifications or shortcomings in the results. To obviate these, the quantity of water employed should be as small as possible, and but little delay in the examination of the contents of the tube permitted Thus the fresher the fluid the better will the colour tests come out. Again, with No 2, while the blood discs in any case will not, as in Roussin's process, be found to have retained their natural size and form, from their imbibition of water and endosmose, they may be expected, if the examination is delayed, to be found of irregular shape, or even altogether broken up. Once more, to render the spectroscope (No. 1) available in this way, the contents of the tube may require previous dilution, or their transference to a tube of very thin glass.

In the detection of blood on weapons or instruments the medical examiner has to guard against some chances of mistake Thus, on steel instruments, the presence of rust spots and certain vegetable salts of iron present very much the aspect of blood. A case in point is adduced by Orfila:—

A man in Paris was suspected of having murdered another; and a knife, apparently spotted with blood, was found in his possession, and regarded as a strong circumstantial proof of his guilt. The weapon was sent to the laboratory of the Faculty for examination, when it was ascertained that the supposed spots of blood were nothing more than citrate of iron. The instrument, it appears, had been used some days previously for the purpose of cutting a lemon, and not having been wiped before it was put aside, a simple chemical action had gone on between the acid and the metal, which gave rise to the appearance in question.

Though, as already pointed out, the distinction is easily established betwixt stains of blood and stains by the salts of iron, when either of these exists singly on weapons, Lesueur and Robin, in 1856, found that some difficulty may be encountered in deciding on the real character of a stain on a weapon compounded of the two To obviate this, in a case in point, they scraped off a portion of the stain, dropped it into a solution of sulphate of soda rendered slightly alkaline by caustic soda or potass, with or without the addition of glycerine, when the substance examined under the microscope resolved itself into blood discs on the one hand, and brownish red particles of carbonate of iron on the other.

Lassaigne found that blood stains on articles of steel, kept for six days in a humid atmosphere, failed to yield albumen or its colouring matter to water, from, as he supposed, the hæmatine and albumen forming with peroxide of iron a compound insoluble in water, and that such stains on wood containing much tannin —such as the common birch—may yield no albumen to water, owing to the previous combination of the two. To obviate this last difficulty, he suggests that the surface of the stain only should be employed; the compound in question originating only with the portion of the blood which has had time to penetrate below the surface of the wood.

The medical jurist may be called on, in some instances, to discriminate betwixt blood and other animal matters, such as cerebral matter, menstrual fluid, etc.

In the case of cerebral matter, Orfila, besides the use of the microscope, proposes that the stain should be moistened, when hydrochloric acid will give a dull reddish-gray with the brain matter, passing ultimately into a Malaga red, and sulphuric acid, a violet colour without any charring. Lassaigne considers the sulphuric acid test sufficiently characteristic: he found that it first yielded a sulphur yellow, speedily passing into a vermilion red, followed in two minutes by violet, which disappeared on exposure in about half-an-hour.

The question of the possibility of distinguishing betwixt menstrual blood and that which has flowed from an ordinary wound was mooted in a trial in France in 1858. In this instance a person had been found dead, at some distance from his own house, with numerous large wounds on the head, shoulders, and other parts. Circumstances, not detailed, led to the suspicion that the murder had been committed in the man's house, and the body subsequently carried to the spot where it had been found. Large spots of blood were found in the bed usually occupied by the man and his wife, who was suspected of the murder; but, on being charged with the crime, the woman affirmed that the blood in the bed had proceeded from herself; and that she had been recently menstruating. This circumstance led, amongst other inquiries, to certain experimental researches on the part of MM. Mannoury, Salmon, and Robin, with the view of deciding as to the true source of the blood in question, the result of which was, that in all their investigations they found —1st, That menstrual blood differed from that drawn from the vessels of the body, in containing a mixture of epithelial cells and mucous globules; the former derived from the utero-vaginal lining, the latter from the mucus covering the genital membrane; 2d, that these bodies were never found in blood issuing directly from the vessels of the body; and 3d, that by comparing the two forms of blood by the microscope, their respective characters could always be distinctly ascertained.

Few experts, however, I imagine, would be disposed to rely on such a test. I have met with epithelial cells in blood stains from different parts of the surface, while mucous globules so closely resemble the colourless blood corpuscles that if not, as held by some, identical, they differ so little from them as to render the discrimination of the two all but impossible.

No difficulty would present itself in the discrimination between the blood on a stain of the mammalia other than the camel, and the blood of fishes, birds, and reptiles, the shapes of the disks differing so much from each other. When, on the other hand, the discrimination has to be made betwixt human blood and that of the mass of the mammalia, the only assistance would be the determination of the respective measurements of the red corpuscles, a task which none but a practised microscopist would be authorised to attempt, even if he could do so successfully, dealing, as he would have to do, not with fresh blood, but with that altered by drying.

In the case of the murder near Kintore, previously referred to, the accused alleged that stains on his coat had been caused by swine which he had been carrying for a flesher a few days before, and we declined to give our opinion on the point raised in consequence, on the precognition.

LECTURE XXXIV.

WOUNDS—(*Concluded*).

PROGNOSIS OF WOUNDS—Distinction of Wounds as slight, severe, dangerous, and fatal—The Situation and the parts involved in the Wound as affecting the Prognosis—Injuries inflicted on the Nervous System—Wounds of the Head—Contusions of the Head—Injuries of the Spinal Cord—Injuries of the Circulatory System—Wounds of the Chest—Injuries of the Abdomen and Pelvis—Wounds of the Organs of Generation—Injuries of the Respiratory System—Injuries of the Nutritive System—Circumstances modifying the Legal Character of Injuries—Age—Sex—Constitutional Peculiarities—Previous Injury or Disease—Subsequent Injury or Disease—Malum Regimen—POST-MORTEM INSPECTION

HAVING concluded what I had to say of the diagnosis of wounds, as the term wound is understood in legal medicine, it now falls to me to notice, in addition, certain other inquiries calling for settlement by the expert in this extensive and important class of injuries.

These inquiries admit of being arranged under two heads; those deducible from, first, the progress of the case in hand during life, where the injuries have not proved immediately or speedily fatal; and secondly, from the inspection of the body where death has resulted from their infliction: or, in other words, the prognosis of wounds, and the post-mortem inspection. These two lines of inquiry, I need scarcely add, may have to be combined in the same case where the party has been seen both before and after the fatal event.

To begin with the prognosis of wounds. Here it behoves the medical jurist to have a familiarity not only with the more usual results of such injuries as they progress in the living, but also to be aware of, and to be prepared to take into account, the circumstances which may be found in certain cases to influence and control, so as to modify, their natural and accustomed course

Taking up in succession these two points, I shall advert, in the first place, to the character and results of injuries in the living under ordinary conditions, or apart from the modifying circumstances to which I have just referred. And here it may be premised that little is to be gained by following the course of some medico-legal writers, especially abroad, of laying down for guidance in their prognosis, arbitrary and artificial schemes of classification founded on the degree of danger of various injuries; such as slight, severe, dangerous, and fatal wounds, characteristics which are of too fluctuating and uncertain a kind to serve as fixed and available bases for reliable distinctive tests. Thus, in practice, it is known that a slight wound may be converted into a dangerous one; a wound not usually considered mortal may terminate life, and *vice versa*, from the occurrence of some of the modifying circumstances previously adverted to. In preference to this, I shall take for my guide in the prognosis the data deducible from the seat of the injury and the parts of the body which it may have involved, or from both sources of information combined.

And *first*, of the prognosis of injuries of the nervous system, including the brain, spinal cord, and the nervous ramifications. Injuries of the nervous system, I need scarcely say, deserve the greatest attention from the expert, as being a frequent cause of both sudden and lingering deaths. Sometimes also they are found closely to resemble the effects of natural disease. Their progress is likewise occasionally influenced by natural causes affecting the same organs. They may prove fatal, too, without leaving any very distinct trace of altered structure in the dead body.

The frequency of railway accidents has, of late, by multiplying this class of injuries, given added importance to them, both as regards the medical jurist, and the profession generally, and, what is to be regretted, has been the occasion of bringing out not a little conflict of professional opinion on the part of witnesses cited on trials originating in such accidents. This undesirable result has arisen from the circumstance of their serious character not being always apparent at the time of their occurrence; and from proper allowance not being always made for the possibility of their giving rise to secondary effects in individual instances.

Wounds of the head are important, chiefly from their liability to disturb the functions of the brain, or to involve that viscus in active disease. When strictly local, they heal without much trouble; but even in these circumstances, they may be complicated with diffuse abscess, erysipelas, or irritative fever.

When the irritation such wounds give rise to is considerable, or even when they appear slight, the brain and its membranes may sympathise with injuries of this sort, or the party may be attacked with tetanus, and in these ways an injury at first inconsiderable may prove unexpectedly fatal. A simple blow on the head, with or without a scalp wound, may sooner or later lead to mischief about the bones of the calvarium. Sometimes the diseased action thus set up ends in hypertrophy of the bones, which may go on for years, and the calvarium thus becomes enormously thickened. Again, the diseased action thus set up may lead to caries and necrosis of the calvarium. Here the disease may be limited to the original seat of the injury, or it may spread widely, affecting either one or both tables of the bone. Again, a blow on the head may be followed by acute inflammation, with its starting point in the diploe, the consequence of extravasation of blood, or of the breaking down of the cancellous tissue without injury to the cranial tables, though liable to spread to these or to induce pyaemia.

In either of these cases, the patient may not appear to suffer much or not at all at first; the illness, when it occurs either in a few days or only after weeks, may assume the chronic form, or it may prove rapidly fatal.

Instances of such effects of apparently slight or trivial injuries, from their occasionally unexpected character are apt to take the practitioner by surprise. They are by no means of very unfrequent occurrence, and such instances have been cited from my own practice in a previous lecture.

Contusions of the head, as a rule, are not dangerous, if unattended with such symptoms of violence as are set down by most surgical writers as the effects of concussion of the brain, but which, as we saw formerly, are by some recent authorities attributed in every case to contusion and mechanical injury of that organ.

Punctures, or even simple fractures of the bones of the head, when unaccompanied by injury of the brain, are not in general followed by bad consequences, though a guarded prognosis should be given, even in apparently slight cases, as the exact state of matters cannot be always known at the time. The brain, however, may be reached in this way, with or without much injury of the soft and hard parts encasing it. Death, as we saw under Infanticide, may be caused in infants by punctures through the fontanelles, or the base of the skull. Again, the brain may be reached by penetrating instruments through the orbits or nostrils.

An interesting case of the last kind led to a trial at Aberdeen in 1855. A person in Peterhead had been thrust at by a walking-stick, not by any means a stout one, but armed with a small iron ferule, having a knob at the extremity about the size of a large pea. The stick had passed through the right lower eye-lid, partially displacing the orbit. The man survived till the third day, at first conscious, and suffering great pain, though afterwards becoming comatose. On dissection, the stick was found to have passed through the orbital plate of the frontal bone, and to have led to unhealthy inflammation of the membranes and surface of the right anterior lobe of the brain, in the vicinity of the fracture

I had an opportunity some years ago of seeing a case at Banchory which terminated favourably, where from the history and symptoms it appeared that a large needle used for making farm sacking had been pushed up the nostrils through the cribriform plate of the ethmoid bone.

In those cases of instantaneous death which are usually known as concussion, but by some as contusion of the brain, death is found to be caused by syncope from the depression of the cerebral functions. Compression of the brain, where death follows more slowly, leads to death by coma or comato-asphyxia, the arrest of the respiration following the depression or arrest of the functions of the brain At a later period, death may follow as the result of inflammation of the brain, originating in the injuries received—superficial injuries; commotion, whether without or with contusion, fractures of the skull, succeeded either by inflammatory or irritative fever, or compression from the products of the inflammation, resolving itself into death by coma. In the same way, death is often produced by disorganisation of the brain, which does not necessarily imply compression of its substance We have seen already that it was till lately held generally, that death may result from the mere commotion of the brain, without either fracture of the skull, effusion of blood within the head, or any other change being observable in dissection; and that this is denied by some later authorities. The dispute, however, is not of much practical importance; since while the latter contend that a structural change has actually occurred in every such instance, the former admit that some such lesion may be inferred, though the suddenness of the fatal event has not allowed time for such subsequent changes as hæmorrhage or inflammation, or for the establishment of reaction Injuries of this sort, whether we term them cases of concussion or of contusion of the brain, may prove fatal instantly and directly, or indirectly, after a lapse of days, weeks, or even still longer periods, from the consequences of the original violence. Thus, chronic inflammation and its sequences may go on progressively and terminate fatally, after the lapse of several weeks, months, or even, it is believed, of years. A case of this sort was given in a previous lecture, p. 432.

Effusion of blood within the cranium, either upon the surface of the brain, into its substance, or into the ventricles, from lacerations of the brain, from rupture of one or more blood-vessels by a fractured bone, or by separation of its membranes, is a very common cause of death from violence producing commotion of the brain. This has even been found to occur when there was no external mark of injury on the head, an occurrence which may lead to a very important medico-legal question in cases of sudden death, namely, Whether the effusion has arisen from violence or from natural disease? In some cases, particularly where the vessels of the brain are in a diseased state, or where there is a tendency to softening of the brain, continued intoxication, a sudden burst of passion, struggling with another person, or a fall, may occasion the bursting of a blood-vessel within the head, and cause a fatal effusion of blood. Such effusions, however, when spontaneous, are most usually in the substance of the brain, while effusion from the effects of violence, is most commonly on its surface, or between the brain and the skull.

Next in importance, though not in frequency, are Injuries of the Spinal Cord. Those which wound, divide, compress, or disorganise any part of the spinal cord, in general prove fatal either immediately, or after an interval of more or less duration, according to the situation, extent, or nature of the injury. When the cord is deeply penetrated or injured at its upper part, death takes place immediately. But if the lesion is superficial, and at a point lower down in the cord, the injury though not immediately fatal, is followed by loss of pain and feeling below the injured parts, and the patient sooner or later dies. Wounds of the medulla oblongata, pressure from effused blood, and fracture or dislocation of the vertebræ, prove instantly fatal in consequence of the circulation and respiration being brought to a stand. Hence the importance in all such cases of a careful inspection of the spine after death, a point too little attended to. It is important, however, to be aware of the fact, that extravasation of blood upon the spinal cord is not necessarily the result of violence, but may occur spontaneously, as has been shown by Dr Abercrombie.

It may be well here to recall your attention to a circumstance noticed under Death (p. 405), which bears chiefly, if not exclusively, on the class of injuries under consideration. I refer to the fact that both sides of the heart in fresh bodies may be emptied of blood, and that so completely, that the endocardium is not wet enough to stain a white cloth applied to it. The first instance of this sort which attracted my attention, was in a man fifty-five years of age, who died instantly from injuries received by the chimney of a house which was being pulled down in Castle Street (Aberdeen) in August 1839, which fell on the back of his head and the upper part of the spine, while in a stooping posture. At the inspection, several fractures of the base of the skull were found radiating upwards from the foramen magnum as a centre. The appearances otherwise were those of death by syncope. I have since met with two cases almost parallel with the above.

The effects on the nerves of concussions received on the trunk, have been already sufficiently illustrated. It may be proper, however, to remark here, that blows on this part may be instantly fatal, by leading to the arrest of the heart's action, and consequently to death by syncope, as in concussion of the brain, without leaving any morbid appearances in the body.

I have now to notice, in the *second* place, the effects of injuries of the circulatory system. Injuries of the circulatory system are frequent causes of sudden death, and are often the subject of medico-legal investigation. The fatal issue arises from the extreme exhaustion and depression of the vital powers, consequent on extensive hæmorrhage; and the death is by syncope. Injuries of the organs of circulation, may, however, prove fatal otherwise. Thus a less effusion of blood than would destroy life may prove fatal from its pressure impeding the functions of organs essential to life; such as the brain, the spinal cord, the heart, or lungs.

A wound of a blood-vessel may instantly destroy life by the admission of air into the veins.

It is impossible to say beforehand what amount of blood may be lost without leading to fatal syncope, as this varies with different states of the constitution, and with the habits of the party. The rupture of a varicose vein, or even the extraction of a tooth, in some spanæmious individuals, will lead to dangerous, or even fatal, hæmorrhage; both of which occurrences I have witnessed in practice. I have twice had the opportunity of examining the bodies of persons who had bled to death from suicidal wounds of the veins at the bend of the arm. One—a seaman—was found dead some years ago in a court in the Gallowgate (Aberdeen), lying in the recumbent position in bed, with the wounded arm hanging down in front of it. The other—a cattle-dealer at Strathdon—in the spring of 1867, was found on a hillside in a pool of blood, with a small superficial wound on the right side of the neck, and the left median basilic vein cut across with a pen-knife, a strap of leather surrounding the arm above the elbow, as in ordinary venesection In the case of Christian Davidson, referred to at p 417, for causing whose death a person was tried at Aberdeen in 1854, the division of the frontal branch of the left temporal artery, with the points of a pair of scissors, had led to fatal syncope

In all these cases the parties were known to have been of very intemperate habits. From the same state of matters, it is notorious that cases of slight wounds of the scalp, or incised wounds in the limbs of no great depth, may lead to so copious a flow of blood that the parties, if they did not perish in this way, as in the three cases above mentioned, when unattended to, would be left thereby in a state of great prostration Such cases are not unfrequent at our police stations or in taverns where fighting has been going on.

The proofs of death from hæmorrhage are deducible from (1) the indications of the wound having been produced during life ; (2) the absence of blood in the larger vessels, and important viscera, and (3) the healthy state of the principal organs of the body

So much for the prognosis of wounds in general I have now to consider the consequences of wounds in different parts of the body

I have nothing to add to what I have said of wounds of the head

Wounds of the neck are often the subject of medico-legal inquiry. Cases of murder by wounds in this situation occasionally occur, though death from this cause is oftener the result of suicide than of homicide. In the Cults case previously adduced (p. 468), the spinal cord was divided through the intervertebral substance betwixt two of the cervical vertebræ, which at once decided that the case was one of homicide It should be borne in mind, however, that the extent of injury inflicted by a determined suicide may sometimes be very considerable

A seaman on board a vessel in Aberdeen harbour, to whom I was called some years ago, was found to have extensively divided the soft parts in front of the vertebræ, and the mark of the edge of the razor was noticeable on the surface of one of these bones, and in a chimney-sweep at Justice Street (Aberdeen) two incisions had been made, and two such impressions were seen on the body of one of the cervical vertebræ.

Punctured wounds are occasionally, though rarely, made in this region with suicidal intent. It was in this way that Castlereagh destroyed himself, by plunging the pen-knife through the carotid artery. In a previous lecture (p. 419), I mentioned a suicidal case which united the characters of an incised and a penetrating wound, on the front of the neck.

Wounds of the chest may prove fatal in different ways. The most frequent cause of death is syncope, from the hæmorrhage they occasion. A less effusion of blood than would destroy life in this way may lead to the same result by compression of the heart, as when effused into the pericardium, or of the lungs, when the effusion is into the pleural cavities. Ruptures of the heart or large vessels within the chest may take place, either from pressure or from a blow, without any appearance of external injury. The same injuries, however, it should be known, may occur spontaneously. I have already related one instance of spontaneous rupture of the aorta in a person free from aneurism or other previous apparent disease. Wounds of the heart and large vessels are not necessarily instantly fatal. Thus, in the case of a woman at Oldmeldrum, in July 1857, for the murder of whom a man (Booth) was tried and executed, the heart had been transfixed with a deer knife, notwithstanding which the victim, after the receipt of the injury, left the apartment (a shop), ran across the street, returned to the shop, and to the back of the counter, before falling down dead.

In injuries of the abdomen and pelvis, death sometimes follows from the division of the arteries of the viscera.

Wounds of the organs of generation occasionally lead to fatal hæmorrhage without any of the larger vessels having been divided. A few years ago several remarkable cases from wounds in the labia of the female occurred in Edinburgh and Glasgow.

In 1826, a person of the name of Pollock was tried at Edinburgh for the murder of his wife, by inflicting two wounds of this sort. Two incisions of the inner side of the right labium and nympha, penetrating to the depth of two-and-a-half inches, were observed on dissection, and the clothes in the vicinity were stained with blood. The woman was intoxicated at the time of receiving these wounds. Pollock was convicted, and condemned to death, but hanged himself before the day of execution.

Two persons were tried at Edinburgh in 1831 for inflicting a wound in the labium of a woman. It was three-quarters of an inch in length, and three inches in depth. She died from loss of blood soon after its infliction. The parties escaped a charge of murder from want of proof as to which of them had given the wound.

Two persons were tried at Glasgow in 1830 and 1831 for causing the death of their wives in this way, and both were convicted and executed.

A case of this sort was tried at Aberdeen in the autumn of 1849, but, from the impossibility of determining which of the two parties tried had inflicted the fatal wound in the vagina, a verdict of not proven was returned. In this instance two incisions were discovered, one at the left labium, the other at the entrance of the vagina at its upper part, and the female, who was pregnant, did not survive above ten minutes

In connection with this subject, it is important to notice that, in a discussion which took place in the Edinburgh Obstetrical Society, it was suggested by the late Sir James Simpson that the spontaneous origin of such wounds in pregnant females was not by any means impossible. In support of this view, he referred to a case reported to him by Dr. Kyle of Dundee, where a pregnant woman died from the rupture of a large vein in one of the labia, produced apparently by straining while on the night-stool. On the same occasion, Dr Thomson brought forward a case from his own practice, where a woman, six weeks after delivery, had nearly perished by hæmorrhage from a wound in the anterior wall of the vagina, at the union of its upper with the middle third, large enough to admit the finger to the depth of about half an inch It was believed by the narrator that the wound had occurred during an intercourse of the woman with her husband without any violence on his part.

Be this as it may it should not be forgotten that it is quite possible that wounds of the labia may be produced accidentally Several years ago I was called to a young woman who, while in drink, had fallen upon a chamber pot and wounded this part, which bled profusely, and required to have the hæmorrhage arrested by pressure.

A curious anomaly occurred in the case of the woman Harvey at Cults in 1854, previously referred to as an instance of homicidal cut-throat The assassin, after the girl's death from the extensive and deep wound in the throat, had inflicted a deep, penetrating wound of the vulva, from which, unlike that on the neck, which had bled copiously, only a little bloody serum had oozed. At the trial in the High Court of Justiciary in Edinburgh, I was asked by the judge (the late Lord Justice-Clerk Hope), how I could account for this genital wound. The only hypothesis I could offer was that the assassin had wished it to be supposed that the woman had been violated, which, in case of the discovery leading in his direction, would avert suspicion from him, as it was known that the girl was his own concubine, whom it would not be supposed he would force

I now come, in the *third* place, to make some remarks on the progress of injuries of the respiratory system. Amongst the most important of these are wounds of the chest and lungs Contusions and fractures of the ribs, and wounds of the pleura and lungs, are not unusual forms of homicide, and prove fatal from the shock, by way of syncope; by the interruption to the functions of respiration, causing death by asphyxia; or they lead to the same result from the consequent hæmorrhage ending in syncope; or the inflammation and pain which are occasioned by the violence may destroy life more gradually In penetrating wounds of the chest, the entrance of the air may cause collapse of the lungs, and death by asphyxia. The lungs may also be compressed from blood or other fluids, in one or both cavities of the pleura. Wounds of the lungs, likewise, by broken ribs or other means, which produce emphysema of these organs, cause death by suffocation. Pneumothorax, from fractured ribs having wounded the lungs, or the decomposition of blood or other fluid effused into the chest, is speedily fatal by asphyxia, when both sides are affected; when confined to one side, the patient may recover. When both sides of the chest are opened by penetrating wounds, even without injury of the lungs, death takes place almost immediately by collapse of the lungs and consequent asphyxia Wounds laying open the larynx and trachea are not necessarily fatal, but they may cause death by asphyxia though no other important part is injured, from the hæmorrhage filling up the air-passages; or in cases of the complete division of the trachea, by the retraction of the lower orifice impeding respiration. When the wound is situated between the os hyoides and the thyroid cartilage, fluids which are being swallowed are apt to fall into the larynx, and cause suffocation Wounds of the larynx, particularly lacerated wounds, may also prove fatal by violent inflammation of the parts Wounds of the larynx and trachea are rendered much more dangerous when the pharynx or œsophagus has also been wounded, in consequence of matters, either attempted to be swallowed or that may be ejected from the stomach entering the trachea. But even injuries of this kind are not necessarily fatal. When death takes place from self-inflicted wounds in the throat, it is in general owing to some of the large blood-vessels or nerves which lie contiguous to the wind-pipe being also wounded in the attempt on life.

This brings me, in the last place, to notice shortly the prognosis in injuries of the abdomen. Homicide has frequently been committed by causing contusions and other wounds on the parts contained in the abdomen and pelvis. These prove fatal in different ways: (1) by the shock or impression made upon the nervous system; (2) by hæmorrhage; (3) by inflammation; and (4) by interfering with the nutrition of the system. To some of these modes of death I have already alluded: to others I shall now briefly advert.

We have seen that blows or other injuries of the abdominal parietes, either without or with lesion of the deep-seated organs, may prove fatal immediately, or after a lapse of some time, without inflammation or other reaction having been set up. We have also seen the effects of loss of blood on the contents of the viscera in leading to death from sinking of the powers of life, without reaction being established, or inflammation being set up in cases where these viscera have been injured seriously. In such instances the death is by way of syncope. Contusions from blows, and other injuries of the belly and pelvis, are likewise sometimes fatal by inducing inflammation, though the internal organs are not injured. Penetrating wounds of the abdomen, even where the intestine is wounded, are not necessarily fatal, for the effusion of their contents into the belly does not necessarily follow, and the consequent inflammation may be inconsiderable. The same remark applies to rupture of the intestines without external wound. It is to be kept in view by the medical jurist that in some cases death happens very suddenly from a spontaneous rupture of some part of the bowels, even without any previous disease. Injuries of the liver, spleen, kidneys, and bladder, are often attended with the same fatal consequences as injuries of the bowels.

This leads me on to the consideration of circumstances which are occasionally found so to interfere with the natural progress of injuries in the living, as to control and modify their accustomed course.

Such of these modifying circumstances as are generally

applicable, more or less, to the whole or the greater number of the injuries which I have included under homicide, were considered under that head. Those which require to be adverted to here are such as refer specially to the one under discussion.

Of the first of these modifying circumstances—age—little need be said It is known that, while on the one hand, children readily succumb to certain forms of violence, on the other, they show a wonderful power of recovery from the consequences of others of them; it is equally well known that adult age presents a better chance of escape than does old age from the severer forms of injury

Equally marked differences distinguish the sexes, particularly during the child-bearing period of the female, who at other times, as a rule, succumbs less readily than the male to many forms of violence.

Certain constitutional peculiarities, natural or acquired, render injuries much more serious to some individuals than the same injuries would be to others Thus, the bones in some are so thin and brittle as easily to be fractured by slight blows or falls In 1833, a workman, in a squabble, received a blow with the fist on the shoulder, which was followed by diffuse abscess, and death in a few days. At the inspection, the head of the humerus was found to be a mere shell, almost without cancelli, and extensively comminuted About the same date, a carter, leaping from the shaft of his cart, on which he had been seated, broke both thigh bones and one of the tibiæ. Several of his long bones had previously been fractured from equally trivial causes. A skull in our museum, extensively fractured on one side by a blow, is that of an old man, and is unusually thin at the seat of the fracture. The case led to the trial of a man in 1848, for the death of his father at Kildrummy (Aberdeenshire), by a blow with a shoemaker's instrument known as a "devil"

Some people are of such a preternaturally phlogistic or hæmorrhagic diathesis, that dangerous inflammation or hæmorrhage may follow trifling blows or wounds. The same serious consequences may follow similar slight injuries in persons of intemperate habits or broken-down constitutions, besides the liability of the one to delirium tremens, and the other to gangrene In such parties, too, and in persons suffering from previous injuries and diseases, death not unusually occurs suddenly in drunken quarrels, in which it may be difficult to say what share should be attributed to the blows which may have been received, and what to passion, intoxication, the struggle, the enfeebled constitution, or previous disease. Cases of this sort might easily be multiplied where dissection has pointed out a ruptured aneurism, apoplexy with diseased state of the arteries at the base of the brain, disease of the heart, advanced phthisis, pneumonia, etc. Subsequent injury or disease may modify the result of the injury, as may the neglect of treatment, or of hygienic precautions on the part of the patient or his medical attendant.

Having now concluded these remarks in regard to the proper diagnosis and prognosis of wounds, and other injuries included in law under that designation, it only remains to treat of the medico-legal inspection after death from wounds. In cases of death from violence, several medico-legal questions may arise which can only be settled by a general survey of the body, and a carefully conducted external examination of the corpse and its accessories, in addition to the ordinary dissection of its internal cavities. The first point for the medical jurist to ascertain in these cases, is the nature of the wound, whether contused, lacerated, incised, or otherwise. Secondly, he should endeavour to ascertain whether the wound has been recently inflicted, or has been of longer standing. Thirdly, he has to determine whether it had been inflicted during life or after death. Fourthly, any weapon found should be compared with the external wound, and with the clothes where they have been penetrated by it. Fifthly, any foreign body found in the wound should be carefully preserved. Sixthly, the length, breadth, and depth of the wound, are to be carefully measured. Seventhly, the situation and direction of the wound demand attention as affording evidence of the intent of the person who inflicted it. The manner in which the wound had been inflicted may indicate the relative position of the individuals concerned at the moment of its infliction. The situation and direction of a wound may be also of importance in ascertaining whether the fatal wound had been inflicted by another, or by the individual himself. Eighthly, the probable manner, force, and weapon employed for their infliction, are often to be ascertained by the nature and extent of the wounds, together with the known effects of certain weapons or wounding bodies, when applied with different degrees of force. Lastly, the question whether death has been the result of accident, suicide, or homicide, may sometimes admit of being decided by the medical examiner.

Many of these various points have been necessarily anticipated; and others of them belong to the legal rather than to the medical proof, though they cannot be properly overlooked by the medical jurist, who is, from his position, best fitted to form a correct estimate of their bearing on the case in hand. General rules, however, cannot be laid down which shall be applicable to the varying circumstances of individual instances of suspected homicide. Still there are some data of a general nature which require the attention of the medical examiner, and are certain to be of essential importance towards the elucidation of the several points I have enumerated. These I shall therefore pass in review, as briefly as possible, not in the precise order in which I have stated them, but as they may be expected to come under the notice of the examiner at the post-mortem examination.

First, then, some preliminary observation may be demanded before proceeding to the examination proper, which may throw light on the case where little or nothing is known of the previous history, and when a body is found under suspicious or doubtful circumstances; such as (*a*) the precise position of the corpse; (*b*) the sex; (*c*) the apparent age; (*d*) the general conformation of the body; (*e*) the clothing, whether complete or otherwise, undisturbed or displaced in any way; if torn, soiled, stained with blood, dirt, mud, etc; (*f*) the locality, whether an open spot, or a concealed place; (*g*) the ground, whether showing traces of a struggle; marks of footprints different from those which might have been left by the deceased, and if so, in what direction they admit of being traced; (*h*) the probable period the corpse may have lain at the place, etc. The data for the settlement of several of these points have been already discussed; as also certain inferences to be drawn from them; while to some of them I shall have to recur presently.

This preliminary observation over, the external examination of the body may be proceeded with, and first, the nature of the wound, whether incised, punctured, contused, etc, is to be determined by the data already laid down. Second, whether it had been inflicted recently or more remotely, and whether during life, or only after death. Third, the weapon, if any has been found near the body, has to be compared with the exterior of the wound, and also with the clothes where they had been penetrated by it; these, along with the weapon, being carefully preserved, labelled, and the label signed for subsequent identification. Fourth, any foreign body found in the wound must be preserved, and note taken of its nature; whether clothes, fragments of wood, wadding, or otherwise. Fifth, the amount of blood which may have escaped from the wound, and *its* distribution round its edges, on the clothes, or on the articles on the ground in the vicinity of the corpse, deserves attention. Sixth, in gunshot wounds, any stains from gunpowder should be looked for and noted if present, either about the lips of the wound, or about the fingers and mouth of the corpse. Seventh, the size of the wound should be carefully measured and noted. Eighth, its direction and depth, points of great importance, demand a methodical course of procedure. For this purpose the inspector should not proceed at random, but in a systematic manner. A circular incision should with this view be carried around, about three or four inches from the wound, taking care not to interfere with it; and the integuments then dissected off, from the circumference to the centre. The same mode of procedure should be adopted with the muscles, blood-vessels, nerves, and bones; in short, all the parts implicated in the course of the wound. In this way only can an accurate idea be formed of the tissues involved in the wound, the direction in which they have been divided, the foreign bodies which may have lodged there, and the relative position of the assassin and his victim at the moment of its infliction. By these means also, the examiner can best ascertain whether the wound has, or has not, been necessarily mortal; how and by what instrument it has been caused; what period of time has probably elapsed between the receipt of the injury and the death of the party; and whether the person has suffered pain to any great extent or otherwise.

This stage of the examination completed, the inspector has only further to proceed to the dissection of the body; for which no special directions require to be given, in so far as the cavities are concerned. The distribution of the blood and the tracing of the extent of the wound or other injury are the chief things to be attended to. By carefully ascertaining the state and distribution of the blood in the heart, lungs, and brain, the mode of death will be learned—a point of some importance.

Lastly, the nature and circumstances under which the body is found may enable the medical examiner sometimes to decide the question whether death has been the result of accident, suicide, or homicide. Thus:— Contusions are very rarely self-inflicted, though exceptions to this occur. Suicide, for instance, is sometimes committed by the party casting himself from a precipice or window, instances of which are met with in maniacs and drunkards. Prisoners and maniacs have also been known to dash themselves against a wall. A fatal accident of this kind occurred at Union

Place, Aberdeen, a few winters ago, by a tradesman, during a snow-storm, while running fast, coming forcibly against a projecting iron railing Although, as a rule, contusions are very rarely self-inflicted, yet it is often very difficult, in many cases, to determine whether they have been the result of accident, or of injury inflicted by another person. The assailant usually strikes about the face or upper part of the chest, but these parts also suffer in an accidental fall. The case is different when the contusion is met with in a part of the body which could not have been injured accidentally, as on the inner side of the arms or legs, on different sides of the legs, and the like

Very severe contusions or lacerations, which could only have been inflicted by means of an axe, hammer, or other such ponderous weapon, are almost always inflicted by another for the purpose of murder. In such cases, accident and suicide are generally both out of the question.

Lacerated wounds, as a rule, are the result of accident, though maniacs have been known to inflict severe injuries of this kind on themselves

A penetrating wound in a concealed part is highly suspicious of murder The part of the body struck at by the assassin will be influenced by the character of the weapon he employs, and the mode in which it is handled by him. Thus, he will strike with a dagger or poniard, which he holds with the point undermost, downwards, and inwards at the root of the neck, or the upper part of the chest of his victim; while, if he stabs with a long knife, he aims at the region of the heart Death by stabbing is generally the deed of another person for the purpose of murder It occurs rarely for the purpose of suicide, and still more rarely by accident

Incised wounds of a serious kind are very infrequent in purely medico-legal practice, except in instances of suicide.

It has been stated that, in cases of suicide, wounds are seldom made steadily, so as to form a clean cut, unless the person is in a state of delirium. But few persons commit suicide who are not either in delirium, or in a state resembling it, at the time. Besides, a very clean cut may be inflicted with a sharp knife by a determined suicide though not delirious; while, on the other hand, a wound made by an assassin may be ragged and uneven from the struggles of his victim. No great reliance, therefore, is to be placed in this indication of suicidal wounds; neither is any confidence to be placed on the evidence deduced from the number of the wounds, which, in suicide, are said to be generally few in number. Suicidal wounds are, as a rule, very seldom inflicted on the back or left side of the body unless the individual is left-handed. Self-inflicted wounds also very rarely occur in a concealed part of the body. In cases of suicide, the situation of the wound varies with the kind of weapon used. Thus, if a suicide shoots himself, he generally shoots himself through the head; if he stabs himself, he does it in the chest or belly; if he effects his purpose by a cutting instrument or incision, he selects the throat. Suicide in females is seldom accomplished by cutting instruments or firearms. If there is a wound upon the body, and no weapon is found near it, or if the weapon is found concealed where it could not have been placed by the deceased, accident and suicide are both out of the question. Murderers often use several weapons to despatch their victims, first employing one to stun, and then another to stab, shoot, or strangle their victims. Suicides, on the other hand, seldom use more than one method, though to this there have been some exceptions. If gun-shot wounds occur on the back, they cannot have been self-inflicted.

LECTURE XXXV.

DEATH BY DROWNING

Death by Asphyxia—Different Stages—Morbid Appearances Death by Drowning—Alleged Modes of its Occurrence—Syncope (Neuro-paralysis)—Coma—Asphyxia—Comato-Asphyxia—Phenomena of Death by Drowning Morbid Appearances in Death by Drowning—Indicative of Death by Asphyxia—Indicative of Death by Submersion—External Appearances.

In the various forms of injury which have been passed under review, as coming under the medico-legal designation of wounds, we have seen the prominent place which syncope occupied as a cause of death—whether from pure loss of blood, the amount of shock at the outset, or the consequent exhaustion. In the class of cases which we have now to consider, the leading form in which death occurs is that of apnœa or asphyxia—a mode of death common, with very few exceptions, to all the instances of drowning, hanging, strangulation, suffocation, and smothering—the subjects in question—though each of these presents certain peculiarities which serve to discriminate and distinguish it.

This being the case, it may be proper, before proceeding to discuss these five forms of death separately, to point out the characteristics of asphyxia generally, as almost equally applicable to each. Three stages, then, may be observed in the phenomena of asphyxia. The first is characterised by the intensity of the sensation which prompts to the acts of inspiration, and the consequently violent and laborious, though ineffectual, attempts to appease that sensation by the action of all the muscles of inspiration, and in some instances by other actions voluntary and instinctive, but still under the guidance of sensibility. The next stage is distinguished by insensibility, rapidly increasing, and attended with irregular spasms or convulsions; and the last by cessation of all effort, and of all outward signs of life, while the heart's action and the circulation are known still to go on for a short time.

As a general rule, it may be assumed that the first two of

these stages are usually over within three minutes, seldom extending to five, and that the circulation through the heart has very generally ceased within less than ten minutes from the commencement of the obstruction

In those cases of hanging and strangulation in which the trachea is completely compressed from the outset, the insensibility is almost instantaneous. In drowning—and, perhaps, in most cases of smothering and suffocation—the first two stages may last for about two minutes on an average, but not longer, unless where the air is only partially excluded from the lungs Contrary to what has been asserted, habit has little or no influence on the length of time for which this privation of air may be borne. There is little reason to believe that life has been restored in any case of asphyxia after from five to ten minutes' arrest of the respiration—the very latest period which can be assigned to the continuance of the heart's action after the entire cessation of the functions of the lungs.

When discussing the different forms or modes of death (Lecture XXIV), I had occasion to lay down the post-mortem appearances which serve to characterise asphyxia generally these being, I need only here remind you, the accumulation of the blood in the veins, and its comparative scantiness in the arteries; congestion of the lungs, right heart, liver, spleen, brain, and kidneys, at times also venous plethora in the intestinal canal, and in portions of the common integuments In these cases on viewing the dead body, the face, except at, or shortly after death, is observed to be rosy, reddish, or somewhat livid, the eyes, though oftenest natural, may be prominent, clear, and fixed, the features are usually calm though occasionally expressive of suffering, the cadaveric lividity of the dependent parts of the body is mostly of a pronounced sort, the cadaveric rigidity is well marked and persistent; the cerebral sinuses are full, and the interior of the brain dotted with bloody points, and accumulation of serum is at times encountered in the cerebral ventricles, the root of the tongue is swollen and red, the trachea and larger bronchi are reddened, and frothy fluid, sometimes reddish, is met with in their interior, the lungs are distended and congested, the right cavities of the heart, the pulmonary artery and venæ cavæ, and their principal branches, are distended with dark fluid blood, as are to a greater or less extent the liver, spleen, and kidneys Little blood is encountered in the left cavities of the heart, or in the aorta and pulmonary veins Congestion to any marked extent of the scalp and face, and of the mucous lining of the alimentary tube, is rarely encountered in cases of rapid asphyxia.

This summary of the appearances in the body after death by asphyxia generally does not, however, include all the peculiarities which may be encountered in some of its special forms or exclude other peculiarities in certain of these, nor are all the appearances I have enumerated constantly encountered in every individual instance of fatal asphyxia, however well marked otherwise. This will come out under the different forms of this mode of death.

These I commence with death by drowning. This form of asphyxia opens up a study of high importance to the medical jurist, and one which will consequently demand a proportionate degree of attention from us. There are circumstances connected with the subject of death by drowning which distinguish it to some extent from other forms of sudden death. There is not, for instance, the same amount of unanimity amongst authors as to the precise mode of death as might have been expected in such a case as is here presented to us, the leading phenomena of which are to such an extent well understood and so uncomplicated in their character. Again, authors have differed as to the appearances to be encountered in the dead body in the case of the drowned, and have assigned a different amount of value and importance to the absence of certain of these, and the presence of others. Hence, the extreme opinions which we encounter in our earlier medico-legal writings, especially as to the facility of determining, from the examination of the body, the cause of death on the one hand, and as to its utter impossibility on the other. Much, however, of this discrepancy comes to disappear on a little consideration given, in the first place, to the circumstances attendant on the last act of life; and, secondly, to the proper appreciation of the influences affecting the body at the period at which it may be presented for examination, whether from the time which has elapsed since the death of the party, or from the character of the medium or media in which the body has lain since death. All this will come out most clearly as we proceed.

Without further preface, then, I go on to remark that the finding of a dead body in water under suspicious circumstances may give rise to the following medico-legal inquiries:—First, whether the person had died by drowning? and secondly, if so, whether the submersion had been the consequence of accident, of suicide, or of homicide? And, first, as to the question whether death arose from drowning. Much unnecessary difficulty has

2 K

been thrown in the way of a satisfactory reply to this inquiry by writers on the subject of death by drowning mixing up the cause of death in drowning with the cause of death in persons found dead in water. A little consideration of this obvious distinction will simplify very much the unnecessary complication of a point in itself not unattended with some inherent difficulties.

The body of a person, then, who has fallen into water and there perished, may, on inspection, present (1) the appearances characteristic of death by syncope, or neuro-paralysis as it has been termed, (2) those of death by coma, (3) those of asphyxia, and (4) those of coma and asphyxia conjoined.—

It has been assumed, rather than proved, that fatal syncope may be brought on by the state of terror into which the individual has been thrown prior to his accidental or violent fall into the water; or, what is more likely, by his coming against some obstacle, either above or below the water, during his fall, with sufficient force to induce concussion of the brain to an extent which, of itself, would destroy life. Now, it would be more philosophical to say that such a person had perished, though in the water, not by drowning, but by syncope—restricting the former term, as we obviously ought, to the primary arrest of the respiration by the exclusion of the atmospheric air from the lungs. In a case of this sort, the syncope, if complete, could not be so far recovered from, as to permit the phenomena of asphyxia to be set up, and the appearances in the body would be those of death by syncope, to which cause the death, though it took place in the water, should be undoubtedly ascribed in every such instance. I am, however, inclined to go somewhat farther than this, and to state that nothing short of complete syncope, such as would be at once fatal in or out of the water, would, in such a case, hinder the phenomena of asphyxia from taking place to some extent in a submerged body I ground this opinion on the following occurrence —

In November 1854, the body of a very stout man was found at the foot of the quay-wall near the mouth of the Aberdeen harbour He was lying on some loose dry blocks of stone, which were covered with water at high tide Besides minor injuries, the inspection showed a comminuted fracture at the base of the skull, and the sternum fractured and depressed near its middle. The nature and extent of these injuries—which were explained by his having, while drunk, fallen over the quay-wall with some added momentum—of themselves would have implied that a concussion sufficient to induce syncope had been sustained by him in his fall, had not the want of effused blood in the vicinity of the fractures indicated this; and yet in this instance the signs of death by asphyxia were sufficiently developed to authorise me to report that his death had been by submersion

I had previously met with a similar case, in which a person, by throwing himself with a considerable momentum—obtained by running some distance—over the parapet of a bridge into the Aberdeenshire Canal, and striking against the retaining wall of the water underneath, had sustained serious injury of the head before his submersion

In this opinion I am glad to find that I am joined by both Drs. Taylor and Caspar, the latter authority especially speaking very decidedly on the point, in opposition to the views of several foreign medical jurists.

It has been suggested by some authors that the congested state of the cerebral vessels, so frequently encountered in the bodies of the drowned, proves that the parties had perished from coma rather than from asphyxia. That a person struggling against an assailant trying to force him into the water may thus bring on a state of apoplexy, or that a person falling into an apoplectic state may accidentally drop into water in his immediate vicinity, are not unlikely occurrences. But in such cases, unless the death was immediate—which is scarcely consistent with known facts,—they would, notwithstanding, if left in the water, perish from asphyxia, not from coma. It will not be pretended that a mere state of oppression of the brain will hinder a person thrown into water from making attempts to save himself, such attempts being less the result of consciousness—of which at such a moment the party is deprived—than of mere instinct, acting blindly but powerfully, like other reflex actions, whenever existence is at stake, in every living creature. I speak from experience when I say that a person in a state of brutal intoxication will struggle powerfully in the water, and that the morbid appearances which indicate such a struggle will be in these cases discovered in the body after death. But the following case seems to me to settle the point in dispute:—

A shipmaster, who had suffered from repeated apoplectiform attacks, was seized with a fresh attack while standing on the edge of a lighter or decked boat, and was seen to fall down insensible, and to roll into the water. Some hours elapsed before his body was recovered. On examining the body afterwards it exhibited all the indications of death from asphyxia, unusually well marked, in addition to the extreme cerebral congestion which was to have been expected

It is not difficult to account for the mixed indications of death by coma and asphyxia occasionally encountered in the bodies of persons who have perished in the water. Such a case as the one I have just referred to would be of this nature. I also met with like mixed appearances on examining the body of a man who, while in the delirium of fever, threw himself into the water and was drowned, and that of a furious maniac who committed suicide in the same way.

But even independently of all this, the duration of the struggle for life, the previous state of the brain, and the vigour of the organs of circulation, and their relative fulness, will influence the amount of the cerebral congestion discoverable after death from that cause, while we should have every reason to believe that the occurrence of this congestion had taken place posterior, not prior, to the final interruption of the respiratory functions,—not to insist on the fact that, in every case, death by coma resolves itself virtually into death by asphyxia.

In this way, then, we get rid of three out of the four ways in which death by submersion has been accounted for. Without denying that a person found in water may have died in any of the three ways specified, all I argue for is that he has not died from drowning, strictly so-called; and that the occurrences enumerated—such as apoplexy, concussion, and ordinary syncope—are merely to be regarded as so many modifying circumstances, known, in certain cases, to attend the act of drowning.

This brings me to notice the only remaining mode to which death by submersion is attributed; and which, if not—as we have seen—the only one adopted by authors, is the one which all agree in considering the most frequent, namely, asphyxia. The following graphic sketch, which I borrow from Devergie, is perhaps as correct an account as can be given of what takes place in most cases of death by drowning.—

The individual sinks in the water, to a depth greater or less according to the height of his fall; then rises again to its surface, under the influence of his specific gravity—rendered less considerable by the air retained in his clothes, and by the position which the body assumes by the effect of his instinctive actions, which have for their object the presentation of a greater surface to the fluid. Then one of two things happens—either the individual can swim, and in this case he instinctively pushes along the surface of the water till he is fatigued, when he comes to the same position as the person who cannot swim: or he finds himself from the outset in this latter predicament, and then he executes irregular movements of the arms and legs, seizes everything within his reach, clutches at the bottom, lays hold on bodies in motion as motionless ones; but inasmuch as his motions are irregular, he appears and disappears successively from the surface of the water It has been observed that at the moment the head comes to the surface, air and water are inspired; the latter is partly swallowed, partly rejected by an involuntary fit of coughing, arising from the contact of the water with the larynx, the liquid reaching this organ at the same time with the air These efforts, however, have caused the expulsion of the inspired air, and the desire to breathe makes itself imperatively felt. If the individual has been able to reach the surface of the water, he profits by his contact with the air to satisfy this desire for breath; but as the head is only partly above or out of the water, he draws in a fresh quantity of air and water, and the cough returns In a short time the person only floats beneath the surface; he again feels the desire to breathe, he opens his mouth, and water alone enters, it is expelled from the trachea, mingled with air, or perhaps swallowed, and a quantity of it—between one and two pounds—may thus reach the stomach A little water always enters the trachea, to form the foam which is found when the body is examined early enough During the whole of these attempts to keep up the respiration, an afflux of blood is taking place towards the brain, which explains the bloody points, and even the gorged state sometimes discovered in that organ, and which is never found in mere asphyxia Finally, the voluntary movements cease, the asphyxia is complete; the individual sinks to the bottom of the water, while at the same time bubbles of air escape from the mouth, on account of the collapse of the walls of the chest and of the diaphragm, under the influence of their elasticity

These successive phenomena have been divided into three stages by Bergeron and Montano, in an elaborate paper in the October number for 1877 of the *Annales d' Hygiène*, which is in substantial agreement with Devergie's description

The morbid appearances after death by drowning are such as naturally follow the closing scenes of life in the way described, namely: (1) those common to this and other forms of asphyxia—or, in rare instances, comato-asphyxia, and (2) in addition to these, certain appearances more or less characteristic of this mode of sudden death

Before proceeding, however, to the formal discussion of the usual signs of death by drowning, it is essential to keep the fact in view that, in some instances, even under favourable circumstances, several of the most characteristic of these may fail to present themselves. In order to their production in a marked form, it is essential, first, that the body had been wholly submerged in the water; secondly, that the person so submerged had not at once sunk to the bottom of the water without having come to the surface again before death; and, thirdly, that the body had been recovered and examined without loss of time.

Now, in practice, this will not be found generally to hold good. In the first place, to cause death by drowning it is only requisite in some instances that the lips and nostrils should have been under water. In 1851 I recorded a case of this sort in a person who had, during an epileptic seizure, fallen with his face downwards into a shallow pool of dirty water, and perished from the occlusion of his mouth and nostrils. I have since met with a parallel instance in a man, who, while intoxicated, and proceeding to cross the channel of the Denburn (Aberdeen), at that time almost dry, was seen to fall on his face, and remain in the recumbent posture. No further notice of the man was taken at the time, and it was not till some hours afterwards that he was found dead, his face in a narrow strip of water at the bottom of the channel. Caspar has referred to similar occurrences as not unfrequent in the case of new-born infants which have been found drowned in shallow vessels containing small quantities of blood, urine, or liquor amnii, as well as instances where intoxicated or epileptic persons have been drowned in shallow brooks and gutters. Such cases, however, can present no difficulties to the medical jurist, as in these all the internal appearances of drowning will be encountered by the inspector.

The position of the medical jurist will be more unfavourable in the second class of cases to which I have referred—where weights, for instance, had been attached to the body, either by a determined suicide, or by a murderer to secure the speedy destruction of his victim. Here, as the buoyancy of the body, which would otherwise have brought it to the surface, is counteracted, many of the indications of death drowning will necessarily be wanting at the inspection. It is but proper, however, to add that Caspar, Taylor, and Bergeron and Montano combat this opinion, as far at least as the froth in the trachea and the water in the lungs are concerned—a point to which I shall have to return by-and-by

Again, it frequently happens that the sinking of the body, which takes place at death, prevents it from being recovered until some time afterwards, the body not coming to the surface until the occurrence of putrefaction has restored its buoyancy. This period will vary, of course, with the seasons,—a few days being sufficient in the summer or in warm weather, while it may be deferred in winter for from three to six weeks, or even longer In these circumstances, the examination of the body, with the view of deciding as to the cause of death, will be conducted under considerable disadvantages, for not only will it be found that time has been afforded for the disappearance of some of the signs on which most reliance is usually placed, but also that putrefaction has obliterated others of them, or rendered it uncertain whether they are to be referred to the asphyxia of which the party may have perished, or to the process of decomposition which has commenced after the immersion

Taking into account these peculiarities liable to be encountered in the examination of the bodies of persons who have perished by drowning, it will be seen at once that room is given for differences of opinion—which at one time prevailed to a considerable extent—as to the value and relative frequency of the individual signs of death by this mode, differences of opinion which, since the subject has been more closely studied, have now mostly disappeared Your attention, however, has been directed to these peculiarities in the examination of the drowned, not so much on this account, as from the circumstance that their existence renders it imperative on the part of the medical jurist engaging in such examinations that he should have previously made himself familiar with the signs of death here, not only in the mass, but also individually, with their relative values, with the fallacies attaching to their individual application and estimation, with the periods which may properly be assigned to each, and with those appearances in the body, after the commencement of decomposition, which are liable to obliterate, mask, or simulate this form of death

Some of the points thus indicated were disposed of under Putrefaction, both as a general process and as modified by the stay of the body in water · most of the others will come in here while discussing, as I now proceed to do, in some detail, the individual signs, or groups of these—first singly, and secondly, as they are to be encountered, in greater or less number, in combination

Taking for guidance my notes of the external appearances

in 272 bodies viewed on removal from the water, and of the internal appearances in 116 of these, in which post-mortem inspection followed, I begin with—

I. The appearances on the *exterior*, taking first the face and general surface of the body. The pallor of the countenance and of the surface generally, whatever their aspect previously, follows the extinction of life in drowning as in other forms of death, as insisted on previously, and persists in this case for from five to twenty-five hours. It must not be assumed, then—as is done by Desgranges and Watson—that such a state of the surface points to a rapid asphyxia, and an opposite state of it to a severe dying struggle and slow asphyxia. A similar state of the surface is usually encountered also in bodies which have remained submerged for considerable periods, where putrefaction has been delayed.

At from sixteen hours to four days after death, an uniform blush of redness, of a more or less bright hue, is commonly seen on the face, if not on the other parts of the surface arising from the action of the oxygen of the atmosphere or of the water. This redness, if it have not taken place previously, will be seen to occur on the exposure of the corpse for a short time to the air.

The redness in the drowned is different from the reddening or lividity of the upper part of the body caused by congestion about the head, which, when present to any marked extent, usually shows itself somewhat earlier—that is, not later than from sixteen to twenty-four hours after death.

Of the green discoloration marking the commencement of putrefaction, I would only remind you that—as previously noticed—in drowning, it usually first makes its appearance over the front of the chest.

Besides the changes of colour on the surface of the body in drowning, the attention of the medical jurist has been called to the roughening of it usually observable, from the prominent state of the papillæ, known as gooseskin, or *cutis anserina*. This state of the surface becomes most perceptible when the fingers are passed over it. The appearance in question is usually best marked on the anterior surfaces of the extremities, and has been generally attributed to the sudden immersion of the warm body in the cold medium of the water; though Caspar, with considerable show of probability, ascribes it rather to the nervous shock experienced at the moment of the immersion; referring, in confirmation of this opinion, to the fact that it is found in the bodies of those drowned in the heat of summer, when the water is of a medium temperature, precisely the same as in the greatest cold of winter. I cannot, however, concur in this last statement, as my experience is the reverse of this, having found the cutis anserina most pronounced in bodies in the winter months, though it is usually encountered at all seasons in fresh bodies.

The circumstance should not be overlooked, that, though rarely absent in the bodies of the drowned, this appearance of the skin may likewise be met with after sudden deaths in other forms, such as hanging, gunshot wounds, etc.—a fact which is testified to by Caspar, and which I have repeatedly verified.

More conspicuous still is an appearance on drowned bodies after a stay of a few hours in water, namely, the blanching and corrugation of parts of the surface. This unnatural whitening and corrugation of the skin first makes its appearance on the palms of the hands and the soles of the feet, whence, when the body has remained for a few days in water, it is found to have spread as far as the wrists and ankles, and subsequently to the backs of the elbows and fronts of the knee-joints. It must be kept in mind, however, that this phenomenon, like the last, is a mere physical effect of the stay of the dead body in water, and has no peculiar connection with this mode of death; while it is sometimes met with in bodies disinterred from the earth, and even in the living, as in the hands of washerwomen.

Some stress has been laid, especially in Germany, on the state of the palms and fingers in the drowned, known as the cholera hand, well represented in Caspar's "Atlas," where the whitening of the surface is modified by the lividity appearing through it. This peculiar aspect of the hand—met with also, as the name implies, in cases of Asiatic cholera—Caspar asserts may be produced by immersing a dead hand, livid from any cause, in water for a certain time, or even by keeping it surrounded by wet cloths. Caspar, however, has pointed out one inference of some value, which may be drawn from the presence of the cholera hand when observed in a body out of water, and which had not been interred, namely, that the body in such a case must have previously lain for some time in that medium. In illustration he refers to the not improbable case of thieves removing a body from the water for the sake of plunder, and leaving it on the banks.

Some other appearances on the exterior of the body after death by submersion have been looked on as characteristic by some writers on this subject, such as excoriations about the knuckles or points of the fingers, dirt or sand under the nails, and foreign bodies grasped in the hands. The finding of such appearances will, of course, depend on the character of the death-struggle, the vicinity of hard bodies struck against by the hands, and the presence of sand or mud below the water or on its banks, or of foreign bodies floating in it. Substances grasped in the hands would, of course, indicate that the party had been alive, and so far conscious at the time of his immersion. The same inference might possibly, but not certainly, be drawn from the discovery of dirt or sand under the nails, and excoriations about the knuckles or points of the fingers. With the exception of this last circumstance, I have never encountered the others, probably from the persons I have examined having been, with few exceptions, drowned in deep water. Such excoriations about the fingers and knuckles I have only once noticed; and these abrasions of the cuticle, as also the slight contusions on the bodies of the drowned, are perhaps more properly to be attributed to the corpse being carried by currents against hard bodies in the water, than to the struggle before death. This at least explains the circumstance that traces of such slight injuries are encountered with nearly equal frequency on various of the more prominent parts of the surface, such as the nose, forehead, face, knees, etc.

Caspar very properly gives no value to the state of the tongue in the drowned. In thirty-six cases I have noticed it pressed against the front teeth, and in a few of these the teeth had left their impressions on it. In only one instance did I find the tongue retracted.

In his "Gerichtliche Leichenoffnungen," Caspar first drew attention to the contraction of the penis, or shortening of this organ, which he states that he has almost never failed to find in recently drowned bodies, while, on the other hand, he did not observe anything similar after any other kind of death. In six males I have met with this appearance pretty well marked, one of these being an infant. On the other hand, I have noted a very different state of the penis, namely, in two cases that of erection, and in twenty-two that of semi-erection.

The only other appearance on the exterior of the body in the drowned is that of froth about the lips and nostrils. But as this sign is connected with the presence of froth in the throat and air-passages, I shall reserve it for notice in connection with the post-mortem appearances observable in the interior of the bodies of the drowned, which next fall to be considered.

LECTURE XXXVI.

DEATH BY DROWNING—(*Concluded*).

INTERNAL APPEARANCES INDICATIVE OF DEATH BY SUBMERSION —Comparative value of the various Appearances.—WHETHER THE DROWNING WAS THE RESULT OF ACCIDENT, SUICIDE OR HOMICIDE.—Moral Evidence—Evidence from Marks of Violence on the Body—Violence inflicted prior to Submersion—Violence inflicted posterior to Submersion — Violence pointing to Accidental Causes, prior or subsequent to Immersion — Violence self inflicted prior to Submersion — Violence pointing to Homicidal Causes prior to Immersion — POST-MORTEM INSPECTION.

RESUMING the subject commenced at last lecture, I now come to notice—

II. The appearances in the *interior* of the body after death by drowning.

Much reliance is properly placed on the finding of a light watery froth, either at the lips and nostrils, or in the mouth, throat, and air-passages simultaneously, or in only one or more of these situations in the same case, as indicative of death by drowning. The presence of this froth about the lips and nostrils is only to be encountered after this mode of death when the body is seen early. In seventy-five instances in which I have noted its presence the period after death averaged twenty-two hours, and ranged from nineteen or twenty minutes to four days. At later periods it was found to have disappeared. In forty of the cases the froth appeared at the lips, and in thirty-five of them at the nostrils.

Contrary to what is generally believed, the froth appears sooner in winter than in the summer. In winter, however, as might be anticipated, it is slower of disappearing than in summer.

Two explanations have been offered to account for this appearance in the drowned—First, that the quantity of froth in summer is so abundant as to fill completely the air-passages and the mouth, and thus to be propelled outwards at the lips and nostrils; Second, that the froth originally present in the air-passages and the mouth is pushed forwards from the latter by the gases formed in the air-cells of the lungs and the bronchi, under the influence of putridity

If the former of these suppositions was the correct one, the froth should be seen earlier in summer than in winter, which we have seen not to be the case. That the latter of these suppositions is untenable, is shown by the circumstance that froth may be encountered at the lips in the freshest bodies—as after only a few minutes' immersion. Would not the phenomenon be more satisfactorily accounted for from the collapse of the walls of the chest on the cessation of the tonic spasm of its muscles, which would then propel the froth from the air-passages outwards and out of the mouth? Without assigning any special value to this conjecture, it seems to be borne out by the fact that the froth about the mouth and nostrils is always most copious shortly after death.

The froth at the lips and nostrils of the drowned is readily affected by the exposure of the body to the air on its removal from the water. I have never met with it at all distinct on the day following such removal, however previously well marked. This disappearance is fortunately not so speedy as regards the froth in the larynx and trachea, where it is often met with after it has gone from the nostrils, mouth, and throat.

There is an opinion and statement advanced by Caspar, and adhered to by Dr. Taylor, in regard to the froth of the drowned, in which it is not possible for me to concur—namely, that it is not requisite to its production that, as contended for by Orfila and Devergie, the individual in drowning should have got his head out of water; and that the froth has been met with in circumstances in which this could not have happened, as where suicides had loaded their bodies with heavy weights before throwing themselves into water. It detracts, however, from the value of this opinion and the facts on which it is based, that neither Caspar nor Taylor seem to discriminate sufficiently betwixt the froth of the drowned and the mixture of air and mucus found in other than drowned bodies —speaking, as Caspar does, of the froth as the product of the mixture of the inhaled fluid in which the drowning has occurred, of the natural mucus of the passages, or even of blood from some ruptured vessel, with the air contained in the lungs and trachea.

Devergie was the first to draw attention to the true character of the froth found in the air-passages of the drowned, and his remarks on this point are of importance to be kept in mind. The froth that forms in the way I have noticed, and which is strictly a vital phenomenon, is usually of a white colour, though in rare cases sanguinolent, and consists of numerous very small air-bubbles, constituting a lather, rather than a froth, properly so-called. It never adheres to the trachea by mucus, but is in immediate contact with its walls All the bubbles that form it have a watery envelope easily broken, and often, in opening the trachea, the greater number of them disappear like soap-bubbles

These characters serve to distinguish the froth found in the air-passages shortly after death by drowning, not only from the frothy mucus found after death by bronchitis or pneumonia, but also from that which is frequently detected in the same situation at long intervals after death by drowning; and which is merely a post-mortem change This last appearance—by no means rare—is solely occasioned by the development of putrid gases in the natural mucus of the air-passages, or on the surface of the water which may be present at the bottom of the trachea in bodies undergoing decomposition I have met with appearances of this last sort at periods after death respectively of seven, twenty-four, twenty-six, thirty-five, and fifty-six days This sign, as thus distinguished from the other appearances which might be confounded with it, I have had occasion to observe to be produced otherwise than in the death-struggle in drowning.

Thus, in a female who perished from an overdose of laudanum in 1836, an attendant poured into her mouth some water containing a few drops of sulphuric ether. This was about an hour before the woman's death, while she was sinking and had lost the power of deglutition The consequence was that the fluid, in place of being swallowed, had entered the windpipe, and been churned up into reddish froth Had the body been found in water, and had no laudanum (which was the case) been found in the stomach, it might readily have been decided that the deceased had died from drowning. The colour of the froth here would have afforded no discriminating mark, as the froth of the drowned, though rarely, has been observed, as stated by Devergie, of a reddish hue

Simultaneously with or after the disappearance of the froth in the air-passages, water is usually found in the trachea and bronchi, of the bodies of the drowned, either with or without the same fluid in the air-cells of the lungs. The froth and water in the air-passages are indeed mutually dependent phenomena Curiously enough, however, up to a comparatively recent period the actual existence of these two signs in the bodies of the drowned was largely contested Thus, we have their presence denied by Wepfer, Conrad, Becker, Littré, Petit, Morgagni, Haller, Unger, Fothergill, and Colman, either singly or in conjunction—an opinion grounded on their failure to detect them in bodies which they had examined. Later observers and experimentalists have shown the fallacy which lurked under these conclusions, by showing, both by experiments on animals and observations on the bodies of the drowned, that these signs are constant when looked for early, and that it is only their disappearance after a time that gives any colour to the denial of their existence in certain instances—points on which all medical jurists are now agreed. In corroboration of this, I may state that, in my own inspections of adults, I found water in the air-passages in 58 per cent, and froth in the larynx or trachea in 59 per cent of these. In all these examinations, however, the bodies were fresh, while in the remaining cases, which had been from four to fifty days in water, both signs had disappeared.

Besides water, particles of ice and several foreign substances have been encountered in the air-passages. Thus, Marc and Orfila both met with ice, which had been drawn in with the water in winter. In a case in the *Gazette Médicale*, sand and pebbles were found in the trachea of an epileptic who had perished from falling with his head in a pool of water. Devergie mentions his finding mud in the trachea, drawn in from foul water in the same way. A case is also published in the *Transactions of the Medical and Physical Society of Bombay*, where mud was found in the bronchi of a Hindoo who had been drowned in a drain. In one instance I found small stalks of decayed leaves, in a second, fragments of seaweed in the air-passages; in a third, sand in the mouth and trachea; in two, sand in the air-cells of the lungs; and in three, sand in the pharynx, trachea, and bronchi. In one of the cases the presence of the sand in the air-cells of the lungs was the only indication of the drowning—the body, that of a fisherman lost in a squall at sea, having been only recovered, in a state of advanced putrefaction and considerable mutilation, after more than a month's stay in the water, in the unusually warm summer of the year 1876.

In connection with the finding of foreign matters in the air-passages of the drowned, this may be the proper place to refer to the discovery of liquor amnii, and even meconium, in the same situation in the bodies of still-born infants; and to the conclusion drawn from this, that the infant in utero may thus die by drowning prior to its birth—a point to which I shall have to recur again under death by smothering. The death of the fœtus in this way has been referred to the arrest of the circulation in the cord, or placenta, by German jurists and accoucheurs, by whom the subject was first mooted, and by whom it has been industriously followed up The consequence of this is by them believed to be, that, by the arrest of the circulation, the fœtus is compelled to attempt to inflate its lungs, and thus the liquor amnii, where it has not previously escaped, is drawn into the air-passages, and, in addition, any meconium which may be found in that fluid In proof of this, Bohr has brought together nine such cases, out of fifty-six fatal instances of arrested placental circulation, collected from different sources, in which these foreign matters were found in the air-passages of the infant. In some of these cases the lungs were partially inflated, and in two, punctiform ecchymoses were encountered

Another sign closely connected with the last is water in the air-cells of the lungs Of course if we admit the entrance of water into the trachea and bronchi, it follows of necessity that it will readily find its way into their extreme ramifications The value of this sign, however, depends altogether on the state in which the water is found in the pulmonary vesicles Nothing is more usual than to meet with a copious watery or bloody froth in such cases, as is at once made evident on compressing the cut portions of the lungs, but this may be met with in the body after death from several morbid states of the heart and lungs, while we have no ready means of distinguishing a mere watery froth in this situation from other frothy matters with which it may be readily confounded When met with unmixed with air, and in any quantity, especially when the corp has not been long in the water, Orfila considers water in the air-cells of the lungs as one of the most valuable indications of death by submersion, and even as the master sign in a case of this sort Some deductions must be made from this statement, however In the first place, it is not always found to be present, it having been wanting in nearly one-half of the cases (48·7 per cent) I have had the opportunity of examining Its absence from the lungs in several of these cases was accounted for by the presence of fluid in the pleural cavities which, from its character and the absence of any indication of its morbid origin, made it evident that it had escaped by transudation or exosmosis from the lungs. In six of these the quantity of watery fluid was small, from one to four and a half ounces, but in the remaining ten, from thirteen to thirty-four ounces

In depreciation of this sign of drowning, it has been suggested that water may enter the lungs of a body after death from other causes, as where it has been kept in a vertical position; or, if

Orfila is to be trusted, where it has lain on its back in water. The further objection—that it might possibly be injected after death—is of such an improbable character as scarcely to require notice.

Water in the stomach is the sign of drowning which next calls for notice. I have met with it in 36.9 per cent of my cases. In ten others this fluid, though absent in the stomach, was met with in the abdominal cavity, but only in sparing quantities, six fluid ounces being the highest quantity noted. The water in the stomach of the drowned was met with in fresh, and but rarely, if at all, in decayed bodies. From the former it is known readily to escape by the mouth in turning the corpse on its face.

Experiments on animals have shown that the water found in the body in drowning enters the stomach during the death-struggle, by the act of deglutition, as the quantity of the fluid was greatest where the animals had been allowed repeatedly to come to the surface to respire; while when they had been kept constantly immersed, and thus in a condition but little favourable to the exercise of deglutition, little or no water entered the stomach. It may be safely assumed that the power of swallowing would be suspended after death, and that the walls of the œsophagus would apply themselves too closely to each other to allow of the passage of water to the stomach in a body immersed in that medium. It has been found, in fact, that no water enters the stomach in animals thrown into water after the extinction of life, prior to the progress, to a considerable extent, of the putrefactive process.

Caspar lays much stress on the increased volume of the lungs after death by drowning—a phenomenon only encountered to a like extent after the most acute œdema of the lungs, and occasionally after suffocation in irrespirable gases. In a few instances this expansion of the lungs is so considerable as to cause them to rise out of the chest on the removal of the sternum. I have met with this in fifteen, or 12.6 per cent, of my inspections; but in seven of these putrefaction was well marked, which leads me to suppose (as stated in Lecture XXVII) that that process has a good deal to do with this great augmentation of the bulk of the lungs. Short of this, expansion of the lungs is so common in the drowned as to strengthen Caspar's conclusion. In only four of my own cases were the lungs found in a state of collapse, and that in bodies much decomposed.

Reddening of the mucous coat of the trachea, a good deal insisted on by Caspar, is not so constant in the drowned as he states, while, as he admits, it is common to other forms of apnœa, and follows the advance of putrefaction

Congestion of the lungs, as might be expected, is very characteristic of this form of asphyxia, and persists even after putrefaction has made great advances Its extent, however, varies In three instances I could not determine its existence, while in the remaining it existed to a greater or less extent. In the former cases the stay of the bodies in water had averaged forty-four days. The lungs were slightly congested, and exhibited some marks of disease. Deducting these, extreme congestion was seen to be less usual than a moderate degree of it.

Congestion of the liver, spleen, and kidneys is common to this and other forms of death by asphyxia and coma, though usually less marked in the latter than in the former of these.

Engorgement of the right cavities of the heart and of the venæ cavæ is one of the most constant of the signs of death by drowning In my cases the right side of the heart was altogether or nearly empty in nine, the left side empty in seventeen, and both sides empty in three; this emptiness was explicable as the effect of decomposition in the bodies, which had been, on an average, thirty-five days in water

Fluidity of the blood, as a sign of death by drowning, and common to this and other forms of asphyxia, as well as coma, is not, however, invariably to be encountered in the drowned In ten cases I have met with blood partly clotted on the right side of the heart The same circumstance has been noticed once by Orfila, and several times by Devergie.

Congestion of the head is more characteristic of death by coma than of this and other forms of apnœa In some cases it is very marked; in others it is not met with to any perceptible extent There is little room for doubt that certain states of the body, as well as the circumstances attendant on this mode of death, favour hyperæmia in this direction — such as previous intoxication, apoplectic and epileptic tendencies, and maniacal excitement, etc In my inspections the congestion has been more frequently met with in the scalp than in the interior of the cranium

Such being the available signs of death by drowning, and their relative frequency and importance, the question now occurs as to how far we can be entitled, from the concurrence of all or the greater number of them in a dead body found in water, or known to have been removed from it, to infer with certainty that these appearances could only have originated in this way.

It may assist in the determination of this point if I separate the signs passed in review into two groups, assuming, at the same time, that nothing else has been met with in the bodies in which the signs in question had been found, which would account for the death in any other way, whether from natural disease or violence inflicted during life.

One such group can readily be made to embrace the appearances common to this and the other forms of death by asphyxia—hyperæmia of the right side of the heart, lungs, liver, kidneys, spleen, and head,

A second group, coming in aid of the former, would take in the appearances peculiar to this particular form of apnœa. The most important of these latter, or special signs, as I may term them, are (1) watery froth about the lips and nostrils, (2) similar froth in the trachea, bronchi, and air-cells of the lungs; (3) water in the trachea and air-cells of the lungs, with or without the admixture of mud, sand, or weeds; and (4) water in the stomach. Then come in, as corroborative signs, the cutis anserina, the cholera hand, the blanched and plaited skin of the hands and feet, excoriations about the knuckles and points of the fingers, dirt or sand under the nails, and foreign bodies grasped in the hands

Of the first three of these, which I place amongst the more certain signs, we may safely assume that they could only have been produced in the living body. In regard to the fourth, or water in the stomach, we encounter the objection that the person may have drunk the water before his immersion, or that it may have entered the dead body from columnar pressure at great depths—both of which are possible, and the latter, if the body had been lying in deep water not improbable Turning, then, to the corroborative signs, it must at once be conceded that, with the exception of the last of them, they only indicate that the body had lain for some time in water

All this, it will be seen, brings me back to the question from which I started—Would the appearances I have thus brought into juxtaposition, authorise the conclusion, that where the whole or the more important of them were encountered in the dead body, the person must have died by drowning?—a question which is answered in the negative by such a high authority as Orfila. In opposition to this conclusion, however, I must bring forward that of Caspar, who on a point of this sort is well entitled to speak with some authority. "I think," says this author, "that by carefully considering in their totality the diagnostic proofs of death by drowning, as actually observed in nature, and setting aside all that subtle scepticism whose ultimate object is mere negation, it is by no means the most difficult task that a medical jurist has to determine, whether or not a man has fallen alive into the water and been drowned" In making this statement, he adds, "of course I suppose that the bodies to be examined are such as, from not being too far advanced in putrefaction, can supply demonstrative evidence in dissection."

To this, though it may be somewhat superfluous, I may be permitted to add, as my own opinion, that, taking in conjunction with the observed absence of appearances indicative of death from any other cause, the combination of the signs of death by asphyxia generally, with the whole or the greater number of the special signs, and in addition, such of the corroborative signs as may be present, a decided opinion may readily be hazarded as to the death having taken place by submersion, and not by any other cause. In connection with this point I would take occasion to repeat once more that it is not by relying on single signs, however valuable, that the medical jurist should reach his conclusions on any of the occasions on which he may be called to resolve questions in medical science. It is only by an enlarged survey of all the available points in the case, and by the concurrence of as many signs and appearances as are obtainable for his purpose, that he can form an opinion which will admit of being defended against all assailants, and which he will be able conscientiously to uphold in the face of the profession and the public

The second point of importance which I stated as liable to call for solution by the medical jurist in cases of death by drowning was the determination of the question—

Whether the death by submersion has been the consequence of accident, of suicide, or of homicide? The solution of this question often rests upon purely moral evidence, with which in general the medical jurist will have nothing to do In other cases the proof will rest upon data of a purely physical character, and of the force and applicability of these the medical practitioner will be the best judge At the same time, it must be admitted that the question seldom permits of being resolved in an absolute manner by the medical jurist, for in fact there does not exist, in many instances at least, any material difference as to consequences between the action of a person who throws himself into the water, and one who falls into it by accident or who is thrown into it by another. In a few instances, however, there are certain indications, which a careful inspection of the body will elicit, and which may enable us to throw some light on the circumstances attending the latest moments of life. Thus, when a person throws himself voluntarily into the water he commonly chooses a deep part of it, leaps from a high bank, and not unfrequently attaches weights to his body. In these circumstances indications of violence will scarcely ever be met with on the body. The same thing will happen from a person falling accidentally into deep water. But, on the other hand, if a man is forcibly thrust into the water, we may expect to find indications of a vigorous struggle for life, unless indeed his assailants have been so numerous as to have overpowered him at once, or he has been taken by surprise, or has been intoxicated, or insensible from narcotics. It is for these indications of violence, therefore, that we have to look in the dead body, and when such are met with it remains for us to determine how they were produced — whether they could have been self-inflicted, whether or not they could have arisen from the struggles of the person in the water, or were produced by the fall into it, or whether they are of such a nature as could only have been produced by the agency of others.

There is no danger of our confounding the marks of violence which may have been inflicted before death in cases of drowning with those injuries which may have caused death before the body was thrown into the water. The absence of the signs of death by drowning in the latter case would obviate any chance of error in this respect. Attention to the nature and character of the injuries found in the body would also facilitate our decision. They would necessarily be such as would be sufficient to account for death independently of the submersion altogether. The danger of such a mistake, however, should not be altogether overlooked, as it is a not uncommon occurrence for murderers, after having despatched their victims by the usual means, to dispose of the body in this way with the view of concealment, or to render it probable that the party had either drowned himself or fallen accidentally into the water, and perished in consequence. Indeed, drowning is a mode of homicide seldom resorted to in the first instance by murderers, from the difficulties in the way of its successful accomplishment, and from the combination of circumstances required to facilitate its execution.

When, on the removal of a body from the water, injuries are found on it of such a nature as to justify the suspicion that they had not been fairly come by, several inquiries must be originated by the medical examiner—Are they of such a character as to account for death prior to submersion? Were they inflicted before or after death? In either case were they the result of accident or of design? If received during life, were they self-inflicted or inflicted by the agency of others?

The data for the correct solution of these inquiries will not require to be entered upon here. There are, however, a few points bearing upon the special circumstances of the present inquiry which will need to be adverted to in this place. Thus, it is of importance to keep in view that injuries of very considerable extent may arise from the circumstances attendant on the decease of the party, even where the drowning was accidental or designed.

In a person of the name of Petrie, who drowned himself at Aberdeen several years ago, numerous bruises, some of them of considerable severity, were observed on the body. He had waded into the Dee, at a spot where the water was shallow, for some distance from the bank, before reaching the deeper channel, and, being intoxicated at the time, he had in all probability fallen repeatedly amongst the rocks which abounded there.

Suicides, by throwing themselves from a high rocky bank, sometimes, in falling, produce severe contusions, dislocations, and fractures. In accidental or suicidal drowning the body is also occasionally carried by the current against mechanical obstacles in a river or canal, and thus the appearance of violence is produced. Even the mechanical resistance offered by the water itself, in falling into it, may give rise to marks of very violent injury on the person. Dr. Smith gives an instance of dislocations of both arms in this way; and a case occurred at Aberdeen in 1833, where the perineum in a female was lacerated by the forcible separation of the thighs on coming into contact with the water, after leaping over the parapet of a swivel-bridge at the harbour. This case reminds me of another remark bearing on this subject. In a tidal harbour the body of a drowned person may float under a ship at high-water, and be crushed below it at the fall of the tide, and thus present very extensive injuries. In a case of this kind in 1855, besides exhibiting some minor injuries, the right clavicle was seen to be dislocated, the left clavicle, the right radius, the bones of the left forearm, and of the right zygoma were fractured, the abdominal cavity widely laid open, and the intestines protruding

It has been remarked that bodies found in the Rhine and other rivers on the Continent, are generally much disfigured and extensively injured from their getting entangled with the wheels of the numerous floating mills stationed along the banks of these streams. A parallel instance occurred in the Aberdeen harbour in 1876. In a putrid body brought up by a dredging-machine, one of the lower extremities had been torn off by the machinery, and the intestines protruded through a rent in the abdominal wall.

Again, it may be observed of these marks of injury that they are sometimes of such a kind as to forbid the idea of their accidental origin after submersion. Thus, there may be severe and extensive bruises about the person, deeply penetrating wounds involving the cavities of the body, gunshot wounds, a deeply ecchymosed circle around the neck, or the marks of violent compression about the larynx or trachea. All these injuries, provided the post-mortem appearances of death by drowning were absent, would afford the strongest presumptive evidence of homicide prior to submersion.

The finding of traces of poisons or of their action in the stomach or intestines, at the inspection, points strongly to the same conclusion. The appearance of vascular fulness in the intestinal canal is not, however, to be hastily assumed as indicative of the action of irritant poisons during life. Discoloration of the alimentary canal from venous congestion is a common feature in death by drowning, and the same appearance arises naturally, and becomes much more marked in the progress of putrefaction. Orfila has also observed that when drowning takes place while the process of digestion is going on, the mucous membrane of the stomach often has a red or violet tint.

Before quitting this part of our subject, I have to remind you that the losses of continuity of portions of the surface sometimes found in bodies which have been long in water, are not to be confounded with wounds or losses of substance during life, or immediately after death; as, independently of their possibly originating in the rapacity of fishes, etc., the erosive action of water, formerly referred to under Wounds, has here to be taken into account. The erosions are found, under these circumstances, most frequently about the scalp and face, or on the hands, feet, knees, and elbows.

With a few observations on the best mode of conducting the medico-legal inspection, I conclude the subject of death by drowning.

Before proceeding to the dissection of a person supposed to have been drowned, the inspector should endeavour to learn what can be ascertained regarding the following points:—First, in what manner the body had been removed from the water. Secondly, whether any, and what, means had been resorted to for the restoration of animation. Thirdly, whether the corpse had been placed on its face after removal from the water. Fourthly, whether it had been suspended by the feet, or the head kept dependent. Fifthly, if conveyed to any distance from the place where it was discovered, what was the mode of its conveyance. Sixthly, what period had elapsed since it was taken out of the water. And lastly,—if the body had been washed or otherwise disturbed—whether any mud, grass, or other substance was observed about the nails, or clutched by the hands. The state of the eyes and mouth should then be noted; the colour of the skin, the expression of the countenance, the state of the joints, and of the hands and feet, should also be observed. Attention should be directed to any marks of violence which may be present on the exterior of the body, such as contusions, ecchymoses, abrasions, or wounds; distinguishing between such as might have been produced during life and those which are of post-mortem origin. In this last case the inspector should examine the spot where the body was found, in order to ascertain, from the nature of the bottom or the banks of the river, etc., whether these injuries could have been readily produced by its stay there. It should be known that from the position of the body in the water, the eyelids, the nose, and the lips are not unfrequently disfigured by abrasions of their surfaces; as are often the integuments over the knees in male, though more rarely in female bodies.

The inspector should next be careful to note the presence or absence of froth about the lips and nostrils, the position of the tongue, and the state of the mouth. He should then proceed to the dissection, attending to the general rules already laid down, directing his attention particularly to the following points:—First, the appearance and distribution of the blood in the principal viscera, especially the brain, lungs, heart, liver, kidneys, spleen, and alimentary canal. Secondly, the state of the larynx, trachea, and bronchi, which should be examined *in situ*. Thirdly, the appearance, quantity, and situation of water or froth present in any part of the air-passages; water containing particles of sand, mud, vegetables, or other foreign bodies in the air-passages, is to be compared with the water in which the body was discovered. Fourthly, the volume, colour, consistence, and feeling of the lungs, and any water or froth which may be present in their cells, and be obvious on compression. Fifthly, the state of the stomach, with the water or other liquids in it. Sixthly, the quantity and colour of any urine in the bladder. Lastly, the condition of the body as to plumpness, leanness, and muscularity, as this may have influenced the nature of the death-struggle, and the speedy sinking or floating of the body at or after death, it being known that, *cæteris paribus*, the body of a person which is much loaded with fat will float more readily than that of one who is thin and emaciated

LECTURE XXXVII.

DEATH BY HANGING

Assigned Causes of Death —Coma—Asphyxia—Syncope—Comato-Asphyxia—Injury to the Spinal Cord —Circumstances Influencing the Mode of Death. Phenomena attendant on Death by Suspension Post-mortem Appearances —External Appearances generally—Appearances about the Neck—Internal Appearances—Relative values of these. Whether the result of Accident, Suicide, or Homicide Post mortem Inspection

Death by hanging is a subject of very considerable importance to the medical jurist, and one the study of which is attended, at times, with difficulties of no ordinary kind Both in its mode of production, and in the effects to which it gives rise, it has much in common with death by strangulation, the differences being— that in the one the constriction of the neck is due to the weight of the body itself, and that in the other the constricting force is foreign to the body, while the amount of violence required to strangle is greater than that required to cause death by hanging

As in the form of asphyxia last considered (Drowning), the points to be determined are—First, the cause of death in hanging; secondly, the proof of the suspension having taken place during life, and thirdly, the determination of the question whether the hanging had been the consequence of accident, suicide, or homicide

And first as to the cause of death The mode in which the fatal event occurs after the suspension of the body has been variously set forth by different writers Thus some have attributed it exclusively to cerebral congestion or apoplexy, others to asphyxia purely, others to a combination of coma and asphyxia, and others still to syncope, or neuro-paralysis (the nervous or simple apoplexy of Remer) either as the effect of severe mechanical injury or shock to the brain or spinal cord, or of mere fright

Now, while there can be no doubt that, after suspension, the body has been known to present appearances characteristic of these four forms of sudden death — coma, asphyxia, comato-asphyxia, and syncope,—I may, by following the course I adopted under drowning, simplify the subject, by transferring one at least of these forms of death to a position different from the mere effects of the suspension.

In those rare and exceptional instances, for example, in which the amount of mental shock has been sufficiently powerful to induce death by syncope, and which consequently have left no positive traces of its operation in the dead body, it would be better, as in the analogous case of a person perishing by syncope in the water, to refer the cause of death to the shock, and not to the suspension.

For all practical purposes, indeed, I may restrict the remaining causes of death in hanging to two factors—coma or asphyxia. For either one of these must be the direct cause of death, or a combination of the two, as in the mixed form of coma and asphyxia. I might have gone farther in simplifying the subject by insisting on the truth that ultimately asphyxia is the immediate cause of death—death by coma, as we saw in a former lecture, resolving itself in every instance into death by apnœa. On this, however, I need not insist, particularly as the statement, now generally received, does not admit of dispute—namely, that in the large majority of instances of hanging the appearances presented by the body after death partake largely of both conditions, and that it is comparatively seldom that coma alone, or asphyxia alone, is indicated by the autopsy. That this should be the case it is not difficult to perceive, when we consider that when a ligature is applied round the neck, and the body has been suspended by it, it can but rarely happen that there will not be, to some extent, both interruption to the return of the blood from the head, inducing cerebral congestion, and compression of the air-tube, interfering with respiration and favouring the occurrence of asphyxia. It must be equally evident, nevertheless, that circumstances may favour the predominence of either the one or the other of these occurrences. Death, for instance, may be slow, and originate in coma, where the ligature is not very tight, and rests in front on the larynx, especially when the larynx is ossified. Again, where the ligature is tight, and firmly compresses the trachea, the death may be almost instantaneous, from sudden asphyxia, with little time afforded for the occurrence of cerebral congestion. It is generally understood that a loose ligature crossing the neck above the os hyoides at once arrests the respiration, inducing rapid asphyxia. Further, it is agreed that

there is a running knot gliding easily upon the ligature, or where the cord or ligature makes more than one turn around the neck, embracing it at every point of its circumference, the stagnation of the blood in the cerebral sinuses occurs promptly, and the stoppage of the respiration only subsequently,—unless at the same time the neck is compressed tightly and forcibly, when death takes place by asphyxia, with or without cerebral congestion. Once more. Whether the ligature has compressed the neck partially or completely, if in addition to this a strong downward or lateral impulse has been communicated to the body, so as to rupture the spinal cord, the death will be instantaneous, either by syncope or asphyxia, from the injury of the cord, with little or no cerebral congestion

We are thus in a position to perceive why the appearances in the dead body, indicative of the mode of death, should present marked differences after suspension, though I am persuaded that these differences have been much exaggerated Still more is this the case, however, as regards the distinctions, laid down so prominently by the earlier writers on this subject, between the appearances respectively of the bodies of suicides and the subjects of violent or forcible suspension It may be the case, for instance, that the death is calm and sudden, as where a person, in a fit of melancholy, has suspended himself with his feet resting on the ground, or on a chair or table, and that the appearances will be those of death by asphyxia; while in another instance the death has been slower, painful, and distressing, and rather the result of coma than asphyxia,—as where a person has suspended himself from a height, or has been forcibly suspended by others, perhaps after a violent resistance. Still, beyond the more marked local effects of the ligature and the greater amount of cerebral congestion in the latter cases, we may look in vain for the other points of difference long believed to characterise cases of this sort—such as the livid and anxious countenance, the distorted features, the starting eyeballs, the protruded tongue, and the clenched jaws. Pictures of this sort have, I believe, been drawn rather from the observation of the vital struggles of animals than from the study of the appearances in the human body after death, with which assuredly they are not found to correspond.

It is mostly in the cases of criminals publicly executed that marked instances of local violence have been encountered, such as displacement or fracture of the odontoid process of the second cervical vertebra; separation of the vertebræ, from rupture of the intervertebral substance; fracture of the bones of the neck, and effusion of blood on the spinal cord. Similar injuries, it is obvious, might likewise occur in a forcible hanging, where the fall had been great, or where much violence had been employed.

Injury to the nerves of the neck by the compression of the ligature has only been encountered in experiments on animals

Of the phenomena attending death by suspension little is known, and much is necessarily left to conjecture. Foderé relates a singular incident of one of his fellow-students. After an argument respecting the cause of death in hanging, this young man resolved personally to gratify his curiosity. He passed a ligature round his neck and attached it to a hook behind the door. To accomplish his purpose he raised himself on tiptoe and gradually brought his heels to the ground. He soon lost all consciousness, but was rescued by a fellow-student in time to L resuscitated by prompt treatment.

A similar incident has been related by Bacon in his "Historia Vitæ et Mortis." A boy in England, who had witnessed a public execution, and who was believed in consequence to have tried what hanging w , was less fortunate, as he was not observed till after the body was cold

Dr Taylor, in his Manual, gives an account of two persons — one in England and the other in America — who, to gratify public curiosity, repeatedly submitted to be hanged for a few minutes. On the last of these occasions the American lost his life by being allowed to hang too long.

Fleischmann tried some experiments on himself to elucidate this subject. When he placed the cord between the lower jaw and the os hyoides, and tightened it moderately, the effect was to disturb in some degree the breathing, which, however, still went on. But then the face reddened, the eyes became somewhat prominent, the heat of the head increased, and he began to experience a sense of weight, a degree of stupefaction, a feeling of distress, and, lastly, a hissing noise in his ears, which warned him that he had carried his experiment to the verge of safety, and he did not venture again to carry it so far.

In another trial, Fleischmann placed the ligature over the larynx, when the same effects followed, but in even less time. The first experiment lasted two minutes. In the second only a minute and a half had passed, when the noise in his ears, and a sensation which he states that he found it impossible to describe, warned him that it was time to desist

In a third experiment, the ligature was placed over the cricoid cartilage, when, almost instantly, the breathing became so enfeebled that he could not support the attempt for even the very shortest period.

These experiments, as far as they go, bear out the usually-received opinion, based upon the very limited number of facts derived from the statements of the parties who have recovered from the effects of temporary, or rather momentary, suspension, as to the differences experienced from the respective positions of the ligature in different cases, while, on the other hand, they give no countenance to the distinctive character of the effects already adverted to as resulting from suicidal and homicidal suspension

The smallness of the number of cases in which resuscitation has been accomplished after suspension of the body is not to be wondered at, owing to the shortness of the period during which life is preserved in every instance, and the rarity of the successful attempts made with this object. A curious instance of this last sort is given by Dr. Gordon Smith in his "Forensic Medicine," from which, perhaps, Sir Walter Scott borrowed the incident in his novel, "The Fair Maid of Perth."

Dr. Smith relates that a surgeon attempted to save a criminal in London from the effects of the gallows, by making an opening in the trachea through which he could breathe freely on the closure of the mouth and nostrils. After hanging for three-quarters of an hour, he showed signs of life, repeatedly opened his mouth and groaned, and blood flowed freely on opening a vein in his arm. But the man could not be further resuscitated. This want of success, Dr Smith thinks, was probably to be attributed to the great weight of the criminal, by which the compression of the vessels of the neck must have become more effectual than in ordinary cases; and that, perhaps, the opening into the trachea was not sufficiently free. This theory, however, does not allow sufficiently for the disturbance of the cerebro-spinal system, which would be even more unfavourable to recovery than those he has condescended on.

However brief the duration of life in any one case of suspension is, that period will obviously be affected in individual instances, by such modifying circumstances, as the degree of constriction of the ligature, the length of the fall, the weight of the individual, and the concomitant injury done to the parts about the neck.

I now come to the point which has next to be considered by

the medical jurist in cases of hanging, namely, the proofs which fall to be adduced by him that the suspension has taken place during life. And here, at the outset, I am compelled to admit that, apart from the moral proof—with which the medical examiner, as such, has but little to do,—the evidence of the mode of death will, in many cases, be of a less decisive character than in most of the other forms of sudden death. The evidence to this effect, apart from the moral proof, is of a twofold character: first, the appearances common to this and some other forms of sudden death; and, secondly, those which have been specially noticed in connection with death by hanging

The first of these appearances need not detain us We have seen that, in hanging, death may take place either by coma or by asphyxia singly, or, what is more frequently found to be the case, by the combination, to a more or less marked extent, of both; now the one predominating, now the other.

Thus, when the mode lecease has been by coma chiefly, the engorgement of the vessels of the head will be best marked, and when it has been chiefly or entirely by asphyxia the lungs and the right side of the heart will usually be most engorged. When, again, death has resulted from the combined operation of both modes, little difference will be observable in the state of the circulation within the head on the one hand, and in that of the chest on the other; both may be expected to present this engorgement to a greater or less extent, according to circumstances.

Of the appearances peculiar to, or characteristic of, death by hanging, the most important are those on the neck which have arisen from the application of the ligature, and the traction exercised on it by the weight of the body on its suspension The appearances thus produced, and the injuries which may show themselves after death in this way, as might be anticipated, are found to differ to a very considerable extent under the varying circumstances in which they are known to originate, such as the nature of the ligature, the weight of the body, the height of the fall, etc The remaining appearances in this class are indirect ones, and are, with one exception, such as may be observed at several parts of the exterior of the body These appearances, both direct and indirect, will be most conveniently passed under review in connection; and in doing so I shall avail myself of forty cases which I have had opportunity of examining after death in this way—thirty-six of these being suicides, and four violent hangings

In twenty-one out of these forty cases, or 52 5 per cent of them, the features had a look of calmness and placidity; while in only one instance, and that a suicidal one, had the face an anxious look. In none of the cases did the colour of the face present anything characteristic. In only one instance, a suicidal one, was prominence of the eyes encountered. In thirty-nine, or 97·5 per cent, the pupils were more or less dilated; while in one they were contracted.

In one instance the external auditory canal on both sides was full of blood.

In fourteen, or 35 per cent of my examinations, the point of the tongue was either protruded beyond the front teeth, or so marked by the teeth as to indicate that it had been pressed against them at the time of death.

In three cases there was frothy mucus at the lips, and in one of these also at the nostrils

Indications of excitement of the genital and urinary organs presented themselves in ten, or one-fourth of the cases under review. The penis was erect in seven, and semi-erect in four. seminal fluid had been discharged in eight of the male subjects, urine in four instances; blood in two—one of these last a male, and the other a female, in the latter set down as menstrual blood; and in two males the urethra was very red

On the exterior of the neck the only uniform appearance was the groove or furrow left by the ligature. Except where the cord had encircled the neck more than once, the mark was not found to be continuous, and where it had made a single turn, it was chiefly confined to the front of the air-tube and the prominences of the sterno-mastoid muscles. (The usual direction of the groove, and the position of the knot, will be reserved for notice under Strangulation) Marked whiteness of the bottom of the furrow was encountered in twenty-seven (or 67 5 per cent) of my observations; in thirteen (or 32 5 per cent) it presented the dry, brown, and horny state known as the parchment skin, in five it was slightly abraded, while only in two were the borders of the groove reddened, and that both above and below

In proceeding to the appearances which present themselves in the interior of the body, in order to prevent misunderstanding it may be well to premise that those which follow are chiefly founded on twenty-two out of the forty cases on which I have been commenting, a complete inspection not having been obtained in some of the others.

The subcutaneous areolar tissue under the groove presented more or less distinctly, in all the inspections, a silvery white and dry streak at the point of the greatest pressure of the cord. At the same point the injection of the skin at the bottom of the groove, or the minute ecchymoses of the cutis vera, noticed by Neyding and Bremme, were encountered in five or 22·7 per cent of the cases; the injection being well marked in four, but the ecchymoses only in one.

In one case a small quantity of clotted blood was found effused below the integuments, under the furrow in front, and on the left side of the neck; in another a like ecchymosis was met with in the interior of the left sterno-mastoid muscle, where the cord had pressed; while in a third a few of the fibres at the anterior border of the same muscle were seen to be ruptured. One case showed slight abrasions of the skin in front of the neck, a little below the mark of the cord. In one the sheath of the carotid artery on one side was a good deal injected. Where the ligature had crossed the right carotid arteries there were, in two of the cases, transverse ruptures of their middle and inner coats. A copious mucous froth was present in the pharynx in nine cases, in the trachea in six, and in the lungs in four; in none of them bloody. In one case there was blood in some quantity in the pharynx and larynx.

Marked redness of the mucous membrane of the trachea was only seen in 36·6 per cent of the cases.

Severe violence was only encountered in two of the bodies inspected, and in those of two criminals viewed on their removal from the scaffold. In one of the bodies inspected the thyroid cartilage had been crushed, and presented a rent on one side of the cartilage from top to bottom; in the other the thyroid cartilage was completely detached from the os hyoides.

The former of these two cases was investigated by the law authorities, but though the hanging was affected by the agency of a second party, the deed was found to have been unintentional. The case was an unusual one. During the breakfast hour at a cotton-mill in Woodside near Aberdeen, one of the men was toying with a female fellow-worker, to whom he was attached, and in sport threw around her neck a loose leather strap suspended from the roof of the apartment. At this moment the machinery was set agoing, and the girl was drawn up to the roof by the strap, and suspended there for a few minutes before the engine could be stopped, too late for saving her life. In the second case there was nothing to account for the injury, as one foot, at the time the body was found, was only a few inches from the ground, and the legs lay across the back of a chair in the vicinity. In one of the executed criminals, fracture of the larynx could readily be felt, and in the other, fracture and dislocation of the atlas was made out.

The only remaining special appearances noted internally in the inspections of the bodies of the hanged were—in four marked expansion, and in two marked collapse of the lungs; in one deep reddening of the interior of the stomach; in one capillary or punctiform ecchymoses of the heart and lungs, in one of the scalp, and in one of the kidneys.

I have adduced these results of my own observation, as they bear out those advanced by Orfila, Remer, and Caspar, in opposition to the views promulgated previous to their time as to the special appearances characteristic of death by hanging I need not insist, in opposition to statements to that effect received and iterated in our earlier writers on this subject, on the not unfrequent absence in the dead body of the greater number of such appearances It is of more consequence to direct your attention to the circumstance that these special appearances would admit of being imitated in the body suspended after death from other causes Frequent and characteristic, for instance, as are the appearances on the neck after death by suspension, too much value should not be placed on their presence as indicative of death in this way. The groove or furrow on the neck, it should be known, being a mere physical effect of the suspension, would be produced by the suspension of the body as readily after as before death, and most of the characters I have assigned to it thus imitated, more or less successfully—facts clearly brought out in the experimental trials undertaken by Orfila and Caspar with the express object of determining this very point. As the result of these experiments, Caspar concludes that the mark of the cord in hanging is a purely cadaveric phenomenon, and that any ligature with which a body may be suspended or strangled, not only with a few hours, but even days after death, especially if the body forcibly pulled downwards, may produce a mark precisely similar to that which is observed in most of those hanged while alive.

The only exceptions which can be safely admitted to such negative conclusions from the appearances about the neck are those instances in which the effects of the drop from a considerable height would leave the severer injuries I have noticed (fractures or dislocations of vertebræ, etc.), co-existing with evident traces of vital reaction. Such injuries as these would, of course, be reliable indications of the suspension having taken place during life, though the rarity of their occurrence would not authorise the opposite conclusion where no traces of them were discovered

Bremme, while he admits the accuracy of Neyding's description of the appearances in the skin at the bottom of the groove when met with, does not with him consider that their presence or absence would suffice to distinguish betwixt suspension before and after death. Bremme (1) did not meet with them at all in his examinations when the death had been instantaneous, and when the cord had been removed immediately after death. (2) He met with them when the death had been instantaneous, and the cord had been left around the neck for a considerable time And (3) when the death had not been instantaneous, the application of the ligature at a subsequent period gave rise to them

Some weight would attach to ecchymoses of the bottom of the groove and in its vicinity, as noticed in two of my cases, but for the circumstance that suspension of the body during life or immediately after death might equally give rise to them, to some extent at least.

We are thus brought to the conclusion that the inspection of the body after death does not furnish any positive proof in the great majority of instances, of the suspension having taken place during life

Were the appearances I have passed under review such as could only happen in death by suspension, and were all, or the greater number of them, invariably to be met with after death in this form, the determination of the character of the fatal issue would be a comparatively easy problem. We have seen, however, that this is not the case in the mass of instances of death by hanging. While the general appearances encountered in the cavities of the body point to one or other of two of the modes of death generally, or to both of these combined, not only do the signs in question, just passed in review, vary in different cases, but many of them may be absent altogether, while several of them, though vital appearances as usually encountered in the hanged, may be imitated by similar appearances producible on the body after death from other causes.

You will, then, perceive that the evidence of death by hanging, derivable from the examination of the body, in some instances, may not be found to amount to more than a mere probability Such a probability, however, may admit of being strengthened by the examiner finding the concurrence of several, if not the whole, of the usual signs in the same case The probability would approach, if it did not reach, to certainty, where such of the few signs as are of a purely vital character were encountered in the body, along with the indications of one or other of the forms of sudden death into which the suspension of the body is known to resolve itself; and where, in addition, none of those morbid appearances which could account for death in any other way were discoverable by the inspector I shall only add here that, by combining, with circumstances such as these last, the moral proof of which the medical examiner is sometimes in a condition to avail himself (as we shall see by and by), the highest certainty may be readily arrived at on the point in question

This brings us, in the next place, to the third of the inquiries opening up to the medical jurist in the investigation of cases of death by hanging, namely—

3. The question, closely allied to that last discussed, the hanging, supposing it proved, had been the result of suicide, or of homicide?

The decision of this question will depend almost wholly, in most instances, on circumstantial evidence The circumstances, however, will not unfrequently be such as will come properly within the cognisance of the medical jurist, and not a few of them will be of a character of which he alone can be the best able to appreciate the value and applicability

Little attention has been paid by medical writers to the possible occurrence of accidental hanging. It should be known, however, that instances of this kind are on record I have already had occasion to refer to one case, given on the authority of Lord Bacon; another is furnished by Dr. Gordon Smith, a third by Dr. Taylor, and Mr. Watson alludes to it as having often been the result of experiments amongst boys and others, though without adducing any other instance than the one recorded by Dr Smith. The discrimination of accidental from suicidal or homicidal hanging must rest in every case on circumstantial evidence

The point of greatest importance for the decision of the medical examiner, will be to determine whether the hanging has been the result of suicide or of homicide, in other words, whether death by hanging has been the act of the person himself, or that of some other. The presumption in every case will be that the hanging has been the act of the person himself; and it will require strong grounds to justify the opinion that murder has been committed in this way. In fact, nothing is more rare than the occurrence, in practice, of homicidal hanging. We must, however, admit that an individual may have been murdered by hanging; and the circumstances which will justify the medical jurist in making this admission are the following:—first, where the person hanged is feeble, and the murderer is a strong, healthy man; secondly, where the person hanged, although usually strong and vigorous, was at the time in a state of intoxication, stupefied by narcotics, asleep, or exhausted by his attempts to defend himself; and, thirdly, murder may be committed by hanging when many are combined against the individual. The possibility of one person hanging another during sleep is shown by a case which was tried at Edinburgh in 1827, where a woman tied a ligature round the neck of her husband while he was asleep, and then pulled him up. With these exceptions, then, the practitioner will be correct in deciding, in a suspected case, in favour of the presumption of suicide, when no marks of violence are present to indicate that a severe struggle has taken place before death, or that severe injuries have been inflicted on the person. For, unless the person had laboured under intoxication or great bodily weakness, at the time, it is not to be expected that he would have resigned himself to his fate, and allowed himself to be murdered without offering the strongest resistance.

The presence of marks of violence, then, on the body of a person hanged is important, and their situation, extent, and direction should be accurately studied, determining whether they are such as could only have been produced during life, and also the probability of their being accidental or not. It should be borne in mind that a suicide might have inflicted some injuries on himself with the view of thus taking his own life, and, not succeeding in these attempts, might have finally had recourse to hanging. A case in point occurred in Aberdeen some years ago. A weaver in Gordon Street cut his throat with a razor, and made a large wound, the blood from which filled a chamber-pot in his room. After this he went into an outhouse and suspended himself.

A case precisely similar is recorded by Dr. Taylor. It should also be kept in view that marks of violence on the body of a hanged person may have been the result of accident, as by the party having thrown himself off articles of furniture, by striking against bodies in his vicinity during the last convulsive struggle, or from the fall of the body by the breaking of the rope.

A considerable degree of importance has been attached by several medical writers to the situation, degree of obliquity, and number of turns of the cord around the neck, as diagnostic of the mode of death by hanging. Thus it has been said that if the mark be circular, and placed at the lower part of the neck, it is an unequivocal proof of murder. Others, who have not gone the same length, have yet stated that it affords strong presumption of that crime when the ligature is found at the lower part of the neck, and when its position is circular and not oblique. But it is absurd to suppose that this want of obliquity in the impression of the cord can afford any evidence in favour of the act having been homicidal. Its course will depend, in a greater degree, upon the fact of the body having been supported or not, for it is the weight of the body which causes the obliquity. It will also depend on the manner in which the cord is adjusted. Orfila records one case in point, and I shall have an opportunity of adducing two other instances when I come to death by strangulation, where this point will be further examined.

Equally ill founded is the assertion that the existence of two impressions on the neck—the one circular, the other oblique—affords positive proof of homicide. One of the first of such cases is reported by Esquirol, that of a female lunatic, who committed suicide by hanging herself, and on whose neck two impressions were seen—the one circular, the other oblique. These appear to have arisen from the circumstance of the cord having been twice passed round the neck, and the body being at the same time partially supported.

The presumption is in favour of homicide when the injuries produced by the cord are considerable, such as severe contusions, laceration of muscles, crushing of the larynx or trachea, and fracture of the vertebræ, provided the body is not corpulent and the fall has not been great. In ninety-nine out of every hundred cases of suicidal suspension no considerable alteration of the tissues is observed. This is accounted for by the fact that life is speedily extinguished in these cases, and that a very slight weight attached to the ligature suffices to bring on speedy insensibility. Thus, in a person whose body I had an opportunity of examining, a few years ago, it was discovered that his toes rested on the ground after death, and that the nail by which he had suspended himself was so loosely fixed in the wall that a very small additional weight would have loosened it; indeed, it could not have borne the whole weight of his body.

In another case, which occurred in the Aberdeen gaol, the person had attached his neckcloth to the bars of the window, and when found dead his knees were within an inch or two of the ground, and his toes touching the floor. He had rested his knees, while fixing the ligature, on a stool, which he had pushed away when all was prepared; and so little struggle had followed that a Bible was found still between his knees, as it had been placed there by him before death.

In a third case, in Marischal Street, Aberdeen, a young woman who had been in a desponding state for some days was found dead in bed one morning, sitting in a reclining posture with a ligature attached to the top frame of the bed. All that had been required to effect her purpose of suicide had been to lean back as the cord was fixed. Two young girls who were in bed with her had not been awakened by the transaction, so quietly must it have been effected.

Excepting the impression of the ligature—slight in the first case,—no marks of injury of the neck existed in the above cases. It should not be forgotten, however, that the same absence of the prominent signs of hanging may be wanting in homicidal cases; as when the person has been hanged in a state of intoxication or stupefaction, or when from feebleness he has been unable to make resistance, or to struggle against his assailants.

In all doubtful cases the examiner should not lose sight of moral and circumstantial evidence. He should ascertain whether the individual had been previously disposed to commit suicide or not; he should observe whether the doors or windows of the apartment had been secured on the outside or inside; whether the dress of the deceased was at all torn or discomposed, or the hair dishevelled; lastly, whether the rope or ligature corresponded to the impression seen around the neck. These points fall, it is true, more within the province of the officers of justice than that of the practitioner; but the latter is generally the first who is called to see the deceased, and therefore, unless such facts were noticed by him on his visit, they might otherwise often remain altogether unknown.

I conclude this subject with a few remarks on the best method of conducting the medico-legal inspection in death by hanging— Before proceeding to the dissection of the body in cases of this sort, the medical inspector should examine the linen, in male bodies, to discover if any spermatic or other stains be present, which, if found, he should describe in detail.

If the ligature has been previously removed it should be asked for, described, and compared with the impression on the neck, to see if it corresponds or otherwise. If the cord has been allowed to remain around the neck, its position should be accurately studied before it is disturbed. Attention should be then turned to the appearance of the face, whether expressive of suffering or otherwise, whether congested or pale, whether swollen or not; to the mouth, whether there be foam about the lips, or this be wanting; to the tongue, whether it projects beyond the teeth, or be drawn back in the mouth; if projecting, whether it has or has not escaped injury from the teeth; its colour, whether natural or injected: and, lastly, to the state of the eyes, whether natural, staring, or projecting. The neck should next be accurately examined, with a view to the appearances already described, such as the groove formed by the ligature, the colour of the borders of the groove, the state of the integuments at the bottom of the furrow, the parchment-like appearance, if present, as also any marks of excoriations or ecchymoses, whether produced by the ligature or by previous manual attempts at strangulation. The depth and extent of the groove should also be noted, as well as its direction on the neck; whether double or single; and any impression which may have been left by the knot. It should also be ascertained if the head is firm on the neck, or is unusually movable on it. The hands should be inspected, to learn the position of the fingers; and the palms, in case of any impression being left on them by the nails. The penis should be compressed, to force out any spermatic fluid which may have existed at the extremity of the urethra.

In proceeding to the dissection, the chief consideration ought to be directed to the examination of the neck. For this purpose two circular incisions should be made, one an inch above, and the other at the same distance below, the groove. These should be connected by a third vertical one at the back of the neck, dissecting away the skin from behind forwards. In this way the silvery or dry yellow line in the connective tissue will come into view, as well as any coagula which may exist in that tissue, or in the thickness of the skin. The cellular substance being then carefully removed the muscles should be exposed one by one, observing if they exhibit the mark of the ligature, or any rent, or clot in their interior. By dividing the superficial muscles at their origin, and dissecting them off from below upwards, the carotid artery may be brought into view as well as the superficial nerves of the neck, and any injury inflicted on these last will be easily perceived, as also any ecchymoses on the outside of the carotid arteries at the point corresponding with the groove, or any rupture of their inner or middle coats at the same point. The larynx, trachea, and os hyoides should next be examined, to ascertain if these have suffered compression, displacement, or fracture. The examiner should look into the interior of the pharynx, larynx, and trachea, to search for any trace of frothy or bloody mucus which may be discoverable there. The points of importance after these are the distribution of the blood in the heart's cavities and the large vessels; the state of the lungs, stomach, liver, and spleen, as to vascular fulness or the reverse; and the presence or absence of food and drink in the stomach. He should examine the vessels of the head, and the state of vascularity of the brain. Lastly, he should never neglect the careful dissection of the back of the neck, noting if the muscles are entire, if there be effusion of blood amongst the muscles, ligaments or bones, if there be any trace of injury to the ligaments of the vertebræ, fractures of their laminæ or processes, if the spinal cord has suffered, or if blood has been effused outside or inside its theca.

LECTURE XXXVIII.

DEATH BY STRANGULATION.

CAUSE OF DEATH. MORBID APPEARANCES.—Local Appearances about the Neck—Internal Appearances—Contrasted with Death by Suspension.—WHETHER THE RESULT OF ACCIDENT, SUICIDE, OR HOMICIDE.

DEATH by strangulation has so much in common with death by hanging, that some writers have treated the subjects in connection. The points of difference, however, betwixt the two are sufficiently obvious to require their separate consideration. In death by hanging, for instance, we have compression of the neck by a ligature of some sort, and the added traction on it by the weight of the body. In strangulation, on the other hand, while the latter element is wanting, the compression on the neck (which is the sole agency employed) may be effected by a ligature—mediate strangulation, so-called,—or by the hand in the so-termed immediate or manual strangulation. Unlike hanging where the mixed form of death is encountered, in strangulation the fatal event is dependent on asphyxia alone. As hanging is most frequently the result of suicide, while strangulation is generally homicidal, it will be understood that the latter is oftener complicated with traces of other injuries than those which have caused death.

Once more: From the relative facility of effecting the two modes of death being different in each, the morbid appearances encountered after strangulation are found—as was to have been anticipated—as a general rule to be of a more marked kind than those usually seen after death by hanging.

All this, however, will come out more clearly as we proceed to consider, as I now propose to do, (1) the cause of death in strangulation, (2) the morbid appearances left by it on the dead body, and (3) the question of its accidental, suicidal, or homicidal origin.

1. Of the cause of death I have little to say, having already stated that this always resolves itself into asphyxia. When the constriction, however employed, is such as perfectly to stop the

ingress of air to the lungs, insensibility and death are believed to follow almost instantly. In circumstances the reverse of this, the asphyxia will be longer in coming on.

2. The morbid appearances after death by strangulation will be those common to this and other forms of asphyxia, with, in addition, those indicative of the special agency which has been employed in effecting it. The former of these have been sufficiently discussed in previous lectures; the latter alone will demand our attention here.

The local or special appearances are liable to considerable variation, according to circumstances. Homicidal strangulation, for instance, is oftenest attempted and successfully accomplished in children, in aged or feeble persons, or in parties previously rendered insensible by blows about the head, or stupefied by intoxication or narcotics. Here, as the compression of the neck would be easily effected, the traces of such compression may neither be very marked nor complicated with other injuries about the neck. On the other hand, while such forcible strangulation has been but rarely found to succeed in young and vigorous persons with all their wits about them, when successfully carried out, it has been known to leave very marked injuries on the neck and other parts of the person. Hence, while in one of these sets of cases the appearances will be mostly those on the neck and organs of respiration, and these not very strongly marked, in the other they will coincide with others on different parts of the body, especially on the head and face, indicating that considerable violence has been employed. Thus, while the head, face, and body generally may be altogether or almost natural, we may have marks of blows or abrasions on the head and face, particularly about the mouth and chin, and, though less constantly, on the trunk and limbs, tumefaction and lividity of the face, the tongue protruded and fixed betwixt the clenched jaws; frothy bloody fluid issuing from the nostrils; numerous minute ecchymosed spots on the conjunctivæ, face, front of the neck, and upper part of the chest. Considerable stress is laid by Tardieu on these punctated effusions, which, though encountered in suffocation from compression of the walls of the chest and abdomen, after prolonged and laborious labours, and violent convulsive attacks, he positively asserts are most frequent, best marked, and most characteristic in death by strangulation

The local appearances met with about the neck are also found to differ according to the agency employed in the strangulation,

amount of the resistance which has been employed. Where the agent has been the ligature, the grooves left by it will most frequently be seen to cross the neck in an almost regularly horizontal direction; they are usually shallow, varying in breadth, either single, double, or multiple, as the ligature has made one or more turns around the neck; and embrace the whole or only a part of its circumference. The bottom of the groove is often pale and well defined, contrasting with the lividity of the surrounding parts. The absence here of the parchment-like state of the skin, the shallowness of the groove, and the lack of the indications of firm compression of the soft parts so usual in hanging, are explained by Tardieu as being due to the circumstance of the ligature, however strongly constricted, being but momentarily applied and speedily relaxed in strangulation, and there not being, as in hanging, the added weight of the body continued after death. In contrast with the less deep and distinct impress of the ligature over the neck in strangulation than in hanging, Tardieu has found ecchymoses more constant in the former than in the latter case, those ecchymoses corresponding with the points where the pressure had been greatest, being well marked, of greater or less, but usually of considerable depth, and of irregular form, but mostly in the direction of the groove

In manual strangulation, again, the external appearances about the neck will differ with the character of the agency employed in effecting it, and are to be looked for on the sides of the larynx, under the lower jaw, and at the lower parts of the neck. The appearances will usually be such as point pretty distinctly to the previous application to the front of the throat of the thumb and one or more fingers, leaving ecchymosed patches corresponding to the points of the fingers, and not unfrequently linear or curvilinear scratches or abrasions caused by the nails of the assailant.

In proceeding to the examination of the deeper-seated parts of the neck, whether in cases of mediate or immediate strangulation, traces of injuries are frequently encountered of a more marked sort and serious character than are usual in hanging, or which might be suspected from the appearances externally. Thus, even where no ecchymoses are visible on the surface, extravasations of blood have frequently been encountered, not only in the subcutaneous areolar tissue, but in the interior of the muscles above and below the hyoid bone, and on the outer surface of the larynx and trachea; and where the strangulation had been manual, extravasated blood has been met with under the lower jaw, over the sternum, and even in the pectoral muscles. These effusions of blood have been found isolated and circumscribed, and corresponding in size with the impressions of the fingers on the surface; at other times diffused, from infiltration of blood through the loose areolar tissue of the neck. The larynx and trachea usually escape serious injury in strangulation, though injuries of these have been met with. A highly congested state of the lining membrane of the trachea is a frequent appearance, and still more so a mucous froth in this canal, with minute air-bubbles, white or sanguinolent, sometimes extending into the bronchial tubes, occasionally replaced by a layer of blood coating the larynx.

The vascular condition of the lungs in this mode of death is not always the same, these viscera being sometimes found congested, sometimes natural. Unless there has been a combination of smothering and strangulation, as is sometimes the case, capillary ecchymoses have not been observed on the surface of the lungs. A characteristic condition of the surface of the lungs in strangulation—according to Tardieu—is the rupture of their superficial air-cells, singly or in groups, giving to the organs, on a superficial examination, the appearance of their being interspersed with pseudo-membranous patches, which on a closer inspection are seen to resolve themselves into emphysema, arising from air-bubbles under the pleura. Equally characteristic with this, though not so constant, according to the same authority, are apoplectic kernels (*noyaux*) in the tissue of the lungs, from well defined and distinct infiltrations or extravasations of blood, varying from the size of a threepenny piece (*pièce de vingt centimes*) to that of a crown (*pièce de cinq francs*) The heart may be found empty, or containing blood either fluid or clotted.

I will only add that, as far as my own experience goes, these pathognomonic appearances in the lungs will be found available in many instances of death by pure strangulation, though less available in the mixed cases which occasionally present themselves in practice—a point to which I shall have to return under Death by Suffocation.

The brain and other organs present no characteristic appearances in death by strangulation beyond those met with ordinarily in death from the other forms of asphyxia.

So much for the post-mortem appearances after death from this form of violence. To one of these (the groove on the neck)

return in order to notice its direction, especially as on this distinction betwixt death by hanging and death by strangulation has been made to hinge — a point which, when treating of hanging, I reserved for this place.

In mediate strangulation, as I have said above, the mark of the ligature is usually circular, and situated at the lower part of the neck; while after hanging it has more or less of obliquity, and its position is high up the neck. It should be kept in mind, however, that these distinctions do not always hold good in practice. In hanging, we have seen, the marks of the ligature may be circular, as where it has been drawn tightly all round the neck, or where it has made several turns around it; while in strangulation it may be oblique, as where the ligature has been applied loosely and from behind, or its loose ends twisted and drawn upwards, the party assailed being in the lying posture. Of this last apparently unlikely occurrence I had an illustrative instance in my own practice. A woman convicted of the homicide of her newly-born infant, in the spring of 1855, had passed a ligature twice round its neck, twisted the loose ends at the left side of the neck, pulling them upwards, so as to give a degree of obliquity to the second turn of the cloth, and to leave the mark of the twisted part of it at the angle of the jaw and on the cheek in front of the ear, as in death by hanging. It usually happens in death by hanging that the weight of the body occasions the knot to be drawn upwards to the highest point on the neck; and the looser the ligature, the higher, and the greater is its consequent obliquity. Too much weight is not, however, to be given to this circumstance. The case of the child just mentioned has some bearing on this point, though less direct than the case which follows.

Several years ago a girl in Loch Street, Aberdeen, committed suicide in the following unusual manner. After making a loop in the middle of a sheet, she attached the two ends of it to the two front posts of her bed. Putting her head through the loop, she then pushed her head and bust over the front of the bed on which she was stretched at the time. The weight of the upper half of her body had thus sufficed to produce death by hanging, as she was found some hours after, in this position, quite dead. Here, consequently, the knot in the ligature was nearest to the centre of the body, instead of being, as usual in hanging, nearer the head than the rest of the cord.

There are further reasons which justify some caution in deciding betwixt death by hanging and strangulation, from the obliquity of the cord in the one case, and its circularity in the other. In the first place, instances have been related where a circular mark has been observed in hanging. Of this I met with an instance in 1874. A weaver at Gilcomston, who had formerly been at sea in the merchant service, was found in a privy, suspended by a thick cord to a beam, the ligature circular and the knot on the same level; the cord having been fastened by what is known as the sailor's knot. It is but fair to state, however, that in this instance the nates were close to the ground and the feet resting on it, as in one of the cases referred to under Death by Hanging. Again, a murderer, who had succeeded in strangling a person, might afterwards drag the body along the ground by the free ends of the cord before leaving his victim, and thus communicate a degree of obliquity, precisely the same as if the individual had been hanged. But what is of still more importance to remark is, that it is quite possible to conceive that, in a person who had strangled himself, this obliquity of the cord might be detected, and that, too, where the body had not been at all interfered with after death.

As this position may be disputed by medical jurists, I shall adduce the proof of it, as it is not an imaginary case, but one which has actually happened in my own practice. As the case illustrates another point to be presently considered, I shall only mention here that an old man whose body was found a few summers ago in the woods at Hazlehead, near Aberdeen, had chosen this mode of committing suicide. In this case his neckcloth was wound more than once around the neck, and a walking-stick had been passed through the open loop of the neckcloth, by means of which the compression had been made, in the way carriers usually tighten the ropes in securing a load upon their carts. On first seeing this body in the wood, where it remained in the precise position in which it had been discovered, my impression, from the obliquity of the outer fold of the neckcloth, was that the body must have been dragged along the ground by the stick. On a careful examination, however, another mode of explaining the circumstance presented itself, which undoubtedly was the correct one. The place where the body was found was in the centre of a thick clump of young trees, set close together. The ends of the walking-stick had got so entangled with the trees on each side as to prevent the uncoiling of the turns of the neckcloth in front of the neck. Consequently, had the individual, in his last convulsive struggle, made an effort to change his position, the weight of the body would have drawn the ligature into the oblique position in which it had remained after death. A case of suicidal strangulation is related by Surgeon-General Francis in the *Medical Times and Gazette* for 1876. A lunatic in an Indian gaol had twisted a stout thread round his neck, attaching the ends to his wrists, when by extending his arms to their utmost limits he effected his purpose.

Taken with the cautions and restrictions I have noticed, the indications derivable from the state of the ligature, and its position in regard to circularity and obliquity, are not to be despised, but, on the contrary, may afford us valuable diagnostics for the determination between the probabilities of death by hanging or strangulation, when the appearances in the body point to one or other of these modes of death.

3. The only remaining point connected with death by strangulation is the question whether it has been the result of accident, suicide, or homicide in any given case. The possibility of accidental strangulation has been entirely overlooked by foreign medical jurists. Three such cases are adduced by British authors—one by Smith, one by Taylor, and one by Watson. In Smith's case a young man paralysed in his arms was accustomed to assist himself in his occupation of moving a heavy weight, by a cord attached to it and passed round his neck. One morning he was found dead, with the cord twisted around his neck. It was supposed that in attempting to move the weight, it had slipped behind his back, and produced fatal compression of the trachea. In the other two cases the strap which supported a weight on the back had slipped over the windpipe.

A case which appeared to me to belong to the same category recently occurred in my own practice. An hostler in an inn at Huntly, Aberdeenshire, in the autumn of 1860, was carried to bed very drunk, and left there with his clothes on. It was supposed that afterwards he had got up so far as to lean over the front of his bed to vomit, with his hands pressed on the pit of his stomach, as he was found dead in this posture in the morning, rigidity having in all probability come on at the moment of death. His neckerchief was so tight around his neck, that the constriction thus caused would have sufficed to produce strangulation, from his inability to change his position in the helpless condition he was in at the time. The inspection, by presenting all the appearances which were to have been expected in such circumstances, left no doubt on my mind as to the mode of death.

The possibility of suicidal strangulation has been denied on purely physiological grounds, inapplicable to the cases of mediate strangulation which, though unusual, have been known to be effected by means of ligatures twisted tightly round the neck by the hand or a stick.

From the admitted rarity of such cases it may be allowed me again to refer to that of the old man who was found in the woods at Hazlehead. That his was a case of suicide was proved to the satisfaction of the law authorities who investigated the case, from the moral evidence alone, which in this instance was unusually strong. It may be worth while to advert to the leading points. This man was insane, having laboured for some time under melancholia. He had some time previous to his death attempted to drown himself, and so afraid was his wife that he would take his own life, that she would not trust him to shave himself, or to have access to a knife. When he was first missing she was quite convinced that he had accomplished his purpose, and did not expect to see him again in life. The examination of the body fully bore out these strong suspicions. The trifling articles which the deceased had in his possession when he left home were found in his pockets. The stick with which the ligature was twisted was the one he had left home with. He usually had in his neckcloth a "stiffener," as it is called, made of carpeting. This stiffener was found carefully folded up in his vest pocket, showing that the neckcloth must have been unloosed, the stiffener taken out and placed where it was discovered, the neckcloth again replaced with a knot at its extremities, through which his own stick had been placed,—an attention to minute proprieties, which no assassin would ever have thought of or hazarded These circumstances, added to the fact of his dress not having been deranged, negative, in a complete way, the possibility of strangulation otherwise than by his own hand.

But what is still more to the point is, that the experiments of Fleischmann, detailed under Death by Hanging, show that it is possible, even with the unassisted fingers, so to compress the windpipe as to produce strangulation.

Homicidal strangulation may take either of the two forms respectively characterised as mediate and immediate. The latter of these forms, immediate or manual strangulation, under the appropriate name of garroting, is unfortunately becoming a trade amongst foot-pads in our large cities, with the intention, on their part, not of taking life, but of producing momentary insensibility to allow the party to be robbed. It is sometimes had recourse to with more fatal effect by the ravisher on his victim, and by the murderer to complete his nefarious purposes after having rendered the person insensible by blows about the head. That the garroter's trade is not a more fatal one than we find it to be, is explicable from the circumstance just referred to, that the object is attained by him short of taking life; and by that mentioned at the outset, that the parties attacked by him do not belong to the class of infants or old and enfeebled subjects, but to the young and vigorous, who present greater powers of resistance to the more serious danger threatened. Murder by strangulation, unless in infants, is oftenest practised by means of the ligature.

A case of this kind was tried at Aberdeen in the spring of 1838, in which a man came by his death in a sudden quarrel at a market. The Crown counsel, however, in this instance failed in his proof of death by this precise mode, in consequence of a difference of opinion between the medical witnesses for the Crown and those for the defence, the latter arguing that, the deceased having fallen undermost in the struggle, some injury might have been done to the spine sufficient to account for death—a circumstance which, though not probable, was not impossible. The objection could not be repelled, in consequence of the medical examiners having neglected to inspect the spine. The anterior border of the sterno-mastoid muscle on one side was lacerated, and blood was effused in the vicinity of the vessels of the neck; but the examination of the cavities of the body appeared to have been conducted in a careless manner, as scarcely anything was said of them in the medico-legal report, and at least one post-mortem change was adduced as a proof of violence inflicted during life. The non-medical witnesses deposed that after the fall the panel sat upon the chest of the deceased, with a leg on each side, while with one hand he grasped the neckcloth or breast of the deceased (it did not clearly come out which) for a sufficient length of time to have produced death by strangulation. I was engaged in this case as a witness for the defence, but was not examined in consequence of my opinion inclining rather to the prosecutor than to the panel, though prepared to give a guarded judgment on a point which was weak from the defective character of the medical examination of the body.

There are few occasions more likely to present themselves, on which the medical jurist would have to make up his mind to encounter frivolous objections, than in a case of this kind, if we may judge from what is known of such trials. Thus it has been suggested on the defence that the deceased might have fallen in a state of intoxication, and have become accidentally strangled by a tight cravat, or by any foreign body exerting pressure on the trachea. In one instance, in which there were finger-marks on the neck, it was attempted to be shown that the deceased might have fallen out of bed, and, his hand being found resting on his neck, the marks there might have thus been produced, and he might have been accidentally strangled. In another instance it was argued that a person believed to have been strangled had died of apoplexy from having gone to bed with a handkerchief tied too tightly around the neck. Difficulties of this kind may in general be pretty easily obviated by attention to circumstances—such as the position in which the body is found; its locality, especially in relation to surrounding objects; the state of the clothes; the local appearances on the neck, how caused, and whether before or after death; the state of the apartment, and of the doors and windows, whether these had been shut from within or from without, the previous state of mind of the party, etc. Any appearances of contusions or wounds should be looked for on every part of the surface. The state of the stomach and intestines should be noted, and any foreign body found there, if suspicious, examined chemically. The use to be made of the moral proofs by the medical practitioner must, however, be left to the decision of the law authorities.

LECTURE XXXIX.

DEATH BY SUFFOCATION.

Suffocation from Natural Causes —Suffocation from Accidental Causes. —Suicidal Suffocation —Homicidal Suffocation —Morbid Appearances —External—Internal—Punctiform or Capillary Ecchymoses.

When the breathing is impeded by any cause, which operates independently of external pressure on the trachea, the person is said to perish by suffocation. This definition distinguishes death by suffocation from death by hanging and strangulation. Properly speaking, it does not exclude death by drowning, which is but a form of suffocation—a subject already disposed of, as deserving, from its importance, a special and independent consideration The definition also takes in smothering as a variety of suffocation —i.e., the exclusion of air from the lungs resulting from the mere covering of the mouth and nostrils

Inclusive, then, of smothering, but excluding death by drowning, suffocation, as thus understood, may be either the consequence (1) of natural disease, (2) of accident, (3) of neglect in infants, or (4) of unintentional or intentional violence

1 The diseased states which may terminate life in this way are—tumours about the throat or fauces; the bursting of abscesses of the tonsils; effusion of lymph in the trachea or about the rima glottidis, the accumulation of the bronchial secretion in the bronchitis of infants; acute pleuritic effusion, where both pleuræ are affected, simultaneous œdema of both lungs, the bursting of an aneurism of the aorta into a bronchus; hæmoptysis, when very copious and sudden; and the so-called pulmonary apoplexy In practice I have on inspection been led on several occasions to notice the fact of the immediate cause of death in infants with bronchitis from the great and rapid accumulation of mucus in the air-passages. Pulmonary œdema has been recognised amongst pathologists as the immediate precursor of death in both acute and chronic diseases of the heart and lungs, by obstructing the flow of blood through large portions of the latter In 1866 I

took occasion to direct attention to the frequency of pulmonary apoplexy as an immediate and direct cause of sudden death in various diseased states of the body in persons advanced in life.

2. This form of sudden death may be purely the result of accident, such as pressure on the chest, sufficiently powerful to prevent the expansion of the lungs, or the inhalation of those of the gases which, though not positively deleterious to the system, deprive the lungs of oxygen. Intoxicated persons not unfrequently perish by suffocation, either from getting into a position which obstructs the free entrance of air into the lungs, or from vomited matters entering the larynx and trachea in sufficient quantity suddenly to interrupt the breathing. I have had opportunities of examining cases of sudden death in both of these ways, in which suspicions of foul play had been entertained. One of these was the woman Paton, previously noticed under "Death" as a case of cadaveric spasm. Instances of accidental suffocation not unfrequently present themselves, from large morsels of solid food getting impacted in the upper part of the œsophagus, and compressing the larynx from behind, or from articles of food either closing the rima glottidis, or getting into the larynx or trachea in the act of being swallowed, or of being rejected by vomiting. Drunkards occasionally perish in this way by smothering in their own vomit. Surgeons are aware of the necessity for administering chloroform on an empty stomach, from the risk to their patients of the contents of the stomach getting into the trachea when vomiting.

In the case of persons who have been rescued from water before life was extinct, death may take place from suffocation in from a few hours to one or two days, the water which had penetrated into the air-cells of the lungs remaining unabsorbed, and interfering with the respiration. Of this I have met with two instances in practice—one the wife of a clergyman, the other a policeman.

We frequently read in the newspapers of persons suffocated in pits, graves, sandbanks, and drains, from the sudden falling in or over them of the soil. I have met with several such cases. A gravedigger at Kintore lost his life in this way at the bottom of a grave a few years ago.

3. Cases of suffocation, as already noticed under "Infanticide," are attributed in infants to carelessness or neglect on the part of the mothers or attendants, in allowing the children at birth to remain under the bedclothes, where there is no access to air, or

leaving a pillow, a bolster, or bedclothes over the child's face. This form of suffocation is what, with one or two others afterwards to be noticed, ought properly to be considered as death by smothering—using the term in its restricted sense as a sub-species of suffocation. As formerly stated, however, under "Infanticide," it is doubtful whether a vigorous child could perish in this way, without putting forth instinctive efforts to change its position, and thus obtaining access to the air

4. Suffocation by violence, unintentional, or intentional, cannot always in practice be readily distinguished from instances of suffocation from accident or misadventure. Thus, overwrapping, whereby an infant has perished, may have been owing to negligence on the side of its attendant, or to design on her part. Again, a mother or nurse, during a heavy or disturbed sleep, may destroy the child by literally overlaying it, and thus compressing its chest, when it may be found difficult or impossible to distinguish betwixt the effects of accident and intentional violence.

Of violent, though accidental and unintentional, suffocation, we have instances in adults from overcrowding in public places, as in theatres, or from sudden alarms of fire in buildings. In this way no fewer than twenty-three persons lost their lives in Paris in 1837, death being occasioned by pressure on the chest. The parties—eleven men and twelve women—died standing, or while being borne along in a crowd. A similar but much more widespread calamity occurred in Paris in 1866, the history of which has been given by Tardieu. The number of victims on this occasion amounted to about forty. In the bodies of those who were inspected, though, as in the previous case, various injuries were detected, the immediate cause of death was traced to suffocation, either at the moment of the pressure of a crowd at the Champ de Mars, or shortly after.

Intentional violence or homicidal suffocation is usually encountered in infants and children. In the majority of cases of infanticide, indeed, suffocation is believed to be the means resorted to for destroying the infant. Tardieu has stated that of 132 judicial inspections of new-born infants which he has been called to undertake, he has satisfied himself that seventy-two had been destroyed by suffocation.

While it is evident that nothing is more easy than to suffocate an infant, to effect this in the case of an adult, it must be equally evident, would, under ordinary circumstances, be a matter of great difficulty. A moderate degree of resistance would suffice to baffle the assailant, unless he had the assistance of others. This, at least, has been the case in two instances of this sort which have come under my notice. An adult, however, in a state of stupefaction, from drink or narcotics, might readily be murdered in this way. The victims of the notorious Burke were destroyed while in a state of intoxication. The evidence adduced in these cases was to the effect that the mouth and nostrils of the parties were closed by one hand of the assailant, the lower jaw fixed by the other, and the expansion of the chest prevented by the weight of his body lying on it. The mode of death, however, was not completely elicited on the trial; and doubts have arisen on this point which we have not the means of clearing up satisfactorily.

An interesting case was tried at Lincoln in 1843, in which a housebreaker, to enable him to rob a house, tied the hands and feet of its inmates—two old women about seventy,—and left them in bed, with the bedclothes tucked up over their heads. Next day one of the women was found suffocated, and the other in an exhausted state, but still alive.

Suffocation, in rare instances, has been resorted to as a mode of committing suicide. Though the possibility of it has been doubted, more than one author has stated that the negroes in the West Indies and in Brazil have been known to choke themselves by doubling back the tongue and swallowing it down into the fauces. Dr. Wagner has stated that a criminal in Austria was found dead in his dungeon, having thrust a shawl into the back part of his mouth and throat. But perhaps the most unique case of suicidal suffocation, or rather smothering, is one which appeared in Henke's *Zeitschrift*. A servant girl had shut herself up in her trunk during the night, and was found dead in the morning, having been suffocated for want of fresh air.

The morbid appearances in this mode of death may or may not be very obvious or characteristic. As a rule, since these cases resolve themselves into death by asphyxia, the indications of this form of sudden death as formerly laid down (Lecture XXIV.) may be looked for in the general case, though these are not so invariable in their occurrence, nor so well marked or obvious in every instance, as might have been expected. Thus, congestion of the lungs, right heart, and brain have been wanting, or but slightly marked, in undoubted cases of suffocation; while Caspar has found the kidneys more strongly congested than the liver, spleen, and other organs.

DEATH BY SUFFOCATION. 551

The previous existence of such diseases as would account for death in this form of asphyxia could scarcely be overlooked by a careful observer, who, with this in view, has attentively examined the state of the throat, larynx, trachea, bronchi, and lungs. Equally obvious would be the presence of foreign bodies lodged in the nostrils, mouth, throat, or gullet, or vomited matters in the trachea or bronchi.

In the case of children buried alive in dunghills, or amongst ashes, bran, or feathers, the foreign substance in which they had been immersed has been found occasionally in the nostrils, mouth, throat, or air-passages, and even in the stomach. Devergie has published a case where the head and face of an adult were forcibly held down into a corn-heap till life was extinct, and in which the grain was found in the back of the mouth, in the pharynx, trachea, œsophagus, stomach, and duodenum.

Some years ago in Aberdeen the life of a boy of eight years was only saved by immediate recourse being had to tracheotomy to obviate threatened suffocation. A mason's labourer had seized the boy and held his face down into a heap of unslaked lime, which had been drawn into the air-passages.

At the inspection of five adults who perished in the smoke of a burning building lined with wood, at Footdee, Aberdeen, in December 1840, and in a subsequent case of the same sort in an old woman, I found the trachea and bronchi lined with a coating of soot.

When death has been caused by mediate occlusion of the mouth and nostrils, unnatural flattening of the nose or lips, or both, will be occasionally found sufficiently well marked. When the throat has been grasped by the assailant's hands to compress the windpipe, scratches, abrasions, or even ecchymoses, may be encountered on the front or sides of the neck. Where, again, suffocation has been brought on by those means which act by compressing the chest and hindering its expansion, marks of such pressure are scarcely to be expected in children, or even in adults, unless where unnecessary violence has been used. None such have been found in animals purposely destroyed in this way.

Certain appearances which the blood presents after suffocation from breathing carbonic acid and carbonic oxide belong to the subject of poisoning by these gases. The most striking of these is the bright-red hue of the blood in cases of poisoning with the carbonic oxide, which persists in the blood kept for a considerable length of time. In one instance of this sort at Aberdeen in 1875 the characteristic hue of this fluid was found to be retained without change three months after the inspection. In cases of death in this way, congestion and minute ecchymoses on the conjunctivæ, and on the front of the face and neck, as also reddening of the interior of the trachea, mucus tinged with blood in the air-passages, and rupture of air-vesicles on the surface of the lungs, are insisted on by Tardieu as characteristic appearances, though none of these are constant or even very frequent.

But a still higher value is claimed by this authority for the so-called punctiform or capillary ecchymoses met with most abundantly on the surfaces of the lungs and thymus gland, less frequently on the inner surface of the scalp and exterior of the pericranium, and occasionally, but still more rarely, on other surfaces. The number of these ecchymoses is found to vary, and they are either few and scattered, or numerous and in clusters; they have a distinctly rounded form and well-defined margin; their size, which is nearly uniform in the same subject, rarely, if ever, exceeds the breadth of a large pin-head;—characters which will usually serve to distinguish the punctiform ecchymoses from the petechiæ met with on the heart and lungs after purpura (*vide* "Drowning"), eruptive and low fevers, and cholera. They also serve to differentiate them from the effusions of blood encountered under the scalp and pericranium in the new-born infant after tedious and difficult labours; the effusions in these cases not having the same uniformity of size and shape, and varying in breadth in the same case, from the diameter of a pea to that of a boy's marble, while they are usually accompanied by redness of the cranial bones, and congestion within the head (*vide* Fig. V. opposite page 256, and Fig. XII.)

Of the frequency and marked character of the punctiform ecchymoses in death by suffocation in infants, as far as the thoracic organs are concerned, there is no room for doubt. They had not escaped the notice of Bernt so early as 1827; they were specially insisted on by Hecker in 1853; Caspar in his *Gerichtliche Leichenöffnungen*, and in his *Forensic Medicine*, has adduced twelve illustrative cases; and Simon in Caspar's *Vierteljahrsschrift* six others; while Maschka and Bohr have largely supplemented Tardieu's cases. I have met with them in eighty-two inspections; twenty-two of which were infants at birth, and forty-five children of from five days to sixteen months. The results of fifty-nine of these inspections were tabulated in 1868 in the *British Medical Journal* of that year.

Simon, Maschka, and Bohr, however, deny the exclusive ap-

Pl XII

PUNCTIFORM ECCHYMOSIS, OF HEART, LUNGS, & THYMUS GLAND.
IN DEATH BY SMOTHERING

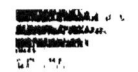

plicability of this test to instances of pure smothering. Simon, in especial, has constantly contended that these punctiform ecchymoses, though almost invariably to be met with in this form of infantile asphyxia, have also been encountered in some instances in other forms of death by apnœa; such as hanging and drowning, of which he has brought forward examples. This is borne out by Skrzeczka, in 1867, who tells us that while he found these appearances in the chest in children at birth or under one year, he met with them also in seven adults who had died from other forms of asphyxia—i.e, in the ratios respectively of 76 6 per cent of the children to 24·3 per cent of the adults.

With this my own experience agrees. Prior to September 1868 I had encountered these ecchymoses in two cases of drowning, one of hanging, one of scarlatina, one of heart disease, one of apoplexy, four of pneumonia, one of pulmonary apoplexy, and two of pulmonary œdema.

Admitting the force of these statements, therefore, I cannot follow the dictum of Tardieu, that the presence of these ecchymoses is an undoubted proof of this form of asphyxia exclusively. Nor can I limit myself to the conclusion argued for by this author, that when found they necessarily imply that the smothering must have occurred in the new-born infant subsequent to its birth.

Various researches on this subject have sufficed to settle beyond doubt that these ecchymoses are encountered in the bodies of stillborn infants, and even in unborn fœtuses where the mothers had perished before the commencement of labour. Instances of such appearances in stillborn infants were met with by Caspar, Schwartz, Elsasser, Maschka, Hecker, and Hoogeweg; while Caspar refers to two instances of this in the unborn fœtus—one in the uterus of a woman who hanged herself in the eighth month of her pregnancy, the other in the uterus of a woman who perished by apoplexy when seven months pregnant. The ecchymoses were found by me in the lungs of a stillborn child; in the lungs of an infant whose chest was felt to expand in utero during an attempt to turn it when delivery could not otherwise be effected, on account of obstruction of the pelvis by a tumour; and in the fœtus in the uterus of a woman, last November (1876), who died from the bursting of an aneurism of the ascending aorta.

It is to be borne in mind, however, that in instances of this sort, the mode of death, where there is no indication of drowning resolves itself into suffocation. In the unborn fœtus, as already explained under "Drowning," the arrest of the fœtal circulation has been shown to induce attempts at inspiration, and the subsequent death of the infant by asphyxia, either by drowning, where the liquor amnii is drawn into the lungs, or by suffocation (properly so called), where the waters had been previously discharged, or where the membranes have been interposed between them and the child's mouth. This circumstance, however, as observed by Caspar, necessitates the greatest care in determining doubtful cases of death by suffocation in new-born infants, though he is of opinion that a careful examination of the body will always afford data sufficient to prevent a case of post-partum suffocation from being confounded with one of suffocation in utero.

In justice to Tardieu, I think it further but fair to state that, as far as my own experience goes, a distinction may be drawn betwixt the ecchymoses met with in infants in these cases, and those in adults perishing from other forms of asphyxia. In the first place, in the latter the ecchymoses were only encountered in one instance on the thymus gland; while in the former class of cases they are usually encountered in greatest abundance on this gland. Secondly, in the cases in which the persons had perished from drowning, hanging, disease, or violence, the ecchymoses were single and scattered, not in numbers and clustered, as in those children whose bodies presented no obvious traces of disease or injury to account otherwise for the death, than by the presumption of suffocation, or rather smothering. Thirdly, while in only one of these infants were the ecchymoses in a marked form wanting in the lungs, in the twenty-two other cases in which they were found in these organs, the spots were few in number and discrete, not in clusters as in the children's cases.

From all this, I am disposed to give a higher value than most of my contemporaries to the punctiform ecchymoses as an indication, which, when present and well marked, if not an infallible one, may be looked on with some confidence, as a strong indication in children of death by smothering, where no other cause of death is obvious or presumable.

LECTURE XL.

DEATH FROM COLD, HEAT, LIGHTNING, AND STARVATION.

Death from Cold—Post-mortem Appearances.—Death by Heat—Cause of—Spontaneous Human Combustion.—Death by Lightning—Cause of—Post-mortem Appearances.—Death from Starvation—Cause of—Post-mortem Appearances

THERE are some subjects which fall to be considered before concluding this division of my course of medical jurisprudence, which have a less direct bearing on the subject than those which have preceded, and whose place amongst the causes of sudden death has not yet been determined with so much precision and unanimity as the others which we have considered. I refer to deaths from cold, heat, lightning, and starvation, to the consideration of which I shall now proceed.

Death by Cold

In the northern part of Europe, deaths from cold are of frequent occurrence, where, as mostly happens, the exposure is combined with intemperance or enfeebled constitution. In temperate climates, death from this cause is more rarely met with; though few winters pass in which there have been snowstorms of unusual severity or continuance without some such cases being encountered.

As far back as the year 1837 my attention was specially called to the subject, from having to investigate an instance of this sort; while again, in 1855, I had occasion to examine the bodies of three individuals who perished in the heavy snowstorm of that inclement winter.

Even at the latter of these dates little or nothing was known of the fatal effects of cold on the human body beyond theoretical views on the subject. In fact, all that was known to the profession, from actual observation of the appearances after death, may be summed up in the following sentence.

Quelmalz found the large veins and arteries filled with polypous concretions; Cappel, the blood and fluids accumulated chiefly in the pectoral and abdominal viscera; Kellie, in two published cases, injection of the intestinal tube; and each of these writers, in addition, more or less cerebral congestion. It does not appear that either Larrey or Beaupré had inspected any of the bodies of the persons who perished in the retreat of the French from Moscow in 1812.

This led me to lay before the profession, in the *British and Foreign Medico-Chirurgical Review* in 1855, and subsequently in Horn's *Zeitschrift* in 1864, the result of my inspection of thirteen cases of this form of death; and to these I have now to add my observations in three more cases, making sixteen in all—ten adults and six children.

In my inspections of the adults, several points of agreement were met with, of so peculiar a kind as to lead me to conclude that, when these were all encountered in the same case, and in the absence of any other obvious cause of death, they pointed, if not with absolute certainty, yet with high probability, to the death having been caused by cold.

These peculiar appearances in adults were:—

(1) An arterial hue of the blood generally, except when viewed in mass within the heart; the presence of this coloration not having been noted in two instances.

(2) An unusual accumulation of blood,—as in Quelmalz and Cappel's cases,—on both sides of the heart, and in the larger blood-vessels of the chest, arterial and venous.

(3.) Pallor of the general surface of the body, and anæmia of the viscera most largely supplied with blood. The only exceptions to this were moderate congestion of the brain in three of the cases, and of the liver in seven of them.

(4) Irregular and diffused dusky-red patches on limited portions of the exterior of the bodies, encountered in non-dependent parts; these patches contrasting forcibly with the pallor of the skin and general surface.

The above appearances were not, however, so universally met with in the children as in the adults. The arterial hue of the blood was absent in one; the anæmia of the larger viscera, in all but one instance; the pallor of the surface was present, nevertheless, in all but one of the children, and the dusky-red patches on the whole of them.

In 1860 there appeared an article in Henke's *Zeitschrift*, by Blosfeld of Kasan, bearing largely on death by cold, in which he that, independently of thirty-eight inspections in which intoxication played the principal part, he examined nine instances of death purely from exposure to cold. In these he encountered the arterial hue of the blood in the blood-vessels and organs external to the heart; the excessive accumulation of the blood on both sides of the heart; and he incidentally mentions the pallor of the surface, except at the parts where dusky-red patches were met with.

In the same journal we find a notice of some researches by Krajewsky on the subject, by which it appears that he had inspected five bodies after death by cold. The first and second of the appearances noted above do not seem to have been encountered by Krajewsky. The third and fourth he notices, though he attributes the last to the effect of the removal of the corpse to a warm temperature after its discovery.

In 1864, Dieberg published in Caspar's *Vierteljahrsschrift* ten cases illustrative of death by cold, though in only three of these has he condescended on details. Some of the parties—the number not stated—by his own admission, had perished rather from intoxication than from exposure to cold. The fourth of the above appearances, termed by this writer frost-erythema, may, he thinks, be caused by the action of cold on the dead body The most important post-mortem sign of death by cold, Dieberg considers to be the second one I have noticed—namely, the excessive congestion, or rather over-distension, of both sides of the heart, and of all its cavities; though, somewhat inconsistently with this, he tells us that he encountered marked hyperæmia of the parenchymatous viscera of the head, chest, and belly; probably in those of his cases where intoxication had played a prominent, if not the principal part. Dieberg mentions incidentally my third sign— the pallid condition of the general surface of the body, as always encountered by him in his cases, but his attention does not seem to have been directed to the first sign—the arterial hue of the blood in the vessels.

In Horn's *Vierteljahrsschrift* for 1865 we have one further case of death by cold given by Dr. Hilty, where he has noticed the crimson hue of the blood, its accumulation on both sides of the heart, and in the large blood-vessels in its vicinity, and the dusky-red patches of the skin on the non-dependent parts of the body.

It is but fair to state, however, that Liman, on passing in review what had been advanced on this subject prior to the appearance of his edition of Caspar's work in 1871, considers that none of the above signs are to be admitted as specific and characteristic of this mode of death. He is inclined to lay most stress, in a case of this sort, on the combination of all the appearances, negative and positive, which may present themselves, particularly in the absence of indications of death from any other than the suspected cause.

I am satisfied, however, that the subject of death by cold, so far as it can be ascertained from the inspection of the dead body, is one which requires further elucidation than has yet been bestowed on it; though I cannot but assign more weight than Liman has done to the data which have been acquired for the solution of the point in question.

Death by Heat

The subject of death by cold is one which is not unattended with difficulties calling for further elucidation. Of the immediate cause of death in the opposite circumstances our ignorance is still great.

Short of such an elevated temperature as would suffice instantly to destroy life, the effects of exposure to heat have been variously explained; though mostly referred to cerebral congestion and its usual consequences. When the heat, on the other hand, is so great as instantly to kill, it has been supposed that the fatal event may be caused, not by apoplexy, but by syncope. This conjecture rests on the experiment of Sir Benjamin Brodie, as reported by Dr. Paris. The former placed a rabbit enclosed in a basket within an oven, the temperature of which was 150° Fahr., when the animal died without any apparent suffering, leaving the heart on both sides distended with blood. This, however, is not borne out by what little we know of the effects of exposure to more elevated temperatures in the human body, which come nearer to such as are set down to sunstroke in tropical climates.

The effects following the application of heat to portions only of the surface of the human body, in its ordinary condition, have been anticipated under "Wounds," where I also briefly referred to what has been loosely designated as—

Spontaneous human combustion. It should be known, however, that under this term we meet with instances, adduced by various authors, chiefly of an earlier date, of what would properly be called spontaneous combustion; while others limit its applicato what is rather a state of preternatural combustibility of the body.

In the former of these two forms of human combustion, we have it alleged that the body, mostly in old and intemperate subjects, has been known to take fire of itself, and the combustion thus self-originated, to proceed nearly to total destruction, leaving only, it may be, the bones, portions of fat, and integuments, on the spot, in a dry and charred, or soft and greasy mass. The latter class of writers, while contending for the occasional occurrence of the same state of the body, and its susceptibility to an equal amount of destruction, assert that for this the contact of some matter in combustion is required.

Arguments against both these conclusions are advanced by medical jurists and chemists of eminence, who contend that, in the first place, the cases of this kind which have been brought forward rest upon too weak evidence to be entitled to confidence. Again, as in the late celebrated case of the Countess of Gorlitz, numerous scientific experiments and facts were adduced by both Liebig and Bischoff, strongly bearing against the possibility of such a state of the human body being encountered in any instance as would support combustion, whether this had arisen from contact with a burning body or not.

The case adduced at page 463 bears not a little in favour of the occasionally preternatural combustibility of the body

A case of the same sort occurred at Aberdeen in September last (1877). A woman, aged 60, was left by her husband in bed, apparently in her usual health, at 5 o'clock in the morning. At 8 A.M. a neighbour, noticing smoke coming from her room, entered it, and found the woman lying dead close to the fireplace, in which there were then only a few nearly extinguished embers, her night-dress, her only clothing, on fire

It was supposed that the deceased had got out of bed at 6 o'clock, to light the fire in her room, in order to prepare breakfast for a lodger, who was then asleep in an adjoining room, and who had not been awakened by any cry or other noise.

The appearances observed at the inspection were —The whole of the right side of the body more or less burned, the burns being in all stages, from mere reddening of the skin to its complete destruction, along with that of the flesh underneath it The flesh of the right arm charred down to the bones, and the elbow-joint laid open. The superficial muscles of the right thigh burned away, the deeper muscles roasted. The right side of the face and head charred The right mamma roasted Burns of the first and second degrees on the left arm and hand. The right arm strongly flexed. The belly much swollen. Serous effusion under the scalp; marked pallor of the brain; congestion and intense œdema of the right lung; the right side of the heart filled with blood, partly fluid, partly loosely clotted, and mixed with minute air-bubbles, its left side nearly empty; and frothy blood in the liver.

In both these instances the combustion appeared to have originated from the ashes left in the fireplaces, but they seemed to me insufficient to account for the extensive destruction of the bodies, without supposing that they were in a state of unusual readiness to support combustion

It seems to me, however, that the subject of preternatural combustibility in certain conditions of the body may perhaps, to say the least of it, be set down as one still *sub judice*. Of one thing there is no room for hesitation—namely, as to the fact of the difficulty of disposing in this way of the body in its usual state. A murderer, seeking to conceal his crime, by heaping up combustible materials around the body, might destroy traces of violence in the body of his victim, if he did not also thereby render its identification more difficult. This, however, could not be accomplished by Professor Parkman, with all the aids of science at his command.

DEATH BY LIGHTNING.

The human body is known to be capable of conducting the electric fluid, which in its passage has been found to give rise to injuries of the material frame, sometimes extending to its coverings and surroundings, and sometimes not. This being the case, it might happen that the discovery of a dead body in a solitary place might give rise to doubts as to the cause of these injuries, while a murderer might allege that his victim had been struck by lightning, in order to cover an act of violence

There is a pretty general agreement among authors as to the cause of death by lightning, when the death, as is not unusual, is instantaneous.

The nervous system is believed to be an excellent conductor of electricity—according to Milne Edwards, almost equal, in this respect, to a rod of metal—hence we have the effects of the electric current primarily manifested on this part of the body, precisely as in death by concussion, *i.e.*, by such an impression on the nervous system generally as seriously to interfere with its functions, or to suspend them entirely.

On this point, the results of experiments on the lower animals are at one with the observed effects of this agent on the human body.

It does not necessarily follow, however, that the passage of the electric fluid through the body will always leave traces of its course, or give rise to appearances which can be set down as characteristic of this agency, either in its lesser or more violent forms.

When the shock has been moderately powerful, but not sufficiently so to destroy life, it has been known to be followed by transient loss of memory, indistinctness or complete loss of sight, insensibility, and paralysis of the muscles; the patient either recovering from these affections of the nervous system, or dying of their consequences

In a boy whom I attended, and who survived a shock of lightning for three days, the power of articulation was entirely lost, and he presented an appearance of dulness and stupidity which approached to stupor. A careful inspection threw no light on the cause of his death, nor did it give any indication of the reality of the occurrence in question

Even where the death has been instantaneous, characteristic appearances are not invariably met with in the body. This remark applies particularly to some of these laid down as constant by the earlier writers on the subject, who give as characteristic such appearances as the following —

Flaccidity of the limbs, the absence or slight character of the cadaveric rigidity, and its speedy disappearance when present, unusual fluidity of the blood, and the early approach of putrefaction—all of these characters having been known to be absent in this form of sudden death.

Our information is not very full or accordant as to the state of the head, and of the viscera of the chest and abdomen after death in this form, observers having limited themselves mostly to certain external appearances, which, though occasionally wanting, are oftener present in some obvious shapes, more or less indicative of their specific origin Such are—linear red streaks or dots on the skin, punctures, contusions, lacerations, burns, and even dislocations and fractures The clothes have been sometimes burned.

The indications of this form of death have been strengthened in such cases by finding in the vicinity of the dead body the effects of the electric current on trees, buildings, and other inanimate objects, or where the same fate has simultaneously overtaken cattle in the vicinity. Coins or other metallic objects in the pockets, or elsewhere about the person of the victim, have been melted or magnetised, yielding a farther corroboration of the nature of the accident.

Death by Starvation

The subject of death by starvation has not hitherto come prominently before the medical jurist.

Of homicidal starvation, with which we have chiefly to concern ourselves, we have the cases recorded by Haller and Fodéré; the evidence, however, in the one instance, is too incomplete to be relied on, while that founded on the other is contradictory and conflicting. In the case of the Jacobs, tried at Caermarthen in 1870, the jury returned a verdict of death by starvation, resulting from criminal neglect in not administering food to their daughter, aged 16, the pretended Welsh fasting-girl. In the Penge case, tried recently, the same verdict was returned against the four persons concerned in the alleged crime, and they were sentenced to death; but this sentence was subsequently commuted.

As regards death by voluntary starvation, our information is both limited and unsatisfactory.

Instances of accidental death in this way are more numerous, though many of these are of a mixed sort. Thus, as in the Penge case, it is not always easy to separate the effects of disease, detected in the body, from those resulting from the deprivation of food, and other neglect, and in cases of shipwreck, and in the garrisons and inhabitants of besieged towns, other depressing causes than abstinence from food are at work, such as mental anxiety, bodily discomfort, and over fatigue. Some such influences are also at work in national famines, such as the Irish potato famine, and the late famines in Persia, Asia Minor, and India.

All this being the case, in the various forms of death by starvation, and in the absence of full and authentic details, it must be admitted that our information, either as regards symptoms during life, or appearances after death, is less satisfactory than could be desired.

The symptoms, in the recorded cases, were mostly as follows:—

DEATH BY STARVATION. 563

Epigastric pains, relieved by pressure; dryness of the mouth and throat; redness of the eyes; intolerable thirst; progressive emaciation; dryness and duskiness of the skin; and prostration, ending in delirium or occasional convulsions.

The character of the morbid appearances, varying somewhat as they do, will be gathered from the cases to be adduced, which are the best we possess

First,—That of a healthy old man, related in the *Lancet*, who was shut up for twenty-three days in a coal-pit, where he could procure nothing but a little foul water. After his discovery and removal, he died in three days from exhaustion. The inspection of the body showed extreme general emaciation, contraction of the intestines, gaseous distension and slight redness of the cardiac portion of the stomach, diminished size of the liver, and distension of the gall-bladder; the remaining viscera being natural. In a case published in the *London Medical Gazette*, which was also a pure case of death by starvation, there were observed—emaciation of the face, toughness of the skin, atrophy of the subcutaneous fat, dryness and roughness of the lips, tongue, and fauces, inflammation of the eyes, shrinking and contraction of the lungs, slight inflammation of the pleuræ, contraction of the stomach and intestines, distension of the gall-bladder, and absence of urine in the urinary bladder, the body exhaling a peculiar odour

The next case is one recorded by Rothamel, in Henke's *Zeitschrift* It was that of a child, six months of age, starved to death by its mother. On inspection, he observed excessive emaciation, the entire absence of fat, with only a small amount of blood in the body; the stomach and intestines closely contracted, with only a little old hardened fœces in the rectum

In the case of a man of 50, examined by Wildberg, who had died after seven days' imprisonment in the ruins of a fallen house, the same extreme emaciation, entire absence of fat, and contraction and emptiness of the intestinal tube, were encountered, as in the previous instances, with, in addition, injection of the eyes, dryness of the mouth and tongue, the lungs shrivelled and yellowish, the liver pale, the gall-bladder distended, the brain anæmic, the heart small and flaccid, with a small quantity of loosely coagulated and highly offensive blood in its cavities, and the body exhaling a peculiar penetrating fœtor, different from that of putrefaction

In an instance of death by starvation from anchylosis of the lower jaw, Caspar found, as in Rothamel and Wildberg's cases, contraction and emptiness of the stomach and intestines, the liver and thoracic viscera pale and anæmic, and the gall-bladder distended, with a small quantity of thick treacly blood in the heart.

In estimating the value of such appearances as the above, the medical jurist would require to be careful not to attribute the emaciation and anæmia met with in the body necessarily to starvation, except in the absence of all traces of wasting disease, with which they would be liable to be confounded. The history of the case would also need to be taken into account in the determination of the question, in every instance where it could be procured.

LECTURE XLI.

GENERAL TOXICOLOGY.

MEDICO-LEGAL RELATIONS OF THE SUBJECT.—Limits to its Application—Proof of Poisoning, when demanded—What constitutes a Poison—Evidence of Poisoning in a general sense—Occasional vagueness of such evidence—Circumstances which modify the action of Poison—Quantity or Dose; Chemical Form; Mechanical Form; Texture acted on; Habit; Constitutional peculiarity, natural or acquired.—INDICATIONS OF POISONING—From Symptoms during Life; Characteristic Symptoms; Diagnostic Symptoms, Pathognomonic Symptoms.

TOXICOLOGY, which has now taken shape as a separate science, dates but a short way back. As a philosophical inquiry it can scarcely be said to have been pursued prior to the middle of the last century; while it was not till the present century that its systematic investigation was fairly entered on. That it has succeeded in so short a time in attaining its present position, has been owing to the circumstances of its having been founded mainly on a basis of observation and experiment; on its cultivators having been careful in keeping fact and hypothesis apart in the pursuit of their inquiries; and in submitting its doctrines to the test of fresh and varied investigation;—points in which it contrasts favourably with the other medical sciences, to whose advance it has not failed to contribute. Thus it has supplied the physiologist with some of his most powerful means of research; some of the soundest principles of therapeutics are based upon it; while it has thrown much of the light we have been able to obtain on the action of not a few of our most important remedies. That the medical practitioner, and especially the medical jurist, should be in possession of an intimate acquaintanceship with this science scarcely needs to be insisted on, since not only has the number of poisonous articles largely increased, a knowledge of their properties been widely spread amongst the vulgar and unprofessional, and their available uses in the arts extended, bringing some of the most powerful of them within the reach of all, but we actually find that we are now called upon to meet and counteract the hidden dangers which surround us in the shape of fictitious or adulterated articles of medicine, food, and drink, of pigments on our walls, and of dyes on our clothing, in addition to the but little less avoidable design of the common poisoner with a largely-increased means of mischief at his hand. Much must here be necessarily left to the sagacity, energy, skill, and information of the medical practitioner in his purely professional character, and still more in his character as an expert. In this position he assumes a more important place than he is called upon to occupy in any other medico-legal proceedings whatever. In trials for poisoning, the medical evidence takes the principal place, and the general evidence comes to be of but secondary importance; the very reverse of what usually happens in other criminal proceedings. What makes the medical evidence in such cases the weightiest part of the proof is, that by establishing the fact of the poisoning, the proof of the intent is thereby also made out; since on trials of this kind it is usually impossible, as on other trials, to entertain the question whether the death was the consequence of deliberate purpose, of sudden fury, or of an act of self-defence.

Since so much depends on the medical jurist on occasions of this sort, as shown by the share which his examination is seen to occupy, the variety of the questions referred to his decision, and the influence allowed to his opinion on the issue of the case, it is fortunate for the interests of the public that his resources are, in not a few instances, so far pretty extensive. Availing himself of the sciences of Semiology, Pathology, Physiology, and Chemistry, the knowledge thence derived has occasionally been brought to bear on individual instances of poisoning with a rare degree of force and precision. But that much remains to be done in this direction it is only fair candidly to admit. Not a little has yet to be accomplished by the toxicologist before he can be allowed to claim for his science the extent and completeness which some of its cultivators have somewhat prematurely boasted that it already possesses. In not a few instances he is unable to discriminate with certainty, during life, betwixt poisoning and ordinary disease; and in an equal number of cases it is found that he is alike incapable of laying down any characteristic distinctions betwixt the appearances left in the dead body by certain diseases, and those resulting from the action of poisons on the tissues. But the deficiencies which we have chiefly to lament, as still attaching to this subject, are those which relate to the chemical proof of the poisoning, particularly in the case of many of the organic poisons.

From circumstances, which I shall have to point out in detail by and by, poisons of the organic class not unfrequently elude detection altogether by chemical means. On no occasion have I been more painfully reminded of the limited nature of the chemical evidence than in the search for traces of some of the opium salts in the dead body, in undoubted cases of rapid poisoning by this drug.

In 1842, for example, the late Professor Gregory and I had to search for traces of muriate of morphia in the body of a woman who had died from an overdose of this salt; and though it was known that no less than from nine to ten grains had been taken on this occasion, and that this person had only survived a few hours; had not ejected any of the poison; and that no remedy had been applied; the most careful search failed in detecting any traces of the morphia in the alimentary tube and elsewhere.

The same failure commonly attends the search for laudanum after its administration in moderately large fatal doses; as also in the case of several of the vegetable acids, and most of the vegetable alkaloids. Even in the case of certain of the inorganic poisons, the proof from chemical analysis, where it does not entirely fail us as in the search for certain of the organic poisons, is yet from a variety of causes peculiar to organic chemistry, too incomplete to allow of our assuming with absolute certainty that the poisonous substance has been received into the body from without, and in a dose sufficient to destroy life. I allude particularly to the search for some of the mineral acids.

When the suspicion of poison having been administered arises on any occasion, the services of the medical jurist may be called for, either on the precognition, or on the trial, or on both of these occasions:—

On the precognition he will be required to prove that death has not arisen from natural causes, but on the contrary, that it has in all probability been occasioned by some active, deleterious agent, the precise nature of which he will be called on to determine. In many instances the suspected poison will be pointed out to him, in which case his duty will be a comparatively easy one.

On the trial the practitioner may be called upon to give evidence as to the possibility, or probability, of poison having been administered so as to cause death, where the public prosecutor is not in a condition to condescend on the particular poison which has been employed. Here nothing short of the most intimate familiarity with the effects of the large majority of the known poisons, in addition to no ordinary acquaintance with the course and termination of acute diseases generally, will suffice to keep the medical witness clear of the risk of falling into dangerous mistakes. Hence it is that I view with some distrust the practice now becoming so common in England, and favourably regarded in Scotland, of separating the two departments of the duty of the toxicologist; assigning to the medical practitioner the investigation of the symptoms and morbid appearances in any given case, and to the mere analytical chemist, the task of isolating the suspected poison. The connection between the poison and its effects is, in many instances, so close that the examiner requires to unite the twofold qualification of pathologist and chemist to be fitted properly to discharge this important duty, a point to which I shall have to return in the sequel.

It may now be considered almost as a settled point, both in law and medicine, that what has been termed poisoning, in a general sense, does not admit of satisfactory proof, or in other words, that poisoning can never be completely substantiated, unless the particular poison be determined. In a very few instances, however, the medical probability may be so high that, in conjunction with other circumstances of general evidence, no room can be left for doubt that poisoning has been perpetrated.

The question, What is a poison? is more easily asked than answered. Not to speak of the vague notions attached by pathologists to the terms *morbid virus* and *specific poisons*, which, in the present state of science, may be at once set aside as mere cloaks for ignorance, in order to obtain a satisfactory answer to our question, we have to consider what limits we are to fix to the term in question, and what are the boundaries which separate poisons, properly so called, from the host of substances which have at times and in certain circumstances, been found to exert injurious or fatal effects on the human system. Some such limitation and discrimination is imperatively called for, unless we are to admit into our lists of toxical agents, not only the far greater number of our drugs and chemicals, but also not a few articles of condiment, food, and drink. The nearest approach we can make to this desirable result will be to restrict the term poison to such substances as, when exhibited in certain quantities to healthy and ordinarily constituted individuals, are capable of producing injurious or fatal effects in a more or less direct and certain way, unless where specially or specifically counteracted. In all such cases, it may be, that the substances are more or less speedy in their actions, that the quantities of them required to be exhibited for this end may vary in each; and that their obvious and direct effects may be more or less clearly traceable to such exhibition; still their essentially noxious characters will be too distinctly manifested on all occasions to admit of their being confounded with other agents whose injurious effects can only admit of being regarded as merely contingent or relative, and not strictly inherent in the substances themselves.

As thus restricted within its proper and recognised province, toxicology may be characterised as the science which treats of poisonous substances, strictly so called; of their varied modes of action; of the morbid effects to which they give rise in the body; of the means available for counteracting or modifying these effects, of the readiest methods for detecting the several poisons in and out of the body, during life or after death; and in addition, of the practical application of all this to the exigencies of society, in guarding it against the insidious arts of the poisoner, or bringing him to condign punishment, and in protecting the public against the deleterious effects of poisons unguardedly swallowed by mistake or accident, or when combined with food or drink in the form of adulterated or fictitious articles. Toxicology will be thus seen to embrace a sufficiently extensive field of study, and to furnish ample scope for the employment of the talent of the most ambitious student in a useful and practical department of his profession.

Taking up in succession the aspects of our subject just noticed, I commence with—

1. *The Action of Poisons* Much of our knowledge in regard to the modes of action of the different poisons is of a purely empirical character, gathered from our observation of the symptoms caused by them in the living, and the morbid traces left by them on the dead body We can gather little or nothing in this way from the chemical composition and the combination of the elements in the toxical agent, and little more from their observed chemical action on inorganic and organic substances out of the body. Nor have we been able to advance very far as yet in our study of the true action of the various poisons, from the experimental inquiries which have been pursued in regard to their physiological effects The chemist is silent when we ask him why it is that the selfsame elements combined in different proportions, may in one case form an article of nutritious food; in another, a powerful remedial agent; and in a third, a deadly poison; or

that by merely altering the arrangement of the elements without alteration of their proportions, we have a dangerous poison converted into an innocuous substance.

There are a few instances, however, in which the chemist has pointed out some actions of certain poisons within the body, the same in kind as those produced by them on organic substances outside the system; such as those which follow the exhibition of sulphuric, nitric, and oxalic acids, and of nitrate of silver, the caustic alkalies, and corrosive sublimate, in their states of concentration.

We are indebted, certainly, to the physiologist for showing us in what way most of our poisons come to reach the organs of the body on which their injurious actions are chiefly exerted, what the organs are which most of our poisons select, as it were, thus to expend their injurious actions, as also, in some cases, through what channels they are thrown out of the body, when they admit of being eliminated from the system, and when time has been afforded for their escape.

But after all, as I have said, it is mainly to clinical observation and post-mortem inspection that we are indebted for our existing information as to the actions of most of our known poisons

From these sources, then, we have come to gather our acquaintance with at least the more obvious and tangible effects of the various poisons. Some few of them destroy the tissues with which they come into immediate contact. A larger number irritate and inflame the parts reached by them A limited number act injuriously on the brain or spinal cord, or both, or on the brain and heart, while a large proportion of poisonous articles act, either simultaneously or successively, both on the mucous surfaces and the cerebro-spinal system; on the former as irritants, on the latter either as stimulants or sedatives. All this has been abundantly confirmed both by observations and by experiments on animals.

To these sources of evidence combined we are indebted for our knowledge of some of the peculiarities in the actions of not a few poisons which had escaped the notice of the earlier observers, some of which results, however, call for further verification than they have as yet received Thus, we have learned to distinguish betwixt the direct action of poisons on the organ or organs to which they are applied, and their indirect action on the system generally, or on some one or more of its remote organs It is only in the case of the concentrated mineral acids and alkalies, and a few of the more powerful irritants, that the local action is sufficiently powerful to destroy life; while even in these, the impression made by them on the system generally, usually plays the most important part in their fatal agency, in other and by far the most numerous instances, the local effects of the irritant and corrosive poisons are the least prominent of their dangerous qualities.

It has also been pretty clearly made out that what have been considered till lately as the purely local effects of several poisons are equally producible, whether the poison in question has been applied directly to the organ affected, or has reached it through the channel of the circulation. Arsenic, for instance, exerts its irritant action on the intestinal tube equally when swallowed in the usual way, or when applied to a wound, or introduced into the veins by injection. And even in the case of the sedatives or irritants acting on the brain, spine, or heart, it is usually necessary for the production of their injurious effects, that time be allowed for the poison, whether in its pure state, or modified by combination with some of the constituents of the body, to arrive at the part which it is found to affect. The time required, however, for this purpose, has been shown by experiments on animals to be so short as to be almost tantamount to instantaneous in certain cases, three or four seconds for example. It is not improbable, however, that a limited number of poisons—alcohol, prussic acid, and strychnia—may act directly on the nervous centres, through the nerves, without entering the current of the circulation at all. Thus, I have noticed in the case of the rabbit, that on introducing alcohol through an œsophageal tube, the fluid had barely time to reach the animal's stomach before it dropped down dead. It militates against this hypothesis, however, that these poisons readily and speedily reach the remotest parts of the body through the circulation.

The affinity which most poisons have for particular organs is a circumstance which, while inexplicable, does not admit of dispute. These affinities may be manifested either on the leading systems of organs, or on special organs, or on both. Thus we have opium, chloroform, and chloral hydrate acting on the cerebrospinal system; strychnia and its congeners, and the African ordeal bean on the spinal cord; coneia, aconitine, and atropine, on both the brain and spine; the Calabar bean, antiarine, and nicotine, on the brain and heart simultaneously; the purer irritants on the intestinal tube; phosphorus on the liver and heart; and arsenic on several organs simultaneously or successively. Again we have what may be considered as more limited agencies of certain poisons, such as hyoscyamus, atropine, and the Calabar bean, on the iris; mercury, iodine, and lead, on the mouth; lead on the extensor muscles of the forearms; cantharides, turpentine, and corrosive sublimate, on the kidneys, etc. Once more, we have blood poisons, nerve poisons, etc.

Such special actions are not invariably witnessed on the organ which most readily attracts the poison, and they are variably influenced by dose, mode of administration, constitutional peculiarities, and proclivity to morbid action or the reverse, in the system. From the selection which has been made, it will have been noticed that the same poison is capable occasionally of affecting more than one organ of the body, a multiplicity of action most remarkable in the case of arsenic, which produces its toxical effects not only on the intestinal canal, but occasionally also on the urinary organs, the brain, the spinal cord, the muscles, the skin, and the conjunctiva.

Inquiries have been instituted, but only with limited success, into the character of the changes which poisons undergo after their absorption, and previously to their leaving the body. The mineral acids combine with alkalies. The vegetable acids are in some cases decomposed; in others, pass off unchanged; while in others still, they combine with the alkalies in the body. The iodide of potassium parts with its base, and escapes in the state of union with lead and mercury when these are present in the tissues. The salts of silver tend to fix themselves permanently in the skin; the salts of lead, and occasionally of mercury or copper, deposit their bases or oxides on the gums, and in the case of lead, in the skin and nails.

Our information as to the channels through which poisons are eliminated from the system is likewise still somewhat limited.

Sulphuric acid and some of its salts, caustic potass, when it has escaped neutralisation, nitrate of potass, the carbonates of soda, the ferrocyanide and sulphocyanide of potassium, chloride of ammonium, and morphia and strychnia in part, pass off by the urine; some of them rapidly. Alcohol, chloroform, and others, pass off quickly by the breath. Arsenic has been found, in large quantities, in the bile and urine; antimony, in quantity, in the urine; the salts of copper, in the bronchial secretion, and sparingly in the urine; lead in the milk and urine; and mercury in the urine and saliva.

The time required for the elimination of these poisons has not been fixed with precision, having been found to vary in different experiments. Though the passage of the inorganic poisons out of the system, as a general rule, is presumed to be slower than that of the organic, probably from the greater aptitude of the former to enter into fixed combinations with the constituents of the body; yet the latter, especially in the fluid form, may be the sooner thrown off. Hence, the greater danger in a long continuance in the use of the more active organic poisons, while symptoms of poisoning in its chronic forms are more seldom met with in the case of the inorganic poisons.

The tendency of certain poisons, such as iodine, digitalis, and lead, to accumulate in the system, in place of being thrown out, is a circumstance which has hitherto admitted of no satisfactory explanation.

To complete this notice of the action of poisons, it remains for me to direct your attention, in some detail, to the modifying circumstances previously alluded to as capable of influencing their effects. These modifying circumstances are one or more of these; (1) quantity of dose; (2) mechanical, or (3) chemical forms; (4) texture directly acted on; (5) habit, and (6) peculiarity of constitution, natural or acquired; by all of which the effects of poisons may be modified, neutralised, or counteracted.

(1.) Quantity of dose effects the result in different ways Thus, there are few poisons which are not innocuous in small doses, while almost all of them are, in moderate doses, medicinal. Some are so active that they can only be safely administered in infinitesimal quantities, such as anhydrous prussic acid, strychnia, coneia, nicotine, veratria, and the oil of tobacco. Other substances again, which are usually harmless, prove injurious or destructive to life, in very large doses; such as nitre, alum, sulphate of potass, cream of tartar, and even table salt.

Again, the very excess of the dose of the poison may occasionally prove the safety of the recipient. In August 1832 three women in a house of ill-fame in Justice Street, Aberdeen, had abstracted from the pocket of a ratcatcher a paper parcel labelled "Arsenic, 4 oz.," and unaccountably mistaking its contents for flour, baked it into a cake with oatmeal, and partook of the greater part of the cake. The effect in all was speedy and copious vomiting, leaving, in one only of the parties, irritability of the stomach for a couple of days One of the women complained that the cake gave her the sensation of pepper in the throat, while in the act of being swallowed. About the same time, an old woman partook of some strawberries in a garden, which, after being carefully hollowed out and the hollows filled with arsenic, had been left exposed by a gardener to poison rats. The impunity in this instance, however, was less complete, as the woman presented the symptoms of irritant poisoning, though in a very mitigated form.

One night in January 1845, a gentleman in Aberdeen swallowed, in mistake for a sedative draught, a liniment containing a quantity of the tincture of aconite, equivalent to four grains of the alkaloid. Here, as with arsenic in the above cases, the dose was instantly rejected, leaving no other effect than a burning heat of the gullet, spasmodic twitchings of the arms, and a sense of drowsiness and exhaustion, which subsided in a few hours

Again, some poisons act on very different parts of the system, according to the extent of dose, such as oxalic acid and arsenic. The former of these, according to the dose, may act upon the alimentary tube, or on the heart, brain, or spine; the latter, on the intestinal canal, or the heart

(2.) The mechanical state of the poison influences its action Some poisons require to be dissolved before they can produce their peculiar effects; others of them act most energetically in the state of vapour, such as the anæsthetic agents, which only produce their specific action on the nervous system in the gaseous form; while, again, the effects of some poisons are weakened by admixture and dilution, though to this there are exceptions.

(3.) The chemical state of the poison materially affects its results. Some substances cease to be poisonous when neutralised; others are rendered more energetic in this way; others still are not in any way affected by this. provided the compound be soluble. As a general rule, as shown by Mr Blake, the effects of the base are little influenced by the acid with which it combines; while, again, as pointed out by Sir Robert Christison, the rule generally holds equally true as to acids, such as the prussic, oxalic, arsenious, and arsenic acids It has also been shown by both these writers that those salts which are isomorphous are closely allied in action

(4.) The texture acted on by poisons influences the results The unbroken cuticle is insensible to the action of most poisons, unless when applied in the state of gas or vapour, or assisted by friction. Introduced into the veins, the action of poisons is the most energetic Scarcely less rapid is their action when brought into contact with the air-cells of the lungs; then follow serous surfaces; lastly, mucous membranes, and perhaps areolar tissue.

Certain vegetable poisons, which are very powerful when directly applied to the wound, may be swallowed with impunity

(5.) Habit has an important influence in modifying the effects of certain vegetable narcotics. Its mitigating effect is most striking in the case of opium and ardent spirits An ounce of laudanum, or a drachm of opium, will produce in the case of those accustomed to the use of this drug, only a moderate degree of exhilaration. I have known a quart of the former consumed in a few weeks by an opium eater, though this was not done with ultimate impunity The same thing is well known to hold good with regard to tobacco, ether, chloroform, and various of the intoxicating substances prepared from plants in various parts of the world. Habit, on the other hand, has no effect in mitigating the action of the inorganic poisons; for notwithstanding the alleged facts which have been brought forward in proof of what is termed the tolerance of increasing doses of certain of these, such as arsenic, tartar emetic, and sulphate of copper, the truth seems to be, that beyond certain limits, undoubtedly pretty wide in the case of arsenic, the system, in the use of these very poisons, comes to be more and more, instead of less and less, susceptible to the same doses, where their administration has been continued for any length of time, and in quantities at all considerable.

(6.) Peculiarity of constitution, or idiosyncrasy, shows itself in the unusual susceptibility of some individuals to the action of certain substances in ordinary medicinal doses, or even in almost infinitesimal quantities, in some of whom the more common articles of food or drink exert a deleterious action Thus, in one case in my own practice, opium in any shape or dose caused distressing nervous irritation; in a second, it led to erythema, and in a third, brought on diarrhœa. In one of these individuals, squill irritated the skin in the same way as the opium; though curiously enough, in the advanced stage of phthisis, opiates could be borne with impunity. One instance occurred in Aberdeen, of a not unusual idiosyncrasy as regards ipecacuan, the smell of which brought on asthmatic attacks in a druggist in weighing out this drug, unless he had previously taken the precaution of covering up his mouth and nostrils. I once witnessed excessive salivation, stomatitis, and glossitis, in a young married lady from a medicinal dose of calomel; a drug which, when given formerly in quantity to children, not unfrequently led to cancrum oris, a disease, happily now almost unknown, since the abandonment of this dangerous practice, once almost universal in cases of real or supposed hydrocephalus. The most noted of the articles of food which are known to act injuriously, in some instances, in certain individuals, are red-fish, shell-fish, mushrooms, bitter almonds, and eggs; while there is scarcely an article of food or drink, except the great staple commodities, beef and mutton, and the simpler kinds of bread, which are not observed occasionally to act poisonously on others.

Sir Robert Christison has adduced instances indicating that this peculiarity of constitution, as regards certain articles of diet, may be an acquired one for a time, and subsequently disappear. Some such alleged peculiarities, I believe, are more imaginary than real. This, at least, was proved in the case of a relative of my own, who was on one occasion cheated into partaking of ling disguised as halibut, the former on this occasion having for once, at least, ceased to bring on severe illness

On the other hand, it occasionally happens that original peculiarity of constitution has the effect of deadening the activity of certain poisons. This is most frequently encountered, however, in some morbid states of the system; such as hydrophobia, tetanus, mania, delirium tremens, and after excessive losses of blood In a case of delirium tremens in 1839, thirty-six grains of opium and an ounce of laudanum had been exhibited within twenty hours, with no other effect than that of temporarily calming the excitement. In this instance the tolerance of the opium was explained by the appearance of a mass of fluid by vomiting, thick with the drug, the torpor of the stomach accounting for the failure of the absorption.

It should be borne in mind that, in a case like the last, the stomach may recover its lost power. This was evident in a person in tetanus, who died from the opium, on the abatement or intermission of the convulsions.

Analogous effects are occasionally witnessed in intoxicated persons, where the alcohol has rendered the system proof against lowering remedies. On one occasion of this sort, where it was desirable to reduce a dislocation of the shoulder, eighteen grains of tartar emetic caused neither nausea nor vomiting, the only effect observed being the calming of the excitement for a little, and the lowering of the force of the circulation.

From this review of the peculiarities in the modes of action of various poisons, and of the modifications which their actions may undergo under different and varying circumstances, an idea will be readily formed of the difficulties necessarily attendant on all the attempts which have been hitherto made by toxicologists to arrange and classify them in a systematic and philosophical manner—a part of our subject which belongs in its details to special and not to general toxicology. I proceed, therefore, in the meantime, to the second source of evidence of poisoning, namely:—

2. The morbid *symptoms* to which poisons give rise. When severe illness is observed suddenly to attack an individual apparently in the possession of robust health, the suspicion of poisoning is very readily awakened in the mind of the party himself, or of his surrounding friends, particularly in the lower ranks of life. Medical men, better informed, distrust a criterion of this loose sort, knowing that the effects of poisons are not always sudden, while they are aware that there are natural diseases which give little or no warning of their approach, and which may come on in the midst of apparent health. Equally unsafe is the criterion of poisoning which occasionally awakens public suspicion, derived from the rapidity of the course of the illness, as contrasted with the effects of natural disease; for the course of the latter may be startlingly rapid, and the progress of the former slow and tedious. Neither is the course of illness from poison, as has been assumed, always steady and progressive, and that of disease slower and less continuous; the reverse of this may take place in some instances of both sorts. Nor is it safe to assume as a guide that alarming symptoms immediately or speedily following the taking of food, drink, or medicine, point necessarily to the having to do with poison rather than with ordinary illness, as exceptions to this occur with poisons, while the outburst of disease may correspond with the date of the last meal.

But though such criteria as these may fail to discriminate betwixt poisoning and disease, it does not necessarily follow that little or no reliance is to be placed on symptoms as evidence of poison having been administered, as had been hastily concluded by some writers. In illustration of the occasional importance of symptoms alone as a guide to us in this direction, Christison speaks of the well-known effects of strychnia and oxalic acid, contending that there are no natural diseases which would successfully mimic such effects as these poisons give rise to, and adds that the suspicions which they would certainly awaken might amount almost to demonstration should it have happened that

2 P

several persons had partaken together of the same articles of food, drink, or medicine, and had been simultaneously attacked with similar symptoms.

It was on hearing the evidence of the symptoms suffered by the victim of the notorious Palmer that Dr. Taylor concluded that strychnia had been administered, though he had previously failed to detect that poison in his examination of the contents of the stomach of the deceased.

The same judgment might, in some instances, be presumably reached from observing the effects of some of the strong mineral acids. It was from the state of the lips and mouth, the impending suffocation from closure of the larynx, the coldness of the surface, and depression of the heart's action, coupled with acid stains on the bed-clothes, that my suspicion of poisoning was aroused in the case of a man of the name of Humphrey, in 1830 It came out in evidence that, while he was drunk in bed, his wife had poured oil of vitriol down his throat, for which crime she was tried and executed in Aberdeen.

But though the evidence from symptoms, except in a few rare instances, may come far short of the actual proof of the administration of poison, the study of these may be of importance to the toxicologist. Their presence, as in Humphrey's case, may arouse suspicion of something deleterious having been given to his patient, and lead him to search for proofs of a less unsatisfactory kind Or they may enable him to say that poisoning was possible, probable, or highly probable, which, when the moral evidence is very strong, may be quite enough to decide the case in the affirmative, or on the contrary, in the absence of this, to pronounce as to its impossibility. Lastly, in those cases in which the chemical or moral evidence has pointed to the administration of poison, the character of the symptoms may require to be taken into account before we are able to decide that the particular poison was the cause of the person's death

On this last point Christison has interposed a caution which it is of importance not to overlook. "It does not follow," he remarks, "because a poison has been given, that it has been the cause of death; hence in every medico-legal inquiry the cause of the first symptoms and the cause of death should be made two distinct questions" This author instances a case in point which was tried at Inverary in 1824, where a person was charged with the crime of poisoning a young woman with whom he cohabited. The girl, as was proved in evidence, though she had suffered severely for twelve days from the administration of arsenic, had subsequently almost completely recovered from its affects, when she was seized with fever, from which she died, and to this disease, and not to the arsenic, the medical witnesses justly attributed the fatal issue in this instructive instance

LECTURE XLII.

GENERAL TOXICOLOGY—*Continued*

INDICATIONS OF POISONING FROM POST-MORTEM APPEARANCES—Characteristic Appearances—Appearances common to Poisoning and Natural Disease—Appearances common to Poisoning and to the Effects of Decomposition—Comparative experiments on Animals—Limits to the Application of such Experiments—Moral Evidence—Chemical Analysis—Importance attached to it—Limits to its employment—Microscopical Examination.—MODE OF CONDUCTING THE POST-MORTEM EXAMINATION—In the case of the recently dead—Preliminary Investigation—External Appearances—Internal Appearances—Preservation of Suspected Articles, etc.—After long Interment.

3. I HAVE now to direct your attention to the evidence of poisoning derivable from the post-mortem appearances in the body after death.

The evidence from this source is either negative or positive. No reliance is now placed, as was once the case, on such appearances in the dead body as unusual lividities, or its rapid decomposition; while it is now admitted that, unless in a very few particular instances, the morbid appearances left by poisons on the corpse do not differ specifically from those following natural disease, or some other kinds of violent death. The entire absence of those morbid appearances on the body, which are indicative of the action of poisons, even if conjoined with the presence of those which result from disease to an extent sufficient to account for death from natural causes, will not always suffice for negativing the possibility of poison having been administered. Christison has collected several cases in which marks of violence, or the existence of natural diseases sufficient to account for death, were observed on dissection, where, notwithstanding, it was known that the parties had died from the operation of poisons which had left little or no trace of their action on the body after death.

The occasional importance of a knowledge of such occurrences as these, on the part of the medical jurist, was well illustrated in a trial in England for poisoning with prussic acid. I allude to the well-known case of Tawell, in which a medico-legal struggle was made in favour of the culprit, and in which much eagerness was shown by those who conducted the defence, to obtain in the cross-examination of the witnesses some sort of admission to the effect that there were marks of disease on the body of the victim. There is usually, in fact, nothing for which a counsel engaged in defending a prisoner more eagerly seeks, than an admission of this kind from a medical witness. The jury are so much in his hands, and so little in the hands of a witness (for long explanations on medical doctrines are never allowed in Court), that it is easy to foresee how, by dexterous management, the verdict may be made to turn. The only chance of the truth being brought to light in such a case is where the symptoms and appearances produced by the disease are widely different from those caused by the poison alleged to have been taken. This being the case, it behoves the medical examiner to be careful to conduct the inspection of the body in such a way as not hastily to assume that because appearances of natural disease are met with, therefore there has been no poisoning in the case, or that these necessarily negative the possibility of such poisoning. He is not entitled to do this unless the appearances met with are such as must, without doubt, have been the cause of death. In any other circumstances, his opinion should be so guarded as not to exclude the possibility of the real cause of death being different from the apparent one. This may appear to some to be playing fast and loose with the law authorities; but it is only doing so in appearance, while in reality it is the only course a conscientious witness can adopt where his science authorises him merely to give an approximation to the truth.

Before coming to a positive decision as to the appearances on the body being necessarily the effects of poison administered during life, the medical examiner should be familiar with the morbid changes which may simulate them. Thus, while we are entitled to look for irritation, inflammation, or corrosion of parts of the alimentary tube after the ingestion of several of the irritant poisons, we must bear in mind that all of these may have arisen from natural causes.

I have already (under Death) directed your attention to the fact of the stomach of drunkards being sometimes met with intensely red, or what is more usual, reddening on exposure to the air.

I have also specially directed your attention (under Infanticide) to appearances of superficial inflammation, or even ulceration, sometimes encountered in the mouth, throat, and stomachs of new-born infants, all of intra-uterine origin. A case of this sort occurred at Aberdeen some years ago under rather embarrassing circumstances. An illegitimate child, a few days old, had died suddenly, and had been left by its mother locked up in her room. Suspicions of foul play having arisen, the door was forced open, and a practitioner in the neighbourhood sent for. This gentleman thought he perceived the odour of turpentine about the child's mouth, which was open, and that some bedding in the apartment smelled strongly of this fluid. At the examination of the body next day, we detected superficial ulceration in the throat and stomach, which was reddened in patches, but could not discover any turpentine either in the mouth or stomach on a careful chemical investigation.

I had also occasion to direct your attention (under Death) to the effect of decomposition in causing redness of the stomach, and the means of discriminating between such pseudo-morbid redness, and that arising from natural causes, or from the action of irritant poisons. Dr. Yellowly has shown that in some cases of sudden death, as in executed criminals, the stomach has been found highly vascular, where no symptoms of irritation or inflammation had existed during life. It is possible, however, that these had been cases of the drunkard's stomach to which I have just alluded.

Severe inflammation or ulcerations in the mouth, throat, or œsophagus observed in the dead body, are much more likely to have been the consequence of previous disease than of any irritant or corrosive poison. Such poisons pass too rapidly over those portions of the alimentary tube to allow of their giving rise to marked local actions. Exceptions to this, however, occasionally occur. Thus, in the case of a young girl in Aberdeen who swallowed by mistake a small quantity of sulphuric acid, inflammation of the pharynx and larynx followed, with the formation of false membranes over the parts. In another case, corrosion of the lower third of the œsophagus was produced by the same poison.

Corrosions of the stomach or smaller intestines from the action of poisons of this class, could scarcely be confounded with ulcerations, the effect of disease, by a competent observer Ulcers, properly so called, are rare after the ingestion of irritant poisons; and, besides, could only be encountered in chronic cases

Softening of the coats of the stomach is common both to disease and to the action of corrosive poisons.

Such softening is also known to take place in a few instances of sudden death, from the solvent action of the gastric juice on the coats of the stomach after death; or it may present itself as an example of the disease termed gelatiniform softening. In both these instances the tissues are completely disorganised, and usually broken up into shreds over considerable portions of the organ In cases of this sort the examiner would not be entitled to attribute the appearances in question to any corrosive poison, unless the poison was actually found in the stomach, as the death would follow the ingestion of the poison almost immediately. Toxicologists, indeed, have pointed out marks for discriminating betwixt the action of corrosives, and both the gelatiniform softening of the stomach, and that caused by the gastric fluid after death: but these are not to be much relied on. Thus, the gelatiniform softening is said to be preceded by well-marked symptoms during life. An exception to this, however, happened in my own practice. The patient, a young lady, though complaining for some days of debility and head symptoms, showed no indications of any affection of the stomach, when she suddenly lay back in bed and instantly expired, the walls of the viscus having suddenly given way Again, in the case of the stomach acted on by the gastric juice, the state of the parts will not always be such as to enable us to say, that the solvent action was limited to the dependent parts of the organ. This, at least, was the fact in the few instances of this occurrence which I have met with.

Rounded perforations of small size, in certain unhealthy states of the stomach or smaller intestines, sometimes destroy life in a few hours, preceded by symptoms not unlike the effects of irritant poisons In these cases, however, the symptoms and death are in general clearly traceable to peritonitis, while the edges of the perforations present some characteristic appearances; being rounded, thickened, and of almost cartilaginous hardness.

In many of the deaths from narcotic and narcotico-acrid poisoning, the inspection of the body fails to yield us any assistance. Either the appearances are such as are common to other cases of death, or the poison has left no trace of morbid action whatever in the dead body. This last may even happen with some of the irritant poisons

I had occasion formerly (under Death) to dwell at sufficient length on the effect of advancing putrefaction in the dead body in obliterating the traces of a large number of those poisons, which produce changes of a sufficiently marked sort in the fresh corpse, and need not recur to this subject. Short of this, however, some poisons leave traces of their morbid action which are not very readily obliterated. Such are the intense phlogosis in the upper part of the alimentary canal, from certain of the irritants, and the destruction of its coats, and even perforation of the tube by the more powerful escharotics, not to speak of the less marked effect on the skin, throat, or œsophagus by some of the mineral acids. It is, however, in connection with the symptoms and the general evidence that the morbid appearances after death furnish decisive proof of poisoning; while, even should the history of the case be unknown, the post-mortem changes present may point out the nature of the previous illness, which information, coupled with the moral evidence, where this is strong, may serve to decide the nature of the case.

The evidence of poisoning in man, from experiments on animals with suspected articles of food, drink, or medicine, was much relied on in the infancy of chemical analysis. Now, however, this line of proof is properly objected to, as a waste of useful material, which might be turned to better account. This objection, however, does not apply to the use of such materials in comparative experiments on animals, where the precise mode of action of the suspected poison happens to be unknown. In some instances accident may even aid us here, as where these materials have been thus partaken of, and produced poisonous effects on the domestic animals.

It must not be taken for granted that the effects of poisons on the lower animals, whether offered by chance, or experimentally obtained, are in all cases precisely the same as in the human subject, or that any general resemblance, which they may present alike in both, will always extend to all their symptoms and consequences. Thus opium, for instance, which in man induces lethargy and coma, in animals brings on tetanic convulsions. Again, animals are not all affected by some of the most powerful poisons known to us. Thus, an elephant at Geneva took first, three ounces of prussic acid in ten ounces of brandy, and afterwards three ounces of arsenic, without any result. Similar immunities from the action of particular poisons are said to be enjoyed by other animals. Thus it is said that, as a general rule, the herbivora are less susceptible to the influence of narcotics than either the carnivora or man; black cattle consume and bear considerable quantities of hemlock; goats and other ruminants feed with impunity on the euphorbiaceæ and pulsatilla, and are insusceptible the presence of antimony; arsenic, the preparations of mercury, and aconite, are but little injurious to the horse; while hyoscyamus and cyclamen are not at all so to the sow; and morphia and other opiates, with belladonna, but to a slight degree, to rabbits On evidence of a more or less loose sort, we have it advanced that cicuta virosa seems to agree well with several aquatic birds, and digitalis with domestic fowls; that cantharides is harmless to swallows; that the caterpillars of various species of butterflies feed with avidity on various poisonous plants; and that parrots have a considerable immunity from the injurious effects of phosphorus. To test the truth of some of these statements, experimental trials have been instituted in America, as to the effect of morphia and other narcotics in pigeons, the result of which was that these birds were insensible to the action of morphia, belladonna, hyoscyamus, stramonium, and atropia. It would be well that the nature of the poisons I have mentioned were also tested in the case of other animals. More than enough, however, is known on this subject to serve as a warning against some late assumptions as to the identity of the effects of poison on man and the lower animals.

Thus, in the case of Bellamy, tried in London in 1844, for the poisoning of his wife, the medical witnesses declared that poisoning by hydrocyanic acid was accompanied by a shriek, as the last act of life, and that this was the immediate precursor of insensibility. In Tawell's case, again, the poetical name of "death shriek" was given by the counsel to this supposed invariable accompaniment of poisoning by prussic acid. It is almost needless to say that there is no foundation whatever for such a statement. The witnesses who spoke of this shriek or cry based their evidence upon some experiments on horses and dogs, and because a cry of pain or a shriek was uttered by these animals, the hasty inference was drawn that the same effect was produced by the poison in the human subject Another improper use of such experiments has been, amongst some witnesses, the inference that because animals generally suffer the most violent tetanic spasms when under the influence of prussic acid, the same effects would be produced in the human subject; ergo, in death from this poison the body of the deceased should always be found in the convulsed attitude, or it must have been interfered with. Such an inference is in opposition to numerous observations; but in the meantime it shows to what hazardous assertions such experiments may lead.

It is curious, by the way, to observe how readily an error in medical opinion obtains currency for a time. The shriek affair, first broached in Bellamy's case, deceived the counsel in Tawell's case; though the correction must now be considered as complete, from the results of subsequent observations.

4. With the *moral aspects* of the case the medical jurist, as such, has usually nothing to do. Yet there are certain moral circumstances, occurring in most cases of actual poisoning, which can only be correctly appreciated by a scientific person, or which actually come prominently before the medical attendant in his professional character: and as they have been admirably summed up by Sir Robert Christison, I cannot do better than lay before you his resumé of these in his own words. As the moral or general proof in charges of poisoning is almost always circumstantial only, the circumstances usually relate—"(1) to suspicious conduct on the part of the prisoner before the event, such as dabbling with poisons, when he has nothing to do with them in the way of his profession, conversing about them, or otherwise showing a knowledge of their properties not usual in his sphere of life; (2) to the purchase or possession of poison recently before the date of the alleged crime, and the procuring it under false pretences, such as for poisoning rats, when there were none on his premises, or for purposes to which it is never applied; (3) to the administration of poison, either in food, drink, medicine, or otherwise; (4) to the intent of the poisoner, such as the impossibility of his having administered the poison ignorantly or by accident, or for beneficial purposes, alleged or not alleged; (5) to the fact of other members of the family besides the deceased having been similarly and simultaneously affected; (6) to suspicious conduct on the part of the prisoner during the illness of the person poisoned, such as directly or indirectly preventing medical advice being procured, or the relations of the dying man being sent for, or showing an over-anxiety not to leave him alone with any other person, or attempting to remove or destroy articles of food or drink, or vomited matters which may have contained the poison, or expressing a foreknowledge of the probability of speedy death; (7) to suspicious conduct after the person's death, such as hastening the funeral, preventing or impeding the inspection of the body, giving a false account of the previous illness, showing an acquaintance with the real or supposed effects of poison on the dead body; (8) to the personal circumstances and state of mind of the deceased, his death-bed declarations and other particulars,

especially such as tend to prove the impossibility or improbability of suicide; lastly, to the existence of a motive or inducement on the part of the prisoner, such as his having a personal quarrel with the deceased or a hatred of him, his succeeding to property by his death, or of being relieved of a burden by it, his knowing that the deceased, if a female, was with child by him"

Several of the above particulars occurred to confirm and strengthen the proof of poisoning in the case of Burnett, tried at Aberdeen in April 1849, for the murder of his wife. The arsenic employed was bought, not at the nearest village, but at a distant town (Fraserburgh). It was purchased shortly before his wife's death. It was procured under the pretence of being required for poisoning rats, which he alleged were very numerous and troublesome, though this was not borne out by the evidence. It was administered, by the culprit himself, as medicine, though he had not been in the habit previously of doing so. He had come to sleep on the night in question with his wife, which for two years previous he had not done, living with an employer at some distance, and for this purpose he had sent away to another part of the house the daughter who usually attended her sick mother. He had not undressed, but had lain down in his clothes, evidently expecting to be disturbed by the illness or death of his victim. When taken ill, he had discouraged the proposal for proper medical assistance, had showed some laxative powders as what he had given to the woman, and which he alleged he had procured to do her good, had destroyed the vomited matters, and had broken the cup which had been used to administer the arsenic. He had previously predicted his wife's death as shortly to be expected. He had hastened the funeral, and refused to allow an inspection of the body when it had been proposed. Lastly, a sufficient motive was apparent in his having cohabited in his wife's lifetime with a younger woman, to whom, within a few days after her death, he was about to be married, at the time of his being taken into custody.

The careful study of the moral aspect of the case in suspected poisoning may be useful to the practitioner in other respects than as affording evidence of the certainty or probability of poison having been exhibited intentionally, for the purpose of murder, in particular instances. It may point, for example, occasionally in the opposite direction. The conclusions which may be thus arrived at by the medical man may suffice to remove any grounds for considering the case as one of murder, and may remove unjust grounds of suspicion against an innocent individual, while in this way suicidal may also be distinguished from accidental, and imaginary from real poisonings.

Once more, attention to the moral aspects of the case will often enable the practitioner to determine directly, and act promptly, in instances of merely suspected poisoning; a duty to which he may be called, not only to secure the ends of justice, but, it may be, the life of his patient, when that has not been already virtually sacrificed. Thus, by watching the conduct of a suspected individual he may be able, on an occasion of this sort, if he can do no more, to protect his patient against the further attempts of the poisoner, or to make sure that nothing is neglected on the part of his attendants, calculated to counteract the evil which may have already been done, or to favour his recovery.

5. The evidence of poisoning derivable from *chemical analysis* Till towards the conclusion of the last century, the proof from this source was very defective, and the modes of analysis resorted to were of the most rude and inefficient kind. In the cases in which this mode of proof is available, it is now justly reckoned the most unexceptionable of all, as it not only establishes poisoning in a general sense, but likewise points out with precision the particular poison which has been employed, and that, when available, occasionally with a degree of accuracy and certainty which is all that could be desired. In competent hands, from a fiftieth to a thousandth part of a grain of a poisonous article may be detected in the most complicated admixtures, in or out of the body; and even in the former situation after months or years have been suffered to elapse since the burial of the party These remarks apply, however, with one or two exceptions, only to a certain number of the inorganic poisons. In a few instances chemical science has altogether failed to determine whether the deleterious effects observed after the ingestion of certain articles, enumerated as poisons, be really owing to any separate ingredient at all. This is the case of certain shell and other fish, where both the chemist and the physiologist have hitherto in vain attempted to discover the cause of their poisonous operation

But what is still more to the point to remark is, that in certain of the poisons which have been isolated, and whose characters, effects, and modes of operation are well known, the proof from chemistry is not available; and these instances are by no means few in number, or of trifling importance in practice. Many of the organic poisons, and even some of the inorganic class, must be numbered in this category.

The failure of the proof, however, is not to be ascribed entirely or chiefly to the defects of the chemical analysis, but to the circumstance of the poison having been removed out of the reach of the examiner before he has had an opportunity of commencing his research. The poison in question may have passed off by the bowels, it may have been thrown off by vomiting, it may have been decomposed, or it may have undergone the processes of digestion or of absorption, and of subsequent elimination, any one of which causes will have sufficed to render the chemical search for poison on the dead body wholly nugatory. One or two illustrations have been already noticed, and others will come before us afterwards.

But even in the case of those poisons, which are not liable to be discharged, to be absorbed, to be digested, or to undergo decomposition in the body, their detection may elude the chemist, from the circumstance of their speedily undergoing neutralisation, or having entered into new combinations. In this latter respect the toxicologist has to encounter difficulties which are almost unknown to the ordinary chemist. Impediments are thrown in his way, even in the case of the inorganic poisons, from the presence, in the organic admixtures in which they have in most instances to be sought for, of colouring, slimy, and other animal or vegetable substances. In the case of the inorganic poisons especially, their detection can often be effected only after the total destruction of the organic admixtures with which they may have been combined, from the circumstances that changes of colour and the formation of precipitates escape the eye in dark coloured fluids, that slimy fluids cannot be filtered, etc.

Many of these difficulties have, however, been of late successfully met and overcome, and every day is extending our resources in this direction. Nothing has marked more the advance which is taking place in the progress of chemical research than the circumstance that, in not a few instances, poisons have been recovered after their entire disappearance from the alimentary canal, the poison itself, or some of its constituents, even in the case of organic poisons, having been successfully traced and recovered from the blood, secretions, excretions, and even the solids of the animal body.

The interesting researches and experiments of Mr Graham have provided us with a ready method of isolation in the case of certain of the poisons most frequently employed for murderous and suicidal purposes. By the aid of the Dialytic method, I have succeeded in readily isolating tartar emetic and strychnia in cases of poisoning in animals, and several of the inorganic poisons from animal admixtures, such as the soluble salts of mercury, lead, and copper.

In the sublimation method advised by Dr Guy, we have a further means for the detection of certain poisons in circumstances under which the resources of the chemist had previously afforded us little or no assistance, a method which has been found best applicable to arsenic, corrosive sublimate, and some other of the inorganic poisons. The sublimation method of Guy has been extended by Helwig to the search for the alkaloids, the detection of which has hitherto been in an unsatisfactory state. This method, however, is so far defective as being only applicable to poisons encountered out of the body, and where they have not entered into combination with animal matters in the organs and tissues.

However interesting the spectrum analysis may be to the physicist and the pure chemist, though proved to be one of exceeding delicacy and certainty in the case of the metallic bases of such of the alkalies and alkaline earths as admit of being readily volatilised, it has not as yet shown much applicability to the purposes of the toxicologist.

But, although chemistry, as now understood and practised, has been successful, to a considerable extent, in overcoming the natural difficulties in the way of the detection and separation of many of the poisons before their escape from the body, whatever direction they may have taken, and wherever they may have to be sought for, the fact still remains as I have said, that a large number of poisonous bodies are known to us, for the detection and separation of which from the fluids and solids of the body, we have as yet been able to devise no adequate or satisfactory methods. I refer particularly to not a few of the vegetable narcotics and narcotico-acrids. In these circumstances the question again occurs, can the evidence from chemical analysis be legitimately dispensed with by the medical jurist in any case of supposed poisoning? To this inquiry opposite answers have been given by toxicologists; one party maintaining that the discovery of poison in the body is not to be held as necessary, in every instance, to the conviction of a person on a charge of poisoning, while others, on the contrary, have gone so far as to maintain, that without the discovery chemically, of poison, either in the body itself, or in the evacuations, no charge of poisoning can be substantiated. That this last position is untenable we have already seen in our review of the sources of evidence previously disposed of. The symptoms and morbid appearances, for instance, coming in support of the moral evidence to the same purport, will occasionally suffice for a conviction, independently altogether of the chemical examination, particularly where the poison is known to be one which usually eludes our search in the dead body This principle, however, must not be carried too far, and the chemical evidence too rashly dispensed with, as has been sometimes done to an unjustifiable extent, particularly in former times

In enumerating the various sources from which evidence of poisoning is to be derived, I have omitted two which have been lately advanced with some show of reason. I refer to the evidence derivable from the employment of the microscope and the spectroscope, both, but to a limited extent, however, available in toxicology. The first of these, the microscope, may occasionally serve to distinguish crystalline poisons, in the pure state, out of the body, or, in rare instances, in the body; while again it may enable us in a very limited number of instances to discriminate the texture of fragments of vegetable matters of a noxious kind found in the stomach But it unfortunately happens, that in the separation of organic and inorganic poisons from organic admixtures, we are unable to obtain these in their characteristic crystalline forms, where the substance in question in ordinary chemical operations is susceptible of being crystallised; while again, few vegetable fragments in the case of poisons of this class, possess any such characteristic structure as would serve to distinguish them from harmless substances.

The use of the spectroscope in the search for poisons is of a still more restricted character By means of this instrument, however, the salts of thallium have been detected in the bodies of animals poisoned by them, where chemical analysis had been unable to do so, from the production of the vivid green band characteristic of the metal, on burning a small portion of the dried liver of the animal The salts of lithium have also been thus detected in the tissues, by the bright red band in the spectrum, characteristic of this metal. The employment of the spectroscope in other cases, where at first it gave promise of usefulness, as in poisoning by oxalic acid and carbonic oxide, has not fulfilled the expectation of toxicologists

A question of considerable importance in relation to the disappearance of poison from the body has been lately broached on several trials both in this country and in France: I allude to the evidence supposed to be derivable from the presence of a quantity of poison in the body, insufficient in amount to account for death, where the gross fallacy has been assumed, that when this has been the case, the proof of the poisoning has failed; in other words that, when the poison is found, in order to bring about conviction for the crime, it is indispensable that the quantity detected should be sufficient to destroy life. From the operation of the causes I have mentioned, the poison may either not have been detected at all, or it may have been detected only in minute fractional proportions; the causes of its eluding research being vomiting, purging, and absorption or decomposition, as the case may be. Facts of this description, known only to medical men, are sometimes kept in the background in a court of law, where a certain purpose is to be served; and a counsel is allowed to use his privilege in defence, so far as not merely to conceal them, but to produce a false impression on the minds of a jury. Thus we find the common argument employed,—there was not sufficient poison found in the stomach to occasion death,—therefore the deceased could not have died from poison! This was an essential point in the defence of Tawell, already more than once alluded to. Orfila quotes no fewer than eight criminal trials, in which this was allowed to become a debated question in France; and it is now almost invariably the practice in England to ask a medical witness whether he found sufficient poison in the stomach to cause death. If he answers in the negative, there is an eloquent appeal for an acquittal to the jury, who are not informed that the poison found in the stomach is only the surplus of that which has really caused death. Of course in circumstances such as these the medical jurist cannot interfere; but the possibility of such an occurrence should induce him to be on his guard, against being made a party to a perversion of medical facts, involving not only a suppression of the truth, but a suggestion of what is so manifestly erroneous as scarcely to require a serious argument for its refutation.

Before leaving this part of our subject it is necessary to warn you against an error of the opposite kind to the one just noticed. If the medical jurist would not be entitled to conclude that death had not occurred from poison in any particular case, because only a trace of it was discovered by him in the body, as little on the other hand would he be justified in assuming that, because poison, whether in greater or less quantity, was found within the body, the death of the party must of necessity have arisen from that cause.

It should always be borne in mind by him, that the poison might have been introduced into the body after death, with a design to impute poisoning; or, although the poison had been swallowed during life, the fatal event might have arisen from natural causes. Instances of such unlikely occurrences are not at all frequent, though sufficiently so to require their being kept in view. It is to be borne in mind, besides, that a large number of our best-known poisons are constantly employed as medicinal agents, and hence it has led to the defence being taken up, that the finding of some of these in the body may be accounted for by their previous employment medicinally. This line of defence has been chiefly resorted to in the cases of arsenic, mercury, and tartar emetic poisonings; as witness the cases of Palmer's second charge, Smethurst's, and more recently that of Dr Pritchard.

Such, then, are the sources of evidence from which in the general case, the proof of poisoning may be derived, though there are limits to the application of each or all of these, and caution is to be observed in our deductions from them. The details into which their formal consideration has led us, will have sufficiently prepared you for the discussion, in the next place, of the duties which usually fall to the medical practitioner in cases of poisoning.

LECTURE XLIII.

GENERAL TOXICOLOGY—*Continued.*

TREATMENT OF POISONING GENERALLY.—Removal of the Poison—Various modes of effecting this—Antidotal Treatment—Cure of resulting Disorders—Various modes of effecting this—In the case of Poisoned Wounds, or Poisons externally applied—Ligature—Ablution—Mechanical Compression—Venesection—Excision of soft parts involved—Caustics and Escharotics—When Inhaled—When Swallowed—Emetics—Diluents—Stomach Pump—Cathartics—Antidotes—Physical and Chemical Antidotes—Tests of their Efficiency—Special indications for Efficient Medicinal Treatment.

IN those instances where the medical practitioner is called in during the lifetime of the party, his duties will be of a twofold kind, namely, those of his ordinary practice as attendant on the sick, and those where, in addition, he will have to give attention to the further investigation of the case, in the event of his patient either dying or recovering. When death has taken place from the poison without opportunity having been afforded for its counteraction or alleviation by treatment, the investigation will be of a purely medico-legal nature; and such are the cases which, in the great majority of instances, come under our notice in actual practice. Keeping this distinction in view, I shall, in the first place, advert to the general principles which regulate the treatment of cases of poisoning, and afterwards consider the special circumstances which demand the notice of the medical practitioner, when called on to speak to the fact of poisoning in any particular instance.

And now, at the outset, in proceeding to speak of the treatment of poisoning in general, I come for the first time to notice the subject of therapeutics, a speciality which attaches to toxicology alone, of all the branches of medical jurisprudence This, however, in regard to this branch of our science, is a course which I am necessitated to pursue for two reasons; first, that the subject is one which is not taken up by any other teacher, and, second, that the treatment of poisoning can not be divorced from the symptoms, mode of action, etc, of poisonous substances without a degree of violence which would be fatal at once to the value and the interest of this very important department of medical science.

Till of late years, the mode of dealing with this class of patients was purely empirical: and the means employed by the practitioner, where not altogether useless, were not unfrequently mischievous, aggravating instead of mitigating the evils they were intended to remedy. In their zeal for sweeping away a mass of inert, and sometimes hurtful agents, the moderns have perhaps gone too far in the opposite direction, and confining their interference too much to treatment based on purely scientific principles, have failed to avail themselves of remedies which experience had shown to be anything but useless, a point which will fall to be noticed by and by.

In order to the methodical and efficient treatment of poisoning, the three following indications present themselves, namely— (1) the removal of the poison, (2) the counteracting of the primary effects, as far as can be done, of such portions of the poison as have got beyond our reach; and (3) the cure of the resulting disorders it may have occasioned.

1. The speedy removal of what of the poison may be accessible to us is obviously the duty which first calls for performance, when required to counteract the effects of its application or administration.

The modes of fulfilling this indication vary according to circumstances; as to whether, for instance, the poison has been applied outwardly or taken inwardly. And, first, of their external application. Some poisons, such as the strong mineral acids and the caustic alkalies, act on the unbroken surface of the body, while others, and these the far larger number of them, require for this purpose to be introduced below the surface. In the first of these instances careful ablution will be all that may be required for the fulfilment of this indication. When, however, the poison has been made to penetrate below the external surface of the body, the following or several of the following steps will require to be taken:—

A ligature should be applied between the wound or sore and the heart, and as far from the wound as possible, taking care to arrest the circulation in the veins, but not in the arteries, as in ordinary venesection. This will prevent the absorption of the poison if adopted in time, or arrest its further absorption if it has already commenced.

The next step to be taken is to wash the wound carefully from every trace of the poison which may be within reach of this operation. When water is not to be readily obtained for this purpose, as in the chase, or on a march, a Dutch contemporary has thrown out the somewhat odd suggestion that, to supply the defect, freshly passed urine may be a good substitute for the pure element.

A further step to be taken is to attempt the withdrawal of what of the poison may be obstinately adhering to the wound, or have entered the current of the circulation at the wounded part. To accomplish this desirable end, various methods have been proposed. Thus Vernière advises that a vein should be opened as near to the ligature as possible, and as much of the local blood withdrawn as is likely to ensure the safety of the patient. Others recommend the manipulation of the soft parts around the wounds, so as by mechanical compression to squeeze out from them as much as possible of the blood they may contain. A further and better procedure is that generally recommended, namely, suction either by the mouth or cupping glasses. The former of these forms of suction has been long and extensively practised, particularly amongst savages, in the cure of the bites of venomous serpents. It was so well known to the ancient Greeks as to have been adopted as a trade, those who engaged in it being designated as "Psylli" (Van Hasselt). Dry cupping has also been extensively employed for poisoned wounds, both as a popular remedy and by scientific practitioners.

With the same object in view, the excision of the soft parts in the vicinity of the wound has been recommended, or even the amputation of the part when the wound is situated in a finger or limb.

Lastly, it has been one of the proposals against the effects of the noxious agent, to ensure the destruction of the poison itself by the application of various caustics or escharotics, such as caustic ammonia or potass, butter of antimony, potash ley, and the actual cautery.

Of these means, those which best deserve to be and are most usually employed are the following:—The application of a ligature; the careful washing of the wound; and suction by the mouth or cupping-glasses; with, in addition, free scarification of the part if necessary.

When poisons have been applied to the unbroken surfaces or the entrances of the various mucous canals—the mouth, nos-

GENERAL TOXICOLOGY.   597

anus, vagina—all that can be done is as speedily as possible to wash out as much as can be got of the noxious substance, and when it admits of it, to neutralise the remainder, as in the case of the mineral acids and alkalies.

When, as in the case of certain of the volatile poisons, these have been drawn into the lungs in inspiration, this indication seldom admits of being satisfactorily fulfilled. So extensive is the surface thus reached, and so rapidly does absorption here take place, that the poison will usually have got beyond our reach, before any attempt having its removal in view can be set up. And were it otherwise, the only resource within our power is the continuance of full and rapid inspirations and expirations to dilute and carry it off. Where the person affected is too insensible to yield to such a direction, it has been advised to set up artificial respiration, with or without the addition of the vapours of ammonia, chlorine, or tobacco.

Notwithstanding that the modes of entrance of poisons into the body, just enumerated, are occasionally encountered, the form with which the toxicologist is called to deal, is, in the vast majority of instances, where the poison has been swallowed, and where his first and most important aim must be to get the poison rejected by the stomach as speedily and as completely as possible.

Many poisons when swallowed, by inducing sickness and vomiting, enable the stomach to rid itself of the noxious substance without assistance. In this way it occasionally happens that the largeness of the dose, or the violent character of the poison, will prove, as previously stated, the safety of the patient. Of this I have, in a previous lecture, adduced several instances in the case of arsenic, and one in that of aconitia. The obvious expedient in these circumstances is to encourage the vomiting by the use of the mildest diluents.

Where vomiting has not thus spontaneously occurred, or where, if it has commenced, it is not sufficiently free, emetics should be at once administered, to ensure, as far as it can be effected, the full discharge of the poison. Of these, the most efficient and speedy must be chosen, and repeated at short intervals, till their full action is obtained.

The choice of the emetic to be given should be regulated by the character of the poison. Thus, as a general rule, the milder vegetable emetics, such as ipecacuan, or the preparations of squill are best adapted for the irritant, and many of the narcotico-acid, poisons; while tartar emetic or sulphate of zinc is called for in the case of the narcotic poisons. The sulphate of zinc should be given in a dose of ten grains, or, what is better, in one of five grains, repeated every ten minutes till it has acted freely

Failing to obtain any of the above drugs, or where too much time would be lost in procuring them, there are a few household substances generally at hand from which an emetic may be readily extemporised on an emergency. Thus table-salt, in the dose of one or two table-spoonfuls, dissolved in 18 or 20 ounces of luke-warm water, will readily act, especially after the swallowing of most of the metallic irritants, or even, as I have found by experience, in the case of opium and other narcotics. One or two tea-spoonfuls, again, of mustard in warm water, though more objectionable on account of its irritant properties, will readily act as an emetic in most cases of poisoning. Snuff has even been recommended in the same circumstances, though we should hesitate to tamper in any case with so dangerous a substance.

Simple diluents freely given will much assist the action of any of the above emetics, whether drugs or domestic articles; and vomiting may be hastened or assisted in most cases by tickling the throat or compressing the epigastrium

There are instances of poisoning, however, in which it would be either unsafe to administer emetics, or where, if administered, they would fail to act. In the first category are those patients who are predisposed to, or have already suffered from apoplexy or hæmoptysis Besides, it occasionally happens that, from the presence of profound stupor, or convulsions, the patient cannot be got to swallow any emetic; while again, some narcotics indirectly, and others, such as opium, directly paralyse the muscular coat of the stomach, rendering it thus insensible to the action of ordinary emetics. In any of these circumstances the stomach pump may be safely substituted, and should be at once had recourse to, and there can be no doubt that previous to its discovery many cases of narcotic poisoning proved fatal from the impossibility of dislodging the poison by emetics

The employment of the stomach pump, however, is sometimes difficult or impossible, as in the case of children, or during the continuance of convulsions or tetanic spasms, while it may be altogether contra-indicated, as after those poisons which corrode or severely irritate the gullet or stomach This last circumstance is too apt to be disregarded by practitioners unfamiliar with the treatment of poisoning Thus I have seen the stomach pump called for in cases where its application would have been very injurious; and only recently I encountered a case where it had actually been used after the swallowing of half-an-ounce of oxalic acid.

I need scarcely add that, in the cases to which the stomach pump is best adapted, it should be had recourse to at once, without waiting for the previous exhibition of an emetic. In those instances where the poison has had time to disappear entirely from the stomach by absorption or otherwise, its use may be dispensed with—a point, however, which should not be too hastily assumed, as some of the poisons may occasionally be detained for some time in this organ

The management of the stomach pump requires a little practical skill on the part of the person employing it. When the jaw of the patient is obstinately or convulsively clenched, this, of course, must be overcome before the œsophageal tube can be introduced. This may be done either by placing an assistant behind the patient's back, with the head of the latter resting on the breast of the former, and getting this person to depress the lower jaw of the other with the thumbs at its back part; or the operator himself, placed in front of the patient, introducing his two thumbs into the mouth and passing them onwards by the outsides of the rami of the jaw towards its angles, may readily effect the same end In practising either of these manœuvres, the operator must take care that his thumbs keep outside the patient's teeth when the jaws open, lest they be caught by their convulsive closure If necessary, to prevent the spasmodic or merely obstinate closure of the jaws subsequently, the gag may be placed betwixt them before the introduction of the œsophageal tube This, however, renders the introduction of the tube more difficult, as the operator cannot then direct it past the bend of the throat, so easily as in the unobstructed mouth Though the gag may not be needed with this object in view, it should nevertheless be slipped over the front end of the œsophageal tube, to prevent it being bitten by the patient during the operation, and thus destroyed It sometimes happens that when the œsophageal tube has reached the stomach it acts as a syphon, and thus secures the emptying of this viscus This can only be expected, however, when the stomach contains much fluid; and in these circumstances, pressure on the epigastrium may assist this spontaneous evacuation On most occasions it is necessary at the outset to throw water into the stomach by the pump, when, on reversing the action of the instrument, the contents thus diluted can be readily withdrawn, and the operation repeated till the fluid comes back as pure as it entered. The previous addition of a little table-salt to the injection occasionally assists in getting it readily to return by the pump. The connection betwixt the œsophageal tube and the pump should be so loose as to admit of their being detached from each other as quickly as possible during the operation, as, whether from the pressure of the tube on the larynx, or the escape of the contents of the stomach by its side during the operation, the patient occasionally threatens suffocation, necessitating the immediate withdrawal of the instrument to avoid this risk. Some poisonous substances in the solid state, or in that of powder, get so entangled amongst the rugæ of the stomach, that the ordinary action of the stomach pump fails to secure their detachment. This failure, however, may be overcome by a little management. In the case of a female who had swallowed two drachms of nux vomica, by introducing the fluid with a jerk and withdrawing it by the same manœuvre, I once succeeded in this, obtaining within five grains of the powder, in the intermissions betwixt the convulsive paroxysms.

There are other means of fulfilling the first indication—the getting rid of as much of the poison as possible—which may occasionally be employed, though far inferior in efficacy to those passed under review. I have already referred to the washing out of the poison from the rectum and the other openings of mucous canals, when it has been introduced into these. There are, again, some of the narcotic poisons of the vegetable class, in which the solid structures readily pass on from the stomach into the intestines, and admit of being expelled per anum by the use of laxative medicines. Again, there are other poisons, such as mushrooms, sausages, etc., which call for the same treatment, on account of their injurious effects continuing, after they have left the stomach and reached the smaller intestines. Where, in cases such as these, cathartics are called for, castor oil is the one usually chosen, on account of the mildness and certainty of its action, the activity of which, when called for by the urgency of the case, may be increased by the addition to it of one or two drops of croton oil.

2. It is seldom, however, that the whole of the poison can be removed from the system by any of the means at our command. When applied to a wound or sore on the exterior of the body, part of it will usually have been absorbed before assistance can arrive. Where it has reached the air-cells of the lungs in a

gaseous state, the activity of the absorption in that quarter is so great that time is not afforded for its dilution and subsequent expulsion by the continuance of respiration. When poison has remained for a short time in the stomach, it will have had time for incorporation with the coats of the viscus in a few cases; in others it will have disorganised its tissues; in other cases still it will have been absorbed, or begun to adhere to its walls so firmly as to render it difficult to be detached by the action of emetics or the use of the stomach pump, or, lastly, it will have passed beyond the pylorus into the smaller intestines. In all of these ways the second indication will come to be called for at our hands—namely, the counteraction of the primary effect, as far as can be done, of such portions of the poison as we have not been able to remove by any of the methods I have noticed, and which may be still within the reach of our preventive means.

To this branch of the treatment of poisoning, the term antidotal has been applied. Not a little vagueness has, however, been attached at various periods, and still continues to attach, to the term antidote, and its English synonym counter-poison, while the sense in which it is now employed, though still somewhat loose, differs essentially from that in which it was used by the ancients. The notion long prevailed, and met with universal acceptance in early times, that there were substances in nature of a character so opposite to that of any one poison whatever, that, preceded or accompanied by them, the poison might be exhibited without any bad effects. Hence the host of so-called universal antidotes, or alexipharmics, both of a simple and compound character contained in the older writings. Thus, amongst simple or uncompounded bodies we have the "toadstone" (lapis Bufonius), the "serpentstone" (lapis serpenarius), the "swine stone" (lapis porcinus), the "rhinoceros stone," and different sorts of "bezoars," from the animal and vegetable kingdoms; the mithridate, diascordium, diatessaron, and theriaca—electuaries compounded chiefly of opium, with the addition of aromatic substances; lizard's flesh, hare's and viper's fat. etc., with, in addition, compounds, the ingredients in which were kept secret, under the names of "orvietan," "euthanasia," etc.

The action of these secret remedies was attributed to the so-called sympathies and antipathies betwixt the antidote and the poison, the innocuous in the one case attracting thus to itself and imparting its own harmless character to the noxious substance; while, in the other, the contrariety betwixt the two was believed to be such that the poison could not remain in the body in the presence of the antidote.

Coming nearer to our own times, we find the earlier chemists engaged, like their predecessors, in the vain search for an universal antidote, the only fruit of whose labours has been the knowledge of a few substances, such as the acetic and tannic acids, magnesia, soap, and charcoal, which long enjoyed a wide reputation, which they still retain as subordinate means in a few instances of actual poisoning, though shorn of the importance attributed to them by their discoverers.

Apart altogether from such fanciful, imaginary, and feeble, if not altogether delusive, antidotes, and short of these to which the term is now most frequently restricted, we are in possession of a limited number of remedies, which are believed on evidence of a more or less satisfactory kind to have the effect to a greater or less extent, of weakening or destroying the injurious action of certain poisons, by exciting in the system an action contrary to that established by these poisons. Mercurial salivation is thus believed to counteract the remote operation of lead; the action of mercury on the salivary glands is in the same way thought to be counteracted by chlorate of potass, or by nauseating doses of tartar emetic; the sedative effects of prussic acid are so far obviated by ammonia and chlorine; and those of opium and alcohol by vinegar and infusions of coffee or green tea; while some remedies are believed to assist in the expulsion of poisons by the emunctories To this class of remedies, for distinction's sake, the term physiological antidotes has been applied.

Within the last few years, the supposed antagonism between poisonous substances has been carried out experimentally in animals, with the expectation of our being enabled to employ one powerful poison to counteract the injurious effects of another As strychnia, for instance, is a powerful excitant of the nervous system, it has been assumed that a poison like curarine, which depresses or annihilates nervous power, would be an efficient antidote for it With the same object, and on the same principle, nicotine, aconitine, and calabar bean (physostigma), have been suggested as antidotes to strychnia, atropia to morphia, and physostigma to atropia, on the ground of the opposite effects of these poisons on the pupils

So far as these experimental trials have as yet gone, some such antagonism has been found betwixt hydrate of chloral and strychnia, sulphate of atropia and calabar bean, chloral and calabar bean, and hydrate of bromal and atropia; while no such antagonism has been shown betwixt atropia and morphia, or morphia and theine, caffeine, and guaranine

How far these supposed counter-agents are likely to be available in poisoning in man yet remains to be seen. Some good grounds for distrust in such cases have been advanced by such eminent physiologists as Bernard and Fraser.

But besides this class of agents antagonistic to poisons there is another class whose remedial powers are found to depend upon some phy... influence, such as an absorbing or suspending agency which t... exert over the poison. To this class of substances which I may term physical antidotes, in preference to that of mechanical, as usually adopted, belong charcoal, the hydrates of iron and magnesia, gruel, fatty substances, oil and water, chalk and water, flour and water, etc, all of which have occasionally been found useful as means of suspending the poisonous agent, and of protecting the coats of the stomach during the time which is lost in the administration of an emetic, or the employment of the stomach pump. Such, in fact, were almost without exception the so-termed antidotes known to our predecessors prior to the rise of modern chemistry; their practice consisting, after the removal of as much of the poison as could be got rid of by various emetic substances, in the exhibition, under this name, of mucilaginous and oleaginous substances, and in a few instances of such stimuli as were likely to counteract the depressing effects of the poison.

Without entirely overlooking the utility, however, of such constitutional and physical counteracting treatment—an error into which our modern writers have been disposed to fall—there can be no doubt that they are so far correct in assuming, as is generally done, that the most efficient, if not the most numerous class of antidotes, are those which are derived from chemistry, and hence termed—

Chemical antidotes, or antidotes strictly so-called. These counter-poisons, in order fully to meet the requirements of the case, should possess the following properties, both of a positive and of a negative kind:

The two most essential qualities of the antidote are that it shall readily unite with the poison within the body, so as thereby to form with it a wholly insoluble, or a nearly insoluble compound and that this compound shall itself be harmless, or at least much less injurious to the system than the substance whose operation it is given to counteract.

Most, though not all, of our poisons, derived from the mineral, and some of them derived from the vegetable kingdom, are, as formerly remarked, only dangerous in solution. Hence our most efficient antidotes are those which form with them insoluble compounds; such as sulphate of magnesia in the case of lead, chalk in the case of oxalic acid, and common salt in that of nitrate of silver. Other antidotes, though not rendering the poison insoluble, are useful by yielding harmless, or nearly harmless compounds; as in the case of very dilute vinegar given to neutralise the caustic alkalies

It should be borne in mind, however, that the mere insolubility of the compound formed under these circumstances is not in every instance to be held as equivalent to its inertness This point has been impressed on our notice by the experiments of Chevallier, undertaken to determine the value of some of the antidotes brought forward for counteracting the noxious effects of strychnia. As the result of his trials on animals, this experimentalist has convincingly shown that, though some of the proposed antidotes for this poison, such as tannin and iodine, have the property of forming with it insoluble compounds, yet these compounds are themselves either redissolved in the stomach, or yield up the alkaloids once more, leaving the poison, after a brief arrest of its violent effects, to resume its injurious action with as much force as if no such arrest had intervened

The further and most important requirement on the part of the chemical antidote, namely, that the counter-poison itself be wholly, or nearly, free from injurious properties, excludes some substances which meet all the demands of our previous proposition Thus, for this reason, we must reject such articles as nitrate of silver for prussic acid, and chloride of platinum for caustic potash. For the same reason, the mineral alkalies cannot be safely given to neutralise the mineral acids, or, conversely, the mineral acids to counteract the mineral alkalies The antidote, in actual practice, must be given in excess, in which case we would only be here throwing in a second poison in addition to the first.

Besides these two leading qualifications, a third requirement is demanded of the chemical antidote, namely, that it be capable of acting speedily on the poison; and a fourth, that this action be of such a kind as can be set up at the ordinary temperature of the stomach These two points are of so obvious a nature that they need not be insisted on. They explain the necessary failures of such proposed antidotes as iron filings for some of the metallic poisons, and common sugar for the salts of copper

Once more the value of an antidote is enhanced when it is

found to be an article readily procurable, without loss of time, in an emergency. It thus not unfrequently happens in actual practice that the readiest antidote is purposely preferred, though it may not equal some other and better one which is not within reach at the moment it is wanted

These obvious considerations, in regard to antidotes, are not sufficiently attended to by chemists and medical practitioners in general. Hence it is that we can scarcely take up a medical journal in which we do not encounter some proposed new antidote, which, on trial, fails to fulfil the conditions required, if it is to be of any efficacy at all, or to be safely had recourse to in practice.

The number of undoubted antidotes—particularly if, with most modern toxicologists, we limit their number to those of the chemical class—is by no means great. In the lists of those given by Devergie and Taylor, it will be found that, with the doubtful exception of prussic acid, the poisons for which we possess chemical antidotes are limited to the inorganic class, leaving us powerless in this respect against the direct toxical operation of the vast array of organic poisons known to us, the number of which is being continually added to.

3. This brings me to the consideration of the last point I proposed to discuss in regard to the treatment of poisoning—namely, the remaining means possessed by us for obviating the effects of poison after the failure or partial operation of these already discussed, or, in other words, the remedies to be adopted for the cure of the resulting disorders it may have occasioned. Few cases occur in practice, even under the most favourable circumstances, in which this last indication does not call for fulfilment, either from the imperfection of our remedial means, or from the period at which assistance has been called for having been too advanced to permit of our best methods being successfully had recourse to, before the poison has got beyond our reach. We may equally fail in removing the poison from the body, and in neutralising it by the proper antidote. Here the toxicologist, it will be seen, comes to be placed, in most respects, in the position of the practitioner called to treat ordinary disease. For, as the injurious effects produced on the body by the exhibition of poisons do not differ specifically from the results of ordinary morbid causes, it is not to be expected that the treatment of the one set of cases will require to be conducted on other than the same general principles, and by the same remedial agencies. There is the speciality, however, in the diseased states induced by the operation of poisons that, when the poison

has once been incorporated with the system or with the organs, which, if not removed in time or counteracted, it may ultimately reach, it renders the induced disease frequently more intractable and less amenable to treatment than if the like disorder had commenced in the ordinary way. Hence the partial success of the practitioner in the treatment of the diseased states induced by poison, in the majority of such instances On the other hand it is to be observed, as a further speciality here, that, as the disorders induced by certain of the poisons are purely functional, and the period during which these disorders continue is often shorter than that of natural disease, it may happen, in this case, that, when the practitioner can succeed in counteracting for a time the functional disorder, ultimate recovery is more certain than when that disorder has been induced by natural causes. To counterbalance this advantage, however, there is a large class of cases where the practitioner has to encounter difficulties which seldom present themselves in ordinary practice. I refer particularly to the effects of the narcotico-acrids, where we have increased action of the vascular with lowered action of the nervous system, and where, in attempting to diminish the one we necessarily increase the other, and *vice versa*. Hence the notorious failure of our resources in many cases of this nature which we are called on to treat with decision and energy

Having thus considered the position of the practitioner as the medical attendant in the case of poisoning, and the leading principles applicable to the treatment medically of such cases generally, I now come to consider the position he may be called on to occupy in such cases in his medico-legal capacity.

When called in during the lifetime of his patient, the first and most obvious duty of the practitioner is to use the utmost diligence to ensure, as far as his resources go, the safety of his patient. This is to be done to the best of his skill and ability, whether successfully or otherwise. Another and equally onerous duty of a twofold kind lies before him, which calls for its conscientious performance: the duty, namely, of doing what he can to counteract the effects of some noxious substance inadvertently or otherwise taken, and that of giving the aid of all his skill and science for the bringing home of crime to the guilty, where poison has been knowingly and wilfully administered

And here, again, I would remind you that, while the practitioner, when called to a suspicious case of this nature, should not officiously or unnecessarily step beyond his proper province, he is not, on the other hand, at liberty to decline doing what he can, when duty calls for his interference, particularly as the proofs of poisoning can only be properly elicited when the medical attendant is sufficiently awake to the importance of his position, and competent to the efficient performance of the work which it may impose on him.

LECTURE XLIV.

GENERAL TOXICOLOGY—*Continued*

DUTIES OF THE MEDICAL PRACTITIONER IN CASES OF POISONING GENERALLY—In his ordinary capacity—As a Medical Jurist—Information deducible from the History of the Patient during life—Information deducible from the Inspection of the Body after death—Information deducible from Chemical Analysis —MODE OF CONDUCTING THE CHEMICAL ANALYSIS—When the poison is in the Pure State—When mixed with Foreign Substances—Preliminary Investigation—Subsequent Investigation

THE particulars which demand the attention of the medical jurist, in a case of suspected poisoning, are deducible from three different sources. 1st, from the history of the patient during life; 2d, from the inspection of the body after death; 3d, from a chemical analysis of remains of suspected articles of food, drink, or medicine, vomited matters, the contents of the alimentary tube, and the fluids, secretions, or tissues of the body, either combined or singly

Much of what would fall to be treated here has been anticipated in the examination I have already had occasion to institute into the nature of poisons, their modes of action, the circumstances modifying their action, the symptoms they give rise to, the traces they leave on the dead body, and their chemical qualities generally All that remains for me to do, in this place, is to bring into juxtaposition the leading points of evidence expected on the part of the medical witness, briefly recalling those which have been already considered, and adding such others as I had no opportunity of previously adducing. In doing so I may premise that, as the investigation which has to be undertaken when a person is supposed to have died by poison, embraces the previous history of the case in the same manner as if recovery had taken place, in order to avoid repetition, I may arrange my remarks under the heads of (1) the post-mortem examination and (2) the chemical analysis

(1.) Of the post-mortem examination in cases of alleged death from poison In proceeding to inspect the body of a person suspected to have been poisoned, it is of the utmost importance for the examiner, before commencing his inspection, to be in possession of all the authentic information which can be procured regarding the previous history of the case. Should he not have been the attendant of the deceased, and acquainted with its particulars, he should at once proceed to supply this desideratum. He should elicit information in regard to the symptoms of the illness during life, the time of their occurrence, their nature, the order of their succession, how far they may have been stationary, intermittent, increasing or diminishing in severity during its course the previous health of the party; the relation of his illness to food, drink, and medicine previously or subsequently taken, whether brought on or aggravated by them, and whether these were partaken of by the patient alone, or shared by others: in the latter case what effects they produced, and whether these articles or vomited matters were preserved or destroyed. The period of the commencement of the illness, and of the fatal event, should also be ascertained and noted down; as well as any particulars bearing on the case which may have been derived from parties who had been present during its course. Such information is of importance to the examiner at the inspection, as it leads him to attend particularly to the state of the organs which are most usually affected by the individual poison or the class of poisons in question; and may prevent his overlooking points and circumstances to which otherwise his search and observation might not have extended.

Before proceeding to the inspection, the examiner should provide himself with ligatures, distilled water, vessels for containing the stomach, the intestines, and any matters which may have been vomited.

If this has not been already done, all the suspected articles, whether of food, drink, or medicine, which may be found in the apartment of the deceased, should be collected, and sealed up for future examination; and great care should be used in doing this necessary duty. If any substances have been spilt on the floor, a new and carefully washed sponge, or a clean cloth, should be used to wipe them up, when they may be preserved in a separate vessel. If the deceased had vomited, the vomited matters—especially those first ejected—should be preserved, and their quantity, odour, colour, and acid or alkaline reaction noted. If the vomiting have taken place on articles of dress, or on the floor or furniture of the room, the stained portion of the clothing, sheet, or carpet should be cut out, and preserved for analysis. If the vomiting have occurred on a deal floor, a portion of the wood may be scraped off or cut out;

or if on a stone pavement, a clean piece of rag or sponge soaked in distilled water, should be used to remove any traces of the substance. In November 1854 I found distinct traces of arsenic, in a small quantity of earthy and other matters taken from the side of a dunghill, in Banffshire, into which vomited fluids had been thrown some days before. The vessel in which vomited matters had been contained will sometimes furnish valuable evidence, since heavy mineral poisons fall to the bottom, or adhere to the sides of the vessel. In the seam at the bottom of a wooden bowl (Scottice, cog) in which poison was said to have been mixed up with oatmeal and beer, at New Pitsligo, in April 1854, I detected a notable quantity of perchloride of mercury. When the vomited substances consist of animal matters liable to run speedily into putrefaction, it has been advised that they be kept in alcohol diluted with about its own weight of water. But the addition of any preservative liquid should be avoided, as it might complicate or embarrass the future chemical analysis. Fœcal matters should also be preserved.

In proceeding to the external examination of the body, the inspector should carefully note down the attitude in which it is found; the appearance of the countenance, whether expressive of suffering or otherwise; any spots which may exist on the skin, the lips, or the fingers, and these should then be removed with the scalpel for future analysis. The same thing should be done with the teeth, when they present any appearance of having been stained or corroded.

In proceeding to open the body, the chief attention must be directed to the alimentary canal. The œsophagus should not be disturbed in the examination of the trachea. The condition of the mouth and pharynx should be first noted down, before the organs in the chest are inspected. The left lung should be reversed upon the heart, to expose the course of the œsophagus, and a ligature placed around it close to the diaphragm; two ligatures should then be tied around the pyloric extremity of the stomach, and the duodenum divided between them, to allow of the removal of the stomach. The same thing is to be done at the termination of the ileum, and the smaller intestines removed. Finally, the extremity of the rectum being secured, the larger intestines are to be removed from the body.

The stomach and intestines should then be opened separately in basins, or other convenient and clean vessels, whose capacity is known, and if regularly graduated, so much the better. Care must be taken to observe the contents of the separate portions of the alimentary tube, the state of their tissues, and the alterations they may have undergone. In regard to the contents of the stomach, it is of importance to note their quantity, odour, colour, acidity or alkalinity; whether luminous or not in the dark, the presence of blood, mucus, or bile, the presence or absence of crystalline matter, foreign substances, or undigested food and spirituous fluid. The appearance of the rugæ of the stomach, and of their interspaces, particularly in the vicinity of the great *cul de sac*, should be remarked, as it is in this situation that traces of poison and its effects are most frequently left. If the stomach is found inflamed, the seat of the inflammation should be exactly specified; as also that of any softening, unusual coloration, ulceration, effusion of blood, corrosion, or perforation, which may be met with. The same minute attention should be paid to the smaller and larger intestines and their contents. The parts of the intestines where morbid appearances are most frequently found, in cases of poisoning, are, the duodenum, upper part of the jejunum, the lower part of the ileum, and the rectum. The comparative intensity of the appearances of irritation at different parts of the alimentary tube should be noticed, as it may throw much light on a suspected case of poisoning, and may sometimes obviate the necessity for any further proceedings. Thus, if the stomach is sound, and the intestines only inflamed, the possibility of irritant poisoning may be pretty safely negatived.

A case of this sort came under my notice in March 1855. A box was sent me for analysis from a distance, containing, besides tea in dry leaves and infusions, and sugars, a piece of human liver, and a stomach and smaller intestines. On examining these last, though the stomach was partially reddened, it was found that the duodenum was the seat of intense inflammation. As was to have been expected, therefore, the search for traces of any of the irritant poisons was unsuccessful.

In the case of a man, who died in 1872, in the parish of Turriff (Aberdeenshire), under suspicious circumstances, at the inspection of the body intense inflammation of the smaller intestines, with a healthy state of the throat, gullet, and stomach, led at once to the abandonment by the law authorities of any further inquiry into the case.

After this examination of the stomach and intestines, the organs are to be put into wide-mouthed vessels, each part by itself, and the basins in which they were opened washed out with distilled water into the bottle appropriated to the morbid part, adding so much water as to cover the contained viscus. When the poison has led to the perforation of the stomach or bowels, the substances effused into the abdominal cavity should be carefully collected and preserved separately. The pharynx and œsophagus, with their contents, if any, should be also preserved. In cases of poisoning by arsenic, the liver and the mass of the blood may require to be preserved, and the poison afterwards sought for in either or both of these. The same thing may require to be done in the case of the greater number of the metallic poisons. Phosphorus alone leaves characteristic appearances in the liver. In instances of suspected poisoning with opium and its salts, and the whole of the vegetable alkaloids, besides portions of the viscera most largely supplied with blood, portions of blood, and the whole of the urine, should be kept, since those poisons have been found in these solids and fluids after death.

The remaining organs of the abdomen must be surveyed, particularly the spleen, kidneys, and rectum; and in the female the uterus and its appendages, including the vagina. No portion of the suspected articles should be wasted at the dissection, or in preliminary trials or testing. A sealed and signed label ought to be attached to each of the vessels before their removal from the apartment.

Suffer me to subjoin a few more directions in regard to the duty of the medical jurist, where articles have to be preserved for chemical analysis, in cases of suspected poisoning. Care must be taken both to preserve these from every source of contamination at the inspection, and to prevent the possibility of their being tampered with subsequently. Supposing, for instance, that during the post-mortem examination the stomach and viscera are removed from the body, they should never be placed on any surface, or in any vessel, until it has been first ascertained that the surface or vessel is perfectly clean. Not only must clean vessels be used for receiving any article destined for subsequent analysis, but care must be taken by the practitioner that its identity be preserved, and that no one but himself has access to it till the chemical examination is brought to a close. The vessels for the removal of viscera or liquids from the body for analysis should be the most suitable for the purpose. They should be wide-mouthed, as I have said, not more than sufficiently large to hold the viscus or liquid, to the exclusion of as much air as possible; and they should be secured with, first, a close-fitting cork, covered with skin or bladder, second, a piece of bladder to embrace the cork and neck of the bottle, third, a layer of tinfoil; and lastly, with white leather

I had occasion, at a previous part of the course, to point out the fact of its being occasionally necessary to examine the body for the remains of poison, even after longer or shorter, but still considerably extended, periods of interment. That putrefaction or decay of the body does not always render the detection of poisons impossible has been satisfactorily proved by the experiments of Orfila and Lesueur. They placed in the dead body, and allowed to remain there for some time, each of the following poisons— namely, sulphuric and nitric acids, arsenic, corrosive sublimate, tartar emetic, sugar of lead, protochloride of tin, sulphate of copper, verdigris, nitrate of silver, chloride of gold, acetate of morphia, chloride of brucia, acetate of strychnia, prussic acid, opium, and cantharides. They found that the acids became neutralised by the ammonia disengaged during the decay of the animal matter, that by the action of the animal matter the salts of mercury, antimony, copper, tin, gold, silver, and likewise the salts of the vegetable alkaloids, undergo chemical decomposition, in consequence of which the bases become less soluble in water, that acids may be detected, after several years' interment, not always however in the free state, that the bases of the decomposed metallic salts may also be found after interment for several years, that arsenic, opium, and cantharides undergo little change after a long interval of time, and are scarcely more difficult to discover in decayed than in recent animal mixtures, but that hydrocyanic acid disappears very soon, so as to be indistinguishable in the course of a few days

I now come to the remaining branch of the duty of the medical practitioner in cases of suspected poisoning, namely—

The chemical analysis of the articles secured and sealed up by him during his previous investigation into the case. And here again, at the outset, the question recurs, Is the medical practitioner the proper party to conduct the chemical analysis on occasions of this sort? Till recently this question would have been settled in the affirmative, if the general practice of the profession and of the legal authorities had been taken as the proper criterion. For some years back, however, a different line of procedure has been adopted in many instances, especially in England, the medical inspectors handing over this part of the investigation to the professional chemist. This at first sight, might seem to be the best course for securing the efficient discharge of the complicated task of collecting the evidence of poisoning in any case. But a little practical acquaintance with the subject will suffice to show that in this way the ends of justice may readily come to be defeated. Amongst the crowd of poisons within the reach of the suicide or the murderer, how is the search of the chemist to be guided, unless he has been previously furnished with a correct account of the symptoms, mode of action, and appearances left by the individual poison which he is required to detect or isolate, and unless by his previous studies he has been enabled correctly to appreciate these, and to act with precision on the information thus obtained. This, it is obvious, no mere chemist, unacquainted with practical medicine, could be expected to be able to do. On the other hand, it must be equally evident that, in the present advanced state of chemical science, the medical practitioner is not qualified to undertake an analysis in a case of suspected poisoning, unless familiar with chemical research, and experienced in the conduct of its leading operations.

To meet the requirements of a case of this sort, it appears to me that the two parties to the investigation should be acquainted with the science of toxicology in its whole extent and be present together throughout the different stages of the inquiry; and that if the one was superior as a pathologist and the other as a chemist, every possible advantage would be secured for the interests of the public.

Till this step in advance is gained, we must be content to address ourselves to what is likely occasionally to be the position of the practitioner under the present imperfect system. After what has been already stated, I would only remind you that, to accomplish his task successfully, the practitioner requires to be possessed of an intimate acquaintance with the nature of the most important individual poisons, their physical and chemical properties, the symptoms they produce, and the morbid appearances they give rise to in the dead body, as well as of some facility in chemical manipulation, and familiarity with the actions of the usual tests on the elementary substances of the body, and the various separate poisons. A good microscope, and some practice in its management, will also be found to be occasionally very useful.

In proceeding to the chemical analysis for the detection of the poisonous ingredient, when the presence of some one poison is rendered probable, the chief difficulty which presents itself to the examiner in not a few instances, is not so much how he has to follow out the search for the individual poison pointed at by the other sources of available evidence, as to determine what that one poison is which he may have to detect and separate. The consideration of this point, unlike the other, which belongs to special, is one which comes under general toxicology, the subject at present engaging our attention.

Let us see then what is the position occupied by the toxicologist where poisoning is probable, but where the poison can only be guessed at, or is wholly unknown, and what are the means possessed by him for meeting this unfavourable conjuncture of circumstances.

In actual practice we may have to undertake the search for poison either out of or in the body, or in both situations. We may have the suspected poison in a separate state without foreign admixture; we may have it mixed with various articles of food or drink, or otherwise disguised by foreign admixture; we may have it in combination, or even altered by its union with the animal fluids, ejected, dejected, or excreted out of the body, or we may have it on its removal from the body after death tolerably pure; mixed with the contents of the alimentary tube, or articles of food or drink incorporated with it there; combined with the tissues of the stomach or duodenum, or of distant organs which it may have reached by absorption; or present, and more or less changed in the blood or secretions.

It will not be necessary here, however, to advert to the search for the poison under each of these varied circumstances. It will be enough if I at present point out the mode of arriving at the determination of the individual poison, first, where it is presented to us in the pure state, and secondly, in combination with foreign matters, either as discovered or suspected, in or out of the body.

1st, When the poison is in the pure or unmixed state. Here both the physical and the chemical characters may assist us, the former enabling us to avail ourselves of the latter. To enable the examiner to condescend on the poison before him in this state, Devergie has drawn out two elaborate tables for guidance, confining himself, however, to inorganic poisons; the one intended for the discrimination of such as are insoluble, and the other for those which are soluble in water. In the former he starts from the colour of the poison under examination—white, red, blue, or green, etc., and in the latter adopts the same guide, as far as this is fitted to conduct the examiner. In addition, this toxicologist adopts other starting-points, such as the smell, acidity, or alkalinity or the effects of hydrogen, sulphide, etc., followed by the usual reagents for the various known inorganic poisons.

2d, When the toxicologist, as most frequently happens, has to search for the supposed poison in combination with foreign matters, within or out of the body, he has often a more difficult task to perform, and one which will occasionally require all his resources to be put forth to meet the emergency. Let us suppose, for instance, that no remains of the suspected poison in the pure state have been obtained, and that the study of the case —its history during life, and the result of the post-mortem inspection subsequently—has failed to indicate the individual poison, and has done no more than yield a vague suspicion of poisoning generally, is the examiner to give up the task of discovery as a hopeless one? Without having gained any clue to direct him what course to take for ascertaining the toxical substance which may be present—in the contents of the stomach for instance— and, having decided that some search is to be made, is he to proceed to seek at random for one after another of the most likely of the popularly known poisons, till he has wasted the whole of his material, and perhaps has missed the poison really contained in it? a circumstance by no means improbable. Thus, in the case of Sarah Hart, tried in England, Mr Cooper having been led to believe that oxalic acid was present in her stomach, sought for it, and failing it, for the mineral poisons, until he had almost exhausted his material, when accident, for it was nothing else, led to the discovery of prussic acid. A similar case lately occurred in France, where the examiner, after some experiments almost at random, stumbled upon the protosulphate of iron in quantity in the contents of a stomach.

In examining, the contents of the stomach or other animal admixtures suspected to contain a poison unknown, some assistance may be gained by observing carefully their colour, odour, or general appearance. Their acidity or alkalinity, if either of these characters prevails in the mass, may direct us to the search for the leading acid or alkaline poisons. If the substances to be examined are contained in, or accompanied with, the stomach or smaller intestines, the presence of traces in these of irritation, inflammation, or corrosion, will point to the probability of irritant or corrosive poisons, their absence to narcotic poisons. To obtain all the aid which this preliminary search is calculated to afford, care should be taken that no insoluble matter present in the mass under examination be overlooked. For this purpose the whole, if fluid, should either be strained through a fine linen cloth, or what is better, poured into a clean, flat, white dish, and left to stand for some time, when, in the one case, the solid matter on the cloth should be examined, or in the other, the supernatant fluid may be poured off, leaving behind it in the dish any solid substance which may have subsided from it, in a state favourable for inspection. The inner surfaces of the stomach or intestines, when they form part of the production, should be carefully examined for any adhering matter which may be attached to them, or in contact with them.

In this manner the examiner may discover the presence of the leaves, berries, etc., of poisonous plants, glittering particles of cantharides, or small pieces of arsenic, or other solid poison. A good lens, and a microscope of moderate power, will sometimes succeed in discriminating the vegetable tissues which may in this way present themselves; or by showing the crystalline forms of saline matters, point out the individual poison of this class. Where inorganic solids can be picked out of the mass on the point of a needle or knife, very small particles may be not unfrequently tested pretty satisfactorily by the blowpipe, in the hands of a competent operator.

When, again, the suspected matter is in a fluid state, and apparently of a homogeneous kind, or where the fluid portion of it has been separated from its more solid part in either of the ways pointed out; its physical characters will occasionally assist in detecting the probable existence of poison in it. By its smell the chemist may be led to seek in it for volatile poisons, such as prussic acid, oil of bitter almonds, savine oil, turpentine, ammonia, and alcohol. The colour may distinguish the poison, as in the case of salts of copper, by the bluish or greenish colour which they usually impart to fluids; nitric acid will sometimes be suspected by the canary yellow hue which it imparts to organic fluids; as also sulphuric acid by the dark colour imparted to same fluids by this poison. Nitrate of silver and corrosive sublimate not only coagulate organic fluids, but also produce in them a whitish colour by combining with the albumen which they contain.

Should no clue be thus gained to the probable poison contained in the fluid—rendered neutral, if not previously so—it may be useful to dip into it a slip of bibulous paper, which should then be placed in a tube in a current of sulphuretted hydrogen, and subsequently, if no change of colour is produced on the paper, in sulphide of ammonium. In this way the presence of some one or other of the following mineral poisons may be shown present in any quantity in the original fluids—namely, arsenic, the proto- and per- salts of tin antimonial salts, the soluble compounds of lead, copper, mercury bismuth, iron, silver, gold, nickel, cobalt, zinc, and the chromates of potass. The advantage of the paper is, that it absorbs the poison in the fluid, sufficiently free from the organic substances in it, to allow the action of the tests, in cases where they would fail to act on portions of the mixture itself.

Should this preliminary investigation have failed to render probable or certain the existence, in the matter under examination, of any particular poison, the further exploratory steps to be taken are as follows.—The whole should be carefully and uniformly mixed as far as possible, solid matters broken up into small portions, and diffused through the more fluid portion, and the whole divided into two equal parts Only on ` these parts should be operated on, the other half being reserv￬ .ther for the verification, if necessary, of the results which may be arrived at by the examiner, or to be handed over to some other and more experienced operator, should the law authorities consider this advisable.

Having fixed upon the half of the material to be operated on, this is next to be subdivided into two equal portions, each of which is to be submitted, separately and in succession, to analytical operations, and with a distinct object in view, for, though such has been worked out in theory, no single method which could well be devised can be made to embrace in one series of operations the detection of all the known poisons, in a practical or satisfactory manner.

One of the sub-divided portions of the material may, however, be made to subserve two series of operations, while the remaining sub-divided portion may be used for the third and last of the series. Taking, then, the first of the sub-divided portions, or the fourth of the original material, it should be introduced into a tubulated retort and a receiver adapted, or, what is better, an alembic and the capital applied, having previously added, if necessary, so much distilled water as to bring the whole to the consistence of a thin pulp The heat of a water-bath should then be applied to the retort or alembic, and continued till a third part, or, if necessary, the whole of the fluid portion, has come over into the receiver The distilled portion is now to be examined for the volatile poisons, such as alcohol, prussic acid, nicotine, hydrochloric acid, ammonia, etc

This first series of exploratory operations being completed, whether with or without satisfactory results, the second series may be proceeded with. With this view, the substance left in the retort or alembic should be mixed with concentrated acetic acid to strongly acid reaction, and the mixture digested for several hours, previously adding, if necessary, a little distilled water. The fluid part is then to be strained off from the solid part, the latter to be washed with water acidulated with acetic acid. The fluids thus obtained are to be evaporated to dryness on the water-bath; the re‑‑‑‑e to be boiled, first with pure spirits of wine, then with a‑‑‑l, containing a little acetic acid, the alcoholic solution thus o‑‑‑‑d evaporated nearly to dryness on the water-bath; the residue, diluted with water, rendered feebly alkaline by carbonate of soda, evaporated to the consistence of syrup, allowed to stand at rest for twenty-four hours, again diluted with water and filtered, the precipitate washed with water, digested with concentrated acetic acid, and decolorised, if necessary, with pure animal charcoal.

The fluid thus obtained is now in a proper state for being tested for the vegetable alkaloids—morphia, strychnia, brucia, veratria, etc. By this process I have succeeded in procuring strychnia from half an ounce of liver, an ounce of blood, and also from putrid matters in the smaller intestines several weeks after death from this poison.

(In connection with the search for the vegetable alkaloids, it might be useful to study the table constructed by Valser, given by Gaultier de Claubry, in the *Annales d' Hygiène*, No 36, p. 43.)

Having thus carried out the second series of exploratory operations on one fourth of the original materials, the second fourth may be employed for the third or concluding series. For this purpose the mass is to be placed in a porcelain basin, and evaporated in a water-bath to a pasty consistence. An amount of pure hydrochloric acid is then to be added, equal at least in bulk to the weight of the matter, and so much distilled water as to bring the whole to the consistence of a thin paste. Successive portions of chlorate of potash are next to be added, till the whole has become of a permanent canary colour and of a fluid consistency. The contents of the basin are afterwards to be cooled and filtered, the residue well washed with hot water, the filtrate and washings mixed and concentrated, an excess of sulphite of soda added, the excess of sulphurous acid driven off by heat, the whole cooled, and sulphuretted hydrogen transmitted through it for twenty-four hours in a warm place.

The precipitate, if any, which has fallen on standing, will be some one of the metallic poisons, none of which will elude detection by this method. This process was first proposed by Fresenius, and admits of being applied to the animal solid as readily as to mixed fluids and the animal fluids and secretion.

The course thus sketched out, when followed in all its details, embraces the search for by far the greater number of the poisons admitting of detection, enables the examiner to form a very correct opinion of the nature of the poison present in the material submitted to him, and permits him with confidence to proceed to the special examination with the remaining half of his original material. This will afford the opportunity of verifying former results, and of determining, where this admits of being done, the amount of the particular poison discovered, while it leaves the examiner at liberty to select the method which experience has shown to be best adapted for the verification and separation of the remains of the particular poison.

Without pretending that this or any other scheme can be looked on as perfect or infallible, or as capable of leading to the detection of more than a large number of our best known and best marked poisons, I have given it as the one which I have myself followed in practice, and which I have found to be capable of being worked out, in whole or in part with tolerable facility. Without claiming for it any originality, being largely indebted to the work of Fresenius, it takes a wider range than the scheme promulgated by Tardieu and Roussin in their work on poisoning, as they leave out the search for the mineral acids, and restrict the number of individual poisons sought for.

To complete this part of his task, one duty remains to be attended to by the medical examiner beyond the chemical investigation, as regards the contents of the stomach and intestines, or it may be, the remains of food out of the body with which poisonous articles may have been found mixed. I refer to the microscopical examination as distinct from the chemical, a subject which I have thought it best to reserve for separate notice.

In the physical examination of the contents of the stomach and intestines which was advised prior to commencing the chemical investigation, you will remember that it was recommended that the matters found in those viscera should be poured into and spread out on a clean flat dish or plate of glass, and examined first with the naked eye and then with a good lens. The detection by this means of any alterations of the tissues, or the presence of any foreign body, will demand the employment of the microscope, beginning with a magnifying power of from 25 to 50 diameters, and rising to one of from 250 to 300 The stomach and intestines may be found to contain alimentary and other matters, more or less broken up or digested, which it may be of importance to the case to be in a condition to discriminate and individualise. The microscope may thus detect certain tissues and elementary organs characteristic of animal or vegetable substances, such as muscular fibres striped or unstriped, adipose tissue, woody fibre, chlorophyll, the fibro-vascular bundles or stomata, or the starch granules of different plants, as found in various alimentary matters, animal or vegetable

LECTURE XLV.

GENERAL TOXICOLOGY—(*Concluded*)

Imaginary Poisoning—Feigned Poisoning—Suspected Poisoning—Imputed Poisoning—Accidental Poisoning—Suicidal Poisoning—Homicidal Poisoning

IN the course of the topics which we have hitherto been called to discuss, you will have observed that I have taken for granted that the evidence from one or more of the different sources which have been pointed out has justified the suspicion, if not the certainty, of poison having been actually in operation on the body. Cases, however, are constantly happening both in ordinary and medico-legal practice, in which a familiarity with the usual effects of poisons is demanded of the practitioner, even although in these no poison has either been actually taken or administered. I allude to cases in which the poisoning is merely imaginary, or feigned, or fictitious, classes of cases often of a very embarrassing kind to have to deal with. Each of these will require to be shortly adverted to here.

First, imaginary, as contradistinguished from real poisoning. So much of the information on the subject of poisons and poisoning which up to a comparatively recent period had been accumulated, is of so uncertain and loose a character, that we are unable, from its study, to separate the real from the imaginary; while but little room is left for doubt that the confounding the effects of natural diseases in ancient and mediæval times, on many occasions, led to deaths being attributed to poisoning, on the most unsatisfactory and insufficient grounds. Such, indeed, was the easy credulity of both earlier and later antiquity on the subject of poisoning, that it rarely happened that the sudden and unexpected death of any eminent person had to be recorded without its being attributed unhesitatingly to poison; while, if there was any one in a position to profit by such an opportune removal, he was almost as a matter of course set down as the agent of the secret destruction. This easy credulity was favoured by the vague, loose, and inaccurate notions universally current on this important and mysterious subject up almost to the end of the last century. Thus it was believed that there were poisons which had the effect of destroying life at any stated period previously determined on, and whose action did not commence till the date thus fixed; that there were others capable of exactly imitating the symptoms and progress of natural disease, or even of occasioning death without any suffering or outward manifestation whatever; that there were substances known and employed, at once so subtle in their operations, speedy in their effects, and at the same time so free from obvious properties, as readily to admit of being disguised in a variety of ways. How small is the grain of truth contained in all this, the modern toxicologist has no difficulty in perceiving. There are, it is true, a few known substances which in small quantities can be taken into the system with impunity for a time, and which, under certain conditions, in larger doses, or when long persevered in, may, by their accumulation, ultimately give rise to severe or fatal effects, as in the cases of lead, mercury, and iodine amongst inorganic, and digitalis, colchicum, and prussic acid amongst organic substances. All this, however, comes far short of the power of lying dormant in the body, without harm, for a certain definite period accurately fixed beforehand. Again, though we have many poisons at once subtle in their operation and speedy in their effects, we have none so entirely free from sensible properties as to mit of being readily disguised. Arsenious acid makes the nearest approach to this, and is believed to be the secret poison known as the aqua tofana, which in the seventeenth century destroyed no fewer than 600 persons in Rome, Palermo, Naples, and Paris.

To what extent imaginary properties were attributed to substances set down as poisonous formerly, we have a further proof, in the undoubting reception in ancient times, of a host of supposed poisons, such as the venom of the live toad, bullock's blood, chopped human hair, curdled milk, the leech when swallowed, the point of the stag's tail, the sweat of different animals, etc, all known now to be inert.

Though the subject of imaginary poisoning has now lost much of its fancied importance, and the once all but universal belief in its frequency and danger, it yet comes before the modern toxicologist not unfrequently in different forms. Nothing is more common, for instance, amongst the lower orders than to suspect that noxious or poisonous substances have been taken by them in certain circumstances. A striking feature of the first epidemic visitation of the malignant cholera in this and other European countries was the belief, almost universally spread, amongst the ignorant portion of the communities, that the disease in question was in every case brought on by poison thrown into the wells for that purpose. In one place it was the rulers, in another the medical men, who were the parties obnoxious to these suspicions. In Edinburgh this notion was extremely prevalent; and in Aberdeen, which was but very lightly visited by the epidemic, it obtained some circulation amongst the credulous in the lower ranks of life.

When an individual in this class is seized with sudden and severe illness after a meal, or after drinking, particularly the latter, he is very apt to suspect that something deleterious has been mixed with his food or drink. When spirituous liquors have been indulged in, it is always the bad quality, and not the quantity, that causes the illness. As an illustration of a very common form of this delusion, I may mention the following case, which occurred to me while writing out the above. A woman, who kept a lodging-house in Aberdeen, came into my room in a highly excited state, crying out that she was poisoned, and that she should be dead before she could detail to me the particulars of her case. It was no easy matter to get her so far assured as to obtain from her an account of the real state of affairs. It was then learned that she had partaken of some porter with a female who came to her lodgings on the previous evening, whose subsequent conduct, she said, had been very strange and suspicious; that she had perceived, at the time, an unusual taste in the porter; and that since that time she had had a burning heat at her stomach, and a very bad taste in her mouth. She had not vomited nor purged; her tongue was much loaded, her face flushed, her manner unsettled, and her pulse rapid and unsteady. There was no evidence, however, to confirm the woman's suspicions, and she was advised to take some castor oil. This advice did not satisfy the applicant, and she left in great haste; most likely to tell her story to some one in the profession who might be more easily satisfied with her account. In this particular instance, there could be no doubt that the sensations of the woman were real, and her sufferings as real, though much exaggerated by her fears. The state of the tongue, skin, and pulse, showed that she was labouring under the effects of intemperance from the excess of the previous evening, which had probably been greater than she was willing to admit. Yet the nature of the case was at once made evident by a host of improbabilities in the narrative of the patient, which I need not point out, as they were chiefly negative.

The following instance may be adduced to illustrate a not unfrequent class of cases of imaginary poisoning. In 1841 a young man of the name of Lawrence presented himself to me and gave me the following history:—He was a schoolmaster, and had some years before his visit connected himself in marriage with a worthless woman, whom he had subsequently been compelled to desert. His wife, he stated, in revenge, endeavoured to poison him, and in consequence he suffered on one occasion from excruciating pains in his bowels after partaking of some articles of food to which she had access. He further stated that, in order to escape a similar danger, he had for some months been moving from place to place; having visited in succession Edinburgh, Glasgow, Liverpool, Manchester, and lastly Aberdeen. He accused his wife of following him everywhere in his wanderings, and conspiring with the people in his lodgings, and the tradespeople from whom he purchased his food, to drug it with arsenic. In confirmation of this statement, he showed me some butter, which he affirmed was thickly studded with particles of arsenic, though the butter, on examination, looked innocent enough of admixed poison. There was no doubt in my mind that this unfortunate individual had been for some time labouring under monomania. He was intelligent and sensible enough upon every subject except the one he dwelt on, the suspicion of poison, doubtless an insane delusion. But so satisfied was he upon this subject that he had lodged information against his wife, as a poisoner, with the law authorities in the towns he had visited, and did so with the public prosecutor in Aberdeen.

Suspected differs from imaginary poisoning in so far as the belief of the poisoning is, in the one case, confined to the party who suffers, and in the other to those about him. Both forms may unite in the same case, and the grounds for the belief may be the same, and usually are so in each.

Although it is not so common now as formerly to look upon the deaths of eminent persons, when sudden or unexpected, and when they have happened opportunely for others, as attributable to poison, there still lingers not a little of this form of credulity in lawless and despotic countries; while even in our own day and land parallel instances are not altogether unknown. In ordinary medico-legal practice, it is no unusual thing to have to investigate cases of suspected poisoning. In one instance, in the summer of

1852, a sudden death, coupled with the early occurrence of cadaveric lividities in the corpse, led a practitioner in Aberdeen to pronounce the case one of death by poison. In another, some years ago, the fact of a gangrenous state of the mouth followed by death, soon after the swallowing of pills prescribed by a medical man, led to a formal investigation of the cause of death in a person in Aberdeenshire. In another case, a disinterment was had recourse to by the law authorities to have the cause of death cleared up, where an irregular practitioner had prescribed for a woman at Ellon. The body of a person was also disinterred at the Spital (Aberdeen) and examined, some years ago, on a groundless suspicion of poisoning.

In the above instances the suspicion arose after death. In the following we have an illustration of suspected poisoning during life. It affords a curious example of the influence of the imagination over the corporeal functions.

In July 1838, H. J. aet. 25, went into a drug shop in Union Street (Aberdeen) to purchase an ounce of laudanum. Suspecting a suicidal purpose, the shopkeeper, instead of laudanum, gave the woman an ounce of tincture of rhubarb, which, without the cheat being detected, was swallowed on the spot. She then went to a second drug shop in the same street, with the intention of procuring a second dose of what she had asked for previously. She was, however, followed by the first druggist, and handed over to the police. When seen soon after at the police office, the woman appeared to be excited, but manifested at times a strong desire for sleep, though the pupils were not contracted and the pulse was strong. Two hours afterwards, in spite of attempts to keep the patient awake, she had fallen into a deep sleep. Conceiving on this that it was possible that the woman had had the opportunity of taking laudanum before swallowing the rhubarb, though the pupils remained natural, the contents of the stomach were drawn off by the pump, but exhaled only a slightly spirituous odour.

Feigned or factitious poisoning occurs mostly amongst the lowest classes of society. A party is detected in some crime, or found to be secretly addicted to drink, and to avoid exposure or punishment, pretends to have taken some deadly poison. Cases of the former sort, in females who have previously borne a good character, often present themselves in police practice. An interesting case of the latter sort is detailed by Sir Robert Christison.

A young married female, in the seventh month of pregnancy,

was discovered to be secretly addicted to dram-drinking. Annoyed at being detected, she pretended to be very ill, and to have swallowed arsenic to destroy herself. It was found that she had bought three drachms of this poison, and a small quantity was found in the bottom of a tea-cup in which she said she had mixed it. The remainder of the powder had been put away. The mildness of the symptoms, however, and the composure with which she complained of her tortures, led her friends to suspect that she was feigning. When examined by Christison, he could discover no proof of poisoning, and her statements and answers to questions were such as to negative the fact of arsenic having been taken. She gradually recovered from some febrile symptoms which were present, and in two days admitted that she was quite well, but continued to insist that she had taken the poison.

Imputed poisoning differs in general from feigned poisoning only in so far as the symptoms which are feigned are imputed to the agency of another.

The imputation of the crime of poisoning, by feigning or actually producing the symptoms, and contriving that poison shall be detected in the quarters where in actual cases it is usually sought for, has been not unfrequently attempted. It is very easy for an artful person to put poison into food and accuse another of having administered it, as well as to introduce poison into the matters vomited or discharged from the bowels. It is not likely however, that such a party should go so far as to swallow poison under these circumstances, owing to the salutary dread of poisons commonly entertained by the vulgar. The atrocious villany of introducing a poisonous substance into the body after death, with the view of accusing an innocent person of the crime of poisoning, is said to have been committed in Sweden; an occurrence, the possibility of which deserves to be kept in view.

Two instances of imputed poisoning are adduced by Sir Robert Christison, of one of which I shall give the outlines. Samuel Whalley was indicted at York in 1821 for administering arsenic to a woman who was pregnant by him. The woman swore that, after in vain proposing means to procure her abortion, Whalley sent her a present of tarts, of which she ate one and part of another, and that half-an-hour afterwards she was seized with symptoms of poisoning, which continued for a long time. Arsenic was found in the remains of the tarts and in some vomited matters. The absence, however, of any symptoms of irritant poisoning, and the inconsistencies in the woman's account, led the examiner to doubt the reality of the alleged poisoning, and the accused was acquitted. It came out afterwards that the woman had conspired with another female to impute the crime, in order to punish the man for deserting her on finding that she was intimate with other men.

The unreal nature of all the above forms of so-called poisoning does not do away with the necessity for great care in their discrimination, while they call for much skill on the part of the toxicologist in pronouncing a decided opinion as to their precise nature. They have several features in common which enable us to judge of them as a class, the most prominent of which may be here adverted to

1. Little reliance is to be placed on the unsupported statements of the patient. In the cases of feigned and of imputed poisoning, the purpose is to deceive and mislead the practitioner. In the case of imaginary poisoning, the party deceives himself, and, unintentionally, would involve his medical attendant in the same error. In suspected poisoning again, facts and circumstances will be misrepresented or distorted in a way which requires a cautious judgment to be formed from them, and a judicious distrust of their accuracy or reality

Hence the importance of proceeding in such inquiries with caution The practitioner, in every case, should proceed as if he had no doubt of the reality of the poisoning When the patient is alive, in any of these cases, the practitioner—allowing him apparently credit for the truth of his statements, and seemingly sympathising with his fears, real, imaginary, or assumed—should request him to give a full history of existing symptoms, of their origin and progress, of their relation in point of time to various meals, and of the mode and vehicle in which the supposed poison was administered The same course should substantially be followed with the attendants, witnesses, or others interested in supporting the patient's statement, either during his lifetime or after his death, in cases of suspected fatal poisoning. No unprofessional person can go through such an ordeal without bringing out many circumstances irreconcilable with the idea of poisoning generally, and still more of the administration of a particular poison

2 The objective features of the case should all be fully and attentively mastered. On such occasions it will seldom or never be found that the party is entirely free from some complaint. Were this not the case, the diagnosis would be an easy task On the contrary, it will usually be seen that there is some illness

present, more or less real, however exaggerated or factitious. In imaginary poisoning there will be disorder of the digestive organs, irritation of the alimentary tube, febrile or inflammatory symptoms, with or without delusions or hallucinations showing that the mind is disordered. In suspected poisoning the same circumstances will have served as the grounds of the suspicion. In feigned and imputed poisoning, if there be no illness to give a colour to the imposture, there will be a fictitious disorder produced. In all these cases, therefore, it should first be settled whether or not there be any actual departure from the state of health. This done, the additional evidence which the ejecta and dejecta, if any such are produced, are capable of affording, should be expiscated, care being taken to ascertain that poison has not been purposely or maliciously added to these. With this view, if necessary, means should be had recourse to for having the patient, or those about him, secretly watched.

Lastly, in none of the cases we are considering is the medical jurist justified, in a case of importance, and where active disease is found to exist, in deciding positively that poison has not been exhibited without a previous chemical examination, both of the suspected articles of food or drink, and of the ejected matters, where these have been preserved. Even then he is only authorised to say that no medical proof exists of the administration of poison, and that it is in the highest degree improbable that such could have been the case. A chemical investigation, in a case of difficulty, will sometimes lead to the proof of the reality of an apparent instance of feigned, suspected, imaginary, or imputed poisoning, which otherwise, from the improbabilities of the circumstances, might appear to be unreal.

Of this I had an illustration at the outset of my practice, in the case of an old man in Aberdeen, whose case seemed to be one of at once imaginary and imputed poisoning. This person accused a relative who lived with him of giving him arsenic in repeated doses, with the view of obtaining his property after his death. His story was so unlikely to be true, his narrative was inconsistent with itself and with circumstances, and he was otherwise such a crack-brained personage, that, in spite of the severity of the symptoms, which were, besides, rather anomalous, I should have been inclined to regard his case as one of imaginary poisoning, but for the detection of arsenic, chemically, in the matters vomited in my presence.

So much for the unreal forms of poisoning. Real poisoning,

as contradistinguished from these, presents itself in three forms:—1st, accidental; 2d, suicidal; and 3d, homicidal poisoning

1. Accidental poisonings are but too common in this country, from the culpable negligence of tradesmen in dispensing from the same shelves articles of food or medicine, and the most deadly drug or poison. The carelessness of parents and nurses too often exposes children to fearful risks in this way while such articles are very freely exposed in the view of the weak, the careless, and the inexperienced, to their occasional detriment or destruction The contamination of water by lead pipes and cisterns, the use of copper vessels in culinary operations, the practice of laying down poisons for the extermination of vermin from fields, gardens, and dwelling-houses, the adulteration of common articles of food and drink, the artificial colouring of pickles and confectionary by poisonous articles, and the sale of tainted or unmarketable fish, flesh, or molluscs, are all so many sources of occasional exposure to accidental poisoning.

We need not go far to seek for illustrations of these remarks. One can scarcely take up a newspaper without encountering some of these forms of accidental poisoning, and if we add to these the vast numbers of deaths in this form from overdoses of alcohol amongst the intemperate, and in the parties—not few—who habituate themselves to the use, or rather abuse, of chloroform and chloral hydrate, a very extended list of such deaths could be readily made up. Of the purely accidental poisonings from mistaking noxious articles for harmless ones, the instances cannot be few, though they must be very far exceeded by those from adulterated or vitiated articles of food or drink. Of the accidents happening in the former of these ways, I have already had occasion to notice some cases where poisons were inadvertently swallowed, and may add a few more of these. The case of the three women in Justice Street, who mistook arsenic for flour, might have seemed a very unlikely occurrence, but it admits of being paralleled A child of eight years mistook for water, and drank, half a cupful of sulphuric acid A labourer at work at an empty house in the Green (Aberdeen), finding in a cupboard a beer bottle containing the same acid, mistaking it for whisky, partook of so much of it as to cause his death on the following day. The same fate overtook a man in the same street, who, getting out of bed during the night after a debauch, drank oil of vitriol standing in a vessel on the table of his bedroom At Tarves (Aberdeenshire) in October 1870 a person, finding in a store a bottle of carbolic acid, kept by a grocer for sale to farmers for washing their sheep, believing that he had to do with bitters, swallowed from one to two ounces of the fluid, and died in fourteen hours. An outline of this case was published at the time by Dr. Alex Ogston in the *British Medical Journal* for 1871. But perhaps a greater instance of combined carelessness, stupidity, and recklessness could scarcely be produced than the following In January 1860 a man, passing the shop of a grocer and druggist at Forgue (Aberdeenshire), gave orders for a dose of "physic powder" (compound powder of jalap), to be called for on his return from a visit in the vicinity. This was about two o'clock afternoon. He came back for his medicine and went home, a distance of about two miles from the shop, and at bedtime swallowed what he believed was the jalap, but which was half a drachm of corrosive sublimate. In the course of the afternoon the vender had discovered his mistake, but gave no notice of this to his customer, who died in great pain on the fourth day.

Much tact and experience is often required on the part of the practitioner in detecting the real nature of these accidental cases, as most of the poisons thus partaken of are slow in their operation, the poisoning being usually of the chronic kind, and closely simulating ordinary disease.

The plea of accidental poisoning may be set up by the poisoner to shield him from the consequences of his crime This can, however, rarely be of any avail to him in a criminal case. As I had already occasion to observe, the medical investigation, set on foot to determine the fact of poisoning, will usually bring out the intention, on his part, with sufficient clearness to cut him off from this line of defence; while, again, the legal investigation will have been directed to the same point; the proof of administration being usually an indispensable part of the evidence to be adduced on the part of the public prosecutor. Where, however, a plea of this sort is likely to be advanced, the practitioner should be careful to confine his evidence to the medical facts of the case, leaving the moral and circumstantial evidence to be dealt with by the court, with whom it properly should rest.

2. Suicidal poisoning frequently comes before the professional man in private, as well as in medico-legal practice For suicidal purposes, such poisons as are best known to the public, and which may be most easily procured, are oftenest chosen; such as arsenic, laudanum, prussic acid, sugar of lead, or oxalic acid A few of the less known and obvious poisons are, however, occasionally resorted to with this view; such as the mineral acids and alkalies.

the protosulphate of iron, nux vomica, or the salts of copper or mercury. The selection of the particular poison on the part of the intending suicide, is often a matter of accident. No doubt the belief that the death is an easy one, has given prominence to one or two poisons in the annals of self-destruction. This has been especially the case with laudanum, and latterly prussic acid in this country, and carbonic acid gas and arsenic on the Continent. The intending suicide, however, does not always calculate thus. The readiest agent is laid hold of, whatever this may be. A particular poison will be the prevailing one for a time, from the notoriety given to it by some celebrated trial, from its employment by some celebrity of the moment, or from its having recently been brought into notice. When the suicidal tendency is strong, it often overcomes the natural dislike to harsh, nauseous, or offensive substances, and the fear of their giving rise to the most hideous tortures. This is most striking in the case of the monomaniac, though the same unusual occurrence may be met with in others. Thus, in the case of a female about 23, whose case I had occasion to notice in the 28th volume of the *British and Foreign Medico-Chirurgical Review*, this person, apparently in her sound mind and sober senses, deliberately swallowed such a quantity of bichromate of potass as to cause her death in less than eight hours.

It is rarely, if ever, that the suicide uses a slow or uncertain poison. Few persons would have courage to use a substance which would require for its effects a frequent repetition of the dose, although it is by no means rare to witness a second or third attempt at self-destruction where the first attempt has failed from the inefficiency of the dose.

3. Homicidal poisoning has been but too common, from an early period of history up to the present time. Many circumstances favour the commission of murder in this way. It requires but little courage to effect it on the part of the criminal, it demands no co-operation with accomplices, and no tedious preparation on his part, while the means are but too accessible, and opportunities usually not very difficult to be found. Nothing in most instances occurs to give warning to the victim, or to put him on his guard against an injury for which he is furnished with no means of defence. No species of murder is, therefore, so base or cowardly as this. The crime too, in itself, shows an amount of coolness and deliberation which aggravates its guilt. It is generally committed in violation of relative or domestic duty and

confidence, and too frequently evinces that unrelenting and barbarous depravity which can witness unmoved the sufferings of its victim for days, nay even months. It is not to be wondered at that society should look on the poisoner with no ordinary horror and disgust; or that the law should doom him on conviction to a severer punishment than other offenders. It is well for society that such feelings exist in the public mind, and that the checks afforded by the stringency and severity of the laws should suffer no relaxation. Something more than this, nevertheless, is imperatively called for to prevent the continuance and extension of this gangrene in the social body. This conviction, which is spreading in our own country, has been acted on for many years past in other European states, where very stringent restrictions have been put on the custody and sale of every kind of known poison. The legislation forced so recently on our own government does not meet the urgency of the case

Nothing appears to me more providential than the circumstance, that the ignorant and the lower classes—by whom crimes against the person are mostly committed—have but a very limited acquaintance with the host of substances accessible to all, and which might with facility be turned to fatal account by them. Were they possessed of but a tithe of the information on this subject placed in the hands of scientific and educated individuals, the facilities of the crime and the chances of escaping detection, would be fearfully increased

Beyond the general notions gathered from the reported cases, we possess little definite information as to the statistics of either criminal or accidental poisonings   As to the relative frequency with which the individual poisons are employed in practice, our knowledge is also very limited, and is in fact confined to the partial and imperfect results deducible from the statistical tables drawn up by the governments of this country and France. From the former source, we gather, taking the Registrar General's returns for England and Wales for the five years, from 1863 to 1867 inclusive, that

Opium and its preparations give	628 cases.
Prussic Acid and its preparations	182 ,,
Arsenic	83 ,,
Oxalic Acid	66 ,,
Strychnia	61 ,,
	1020 cases

		1020 cases
The Mineral Acids	. .	77 ,,
Mercurial preparations	. .	28 ,,
Phosphorus	. .	16 ,,
Carbolic Acid	. . . .	5 ,,
Remaining poisons	. . .	95 ,,
	Total cases .	1241

The results of the French tables do not differ much from the above

It is to be regretted that similar tables are not issued yearly; although we must admit that they convey rather an imperfect idea of the extent to which—at least as far as this country is concerned—the crime of poisoning prevails. In the first place, these returns only comprise the deaths from poison, while again, they are manifestly defective with respect to the individual poisons. Some recent disclosures have shown that under the present system of conducting coroners' inquests in England, where post-mortem inspections are rarely performed unless the rumour of poisoning be so strong that it would become a public disgrace to neglect it —persons die from poison, they are buried, and their deaths are registered as having occurred from natural disease.

On this point the remarks borrowed from Dr Davies' pamphlet on burgh reform, published several years ago, are as apposite at the present time as when they were offered, and the following cases which he gives from his own knowledge of Manchester deserve repetition.

1. A person was found either dead or dying More than one medical man of eminence seeing the body within a few minutes of the seizure, pronounced the party to have fallen a victim to apoplexy. It was subsequently proved that the death arose from drinking hydrocyanic acid.

2. A person died in what was considered by the surgeon and the physician attending to have been a fit. Opium was found in the stomach.

3. A person was attended by a physician and a surgeon for some hours The illness and death were ascribed to, and treated by them as apoplexy, but it was proved beyond all doubt that he died from laudanum

Such cases as these strongly establish the necessity for not suffering the consideration of expense to deprive the act of suicide or murder of that salutary check—the certainty of detection

They also point to the imperative necessity that exists for medical men being better acquainted with the effects of poisons, than unfortunately is yet the case. In the above instances the grossest ignorance was displayed by the practitioners in attendance, there being very obvious points of distinction between the symptoms of apoplexy, or convulsions, and those produced by prussic acid or opium.

APPENDIX I.

CERTIFICATES OF INSANITY

In the ordinary case the following, filled up in duplicate, is all that is required in Scotland :—

MEDICAL CERTIFICATE, No. I.

I, the undersigned,
being a (1)

and being in actual practice as a (2)
hereby certify, on soul and conscience, that I have this day, at (3)

in the County of
separately from any other Medical Practitioner, visited and personally examined (4)

and that the said   is a (5)
and a proper person to be detained under Care and Treatment, and that I have formed this opinion upon the following grounds, viz.—

1. Facts indicating Insanity observed by myself (6)

2. Other facts (if any) indicating Insanity communicated to me by others (7)

Name and Medical Designation, _____
Place of Abode, _____

DATED this   day of   One thousand Eight hundred and

---

(1) Set forth the qualification entitling the person certifying to grant the certificate, e.g. Member of the Royal College of Physicians in Edinburgh
(2) Physician or Surgeon, or otherwise as the case may be.
(3) Insert the street and number of the house (if any), or other like particulars

(4) Insert Designation and Residence, and if a Pauper state so
(5) Lunatic or an insane person, or an idiot, or a person of unsound mind.
(6) State the facts
(7) State the information, and from whom derived

When the case is pressing, as where the patient is violent, or makes determined attempts on his life, etc., the following certificate, signed by *one* medical practitioner, may be used, and the patient committed at once to an asylum, without waiting for the usual forms to be gone through:—

CERTIFICATE OF EMERGENCY.

(This Certificate authorises the detention of a Patient in an Asylum, for a period not exceeding three days, without any order by the Sheriff.)

I, the undersigned,
being (¹)
hereby certify, on soul and conscience, that I have this day, at (²)
    , in the County of   , seen and personally examined
    , and that the said person is of unsound mind, and a proper Patient to be placed in an Asylum

And I further certify that the case of the said person is one of Emergency.

DATED this   day of   One thousand eight hundred and

(1) State medical qualification.   (2) State place of examination

CERTIFICATE IN CASES WHERE LUNATICS HAVE BEEN CHARGED WITH ASSAULT, ETC., UNDER 25 AND 26 VICTORIA, CAP. 54

I hereby certify, on soul and conscience, that I have this day, within the Aberdeen Prison, visited and examined C. M——, presently a prisoner there, and that I consider him a Lunatic, and in a state threatening danger to the lieges (or, offensive to public decency).

    (Signed)   ——— M D

ABERDEEN, 27th September 18—.

In England the certificates differ only in a few words from those used in Scotland, but there is no such thing as the Certificate of Emergency. I append one of the usual English forms:—

CERTIFICATES OF INSANITY. 639

MEDICAL CERTIFICATE.

Sched (F) No 3

I, the undersigned,
being a (a)
and being in actual practice as a (b)   hereby Certify,
That I, on the   day   at (c)
in the County of
(d) separately from any other medical practitioner, personally examined (e)
and that the said   is a (f)
and a proper person to be taken charge of and detained under Care and Treatment, and that I have formed this opinion upon the following grounds, viz—

1. Facts indicating Insanity observed by myself (g)

2. Other facts (*if any*) indicating Insanity communicated to me by others (h)

SIGNED   Name,_____

Place of Abode,_____

DATED this   day of   One Thousand Eight Hundred and Seventy

(a) *Here set forth the qualification entitling the person certifying to practise as a physician, surgeon, or apothecary, ex gra.*—Fellow of the Royal College of Physicians in London.
(b) Physician, Surgeon, or apothecary, *as the case may be*
(c) *Here insert the street and number of the house (if any), or other like particulars*
(d) *In any case where more than one medical certificate is required by this Act, here insert separately from any other medical practitioner*
(e) *A B of ———, insert residence and profession, or occupation (if any)*
(f) Lunatic, or an idiot, or a person of unsound mind
(g) *Here state the facts*
(h) *Here state the information, and from whom.*

Full information on these and other points of Insanity may be obtained from the study of Dr. Lyttleton S Winslow's *Manual of Insanity*, which contains much information on the subject arranged in a very handy form

APPENDIX II.

VARIOUS FORMS OF MEDICO-LEGAL REPORTS,

AS REQUIRED IN SCOTLAND, IN CASES OF

I Assault.
II Sudden death from natural causes
III Death from non-natural causes
    a When nothing suspicious is found on the inspection
    b. When marks of violence are observed.
IV. Infanticide.
V. Recent delivery
VI Rape.
    a Examination of the woman.
    b Examination of the man

I.—MEDICO-LEGAL REPORT ON A CASE OF ASSAULT (No. 1251).

I hereby certify, on soul and conscience, that on Thursday, the second day of March 18—, I visited and examined M. A M‘L——, residing in Number seventeen —— Lane, Aberdeen, that I observed a wound with sharp edges on the left cheek, an inch below and in a direction parallel to the eye, three-quarters of an inch in length, and extending, at its deepest part, down to the bone; that I consider it such a wound as might be produced by a pocket-knife; that I also observed a bruise, two inches in greatest diameter, on the back of the left forearm; that I visited her again this day, and found her almost recovered from her injuries, and that I do not consider her life to have been in any danger from them.

                    (Signed)   —— M D

ABERDEEN, *7th March* 18—.

II.—MEDICO-LEGAL REPORT IN A CASE OF SUDDEN DEATH FROM NATURAL CAUSES (No 1322).

We hereby certify, on soul and conscience, that on Saturday, the thirtieth day of December 18—, we inspected the dead body of S K——, aged sixty-five, residing in Number —, —— Street, Strichen, Aberdeenshire, and then lying there, when the following appearances presented themselves, viz—

Externally—The joints rigid The pupils of the eyes natural. The front of the body generally pale, the back parts purplish. Green discoloration on the front of the belly. Nothing else unusual observable on the exterior of the body.

Internally—The outer covering of the brain (dura mater) adherent to the skull. The blood-vessels at the base of the brain fatty. The mouth, throat, and gullet natural The substance of the heart fatty, its right cavities filled with blood, partly fluid and partly as black and yellow clots, its left cavities containing only a little fluid blood

The left lung adherent to the walls of the chest by old adhesions; the right lung and the lining membrane of the right cavity of the chest coated with yellow fleshy matter (fibrine), and the right lateral cavity of the chest containing thirteen ounces by measure of yellow opaque fluid. The upper division of the left lung of a red colour, dense and firm (carnified), its lower division loaded with dark blood and white frothy fluid (œdematous); the upper and lower divisions of the right lung in similar conditions, though to a less degree.

The liver, spleen, and kidneys fatty, and loaded with dark blood

Nothing else unusual observable within the cavities of the head, chest, or belly, or about the top of the spine

We further certify, on soul and conscience, that from this inspection we concluded that S K—— had died from disease of the lungs, and of their investing membrane (pleuro pneumonia)—the result of natural causes.

(Signed) —————— M.D.
do —————— M.D.

STRICHEN, 30th December 18—

III.A.—MEDICO-LEGAL REPORT IN A CASE OF DEATH BY DROWNING—CIRCUMSTANCES UNKNOWN (No. 1296)

We hereby certify, on soul and conscience, that on Monday, the eighteenth day of October 18—, we inspected the dead body of A. B——, then lying in his house, Number ten —— Street, Aberdeen, when the following appearances presented themselves, viz.—

Externally—The body was fully clothed, the clothes being undisturbed. It was that of a well-formed and well-developed person, apparently about thirty years of age. The front of the body generally pale. A faint blush of redness over the face. The back parts of the head and trunk of a deep red, interspersed with rounded patches of reddish purple The expression of the features calm. The pupils of the eyes widely opened White watery froth at the lips and nostrils The joints stiff. The skin of the palms of the hands and the soles of the feet bleached and wrinkled. The male organ semi-erect. The appearance known as "gooseskin" on the front of the thighs Nothing else unusual observable on the exterior of the body.

Internally—The scalp bloody. A slight excess of fluid blood in the veins on the surface of the brain. The point of the tongue pressed against and marked by the front teeth. The mouth, throat, and gullet, natural. Light watery froth in the windpipe, the lining membrane of which was slightly reddened throughout. Water in the lower part of the windpipe and in its larger subdivisions. Four ounces by measure of red watery fluid in each of the lateral cavities of the chest. The lungs expanded, loaded with dark fluid blood, and giving out from their cut surfaces a copious light watery froth. Dark fluid blood in quantity in the right, and sparingly in the left, cavities of the heart. Liver, spleen, and kidneys, loaded with dark blood Water, mixed with alimentary matters, in some quantity in the stomach. Nothing else unusual observable within the cavities of the head, chest, or belly, or about the top of the spine

We further certify, on soul and conscience, that from this inspection of the body of A. B——, we are of opinion that he had recently died by drowning.

(Signed) ——— M D
do. ——— M D.

ABERDEEN, 18*th October* 18—

IIIB.—MEDICO-LEGAL REPORT IN A CASE OF DEATH BY EXTERNAL VIOLENCE (No. 1223).

We hereby certify, on soul and conscience, that on Monday, the first day of January 18—, we inspected the dead body of H. C——, residing in ——— Street, Aberdeen, and then lying there, when the following appearances presented themselves, viz.—

Externally—Minute abrasions of the skin on the prominent parts of the left temple and cheek, and on the back of the left elbow. The body emaciated. The surface of the body pale. The joints flaccid. The pupils of the eyes natural. Nothing else unusual observable on the exterior of the body.

Internally—The scalp bloody A thin layer of fluid blood under the investment (fascia) of the muscle of the left temple. Rather more blood than usual on the surface of the brain, particularly on its left side, and over the right side of the little brain (cerebellum).

The mouth, throat, gullet, and air-passages, natural. The heart and its valves healthy, and containing only a little fluid blood, in equal quantities, in its lateral cavities. The lungs pale, containing little blood, but a considerable quantity of white frothy fluid (œdematous).

Several superficial rents, mostly in a longitudinal direction, in the spleen.

A large irregular rent in the urinary bladder, with blood effused around its edges. Twenty ounces by measure of bloody fluid in the cavity of the belly, collected at its lower part (pelvis), containing clots of blood, and exhaling a urinous smell.

Nothing else unusual observable within the cavities of the head, chest, or belly, or about the top of the spine

We further certify, on soul and conscience, that from this inspection we concluded that H. C—— had died from injuries to the head, spleen, and bladder, the result of external violence.

(Signed) ——— M D.
do ——— M D

ABERDEEN, 1st January 18—

IV.—MEDICO-LEGAL REPORT IN A CASE OF INFANTICIDE (No. 1361).

We hereby certify, on soul and conscience, that on Tuesday, the fourth day of September 18—, we examined the contents of a deal box, handed over to one of us by Constable George D——, of the Aberdeenshire police force, and then lying in the police deadhouse of Aberdeen, when the following appearances presented themselves, viz.—

The box, when opened, was found to contain a brown wincey petticoat, stained with blood, partly fluid and soaked into it, and partly clotted and lying on it, there was also a patch of greenish matter (meconium) on the petticoat it further contained a red flannel petticoat, also stained with blood. To both these articles we affixed sealed labels, which we signed.

Wrapped closely in these petticoats was the body of a female child, which was found to weigh six and three-quarter pounds imperial weight, and to measure twenty inches, the navel being in the centre of its length It was plump and well-formed. The surface of the body pale and slightly mottled with purple, mostly on the back, face, and head. White cheesy matter in the groins and armpits. Twelve inches of the navel-string remained attached to the belly, its free extremity appearing to have been irregularly divided, and unsecured by any ligature. The navel-string flabby, somewhat flattened, and partly untwisted. The surface of the body smeared with blood The joints stiff The fingers and toes bent, and their nails blue. The skin of the palms of the hands bleached and wrinkled The pupils of the eyes slightly dilated. Nothing else unusual observable on the exterior of the body.

Internally —The scalp containing rather more blood than usual. Two minute rounded dots of effused blood on the inner surface of the scalp. The mouth, throat, and gullet natural. The windpipe containing watery froth. The lungs expanded, partly covering the heart-bag, and the part known as the "thymus gland;" their margins partly rounded partly sharp; their surfaces of a pink colour, slightly mottled with darker patches; the air-cells on their surfaces expanded—they floated buoyantly in water, in whole and in every part, before and after firm compression, and with the other contents of the chest attached; they crepitated on being cut and handled; abundance of minute air-bubbles escaped from them when compressed under water, and when compressed in the air frothy fluid and blood issued from them. Numerous minute rounded dots of effused blood on the surfaces of the heart, lungs, and the part known as the "thymus gland."

The heart containing fluid blood. The blood channels peculiar to the infant, at and before birth, open and uncontracted.

The liver, spleen, and kidneys loaded with blood, the kidneys containing one or two gritty particles (uric acid).

The stomach containing a few air-bubbles, mixed with glairy matter (mucus). The small gut floating in water. The urinary bladder empty. The right middle ear containing red fluid, the left filled with air. A bony point in the gristle at the lower end of the thigh-bone. Nothing else unusual observable within the cavities of the head, chest, or belly, or about the top of the spine.

We further certify, on soul and conscience, that from this inspection we concluded that the child had been born at or near the full term of its mother's pregnancy; that it had been alive and had breathed at or about the time of its birth, and that it had died from smothering.

(Signed) ——— M.D
do. ——— M.D

ABERDEEN, 5th September 18—

V.—MEDICO-LEGAL REPORT IN A CASE OF RECENT DELIVERY (No. 1312)

We hereby certify, on soul and conscience, that on Monday, the twentieth day of November 18—, we visited and examined M. M———, residing in number fifty-one ——— Street, Aberdeen, that we found her in bed; her face pale, a dark brown circle around her nipples, a thin yellowish fluid issuing from her breasts, which were somewhat knotty and swollen, on compressing them; a narrow brown line on the front of her belly, extending between the pit of the stomach and the centre of the share bone (pubes); the walls of the belly relaxed, and streaked with pink lines; a rounded tumour, varying in size from time to time, under the surface at the lower part of the belly, her forebirth bloody, relaxed, and presenting a recent rent at its entrance; the mouth of the womb admitting of the introduction of the forefinger, which, on removal from the forebirth, was coated with a fluid having a peculiar smell; —and that, from the above appearances, we were of opinion that she had recently given birth to a child at or near the full term of her pregnancy.

(Signed) —— M.D.
do.   —— M.D.

ABERDEEN, 20th November 18—.

VIA.—MEDICO-LEGAL REPORT IN A CASE OF RAPE
(No. 1349)

Examination of the Woman.

We hereby certify, on soul and conscience, that at two o'clock on the afternoon of Wednesday, the twenty-third day of May 18—, we examined the person of J. R——, then in the farmhouse of ——, parish of ——, Aberdeenshire, when the following appearances presented themselves, viz.—

The skin under the eyes discoloured and reddish brown. Dried blood in the right nostril, within and at the back of the right ear. Bluish discoloration and swelling at the back of both ears, on the side of the neck below them, and on the cheek in front of the left ear. A minute wound on the left side of the tongue, at a point opposite the upper eye-tooth. A linear scratch, an eighth of an inch in length, on the front of the left wrist near the ball of the thumb; and a similarly-sized scratch on the front of the right thigh, immediately above the knee-pan.

The parts at the entrance of the forebirth (labia majora and minora) bruised and swollen. And the structure known as the "hymen" torn and bloody at its hinder part. A semi-transparent jelly-like substance about the entrance and in the canal of the forebirth, which, on being examined under the microscope, was found to contain the bodies known as seminal animalcules, and abundance of minute rounded bodies (pus cells).

We also examined the chemise of the said J. R——, and observed on its front part two irregularly rounded spots of a grayish colour, stiff, as if starched, with slightly thickened borders, and which, on being breathed upon, exhaled a characteristic odour. These spots on being examined microscopically, were found to contain seminal animalcules.

We further certify, on soul and conscience, that from this examination of the person and chemise of J. R—— we came to the conclusion that she had recently had sexual connection with a man, and that in all probability the connection had not been voluntary on her part.

(Signed) —— M.D.
do.   —— M B.C M.

ABERDEEN, 24th May 18—

VI_B.—MEDICO-LEGAL REPORT IN A CASE OF RAPE (No. 71).

Examination of the Man.

I also certify, on soul and conscience, that I this day examined A. F——, then in the watch-house of Aberdeen, that I found on different parts of his face, and on his left hand, scratches and spots of blood, as also a scratch on his penis

(Signed) ——— M.D

ABERDEEN, 16*th October* 1837.

LIST OF SOME OF THE AUTHORITIES MADE USE OF.

Alison, (Sir A.) Principles of the Criminal Law of Scotland	Edin 1832
Practice of the Criminal Law of Scotland	Edin 1833
Alison, (W. P.) Cyclopedia of Anatomy—Art. "Asphyxia."	
Beatty, (P. E.) Cyclopedia of Anatomy—Art. "Impotence."	
Beaupré (M) On the Properties and Effects of Cold, by Clendinning	Edin. 1826.
Beck, (P. R.) Medical Jurisprudence, by Darwell	Lond. 1829
Elements of Medical Jurisprudence	Albany, 1853
Briand (J) Manuel Complet de Médecine Legale	Paris, 1863
and Chaudé, Manuel Complet de Médecine Legale	Paris, 1873.
Capuron (J.) La Médecine Legale, relat. á l' Art. des "Accouchements"	Paris, 1821.
Caspar, (J. L) Pract. Handbuch der Gerichtlichen Medicin	Berlin, 1857-8
" " " (Liman)	Berlin, 1871.
Forensic Medicine—Sydenham Society	
Klinische Novellen, z. Gerichtlichen Medicin	Berlin 1863
Gerichtliche Leichenoffnungen	Berlin, 1853-57.
Chitty (J) Practical Treatise on Medical Jurisprudence	Lond. 1834.
Christison, (Sir R.) Treatise on Poisons	Edin 1835, 1845
Cummin (W) Lectures on Medical Jurisprudence	Med. Gazette, 1836.
Devergie, (A.) Médecine Legale, theoretique et pratique	Paris, 1836.
Esquirol (E.) Des Maladies Mentales	Bruxelles, 1838
Fodéré, (F. E) Traité de Médecine Legale et d'Hygiène publique	Paris, 1813
Fresenius, (C R.) Instruction in Chemical Analysis	Lond. 1850
Georget, (D. G.) Discussion Médico-legale sur la Folie	Paris, 1826.
Griesenger, (W.) Mental Pathology and Therapeutics—Syden Society	
Guy, (W.) Ferrier, (D) Principles of Forensic Medicine	Lond. 1844, 1868 [1876
Haslam, (J) Medical Jurisprudence as it relates to Insanity	Lond. 1817
Hasselt, (A. W M. van) Allgemeine Giftslehre	Braunschweig, 1862.
Thiergifte u Mineralgifte	Braunschweig, 1862
Henke, (A.) Lehrbuch f. d. Staatsarzneikunde	Berlin, 1851
Hoffbauer, (J. C) Médecine Legale, relat. aux "Aliénés	Paris, 1827.
Mahon, (P A. O.) Médecine Legale et Police Medicale	Paris, 1801.
Male, (G E) Epitome of Juridical or Forensic Medicine	Lond. 1816
Marc, (C. C. H) De la Folie dans des Rapports avec les Questions Medico-judiciaires	Paris 1840.
Marshall, (H) On the Enlisting and Pensioning of Soldiers	Lond 1832.
Maschka, (J) Sammlung der Gerichtsarzlichen Gutachten	Leipsig. V D
Meckel, (J F) Manuel d' Anatomie	Paris, 1825
Montgomery, (W. P.) Exposition of the Signs and Symptoms of Pregnancy	Lond. 1863.
Cyclopedia of Medicine—Art. "Personal Identity."	

LIST OF AUTHORITIES.

Morrison, (Sir A.) Lectures on Insanity	Lond. 1856
Most, (G. F.) Encyclopædia der Staatsarzneikunde	Leipzig, 1838-40
Orfila, (M.) Traité de Médecine Legale, et des Exhumations Juridiques	Paris, 1836
Pagan, (J. M.) Medical Jurisprudence of Insanity	Lond. 1840
Paris and Fonblanque, Medical Jurisprudence	Lond. 1823
Percival, (T.) Medical Ethics	Manch. 1803.
Percy et Laurent, Dictionnaire des Sciences Médicales, Tom. 41.	
Pinel, (Th.) Sur l' Alienation Mentale	Paris, 1809
Posner u. Simon, Handbuch der spec. Arznei-Verordnungslehre	Berlin, 1862
Ray, (J.) Medical Jurisprudence of Insanity	Edin. 1839
Regulations for Procurators-Fiscal in Criminal and other Investigations	Crown Office, Edin. 1868
Ritchie, (G. G.) Ovarian Physiology and Pathology	Lond. 1865
Roth, (A. H. T.) Der Tod durch Ertrinkung	Berlin, 1865
Russel, (W. O.) On Crimes and Misdemeanours	Lond. 1826-28
Ryan, (M.) Manual of Medical Jurisprudence	Lond. 1831
Scott, Forbes, and Marshall, Cyclopedia of Medicine—Art. " Feigned Diseases"	
Simpson, (Sir J. Y.) Cyclopedia of Anatomy—Art. " Hermaphrodism."	
Smith, (J. Gordon) Principles of Forensic Medicine	Lond. 1821
Syme, Christison, and Traill, Suggestions for the Examination of dead bodies	Crown Office, Edin 1839
Symonds, (J. A.) Cyclopedia of Anatomy—Art. " Death"	
Tardieu (A.) Etude Médico-legale sur l' Infanticide	Paris, 1868
Etude Médico-legale sur l' Avortment	Paris, 1868
Etude Médico-legale sur la Pendaison, la Strangulation et la Suffocation	Paris, 1870
Etude Médico-legal-sur les attentats aux mœurs	Paris, 1873
Tardieu et Roussin, Etude Médico-legale et Clinique sur l' Empoisonnement	Paris, 1867
Taylor, (A. S.) Elements of Medical Jurisprudence	Lond. 1836, 1861
Manual of Medical Jurisprudence	Lond. 1832, 1871
Principles and Practice of Medical Jurisprudence	Lond. 1865, 1873
Lectures on Medical Jurisprudence, London Medical Gazette, vols. 2, 3, 4	
On Poisons	Lond. 1849, 1859, 1865
Medical Jurisprudence	Lond. 1861
Traill, (T. S.) Outlines of a Course of Lectures on Medical Jurisprudence	Edin. 1840-41.
Trébuchet, (A.) Jurisprudence de la Médecine et de Chirurgie	Paris 1834
Vernois, (M.) De la Main des Ouvriers et les Artisans, au point de vue de l' Hygiène et de la Médecine legale	Paris, 1867
Watson, (A.) Medico-legal Treatise on Homicide by External Violence	Edin 1837
Wharton and Stillé, Treatise on Medical Jurisprudence	Philadelphia, 1855, [1873.
Wormley, (T. G.) Micro-chemistry of Poisons	New York, 1867.

INDEX.

ABDOMEN, wounds of, 488.
Abortion, cases of attempted, 200.
 cases of, where child not produced, 205.
 consequences of the induction of, 199
 dangers from mechanical, 199
 evidences of criminal intention, 201
 legal definition of, 34, 192
 modes of criminal, 196
 diseased states causing, 196
 exciting causes of, 195
 mechanical causes of, 198
 medicinal causes of, 197
 natural causes of, 194
 occasional causes of, 196.
 occult causes of, 196
 period of inducing, in criminal cases, 194.
 predisposing causes of, 195
 proofs of its having occurred, 201.
 proofs of, from the woman's history, 201
 proofs of, from the examination of the woman, 202
 proofs of, in the living female, 202
 proofs of, in the dead female, 203
 proofs of, from the inspection of the child, 205
 necessity for early examination of the woman in cases of, 202
 questions raised in cases of, 194
 risks attending artificial, 194
 signs of, 161
 with the woman's consent, 192
Abortives, true, 196
 doubtful, 198
Actea racemosa (squaw root), 198
Active movements of the foetus, character of, 141
 diagnosis of, 142
 late appearance of, 143.
 simulation of, 143
Adipocere, 394
Affiliation of the child, 191.
Age, legal questions respecting, 34
 data for determining the, 36.
 from the colour of the skin, 216
 from the dentition, 39, 43

Age from the desquamation of the cuticle, 216.
 from the ossification, 39, 43.
 at which foetus may survive birth, 36.
Agent for the defence, precognition by, 15.
Air as a proof of live birth, 240
 in the intestines, 240
 in the middle ear, 241
 in the stomach, 39, 240
 in the veins, effects of, 483.
Alexipharmics, 601
Alison on law of homicide, 412
 on proofs of insanity, 321
Amenorrhoea, sterility from, 86
America, United States of, criminal institutions of, 7.
American courts, position of medical man in, 12
Ammonia injection, test of death, 386.
 test for blood, 474
Amniotic fluid in the air-passages of infants, 510
Anaemia, death by, 354.
Analysis chemical, fees for, 12
Androgynae, 49
Aneurisms in the new-born, 262
Antagonism of poisons, 602
Antidotes, chemical, 603
 physical, 603
 treatment of poisoning by, 601
Aorta, ruptures of, 448
Apnoea, death by, 355
Apoplexia neonatorum, 256
Apparent death, 361
 cases of, 362
 explanation of cases of, 362
Aqua tofana, 623.
Arteries, ruptures of, 448
Arteriosus, ductus, 215.
Asexual child, case of, 44.
Asphyxia, death by, 355
 phenomena of, 495
 duration of life after beginning of, 495
 post mortem appearances of, 496
 in utero, 260.
Asthenia, death by, 354
Attrition, 442
Authorities, list of, 647.
 use of, in the witness box, 26

BALLOTEMENT, value of, 144.
    period for performing, 144.
    mode of performing, 145.
    mistakes in performing, 145.
    failure of, 144.
Basilar artery, rupture of, 448.
Bicorned uterus, 86.
Bifurcation of the penis, impotence from, 80
Birth, concealment of, 85, 158.
    concealment of, punishment for, 208
    immaturity, 171
    legitimacy, 185.
    monstrous, 177.
    prematurity, 178
    retardation, 177.
    single and plural, 179.
    viability, 182.
    legal definition of, 180
    legal relations of, 180.
    live, proofs of, 180, 220
    live, summary of the proofs of, 242.
    live, signs of, in Scotch law, 182.
    live, signs of, in English law, 182.
    live, proofs of, in criminal cases, 182.
    live, English laws relating to, 181.
    live, Scotch laws relating to, 182
    proof of survival of, 182, 212.
    respiration before entire, 245
    proofs of still, 180.
    still, proofs of, from the examination of the child, 217.
    still, proofs of, from the examination of the mother, 219
    still, summary of proofs of, 242
    unaided, cases of, 158.
Bismuth, preparations of, used for dyeing the hair, 60.
Bladder, urinary, rupture of 446
    state of, in the new-born infant, 39, 241.
Blisters, post mortem, 394.
Blood in carbonic oxide poisoning, 551
    corpuscles, effects of water on, 475
    crystals, 471
    discrimination between human and other, 477
    effects of loss of, 483
    menstrual, discrimination of, 476
    post mortem coagulation of, 367, 427.
    tests for, 471
        ammonia, 474.
        by boiling, 471.
        caustic potash (liquor potassæ), 471.
    microscopic test for, 473.
    Schonbein's test for, 472
    spectral test for, 472
    Taylor's test for, 472
    Teichmann's test for, 471
    tests, judgment of, 472
    stains while life exists, 468
    stains after life extinct, 468.
    stains from arteries, 468
    stains, age of, 469.

Blood stains, recent, discrimination of, 467
    stains, verification of, 467.
    stains, verification of doubtful, 471.
    stains, Roussin's mode of examining, 473.
    stains, Ogston's mode of examining, 473.
    stains, appearances of, 467, 470.
    stains, appearances similar to, 470
    stains, characterising spot where injury inflicted, 468.
    stains, where to look for, 470
    stains on various articles, 469.
    stains on iron, 476.
    stains, discrimination of, from rust, etc., 476
    stains, discrimination of, from those of cerebral matter, 476.
    stains on wood, 476
    stains in cases of rape, 107
    vessels, ruptures of, 448
Bloody footprints, identification by, 63
Blows, effects of, 430
    on the belly, 430.
    on the head, 432
    on the præcordia, 432.
Bones, discrimination of human from other animals, 48.
    fractures of, 449.
Brain, concussion of, 481.
    contusion of, 439
    rupture of, from violence, 447
    injuries of, prognosis in, 481
    injuries of, results, 481.
    injuries of, violence or disease, 482.
Breslau on the state of the intestinal canal in the new-born, 240
British Colonies, criminal institutions of, 7
Bullet, traject of, through various media, 456
Burking, 550
Burns, 460.
    cause of death after, 461.
    in the living body, 461
    occasional failure of vital signs of, 462.

CADAVERIC lividity, 378
    rigidity, 374
    rigidity, period of, 374
    rigidity of the heart, 375
    spasm, 375
    softening, 373
Caput succedaneum, 256.
Carbonic acid and oxide poisoning, 551.
Carnal knowledge of children under puberty, 35
    above puberty, 35.
Carunculæ myrtiformes, 103
Caspar on signs of drowning, 514.
Castration, effects of, 78.
Cauvet on identification by the flash produced by firearms, 65
Cephalhæmatoma, 257
Cerebellum, rupture of, 448

INDEX.

Cerebral arteries, ruptures of, 448.
    matter, stains from, 476
Certificates of insanity, 333, 637.
Chancres, hard, disappearance of scar left by, 60
    in cases of suspected rape, 113
Chest, wounds of, 485
Chitty on the legal test of insanity, 315
    on lucid intervals, 320
Children, appearance of hymen in, 102
Child-murder and homicide, distinction between, 253
Chloasmata uterina, 137
Chlorine as a means for making dark hair light, 61
Cholera hand in the drowned, 505
Cholesterine, 212
Cicatrices of wounds, 425
Circulatory system, injuries of, effects of, 483.
    injuries of, prognosis in, 483.
Cirrhosis of the liver in the new-born, 262.
Civil courts, position of the medical jurist in, 10.
Clitoris, state of, in virgins, 101
    hypertrophy of, 50
Cognition in cases of weak mind, 295
    degree of weak-mindedness warranting, 298
Coition without rupture of hymen, 103
Coke, Lord, on lucid intervals, 320.
Cold, death by, 555
Colonies, criminal institutions of, 7.
Colostrum, 160
Coma, death by, 357
    signs of, in persons falling into water, 499
Comato asphyxia, death by, 358
Combustibility, preternatural, of the body, 463
Combustion, spontaneous human, 463
Compulsory attendance of medical men at coroner's inquest, 11
    attendance at precognition, 11
Concealed insanity, 325
    sex, investigation of cases of, 55
Concealment of birth, 85
Conciseness in giving evidence, 27
Concussion, effects of, 429
    of the brain, 431
    of the brain, prognosis in, 481
    of the spine, 431.
    without local marks of injury, 430.
Concussions of the trunk, prognosis in, 483
Consultations between medical men before the trial, 25
Contusion, 429
    definition of, 433
    appearances of, 433
    without ecchymosis 437
    effects of, 429
    of the brain, 431
    of brain, appearance of, 439

Contusions of the scalp, prognosis in, 480
    appearance of, in the parenchymatous viscera, 439
    consecutive injuries from, 443
    in dead bodies, 349.
    inflicted during life, 440.
    inflicted after death, 440
    relative size of, to weapon, 439.
Contused wounds, 441.
Cooling of the body after death, 363
Coroner's inquest, examination at, 15
    fees for attendance, 11.
    position of medical man at, 11.
Corpus glandulosum, 165
    luteum, 164
    luteum, spurious or false, 165
    luteum, true, 165.
    luteum, valuation of, 166
    menstruale, 166
Cretins, semi-cretins, 288
Criminal institutions of Scotland, 4
    institutions of England, 6.
    institutions of India, 7
    institutions of British colonies, 7
    institutions of the United States of America, 7
    institutions of France, 7
    institutions of Germany, 8
    causes of infant's death, 266
Criminating evidence, 21
Crypsorchides, 78, 80
Cupping, disappearance of the marks from, 58
Cuticle, post-mortem detachment of, 388
Curator bonis, appointment of, to persons of weak mind, 295
Cutis anserina after sudden death, 505
    in the drowned, 504
Cut throat, homicidal, 423
    suicidal, 423

DEAF MUTISM in its medico legal relations, 327
Deas, Lord, on dypsomania, 310
    on the legal test of insanity, 317.
Dead bodies, question of abortion in, 350.
    question of delivery in, 350
    identity of, 350
    traces of violence in, 350.
    directions for retarding decomposition of, 383
Death, medico legal relations of, 346
    definition of, 360
    signs, 363
    tests of, 365
    reality of, 347
    immediate causes of, 351
    immediate precursors of, 351
    modes of, 351
    by syncope, 354
    by anæmia, 354
    by asthenia, 354
    by neuro-paralysis, 354
    by asphyxia (apnœa), 355

652 INDEX.

Death by coma, 357
    by comato asphyxia, 358.
    from syncope, after falling into water, 498.
    from coma, after falling into water, 499.
    summary of causes of, 357
    forms of, 358.
    from burns, 461.
    by cold, 555
    by drowning, 497
    by hanging, 521
    by heat, 558.
    by hæmorrhage, 484
    by lightning, 560.
    by mechanical violence, 354
    by misadventure, 412.
    by overlaying, 265
    by smothering, 547.
    by starvation, 562.
    by strangulation, 587
    by suffocation, 547.
    apparent, 361.
    simulated, 364
    morbid states simulating, 363
    changes in the body after, 360.
    data for determining the period of, 348, 395.
    examination of the suspected murderer, 400
    extinction of the vital functions as a sign of, 363.
    in the uterus, signs of, 218
    causes of, in the fœtus in utero, 254
    by fractures in utero, 268
    by wounds in utero, 269
    by dislocation in utero, 270
    of the infant, during birth, from accidental causes, 255
    of the infant, during labour, from criminal causes, 266
    of the infant, during labour, from natural causes, 256
    of the infant, after delivery, from accidental causes, 261
    of infant, after delivery, from criminal causes, 270
    of infant, after delivery, from natural causes, 261
Declaration, examining children on, 35
Decomposition of the dead body, 382
    agents modifying, 382.
    modified by disease, 383.
    data for estimating the stage of, 395.
Defective ossification of infant's skull, 259
Defence, agent for, precognition by, 15
Defloration, definition of, 88.
    signs of, in adults, 105.
    signs of, in old females, 106.
    signs of, at remote periods, 115
Defloration, seminal stains in, 105
    Scotch law regarding, 115.
    English law regarding, 116.

Delirium in its medico-legal relations, 326.
    tremens in its medico-legal relations, 326.
Delivery, questions relating to, 150
    operative interference during, 150.
    duty of accoucheur during, 150.
    legal responsibility of the accoucheur during, 150.
    malpraxis during, 150
    feigned 152
    proofs of recent, at full time, 153.
    proofs of recent, from the woman while alive, 154.
    proofs from the infant; vide Birth, Abortion, and Infanticide.
    duration of appearances of recent 157.
    occasional absence of marks of recent, 158
    valuation of signs of recent, 160
    signs of, in the dead body, 163
    diseases in the uterus which might be mistaken for the signs of previous, 167.
    previous, at remote periods, 162.
    proofs of premature, 154, 162
    signs of early abortion, 161
    without woman's knowledge, 168
    during sleep, 168.
    after the woman's death, 168
De lunatico inquirendo, writ, 312
Dementia, meaning of, 323
    diagnosis of, 323
    legal consequences of, 323
    restraint in, 324
    adventitia, 301
Dentition, first commencement of, 36
    second commencement of, 36
Destructive monomania, 308
Dialysis of poisons, 589
Diaphragm, rupture of, 449
Dipsomania, 309.
Direct testimony, 19
Discoloration, post-mortem, 386
    of skin after contusion, 135
Disease, factitious, 338
    feigned, 334.
    latent, 342
    in fœtal lungs, effects of, 237
Disinterment of bodies, 406.
Dislocations, 464
    in utero, 270
Disorganisation, 442.
Down on new-born infants, 38.
Dropsy in the new-born infant, 262
Drowning, death by, 497
    modes of dying from, 498
    phenomena of, 500
    post-mortem signs of, 501
    external signs of, 501.
    internal signs of, 507
    special signs of, 514
    review of signs of, 513.
    of infants in the uterus, 510

INDEX. 653

Drowning, whether accidental, suicidal, or homicidal, 515
 post-mortem inspection in, 518.
Drowned bodies, erosions on, 518
 bodies, marks of violence on, 516.
 bodies, poisons in, 518.
Drunkenness in the prognosis of wounds, 484
Ductus arteriosus, period of closure of, 215
Duels, medical evidence in, 21.
Dupont's test of death, 366
Duties of medical attendant in suspicious cases, 30
Dyeing the hair, methods for, 60
Dying, process of, 352.
 declarations, 19.
Dysæmic death, 354

Ear, state of the middle, in new-born children, 241
Ecchymosis after contusion, 434.
 situation of, 437
 absence of, after injuries, 437
 from natural causes, 437
 subcutaneous appearance of, 439
 variations in disappearance of, 436.
 latent, 436.
 punctiform, of scalp, 256
 punctiform, in smothering, 552
 punctiform, in still-born children, 553
 punctiform, valuation of, 554
 on child's neck caused by the navel string, 260
Ecclesiastical courts, position of the medical jurist in, 10
Emetics, use of, in poisoning, 597.
Emphysema of fœtal lungs, 232.
England, criminal institutions of, 6.
English law, regarding complete birth, 246.
 law, definition of insanity in, 286
 procedure in cases of weak mind, 295
Ephilis, 137
Epispadia, characters of, 80
Epispadians, impotence of, 80.
Ergot of rye, 197.
Erosions on drowned bodies, 518
Erotomania, 309.
Erskine on the legal test of insanity, 316
Eunuchs, characters of, 78.
 impotence of, 78.
Evidence expected from the medical jurist in law courts, 10
 of medical jurist on the precognition, nature of, 12
 conciseness in giving, 27
 imperfect, 27
Examination at coroner's inquest, 15
 at precognition, 13
 of infants in cases of infanticide, 273
Exhumation of bodies, directions for, 406
 of bodies, dangers attending the, 406.
Extra uterine pregnancy, 147.

Extra-uterine pregnancy, diagnosis of, 148
Extrophy of the bladder, appearance of, 79
 of the bladder, impotence from, 79
Extroversion of the bladder, 51

Facies Hippocratica, 381.
Factitious diseases, 338.
 poisoning, 626.
Factory Acts referring to age of children, 35
Facts, inference drawn from, 2
Fallopian tubes, obliteration of, 86.
Faults in medical witnesses, 31.
Fees for attendance at coroner's inquest, 11.
 for attendance at precognition, 11
 for attendance at the trial, 18
 for chemical analysis, 12.
Feigned diseases, 334
 insanity, 325
 poisoning, 626
Fine for non appearance at the trial, 18
Fingers, flexed state of, after death, 381
Firearms, wounds by, 451
Fleischmann's experiments in hanging, 504
Fl... ..ns simulating those from blood, 1.
Fœtal heart sounds in pregnancy, 146
 vessels, closure of, 215
Fœtus, active movements of, 141
 active movements of, diagnosis of, 142
 active movements, simulation of, 143
 passive movements of, character of, 144
Folie raisonnante, 306
Food in the new born infant's stomach, 239
Footprints, identification by, 62
 size of, 62
 bloody, identification by, 63.
 methods of preserving, 62
Foramen ovale, period of closure of, 215
Fossa navicularis, state of, in virgins, 101.
Foubert's test of death, 366
Fourchette, state of, in virgins, 101
 causes of rupture of, 101.
Fractures, 464
 spontaneous, 464.
 from slight causes, 465
 in utero, 269
 of the skull in the new-born infant, 258
 of the ribs, prognosis of, 487
 of skull, prognosis in, 480
 signs of production during life, 465
 signs of production after death, 465
 without effusion of blood, 419
 diagnosis of weapon producing, from shape of, 466
France, criminal institutions of, 7.
Frost erythyms, 380, 557.

GALL-BLADDER, detachment of, from liver, 445
    rupture of, 446.
Gall-duct, occlusion of, in the new-born, 282
Gardiner Peerage cause, 190.
Garroting, 544
Generative organs, external, want of the, 83
Genital malformations, 45
    injuries produced by other bodies than the penis, 106
Genitals, diseases of in children, 94
    state of, in prostitutes, 100.
    state of, in virgins, 100
Germany, criminal institutions of, 8
Gonorrhœa following rape, 91
    diagnosis between, and other discharges, 114
    spurious, in children, 95
    spurious, diagnosis of, 96
Graafian vesicles, 164
Gravidine, 188
Gravis odor puerperii, 156.
Guaiacum test for blood, 471
    test with sweat stains, 473
Gunshot wounds, 451
Gynandri, 51.

HAEMINE CRYSTALS, 471
Hæmorrhage, proofs of death from, 484
Hair, dyeing the, 60
Hall, Dr Marshall's, test of death, 365
Hanging, 521.
    cause of death in, 521.
    asphyxia in, 522
    coma in, 522
    syncope in, 522
    phenomena of death by, 524.
    modifying circumstances in, 525.
    effects of weight of body in, 523
    external appearances in, 527
    effects of ligature in, 522.
    groove on neck in, 527-533
    internal appearances in, 527
    during life, proofs of, 525
    valuation of signs of vital, 529
    circumstantial evidence in, 534
    marks of violence in, 532
    whether accidental, suicidal, or homicidal, 531.
    suicidal, cases of, 533.
    appearance in judicial, 523.
    post-mortem inspection in, 534.
    examination of groove on neck in, 535.
    and strangulation, diagnosis between, 540.
    resuscitation after, 525
Head, measurements of the, in new-born infants, 38
    wounds of, prognosis in, 479
Hearsay evidence, 19
Heart, ruptures of, 417, 485
    wounds of, 485

Heart, sounds of the fœtal, 146
    state of, after fatal spinal injuries, 482
Heat, death by, 558
    increase of, after death, 370
    loss of, after death, 368
Hermaphrodites, impotence of, 79
    marriage of, 54
Hermaphrodism, meaning of the term, 49
    classification of, 49
    causes of, 50
    in the female (androgynæ), 50
    in the male (gynandri), 51
    legal questions relating to, 54
    rules for the examination in cases of, 54.
Hernia as a cause of impotence, 80.
Homicide, definition of, 409
    divisions of, 409
    causes of death in case of, 411
    circumstances modifying, 410
    limit of fatal illness, 412
    laws of (Alison), 412
    medical evidence in cases of, 411
    and child murder, distinction between, 253
    Kebbaty, case of, 417
Homicidal cut throat, diagnosis of, 423.
    monomania, 310
Hydrocele as a cause of impotence, 80
Hydrostatic test, 229
    mode of performing, 230
    objections to, 230
    positive inference from, 230
    negative inference from, 237
Hymen, appearance of, in virgins, 102
    appearance of, at puberty, 102
    appearance of, in children, 102
    position of, in adults, 105
    accidental rupture of, 103
    rupture of, in coition, 102
    unruptured by coition, 103
Hypertrophy of heart, etc., in the new born, 262
Hypospadians, 51
    impotence of, 80,
Hypostases, external, 378.
    internal, 381
Hypostatic injection of the dura mater, 391
Hysteria after blows, 432

IDENTITY, questions where a medical man is concerned, 57.
    in the living, 57.
    means for concealing, 58
    means for establishing, 63
    in the dead, 65
    mistaken, cases of, 67
Identification of articles produced, 15
    from momentary light, 64
    by footprints, 62
    from the mark left by a blow with a key, 65

Identification from the mode of cutting the throat, 65
   from being left-handed, 65
   after decomposition has begun, 68
   where body is mutilated or incomplete, 69.
   from teeth, 65, 70
   of the skeleton, 70, 72.
   from the presence of supernumerary mammæ, 72.
   from wrappings of body, 70
   earliest period of, in the foetus, 73
   of human bones mixed with those of oxen, etc, 73
   summary of the means of, 74
Idiocy, 287.
   medico-legal relations of, 289
   plea of, in criminal cases, 289
   plea of, in civil cases, 294.
   legal responsibility of, 290
   Scotch law regarding, 294
   English law regarding, 294.
Illness, legal limit of fatal, 412.
Imaginary poisoning, 622
Imbeciles, legal responsibility of, 290
Imbecility, 288
   medico-legal relations of, 289
   plea of, in criminal cases, 289.
   plea of, in civil cases, 294
   Scotch law regarding, 294.
   English law regarding, 294
   degree of, which would invalidate a marriage, 299.
   degree of, which would invalidate a will, 299
   justifying restraint, 300
Imperfect evidence, 14, 27
Importance of medical testimony, 28
Impotence, definition of, 75
   causes of, 76
   functional causes of, 81
   moral causes of, 81
   occult causes of, 82.
   physical causes of, 77
   relative, 81
   temporary, 82
   from old age, 81.
   from youth, 81
   as a bar to marriage, 76
   in the female, 82.
Impulsive monomania, 310.
Imputed poisoning, 627.
Incorrect evidence at the precognition, 14
Incised wounds, characters of, 420
Incubation stage of insanity, 302
India, criminal institutions of, 7
Infanticide, legal meaning of, 207.
   cause of death in cases of, 253
   character of the proofs of, 206
   proofs of survival of birth, 211.
   the plea of temporary insanity in cases of, 207
   before the full birth of the child, 207
   production of the body, 208.

Infanticide by exposure, 209
   without intention, 207
   how to secure conviction for, 208.
   proofs of maternity, 209
Inflation, artificial, of foetal lungs, 232
   of foetal lungs, judgment on, 235.
Injuries against the person, 88
   of the nervous system, prognosis of, 479.
   of the circulatory system, prognosis in, 483
   modifying circumstances in prognosis of, 488
   modifying putrefaction, 383
   in the infant's body as proofs of live birth, 242
Insane, examination of the, 328
Insanity, 277
   medical views of, 277
   legal views of, 277.
   discrimination of, 278
   classification of, medical, 285
   classification of, legal, 286.
   varieties of, 282
   moral proofs of, 318
   medical evidence in cases of, 279
   legal test of, 315.
   legal test of medical objections to, 316
   plea of, in criminal cases, 281
   plea of, in civil cases, 281.
   tests of, in civil cases, 281
   tests of, in criminal cases, 281
   evidence of design in cases of, 321
   stage of incubation of, 302
   lucid intervals in, 320
   certificates of, 333 and 637
   feigned, 325.
   examination of feigned, 331
   concealed, 325
   examination of concealed, 332
   in cases of infanticide, 207
Inquest, coroner's, position of medical man at, 11
   in cases of weak mind, 295
Instinctive monomania, 310
Intercourse, sexual, signs of previous, 100
Interdiction in cases of weak mind, 297.
Intestines, state of, in new-born infant, 39
   air in the, of new-born children, 240.
   rupture of, 446, 488
Intra uterine diseases, 261
   maceration, 218
   petrifaction, 219
   saponification, 219
Investigation entrusted to the medical expert, 10
Irresponsibility, legal test of, in idiots, 290
   legal test of, in imbeciles, 290
Irritability of the genitals, sterility from, 85.

JAUNDICE in the new-born, 262

KIDNEYS, state of, in the new-born infant, 241.
Kiestine, 138
Kleptomania, 307.

LABIA, adhesion of, 85
    state of, in virgins, 100
Laborde's test of death, 366
Labour, tedious, effects of, on scalp, 256
Lacerated wounds, 450
Lansdowne Act, 153
Larynx, wounds of, 487.
Latent diseases, 342
Law of child murder, 253
    (English), concealment of the birth, 153.
    (Scottish), concealment of the birth, 153
    de custodiendo partu, 152
Lead, preparations of, used for dyeing the hair, 60
Legal classification of insanity, 286
    question of entire birth, 245
Legitimacy, English laws of, 185
    French laws of, 185.
    German laws of, 185
    Scotch laws of, 185
    proof of immorality of the female, 190
    proof of incapacity of the male, 190
    proof of sterility in the female, 190
    proof of non-access to the woman, 190.
Length of new-born infant, 37.
Life in infants without respiration, 238
Lightning, death by, 560
    death by, cause of, 560.
    death by, appearances in, 561
    death by, corroborative evidence in, 561
    effects of strokes of, 561.
Lineæ albicantes, 155.
Liquor amnii 156
Live birth, proofs of, 220.
    proofs of, from the inspection of the stomach, 239
    doubtful cases of, 244
    summary of the proofs of, 242.
Liver, rupture of, 444
    spots, 137
Lividity, cadaveric, 378
Lochia, 156
Lucid intervals in insanity, 320
    proof of, 320
    legal views of, 321
    medical views of, 321
Lunacy, 301
    regulation Act, 279
Lunatics, examination of, 328
Lungs, functions of the, 222.
    alterations in, after birth, 223
    changes produced by inspiration, 223, 226.

Lungs, time required for the expansion of the infant's, 222
    imperfectly breathed, 238
    artificial inflation of, 223, 232
    changes produced by inflation, 226
    specific gravity (hydrostatic) test of, 224, 229.
    static test of, 227.
    pressure test of infants, 227
    effects of pressure on inflated, 231
    colour of respired, 225
    marbling of respired, 226
    consistence of respired, 225
    shape of respired, 225
    colour of fœtal, 225
    consistence of fœtal, 225.
    shape of fœtal, 225.
    situation of the fœtal, 224
    size of the fœtal, 224
    collapse of, 487.
    effects of putrefaction in the infant's, 223, 227
    ruptures of, 444.
    wounds of, 487.
    entrance of water into the, after death, 511
    water in the air cells of the, in drowning, 511.
    afflux of blood to the infant's from disease, 223
    tubercles in infants', 227
    red hepatization of infant's, 227
    emphysema of fœtal, 232

MACERATION intra uterine, 218
Madschenschander, 308
Malignant diseases in the new-born, 262
Malum regimen, 410
Mania, 301.
    classification of, 301
    general intellectual, 302
    partial intellectual, 303
    moral, 304.
    general moral, 305
    partial moral, 306
    diagnosis of, 302
    active stage of, 303
    sine delirio, 306
    legal proof of, 312
    legal consequences of, civil, 312
    legal consequences of, criminal, 315
    procedure in cases of, Scottish, 312
    procedure in cases of, English, 312
    duties of medical men in cases of, 313.
    restraint in cases of, 314
Manslaughter by a doctor, 412
Marks on the neck in fat children, 261.
Marriage, validity of, 44
    invalidated by mania, 314
    degree of imbecility which would invalidate a, 299
Masturbation, signs of, in females, 101

INDEX. 657

Maternity of a child, proofs of, *vide* Delivery and 211
Measurements of head in a new born infant, 38
Mechanical violence, death by, 354.
Meconium, 212
    a sign of live birth, 212.
    as a sign of recent birth, 240
    in the air-passages of infants, 510
Mediastinal abscess, 262
Medical evidence, scope of, 3
Medical evidence in duels, 21
Medical report, character of, 12
Medico-legal reports, forms of, 640
Melancholia, 301
Melanosis of heart, etc., in the new born, 262.
Memoranda, use of, on the trial, 22
Menstrual blood, discrimination of, 476
Menstruation during pregnancy, 175
Methods for preserving footprints, 62
    of darkening the hair, 60
    for dyeing the hair light, 61
    for detecting the change of colour of the hair, 61
Microscopic test for blood, 473
Middle point of body in the new born infant, 38
Milk after recent delivery, 159
    in the new born infant's breasts, 39
    in the new born infant's stomach, 239
Milk fever, 156
Misadventure, death by, 412
Miscarriage, legal meaning of, 34
Mistaken identity, cases of, 67
Moles, uterine, 149
Monomania, 303
    destructive, 308
    homicidal, 310
    impulsive, 310
    instinctive, 310
    suicidal, 311
Monomanie de l'ivresse, 309
Monorchides, 80
Monsters, classification of, 178
    laws relating to, 177
    destruction of, 177
Moral mania, 304
Mummification of the dead body, 69, 382
Murder, or wilful homicide, 409
    by hanging, 532
    by strangulation, 544
    classification of, in the United States, 409
Muscular contractility, loss of, 367.
Muscles, ruptures of, 449

Nails, state of, in new-born infants, 38
Navel, state of, during pregnancy, 140
    string, appearance in natural division of, 214
    string, appearance in violent division of, 214

Navel string, comparison of the divided portions of, 164
    string, mark caused by, on neck of infant, 271.
    string, prolapse of the, 260.
Neck, wounds of, 484
Nervous system, prognosis of injuries, 479
Neuro-paralysis, death by, 354.
New born infant, length of, 37
    infant, middle point of body in, 38
    infant, weight of, 37
    infant, measurement of head, 38
    infant, points of ossification, 82
    infants, down on, 88
    infants, state of the nails, 38
    infants, condition of the umbilical cord, 38.
    infants, vernix caseosa, 38
    infant, pupillary membrane, 38
    infant, changes taking place after birth, 38
    infant, air in stomach, 39
    infant, saliva in stomach, 39
    infant, state of intestines, 39.
    infant, state of bladder, 39
    infant, milk in the breasts, 39
Non-attendance at courts, fines for, 11
Non-viability, of infants, causes of, 183
    proofs of, 184
Nostril, puncture of brain through, case of, 481
Notes of inspections, use of, in court, 22, 406
    of statements at precognition, 13
Nymphæ, state of, in virgins, 101

Oath, putting child on, 35
Occlusion of the gall duct in the new-born, 262
    of infant's mouth by the membranes, 262
Oikeiomania, 309
Onanism, signs of, in females, 104
Orbit, puncture of brain through, case of, 480
Ordinary witness, evidence of, 2
Orfila on signs of drowning, 514
Ossification of skeleton at different ages, 39.
    defective, of skull in infants, 259
Ossific points in the new-born infant, 38
Ova, 164
Overlaying, 265

Pæderastia, 128
Paraphymosis as a cause of impotence, 80
Parchment skin, 433
Partial inspiration in infants, 238
Passive movements of fœtus, 144
Paternity, proof of, 191
Pemphigus simulating burns, 462
Penetrating wounds, 416
Penge case of starvation, 562
Penis, abnormal direction of, 80.
    absence of, 77.

2 U

Penis, adhesion of, to the abdomen, 80
    adhesion of, to the scrotum, 51, 80
    bifurcation of, 80.
    excessive size of, 80
Phymosis as a cause of impotence, 80
Piqueurs, 308.
Pistol fired off, pressed against the body, 454
Pityriasis gravidarum, 137.
    versicolor, 137
Placental soufflé, 145
Pleura, wounds of, 487.
Ploucquet's test, 227
Pneumothorax, prognosis of, 487
Points of ossification in foetus, 38
Poisoned wounds, 460
Poison, definition of a, 568
    means for removal of, 595
    proof that death was caused by a particular, 593
    proof that the, was the cause of death, 593.
Poisoning, accidental, 630.
    homicidal, 632.
    suicidal, 631.
    factitious, 626.
    feigned, 626
    imaginary, 622
    imputed, 627
    suspected, 625
    detection of imaginary, etc., 628
    statistics of, 633
    duties of medical man during life, in cases of, 606
    collection of suspected matters in cases of, 609
    proof of, 568
    moral proof of, 586
    proof of, from chemical analysis, 588
    proof of, from experiments on animals, 584.
    proof of sufficient quantity of poison in, 591
    symptoms of, 577.
    discrimination of, from natural disease, 580.
    effects of, masked by putrefaction, 583
    treatment of, 594
    use of emetics in, 597
    use of stomach pump in, 598
    treatment by antidotes, 601
    after-treatment of, 605
    preservation of viscera in cases of, 612
    post-mortem inspection in cases of, 608
    external examination of body in, 610.
    internal examination of body in, 610.
    evidence of on post-mortem inspection, 580.

Poisoning, medical evidence in cases of, on precognition, 567
    medical evidence in cases of, on the trial, 567
Poisons, chemical analysis of, 613
    chemical analysis of, when in a pure state, 615
    chemical analysis of, when mixed with organic matter, 616
    sublimation method of isolating, 590
    dialytic method of isolating, 589.
    microscopic test for, 591, 620
    test for, by spectrum analysis, 590
    search for volatile, 618
    search for vegetable, 619
    search for mineral, 619
    action of, 569
    affinities for particular organs, 571
    changes after absorption, 572
    elimination of, 572
    cumulative properties of, 573
    dose of, 573
    mechanical state of, 574
    chemical state of, 574
    texture acted on, 574
    effects of habit on, 575
    peculiarity of constitution, 575
    antagonism of, 602
    in drowned bodies, 518
    search for, some time after death, 613
Polyorchides, 80
Polysarcia as a cause of impotence, 80.
Position of the medical jurist in civil courts, 10
    of the medical jurist in ecclesiastical courts, 10
    of medical man at the coroner's inquest, 11
    of the medical jurist in France and Germany, 9.
Possessio fratris, 181
Post mortem bleaching, 394
    blisters, 394
    changes of the muscles, 367
    coagulation of the blood, 367
    cooling of body, 368
    change of the eyes, 366
    detachment of cuticle, 388.
    discoloration, 386.
    effusions of fluid, 391
    effusion of serum, 388
    erosions, 392
    generation of gas, 386
    redness, external, 387
    redness, internal, 388
    rigidity, 374
    softening, 392
    inspections, 397
    inspections, period for conducting, 398.

INDEX. 659

Post-mortem inspection where body previously opened, 399
  inspection by one doctor, 399
  inspection by more than one doctor, 399
  inspections where suspicious facts unexpectedly appear, 399
  inspection, examination of the surroundings, 398, 401
  inspection, nature of warrant (remit) for, 400
  inspection, presence of friends at the, 400
  inspection, exclusion of suspected parties from the, 400
  inspection, admission of medical men to the, 400
  inspection, refusal to allow the, 400
  inspection, instruments required at the, 400
  inspection, assistance from circumstances attending the death, 401
  inspection, means for identifying clothes, etc, removed from body, 401
  inspection, external examination, 402
  inspection, written notes of appearances, 402
  inspection, marks of identity, 402.
  inspection, injuries on surface of body, 403.
  inspection, what to examine, 403
  inspection, internal examination, 404
  inspection, how to conduct the internal examination, 404
  inspection, report of, 406
  inspection of infants, 273
  inspection in the drowned, 518
  appearances of asphyxia, 496
Præcordia, effects of blows over the, 432
Precognition, medical jurist on the, 10
  citation to, 11
  compulsory attendance at, 11
  fees for attendance at, 11
  by the defender, 15
Pregnancy, circumstances under which it may have to be determined, 131.
  plea of, 132
  Scotch law regarding, 132
  English law regarding, 132
  signs of, 133
  early signs of, 133
  signs of natural, 133
  subjective signs of, 133
  rational signs of, 133
  sensible signs of, 133
  uncertain signs of, 134
  objective signs of, 134
  certain signs of, 141
  active movements of the fœtus, 141
  passive movements of the fœtus, 144

Pregnancy, certain signs of ballotement, 144
  quickening, 141
  stethoscopic signs of, 145
  certain signs of, value of, 147
  concealment of, proofs of, 209
  methods for estimating the duration of, 173
  cessation of the catamenia, 174
  conception, 173
  single coitus, 176
  quickening, 175
  longest period of protraction of, 187.
  contractions of uterus during, 140
  menstruation during, 175
  complicated, 148.
  extra-uterine, 147
  false, 148
  false, from moles, 149
  false, from retention of the menses, 149
  spasmodic or nervous, 148
  without delivery, 169
  unknown to the woman, 149.
  irresponsibility for actions during, 149
  as a proof of rape, 114
Pregnancies, protracted, tables of, 188 9
Premature birth, legal meaning of, 34
  labour, induction of, position of medical men in regard to, 192
  labour, propriety of inducing, 193
  labour, precautions to be observed in bringing on, 193.
Preternatural combustibility, cases of, 463, 559
Private nature of evidence given at the precognition, 14
Professional secrets, 21
Prostitutes, state of genitals in, 100
  under age of puberty, diagnostic marks of, 97
Pseudo morbid redness, 390
  discolorations, 390
Pseudonomania, 309
Puberty, age of, 36, 37
  determination of, 40
Punctiform ecchymosis of lungs, 257, 552
  ecchymosis of scalp, 256
Punctured wounds, 416
  wounds of neck, 485
Punctures of the head, prognosis in, 480
Pupillary membrane in new-born infants, 38
Putrefaction, occurrence of, in the dead body, 382
  in the earth, 383
  in water, 383
  advanced stages of, 394
  influence of, on the proofs of respiration, 215
Pyromania, 307

QUICKENING, laws relating to, 35
  period of, 141, 175

RAILWAY accidents, injuries from, 479
Rape, definition of, 88
    law regarding, 90
    by moral force, 88.
    proofs of, 94
    physical proofs of, 116
    genital appearances after, 94.
    gonorrhœa in cases of, 91.
    marks of injury on genitals, 91.
    marks of violence on the body in charges of, 91.
    characteristic discharge after, 94
    followed by bubo in groin, 97.
    discovery of semen in the vagina, 107.
    seminal stains on the chemise, position of, 107.
    seminal stains on the chemise, characters of, 107
    means of isolating the zoosperm in cases of, 109
    blood stains on female's linen in cases of, 107.
    various stains on woman's linen in cases of, 107.
    stains from urine in cases of, 107.
    chancres in a case of suspected, 113.
    syphilis in a case of suspected, 113
    gonorrhœa in a case of suspected, 113
    genital diseases in children leading to suspicions of, 94.
    spurious gonorrhœa in children, in cases of suspected, 95
    pregnancy as a proof of, 114
    moral proofs of, 119.
    proofs of, from insensibility in the woman, 119
    proofs of, from the woman's character, 119
    proofs of, from relative age of the parties, 123
    proofs of, from narrative of the complainant, 123.
    proofs of, from bruises, etc., on the body, 117
    proofs from the relative strength of the parties, 123.
    proofs of, from cries, etc., 122.
    proofs of, from examination of the man, 118
    proofs of, from post-mortem examination, 117
    negative indications in cases of, 93, 112
    proofs of, in married women, etc., 124
    summary of proofs of, 126
    false charges of, 92
    without penetration, 92
    where penetration not complete, 90
    with female's consent, 89.
    of infants, 92
    of females under ten years, 91.
    of females under puberty, 91
    in virgins after puberty, proofs of, 99.
    on a concubine, 89.

Rape of a prostitute, 89.
    in females who have borne children, 106.
    on insane persons, 121
    during sleep, 121.
    while under narcotics, etc., 120
    by females on males, 127.
Ravish, attempt to, 90
Refusal to answer questions, 22
Report at the trial, 22
    of post mortem inspection 406
    medico-legal, character of, 10.
Reports, medico-legal, forms of, 10, 640
Respiration before entire birth, 245
    within the uterus, 246
    within the vagina, 251.
    doubtful cases of, 244
    life without, in infants, 238
Respiratory system, injuries of, 487
Restraint in cases of imbecility, 300
Rigor mortis, 374.
Roussin's fluid for dissolving blood, 473
    mode of examining blood stains, 473
Ruptures of blood-vessels, 448.
    of muscles, 449
    of viscera, 444
Russel on proofs of insanity, 321.

SALIVA in the stomach of new-born infants 39
Saponification, intra-uterine, 219
Sarcocele as a cause of impotence, 80
Scars of wounds, 425
    disappearance of, 58.
Schlaftrunkenheit (sleep-drunkenness), 327
Schmidt's test, 228
Schonbein's test for blood, 472.
Scientific terms, use of, in court, 28
Scleroderma (sclerema), 183, 262
Scotch law, definition of insanity in, 286
    procedure in cases of weak mind, 295
Scotland, criminal institutions of, 4
Sebaceous coating on new-born infants, 38
Secale cornutum, 197.
Semen in the vagina in cases of rape, 107
Seminal stains on the chemise, 107
    animalcule, means of isolating, 109
    animalcule, bodies resembling, 112
Sex, questions relating to, 44
    determination of, in the fœtus, 46
    determination of, before puberty, 46
    determination of, after puberty, 46.
    determination of, from the pelvis, 48.
    determination of, from the skeleton, 47
    determination of, in cases of imperfect development, 44.
    determination of, in cases of genital malformation, 48
    determination of, in mutilated bodies, 44.

INDEX. 661

Sex, earliest period at which it can be discriminated, 46
    concealed, investigation of cases of, 55
Shock, nervous, after blows, 432
Silver, preparations of, used for dyeing the hair, 60
Size of the footprint, 62.
Skeleton, ossification of, at different ages, 39
Skilled witness, evidence of, 2
Skinbound, 183, 262
Skull, fractures of, in the new born infant, 258
    fracture of, in the infant, cases of, 259
    fractures of, prognosis in, 480
Smothering, death by, 547.
    from natural causes, 265
    punctiform ecchymosis in, 552
Sodomy, 128
    signs of, in the male (Tardieu), 129
    signs of, in the female (Tardieu), 129.
    signs of (Caspar), 130.
Softening, vital or cadaveric, 393
Somnambulism, medico legal relations of, 327.
Spasm, cadaveric, 375
    tetanic, 378
Special nature of medico legal questions, 14
Specific gravity, test of respiration, 229
Spectrum analysis of blood, 472
    analysis of poisons, 590
Spinal injuries, prognosis in, 482
    injuries, results of, 482
    injuries, state of blood in heart, 482
Spine, concussion of, 431
Spleen, rupture of, 446
Spontaneous human combustion, 463, 558
    human combustion, cause of, 559
    fractures, 465
Squaw root, 198
Starvation, death by, 562
    accidental, 562
    homicidal, 562
    voluntary, 562
    symptoms of, 563
    post mortem signs of, 563
    signs of, valuation of, 564.
Static test of the lungs, 227
Sterility, definition of, 75
    in the female, 82
    certain causes of, 82
    doubtful causes of, 84
    from youth, 84
    from age, 84
    occult causes of, 86
    summation of causes of, 87
Stethoscopic signs of pregnancy, 145
    signs of pregnancy, value of, 147.
Still birth, proofs of, 217
    summary of the proofs of, 242

Stomach, signs of live birth in the, 239.
    air in the new-born infant's, 240
    drugs in the new-born infant's, 240
    saliva in the new-born infant's, 240
    ruptures of, 446
    ulceration of, in infants, 272
    water in the, in drowning, 512.
Stomach-pump, use of in poisoning, 598
Strangulation, death by, 537
    cause of death in, 537.
    immediate, 537
    mediate, 537
    general morbid appearances in, 538
    state of brain in, 540
    state of heart in, 540
    state of lungs in, 540
    apoplectic kernels in lungs, 540
    rupture of air-cells of lungs in, 540
    capillary ecchymosis of lungs in, 540
    mucous froth in air-tubes, 540
    appearance of trachea in, 540
    special morbid appearances in, 538.
    appearances on neck in, 538
    immediate, marks on neck in, 539
    mediate, mark of cord on neck in, 539
    deep injuries on the neck in, 539
    direction of groove on neck in, 540
    whether accident, suicide, or homicide, 543
    accidental cases of, 543
    homicidal, 544
    suicidal, cases of, 542
    appearances of violence in, 538
    external ecchymosis in, 538
    and hanging, diagnosis between, 540
    by the navel string, 260, 271.
    peculiar cases of, 541
    lawyers' objections in cases of, 545
    circumstantial evidence in, 546
Sublimation of poisons, 595
Suffocation, definition of, 547
    death by, 547
    accidental causes of, 548
    after removal from the water, 548
    under chloroform, 548
    by neglect of infants, 548
    natural causes of, 547
    of infants from bronchitis, 547.
    from impaction of food in throat, 548
    by carbonic acid and oxide, 551
    suicidal, 550
    by violence, unintentional and intentional, 549
    foreign bodies in air-passages in, 551
    marks of violence in, 551
    punctiform ecchymosis in, 552
    post mortem signs of, 550
Suggilations, 380, 435
Suicidal cut throat, diagnosis of, 423
    monomania, 311

INDEX.

Suicidal venesection, 483
Summons to appear at the trial, 18
Superfœtation, 179
Suspected poisoning, 625
Suspicious cases, duties of medical attendant in, 80
Sweat-stains, with guiacum test, 473
Symonds on modes of dying, 352
Syncope, death by, 354.
    appearances of death by, 355
    signs of, in persons falling into water, 498

TARDIEU's spots in smothering, 257, 552
    test of live birth, 240
Tattooing, disappearance of marks of, 58
Tattooed marks, methods for effacing, 59
    marks, influence of the substance employed in the disappearance of, 59
    marks as a means of determining the trade of the person, 59
Taylor's test for blood, 472
Teichmann's test for blood, 471
Tenancy by the courtesy, 44
    by the courtesy, legal conditions of, 181
Testes, period of the descent of, 46
    congenital absence of, 77
    absence of, causing impotence, 77
Tests for blood, 471
Tetanic spasm, 378
Thymus gland, suppuration of, 261
Toxicology, general, 565
    scope of, 569
    deficiencies in, 566
Trachea, redness of, in drowning, 512
    wounds of, 487
Trial, fees for attendance at the, 18.
    summons to appear at the, 18
    appearance of the medical expert on the, 10
Trichomonas vaginæ, 112
Trunksucht, 309
Tubercles in the lungs of infants, 227

ULCERATION of stomach in infants, 272
    of intestines in infants, 273
Umbilical arteries, period of closure of, 215
    cord in new-born infants if tied or not, 38
    cord, state of, at birth, 213
    cord, desiccation of, 213
    cord, period of fall of, 214
    cord, spiral state of, 214
    cord in the dead child, 213
    vein, period of closure of, 215
Unchastity, signs of, 100
United States of America, criminal institutions of, 7
United States of America, position of medical man in courts, 12
Urethra, contraction of the, causing impotence, 80

Uric acid infarction in the kidneys of the new-born infant, 241
Urinary bladder, state of, in the new-born infant, 241.
Urine, character of stains of, 107
Uterine souffle, 145
Utero-gestation, longest duration of, 187
Uterus, absence of, 83
    enlargement of, from pregnancy, 140
    enlargement of, from other causes, 141
    obliteration of cavity of, 86.
    prolapse of, 51, 87
    bicornis, 86
    respiration within the, 216

VAGINA in virgins, size of, 103
    in virgins, causes of enlargement of, 104
    absence of, 82
    constriction of, 85
    double, 86
    irregular course of, 84
    occlusion of, 85
    prolapse of, 87
    respiration within the, 251
Vagitus uterinus, 181, 246
    uterinus, cases of, 247
    vaginalis, 181, 251
    vaginalis, cases of, 251
Veins, admission of air into, 483
    ruptures of, 449
Venesection, suicidal, 483
Venosus, ductus, period of closure of, 215
Vernix caseosa in new born infants, 38
Viability, proofs of, 183
    earliest period of, 186
    French laws regarding, 182
    German laws regarding, 182
Violence, marks of, on drowned bodies, 516
Virginity, signs of, 99
    narrow outlet of pubes as a sign of, 104.
Virgins, state of genitals in young, 100
Vital processes, continuance of, after death, 371
Volunteering evidence, 23
Vulva, absence of, 83

WASHERWOMEN's hand in the drowned, 505
Weak mind, cognition in cases of, 295
    mind, interdiction in cases of, 297
    mind, inquest in cases of, 295
    minded persons, 290
    mindedness, legal dictum on, 393
    mindedness, degree of, to warrant cognition, 298
Weight of new-born infant, 37
Will, earliest age at which valid, 36
    degree of imbecility which would invalidate a, 299
Wills invalidated by mania, 314
Wind contusions, 458.

INDEX.

Winslow's test of death, 365
Withholding evidence, 21
Wound, legal definition of, 414
   medical definition of, 415
Wounds, classification of, 414.
   diagnosis of their cause from their appearance, 419
   contused, 441
   contused, mode of production of, 441
   gunshot, characters of, 451
   gunshot, appearance of exit, 451, 455
   gunshot, appearance of entrance, 451, 455
   gunshot, track of ball, 451
   gunshot, of skull, 452
   gunshot, modifying circumstances in, 453
   gunshot, varying appearances of entrance opening, 453
   gunshot, blackening at entrance of, 458
   gunshot, burning of clothes in, 453
   caused by weapons loaded with gun powder alone, 454
   gunshot, effects of varying momentum, 455
   gunshot, effects of various projectiles, 455
   gunshot, conclusions regarding, 455
   gunshot, in clothes, 458
   gunshot, anomalous cases of, 458
   gunshot, period at which weapon discharged, 459
   incised, characters of, 420
   incised, state of edges of, 421
   incised, variations of, 421
   incised, apparent, by blunt bodies, 421
   incised, appearance of commencement of, 422
   incised, appearance of termination of, 422
   incised, of the throat, 423
   incised, interrupted, 424
   incised, in clothes, 424
   incised appearances in healing, 425
   incised, influences modifying healing of, 425
   incised, whether inflicted during life, 424, 426

Wounds, incised, inflicted after death, 426
   contused, 429
   lacerated, 450
   lacerated, state of edges of, 450
   lacerated, bleeding of, 450
   lacerated, signs of vital origin, 451
   poisoned, 460
   punctured, 416
   punctured, diagnosis of instrument from shape of, 416
   punctured, relative size of, to instrument, 417
   prognosis of, 478
   of the abdomen, prognosis of, 488
   of generative organs, prognosis of, 485
   of the head, prognosis in, 479
   of the heart, prognosis of, 485
   of the larynx, prognosis in, 487
   of the lungs, prognosis of, 487
   of the pleura, prognosis of, 487
   of the trachea, prognosis of, 487
   effects of intemperance on prognosis of, 484
   cause of death in, 492
   of the abdomen, cause of death in, 488.
   of chest, causes of death in, 485, 487
   of neck, cause of death in, 484
   of the genitals, motives for causing, 487
   of genitals, spontaneous origin of, 486
   cicatrices of, 425
   traces of blood from, on furniture, etc., 418
   traces of in clothes, 419
   in dead bodies, 348
   distance of, from each other, 418
   apparently more than one, 419
   with Y-like spur, 420.
   medico-legal inspection after death by, 490
   post-mortem examination of, 492
Wreden's test of live birth, 241
Written evidence on the trial, 22

ZOOSPERM, means for isolating the, 109
   bodies resembling, 112

THE END

Printed by R. & R. CLARK, Edinburgh

London, New Burlington Street.
November, 1877.

SELECTION

FROM

MESSRS J. & A. CHURCHILL'S

General Catalogue

COMPRISING

ALL RECENT WORKS PUBLISHED BY THEM

ON THE

ART AND SCIENCE

OF

MEDICINE

INDEX

	PAGE
Acton on the Reproductive Organs	8
Adams (W) on Clubfoot	6
— (R) on Rheumatic Gout	18
Allen on Aural Catarrh	6
Allingham on Diseases of Rectum	7
Anatomical Remembrancer	11
Anderson (McC) on Eczema	19
— (McC) on Parasitic Affections	19
Arnott on Cancer	19
Aveling's English Midwives	14
Balfour's Diseases of the Heart	16
Barclay's Medical Diagnosis	11
Barker's Puerperal Diseases	13
Barnes' Obstetric Operations	14
— Diseases of Women	14
Basham on Renal Diseases	8
— on Diseases of the Kidneys	8
Beale on Kidney Diseases	8
Bellamy's Guide to Surgical Anatomy	10
Bennet's Winter and Spring on the Mediterranean	16
— Pulmonary Consumption	16
— Nutrition	18
Bennett (J. R) on Cancerous Growths	19
Bigg's Orthopraxy	6
Black on the Urinary Organs	8
— on Bright's Disease	8
Braune's Topographical Anatomy	11
Brodhurst's Orthopædic Surgery	6
Bryant's Practice of Surgery	4
Bucknill and Tuke's Psychological Medicine	21
Burdett's Cottage Hospital	14
Buzzard on Syphilitic Nervous Affections	9
Carpenter's Human Physiology	10
Carter on Mycetoma	20
Cauty on Diseases of the Skin	20
Chapman on Neuralgia	18
Charteris' Practice of Medicine	11
Clark's Outlines of Surgery	4
— Surgical Diagnosis	5
Clay's Obstetric Surgery	13
Cobbold on Worms	20
Coles' Dental Mechanics	23
Cooper's Surgical Dictionary	4
Cormack's Clinical Studies	12
Cottle's Hair in Health and Disease	20
Coulson on Syphilis	9
— on Stone in the Bladder	9
Cullingworth's Nurse's Companion	14
Curling's Diseases of the Rectum	7

	PAGE
Dalby on the Ear	6
Dalton's Human Physiology	9
Day on Children's Diseases	13
— on Headaches	18
De Valcourt on Cannes	16
Dobell's Lectures on Winter Cough	15
— First Stage of Consumption	15
Domville's Manual for Hospital Nurses	14
Druitt's Surgeon's Vade-Mecum	4
Dunglison's Medical Dictionary	22
Ellis's Manual of Diseases of Children	12
Fayrer's Observations in India	4
Fergusson's Practical Surgery	4
Fenwick's Guide to Medical Diagnosis	11
— on the Stomach, &c	18
Flint on Phthisis	15
— on Percussion and Auscultation	15
Flower's Nerves of the Human Body	10
Foster's Clinical Medicine	12
Fox (T) Atlas of Skin Diseases	19
Fox and Farquhar's Skin Diseases of India	20
Frey's Histology	9
Gamgee on Fractures of the Limbs	6
Gant's Science and Practice of Surgery	4
— Diseases of the Bladder	8
Gaskoin on Psoriasis or Lepra	20
Glenn's Laws affecting Medical Men	20
Godlee's Atlas of Human Anatomy	11
Gordon on Fractures	6
Habershon on Diseases of the Liver	17
— on Diseases of the Stomach	17
— on the Pneumogastric Nerve	17
Hancock's Surgery of Foot and Ankle	6
Harris on Lithotomy	7
Hayden on the Heart	15
Heath's Minor Surgery and Bandaging	5
— Diseases and Injuries of Jaws	5
— Operative Surgery	5
— Practical Anatomy	11
Higgens' Ophthalmic Practice	23
Holden's Landmarks	10
Holt on Stricture of the Urethra	7
Hood on Gout, Rheumatism, &c	19
Hooper's Physician's Vade Mecum	11
Horton's Tropical Diseases	17
Hutchinson's Clinical Surgery	5
Huth's Marriage of Near Kin	10
Ireland's Idiocy and Imbecility	21
Jones (C H.) and Sieveking's Pathological Anatomy	10
— (C H) on Functional Nervous Disorders	17

INDEX

	PAGE
Jones (Wharton) Ophthalmic Medicine and Surgery	23
Jordan's Surgical Inflammations	6
— Surgical Inquiries	6
Kennion's Springs of Harrogate	16
Lawson on Sciatica, &c.	18
Lee (H.) Practical Pathology	8
— on Syphilis	8
Leared on Imperfect Digestion	18
Liebreich's Atlas of Ophthalmoscopy	22
Liveing on Megrim, &c.	18
Macdonald's Examination of Water	22
Mackenzie on Growths in the Larynx	15
Macnamara on Diseases of the Eye	22
Madden's Health Resorts	16
Marsden on certain Forms of Cancer	19
Mason on Harelip and Cleft Palate	5
Maunder's Operative Surgery	4
— Surgery of Arteries	4
Mayne's Medical Vocabulary	22
Meryon's System of Nerves	18
Moore's Family Medicine for India	17
Parkes' Manual of Practical Hygiene	21
Parkin's Epidemiology	23
Pavy on Food and Dietetics	18
Peacock's Valvular Disease	15
Phillips' Materia Medica	12
Pirrie's Surgery	4
Ramsbotham's Obstetrics	13
Reynolds' Uses of Electricity	22
Roberts' Practice of Midwifery	13
Roussel's Transfusion of Blood	5
Routh's Infant Feeding	12
Roy's Burdwan Fever	17
Royle and Harley's Materia Medica	12
Rutherford's Practical Histology	10
Sabben and Browne's Handbook of Law and Lunacy	21
Salts' Medico Electric Apparatus	22
Sanderson's Physiological Handbook	9
Sansom's Diseases of the Heart	16
Savage on the Female Pelvic Organs	5
Savory's Domestic Medicine	14
Sayre's Orthopædic Surgery	6
Schroeder's Manual of Midwifery	13
Semple on the Heart	15
Sewill's Dental Anatomy	23
Shapter's Diseases of the Heart	16
Shaw's Medical Remembrancer	12
Sheppard on Madness	21
Sibson's Medical Anatomy	11
Sieveking's Life Assurance	21
Smith (E.) Wasting Diseases of Children	12
— Clinical Studies	12
Smith (Henry) Surgery of the Rectum	8
Smith (Heywood) Gynæcology	13
Smith (J.) Dental Anatomy	23
Smith (W. R.) Nursing	14
Spender's Bath Waters	16
Steiner's Diseases of Children	13
Stowe's Toxicological Chart	20
Sullivan's Tropical Diseases	17
Swain's Surgical Emergencies	5
Swayne's Obstetric Aphorisms	13
Taft's Operative Dentistry	23
Tait's Hospital Mortality	14
Taylor's Principles of Medical Jurisprudence	20
— Manual of Medical Jurisprudence	20
— Poisons in relation to Medical Jurisprudence	20
Thompson's Stricture of Urethra	7
— Practical Lithotomy and Lithotrity	7
— Diseases of Urinary Organs	7
— Diseases of the Prostate	7
— Calculous Disease	7
Thornton on Tracheotomy	16
Thorowgood on Asthma	15
— on Materia Medica	12
Thudichum's Pathology of Urine	9
Tibbits' Medical Electricity	22
— Map of Motor Points	22
Tilt's Uterine Therapeutics	13
— Change of Life	13
— Health in India	17
Tomes' (C. S.) Dental Anatomy	23
— (J. and C. S.) Dental Surgery	23
Tufnell's Internal Aneurism	7
Tuke on the Influence of the Mind upon the Body	21
Van Buren on Diseases of the Genito-Urinary Organs	9
Veitch's Handbook for Nurses	14
Virchow's Post-mortem Examinations	10
Wagstaffe's Human Osteology	10
Walton's Diseases of the Eye	22
Ward on Affections of the Liver	17
Waring's Practical Therapeutics	12
— Bazaar Medicines of India	17
Waters on Diseases of the Chest	15
Wells (Soelberg) on Diseases of the Eye	23
— Long, Short, and Weak Sight	23
Wells (Spencer) on Diseases of the Ovaries	13
Wife's Domain	14
Wilks' Pathological Anatomy	10
Wilson's (E.) Anatomist's Vade-Mecum	11
— Diseases of the Skin	19
— Lectures on Eczema	19
— Lectures on Dermatology	19
Wilson's (G.) Handbook of Hygiene	21
Woodman & Tidy's Forensic Medicine	21

THE PRACTICE OF SURGERY.

a Manual by THOMAS BRYANT, F.R.C S., Surgeon to Guy's Hospital. Second Edition, 2 vols., crown 8vo, with 559 Engravings 25s [1876]

THE PRINCIPLES AND PRACTICE OF SURGERY,

by WILLIAM PIRRIE, F.R.S.E., Professor of Surgery in the University of Aberdeen. Third Edition, 8vo, with 490 Engravings, 28s [1873]

A SYSTEM OF PRACTICAL SURGERY,

by Sir WILLIAM FERGUSSON, Bart., F.R.C.S., F.R.S. Fifth Edition, 8vo, with 463 Engravings, 21s [1870]

OPERATIVE SURGERY,

by C. F. MAUNDER, F R C.S, Surgeon to the London Hospital, formerly Demonstrator of Anatomy at Guy's Hospital. Second Edition, post 8vo, with 164 Engravings, 6s. [1873]

BY THE SAME AUTHOR.

SURGERY OF THE ARTERIES

Lettsomian Lectures for 1875, on Aneurisms, Wounds, Hæmorrhages, &c Post 8vo, with 18 Engravings, 5s. [1875]

THE SURGEON'S VADE-MECUM,

by ROBERT DRUITT. Eleventh Edition, fcap. 8vo, with numerous Engravings. [In the press]

THE SCIENCE AND PRACTICE OF SURGERY:

a complete System and Textbook by F. J. GANT, F.R.C.S., Senior Surgeon to the Royal Free Hospital. 8vo, with 470 Engravings, 24s. [1871]

OUTLINES OF SURGERY AND SURGICAL PATHOLOGY,

including the Diagnosis and Treatment of Obscure and Urgent Cases, and the Surgical Anatomy of some Important Structures and Regions, by F. LE GROS CLARK, F.R.S., Consulting Surgeon to St. Thomas's Hospital. Second Edition, Revised and Expanded by the Author, assisted by W. W. WAGSTAFFE, F.R C S, Assistant-Surgeon to, and Lecturer on Anatomy at, St. Thomas's Hospital. 8vo, 10s 6d. [1872]

CLINICAL AND PATHOLOGICAL OBSERVATIONS IN INDIA,

by Sir J. FAYRER, K.C.S.I., M.D., F.R.C P. Lond., F R S.E., Honorary Physician to the Queen. 8vo, with Engravings, 20s. [1873]

DICTIONARY OF PRACTICAL SURGERY

and Encyclopædia of Surgical Science, by SAMUEL COOPER. New Edition, brought down to the present Time by SAMUEL A. LANE, Consulting Surgeon to St. Mary's and to the Lock Hospitals, assisted by various Eminent Surgeons. 2 vols. 8vo, 50s. [1861 and 1872]

SURGICAL EMERGENCIES

together with the Emergencies attendant on Parturition and the Treatment of Poisoning a Manual for the use of General Practitioners, by WILLIAM P SWAIN, F R C.S., Surgeon to the Royal Albert Hospital, Devonport. Second Edition, post 8vo, with 104 Engravings, 6s 6d. [1876]

TRANSFUSION OF HUMAN BLOOD·

with Table of 50 cases, by Dr ROUSSEL, of Geneva. Translated by CLAUDE GUINNESS, B.A With a Preface by SIR JAMES PAGET, Bart Crown 8vo, 2s 6d. [1877]

ILLUSTRATIONS OF CLINICAL SURGERY,

consisting of Coloured Plates, Photographs, Woodcuts, Diagrams &c, illustrating Surgical Diseases, Symptoms and Accidents, also Operations and other methods of Treatment. By JONATHAN HUTCHINSON, F R.C.S, Senior Surgeon to the London Hospital In Quarterly Fasciculi Fasc I to IX already issued 6s. 6d. each. [1876-7]

PRINCIPLES OF SURGICAL DIAGNOSIS

especially in Relation to Shock and Visceral Lesions, by F LE GROS CLARK, F.R.C.S., Consulting Surgeon to St. Thomas's Hospital 8vo, 10s. 6d [1870]

MINOR SURGERY AND BANDAGING

a Manual for the Use of House-Surgeons, Dressers, and Junior Practitioners, by CHRISTOPHER HEATH, F R C S., Surgeon to University College Hospital, and Holme Professor of Surgery in University College. Fifth Edition, fcap 8vo, with 86 Engravings, 5s 6d [1875]

BY THE SAME AUTHOR,

INJURIES AND DISEASES OF THE JAWS

JACKSONIAN PRIZE ESSAY. Second Edition, 8vo, with 164 Engravings, 12s [1872]

BY THE SAME AUTHOR.

A COURSE OF OPERATIVE SURGERY.

with 20 Plates drawn from Nature by M. LÉVEILLÉ, and coloured by hand under his direction. Large 8vo. 40s [1877]

HARE-LIP AND CLEFT PALATE,

by FRANCIS MASON, F.R.C.S., Surgeon and Lecturer on Anatomy at St. Thomas's Hospital With 66 Engravings, 8vo, 6s. [1877]

THE FEMALE PELVIC ORGANS,

their Surgery, Surgical Pathology, and Surgical Anatomy, in a Series of Coloured Plates taken from Nature with Commentaries, Notes, and Cases, by HENRY SAVAGE, M.D Lond, F R C S., Consulting Officer of the Samaritan Free Hospital Third Edition, 4to, £1 15s. [1875]

FRACTURES OF THE LIMBS
and their Treatment, by J. SAMPSON GAMGEE, Surgeon to the Queen's Hospital, Birmingham. 8vo, with Plates, 10s. 6d. [1871]

FRACTURES OF THE LOWER END OF THE RADIUS,
Fractures of the Clavicle, and on the Reduction of the Recent Inward Dislocations of the Shoulder Joint. By ALEXANDER GORDON, M.D., Professor of Surgery in Queen's College, Belfast. With Engravings, 8vo, 5s. [1875]

DISEASES AND INJURIES OF THE EAR,
by W. B. DALBY, F.R.C.S., M.B., Aural Surgeon and Lecturer on Aural Surgery at St. George's Hospital. Crown 8vo, with 21 Engravings, 6s 6d. [1873]

AURAL CATARRH,
or, the Commonest Forms of Deafness, and their Cure, by PETER ALLEN, M.D., F.R.C.S.E., late Aural Surgeon to St Mary's Hospital. Second Edition, crown 8vo, with Engravings, 8s. 6d. [1876]

CLUBFOOT.
its Causes, Pathology, and Treatment; being the Jacksonian Prize Essay by WM ADAMS, F.R.C.S., Surgeon to the Great Northern Hospital. Second Edition, 8vo, with 106 Engravings and 6 Lithographic Plates, 15s. [1873]

ORTHOPÆDIC SURGERY:
Lectures delivered at St. George's Hospital, by BERNARD E BRODHURST, F.R.C.S., Surgeon to the Royal Orthopædic Hospital. Second Edition, 8vo, with Engravings, 12s 6d. [1876]

OPERATIVE SURGERY OF THE FOOT AND ANKLE,
by HENRY HANCOCK, F.R.C.S., Consulting Surgeon to Charing Cross Hospital. 8vo, with Engravings, 15s. [1873]

ORTHOPÆDIC SURGERY.
and Diseases of the Joints. Lectures by LEWIS A. SAYRE, M.D., Professor of Orthopædic Surgery, Fractures and Dislocations, and Clinical Surgery, in Bellevue Hospital Medical College, New York With 274 Wood Engravings, 8vo, 20s. [1876]

THE TREATMENT OF SURGICAL INFLAMMATIONS
by a New Method, which greatly shortens their Duration, by FURNEAUX JORDAN, F.R.C.S., Professor of Surgery in Queen's College, Birmingham. 8vo, with Plates, 7s. 6d. [1870]

BY THE SAME AUTHOR,

SURGICAL INQUIRIES
With numerous Lithographic Plates. 8vo, 5s [1873]

ORTHOPRAXY
the Mechanical Treatment of Deformities, Debilities, and Deficiencies of the Human Frame, by H. HEATHER BIGG, Associate of the Institute of Civil Engineers. Third Edition, with 319 Engravings, 8vo, 15s [1877]

INTERNAL ANEURISM.

Its Successful Treatment by Consolidation of the Contents of the Sac. By T Joliffe Tufnell, F R.C.S.I., President of the Royal College of Surgeons in Ireland. With Coloured Plates Second Edition, royal 8vo, 5s. [1875]

DISEASES OF THE RECTUM,

by Thomas B. Curling, F.R S., Consulting Surgeon to the London Hospital Fourth Edition, Revised, 8vo, 7s. 6d [1876]

STRICTURE OF THE URETHRA

and Urinary Fistulæ; their Pathology and Treatment. Jacksonian Prize Essay by Sir Henry Thompson, F.R C S, Emeritus Professor of Surgery to University College Third Edition, 8vo, with Plates, 10s [1869]

BY THE SAME AUTHOR,

PRACTICAL LITHOTOMY AND LITHOTRITY;

or, An Inquiry into the best Modes of removing Stone from the Bladder. Second Edition, 8vo, with numerous Engravings. 10s [1871]

ALSO,

DISEASES OF THE URINARY ORGANS.

(Clinical Lectures) Fourth Edition, 8vo, with 2 Plates and 59 Engravings, 12s. [1876]

ALSO,

DISEASES OF THE PROSTATE.

their Pathology and Treatment. Fourth Edition, 8vo, with numerous Plates, 10s [1873]

ALSO,

THE PREVENTIVE TREATMENT OF CALCULOUS DISEASE

and the Use of Solvent Remedies Second Edition, fcap 8vo, 2s 6d. [1876]

STRICTURE OF THE URETHRA

and its Immediate Treatment, by Barnard Holt, F R C S., Consulting Surgeon to the Westminster Hospital Third Edition, 8vo, 6s [1868]

LITHOTOMY AND EXTRACTION OF STONE

from the Bladder, Urethra, and Prostate of the Male, and from the Bladder of the Female, by W Poulett Harris, M.D ,[Surgeon-Major H.M Bengal Medical Service. With Engravings, 8vo, 10s 6d. [1876]

FISTULA, HÆMORRHOIDS, PAINFUL ULCER,

Stricture Prolapsus, and other Diseases of the Rectum- their Diagnosis and Treatment, by Wm. Allingham, F.R C S, Surgeon to St. Mark's Hospital for Fistula, &c., late Surgeon to the Great Northern Hospital. Second Edition, 8vo, 7s. [1872]

THE SURGERY OF THE RECTUM.
    Lettsomian Lectures by HENRY SMITH, F.R.C.S., Professor of Surgery in King's College, Surgeon to King's College Hospital. Fourth Edition, fcap. 8vo, 5s. [1876]

THE URINE AND ITS DERANGEMENTS,
    with the Application of Physiological Chemistry to the Diagnosis and Treatment of Constitutional as well as Local Diseases. Lectures by GEORGE HARLEY, M.D., F.R.S., F.R.C.P., formerly Professor in in University College. Post 8vo, 9s. [1872]

KIDNEY DISEASES, URINARY DEPOSITS,
    and Calculous Disorders by LIONEL S. BEALE, M.B., F.R.S., F.R.C.P., Physician to King's College Hospital. Third Edition, 8vo, with 70 Plates, 25s. [1869]

DISEASES OF THE BLADDER,
    Prostate Gland and Urethra, including a practical view of Urinary Diseases, Deposits and Calculi, by F. J. GANT, F.R.C.S., Senior Surgeon to the Royal Free Hospital. Fourth Edition, crown 8vo, with Engravings, 10s. 6d. [1876]

RENAL DISEASES:
    a Clinical Guide to their Diagnosis and Treatment by W. R. BASHAM, M.D., F.R.C.P., late Senior Physician to the Westminster Hospital. Post 8vo, 7s. [1870]

BY THE SAME AUTHOR,
THE DIAGNOSIS OF DISEASES OF THE KIDNEYS,
    with Aids thereto. 8vo, with 10 Plates, 5s. [1872]

THE REPRODUCTIVE ORGANS
    in Childhood, Youth, Adult Age, and Advanced Life (Functions and Disorders of), considered in their Physiological, Social, and Moral Relations, by WILLIAM ACTON, M.R.C.S. Sixth Edition, 8vo, 12s. [1875]

URINARY AND REPRODUCTIVE ORGANS
    their Functional Diseases, by D. CAMPBELL BLACK, M.D., L.R.C.S. Edin. Second Edition. 8vo, 10s. 6d. [1875]

BY THE SAME AUTHOR,
LECTURES ON BRIGHT'S DISEASE,
    delivered at the Royal Infirmary of Glasgow. 8vo, with 20 Engravings, 6s. 6d. [1875]

PRACTICAL PATHOLOGY.
    containing Lectures on Suppurative Fever, Diseases of the Veins, Hæmorrhoidal Tumours, Diseases of the Rectum, Syphilis, Gonorrheal Ophthalmia, &c., by HENRY LEE, F.R.C.S., Surgeon to St. George's Hospital. Third Edition, in 2 vols 8vo, 10s. each. [1870]

BY THE SAME AUTHOR,
LECTURES ON SYPHILIS,
    and on some forms of Local Disease, affecting principally the Organs of Generation. With Engravings, 8vo, 10s. [1875]

PATHOLOGY OF THE URINE,
 including a Complete Guide to its Analysis, by J. L. W. Thudichum, M.D. Second Edition, rewritten and enlarged, with Engravings, 8vo, 15s. [1877]

GENITO-URINARY ORGANS, INCLUDING SYPHILIS.
 A Practical Treatise on their Surgical Diseases, designed as a Manual for Students and Practitioners, by W. H. Van Buren, M.D., Professor of the Principles of Surgery in Bellevue Hospital Medical College, New York, and E. L. Keyes, M.D., Professor of Dermatology in Bellevue Hospital Medical College, New York. Royal 8vo, with 140 Engravings, 21s. [1874]

SYPHILIS
 A Treatise by Walter J. Coulson, F.R.C.S., Surgeon to the Lock Hospital. 8vo, 10s. [1869]

BY THE SAME AUTHOR,

STONE IN THE BLADDER
 Its Prevention, Early Symptoms, and Treatment by Lithotrity. 8vo, 6s. [1868]

SYPHILITIC NERVOUS AFFECTIONS
 Their Clinical Aspects, by Thomas Buzzard, M.D., F.R.C.P. Lond., Physician to the National Hospital for Paralysis and Epilepsy. Post 8vo, 5s. [1874]

HISTOLOGY AND HISTO-CHEMISTRY OF MAN
 A Treatise on the Elements of Composition and Structure of the Human Body, by Heinrich Frey, Professor of Medicine in Zurich. Translated from the Fourth German Edition by Arthur E. J. Barker, Assistant-Surgeon to University College Hospital. And Revised by the Author. 8vo, with 608 Engravings, 21s. [1874]

HUMAN PHYSIOLOGY.
 A Treatise designed for the Use of Students and Practitioners of Medicine, by John C. Dalton, M.D., Professor of Physiology and Hygiene in the College of Physicians and Surgeons, New York. Sixth Edition, royal 8vo, with 316 Engravings, 20s. [1875]

HANDBOOK FOR THE PHYSIOLOGICAL LABORATORY,
 by E. Klein, M.D., F.R.S., Assistant Professor in the Pathological Laboratory of the Brown Institution, London, J. Burdon-Sanderson, M.D., F.R.S., Professor of Practical Physiology in University College, London, Michael Foster, M.D., F.R.S., Prælector of Physiology in Trinity College, Cambridge, and T. Lauder Brunton, M.D., D.Sc., Lecturer on Materia Medica at St. Bartholomew's Hospital, edited by J. Burdon-Sanderson. 8vo, with 123 Plates, 24s. [1873]

§

PRINCIPLES OF HUMAN PHYSIOLOGY,
by W. B. CARPENTER, C.B., M.D., F.R.S. Eighth Edition by HENRY POWER, M.B., F.R.C.S., Examiner in Natural Science, University of Oxford, and in Natural Science and Medicine, University of Cambridge. 8vo, with 3 Steel Plates and 371 Engravings, 31s. 6d [1876]

PRACTICAL HISTOLOGY.
By WILLIAM RUTHERFORD, M.D., Professor of the Institutes of Medicine in the University of Edinburgh Second Edition, with 63 Engravings. Crown 8vo (with additional leaves for notes), 6s [1876]

THE MARRIAGE OF NEAR KIN,
Considered with respect to the Laws of Nations, Results of Experience, and the Teachings of Biology, by ALFRED H. HUTH 8vo, 14s [1875]

STUDENTS' GUIDE TO HUMAN OSTEOLOGY,
By WILLIAM WARWICK WAGSTAFFE, F.R.C.S., Assistant-Surgeon and Lecturer on Anatomy, St. Thomas's Hospital. With 23 Plates and 66 Engravings Fcap. 8vo, 10s 6d [1875]

LANDMARKS, MEDICAL AND SURGICAL,
By LUTHER HOLDEN, F.R.C.S., Surgeon to St. Bartholomew's Hospital. Second Edition, 8vo [In the Press]

PATHOLOGICAL ANATOMY.
Lectures by SAMUEL WILKS, M.D., F.R.S., Physician to, and Lecturer on Medicine at, Guy's Hospital, and WALTER MOXON, M.D., F.R.C.P., Physician to, and Lecturer on Materia Medica at, Guy's Hospital. Second Edition, 8vo, with Plates, 18s. [1875]

PATHOLOGICAL ANATOMY.
A Manual by C. HANDFIELD JONES, M.B., F.R.S., Physician to St. Mary's Hospital, and EDWARD H. SIEVEKING, M.D., F.R.C.P., Physician to St. Mary's Hospital. Edited by J. F. PAYNE, M.D., F.R.C.P., Assistant Physician and Lecturer on General Pathology at St Thomas's Hospital Second Edition, crown 8vo, with 195 Engravings, 16s [1875]

POST-MORTEM EXAMINATIONS
a Description and Explanation of the Method of Performing them, with especial Reference to Medico-Legal Practice By Professor RUDOLPH VIRCHOW, of Berlin. Fcap 8vo, 2s. 6d. [1876]

STUDENT'S GUIDE TO SURGICAL ANATOMY
a Text-book for the Pass Examination, by E. BELLAMY, F.R.C.S., Senior Assistant-Surgeon and Lecturer on Anatomy at Charing Cross Hospital Fcap 8vo, with 50 Engravings, 6s 6d. [1873]

DIAGRAMS OF THE NERVES OF THE HUMAN BODY,
Exhibiting their Origin, Divisions, and Connexions, with their Distribution, by WILLIAM HENRY FLOWER, F.R.S., Conservator of the Museum of the Royal College of Surgeons Second Edition, roy 4to, 12s. [1872]

AN ATLAS OF HUMAN ANATOMY

illustrating most of the ordinary Dissections, and many not usually practised by the Student. To be completed in 12 or 13 Bi-monthly Parts, each containing 4 Coloured Plates, with Explanatory Text. By RICKMAN J. GODLEE, M.S., F.R.C.S., Assistant Surgeon to University College Hospital, and Senior Demonstrator of Anatomy in University College. Imp 4to, 7s 6d each Part [1877]

THE ANATOMIST'S VADE-MECUM

a System of Human Anatomy by ERASMUS WILSON, F.R.C.S., F.R.S. Ninth Edition, by G. BUCHANAN, M.A., M.D., Professor of Clinical Surgery in the University of Glasgow, and HENRY E. CLARK, F.F.P.S., Lecturer on Anatomy at the Glasgow Royal Infirmary School of Medicine. Crown 8vo, with 371 Engravings, 14s [1873]

PRACTICAL ANATOMY

a Manual of Dissections by CHRISTOPHER HEATH, F.R.C.S., Surgeon to University College Hospital, and Holme Professor of Surgery in University College. Fourth Edition, crown 8vo, with 16 Coloured Plates and 264 Engravings, 14s [1877]

MEDICAL ANATOMY,

by FRANCIS SIBSON, M.D., F.R.C.P., F.R.S. Imp folio, with 21 coloured Plates, cloth, 42s, half-morocco, 50s [1869]

ATLAS OF TOPOGRAPHICAL ANATOMY,

after Plane Sections of Frozen Bodies. By WILHELM BRAUNE, Professor of Anatomy in the University of Leipzig. Translated by EDWARD BELLAMY, F.R.C.S., Senior Assistant-Surgeon to, and Lecturer on Anatomy, &c., at, Charing Cross Hospital. With 34 Photo-lithographic Plates and 46 Woodcuts. Large Imp 8vo, 40s [1877]

THE STUDENT'S GUIDE TO THE PRACTICE OF MEDICINE,

by MATTHEW CHARTERIS, M.D., Professor of Medicine in Anderson's College, and Lecturer on Clinical Medicine in the Royal Infirmary, Glasgow. With Engravings on Copper and Wood, fcap 8vo, 6s 6d [1877]

THE STUDENT'S GUIDE TO MEDICAL DIAGNOSIS,

by SAMUEL FENWICK, M.D., F.R.C.P., Physician to the London Hospital. Fourth Edition, fcap 8vo, with 106 Engravings, 6s 6d [1876]

A MANUAL OF MEDICAL DIAGNOSIS,

by A. W. BARCLAY, M.D., F.R.C.P. Physician to, and Lecturer on Medicine at, St George's Hospital. Third Edition, fcap 8vo, 10s. 6d [1870]

THE ANATOMICAL REMEMBRANCER,

or, Complete Pocket Anatomist. Eighth Edition, 32mo, 3s 6d [1876]

HOOPER'S PHYSICIAN'S VADE-MECUM,

or, Manual of the Principles and Practice of Physic, Ninth Edition by W. A. GUY, M.B., F.R.S., and JOHN HARLEY, M.D., F.R.C.P. Fcap 8vo, with Engravings, 12s 6d [1874]

THE MEDICAL REMEMBRANCER,
or, Book of Emergencies. By E. SHAW, M.R.C S Fifth Edition by JONATHAN HUTCHINSON, F.R.C S., Senior Surgeon to the London Hospital. 32mo, 2s. 6d [1867]

MATERIA MEDICA AND THERAPEUTICS:
(Vegetable Kingdom), by CHARLES D F. PHILLIPS, M D., F R C S.E. 8vo, 15s [1874]

CLINICAL MEDICINE·
Lectures and Essays by BALTHAZAR FOSTER, M D, F.R C.P Lond., Professor of Medicine in Queen's College, Birmingham. 8vo, 10s. 6d. [1874]

CLINICAL STUDIES
Illustrated by Cases observed in Hospital and Private Practice, by Sir J ROSE CORMACK, M D, F R.S.E, Physician to the Hertford British Hospital of Paris 2 vols., post 8vo, 20s [1876]

ROYLE'S MANUAL OF MATERIA MEDICA AND THERAPEUTICS
Sixth Edition by JOHN HARLEY, M.D., Assistant Physician to, and Joint Lecturer on Physiology at, St Thomas's Hospital. Crown 8vo, with 139 Engravings, 15s. [1876]

PRACTICAL THERAPEUTICS
A Manual by E J. WARING, M D., F.R C P. Lond Third Edition, fcap 8vo, 12s 6d [1871]

THE STUDENT'S GUIDE TO MATERIA MEDICA,
by JOHN C THOROWGOOD, M.D. Lond., Physician to the City of London Hospital for Diseases of the Chest. Fcap 8vo, with Engravings, 6s. 6d [1874]

THE DISEASES OF CHILDREN:
A Practical Manual, with a Formulary, by EDWARD ELLIS, M D, Physician to the Victoria Hospital for Children Third Edition, crown 8vo [In the Press]

THE WASTING DISEASES OF CHILDREN,
by EUSTACE SMITH, M.D. Lond., Physician to the King of the Belgians, Physician to the East London Hospital for Children. Second Edition, post 8vo, 7s. 6d. [1870]

BY THE SAME AUTHOR,
CLINICAL STUDIES OF DISEASE IN CHILDREN
Post 8vo, 7s 6d [1876]

INFANT FEEDING AND ITS INFLUENCE ON LIFE,
or, the Causes and Prevention of Infant Mortality, by CHARLES H F. ROUTH, M D., Senior Physician to the Samaritan Hospital for Women and Children. Third Edition, fcap 8vo, 7s 6d [1876]

COMPENDIUM OF CHILDREN'S DISEASES
A Handbook for Practitioners and Students, by JOHANN STEINER, M.D., Professor in the University of Prague. Translated from the Second German Edition by LAWSON TAIT, F.R.C S., Surgeon to the Birmingham Hospital for Women. 8vo, 12s. 6d. [1874]

THE DISEASES OF CHILDREN
Essays by WILLIAM HENRY DAY, M.D., Physician to the Samaritan Hospital for Diseases of Women and Children. Fcap 8vo, 5s. [1873]

PUERPERAL DISEASES:
Clinical Lectures by FORDYCE BARKER, M.D., Obstetric Physician to Bellevue Hospital, New York. 8vo, 15s [1874]

THE STUDENT'S GUIDE TO THE PRACTICE OF MIDWIFERY,
by D LLOYD ROBERTS, M.D., Physician to St Mary's Hospital, Manchester Fcap 8vo, with 95 Engravings, 6s. 6d. [1875]

OBSTETRIC MEDICINE AND SURGERY,
Their Principles and Practice, by F H RAMSBOTHAM, M D, F R C P. Fifth Edition, 8vo, with 120 Plates, 22s [1867]

OBSTETRIC APHORISMS.
for the Use of Students commencing Midwifery Practice by J. G SWAYNE, M.D, Consulting Physician-Accoucheur to the Bristol General Hospital, and Lecturer on Obstetric Medicine at the Bristol Medical School Sixth Edition, fcap 8vo, with Engravings, 3s 6d [1876]

OBSTETRIC SURGERY
A Complete Handbook, giving Short Rules of Practice in every Emergency, from the Simplest to the most Formidable Operations connected with the Science of Obstetricy, by CHARLES CLAY, Ext L R C P Lond, L R C S E, late Senior Surgeon and Lecturer on Midwifery, St Mary's Hospital, Manchester Fcap 8vo, with 91 Engravings, 6s. 6d [1874]

SCHROEDER'S MANUAL OF MIDWIFERY,
including the Pathology of Pregnancy and the Puerperal State Translated by CHARLES H. CARTER, B A., M D 8vo, with Engravings, 12s 6d [1873]

A HANDBOOK OF UTERINE THERAPEUTICS,
and of Diseases of Women, by E. J TILT, M D, M R C.P. Third Edition, post 8vo, 10s [1868]

BY THE SAME AUTHOR,

THE CHANGE OF LIFE
in Health and Disease · a Practical Treatise on the Nervous and other Affections incidental to Women at the Decline of Life Third Edition, 8vo, 10s 6d [1870]

DISEASES OF THE OVARIES
their Diagnosis and Treatment, by T. SPENCER WELLS, F.R.C.S, Surgeon to the Queen's Household and to the Samaritan Hospital 8vo, with about 150 Engravings, 21s. [1872]

PRACTICAL GYNÆCOLOGY
A Handbook of the Diseases of Women, by HEYWOOD SMITH, M D Oxon, Physician to the Hospital for Women and to the British Lying-in Hospital With Engravings, crown 8vo, 5s 6d. [1877]

OBSTETRIC OPERATIONS,
including the Treatment of Hæmorrhage, and forming a Guide to the Management of Difficult Labour, Lectures by ROBERT BARNES, M D, F.R.C P , Obstetric Physician and Lecturer on Obstetrics and the Diseases of Women and Children at St George's Hospital Third Edition, 8vo, with 124 Engravings, 18s [1875]

BY THE SAME AUTHOR,

MEDICAL AND SURGICAL DISEASES OF WOMEN
a Clinical History Second Edition, 8vo, with many Engravings [In the Press]

HANDBOOK FOR NURSES FOR THE SICK,
by ZEPHERINA P. VEITCH. Second Edition, crown 8vo, 3s 6d. [1876]

A MANUAL FOR HOSPITAL NURSES
and others engaged in Attending on the Sick by EDWARD J. DOMVILLE, L.R C P., M R.C.S. Second Edition, crown 8vo, 2s 6d [1875]

THE NURSE'S COMPANION
A Manual of General and Monthly Nursing, by CHARLES J CULLINGWORTH, Surgeon to St. Mary's Hospital, Manchester Fcap 8vo, 2s 6d [1876]

LECTURES ON NURSING,
by WILLIAM ROBERT SMITH, M B , late Resident Surgeon, Royal Hants County Hospital, Winchester Second Edition, with Engravings Post 8vo [In the Press]

THE COTTAGE HOSPITAL
Its Origin, Progress, Management, and Work, by HENRY C BURDETT, the Seaman's Hospital, Greenwich. With Engravings, crown 8vo, 7s 6d. [1877]

HOSPITAL MORTALITY
being a Statistical Investigation of the Returns of the Hospitals of Great Britain and Ireland for fifteen years, by LAWSON TAIT, F R C S , F S S 8vo, 6s [1877]

ENGLISH MIDWIVES.
their History and Prospects, by J H AVELING, M D., Physician to the Chelsea Hospital for Women, Examiner of Midwives for the Obstetrical Society of London Crown 8vo, 5s. [1872]

A COMPENDIUM OF DOMESTIC MEDICINE
and Companion to the Medicine Chest, intended as a Source of Easy Reference for Clergymen, and for Families residing at a Distance from Professional Assistance, by JOHN SAVORY, M S A Eighth Edition, 12mo, 5s. [1871]

THE WIFE'S DOMAIN
The Young Couple—The Mother—The Nurse—The Nursling, by PHILOTHALOS. Second Edition, post 8vo, 3s 6d [1871]

WINTER COUGH:

(Catarrh, Bronchitis, Emphysema, Asthma), Lectures by HORACE DOBELL, M.D., Consulting Physician to the Royal Hospital for Diseases of the Chest. Third Edition, with Coloured Plates, 8vo, 1s 6d. [1875]

BY THE SAME AUTHOR,

THE TRUE FIRST STAGE OF CONSUMPTION

(Lectures.) Crown 8vo, 3s 6d. [1867]

DISEASES OF THE CHEST.

Contributions to their Clinical History, Pathology, and Treatment, by A. T. H. WATERS, M.D., F.R.C.P., Physician to the Liverpool Royal Infirmary. Second Edition, 8vo, with Plates, 15s. [1873]

NOTES ON ASTHMA;

its Forms and Treatment, by JOHN C. THOROWGOOD, M.D. Lond., F.R.C.P., Physician to the Hospital for Diseases of the Chest, Victoria Park. Second Edition, crown 8vo, 4s 6d. [1873]

PROGNOSIS IN CASES OF VALVULAR DISEASE OF THE

Heart, by THOMAS B. PEACOCK, M.D., F.R.C.P., Honorary Consulting Physician to St. Thomas's Hospital. 8vo, 3s 6d. [1877]

DISEASES OF THE HEART.

Their Pathology, Diagnosis, Prognosis, and Treatment (a Manual), by ROBERT H. SEMPLE, M.D., F.R.C.P., Physician to the Hospital for Diseases of the Throat. 8vo, 8s 6d. [1875]

DISEASES OF THE HEART AND AORTA,

By THOMAS HAYDEN, F.K.Q.C.P. Irel., Physician to the Mater Misericordiæ Hospital, Dublin. With 80 Engravings. 8vo, 25s. [1875]

PHTHISIS

In a series of Clinical Studies, by AUSTIN FLINT, M.D., Professor of the Principles and Practice of Medicine and of Clinical Medicine in the Bellevue Hospital Medical College. 8vo, 16s. [1875]

BY THE SAME AUTHOR,

A MANUAL OF PERCUSSION AND AUSCULTATION,

of the Physical Diagnosis of Diseases of the Lungs and Heart, and of Thoracic Aneurism. Post 8vo, 6s 6d. [1876]

GROWTHS IN THE LARYNX,

with Reports and an Analysis of 100 consecutive Cases treated since the Invention of the Laryngoscope, by MORELL MACKENZIE, M.D. Lond., M.R.C.P., Physician to the Hospital for Diseases of the Throat. 8vo, with Coloured Plates, 12s 6d. [1871]

DISEASES OF THE HEART
and of the Lungs in Connexion therewith—Notes and Observations by THOMAS SHAPTER, M.D., F R.C P Lond., Senior Physician to the Devon and Exeter Hospital. 8vo, 7s. 6d. [1875]

DISEASES OF THE HEART AND AORTA
Clinical Lectures by GEORGE W. BALFOUR, M.D., F R.C P, Physician to, and Lecturer on Clinical Medicine in, the Royal Infirmary, Edinburgh. 8vo, with Engravings, 12s. 6d. [1876]

PHYSICAL DIAGNOSIS OF DISEASES OF THE HEART
Lectures by ARTHUR E SANSOM, M.D., Assistant Physician to the London Hospital. Second Edition, with Engravings, fcap. 8vo, 4s 6d [1876]

TRACHEOTOMY,
especially in Relation to Diseases of the Larynx and Trachea, by PUGIN THORNTON, M R C S, late Surgeon to the Hospital for Diseases of the Throat. With Photographic Plates and Woodcuts, 8vo, 5s 6d [1876]

SKETCH OF CANNES AND ITS CLIMATE,
by TH DE VALCOURT, M.D. Paris, Physician at Cannes Second Edition, with Photographic View and 6 Meteorological Charts Crown 8vo, 2s. 6d. [1873]

WINTER AND SPRING
on the Shores of the Mediterranean, or, the Genoese Rivieras, Italy, Spain, Greece, the Archipelago, Constantinople, Corsica, Sardinia, Sicily, Corfu, Malta, Tunis, Algeria, Smyrna, Asia Minor, with Biarritz and Arcachon, as Winter Climates By HENRY BENNET, M D Fifth Edition, post 8vo, with numerous Plates, Maps, and Engravings, 12s 6d. [1871]

BY THE SAME AUTHOR,
TREATMENT OF PULMONARY CONSUMPTION
by Hygiene, Climate, and Medicine. Second Edition, 8vo, 5s [1871]

PRINCIPAL HEALTH RESORTS
of Europe and Africa, and their Use in the Treatment of Chronic Diseases A Handbook by THOMAS MORE MADDEN, M D, M R I A, Vice-President of the Dublin Obstetrical Society. 8vo, 10s [1876]

MINERAL SPRINGS OF HARROGATE,
By Dr KENNION Revised and enlarged by ADAM BEALEY, M A, M.D Cantab, F R C.P. Lond Seventh Thousand. Crown 8vo, 1s [1875]

THE BATH THERMAL WATERS
Historical, Social, and Medical, by JOHN KENT SPENDER, M D, Surgeon to the Mineral Water Hospital, Bath. With an Appendix on the Climate of Bath by the Rev L. BLOMEFIELD, M.A, F.L S, F G S 8vo, 7s. 6d. [1877]

FAMILY MEDICINE FOR INDIA:
A Manual, by WILLIAM J. MOORE, M.D., Surgeon-Major H.M Indian Medical Service. Published under the Authority of the Government of India Third Edition, post 8vo, with 60 Engravings [in the press]

DISEASES OF TROPICAL CLIMATES
and their Treatment with Hints for the Preservation of Health in the Tropics, by JAMES A. HORTON, M.D., Surgeon-Major, Army Medical Department. Post 8vo, 12s 6d. [1874]

ENDEMIC DISEASES OF TROPICAL CLIMATES,
with their Treatment, by JOHN SULLIVAN, M.D., M.R.C P. Post 8vo, 6s. [1877]

HEALTH IN INDIA FOR BRITISH WOMEN
and on the Prevention of Disease in Tropical Climates by EDWARD J. TILT, M.D, Consulting Physician-Accoucheur to the Farringdon General Dispensary Fourth Edition, crown 8vo, 5s. [1875]

BURDWAN FEVER,
or the Epidemic Fever of Lower Bengal (Causes, Symptoms, and Treatment), by GOPAUL CHUNDER ROY, MD, Surgeon Bengal Establishment New Edition, 8vo, 5s. [1876]

BAZAAR MEDICINES OF INDIA
and Common Medical Plants Remarks on their Uses, with Full Index of Diseases, indicating their Treatment by these and other Agents procurable throughout India, &c , by EDWARD J. WARING, M.D., F R C P. Lond., Retired Surgeon H.M. Indian Army Third Edition Fcap 8vo, 5s [1875]

SOME AFFECTIONS OF THE LIVER
and Intestinal Canal; with Remarks on Ague and its Sequelæ, Scurvy, Purpura, &c , by STEPHEN H WARD, M D Lond , F R C P , Physician to the Seamen's Hospital, Greenwich. 8vo, 7s [1872]

DISEASES OF THE LIVER·
Lettsomian Lectures for 1872 by S O. HABERSHON, M.D, F.R.C P., Senior Physician to Guy's Hospital. Post 8vo, 3s 6d [1872]

BY THE SAME AUTHOR,
DISEASES OF THE STOMACH DYSPEPSIA.
Second Edition, crown 8vo, 5s.

BY THE SAME AUTHOR,
PATHOLOGY OF THE PNEUMOGASTRIC NERVE,
being the Lumleian Lectures for 1876. Post 8vo, 3s. 6d. [1877]

FUNCTIONAL NERVOUS DISORDERS·
Studies by C. HANDFIELD JONES, M.B., F.R.C P, F.R.S., Physician to St. Mary's Hospital Second Edition, 8vo, 18s. [1870]

NUTRITION IN HEALTH AND DISEASE:
 A Contribution to Hygiene and to Clinical Medicine. By HENRY BENNET, M.D. Third Edition. 8vo, 7s. [1877]

THE STOMACH AND DUODENUM
 Their Morbid States and their Relations to the Diseases of other Organs, by SAMUEL FENWICK, M.D., F.R.C.P., Physician to the London Hospital. 8vo, with 10 Plates, 12s. [1868]

FOOD AND DIETETICS,
 Physiologically and Therapeutically Considered. By FREDERICK W. PAVY, M.D., F.R.S., Physician to Guy's Hospital. Second Edition, 8vo, 15s. [1875]

HEADACHES:
 their Causes, Nature, and Treatment. By WILLIAM H. DAY, M.D., Physician to the Samaritan Free Hospital for Women and Children. Crown 8vo, with Engravings. 6s. 6d. [1877]

IMPERFECT DIGESTION:
 its Causes and Treatment by ARTHUR LEARED, M.D., F.R.C.P., Senior Physician to the Great Northern Hospital. Sixth Edition, fcap 8vo, 4s. 6d. [1875]

MEGRIM, SICK-HEADACHE,
 and some Allied Disorders a Contribution to the Pathology of Nerve-Storms, by EDWARD LIVEING, M.D. Cantab., Hon. Fellow of King's College, London. 8vo, with Coloured Plate, 15s. [1873]

NEURALGIA AND KINDRED DISEASES
 of the Nervous System their Nature, Causes, and Treatment, with a series of Cases, by JOHN CHAPMAN, M.D., M.R.C.P. 8vo, 14s. [1873]

THE SYMPATHETIC SYSTEM OF NERVES,
 and their Functions as a Physiological Basis for a Rational System of Therapeutics by EDWARD MERYON, M.D., F.R.C.P., Physician to the Hospital for Diseases of the Nervous System. 8vo, 3s. 6d. [1872]

RHEUMATIC GOUT,
 or Chronic Rheumatic Arthritis of all the Joints, a Treatise by ROBERT ADAMS, M.D., M.R.I.A., late Surgeon to H.M. the Queen in Ireland, and Regius Professor of Surgery in the University of Dublin. Second Edition, 8vo, with Atlas of Plates, 21s. [1872]

SCIATICA, LUMBAGO, AND BRACHIALGIA.
 Their Nature and Treatment, and their Immediate Relief and Rapid Cure by Hypodermic Injection of Morphia. By HENRY LAWSON, M.D., Assistant-Physician to St Mary's Hospital, and Lecturer on Physiology in its School. Second edition, crown 8vo, 5s. [1877]

GOUT, RHEUMATISM,

and the Allied Affections, a Treatise by PETER HOOD, M D. Crown 8vo, 10s 6d [1871]

CANCER

its varieties, their Histology and Diagnosis, by HENRY ARNOTT, F.R.C S , late Assistant-Surgeon to, and Lecturer on Morbid Anatomy at, St Thomas's Hospital. 8vo, with 5 Plates and 22 Engravings, 5s 6d [1872]

CANCEROUS AND OTHER INTRA-THORACIC GROWTHS

their Natural History and Diagnosis, by J RISDON BENNETT, M.D., F.R.C P , Member of the General Medical Council Post 8vo, with Plates, 8s [1872]

CERTAIN FORMS OF CANCER,

with a New and successful Mode of Treating it, to which is prefixed a Practical and Systematic Description of all the varieties of this Disease, by ALEX MARSDEN, M.D., F R C.S E., Consulting Surgeon to the Royal Free Hospital, and Senior Surgeon to the Cancer Hospital. Second Edition, with Coloured Plates, 8vo, 8s 6d. [1873]

ATLAS OF SKIN DISEASES

a series of Illustrations, with Descriptive Text and Notes upon Treatment By TILBURY FOX, M D , F R C P , Physician to the Department for Skin Diseases in University College Hospital. With 72 Coloured Plates, royal 4to, half morocco, £6 6s [1877]

DISEASES OF THE SKIN

a System of Cutaneous Medicine by ERASMUS WILSON, F R C S, F R S Sixth Edition, 8vo, 18s , with Coloured Plates, 36s. [1867]

BY THE SAME AUTHOR,

LECTURES ON EKZEMA

and Ekzematous Affections with an Introduction on the General Pathology of the Skin, and an Appendix of Essays and Cases. 8vo, 10s 6d. [1870]

ALSO,

LECTURES ON DERMATOLOGY.

delivered at the Royal College of Surgeons, 1870, 6s , 1871-3, 10s. 6d., 1874 5, 10s 6d.

ECZEMA

by McCALL ANDERSON, M.D , Professor of Clinical Medicine in the University of Glasgow Third Edition, 8vo, with Engravings, 7s 6d [1874]

BY THE SAME AUTHOR,

PARASITIC AFFECTIONS OF THE SKIN

Second Edition, 8vo, with Engravings, 7s 6d [1868]

PSORIASIS OR LEPRA,
    by George Gaskoin, M.R.C S., Surgeon to the British Hospital for Diseases of the Skin. 8vo, 5s. [1875]

MYCETOMA;
    or, the Fungus Disease of India, by H Vandyke Carter, M D, Surgeon-Major H M. Indian Army. 4to, with 11 Coloured Plates, 42s [1874]

CERTAIN ENDEMIC SKIN AND OTHER DISEASES
    of India and Hot Climates generally, by Tilbury Fox, M.D, and T. Farquhar, M.D. (Published under the sanction of the Secretary of State for India in Council). 8vo, 10s. 6d. [1876]

DISEASES OF THE SKIN,
    in Twenty-four Letters on the Principles and Practice of Cutaneous Medicine, by Henry Evans Cauty, Surgeon to the Liverpool Dispensary for Diseases of the Skin, 8vo, 12s. 6d. [1874]

THE HAIR IN HEALTH AND DISEASE,
    by E. Wyndham Cottle, F.R C.S, Senior Assistant Surgeon to the Hospital for Diseases of the Skin, Blackfriars. Fcap. 8vo, 2s 6d. [1877]

WORMS:
    a Series of Lectures delivered at the Middlesex Hospital on Practical Helminthology by T. Spencer Cobbold, M.D, F R.S. Post 8vo, 5s. [1872]

THE LAWS AFFECTING MEDICAL MEN.
    a Manual by Robert G. Glenn, LL B, Barrister-at-Law; with a Chapter on Medical Etiquette by Dr A Carpenter 8vo, 14s. [1871]

MEDICAL JURISPRUDENCE,
    Its Principles and Practice, by Alfred S Taylor, M.D., F R C P., F.R S Second Edition, 2 vols., 8vo, with 189 Engravings, £1 11s. 6d. [1873]

BY THE SAME AUTHOR,

A MANUAL OF MEDICAL JURISPRUDENCE
    Ninth Edition. Crown 8vo, with Engravings, 14s [1874]

ALSO,

POISONS,
    in Relation to Medical Jurisprudence and Medicine Third Edition, crown 8vo, with 104 Engravings, 16s. [1875]

A TOXICOLOGICAL CHART,
    exhibiting at one View the Symptoms, Treatment, and mode of Detecting the various Poisons—Mineral, Vegetable, and Animal: with Concise Directions for the Treatment of Suspended Animation, by William Stowe, M.R.C.S E. Thirteenth Edition, 2s, on roller, 5s. [1872]

A HANDY-BOOK OF FORENSIC MEDICINE AND TOXICOLOGY,
by W. BATHURST WOODMAN, M.D., F.R.C.P., Assistant Physician and Co-Lecturer on Physiology and Histology at the London Hospital; and C MEYMOTT TIDY, M D , F.C.S., Professor of Chemistry and of Medical Jurisprudence and Public Health at the London Hospital. With 8 Lithographic Plates and 116 Engravings, 8vo, 31s. 6d. [1877]

THE MEDICAL ADVISER IN LIFE ASSURANCE,
by EDWARD HENRY SIEVEKING, M.D., F.R.C P., Physician to St. Mary's and the Lock Hospitals, Physician-Extraordinary to the Queen; Physician-in-Ordinary to the Prince of Wales, &c. Crown 8vo, 6s [1874]

IDIOCY AND IMBECILITY,
by WILLIAM W. IRELAND, M D., Medical Superintendent of the Scottish National Institution for the Education of Imbecile Children at Larbert, Stirlingshire. With Engravings, 8vo, 14s [1877]

PSYCHOLOGICAL MEDICINE
a Manual, containing the Lunacy Laws, the Nosology, Ætiology, Statistics, Description, Diagnosis, Pathology (including Morbid Histology), and Treatment of Insanity, by J C. BUCKNILL, M D, F.R.S, and D. H. TUKE, M D., F R C P Third Edition, 8vo, with 10 Plates and 34 Engravings, 25s. [1873]

MADNESS.
in its Medical, Legal, and Social Aspects, Lectures by EDGAR SHEPPARD, M D., M R.C P, Professor of Psychological Medicine in King's College; one of the Medical Superintendents of the Colney Hatch Lunatic Asylum. 8vo, 6s 6d. [1873]

HANDBOOK OF LAW AND LUNACY;
or, the Medical Practitioner's Complete Guide in all Matters relating to Lunacy Practice, by J. T. SABBEN, M.D., and J. H BALFOUR BROWNE, Barrister-at-Law. 8vo, 5s. [1872]

INFLUENCE OF THE MIND UPON THE BODY
in Health and Disease, Illustrations designed to elucidate the Action of the Imagination, by DANIEL HACK TUKE, M.D., F.R.C.P. 8vo, 14s. [1872]

A MANUAL OF PRACTICAL HYGIENE,
by E. A. PARKES, M.D, F.R.C.P., F R.S. Fifth Edition. Edited by F. DE CHAUMONT, M.D , Professor of Military Hygiene in the Army Medical Service. 8vo, with Plates and Engravings. [In the press]

A HANDBOOK OF HYGIENE AND SANITARY SCIENCE,
by GEORGE WILSON, M.A , M.D., Medical Officer of Health for Mid-Warwickshire. Third Edition, post 8vo, with Engravings, 10s. 6d. [1877]

MICROSCOPICAL EXAMINATION OF DRINKING WATER·
A Guide, by JOHN D MACDONALD, M.D., F.R.S., Assistant Professor of Naval Hygiene, Army Medical School. 8vo, with 24 Plates, 7s. 6d. [1875]

HANDBOOK OF MEDICAL AND SURGICAL ELECTRICITY,
by HERBERT TIBBITS, M.D, F R C.P E, Medical Superintendent of the National Hospital for the Paralysed and Epileptic. 8vo, with 95 Engravings, 9s [1877]

BY THE SAME AUTHOR.

A MAP OF ZIEMSSEN'S MOTOR POINTS OF THE HUMAN BODY
a Guide to Localised Electrisation. Mounted on Rollers, 35 × 21. With 20 Illustrations, 5s. [1877]

CLINICAL USES OF ELECTRICITY,
Lectures delivered at University College Hospital by J RUSSELL REYNOLDS, M.D Lond., F R.C.P, F R S., Professor of Medicine in University College. Second Edition, post 8vo, 3s. 6d. [1873]

MEDICO-ELECTRIC APPARATUS
A Practical Description of every Form in Modern Use, with Plain Directions for Mounting, Charging, and Working, by SALT & SON, Birmingham. Second Edition, revised and enlarged, with 33 Engravings, 8vo, 2s. 6d. [1877]

A DICTIONARY OF MEDICAL SCIENCE;
containing a concise explanation of the various subjects and terms of Medicine, &c, Notices of Climate and Mineral Waters, Formulæ for Officinal, Empirical, and Dietetic Preparations; with the Accentuation and Etymology of the terms and the French and other Synonyms, by ROBLEY DUNGLISON, M D, LL D. New Edition, royal 8vo, 28s [1874]

A MEDICAL VOCABULARY;
being an Explanation of all Terms and Phrases used in the various Departments of Medical Science and Practice, giving their derivation, meaning, application, and pronunciation, by ROBERT G MAYNE, M D, LL D Fourth Edition, fcap 8vo, 10s. [1875]

ATLAS OF OPHTHALMOSCOPY,
by R. LIEBREICH, Ophthalmic Surgeon to St Thomas's Hospital. Translated into English by H ROSBOROUGH SWANZY, M.B Dub Second Edition, containing 59 Figures, 4to, £1 10s [1870]

DISEASES OF THE EYE
a Manual by C MACNAMARA, Surgeon to Westminster Hospital Third Edition, fcap, 8vo, with Coloured Plates and Engravings, 12s 6d. [1876]

DISEASES OF THE EYE
A Practical Treatise by HAYNES WALTON, F.R.C S, Surgeon to St. Mary's Hospital and in charge of its Ophthalmological Department. Third Edition, 8vo, with 3 Plates and nearly 300 Engravings, 25s
[1875]

HINTS ON OPHTHALMIC OUT-PATIENT PRACTICE,
by CHARLES HIGGENS, F R C S., Ophthalmic Assistant Surgeon to, and Lecturer on Ophthalmology at, Guy's Hospital. 87 pp , fcap 8vo, 2s. 6d [1877]

OPHTHALMIC MEDICINE AND SURGERY
a Manual by T WHARTON JONES, F R S, Professor of Ophthalmic Medicine and Surgery in University College. Third Edition, fcap 8vo, with 9 Coloured Plates and 173 Engravings, 12s 6d [1865]

DISEASES OF THE EYE
A Treatise by J SOELBERG WELLS, F R C S, Ophthalmic Surgeon to King's College Hospital and Surgeon to the Royal London Ophthalmic Hospital Third Edition, 8vo, with Coloured Plates and Engravings, 25s [1873]

BY THE SAME AUTHOR,

LONG, SHORT, AND WEAK SIGHT,
and their Treatment by the Scientific use of Spectacles Fourth Edition, 8vo, 6s [1873]

A SYSTEM OF DENTAL SURGERY,
by JOHN TOMES, F R S , and CHARLES S TOMES, M.A , Lecturer on Dental Anatomy and Physiology at the Dental Hospital of London Second Edition, fcap 8vo, with 268 Engravings, 14s [1673]

DENTAL ANATOMY, HUMAN AND COMPARATIVE
A Manual, by CHARLES S TOMES, M.A, M R C.S, Lecturer on Anatomy and Physiology at the Dental Hospital of London With 179 Engravings, crown 8vo, 10s. 6d [1876]

A MANUAL OF DENTAL MECHANICS,
with an Account of the Materials and Appliances used in Mechanical Dentistry, by OAKLEY COLES, L D S , R C S, Surgeon-Dentist to the Hospital for Diseases of the Throat Second Edition, crown 8vo, with 140 Engravings, 7s 6d [1876]

HANDBOOK OF DENTAL ANATOMY
and Surgery for the use of Students and Practitioners by JOHN SMITH, M D , F R S Edin , Surgeon-Dentist to the Queen in Scotland Second Edition, fcap 8vo, 4s 6d [1871]

STUDENT'S GUIDE TO DENTAL ANATOMY AND SURGERY,
by HENRY SEWILL, M R C S , L D S , Dentist to the West London Hospital With 77 Engravings, fcap 8vo, 5s 6d [1876]

OPERATIVE DENTISTRY
A Practical Treatise, by JONATHAN TAFT, D.D S., Professor of Operative Dentistry in the Ohio College of Dental Surgery Third Edition, thoroughly revised, with many additions, and 134 Engravings, 8vo, 18s [1877]

EPIDEMIOLOGY;
or, the Remote Cause of Epidemic Diseases in the Animal and in the Vegetable Creation by JOHN PARKIN, M D , F R C S. Part I, Contagion—Modern Theories—Cholera—Epizootics. 8vo, 5s [1873]

The following CATALOGUES issued by Messrs CHURCHILL will be forwarded post free on application:

1. *Messrs Churchill's General List of nearly 600 works on Medicine, Surgery, Midwifery, Materia Medica, Hygiene, Anatomy, Physiology, Chemistry, &c., &c., with a complete Index to their Titles, for easy reference.*

N.B.—This List includes Nos. 2 and 3.

2. *Selection from Messrs Churchill's General List, comprising all recent Works published by them on the Art and Science of Medicine.*

3. *A descriptive List of Messrs Churchill's Works on Chemistry, Pharmacy, Botany, Photography, Zoology, and other branches of Science.*

4. *Messrs Churchill's Red-Letter List, giving the Titles of forthcoming New Works and New Editions.*

[Published every October.]

5. *The Medical Intelligencer, an Annual List of New Works and New Editions published by Messrs J. & A. Churchill, together with Particulars of the Periodicals issued from their House.*

[Sent in January of each year to every Medical Practitioner in the United Kingdom whose name and address can be ascertained. A large number are also sent to the United States of America, Continental Europe, India, and the Colonies.]

MESSRS CHURCHILL have a special arrangement with MESSRS LINDSAY & BLAKISTON, OF PHILADELPHIA, in accordance with which that Firm act as their Agents for the United States of America, either keeping in Stock most of Messrs CHURCHILL'S Books, or reprinting them on Terms advantageous to Authors. Many of the Works in this Catalogue may therefore be easily obtained in America.

PRINTED BY J. E. ADLARD, BARTHOLOMEW CLOSE.